Management of Serials in Libraries

Management of Serials in Libraries

Thomas E. Nisonger

Associate Professor
Indiana University
School of Library and Information Science

This book is dedicated to my wife, Claire J. Nisonger.

Libraries Unlimited, Inc.
P.O. Box 6633
Englewood, CO 80155-6633
1-800-237-6124
www.lu.com

Production Editor: Kay Mariea
Copy Editor: Eloise Kinney
Proofreader: Natalie J. Johnson
Indexer: Christine J. Smith
Design and Layout: Pamela J. Getchell

Library of Congress Cataloging-in-Publication Data

Nisonger, Thomas E.
    Management of serials in libraries / Thomas E. Nisonger.
    xxviii, 433 p. 19x26 cm.
    Includes bibliographical references (p. 361) and index.
    ISBN 1-56308-213-6 (cloth)
    1. Serials control systems--United States.   I. Title.
Z692.S5N57   1998
025.17'32'0973--dc21
                              98-28879
                              CIP

Contents

Acknowledgments

The author would like to thank the following individuals who contributed to the completion of this book. My deceased parents, Irvin J. and Mary C. Nisonger, always encouraged all my intellectual endeavors. My wife, Claire, and my daughter, Suzanne, displayed incredible patience throughout the project's duration.

I would also like to thank numerous present and former Libraries Unlimited staff members, including David V. Loertscher, who helped conceptualize the book's content; Bohdan S. Wynar, who provided useful input; Kim Dority, who provided feedback on my sample submission; Stacey Ennis Chisholm, who served an important liaison function; Ronald Maas, my final editor; Kay Mariea, my production editor; Eloise Kinney, my copy editor; Barbara Ittner for marketing assistance; and numerous unnamed staff members who contributed to the book's editing and final production.

The assistance of the following people is also gratefully acknowledged. Judith Serebnick, Associate Professor Emeritus, Indiana University's School of Library and Information Science, gave me many useful source materials on serials when she retired and offered advice and encouragement during completion of the project. Kenneth D. Crews, Associate Professor, Law and Library and Information Science, and Director, Copyright Management Center, Indiana University–Purdue University at Indianapolis, gave helpful advice on copyright; and Howard Rosenbaum, Assistant Professor, Indiana University's SLIS, offered similar advice on the World Wide Web. Kathy Coleman and Ying Li, students at Indiana University, SLIS, conducted DIALOG searches on electronic journals and copyright, respectively. My graduate assistants at Indiana University's SLIS provided considerable clerical support: Cynthia Berquist photocopied articles; Louann Marcelin-Salinas identified, photocopied, and helped organize pertinent articles; Kenneth Thompson photocopied articles and word processed tables; and Scott Walter verified WWW addresses and other citations. The following individuals read sections of the manuscript and provided valuable feedback: Kenneth D. Crews; Stephen P. Harter, Professor, Indiana University's SLIS; Judith Serebnick; and Stephen E. Wiberley, Bibliographer for the Social Sciences, the University of Illinois at Chicago library. I would also like to thank the SLIS Library Staff for their excellent services. Any deficiencies of this volume are the author's own responsibility.

Introduction

As we approach the twenty-first century, serials offer one of the greatest challenges confronting library and information science professionals. For more than a decade, serial prices have continuously increased at a rate far higher than general inflation and library funding levels, placing genuine financial pressure on most libraries. During 1995-96, the collective expenditures of all Association of Research Libraries (ARL) university libraries for current serial subscriptions exceeded $380 million,[1] and reported periodical expenditures by all U.S. public, academic, special, and governmental libraries approached $600 million for 1995-96.[2] That same year, the median expenditure of ARL university libraries on serial subscriptions was greater than $3.3 million—more than twice the amount spent on books.[3]

For years, talk has abounded about a so-called serials crisis brought on by budgetary concerns. Recent technological developments such as electronic journals, CD-ROMs, listservs, the Internet, and the World Wide Web (WWW) both present opportunities and create unresolved problems. The library profession has for some time been experiencing a paradigm shift from ownership to a mixture of ownership and access in which the ultimate proportion of each is still unforeseen. A few years ago, a serials collection manager usually faced a relatively straightforward decision: to subscribe or not to subscribe. Now, for many periodical titles, at least four options are available: a print subscription only; an electronic subscription only; both a print and an electronic subscription; or reliance on a document delivery service. Moreover, as G. E. Gorman has observed, "every area of library practice is impinged upon by serials:

1. collection development

2. acquisitions

3. cataloging

4. collection maintenance and preservation

5. public service

6. circulation

7. general management (i.e., budgeting)."[4]

The voluminous serials literature testifies to this format's perceived importance. A keyword search under the term *serial*[5] in the *Library Literature* database on CD-ROM retrieved 2,884 items published between December 1984 and April 24, 1997. Similar searches in early 1997 retrieved 5,758 entries published since 1968 from *LISA Plus* (which combines on CD-ROM the *Library and Information Science Abstracts* and the *Current Research in Library and Information Science* databases) and 1,219 published since 1966 from *Information Science Abstracts*.

In light of the ever-increasing challenges that serials present to librarians, this textbook analyzes the management of serials in libraries. The book is addressed to library practitioners whose professional duties involve serials—that is, serials, reference, collection development, and technical services librarians as well as library and information science teachers and researchers. This book stresses the handling of serials in libraries but also addresses serials as a scholarly communications medium apart from the library context. Accordingly, discussion includes the historical development of both print and electronic serials.

Certain topics are beyond this book's scope. Although serial publications are frequently the target of censors, censorship is not addressed in this volume. A distinct literature exists concerning censorship. Moreover, because the fundamental censorship issues (e.g., definition of obscenity, First Amendment rights, or protection versus access) are normally not affected by the monograph vs. serial format, a separate discussion in regard to serials seems unnecessary.

When informed the author was writing a serials textbook, more than one librarian commented, "We need your book to solve all our problems with serials." This book is not intended to solve all serials problems. Rather than provide definitive answers, it attempts to review major options for handling serials problems as well as to clarify fundamental issues.

Any textbook author confronts a fundamental dichotomy between the descriptive (describing how things actually are done) and the prescriptive (prescribing how things ought to be done). This book seeks to balance the two approaches.

This book addresses serials management in the four major categories of libraries: academic, public, school, and special. Nonetheless, the strong bias toward academic libraries reflects the author's background and interests as well as the published literature. The literature's skew toward academic libraries may reflect that in recent years academic libraries have been affected by serials more than other types of libraries.

The volume illuminates the major serials management issues. No attempt has been undertaken to comprehensively survey the fairly voluminous serials literature, although important publications and research are discussed. Information sources include the following:

- the author's experience as a library practitioner, teacher, and researcher;

- CD-ROMs of the major indexing tools relevant to library and information science (e.g., *Library Literature*, *ERIC*, and *Library and Information Science Abstracts)* to identify pertinent literature;

- printed serials bibliographies;

- subscriptions to electronic journals and listservs pertaining to serials, such as the *Newsletter on Serials Pricing Issues*, SERIALST (Serials in Libraries Discussion Forum), SERCITES (Citations for Serial Literature), ACQNET (for acquisitions), COLLDV-L (for collection development), ARL-EJOURNAL (for electronic journal management), VPIEJ-L (for electronic journal publishing), DOCDEL-L (dealing with document delivery issues), the International Society for Scientometrics and Informetrics (ISSI) Distribution List (for informetrics, scientometrics, and bibliometrics), GIFTEX-L (covering gift and exchange issues), and JESSE (for library and information science education)—although not all these listservs were subscribed to during the entire four years spent working on this volume;

- scanning shelf runs of major serials journals (e.g., *Serials Librarian* and *Serials Review*);

- current developments reported in the national press, such as the *New York Times* and *USA Today*;

- the Internet, to view WWW home pages relevant to serials;

- vendor advertisements, which often offer the most current information that is not necessarily available from other sources, even though they must be critically evaluated for self-promotional biases;

- attendance at professional and scholarly meetings, such as the American Library Association (ALA), the American Society for Information Science (ASIS), the Association for Library and Information Science Education (ALISE), the International Federation of Library Associations (IFLA), and the ISSI;

- "serendipity," as relevant information about serials may be found in a variety of unexpected sources. For example, the author read an article about electronic newspapers in Delta Airlines's *Sky Magazine* [6] when returning from the 1995 ALA Midwinter meeting in Philadelphia.

ORGANIZATION OF THE BOOK

Following this introduction, the book is organized into 10 chapters. The first chapter defines a serial, discusses various types of serials and electronic publications, and reviews some serials classification schemes. The history of serials—emphasizing electronic publications and the impact of serials costs on libraries—is examined in chapter 2. The collection management of serials is covered in the next two chapters. Chapter 3 addresses serials microevaluation criteria, selection, deselection, document delivery, and budgeting for serials. Chapter 4 discusses other serials collection management functions, serials decision models, core serial lists, and approaches to serials macroevaluation.

Chapter 5 examines the application of citation analysis to serial collection management, with emphasis on the *Journal Citation Reports* (JCR) and Bradford distribution. The analysis of periodical use is examined in chapter 6. Chapter 7 focuses on journal ranking methods. Serials processing in libraries—including acquisition, check-in, housing, circulation, and cataloging—is covered in chapter 8. Chapter 8 also discusses duplicate exchange of serials, serial subscription agents, vendor evaluation, organization of serials work, and copyright issues. Chapter 9 discusses electronic journals, the Internet, and the WWW. Chapter 10 addresses serials automation, including the role of automation standards. Finally, the epilogue offers a brief summary, with speculation about future trends.

Abbreviations and acronyms are spelled out in a section at the beginning of the volume. An unannotated bibliography follows each chapter. These bibliographies are by no means comprehensive, but they list the most important works pertinent to the chapter's subject matter. Occasionally, the same item may be in the bibliographies of more than one chapter, when it supports the content of both. A collective bibliography on serials in general appears at the end of the book.

A glossary is unnecessary because terms requiring definition are explained when they are introduced in the text. Readers should consult the *Serials Acquisitions Glossary*,[7] published in 1993 by the ALA's Association for Library Collections and Technical Services (ALCTS), for authoritative and relatively current definitions of serials terminology.

Three appendixes follow the text. The first appendix provides an annotated guide to sources of statistical data about serials, including prices, serial production, and library holdings. The second appendix is an annotated bibliography of serial bibliographies. The final appendix is a listing of World Wide Web resources pertaining to serials. The indexes at the end of the volume were prepared by a professional indexer.

EARLIER BOOKS ON SERIALS

According to Robert L. Migneault, the first book devoted to serials was Pearl Holland Clark's *The Problem Presented by Periodicals in College and University Libraries*, published by the University of Chicago Press in 1930.[8] Other early serials textbooks include J. Harris Gable's *Manual of Serials Work*,[9] David Grenfell's *Periodicals and Serials: Their Treatment in Special Libraries*,[10] D. E. Davinson's *The Periodicals Collection: Its Purpose and Uses in Libraries*,[11] and *Serial Publications in Large Libraries*, edited by Walter C. Allen.[12] Andrew D. Osborn's *Serial Publications: Their Place and Treatment in Libraries*, issued by the ALA in three editions spanning 1954 to 1980, is undoubtedly the classic serials textbook.

Other serials management textbooks include Clara D. Brown and Lynn S. Smith's *Serials: Past, Present and Future*;[13] *Serials Librarianship*, edited by Ross Bourne;[14] Marcia Tuttle's *Introduction to Serials Management*;[15] *Projects and Procedures for Serials Administration*, compiled and edited by Diane Stine;[16] *Serials Management: A Practical Handbook*, edited by Margaret E. Graham and Fiona Buettel;[17] Chiou-sen Dora Chen's *Serials Management: A Practical Guide*;[18] and *Managing Serials*, by Marcia Tuttle, with contributions by Luke Swindler and Frieda B. Rosenberg.[19] *Serials Management in the Electronic Era: Papers in Honor of Peter Gellatly, Founding Editor of the "Serials Librarian,"* edited by Jim Cole and James W. Williams, presents the articles from *Serials Librarian*, volume 29, numbers 3/4, 1996, issued in monographic form rather than a unified textbook.[20] Note, however, that only a few of the *Serials Librarian* numbers simultaneously issued as monographs will be mentioned in this section. Finally, note that Jean Walter Farrington's *Serials Management in Academic Libraries: A Guide to Issues and Practices*[21] was not available to me before the submission of this manuscript.

Books on special aspects of serials are too numerous to be comprehensively surveyed. However, some of the most important, though outdated, should be mentioned. Serials cataloging has been addressed in Lynn S. Smith's *A Practical*

Approach to Serials Cataloging,[22] Carol L. H. Leong's *Serials Cataloging Handbook: An Illustrated Guide to the Use of AACR2 and LC Rule Interpretations*,[23] and *Serials Cataloging: Modern Perspectives and International Developments*, edited by Jim E. Cole and James W. Williams.[24] Regarding reference, note Joseph A. Puccio's *Serials Reference Work*[25] and *Serials and Reference Services*, edited by Robin Kinder and Bill Katz.[26] N. Bernard Basch and Judy McQueen's *Buying Serials: A How-to-Do-It Manual for Librarians* addresses library use of serial subscription agents.[27] Serials standards are covered in *Library Serials Standards: Development, Implementation, Impact*, edited by Nancy Jean Melin.[28] Also note *Magazine Selection: How to Build a Community-Oriented Collection*, by Bill Katz, which focused on the selection of periodicals for public libraries,[29] and *Scientific Journals: Issues in Library Selection and Management*, edited by Tony Stankus.[30] The journal's role in science is explored in *The Scientific Journal*, edited by A. J. Meadows.[31]

Some recent books address various aspects of electronic journals, including Jan Olsen's *Electronic Journal Literature: Implications for Scholars*;[32] *The Electronic Journal: The Future of Serials-Based Information*, edited by Brian Cook;[33] and *Scholarly Journals at the Crossroads: A Subversive Proposal for Electronic Publishing*, edited by Ann Shumelda Okerson and James J. O'Donnell.[34] However, no book yet published thoroughly covers the management of electronic journals by libraries.

A question arises: Why another book on serials? What does this present book offer that is not available in the previously published monographs?

This is not a practical, "how to" guide on serials. It seeks to educate rather than train. Because this volume is more current than any of the titles noted above, the most recent information about electronic publications, the Internet, and the WWW is included. Moreover, electronic sources that offer information often not available in traditional print format (e.g., listservs, electronic journals, and Web sites) have been used in writing the text. This volume emphasizes collection management rather than processing issues. Unlike most earlier general serials monographs, which include just a single chapter on serials collection management, this text contains chapters on use studies, journal ranking, and the application of citation analysis to serials management. Finally, this book offers the perspective of a library and information science educator rather than a library practitioner.

This book complements rather than competes with Tuttle's excellent *Managing Serials*, which was issued about one year before this final draft was completed. This volume emphasizes collection management issues and includes separate chapters on electronic journals and serials automation.

NOTES

1. Martha Kyrillidou, Ken Rodriguez, and Kendon Stubbs, comps. and eds., *ARL Statistics; 1995-96: A Compilation of Statistics from the One Hundred and Twenty Members of the Association of Research Libraries* (Washington, D.C.: Association of Research Libraries, 1997), 36. The precise figure was $386,356,960.

2. *Bowker Annual: Library and Book Trade Almanac; 1997*, 42d ed. (New Providence, N.J.: R. R. Bowker, 1997), 437, 439, 441, 443. Based on my calculations from Bowker's data,

1995-96 periodical expenditures by public, academic, special, and government libraries amounted to $595,163,184. Data were not reported for school library media centers.

3. Kyrillidou, Rodriguez, and Stubbs, *ARL Statistics; 1995-96*, The median expenditure for serials by 109 ARL university libraries was $3,384,928 contrasted to $1,430,040 for monographs.

4. G. E. Gorman, "The Education of Serials Librarians in Australia: A Proposed Course in Serials Librarianship," *Serials Librarian* 17, nos. 1/2 (1989): 53.

5. The truncated search strategy "serial#" was used to retrieve records that contained either the word's singular or plural form.

6. David Noack, "The Cyber Papers," *Sky Magazine* (February 1995): 112.

7. Association for Library Collections and Technical Services, *Serials Acquisitions Glossary* (Chicago: Association for Library Collections and Technical Services, 1993).

8. Robert L. Migneault, "Serials: An Introductory Perspective," in *Projects and Procedures for Serials Administration*, comp. and ed. Diane Stine (Ann Arbor, Mich.: Pierian Press, 1985), 6.

9. J. Harris Gable, *Manual of Serials Work* (Chicago: American Library Association, 1937).

10. David Grenfell, *Periodicals and Serials: Their Treatment in Special Libraries,* 2d ed. (London: Aslib, 1965).

11. D. E. Davinson, *The Periodicals Collection: Its Purpose and Uses in Libraries* (London: Andre Deutsch, 1969).

12. Walter C. Allen, ed., *Serial Publications in Large Libraries* (Urbana, Ill.: University of Illinois, Graduate School of Library Science, 1970).

13. Clara D. Brown and Lynn S. Smith, *Serials: Past, Present and Future,* 2d rev. ed. (Birmingham, Ala.: EBSCO, 1980).

14. Ross Bourne, ed., *Serials Librarianship* (London: The Library Association, 1980).

15. Marcia Tuttle, *Introduction to Serials Management* (Greenwich, Conn.: JAI Press, 1982).

16. Diane Stine, comp. and ed., *Projects and Procedures for Serials Administration* (Ann Arbor, Mich.: Pierian Press, 1985).

17. Margaret E. Graham and Fiona Buettel, *Serials Management: A Practical Handbook* (London: Published by Aslib in collaboration with the United Kingdom Serials Group, 1990).

18. Chiou-sen Dora Chen, *Serials Management: A Practical Guide* (Chicago: American Library Association, 1995).

19. Marcia Tuttle, *Managing Serials* (Greenwich, Conn.: JAI Press, 1996).

20. Jim Cole and James W. Williams, eds., *Serials Management in the Electronic Era: Papers in Honor of Peter Gellatly, Founding Editor of the "Serials Librarian"* (New York: Haworth Press, 1996). Also issued as *Serials Librarian* 29, nos. 3/4 (1996).

21. Jean Walter Farrington, *Serials Management in Academic Libraries: A Guide to Issues and Practices* (Westport, Conn.: Greenwood Press, 1997).

22. Lynn S. Smith, *A Practical Approach to Serials Cataloging* (Greenwich, Conn.: JAI Press, 1978).

23. Carol L. H. Leong, *Serials Cataloging Handbook: An Illustrative Guide to the Use of AACR2 and LC Rule Interpretations* (Chicago: American Library Association, 1989).

24. Jim E. Cole and James W. Williams, eds., *Serials Cataloging: Modern Perspectives and International Developments* (New York: Haworth Press, 1992). Also issued as *Serials Librarian*. 22, nos. 1/2 and 3/4 (1992).

25. Joseph A. Puccio, *Serials Reference Work* (Englewood, Colo.: Libraries Unlimited, 1989).

26. Robin Kinder and Bill Katz, eds., *Serials and Reference Services* (New York: Haworth Press, 1990). Also issued as *The Reference Librarian*, nos. 27/28 (1990).

27. N. Bernard Basch and Judy McQueen, *Buying Serials: A How-to-Do-It Manual for Librarians* (New York: Neal-Schuman, 1990).

28. Nancy Jean Melin, ed., *Library Serials Standards: Development, Implementation, Impact: Proceedings of the Third Annual Serials Conference* (Westport, Conn.: Meckler Publishing, 1984).

29. Bill Katz, *Magazine Selection: How to Build a Community-Oriented Collection* (New York: R. R. Bowker, 1971).

30. Tony Stankus, ed., *Scientific Journals: Issues in Library Selection and Management* (New York: Haworth Press, 1987).

31. A. J. Meadows, *The Scientific Journal* (London: Aslib, 1979).

32. Jan Olsen, *Electronic Journal Literature: Implications for Scholars* (Westport, Conn.: Mecklermedia, 1994).

33. Brian Cook, ed., *The Electronic Journal: The Future of Serials-Based Information* (New York: Haworth Press, 1992). Also issued as *Australian and New Zealand Journal of Serials Librarianship* 3, no. 2 (1992).

34. Ann Shumelda Okerson and James J. O'Donnell, eds., *Scholarly Journals at the Crossroads: A Subversive Proposal for Electronic Publishing* (Washington, D.C.: Office of Scientific and Academic Publishing, Association of Research Libraries, 1995).

Abbreviations and Acronyms

AAAS	American Association for the Advancement of Science
AACR	*Anglo-American Cataloguing Rules*
AACR2	*Anglo-American Cataloguing Rules,* published in 1978 and implemented by the LC in 1981
AACR2R	*Anglo-American Cataloguing Rules*, 2nd edition, 1988 revision.
AACSB	American Assembly of Collegiate Schools of Business
AASL	American Association of School Librarians
ACRL	Association of College and Research Libraries
AECT	Association for Educational Communications and Technology
ALA	American Library Association
ALCTS	Association for Library Collections and Technical Services (an ALA division)
ALISE	Association for Library and Information Science Education
ANSI	American National Standards Institute
APA	American Psychological Association
APSA	American Political Science Association
ARL	Association of Research Libraries
ARIA	American Risk and Insurance Association
ARPA	Advanced Research Projects Agency
ASC	Accredited Standards Committee
ASCII	American Standard Code for Information Interchange
ASEE/ELD	American Society for Engineering Education/Engineering Libraries Division
ASIS	American Society for Information Science
Aslib	Association of Special Libraries and Information Bureaux
BISAC	Book Industry Systems Advisory Committee
BLEND	Birmingham Loughborough Electronic Network Development
CCC	Copyright Clearance Center
CEO	Chief Executive Officer

CERN	European Particle Physics Laboratory (abbreviation is based on the French name)
CIC	Committee on Institutional Cooperation
CISTI	Canada Institute for Scientific and Technical Information
CPI	Consumer Price Index
CONSER	Cooperative Online Serials Program (until 1986, Conversion of Serials Project)
CONTU	Commission on New Technological Uses of Copyrighted Works
CORE	Chemistry Online Retrieval Experiment
CSISAC	Canadian Serials Industry Systems Advisory Committee
DARPA	Defense Advanced Research Projects Agency
DDC	Dewey decimal classification
DDT	document delivery test
DEU	Duplicates Exchange Union (sponsored by ALA's ALCTS)
DOI	Digital Object Identifier
EDI	Electronic Data Interchange
EDIFACT	Electronic Data Interchange for Administration, Commerce, and Transport
EFT	Electronic Funds Transfer
EIES	Electronic Information Exchange System
EJC	Electronic Journal Collection (of the CIC)
e-mail	Electronic mail
EPPP	Electronic Publications Pilot Project (of the National Library of Canada)
ERIC	Educational Resources Information Center
ESP	*Electronic Social Psychology*
FTE	Full Time Equivalent
ftp	File Transfer Protocol (on the Internet)
HTTP	Hypertext Transfer Protocol (on the World Wide Web)
ICEDIS	International Committee on Electronic Data Interchange for Serials
IFLA	International Federation of Library Associations
ILL	interlibrary loan
ISBD	International Standard Bibliographic Description
ISDS	International Serials Data System

ISI	Institute for Scientific Information
ISO	International Organization for Standardization
ISSI	International Society for Scientometrics and Informetrics
ISSN	International Standard Serial Number[1]
JCR	*Journal Citation Reports*
JSTOR	Journal storage
LC	Library of Congress
LCRI	*Library of Congress Rule Interpretations*
LIS	library and information science
MARC	machine readable cataloging
MARC-S	machine readable cataloging serials format
NASIG	North American Serials Interest Group
NISO	National Information Standards Organization
NLC	National Library of Canada
NSDP	National Serials Data Program
NSF	National Science Foundation
OCLC	Online Computer Library Center
OJCCT	*Online Journal of Current Clinical Trials*
OPAC	Online Public Access Catalog
PACS Review	*Public-Access Computer Systems Review*
PII	Publisher Item Identifier
RFP	Request for Proposal
RLG	Research Libraries Group
RLIN	Research Libraries Information Network
SCI	*Science Citation Index*
SCONUL	Standing Conference of National and University Libraries (in the United Kingdom)
SDI	Selective Dissemination of Information
SERIALST	Serials in Libraries Discussion Forum
SGML	Standard Generalized Markup Language
SICI	Serial Item and Contribution Identifier
SISAC	Serials Industry Systems Advisory Committee
SLIS	School of Library and Information Science

SPSS	Statistical Package for the Social Sciences
SSCI	*Social Sciences Citation Index*
STM	Science, Technical, and Medical
SUNY	State University of New York
UKSG	United Kingdom Serials Group
TULIP	The University Licensing Project
UCRI	Usage/Cost Relational Index
UMI	University Microfilms International
UNESCO	United Nations Educational, Scientific, and Cultural Organization
URL	Uniform Resource Locator (on World Wide Web)
USBE	United States Book Exchange
UTLAS	University of Toronto Library Automation System
WLN	Western Library Network
WWW	World Wide Web

NOTES

1. The ISSN stands for both the singular and plural form. See Jim E. Cole, "ISDS: The Unfinished Revolution," in *Advances in Serials Management: A Research Annual*, vol. 4, ed. Marcia Tuttle and Jean G. Cook (Greenwich, Conn.: JAI Press, 1992), 66.

Chapter One

The Serials Format

This chapter defines the term *serial,* describes different types of serials, examines some serials classification schemes, and finally, discusses definitional issues about electronic publications. The history of serials is covered in chapter 2.

DEFINITION OF A SERIAL

What is a serial? It is not something one eats for breakfast. Definitions, although sometimes boring, are essential—especially because over the years many key terms, such as *periodical* and *serial,* have been used inconsistently. Moreover, many other terms, such as *magazine, little magazine, zine, review, journal, newspaper, underground press,* and *newsletter* need clarification.

The precise definition of terminology is not simply an academic question, although some have questioned its usefulness.[1] Bill Katz has said, "Obviously, the child next door can tell a librarian what a magazine is, or is not, and the average adult doesn't confuse the *Reader's Digest* with a new edition of *Tarzan of the Apes,* so why all the fuss?"[2] Nevertheless, defining terms is significant. In a practical sense, definitions might affect the organization of work flow, budgeting, the division of staff responsibilities, how an item is cataloged, and what is included in a union list. Theoretically, a serials textbook should explain what a serial is and address the conflicting terminology.

The 1988 revision of the *Anglo-American Cataloguing Rules* second edition (AACR2R) defines a serial as "A publication in any medium issued in successive parts bearing numeric or chronological designations and intended to be continued indefinitely. Serials include periodicals; newspapers; annuals (reports, yearbooks, etc.); the journals, memoirs, proceedings, transactions, etc. of societies; and numbered monographic series."[3]

This definition has nearly achieved general acceptance in North America. It has been adopted by the *ALA Glossary of Library and Information Science,*[4] the Association for Library Collections and Technical Services (ALCTS) *Guidelines for Handling Library Orders for Serials and Periodicals,*[5] and the ALCTS *Serials Acquisitions Glossary.*[6]

Three key elements form the definition of a serial: the item is issued in separate parts on an ongoing basis, the parts are numbered or contain a chronological designation, and no discernible end is in sight—that is, it is "intended by the producer to continue indefinitely." The producer's intention is critical because even a single piece would be considered a serial if the publisher had originally intended it to continue indefinitely.[7] If a definite end is in sight (e.g., an encyclopedia issued in separate volumes, each covering one letter of the alphabet), it is not a serial. The very word *serial* implies continuation, such as an old-time "serial movie" or, as a more ghoulish example, a serial killer. Arguably, ongoing television shows, such as the nightly news or soap operas, are serials.[8] As G. E. Gorman states, "It is the 'intended to continue indefinitely' aspect which contributes most to the uniqueness of serial literature and which is the source of most problems associated with serials librarianship."[9]

What is the relationship between the terms *periodical* and *serial?* The precise meaning of these terms varies depending on time period, country, author, library, or purpose for which the terms are used. Depending on the context, at least four relationships exist between the terms *periodical* and *serial*:

1. They are synonyms.

2. Periodicals are a subset of serials.

3. Serials are a subset of periodicals.

4. Periodicals and serials are mutually exclusive phenomena.

In popular usage, among nonspecialists, the terms *serial* and *periodical* are sometimes used as synonyms because the difference between the two is not fully understood. Specialists almost always differentiate between serials and periodicals but often not consistently.

Most current North American usage tends to conform to the second relationship outlined above—that periodicals are a subset of serials. Although the AACR2R's glossary does not define *periodical* per se, its above-cited definition of *serial* specifically lists periodical as a category of serial. Likewise, the *ALA Glossary of Library and Information Science* defines periodical as a type of serial:

> A serial appearing or intended to appear indefinitely at regular or stated intervals, generally more frequently than annually, each issue of which is numbered or dated consecutively and normally contains separate articles, stories, or other writings. Newspapers disseminating general news, and the proceedings, papers, or other publications of corporate bodies primarily related to their meetings, are not included in this term.[10]

Magazines and journals (the distinctions between the two are analyzed in the next section) are almost invariably considered periodicals, but much inconsistency exists about whether newspapers are periodicals or a different type of serial. The *ALA Glossary of Library and Information Science*, quoted in the above paragraph and in the *Serials Acquisitions Glossary*,[11] explicitly excludes general newspapers from the definition of a periodical. Yet many authorities, including Marcia Tuttle,[12] classify newspapers as a major category of periodical.

The third logical relationship, serials as a subset of periodicals, has been used in the past in the United Kingdom. Tuttle wrote in 1996, "In the United Kingdom, until recently, *serial* was a specific term, comparable to what Americans know as *periodical*. British librarians used periodical as the broad term."[13] Now British usage is essentially in agreement with North American terminology, as indicated by the definitions in the 1995 edition of the British publication *Harrod's Librarians' Glossary*.[14]

Some uses conform to the fourth relationship, applying the term *periodical* to periodical serials and reserving the term *serial* for nonperiodical serials. (The distinction between periodical and nonperiodical serials is explained below.) For example, an article describing binding expenditures at the Georgia Institute of Technology library reported them separately for periodicals and serials as if they were two totally separate categories.[15]

The terminology used in this book conforms to the definition outlined in AACR2R, with periodicals considered a subset of serials. However, throughout the text the terms are sometimes used interchangeably for stylistic variation when the concept under discussion is equally applicable to both serials and periodicals.

Many experts, including N. Bernard Basch and Judy McQueen, differentiate between periodical serials and nonperiodical serials. According to Basch and McQueen, the former are issued on a regular basis at an annual or greater frequency and include periodicals, newspapers, and legal and business services. The latter, which "are issued less regularly and more infrequently," include proceedings, biennials, sets, and monographic and multivolume series. In contrast, many authorities consider annuals to be serials but not periodicals. Basch and McQueen assert that annuals "straddle" the two categories. They explain that annuals regularly issued in the same month (e.g., April 1995, April 1996, etc.) "behave like periodical serials," whereas ones issued in different months (e.g., March 1995, June 1996) correspond to nonperiodical serials.[16]

Andrew D. Osborn identified three types of what Tuttle terms "near serials":[17] "continuations," "provisional serials," and "pseudoserials." In Osborn's scheme, a continuation is a nonserial set for which a library places a continuing order, for example, a multivolume monographic title. A provisional serial refers to a monographic set with ongoing supplements, such as the yearbook for an encyclopedia. "A pseudoserial is a frequently reissued and revised publication which quite properly may be, and on first publication generally is, considered to be a monograph"[18]—in other words, a work issued in repeated editions, such as *Burke's Peerage*.

The relationship between a serial and a series is somewhat complex and requires examination. AACR2R defines a *series* as follows:

1. A group of separate items related to one another by the fact that each item bears, in addition to its own title proper, a collective title applying to the group as a whole. The individual items may or may not be numbered. 2. Each of two or more volumes of essays, lectures, articles, or other writings, similar in character and issued in sequence (e.g., Lowell's *Among my books*, second series). 3. A separately numbered sequence of volumes within a series or serial (e.g., *Notes and queries*, 1st series, 2d series, etc.).[19]

Definition one covers a monographic series. If numbered, a monographic series meets the criteria for being considered a serial; but if unnumbered, it does not. As indicated in the AACR2R's third definition, a serial can be suborganized into separate series.

Serials are often thought of as a distinct format. Yet periodicity—being regularly recurrent—rather than format is crucial to the definition. The AACR2R explicitly states that a serial is "a publication in any medium."[20] Accordingly, a serial can assume a paper, microfiche or film, online, or CD-ROM format.

TYPES OF SERIALS

The major types of serials are discussed in this section. Some of the distinctions between specialized types may not be especially significant for processing purposes but might be useful in collection development and for a full understanding of the diverse range of serials.

One must distinguish between a definition and a characteristic. Men generally weigh more than women, but weight is clearly not the defining difference between a man and a woman. A review of the pertinent literature indicates that many types of serials are described by their major characteristics rather than precisely defined.

The *ALA Glossary of Library and Information Science* defines a *journal* as "a periodical, especially one containing scholarly articles and/or disseminating current information on research and development in a particular subject field."[21] The *American Political Science Review*, the *American Historical Review*, *Signs: Journal of Women in Culture and Society*, and *Journal of Applied Physics* are typical examples of journals.

A *magazine* is defined by the *ALA Glossary of Library and Information Science* as "a periodical for general reading, containing articles on various subjects by different authors."[22] *Time*, *Sports Illustrated*, *People*, or *Playboy* are examples of magazines. Ironically, not all magazines meet the technical definition of a serial. A phenomenon, termed a "temporary magazine," is geared toward a specific event. One can cite the *Sports Illustrated Olympic* marketed only in Atlanta at the 1996 Olympics or the *Ryder Cup Journal* sold at the biannual Ryder Cup international golf competition. When the event is finished, the magazine ceases, thus failing to meet the "intended to be continued indefinitely" criterion. Temporary magazines produce lucrative advertising revenue and are often "thick and glossy, coffee-table worthy,"[23] but are seldom collected by libraries.

What is the difference between a magazine and a journal? Chuck Dintrone outlined nine criteria for distinguishing between the two: authors, notes, style, editors, audience, advertisements, look, the contents, and index coverage. A magazine's authors are journalists or laypersons who write in a journalistic style for the general public on current events or general-interest topics. A journal's authors are experts who write in a scholarly style for a specialized audience on research topics. A magazine tends to have a glossy look and few, if any, footnotes; but it is likely to include advertisements and pictures (often in color) and to be covered by general indexes such as the *Readers' Guide to Periodical Literature*. In contrast, a journal tends to have a sedate look, footnotes and bibliographies, an editorial board, and outside reviewers as well as to be covered in specialized subject indexes; but it is less likely to have advertising or pictures.[24] Although not mentioned by Dintrone, magazines tend to have larger circulations than journals.

The preceding discussion focused on characteristics. At the risk of over-simplification, the defining difference is that a journal disseminates information to scholars, whereas a magazine entertains or informs the general public or a specialized interest group. Whether a particular title is a magazine or a journal is not always clear-cut and, in fact, might not make any difference for many library-processing functions. The Katzes's *Magazines for Libraries* contains many titles that are without doubt journals (e.g., *Libraries and Culture: A Journal of Library History).*[25]

According to the *ALA Glossary of Library and Information Science*, a *newspaper* is "a serial issued at stated, frequent intervals (usually daily, weekly, or semiweekly), containing news, opinions, advertisements, and other items of current, often local, interest."[26] Practically every community has a local newspaper. Several U.S. newspapers with circulations extending far beyond their local communities have achieved status as "national newspapers," for example, the *New York Times*, the *Washington Post*, or the *Los Angeles Times*. Other national newspapers, such as the *Wall Street Journal, USA Today*, or the *Christian Science Monitor*, do not serve a specific geographic locality. Ethnic newspapers, such as the *China Daily News* or *Novoe Russkoe Slovo*, represent another distinct type. Lubomyr R. Wynar and Anna T. Wynar define the American ethnic press "as consisting of newspapers and periodicals published either in English, in non-English, or bilingually, published by ethnic organizations or individuals in the United States, and specifically aimed at an ethnic readership."[27] In mid-1996 several hundred ethnic newspapers in at least 40 languages were published in the United States.[28] Although many people would consider *Computerworld* and the *Daily Racing Form* to be newspapers because of their appearance, they do not, according to Joseph A. Puccio, meet the technical definition. Puccio writes "to the library world, any publication that has a subject orientation and is reporting something other than general news is not a newspaper."[29]

The term *tabloid*, which is often used in association with newspapers, can have two meanings. One refers to physical format; the other is a derisive term applied to the sensation-seeking (some might even say "sleazy") news items frequently seen at grocery store checkout lines that proclaim Elvis sightings and alien abductions.

A *newsletter* is defined by the *ALA Glossary of Library and Information Science* as "a serial consisting of one or a few printed sheets containing news or information of interest chiefly to a special group."[30] The *Oxbridge Directory of Newsletters*, which in 1994 listed more than 20,000 newsletters published in the United States and Canada, states that newsletters raise revenue primarily through subscription sales rather than advertising "but there are many exceptions."[31]

A *house magazine* is defined in *Free Magazines for Libraries* as "a publication available without charge to its readers, carrying no paid advertising, and produced . . . with the intention of promoting the sponsor's interest." It can be distinguished from a trade publication, which deals with an entire industry, carries advertising, and charges a subscription fee. A house magazine may be "internal" (for employees only), "external" (for outsiders), or "combination" (for both employees and outsiders). Such publications are issued by both commercial entities—especially in the areas of manufacturing, banking, insurance, and utilities—and by the nonprofit sector—including government agencies, trade associations, universities, libraries, and foundations. Self-promotion of the sponsoring agency is often a prime motivation for publication. Examples of a house magazine would be the *Dartmouth College Library Bulletin* and the *Statistical Review of the Arkansas Employment Security Department*. This category often overlaps with newsletters.[32]

Little magazines form another genre. A little magazine may be viewed as the periodical equivalent of a small press monographic publication. They are "little" from two perspectives: circulation and the number of pages in an issue. "Their format is usually characterized by eccentricities in size, illustrations, and printing—all the way from mimeographed to conventional."[33]

A chapter in Katz's text on magazine selection lists six "principle characteristics" of little magazines:

1. Circulation seldom exceeds 500 to 2,000.

2. Financial support is primarily from subscription and donation with minimum advertising.

3. Most seldom survive more than a year or two due to poor financial support.

4. They are often difficult for librarians to deal with from a business perspective.

5. They may have unusual sizes and formats as well as inconsistent numbering.

6. They "are 'little' only in terms of circulation, not physical size . . . [which is] a far cry from the standard sizes" (somewhat repetitive of the previous point). Katz carefully distinguishes little magazines from literary reviews, the underground press, and established sociopolitical magazines such as the *National Review* or the *New Republic*.[34] *Formalist: A Journal of Metrical Poetry*, *Mississippi Mud*, and *Exquisite Corpse: A Journal of Books and Ideas* serve as examples of contemporary little magazines.

Literary reviews (sometimes simply called *reviews*) can be difficult to distinguish from little magazines. According to the Katzes, *literary reviews* contain "critical analysis and evaluation . . . [and] fiction, poetry, drama, interviews, and graphics, and they may extend their boundaries beyond pure literature to the arts, social commentary, politics, history, and other areas."[35] Some of the best-known literary reviews include the *Antioch Review*, the *Paris Review*, *Partisan Review*, and the *Southern Review*.

What is the difference between a little magazine and a review, as both contain literature as well as sociopolitical commentary? According to Clara D. Brown and Lynn S. Smith, reviews are such "close relatives" of little magazines that they may be called "hybrid littles." Brown and Smith note that reviews are usually published by colleges or universities and contain the word *review* in the title.[36]

Another closely related genre is the "underground press." Writing in the context of the 1960s, Katz asserted, "There is no completely satisfactory definition of the underground press," but then he stated they tended to be

- antiestablishment,

- opposed to the Vietnam War,

- in favor of "legalization of marijuana, but not necessarily all drugs,"

- "politically to the left,"

- culturally avant-garde,

- representative of the "under thirty" generation, and

- staffed by volunteers or poorly paid workers.[37]

The *East Village Other*, the *Berkeley Barb*, and the *Great Speckled Bird* were among the most famous underground press periodicals of the 1960s.

Another category sometimes confused with little magazines or the underground press are the "fanzines"—an obvious combination of the terms *fan* and *magazine*. Fredric Wertham defines *fanzines* as "uncommercial, nonprofessional, small-circulation magazines which their editors produce, publish, and distribute. They deal primarily with what they call fantasy literature and art."[38] Wertham defines some terms used in the fanzine world of the 1970s. A "poorly done" fanzine was a "crudzine" contrasted to a more professional looking "ultrazine." A "Gerzine" was a German fanzine, and underground comics were know as "undies."[39]

Zines developed from fanzines or fan magazines. Precise definitions of a zine are elusive. Even Mike Gunderloy and Cari Goldberg Janice, authors of a guide to zines, admit, "It's hard to say what defines a zine."[40] However, zines are characterized by self-publication on a nonprofit basis and typically focus on a specific subject.[41] They have been compared to the "low-tech print equivalent"[42] of a World Wide Web (WWW) home page where the creator has almost total autonomy. In 1995 the average zine was reported to have a run of 200 copies and a production cost of $500.[43] According to Chris Dodge, zines are "Notorious for their ephemeral nature . . . sloppy production values and dubious credibility."[44] Dodge further states, "Often produced by disaffected sorts, zines' contemporary audience is the same: marginalized people of all kinds."[45] Zines about their publishers' lives have been appropriately termed "personal zines." An example would be *Pathetic Life: Diary of a Fat Slob*, by Doug Holland.[46] Other categories of zines, as listed in Gunderloy and Janice's guide, include "fringe culture," comics, sports, hobbies, music, reviews, politics, literary, people, "love, sex & relationships," travel, spirituality, and "movies & television."[47]

Traditionally, most libraries have not collected zines to any appreciable extent. However, the New York State Library, the State Historical Society of Wisconsin, Michigan State University, and Washington State University reportedly have strong zine collections.[48] In any case, zines represent a significant cultural phenomenon that needs to be addressed in a survey of serial genres.

The term *newsstand magazine* has been used for magazines sold at newsstands, smoke shops, drug stores, groceries, or supermarkets.[49] Different categories of "newsstand magazines" have been identified as "sports,"[50] "detective,"[51] "bridal,"[52] "humor,"[53] and "confession"[54] magazines plus "superhero comic books."[55] Other types could also be named.

A *trade journal,* as discussed earlier, is devoted to a particular business or industry, carries advertising, and charges a subscription fee. An example would be *Blood-Horse,* which covers the thoroughbred horse racing industry. *Bank Card Industry Report* and *Drug Store Market Guide* are also trade journals.

Serials that support the reference function are called *reference serials*. Many of the most important sources in a reference department, such as abstracts, indexes, yearbooks, and almanacs, would be included in this category. In 1984 the journal *Reference Services Review* stated two criteria for defining reference serials:

1. they must be useful as reference sources, and

2. they must be issued as serials or be titles superseded periodically by new editions.[56]

One sometimes hears the term *controlled circulation* applied to a journal or serial. The *ALA Glossary* states these serials are "available (usually without charge) only to those specified by the authors or publisher."[57] They are usually intended for "designated market sectors at predetermined circulation levels."[58] *Ulrich's International Periodicals Directory* lists more than six thousand controlled-circulation serials.[59] Examples would be college or university alumni magazines (e.g., *Columbia College Today*), professional publications (e.g., the *Florida Independent Accountant*), state publications (such as *North Dakota's Highway Safety Plan*), or serials for hobbyists (such as the *Green Thumb Gardening Newsletter*). Controlled-circulation serials, contrary to what the term implies, are frequently available to libraries.[60]

Standing orders are sometimes confused with serials, yet the two are distinct concepts. A *standing order* is not a type of serial, but, as logically implied, a type of order. (Most serials are acquired by an order type known as "subscription.") Most, but not all, standing orders are for certain types of serials. For example, annuals (e.g., the *World Almanac* or the *UNESCO Yearbook*), are serial types that are commonly acquired through standing order. In library budgeting, serials and standing orders are sometimes grouped together because both represent continuing financial obligations on the library's part. The distinction between serials and standing orders can critically affect budgeting and technical services organization. For more detailed discussions of budgeting, see chapter 3.

SERIALS CLASSIFICATION SCHEMES

A serials or periodicals classification scheme systematically defines the categories of publications that compose the serials universe or a particular type of periodical. Theoretically, one should be able to place every title within a single category, although some schemes have overlapping, nonmutually exclusive categories. Over the years, many schemes have been proposed for serials in general or for various serial types. Because classification schemes can illustrate the functions serials perform and help impose order on the sometimes chaotic world of serial publications, this section reviews some representative examples.

As far back as 1937, J. Harris Gable classified periodicals into three broad categories: "Those intended to foster the interest of knowledge," such as professional journals; "those intended to foster the interests of a trade, profession, or society;" and "money-making ventures," for a popular audience, which Gable subdivided into ten groups: literary, fiction and short story, features, news and comment, family or women's magazines, reviews, juvenile, humorous, cheap story, and sex.[61]

G. Edward Evans, citing the work of F. Machlup and others, identifies the following serial categories: reports (annual, semiannual, quarterly, or occasional) of corporations or business organizations; society and association publications, "including yearbooks, almanacs, proceedings, transactions, memoirs, directories and reports;"[62] superseding serial services (e.g., telephone books and airline schedules); nonsuperseding serial services; newspapers; newsletters, news releases, and leaflets; news magazines, either weekly or monthly; popular magazines covering sports, fashion, sex, travel, humor, etc.; magazines offering a popular treatment of scholarly topics; magazines providing social, political, literary, artistic, or religious criticism; other magazines; nonspecialized journals for the well-informed intelligentsia; primary research journals for specialists; secondary research journals for specialists (i.e., reviews, literature surveys, and abstracts); professional journals in applied fields; parochial journals addressed to a local or regional audience; and government documents. Another of Machlup and others' category, "other serials," was rejected by Evans because he believes all serials can fit into the preceding scheme.[63]

Benjamin M. Compaine divides magazines into two categories: general interest, which appeal to a mass audience, and special interest, which are devoted to a specific topic.[64] E. W. Hildick also distinguishes between general and specialist magazines. He identifies four categories of the former (news, family, women's, and children's) and six of the latter (political, fan, hobbies and pastime, trade and professional, house, and literary).[65] Katz has divided magazines into three types:

1. general, "which attempts to be all things" to all people;

2. "less general special magazines," which focus on more limited groups; and

3. "highly specialized," which require specialized knowledge or interest on the part of readers.[66]

D. E. Davinson categorizes periodicals into four classes: those from learned and professional societies, house journals, "commercial ventures," and newspapers.[67]

Bernard Houghton identifies ten categories of scientific and technical journals:

1. primary journals of learned societies or professional institutions,

2. communications journals of learned societies or professional institutions,

3. general purpose journals of learned societies or professional institutions,

4. review journals of learned societies or professional institutions,

5. primary commercially published journals,

6. technical and trade commercially published journals,

7. "controlled-circulation" commercially published journals,

8. "prestige" house journals,

9. "information on products" house journals, and

10. internal house organs.[68]

Even fairly narrow periodical categories, such as ethnic publications, have been classified. In addition to general ethnic newspapers and periodicals, Wynar and Wynar identify 12 specific types: political and ideological, fraternal, religious, scholarly and academic, educational, professional and trade, cultural, youth-oriented, women-oriented, sports and recreational, veterans', and bibliographical periodicals.[69]

Apparently, a variety of schemes, often quite different, have been proposed, thus testifying to the variety and elusiveness of the serials format. The schemes typically merge such factors as audience, publisher, purpose, frequency, and subject. Most serials classification schemes do not address electronic publications, which are discussed in the next section.

ELECTRONIC JOURNALS AND OTHER ELECTRONIC PUBLICATIONS

In recent years, electronic journals have grown explosively, as have a variety of other electronic phenomena—including listservs—that have some of the characteristics of a serial. Accordingly, several important definitions should be addressed. What is an electronic serial? Are all titles termed "electronic journals" genuine serials? Is a listserv a serial?

No generally accepted standard definition exists for electronic serial publications. The terminology itself and the definitions have varied over time. Before the terms *electronic journal* and *e-journal* came into vogue, a variety of terms, including the "virtual journal," the "paperless journal," and the "online journal," were used.[70]

In 1992, D. Scott Brandt offered a definition applicable to early generation electronic journals: "In its broadest definition, an e-journal is some grouping of information which is sent out in electronic form with some periodicity."[71] Some definitions limit the concept to networked journals. For example, Gail McMillan defines electronic journals as "any serials produced, published, and distributed nationally and internationally via electronic networks such as Bitnet and the Internet."[72] Lawrence R. Keating II, Christa Easton Reinke, and Judi A. Goodman use "a scholarly journal delivered electronically over networks" as the definition.[73]

According to other definitions, an electronic counterpart of a print journal is not considered a genuine electronic journal. For instance, Marian Dworaczek and Victor G. Wiebe "consider a true e-journal to be a serial whose creation and distribution to the public is entirely in electronic format."[74] Tom Moothart reserves the term electronic journal for "those titles only available electronically" and uses the phrase "online journal" for "titles that have a print counterpart."[75] Other analysts use the term *networked* to distinguish journals available on the Internet from those that are on CD-ROMs.[76] Hazel Woodward and Cliff McKnight differentiate three types of electronic journals: online (which are available through a host such as DIALOG), CD-ROM, and networked, (i.e., on the Internet).[77] One might conclude that the terminological inconsistency reflects the fact that electronic journals themselves are in a state of flux, yet terminology for print serials and periodicals that have been in existence for centuries is still sometimes used inconsistently.

This book uses a broad definition of *electronic journal* to cover any serial or serial-like publication available in an electronic format. Accordingly, networked, nonnetworked, electronic only, and dual print and electronic titles are considered electronic journals. Conforming to Woodward and McKnight's terminology, this book uses *online* for journals available through such services as DIALOG and *networked* for journals on the Internet.

Note that many titles that call themselves and are generally referred to as "electronic journals" do not meet all the requirements of the AACR2R serial definition. Marilyn Geller states that many so-called electronic journals such as the *Journal of Electronic Publishing* or *Olive Tree* are really cumulative electronic archives to which articles are continuously added. However, they lack chronological or numeric order and the grouping of articles into issues.[78] In a similar vein, Ed Jones terms electronic indexing and abstracting services, such as *Library Literature,* "dynamic databases, in a perpetual state of cumulation (and not serial cumulation)."[79] In the online version, the new entries that are continuously added lead to new cumulations of the entire database without producing separate parts. Likewise, each quarterly *Library Literature* CD-ROM disk contains a total cumulation of the database back to 1984. In contrast, the print versions of indexes and abstracts are genuine serials because each issue represents a separate part. Print cumulations usually compile several previous issues but seldom the entire backrun of the service.

A related question concerns the classification of listservs. According to Sharon H. Domier's thoughtful analysis, electronic conferences and listservs share with serials the intention to continue indefinitely and a list of subscribers. A serial and an electronic conference are similar in that a serial has a publisher and an electronic conference has a host computer; a serial has an editor and an electronic conference has a list owner; and a serial is characterized by numerical or chronological numbering, while an electronic conference contains messages with a time and date. But Domier concludes that many electronic conferences "would seem to fail the 'serials' test because they do not have consecutive numbering schemes." She notes, however, that an electronic conference digest, which compiles and sends messages on a daily basis to designated users, could be considered a serial because of its consistent chronological organization.[80]

Crystal Graham and Rebecca Ringler have, perhaps facetiously, used *bibliographic hermaphrodite* to describe publications that display both monographic and serial features. They state that a bibliographic hermaphrodite possesses three characteristics: completeness in one part, the potential for updating, and the potential for indefinite continuation. Included in this category are listservs and electronic bulletin boards; WWW, gopher, and ftp (File Transfer Protocol) sites; online indexing and abstracting services; and Online Public Access Catalogs (OPACs). These publications are monographic by virtue of being complete in one part but serial in that they can continue indefinitely through limitless updating.[81]

The question of whether the AACR2R serials definition should be expanded was debated in *Serials Review*'s spring 1996 issue.[82] Geller argues that the profession should "start stretching the definition of a serial" to accommodate continuing electronic publications that are essentially serial even if they do not meet all the requirements of the AACR2R definition, (e.g., numbered parts that package articles).[83] Arguing that expanding the AACR2R definition would confuse the treatment of print serials, Graham and Ringler advocate a third category in addition to serials and monographs, based on Adele Hallam's *Cataloging Rules for the Description of Looseleaf Publications,* for items displaying both serial and monographic characteristics.[84]

Authoritative but probably not final answers to several of these issues are provided in the *CONSER Cataloging Manual, Module 31*, which addresses the cataloging of electronic serials. This document explicitly asserts that OPACs, gophers, listservs, WWW home pages, online services such as DIALOG, and listserv digests should not be considered serials. It also states that the "current serial/monograph distinctions may need reconsideration" because "the transition from print to online format may result in a serial becoming a monograph. For example, a directory issued semiannually in print can be updated continuously online without the existence of distinct issues or editions."[85]

In conclusion, a technical discussion of whether various electronic entities are authentic serials might appear somewhat academic. However, resolving these definitional issues can have practical implications for library operations, determining how and by whom electronic phenomena are cataloged and processed.

NOTES

1. Mary Ellen Soper, Larry N. Osborne, and Douglas L. Zweizig, with the assistance of Ronald R. Powell, *The Librarian's Thesaurus*, ed. Mary Ellen Soper (Chicago: American Library Association, 1990), 35-36. They state: "Many terms have been used to describe various kinds of serials, such as 'periodicals,' 'magazines,' 'newspapers,' 'annuals,' 'journals,' 'bulletins,' 'memoirs,' 'proceedings,' 'transactions,' 'papers,' and so on. But a closer look at these terms' overlapping definitions supports the contention that there are really few useful distinctions among these serial types."

2. Bill Katz, *Magazine Selection: How to Build a Community-Oriented Collection* (New York: R. R. Bowker, 1971), 1.

3. Michael Gorman and Paul W. Winkler, eds., *Anglo-American Cataloguing Rules*, 2d ed., 1988 revision (Ottawa: Canadian Library Association; London: Library Association Publishing; Chicago: American Library Association, 1988), 622.

4. Heartsill Young, ed., *ALA Glossary of Library and Information Science* (Chicago: American Library Association, 1983), 203.

5. Association for Library Collections and Technical Services, *Guidelines for Handling Library Orders for Serials and Periodicals*, rev. ed. (Chicago: American Library Association, 1992), 1.

6. Association for Library Collections and Technical Services, *Serials Acquisitions Glossary* (Chicago: Association for Library Collections and Technical Services, 1993), 27.

7. Soper, Osborne, and Zweizig, *The Librarian's Thesaurus*, 35.

8. Brian O'Connor, "Moving Image-Based Serial Publications," *Serials Review* 12 (summer and fall 1986): 20.

9. G. E. Gorman, "The Education of Serials Librarians in Australia: A Proposed Course in Serials Librarianship," *Serials Librarian* 17, nos. 1/2 (1989): 53.

10. Young, *ALA Glossary*, 166.

11. Association for Library Collections and Technical Services, *Serials Acquisitions Glossary*, 23.

12. Marcia Tuttle, *Managing Serials* (Greenwich, Conn.: JAI Press, 1996), 5.

13. Ibid., 3.

14. Ray Prytherch, comp., *Harrod's Librarians' Glossary: 9,000 Terms Used in Information Management, Library Science, Publishing, the Book Trades, and Archive Management*, 8th ed. (Aldershot, U.K.: Gower; Brookfield, Vt.: Ashgate, 1995), 580-81, defines a serial as "Any publication issued in successive parts, appearing at intervals . . . intended to be continued indefinitely. The term includes periodicals. . . ."

15. Dorothy C. Bailey, "Coping with a Binding Crisis," *Serials Review* 13 (winter 1987): 60.

16. N. Bernard Basch and Judy McQueen, *Buying Serials: A How-to-Do-It Manual for Librarians* (New York: Neal-Schuman, 1990), 3.

17. Marcia Tuttle, *Introduction to Serials Management* (Greenwich, Conn.: JAI Press, 1983), 8.

18. Andrew D. Osborn, *Serial Publications: Their Place and Treatment in Libraries*, 3d ed. (Chicago: American Library Association, 1980), 16-22.

19. Gorman and Winkler, *Anglo-American Cataloguing Rules*, 622.

20. Ibid.

21. Young, *ALA Glossary*, 125.

22. Ibid., *137*.

23. Stacy Lu, "Magazines You Won't Find in Publishers Clearinghouse," *New York Times* 145 (July 22, 1996): D7.

24. Chuck Dintrone, *What Is a Scholarly Journal?* Available: http://www.winona.msus.edu/is-f/library-f/scol-jou.txt (Accessed February 15, 1998).

25. Bill Katz and Linda Sternberg Katz, *Magazines for Libraries*, 8th ed. (New Providence, N.J.: R. R. Bowker, 1995), 766.

26. Young, *ALA Glossary*, 153.

27. Lubomyr R. Wynar and Anna T. Wynar, *Encyclopedic Directory of Ethnic Newspapers and Periodicals in the United States*, 2d ed. (Littleton, Colo.: Libraries Unlimited, 1976), 15.

28. Sreenath Sreenivasan, "As Mainstream Papers Struggle, the Ethnic Press Is Thriving," *New York Times* 145 (July 22, 1996): D7.

29. Joseph A. Puccio, *Serials Reference Work* (Englewood, Colo.: Libraries Unlimited, 1989), 16.

30. Young, *ALA Glossary*, 153.

31. *Oxbridge Directory of Newsletters, 1994* (New York: Oxbridge Communications, 1994), unnumbered preface.

32. Diane Jones Langston and Adeline Mercer Smith, *Free Magazines for Libraries*, 4th ed. (Jefferson, N.C.: McFarland, 1994), 1.

33. Clara D. Brown and Lynn S. Smith, *Serials: Past, Present and Future*, 2d rev. ed. (Birmingham, Ala.: EBSCO Industries, 1980), 7-8.

34. Katz, *Magazine Selection*, 100-102.

35. Katz and Katz, *Magazines for Libraries*, 709.

36. Brown and Smith, *Serials: Past, Present and Future*, 8.

37. Katz, *Magazine Selection*, 105-6.

38. Fredric Wertham, *World of Fanzines: A Special Form of Communication* (Carbondale, Ill.: Southern Illinois University Press, 1973), 33.

39. Ibid., *63-65.*

40. Mike Gunderloy and Cari Goldberg Janice, *World of Zines: A Guide to the Independent Magazine Revolution* (New York: Penguin Books, 1992), 2.

41. Ibid.

42. David M. Gross, "Zine Dreams," *New York Times Magazine* 145 (December 17, 1995), 72.

43. Ibid.

44. Chris Dodge, "Pushing the Boundaries: Zines and Libraries," *Wilson Library Bulletin* 69 (May 1995): 26.

45. Ibid., *28.*

46. Doug Holland, *Pathetic Life: Diary of a Fat Slob*, cited in J. Peder Zane, "Now, the Magazines of 'Me,' " *New York Times* 144 (May 14, 1995): sec. 4, p. 4.

47. Gunderloy and Janice, *World of Zines*, unnumbered table of contents.

48. Dodge, "Zines and Libraries," 27.

49. David Walter Lupton, "Newsstand Magazines: A Select Guide to Short Reviews," *Serials Review* 3 (October/December 1977): 59-60.

50. Jeffrey Levine, "Sports Magazines," *Serials Review* 7 (October/December 1981): 39-41.

51. Michael H. Randall, "Detective Magazines," *Serials Review* 6 (October/December 1980): 27-30.

52. Michael H. Randall, "Bridal Magazines," *Serials Review* 8 (summer 1982): 29-31.

53. Michael H. Randall, "Humor Magazines," *Serials Review* 7 (July/September 1981): 69-72.

54. Michael H. Randall, "Confession Magazines," *Serials Review* 7 (January/March 1981): 43-47.

55. Emily Alward, "Superhero Comic Books," *Serials Review* 8 (spring 1982): 33-38.

56. "Column Descriptions: Reference Serials," *Reference Services Review* 12 (fall 1984): 95.

57. Young, *ALA Glossary*, 58.

58. Association for Library Collections and Technical Services, *Serials Acquisitions Glossary*, 8.

59. *Ulrich's International Periodicals Directory, 1998*, 36th ed. (New York: R. R. Bowker, 1997), 5:10, 289-414.

60. Association for Library Collections and Technical Services, *Serials Acquisitions Glossary*, 8.

61. J. Harris Gable, *Manual of Serials Work* (Chicago: American Library Association, 1937), 19.

62. Several of these categories (e.g., yearbooks, almanacs, or directories) are also issued by commercial publishers.

63. G. Edward Evans, *Developing Library and Information Center Collections*, 2d ed. (Littleton, Colo.: Libraries Unlimited, 1987), 165-68, citing F. Machlup and others, *Information Through the Printed Word* (New York: New York University, 1978).

64. Benjamin M. Compaine, *The Business of Consumer Magazines* (White Plains, N.Y.: Knowledge Industry Publications, 1982), 16, cited in Puccio, *Serials Reference Work*, 18.

65. E. W. Hildick, *A Close Look at Magazines and Comics* (London: Faber Educational, 1966), cited in D. E. Davinson, *The Periodicals Collection: Its Purpose and Uses in Libraries* (London: Andre Deutsch, 1969), 35.

66. Katz, *Magazine Selection*, 2.

67. Davinson, *The Periodicals Collection*, 39-47.

68. Bernard Houghton, *Scientific Periodicals: Their Historical Development, Characteristics and Control* (Hamden, Conn.: Linnet Books, 1975), 32-41.

69. Wynar and Wynar, *Encyclopedic Directory*, 19-21.

70. Margo Sassé and B. Jean Winkler, "Electronic Journals: A Formidable Challenge for Libraries," *Advances in Librarianship* 17 (1993): 150.

71. D. Scott Brandt, "Campus-Wide Computing: Accessing Electronic Journals," *Academic and Library Computing* 9 (November-December 1992): 17-20.

72. Gail McMillan, "Embracing the Electronic Journal: One Library's Plan," *Serials Librarian* 21, nos. 2/3 (1991): 97.

73. Lawrence R. Keating II, Christa Easton Reinke, and Judi A. Goodman, "Electronic Journal Subscriptions," *Library Acquisitions: Practice and Theory* 17 (winter 1993): 456.

74. Marian Dworaczek and Victor G. Wiebe, "E-Journals: Acquisition and Access," *Acquisitions Librarian,* no. 12 (1994): 106.

75. Tom Moothart, "Migration to Electronic Distribution Through OCLC's Electronic Journals Online," *Serials Review* 21 (winter 1995): 61.

76. J. W. T. Smith, "Ejournal Def'n," *VPIEJ-L* (July 31, 1997).

77. Hazel Woodward and Cliff McKnight, "Electronic Journals: Issues of Access and Bibliographic Control," *Serials Review* 21 (summer 1995): 71.

78. Marilyn Geller, "A Better Mousetrap Is Still a Mousetrap," *Serials Review* 22 (spring 1996): 72-73.

79. Ed Jones, "Serials in the Realm of the Remotely-Accessible: An Exploration," *Serials Review* 22 (spring 1996): 77.

80. Sharon H. Domier, "Listservs Within the Pantheon of Written Materials," in *Advances in Serials Management: A Research Annual*, vol. 5, ed. Marcia Tuttle and Karen D. Darling (Greenwich, Conn.: JAI Press, 1995), 129-30.

81. Crystal Graham and Rebecca Ringler, "Hermaphrodites and Herrings," *Serials Review* 22 (spring 1996): 73-77.

82. Ellen Finnie Duranceau, "Old Wine in New Bottles? Defining Electronic Serials," *Serials Review* 22 (spring 1996): 69-79. This is the collective title for the entries listed in this chapter's "Further Reading" section by Marilyn Geller, Crystal Graham and Rebecca Ringler, Ed Jones, and Erik Jul.

83. Geller, "A Better Mousetrap Is Still a Mousetrap," 73.

84. Adele Hallam, *Cataloging Rules for the Description of Looseleaf Publications: With Special Emphasis on Legal Materials*. Washington, D.C.: Library of Congress, Office for Descriptive Cataloging Policy, 1986, cited in Graham and Ringler, "Hermaphrodites and Herrings," 76.

85. Melissa Beck, with the assistance of Bill Anderson, Les Hawkins, and Regina Reynolds, *CONSER Cataloging Manual, Module 31: Remote Access Computer File Serials*. Available: http://lcweb.loc.gov/acq/conser/module31.html (Accessed February 15, 1998).

FURTHER READING

Association for Library Collections and Technical Services. *Serials Acquisitions Glossary*. Chicago: Association for Library Collections and Technical Services, 1993.

Basch, N. Bernard, and Judy McQueen. "What Is a Serial?" In *Buying Serials: A How-to-Do-It Manual for Librarians*, 2-3. New York: Neal-Schuman, 1990.

Carson, Doris M. "What Is a Serial Publication?" *Journal of Academic Librarianship* 3 (September 1977): 206-9.

Geller, Marilyn. "A Better Mousetrap Is Still a Mousetrap." *Serials Review* 22 (spring 1996): 72-73.

Graham, Crystal, and Rebecca Ringler. "Hermaphrodites and Herrings." *Serials Review* 22 (spring 1996): 73-77.

Jones, Ed. "Serials in the Realm of the Remotely-Accessible: An Exploration." *Serials Review* 22 (spring 1996): 77-79.

Jul, Erik. "Revisiting Seriality and Periodicity." *Serials Review* 22 (spring 1996): 70-71.

Osborn, Andrew D. "Definition of a Serial." In *Serial Publications: Their Place and Treatment in Libraries*, 3-23. 3d ed. Chicago: American Library Association, 1980.

Prytherch, Ray, comp. *Harrod's Librarians' Glossary: 9,000 Terms Used in Information Management, Library Science, Publishing, the Book Trades, and Archive Management*. 8th ed. Aldershot, U.K.: Gower; Brookfield, Vt.: Ashgate, 1995.

Soper, Mary Ellen, Larry N. Osborne, and Douglas L. Zweizig, with the assistance of Ronald R. Powell. *The Librarian's Thesaurus*. Edited by Mary Ellen Soper. Chicago: American Library Association, 1990.

Tuttle, Marcia. "The Nature of Serials." In *Managing Serials*, 1-14. Greenwich, Conn.: JAI Press, 1996.

———. "The Serial: Its Definition and Place in the Library." In *Introduction to Serials Management*, 1-15. Greenwich, Conn.: JAI Press, 1983.

Young, Heartsill, ed. *ALA Glossary of Library and Information Science*. Chicago: American Library Association, 1983.

Chapter Two

History and Statistics

This chapter covers the historical development of serials, with special emphasis on electronic journals. It also addresses statistical data on serial output and prices, the effect of serial costs on library budgets, and the factors responsible for serial price increases.

THE HISTORICAL DEVELOPMENT OF SERIALS

Although Andrew D. Osborn's discussion of early serials history still stands as a valuable account (and is frequently cited in this chapter), the best historical work on serials appears to have been written by authors outside the field of library and information science. Allen Veaner's comment, made 13 years ago, that despite the "vast" literature on serials "surprisingly little has been published that deals comprehensively and universally with the history of the serial as a form per se,"[1] still remains essentially correct. However, some book-length historical studies have been written for specific types of serials, such as magazines (discussed in a subsequent section) and scientific journals, by David A. Kronick[2] and Bernard Houghton.[3] Greenwood Press has an important series, "Historical Guides to the World's Periodicals and Newspapers." Each volume, devoted to a particular category such as children's[4] or religious periodicals,[5] contains historical narratives and profiles for the genre's major titles.

This section covers the history of serials in general, the two major types of periodicals (scholarly journals and magazines), and some key events in dealing with and controlling serials. The description is based on secondary sources, with no attempt at comprehensive coverage.

General History of Serials

The origin of serials has been traced to antiquity. According to Osborn, annals written on the tombs of Egyptian kings during the first dynasty (2750–2625 B.C.) may possibly be considered the world's earliest known serials. He also mentions a decree by Julius Caesar in 60 B.C. requiring the proceedings of the Roman Senate to be published.[6]

Osborn divides serials history into four broad periods. The initial period, to 1700, witnessed "numerous forerunners of serial publications," including almanacs, annual book catalogs, and newsbooks. Weekly newspapers and periodicals arose during this period's latter part. In the second period, 1700 to 1825, daily newspapers replaced weeklies; and literary periodicals, gentleman's magazines, "proceedings" of learned societies, scientific periodicals, law reports, and parliamentary papers flourished. The third period, 1825 to 1890, was characterized by great expansion in the number of periodicals and their circulation, especially in the post-Civil War era. This growth was fueled by technological developments leading to high-speed printing and an adequate paper supply and such cultural factors as the "popularization of knowledge" and the growth of science and technology. The period witnessed the origin of illustrated magazines, and trade publications, children's magazines (e.g., *Youth's Companion*), and women's periodicals (e.g., *Godey's Lady's Book*) flourished. Moreover, "there were innumerable . . . government publications at the local, state, and federal level. This was also the golden age of the newspaper." Osborn's fourth period, from 1890, saw a "vast . . . proliferation" of periodicals in an "era of mass communications . . . made possible by cheap paper." Tabloid newspapers, pulp magazines, sports magazines, and periodicals for men grew in number. "Little magazines," the "underground" press, and radical political publications were typical of this period, and technical reports, indexing and abstracting services, and publications from international organizations played an increasingly important role.[7] Published in 1980, Osborn's scheme obviously predates the electronic journal.

The existence of journals and magazines inevitably resulted in the need to access their content. Accordingly, what might be termed *secondary serials,* consisting of indexes and abstracts, developed to facilitate use of the primary literature. The first cumulative index, was published in Holland in 1683 to what many consider the world's first scholarly journal, *Journal des Sçavans.*[8] The initial serial abstracting service began in 1830. By 1950 there were 300 abstracting journals worldwide,[9] and the 1998 edition of *Ulrich's International Periodicals Directory* notes the existence of 800 indexing and abstracting services.[10] The *Index to Periodical Literature* was begun by William Frederick Poole in 1848 and continued publication until 1907. In 1900 H. W. Wilson began publishing the *Readers' Guide to Periodical Literature.*[11] Carolyn Ulrich, the former head of the New York Public Library's periodicals division, published in 1932 *Periodicals Directory: A Classified Guide to a Selected List of Current Periodicals Foreign and Domestic*, forerunner of the illustrious *Ulrich's International Periodicals Directory.*[12]

The footnote as a scholarly convention dates to the nineteenth century.[13] During the 1920s scholars began counting footnotes (technically termed *citations* or *references*) for journal ranking and other purposes. The Institute for Scientific Information (ISI) founded the *Science Citation Index* in 1961, the *Social Sciences Citation Index* in 1973, and the *Arts and Humanities Citation Index* in 1978. See chapters 5 and 7 for further details.

Impact of Technology on Serials

Technology has affected serials from several perspectives, and its role in the historical development of serials is briefly discussed here.

The invention of movable print typesetting in the fifteenth century, attributed to Johannes Gutenberg, undoubtedly helped lay the groundwork for the earliest journals. Since the 1820s, when machine-driven typesetting began development, increasingly sophisticated technology has contributed to the production of print serials. By the mid-twentieth century, photographic typesetting was playing a major role, and powerful computerized methods have developed in recent decades.[14] During the 1980s, authors began submitting journal articles in word-processed format, and in the 1990s, via the Internet.

Microform technology, invented in 1839 by John Benjamin Dancer,[15] has had profound implications for serials. According to William F. Birdsall, by the 1920s, microform technology was "attracting the interest of many of the most innovative librarians, scholars, scientists and engineers."[16] During the 1930s, the esteemed scientist Vannevar Bush proposed and developed a "rapid selector" machine for speedy retrieval of microformat documents—apparently a forerunner of the famous Memex that Bush described in the July 1945 *Atlantic Monthly*.[17] The *Journal of Wildlife Diseases* is somewhat noteworthy in periodical history because it was published on microfiche. This journal was produced from typewritten manuscripts to avoid typesetting costs.[18]

During the technological explosion of the 1980s, serials often appeared in nonprint formats. For example, the *Journal of Cell Motility* included a videodisc supplement,[19] and some magazines were issued on disk, such as *I.B. Magazette*, *Loadstar*, *Microzine*, *Softdisk*, and *OCLC Micro*, which was also issued in a print format.[20] The historical evolution of electronic journals is discussed in following sections.

History of Scholarly Journals

The journal dates from the mid-seventeenth century. As noted by Derek J. de Solla Price, prior to that time, "the device of the scientific paper had not yet been invented, and men did not publish until they thought they had mastered completely some whole department of science and could produce a definitive book."[21]

A major impetus to the origin of scholarly journals was the founding of national academies devoted to the study of science. Between 1635 and 1752, at least 11 such academies were founded in Paris, London, Bologna, Berlin, Lyons, Milan, Uppsala, St. Petersburg, Philadelphia, and Göttingen. Perhaps the most famous of these is the Royal Society of London, founded in 1645 and officially chartered in 1662.[22] The origin of the modern university, the experimental method's widespread adoption by scientists,[23] and the development of a dependable European postal system[24] were other factors during the sixteenth and seventeenth centuries that helped lay the groundwork for scholarly journals.

On January 5, 1665, a weekly publication called *Journal des Sçavans*, considered "the first true scholarly journal"[25] by many authorities, began in Paris[26] under the direction of Denis de Sallo.[27] Osborn reports that the first issue's preface stated five objectives, including listing major European books, publishing obituaries, recording advances in the sciences, and citing civil and ecclesiastical court decisions.[28] In its early years, the primary emphasis was on the listing and reviewing of books. Publication was suspended during the French Revolution in December 1792; when publication resumed in August 1816, the periodical was renamed *Journal des Savants*.[29]

In March 1665, the Royal Society of London began publishing a monthly periodical titled *Philosophical Transactions: Giving Some Account of the Present Undertakings, Studies, and Labours of the Ingenious in Many Considerable Parts of the World*, edited by Henry Oldenburg.[30] Thankfully, the subtitle was dropped after a short time! Oldenburg's extensive correspondence with European scientists, based on his travels, international connections, and position as Royal Society secretary, formed the journal's "raw material,"[31] thus illustrating, in Osborn's words, "the historical connection between scholarly correspondence and the periodical press."[32] David C. Taylor humorously comments, "I like to imagine the librarian at the Bodleian Library in Oxford receiving the first issue of *Philosophical Transactions* in March 1665 with great displeasure. 'What, another journal? What purpose can possibly be served by another scholarly periodical when we already have one!' "[33]

Other academies and societies began publishing scholarly journals. In 1684, an academy in Holland issued *Nouvelles de la Republique des Lettres. Memoires* of the Academy of Sciences in Russia began in 1728. Benjamin Franklin founded the *Transactions of the American Philosophical Society* in 1771.[34] Yet many of the journals founded during the seventeenth and eighteenth centuries ceased existence after a year or two.[35]

Although the earliest journals dealt with science or scholarship in general, Veaner notes that journals eventually appeared for specific disciplines—the initial step in what is now called *twigging*[36]—the division of knowledge into smaller and smaller units. Kronick identifies *Medicina Curiosa, or a Variety of New Communications in Physick, Chirurgery and Anatomy*, of which two issues were published in 1684, as Great Britain's first medical journal.[37] Veaner cites as examples of early disciplinary journals the *Transactions of the Geological Society of London*, founded in 1811; the *Memoirs of the Royal Astronomical Society*, which began in 1825; and the Chemical Society's *Journal*, started in 1848.[38]

Charles B. Osburn comments that the "increasing importance" of universities during the last half of the seventeenth century through the end of the nineteenth century helped shape scholarly journal output. He states that "in the bureaucratic structure of academia, areas of specialization were developed in ever-narrowing subfields," leading to the creation of new journals in these specializations. Moreover, by the mid-1800s most journals were aimed at specialized audiences of scientists[39]—a trend that has intensified in the twentieth century. In 1989, the Association of Research Libraries (ARL) Serials Prices Project identified the academic promotion and tenure system as a major cause of serials proliferation.[40]

The so-called critical reviews, which appeared in the early nineteenth century, might be viewed as forerunners of humanities journals. According to Donald Davinson, the *Edinburgh Review*, first published in 1802, served as a model for others, including the *Quarterly Review*, founded in 1809; *Westminster Review*, started in 1824; and the *Athenaeum*, which began in 1826. Although their chief function was entertainment, these reviews were generally characterized by lower circulations and more scholarly content (literature plus social and political commentary) than mere magazines.[41] Osburn speculates that by the 1850s "the humanities journal evolved from one serving the tastes of the amateur of letters into a form serving the more scientifically oriented needs of specialist scholars."[42]

In 1975 Houghton outlined the rapid growth in the number of scientific journals during the three centuries after the first ones were founded. Citing various authoritative sources, Houghton estimated the number of published scientific periodicals at 30 in 1700, 330 in 1730, 750 in 1800, 5,100 in 1885, 8,600 in 1895, 25,000 in

1920, 36,000 in 1930, 50,000 in 1950, 60,000 in 1960, and 75,000 in 1970.[43] In 1984, Osburn estimated there were 100,000 scientific and technical journals.[44]

Although his figures vary from Houghton's, Price observed in 1961 that the growth in the number of scientific journals follows an exponential pattern. He estimated their number multiplies by a factor of ten roughly every half century. Starting with the initial journal in 1665, he calculated there were 10 scientific journals by 1750, 100 by 1800, 1,000 by the mid-nineteenth century, 10,000 by 1900, and 100,000 sometime in the middle of the twentieth century. Price projected 1,000,000 journals by the year 2000, further reckoning that the number of scientific journals doubles approximately every 15 years.[45] Ironically, Price commented that the number of journals had "reached a point of absurdity" around 1830, as no scientist could possibly read everything of interest![46] Although frequently cited, Price's data have been questioned by some. K. P. Barr points out that Price's figures represent the total number of journals that had been founded without considering cessations.[47]

The role scholarly journals played as a formal communications device among scientists is clear from the earlier discussion. Previously, the primary means of communication among scientists were such informal mechanisms as letters and travel for personal meetings.[48] In 1995—more than three centuries after the *Journal des Savants* and *Philosophical Transactions* were founded—Pieter A. van Brakel outlined four functions performed by scholarly journals: building a collective knowledge base; communicating information; distributing such rewards as recognition, priority, and funding; and building scientific communities.[49]

History of Magazines

The history of magazines has been documented in more detail than has scholarly journal history, perhaps due to the former's contribution to social history and popular culture. Book-length general histories of magazines have been written by Frank Luther Mott,[50] James Playsted Wood,[51] John Tebbel,[52] John Tebbel and Mary Ellen Zuckerman,[53] and Theodore Peterson;[54] the history of early American magazines has been addressed by Lyon N. Richardson.[55] Greenwood Press's "Historical Guides to the World's Periodicals and Newspapers" includes volumes on Southern U.S. magazines,[56] humor and comic magazines,[57] and U.S. popular religious magazines.[58]

Although the first periodicals disseminated scholarly knowledge, periodicals whose chief purpose was to entertain (what would now be termed *magazines*) emerged during the late seventeenth and early eighteenth centuries. Davinson names *Athenian Mercury*, founded about 1690, and *Ladies Mercury*, began a few years later, as the earliest popular periodicals.[59] *The Tatler*, a periodical founded in England by Richard Steele in 1709, has been identified by Clara D. Brown and Lynn S. Smith as "the first popular magazine."[60] Two years later, in 1711, Joseph Addison founded his equally famous *Spectator*.[61] *The Gentleman's Magazine*, founded in 1731, was supposedly the first periodical to use the word *magazine* in its title.[62] The late eighteenth century witnessed the creation in industrialized nations of "periodical clubs" whose members pooled financial resources to purchase periodicals to share among themselves.[63]

The history of magazine publishing in America is usually dated to 1741. On February 13 of that year Andrew Bradford, a Philadelphia printer, first published *American Magazine, or A Monthly View of the Political State of the British Colonies*. Three days later, Benjamin Franklin brought out *The General Magazine, and Historical Chronicle, for All the British Plantations in America*, although he apparently conceptualized the idea in 1740.[64]

The post-Civil War period saw the development of mass-market magazines. Major magazines founded in the late nineteenth century were the *Saturday Evening Post* and the *Ladies Home Journal*. For a detailed analysis of American magazine history from 1741 to 1905, see Mott's excellent multivolume study, *A History of American Magazines*, which is often considered a classic.

The number of magazines and their circulation continued to expand throughout the twentieth century. The total circulation of all U.S. magazines increased from 65 million in 1900 to more than 391 million by 1958.[65] Contributing factors included an increasing population, a higher level of education, more affluence, more leisure time, and the impact of advertising revenue.[66] During the twentieth century, several magazine publishers built financial empires and became major social or political personalities, such as Henry Luce (*Time* and *Life*), DeWitt Wallace (*Reader's Digest*), and Hugh Hefner (*Playboy*).

A major historical trend is the development of specialized magazines for hobbies, professions, reading interests, types of people, etc. Examples of magazine genres include sports, humor, regional interest, mystery, detective, confession, and western. The *National Directory of Magazines* recently listed magazines in more than 200 subject categories.[67] Tebbel and Zuckerman exaggerate only slightly when they state " there is no interest known to mankind which does not have at least one magazine to serve it."[68] A few types of magazines are discussed below.

The post-World War I era witnessed the development of an avant-garde literary genre known as "little magazines." Bill Katz asserts that little magazines were devoted to "idealistic radicalism" during the 1930s, "new criticism" in the 1940s, the Beats in the 1950s, and "politically oriented criticism and more controversial literary expression" during the tumultuous 1960s.[69] The number of little magazines in the United States reportedly increased from fewer than 200 in 1952 to more than 5,000 by 1995.[70]

A related genre that emerged in the 1960s was the "underground press." The *Village Voice*, first published in New York City's Greenwich Village on October 26, 1955, "marked the official birth of the underground newspaper."[71] Other prominent underground newspapers of the 1960s were the *Los Angeles Free Press*, the *Berkeley Barb*, and the *East Village Other*.

Yet another genre somewhat comparable to little magazines and the underground press is the "fanzines" that developed during the 1930s. Fredric Wertham asserts that the first fanzine was *The Comet*, published in 1930 and dealing with science and science fiction.[72]

Zines, small underground publications that defy easy definition, "emerged from the punk rock scene of the 1970s."[73] During the 1980s, a so-called zine revolution took place, no doubt aided by technological developments (e.g., the personal computer and desktop publishing software) that made self-publication easy. The historical origin of zines has been linked by Chris Dodge to the 1930s fanzines, high school underground newspapers, minicomics, and literary small-press publications. *Factsheet Five*, founded in 1982 by Mike Gunderloy, played a major role in the proliferation of this genre during the 1980s by publishing reviews of other zines.[74] Noteworthy contemporary zines include *Subterranean Pop* and *Ersatz*. In mid-1995 the number of zines was estimated to range from 20,000 to 50,000, approximately double the number that existed in 1990.[75] Due to their ephemeral nature, calculating the precise number of zines is difficult. By the mid-1990s, zines obtained a degree of mainstream acceptance, as Barnes & Noble was "selling zines with bar codes."[76]

Important trends in magazine publishing during the 1990s include competitive pressures that in combination with other factors often resulted in declining circulation; decreasing newsstand sales; mergers, acquisitions, and consolidation within the industry; an increasingly international market with separate language and national editions; and the creation of magazine World Wide Web (WWW) pages. The Electronic Newsstand, for marketing magazines over the Internet, was launched in July 1993.[77] Tebbel and Zuckerman state that in 1990 there were 22,000 magazines "deserving of the name" in the United States, although they acknowledge other estimates vary widely from this figure.[78] The number of newsstand magazines was reported as 3,300 in 1994.[79]

Each year during the 1990s, Samir Husni, a journalism faculty member at the University of Mississippi, calculated the number of newly founded magazines based on weekly surveys of bookstores and newsstands in Memphis, Tennessee—a seemingly unscientific method, but Husni claims, "There is no other way."[80] He calculated the number of newly founded magazines in the United States at 679 in 1992, 789 in 1993,[81] and 832 in 1994. For each year from 1990 through 1993, the largest category of new magazines dealt with sex, but in 1994 sexually oriented magazines fell into second place after sports.[82] More recent data are not available.

Organizational Responses to Serials

Besides serials themselves, another historical aspect concerns actions taken in response to the growing number of serials, their perceived importance to libraries and the scholarly communications process, and increasing awareness of associated problems such as cost and bibliographical control. These actions might be termed the *organizational response* to serials. A select number of key developments are addressed in this section.

Serial Subscription Agents

Serial subscription agents originated during the nineteenth century. William H. Huff states, "The beginnings may be found in the development of specialization in handling reviews and journals by certain booksellers early in the nineteenth century."[83] Gustav E. Stechert, headquartered on East Sixteenth Street in New York City, began marketing foreign serials in 1872. According to Huff, who scanned advertisements in *Library Journal*, other periodical sellers of the 1870s were Lemcke & Buechner and A. S. Clark—both also located in New York City.[84] The F. W. Faxon company traces its origin to the Boston Book Company, which was founded in 1881 as a publisher of law books. It later developed a library department, which specialized in journal subscriptions and back issues. Frederick W.

Faxon purchased the library department in 1918, thus founding the Faxon company.[85] Founded in 1879 as a bookshop at Oxford in the United Kingdom, the B. H. Blackwell company began providing periodical services to libraries in 1919.[86] By the mid-1990s, more than 250 serial subscription agents were listed in a standard directory.[87] The functions performed by contemporary subscription agents are covered in chapter 8.

The ISSN System

The development of the International Standard Serial Number (ISSN) and the ISSN Network during the late 1960s and early 1970s represented a major step toward achieving bibliographical control of serial titles and was termed by Marcia Tuttle "one of the top two or three most crucial events in the world of serials."[88] Jim E. Cole has written about this system's historical development.[89]

The ISSN is an internationally accepted code for identifying a specific serial title and distinguishing serials with similar titles. It has recently been incorporated into bar codes for identifying specific issues and articles. ISSN is linked with a key title, "a standardized form of the title derived from information in the serial issue,"[90] created at the time the number is assigned. The ISSN is used by publishers, libraries, serial subscription agents, copyright centers, and post offices. If a serial title changes, a new ISSN is required. An ISSN consists of eight characters separated by a hyphen and preceded by the letters "ISSN." The first seven characters are always digits zero through nine; the eighth character, a control digit, can sometimes be an X.[91] A typical ISSN, found on the cover of *Library Acquisitions: Practice and Theory*, is ISSN 0364-6408. An ISSN can be assigned to a serial in any format (e.g., paper, CD-ROM, electronic, microformat, etc.).[92]

The ISSN Network, originally referred to as the International Serials Data System (ISDS), is composed of an international center in Paris and national centers throughout the world[93]—67 as of the summer of 1997.[94] The ISDS International Centre in Paris was established in a series of agreements between the French government and the United Nations Educational, Scientific, and Cultural Organization (UNESCO) in the early and mid-1970s. The International Centre's responsibilities include assigning numbers to serials issued by international organizations or published in countries without international centers, assisting with establishing and operating national centers, and coordinating the work of the entire system.[95] In early 1995 the ISSN International Centre set up a bilingual English-French ISSN Home Page on the WWW.[96] By December 31, 1996, ISSNs had been assigned to 801,522 serials, of which 516,918 were periodicals.[97]

The U.S. center of the ISSN Network is represented by the National Serials Data Program (NSDP), created in 1972. It is administered through the Library of Congress as a section in the Processing Department's Serial Record Division.[98] The program registers and assigns ISSNs to all serials cataloged by the three U.S. national libraries: the Library of Congress, the National Library of Medicine, and the National Agricultural Library, or added to the Cooperative Online Serials Program (CONSER) database.[99]

The National Periodicals Center

During the 1970s, a strong movement developed within the United States for the creation of a National Periodicals Center to be modeled after the British Library Lending Division. In fact, a site for the center was selected in Dallas, Texas. The plan envisaged maintaining a large periodical collection from which articles requested by libraries would be rapidly supplied for only a nominal processing fee. Opposition to the concept developed among some librarians and publishers, and the necessary legislation was never enacted by Congress. By 1986, Judith Segal, a serials specialist, wrote that the National Periodicals Center "seems to have been dropped from all agendas."[100] Currently, technology rather than a national warehouse is generally viewed as the most promising potential solution to the serials problem. See Susan J. Webreck's encyclopedia article for a full history of the National Periodicals Center.[101]

Serials Groups

During the last two decades, some "serials groups" have formed to promote discussion among librarians, publishers, and serials agents about the problems posed by serials. The United Kingdom Serials Group (UKSG) was officially founded in 1978 during its first annual conference at St. John's College in York.[102] The UKSG holds annual conferences, publishes *Serials: The Journal of the United Kingdom Serials Group*, and, in cooperation with other organizations, has promoted seminars and European Serials Conferences.

The North American Serials Interest Group (NASIG) was "patterned after" UKSG. An organizational meeting for the creation of NASIG took place at the 1985 ALA annual conference in Chicago, and the first NASIG meeting was conducted at Bryn Mawr College in June 1986.[103] Since then, it has held annual conferences. NASIG's publications include the NASIG *Newsletter* and the conference proceedings, which have also been published in *Serials Librarian*. NASIG also operates a WWW site (see appendix 3). Tuttle reports that organizations comparable to the UKSG and NASIG have been formed in Australia, China, Europe, and South Asia.[104]

The ARL Serials Prices Project

In response to a concern about the effects of rising serials costs on library budgets, the ARL began its Serials Prices Project in spring 1988. The project commissioned two separate studies of serials prices, by the Economic Consulting Services and by Ann Okerson.[105] Okerson compiled useful data about serials pricing and library budget trends. Her study concluded by recommending three policies for the ARL: to publicize the serious impact of the serials crisis; to encourage the creation of non-profit alternatives to commercial publishers; and to advocate changing promotion, tenure, and grant-funding policies to minimize current pressure for excessive publication.[106] Findings from the ARL Serials Prices Project are cited later in the chapter.

HISTORY AND GROWTH OF THE ELECTRONIC JOURNAL

Because the electronic journal is arguably the most exciting recent development in the serials arena, its history deserves an in-depth examination.

Early History

The electronic journal's historical evolution has been traced to a 1960 UNESCO report that advocated use of computer technology to help solve the problems of traditional journal publishing.[107] *Mental Workload*, dealing with human-machine interactions in complex systems, has been identified as the first full-fledged electronic journal. It was issued in 1980 at the New Jersey Institute of Technology and funded by the National Science Foundation. *Mental Workload* was refereed, edited, and copyrighted the same as a print journal. However, articles separately became available as soon as they were published. An author-title index and article abstracts were available online, and readers could print the full text of an article. The editors planned to attach readers' commentary to articles, although this idea was apparently never implemented. According to Margo Sassé and B. Jean Winkler, its relatively quick failure can be attributed to software problems, the reluctance of scholars to submit manuscripts, and the fact it was distributed only in the United States due to a disagreement with the British Post Office concerning transatlantic telecommunications. This experiment is sometimes called the Electronic Information Exchange System (EIES) project after the computer conferencing system at the New Jersey Institute of Technology on which it was published.[108]

The Birmingham Loughborough Electronic Network Development (BLEND) project, a transatlantic counterpart to EIES, took place in the United Kingdom during the early 1980s. The project—a cooperative venture between the University of Loughborough and the University of Birmingham—produced a journal entitled *Computer Human Factors*, which was "designed to accept, referee, edit, and archive articles electronically."[109] The BLEND project resulted in two issues of *Computer Human Factors,* each containing two refereed articles. However, it failed for essentially the same reasons that lead to the demise of *Mental Workload*.[110] Both the EIES and BLEND projects illustrated the importance of "human factors" (i.e., although the electronic medium allowed more rapid editing and refereeing, there were still "human delays in getting down to work").[111]

In 1982, based on the EIES project experience, Murray Turoff and Starr Roxanne Hiltz outlined four potential forms for the electronic journal of the future:

1. an informal newsletter;

2. an unrefereed "Paper Fair" to which any member of an electronic conference system can submit a paper that can be read and commented upon by other members;

3. an electronic form of the traditional print journal; and

4. "a highly structured inquiry-response system" in which a member of an electronic network submits an "inquiry," receives "responses"

from other members, and compiles the responses into a "brief" for distribution to other members.[112]

Fifteen years later, apparently all four of these forms evolved to some degree. Electronic newsletters and equivalents of traditional print journals now abound. The "Paper Fair" is quite similar to a contemporary preprint server, and "a highly structured inquiry-response system" bears a remarkable resemblance to what often takes place on a listserv or electronic conference.

In the mid-1980s, *Electronic Social Psychology* (ESP), covering a wide range of social psychology topics, was described in the literature. Subscribers to this fee-based journal required a modem and membership in the Source, a commercial computer network that maintained ESP on a mainframe computer. Subscribers also received electronic mail (e-mail) services, access to a bulletin board and a computer conference, and the opportunity to communicate with each other through the Source's Chat service. ESP was not refereed, but readers rated each article on a one-to-nine scale and added a single line of commentary. A printed version was distributed to subscribers twice a year for archival purposes.[113]

New Horizons in Adult Education, a refereed electronic journal, was first issued in fall 1987. Initiated and run by Syracuse University graduate students, it was distributed for free on a BITNET listserv.[114] This title was recently called "the first widely recognized scholarly electronic journal."[115]

Several electronic journals—some of which are now quite well-known—began publication in 1990. These early generation journals often used e-mail or listservs to send issues to subscribers. The *Public-Access Computer Systems Review*, a free, nonpeer-reviewed journal, was first published by the University of Houston Libraries in January 1990, and the second issue appeared in June. The table of contents for each of the three yearly issues was sent to members of PACS-L, a BITNET computer conference established by the University of Houston Libraries in 1989, as well as other subscribers. They would then issue appropriate commands to obtain specific articles by file transfer. A companion volume focusing on vendor releases and current news items, the *Public-Access Computer System News*, began publication in March 1990.[116]

The first issue of the *Journal of the International Academy of Hospitality Research*, a peer-reviewed publication in hotel, restaurant, and institutional management and tourism, was released via listserv over BITNET and the Internet on November 26, 1990, with the second on February 20, 1991. This subscription-based title was published by the Scholarly Communications Project of Virginia Polytechnic Institute and State University. Each issue consisted of a single article.[117]

Also founded in 1990, at North Carolina State University, was the now well-known journal *Postmodern Culture*. Dealing with contemporary literature and culture, this journal's table of contents was distributed via e-mail three times a year. Subscribers could then issue listserv commands to receive one or more articles or the entire issue free of charge. For a subscription price, the journal was also available on a computer disk or microfiche.[118]

Ejournal, which addressed the implications of electronic publishing for an audience of humanists, was first published at the State University of New York at Albany in spring 1991 using listserv technology.[119] *Current Cites*, composed of citations to recent articles dealing with information technology, began electronic distribution through the University of California's MELVYL system in February 1991 and through PACS-L in fall 1991.[120]

The Online Journal of Current Clinical Trials (OJCCT), sponsored jointly by the American Society for the Advancement of Science (AAAS) and OCLC Online Computer Library Center was founded, among other reasons, in response to the need for the rapid dissemination of information in clinical medicine. OJCCT, launched on July 1, 1992, was reportedly the first electronic journal in the area of science to be peer-reviewed. Unlike most of the earliest electronic journals, which were free, in 1993 a subscription to OJCCT cost $110 per year.[121] This was the beginning of OCLC's Electronic Journals Online program, which included *Online Journal of Knowledge Synthesis for Nursing*, *Applied Physics Letters Online*, and *Immunology Today Online*.[122]

Developments during the early 1990s testify to the burgeoning interest in electronic journals. The first meeting of the Association of Electronic Scholarly Journals took place in October 1990 at North Carolina State University.[123] *VPIEJ-L*, an online discussion group devoted to electronic journals, was founded in the mid-1990s at the Virginia Polytechnic Institute and State University.[124] Also during the early 1990s, some seminars or conferences devoted to electronic journals were organized. Typical examples include a seminar at Bond University in May 1992, sponsored by the Australian Serials Special Interest Group and the Australian Council of Libraries and Information Services,[125] or the "International Conference on Refereed Electronic Journals," held at the University of Manitoba in Winnipeg, Manitoba, Canada, during October 1993.[126] By the late 1990s, too many conferences to enumerate had been held on the topic of electronic journals.

Perhaps the best-known electronic journal within the discipline of library and information science is the *Newsletter on Serials Pricing Issues*, whose history has been chronicled by its editor, Marcia Tuttle.[127] This newsletter was first issued on February 27, 1989, in both paper and electronic format.[128] Due to the high cost of producing the paper copy as well as its "lack of timeliness," the paper format was discontinued at the end of 1989, and the *Newsletter on Serials Pricing Issues* converted to an electronic-only format with number 14 in 1990.[129] Of considerable relevance to this book's subject is the Serials in Libraries Discussion Forum (SERIALST), founded in October 1990 at the University of Vermont. It is devoted to almost all topics pertinent to serials management in libraries. On November 25, 1991, SERIALST converted from an unmoderated to a moderated forum.[130] Also worth noting is NewJour, a moderated discussion list for announcing "newly planned, newly issued, or revised" electronic journals or newsletters. It also covers new electronic versions of previously established print periodicals. NewJour, administered by the ARL , was founded in August 1993.[131] The Web site where it is archived is discussed in appendix 3.

Electronic Journal Projects

The electronic journal's relative newness generated many experimental projects during the past decade to address both technical and user issues. Some of these projects are discussed in the following paragraphs.

Project QUARTET, conducted in the United Kingdom during the late 1980s and early 1990s, created on an experimental basis the world's first hypertext-based electronic journal, entitled *HyperBit*. This journal, a version of Taylor and Francis's established print serial *Behavior and Information Technology*, was designed and constructed by Cliff McKnight, Andrew Dillon, and John Richardson, and Project QUARTET was funded by the British Library Research and Development Department. *HyperBit* was intended for personal use rather than providing archival copy for libraries.[132]

The Chemistry Online Retrieval Experiment (CORE) project was a collaborative effort on the part of the American Chemical Society, Bellcore, the Chemical Abstracts Service, Cornell University's Mann Library, and OCLC. Twenty print journals published by the American Chemical Society were digitized to provide online access for the 1991-1994 issues to faculty and students at Cornell University. A total of 400,000 pages were digitized. Actual testing by users took place between April 1993 and May 1995.[133] Initial evaluation of the experiment indicated that users were most satisfied with the "ease of access" provided by the online format. In contrast, dissatisfaction was expressed about the perception that scrolling through screens is more cumbersome than flipping through pages, that the print format allowed the reader to assume a more comfortable position, and that it was impossible to highlight, underline, or annotate on the terminal screen.[134]

A similar electronic journal experiment, termed Red Sage, originated in an August 1992 agreement among AT&T Bell Laboratories, Springer Verlag, and the University of California at San Francisco.[135] Following a one-year pilot project, it was announced at the 1993 Frankfurt Book Fair that more than 40 print journals, including the prestigious *New England Journal of Medicine*; 16 biology journals published by Wiley; and 24 Springer-Verlag molecular biology and radiology journals would be made available for a two-year period beginning January 1, 1994, to students and faculty at the University of California at San Francisco Medical School. The journals were distributed through the Unix computer operating system using AT&T's Right Pages software, which automatically processes fees for printed copies.[136]

TULIP, an acronym for The University Licensing Project, is possibly the best-known electronic journal project. Begun in 1991 and fully operational in January 1993, TULIP was carried out by Elsevier Science and ten university libraries—all libraries in the University of California system plus Carnegie Mellon, Cornell, the Georgia Institute of Technology, the University of Michigan, the Massachusetts Institute of Technology, the University of Virginia, Virginia Polytechnic, the University of Washington, and the University of Tennessee.[137] More than 40 Elsevier Science and Pergamon Press materials science and engineering journals were digitized, beginning with the 1992 volumes, so that a total of four years were available online at the project's completion at the end of 1995. The participating university libraries received the full electronic text of the journals free but continued their paid paper subscriptions. With the exception of one library, the electronic text was mounted on local file servers. The project's purpose was to compare use of the online and paper versions as well as to address some technical questions.[138] A 1995 issue of *Library Hi Tech* contains reports from almost all the participating libraries.[139] Karen Hunter, an Elsevier Science vice president, concluded that the TULIP experiment indicated "at the moment, managing large digital collections locally is harder and more expensive than managing a comparable print collection," and "not everyone is ready for digital collections, nor will they be soon."[140, 141]

In the mid-1990s, the University of California Press and the University of California at Berkeley Library undertook a joint initiative, Project SCAN (Scholarship from California on the Net), to make humanities journals and books available on the Internet. The established print journals *Nineteenth Century Literature* and *Classical Antiquity* were the first to be offered in an electronic format by the project. For 1995, the electronic issues of these two journals were scheduled to appear a month before the print version, yet the electronic subscription cost 20 percent less than the print price. A spokesperson for the University of California Press asserted that combination print and electronic subscriptions would probably be sold for five years "as a way of easing scholars through the transition to electronic publication and meeting libraries' hard-copy archival needs."[142]

In the United Kingdom, the Institute of Physics Publishing Limited, the Standing Conference of National and University Libraries (SCONUL), and Loughborough University cooperated in the ELVYN (Electronic Version whY Not) Project, funded by the British Library, to test the cost of setting up, running, and distributing to research libraries an electronic version of the print journal, *Modelling and Simulation in Material Science and Engineering*. Completed in 1994, the project concluded that the cost, effort, and computer skills were "considerable."[143]

Also in the United Kingdom, the "SuperJournal project" experimented during 1993 with four different interfaces for electronically transmitting articles from 13 scholarly print journals over SuperJANET, a high-speed computer network. The project demonstrated the feasibility of transmitting color images and mathematical equations over high-speed networks, even though other technical issues remain to be resolved.[144]

Potentially quite significant is the JSTOR (an abbreviation for Journal Storage) project, "originally conceived" by the Andrew W. Mellon Foundation's President, William G. Bowen. This project seeks to convert scholarly journal back-runs to an electronic format, maintain them in a permanent electronic archive, and license access rights to libraries. A 1994 Melon Foundation grant underwrote the test archiving of five history and five economics journals, and database access was originally tested in seven academic libraries: Bryn Mawr, Denison, Harvard, Haverford, Swarthmore, the University of Michigan, and Williams.

JSTOR, a not-for-profit organization headquartered in New York City, was officially launched on January 1, 1997. According to its Web page, JSTOR's objectives include creating a "reliable and comprehensive" archive of scholarly journal literature; helping fill the gaps in existing library journal collections; addressing mutilation and paper deterioration; and studying the effects of electronic access on journal use. To avoid jeopardizing publishers' revenue, current issues are not archived. Although its initial audience is academic libraries, JSTOR should eventually be accessible to other types of libraries as well as individuals. Present pricing for academic libraries uses a differential structure based on academic library size and the extent to which the institution focuses on research, according to the 1994 Carnegie Classification of Institutions of Higher Education. Through January 1, 2000, academic library site license fees will include a $10,000 to $40,000 one-time start-up charge for database development plus a $2,000 to $5,000 annual access fee. Twenty-two libraries participated as of January 31, 1997, but JSTOR estimates that the financial break-even point will be reached when 750 libraries take part.[145] Although its ostensible purpose is retrospective conversion from print to the electronic format, JSTOR could conceivably serve as a model for archiving electronic journals.

Further Growth and Development of Electronic Journals

A major trend beginning in the mid-1990s has been for commercial and university presses to offer simultaneous electronic versions of their established print journals. For example, during the summer and fall of 1993, Johns Hopkins University Press, the Johns Hopkins University library, and the Johns Hopkins University Computing Center instigated Project Muse to market on the WWW electronic versions of the press's 42 scholarly journals, mostly in the humanities and social sciences. Subscribers are offered a print subscription, an electronic subscription, or both. A prototype providing free access to four sample issues was mounted on the WWW in early 1994.[146] As of July 1997, the Web site contained sample electronic issues and other information for all titles in the project, although access to the full text was restricted to individuals associated with subscribing institutions.[147]

By the early 1990s, commercial online computer information services were providing full text (and sometimes graphics) from popular magazines to end users. For example, in 1993 America Online offered 22 magazines, including the *Atlantic Monthly*, *Consumer Reports*, *National Geographic*, and *Time*; CompuServe provided 16, including *U.S. News & World Report*; and Prodigy offered 9, among which was *Kiplinger's Personal Finance Magazine*.[148]

New, multimedia magazines were beginning to appear in CD-ROM format by the mid-1990s. *Newsweek Interactive*, issued quarterly on CD-ROM, included, among other items, the complete text of *Newsweek* for the last three months as well as 200 recent *Washington Post* articles. First issued in 1994 were *Medio Magazine*, a monthly that included movie clips, children's games, audio CD reviews, and Associated Press dispatches; *substance.digizine*, a quarterly focusing on books, movies, music, and technology for "twenty-somethings"; and *Blender*, a monthly "youth-oriented pop culture journal."[149] *Launch*, aimed at the "computer-literate 18- to 34 year olds" and launched in May 1995, was described by the *New York Times* as "a CD-ROM magazine with a difference: more ads."[150] *Ulrich's International Periodicals Directory, 1988-89* noted 84 serials or periodicals available on CD-ROM,[151] but the 1998 *Ulrich's* listed 2,240.[152]

A significant trend during the last half of the 1990s was the creation of Web-based electronic journals. The 1994 *Directory of Electronic Journals, Newsletters and Academic Discussion Lists* listed approximately 35 electronic publications "created for Web reading/distribution"—a number that had increased to about 140 in the 1995 *Directory*. Counting publications also available through gophers or listservs, almost 350 journals were available on the Web or through Web links in 1995.[153] Reportedly the initial refereed library and information science journal on the WWW was *The Olive Tree*, published by the School of Library Science at the University of Arizona and first issued in January 1995.[154]

The number of scholarly, peer-reviewed journals also increased in the 1990s. Sassé and Winkler estimated there were more than 30 scholarly electronic journals published in 1992.[155] At the end of 1995, Stephen P. Harter and Hak Joon Kim identified 77 scholarly, peer-reviewed electronic journals.[156]

By the mid-1990s, authorities were distinguishing between first-generation and second-generation electronic journals. In 1995 Ellen Duranceau and colleagues used the following generalizations to characterize the first-generation:

1. based on ASCII text files and used a simple file structure

2. published by individuals or groups of scholars rather than commercial or university presses

3. disseminated through e-mail—thus making check-in easy

4. copyright restrictions waived by the publishers

5. because of "small file sizes, ASCII text format, and lack of access restrictions," local library storage cost relatively little in file space and staff time

6. "uncertainty about server and archive stability"

In contrast to the first generation, second-generation electronic journals are more likely to

1. be based on HTML or "specially formatted files" for distribution on the WWW rather than on ASCII text,

2. have more complex file structures (especially for multimedia),

3. require more storage space,

4. be fee-based rather than free and thus concerned with copyright,

5. not use e-mail for delivery,

6. be difficult to check-in due to links to other sources on the Internet, and

7. be published by university presses or commercial publishers rather than individuals or groups of scholars.[157]

The number of electronic journals grew rapidly throughout the early and mid-1990s. The 1989-90 *Ulrich's* listed 2,131 serials in an online format (either exclusively online or simultaneously with a print version);[158] the 1998 edition contained 8,762.[159] In December 1993 *Time* magazine estimated 2,500 electronic newsletters and 5,000 discussion groups were available on the Internet.[160] On August 1, 1997, William Miller estimated the number of electronic journals "available to scholars worldwide" as approaching 4,000.[161] The number of items listed in the *Directory of Electronic Journals, Newsletters and Academic Discussion Lists'* annual editions, summarized in table 2.1, illustrates the growth of these phenomena. Journals and newsletters increased from 110 in 1991 to 1,689 in 1996, and the number of discussion lists rose from 517 in 1991 to 3,118 by 1996.[162]

Table 2.1.
Growth of Electronic Publications Listed in the *Directory of Electronic Journals, Newsletters and Academic Discussion Lists*

Year	Journals and Newsletters	Discussion Lists
1991	110	517
1992	133	769
1993	240	1,152
1994	443	1,785
1995	675	2,480
1996	1,689	3,118

These figures may partially reflect the *Directory's* expanded coverage rather than the absolute number of electronic journals and discussion groups, although the genuine growth in their numbers is indisputable.

In summary, the history of electronic journals is undeniably in its early stages. One can easily imagine there will be third-, fourth-, and later-generation electronic journals.

SERIALS OUTPUT, COST, AND LIBRARY COLLECTING STATISTICS

This section summarizes statistics about serials output as well as library collecting and expenditures. Although sometimes boring, statistics can provide perspective on a subject. For an annotated guide to sources for serial statistics see appendix 1.

Serials Production and Costs

Many people wonder how many serials there are. In 1980 Osborn estimated that more than 500,000 serial titles were published throughout the world and that more than a million titles had been published from 1609 to 1979.[163] Luke Swindler reports that the number of titles listed in *Ulrich's International Periodicals Directory* increased from 14,000 in 1953 to 140,000 in 1993-94; he notes that about 3,000 new serial titles were created each year during the 1990s.[164] The 1994-95 edition of *Ulrich's International Periodicals Directory* listed more than 147,000 serials published world wide,[165] and the 1998 edition stated that 3,571 new serial titles are known to have been published since January 1, 1995.[166] In mid-1997 Miller estimated the number of scholarly journals worldwide as "perhaps 150,000."[167]

Not only has the number of serial titles increased, but so has their cost. According to the U.S. Periodical Price Index, the average annual cost of a U.S. periodical rose from $24.59 in 1977 to $165.61 in 1996. The index also indicates that the average cost of chemistry and physics journals rose from $93.76 in 1977 to $957.36 in 1997, thus illustrating the well-known inflationary spiral for science, technical, and medical (STM) journals.[168] The more recently developed Public Library Price Index reveals that between 1992 and 1995 the yearly cost of a U.S. periodical for a hypothetical average library increased from $45.18 to $50.67, the cost of a foreign periodical increased from $117.71 to $139.08, and a newspaper's cost rose from $222.68 to $270.22.[169] A similar serials price trend can be observed in the United States's neighbor to the north. The cost of an average title in the Foreign and Domestic Periodicals Price Index for Canada rose from $203.44 in 1989 to $435.52 in 1995.[170] Findings from several other notable serials cost indexes will be incorporated in subsequent sections.

Library Serial Collections and Expenditures

Beginning with the 1961-62 academic year, the ARL issued an annual statistical report that includes the holdings and expenditures of its members. The ARL statistical series is often viewed as a continuation of the so-called Gerould or Princeton statistics, begun for 1907-08 by James Thayer Gerould, a librarian at the University of Minnesota and later Princeton, and continued after his retirement by the Princeton library through 1961-62. The Gerould series contained data on holdings and expenditures for select North American academic libraries, but separate serials data were not included.[171]

The ARL began reporting data on periodical subscriptions in 1971-72, when the number of current periodical subscriptions ranged from 4,838 at the lowest ranking library to 98,458 at the University of California at Berkeley. The median number was 17,160, with 1,659,909 periodicals subscribed to by all members.[172] A quarter of a century later, ARL university libraries were actually receiving a larger number of serials. In 1995-96 the median number of current serial subscriptions at ARL university libraries was 21,107, ranging from 97,568 at Harvard to a low of 9,591. ARL university libraries had a total of 2,999,951 serial subscriptions, and all ARL libraries subscribed to 3,482,074.[173]

Not until 1975-76 were current periodical expenditures reported separately from expenditures for all library materials. That year Harvard ranked number one in the ARL in periodical expenditures, spending $1,320,000. The lowest reported figure was $171,565. The median expenditure by ARL university libraries was $526,594. A total of $50,884,028 was spent by ARL university libraries and $54,094,273 by all ARL members.[174] By 1995-96 the median current serials expenditure by ARL university libraries had reached $3,384,928; the total stood at $386,356,960 for ARL university libraries and $410,177,992 for all ARL institutions. Michigan ranked first, spending $7,429,048, and the lowest reported figure was $1,611,864. These sums do not include binding expenditures.[175]

Serials statistics pertaining to other types of libraries should be briefly mentioned. Robert E. Molyneux's study of 1988-89 statistics from historically black college and university libraries revealed that total expenditures for current serials was $8,020,870, ranging from a low of $4,131 to $2,694,799 at Howard University library, with a $42,816 median. The number of subscriptions ranged from a low of 16 to 27,931 at Howard; the median was 706.[176]

Total serial expenditures in 1978-79 by Association of College and Research Libraries (ACRL) libraries (i.e., smaller university libraries that do not belong to the ARL) amounted to $30,888,662, with the median library spending $312,514 for 7,080 subscriptions.[177] By 1994-95 total serial expenditures by ACRL libraries had grown to $133,405,078, and the median figures for serial expenditures and total subscriptions stood at $1,062,668 and 5,985, respectively.[178] Thomas G. Kirk reported data for libraries of colleges "highly selective in their student admissions" (institutions smaller than ACRL universities). In 1973-74 the average library in this group spent $32,268 for 1,224 periodical titles at a mean cost of $26.77 per title. By 1988-89 the average library spent $186,538 for 1,535 titles at an average cost of $105.72. Kirk concluded that college libraries had been affected by rising periodical costs to a lesser degree than had large university libraries.[179]

In 1979-80 the average library of an accredited North American medical school paid $172,099 for 2,319 serial subscriptions.[180] By 1995-96 the mean expenditure had increased to $694,881, yet the number of subscriptions declined to 2,009.[181] Considerably less has been published about periodical expenditures in public and school libraries than in academic libraries. The 1978 *Bowker Annual of Library and Book Trade Information* reported an annual expenditure of $13,629,604 by U.S. public libraries for periodicals,[182] a figure that rose to $89,432,373 in the 1995 *Bowker Annual: Library and Book Trade Almanac*.[183] Since then expenditures have decreased two consecutive years—to $69,400,126 in the 1996 *Bowker Annual*[184] and $64,416,879 in the 1997 edition.[185] The Public Library Price Index estimates that during 1991-92 the typical public library spent 18 percent of its materials budget on serials.[186] The median expenditure for periodicals in U.S. school library media centers increased from $560 in 1984 to $1,000 in 1994.[187]

Note that data from such organizations as ARL or ACRL do not lend itself to precise longitudinal comparison because the membership varies over time. Even within the same year, the number of responding libraries will vary from question to question on the survey form. Nevertheless, there can be little doubt that libraries are spending more money for serial subscriptions.

Impact on Library Budgets

Statistics on the impact of serial costs on libraries have been extensively reported. Although the precise impact naturally varies from library to library, general trends are discernible.

Since 1965 Alfred N. Brandon and Dorothy R. Hill have been publishing biannually in the *Bulletin of the Medical Library Association* the so-called Brandon-Hill list of recommended books and serials for small medical libraries. Brandon and Hill calculate that the annual subscription cost for all journals on their list rose from $7,080 in 1965 to $101,700 in 1997.[188] Michael R. Kronenfeld calculates that the average journal on the Brandon-Hill list of recommended titles for small medical libraries increased in cost more than 1,000 percent from 1967 to 1995, from $14.85 to $181.40—based on the 115 journals continuously published since 1967. Consequently, a hospital library whose budget had increased at the same rate as the Consumer Price Index (CPI) would have only 37 percent of its 1967 periodical purchasing power by 1995.[189] Naomi P. Fackler reports that the average cost of a core veterinary medicine journal from the "Basic List of Veterinary Medical Serials"[190] (compiled by the Veterinary Serials Committee of the Veterinary Medical Libraries Section of the Medical Library Association) increased from $69.07 in 1983 to $258.77 in 1996, amounting to an average annual increase of 11.04 percent. The total cost for all core titles increased from $5,802.25 in 1983 to $21,736.45 in 1996.[191]

Numerous studies conducted at individual libraries have also indicated inflation in serials cost. For example, John O. Christensen reports that at the Brigham Young University library, a chemistry journal's average yearly cost increased from $268.63 in 1980 to $751.33 in 1990, amounting to a yearly average increase of 10.9 percent.[192]

Even though many librarians appear to perceive their budgets as inadequate, the ARL Serials Prices Project revealed that from 1971-72 through 1987-88 expenditures by ARL libraries increased at a rate notably higher than the CPI: 234 percent compared to 182.5 percent. The mean percentage of ARL library budgets devoted to materials increased from 29.2 percent in 1971-72 to 33.1 percent in 1987-88, and the percentage of the materials budget devoted to serials rose from 40.4 percent in 1975-76 to 56.2 percent in 1987-88.[193] By 1995-96 the percentage of ARL materials budgets devoted to serials stood at 60 percent.[194] Kirk's survey of college libraries revealed that the average percentage of the materials budget devoted to serials rose from 31.13 percent in 1973-74 to 42.12 percent in 1988-89.[195] In effect, libraries have been shifting funds from other materials to pay for escalating serials costs.

The ARL Serials Prices Project also demonstrated that research libraries are collecting a smaller segment of the serials universe. The average serials holdings of an ARL university library as a portion of the titles listed in *Ulrich's* declined from 33 percent in 1973-74 to 26 percent in 1987-88.[196] My calculation found the proportion to be 14 percent in 1995-96,[197] although it is uncertain whether my methodology is identical to the ARL Serials Prices Project's.

In 1994 Chandra Prabha and John E. Ogden wrote that for ARL libraries, "serials expenditures started an explosive growth around 1986." Using 1986 data as a baseline of 1.00, by 1992 ARL serials expenditures reached 1.87 contrasted to 1.48 for total library expenditures, 1.56 for all materials expenditures, and 1.28 for monographic expenditures. From 1986 to 1992, the CPI increased from 1.00 to 1.27; and the Public Library Price Index, which considers inflation in librarian salaries and materials costs increased to 1.40.[198]

The ARL, using time series analysis, reports that median serials expenditures by its members more than doubled between 1986 and 1996, increasing at an 8.4 percent annual rate, from $1,517,724 to $3,393,307. Also, the median serial unit price rose from $88.81 in 1986 to $219.46 in 1996, a 147 percent total increase at an annual rate of 9.5 percent. During this time, the median monograph unit cost increased only 63 percent, from $28.65 to $46.73—an annual rate of 5 percent. From 1986 to 1996, the total number of students increased 10 percent and the number of faculty, rose 11 percent. However, 7 percent fewer serial subscriptions were purchased, even though total expenditures for serials increased by 124 percent. In

1986, 910 serial titles were purchased for every 1,000 students, a figure that had declined to 780 per 1,000 students by 1996.[199]

The effect of serials prices on budgets varies among library types. Academic libraries—especially those attached to research-oriented universities—have been affected more than public or school libraries. Even within a specific type of library, the impact will vary significantly from one institution to another. Molyneux reports that among historically black U.S. college and university libraries, in 1988-89 the materials budget's proportion devoted to serials ranged from 3 to 89 percent.[200]

Kendon Stubbs stated in January 1994 that "just as there is recognized to be a 'serials crisis,' equally or even more is there a monographs crisis."[201] This is illustrated by Anna H. Perrault's prizewinning Ph.D. dissertation, based on the *OCLC/AMIGOS Collection Analysis CD*, which contains library holdings records from the OCLC database. Her research revealed that 72 ARL libraries collected a total of 144,879 monographs with 1985 imprints compared to 104,664 1989 imprints—a decline of 27.7 percent in just four years.[202] Likewise, the median number of monographs purchased by ARL libraries decreased from 33,210 in 1986 to 26,262 in 1996, an overall decline of 21 percent. On a per-student basis, the decline was 33.3 percent, with 2.22 monographs purchased for each student in 1986 contrasted to 1.48 in 1996. Not surprisingly, interlibrary loan (ILL) borrowing by faculty and students more than doubled between 1986 and 1996.[203] In their article "The Library 'Doomsday Machine,'" Ann Okerson and Kendon Stubbs wrote that increasing serial costs "have occurred at the expense of other library services—most visibly monograph purchases."[204] Awareness of the problem extends beyond the library profession: a front-page article in the November 18, 1996, *New York Times* exclaimed, "[research library] budgets are being eaten up by the cost of journals at the expense of books."[205]

Summary

The following generalizations can be made:

1. Serials prices have increased at a rate far higher than the costs of books or the general inflation rate.

2. The number of serial publications is continuing to increase.

3. The "crisis" has been caused by the cost of serials rather than the inadequacy of library budgets.

4. Serials are consuming an increasing portion of library materials budgets, thus eroding support for other formats.

5. Libraries are collecting a smaller portion of the total serials universe.

The cost of electronic resources is also placing pressure on library budgets. It has recently been contended that the CPI overstates the actual inflation rate because it fails to take into consideration increases in product quality. One wonders what implications this assertion has for serials. If correct, a pessimist might argue that serials inflation is worse than most observers believe because the difference between it and the general inflation rate would be greater than the CPI indicates. Alternatively, an optimist might argue that serials inflation figures, similar to the allegation concerning the CPI, also fail to take into consideration an increasing research quality in scholarly journals.

Factors Responsible for Serials Price Increases

Innumerable theories and hypotheses have offered explanations for the long-term increase in serial prices. It is beyond this book's scope to provide a definitive explanation for serials price inflation. However, this section will summarize the variables affecting serials price increases.

The ARL Serials Prices Project's report outlined seven major factors that contribute to the perceived serials crisis.

1. Publishers' Behavior—this includes increases in journal size and the number of new journals, and a two-tiered pricing structures by non-U.S. publishers who charge U.S. libraries more than libraries in the country of publication.

2. Exchange Rate Fluctuation—a weaker U.S. dollar increases the price of international journals for U.S. libraries. Yet ARL research demonstrates that "prices have risen well beyond what can be attributed to exchange rate fluctuations.

3. Growth in Volume of Published Research—this factor is accentuated by an increased need for international research by North American scientists.

4. Competition in Academe—increased competition for promotion, tenure, and grants results in a proliferation of published articles.

5. Market Dominance—a small number of profit-oriented publishers dominates the STM market.

6. Journal Publishing Economics—many specialized journals have a narrow market consisting primarily of libraries, so a relatively small number of subscribers provides most of the revenue.

7. Role of Commercial Publishers—commercial publishers, who charge higher prices than do society and association publishers, "have now assumed a commanding position" in the academic journal market.[206]

Another factor involves the vicious cycle of price increases, subscription cancellations, more price increases, more cancellations, and so forth. As publishers confront a diminishing subscription base, prices must be increased to generate an equivalent amount of revenue.

Some observers have attributed the serials crisis to excessive price increases by a relatively small number of important publishers.[207] Research demonstrates that serials from commercial publishers are generally more expensive than those published by nonprofit societies and associations.[208] The Economic Consulting Services, commissioned for the ARL Serials Prices Project, concluded that from 1973 through 1987 the percentage increase in price per published page exceeded the percentage increase in cost by a significant differential for each of four major publishers: Elsevier Science, Pergamon Press, Plenum Press, and Springer-Verlag. Herbert S. White cogently argues that librarians find themselves in a weak bargaining position vis-à-vis serials publishers because they act as purchasing agents who merely order the serial titles selected by faculty.[209]

Early each year, leading serial subscription agents issue preliminary projections (which may be revised as the year progresses) of the serials inflation rate for the next year. For example, in January 1995 Faxon projected a 1996 serials price increase of 10.5 percent for North American titles and 18.5 percent for European titles. These projections were subdivided into five major components, which, for European titles, were page inflation—3.0 percent; paper or postage or both—3.0 percent; general inflation—2.0 percent; cancellations—3.0 percent; and currency changes—7.5 percent.[210] This revealing breakdown represents a major serial subscription agent's assessment of the factors causing serials inflation and the relative importance of each factor during that year.

NOTES

1. Allen B. Veaner, "Into the Fourth Century," *Drexel Library Quarterly* 21 (winter 1985): 4.

2. David A. Kronick, *A History of Scientific and Technical Periodicals: The Origins and Development of the Scientific and Technical Press, 1665-1790*, 2d ed. (Metuchen, N.J.: Scarecrow Press, 1976).

3. Bernard Houghton, *Scientific Periodicals: Their Historical Development, Characteristics, and Control* (London: Clive Bingley, 1975).

4. R. Gordon Kelly, ed., *Children's Periodicals of the United States* (Westport, Conn.: Greenwood Press, 1984).

5. Charles H. Lippy, ed., *Religious Periodicals of the United States: Academic and Scholarly Journals* (Westport, Conn.: Greenwood Press, 1986).

6. Andrew D. Osborn, *Serial Publications: Their Place and Treatment in Libraries*, 3d ed. (Chicago: American Library Association, 1980), 24-25.

7. Ibid., 31-34.

8. Ibid., 29-30.

9. Veaner, "Into the Fourth Century," 8.

10. *Ulrich's International Periodicals Directory, 1998*, 36th ed. (New Providence, N.J.: R. R. Bowker, 1997), 1:v.

11. D. E. Davinson, *The Periodicals Collection: Its Purpose and Uses in Libraries* (London: Andre Deutsch, 1969), 29.

12. Charles D. Patterson, "Origins of Systematic Serials Control: Remembering Carolyn Ulrich," *Reference Services Review* 16, nos. 1/2 (1988): 79-80.

13. Veaner, "Into the Fourth Century," 12.

14. Ibid., 5-6.

15. Ibid., 16.

16. William F. Birdsall, *The Myth of the Electronic Library: Librarianship and Social Change in America* (Westport, Conn.: Greenwood Press, 1994), 8.

17. Ibid., 8-10.

18. Donald Davinson, *The Periodicals Collection*, rev. and enl. ed. (Boulder, Colo.: Westview Press, 1978), 24.

19. Brian O'Connor, "Moving Image-Based Serial Publications," *Serials Review* 12 (summer and fall 1986): 20.

20. David J. Bertuca and Cynthia A. Bertuca, "Is There a Disk Magazine in Your Future?" *Serials Review* 12 (summer and fall 1986): 41-45.

21. Derek J. de Solla Price, *Science Since Babylon* (New Haven, Conn.: Yale University Press, 1961), 52.

22. Veaner, "Into the Fourth Century," 7-8.

23. Ibid., 7.

24. Ann C. Schaffner, "The Future of Scientific Journals: Lessons from the Past," *Information Technology and Libraries* 13 (December 1994): 239-40.

25. David C. Taylor, *Managing the Serials Explosion: The Issues for Publishers and Libraries* (White Plains, N.Y.: Knowledge Industry Publications, 1982), 10.

26. Davinson, *The Periodicals Collection*, rev. and enl. ed., 20.

27. Taylor, *Managing the Serials Explosion*, 10.

28. Osborn, *Serial Publications*, 29.

29. Ibid., 29.

30. Davinson, *The Periodicals Collection*, rev. and enl. ed., 20.

31. Ibid.

32. Osborn, *Serial Publications*, 30.

33. Taylor, *Managing the Serials Explosion*, 10-11.

34. Veaner, "Into the Fourth Century," 8.

35. Kathy G. Tomajko and Miriam A. Drake, "The Journal, Scholarly Communication, and the Future," *Serials Librarian* 10 (fall 1985/winter 1985-1986): 290.

36. Veaner, "Into the Fourth Century," 12.

37. David A. Kronick, "Medical 'Publishing Societies' in Eighteenth-Century Britain," *Bulletin of the Medical Library Association* 82 (July 1994): 277.

38. Veaner, "Into the Fourth Century," 12.

39. Charles B. Osburn, "The Place of the Journal in the Scholarly Communications System," *Library Resources and Technical Services* 28 (October/December 1984): 317-18.

40. Ann Okerson, "Of Making Many Books There Is No End," in *Report of the ARL Serials Prices Project* (Washington, D.C.: Association of Research Libraries, 1989), 45.

41. Davinson, *The Periodicals Collection*, rev. and enl. ed., 23-24.

42. Osburn, "The Place of the Journal," 318-19.

43. Houghton, *Scientific Periodicals*, 102.

44. Osburn, "The Place of the Journal," 319.

45. Price, *Science Since Babylon*, 95-100.

46. Ibid., 96-97.

47. K. P. Barr, "Estimates of the Number of Currently Available Scientific and Technical Periodicals," *Journal of Documentation* 23 (June 1967): 110.

48. Veaner, "Into the Fourth Century," 7.

49. Pieter A. van Brakel, "Electronic Journals: Publishing via Internet's World Wide Web," *Electronic Librarian* 13 (August 1995): 391-92.

50. Frank Luther Mott, *A History of American Magazines* (Cambridge, Mass.: Harvard University Press, 1938-68).

51. James Playsted Wood, *Magazines in the United States: Their Social and Economic Influence* (New York: Ronald Press, 1949).

52. John Tebbel, *The American Magazine: A Compact History* (New York: Hawthorn Books, 1969).

53. John Tebbel and Mary Ellen Zuckerman, *The Magazine in America, 1741-1990* (New York: Oxford University Press, 1991).

54. Theodore Peterson, *Magazines in the Twentieth Century* (Urbana, Ill.: University of Illinois Press, 1964).

55. Lyon N. Richardson, *A History of Early American Magazines, 1741-1789* (New York: Octagon Books, 1966).

56. Sam G. Riley, *Magazines of the American South* (New York: Greenwood Press, 1986).

57. David E. E. Sloane, ed., *American Humor Magazines and Comic Periodicals* (Westport, Conn.: Greenwood Press, 1987).

58. P. Mark Fackler and Charles H. Lippy, eds., *Popular Religious Magazines of the United States* (Westport, Conn.: Greenwood Press, 1995).

59. Davinson, *The Periodicals Collection*, 17.

60. Clara D. Brown and Lynn S. Smith, *Serials: Past, Present and Future*, 2d rev. ed. (Birmingham, Ala.: EBSCO, 1980), 5.

61. Davinson, *The Periodicals Collection*, 18.

62. Joseph A. Puccio, *Serials Reference Work* (Englewood, Colo.: Libraries Unlimited, 1989), 16, citing *The Compact Edition of the Oxford English Dictionary* (Oxford: Oxford University Press, 1971), 1690.

63. Rosalee McReynolds, "Serials Librarianship," in *Encyclopedia of Library History*, ed. Wayne A. Wiegand and Donald G. Davis Jr. (New York: Garland, 1994), 574.

64. Tebbel and Zuckerman, *The Magazine in America*, 3.

65. Peterson, *Magazines in the Twentieth Century*, 59.

66. Ibid., 55, and *passim*.

67. *National Directory of Magazines, 1994* (New York: Oxbridge Communications, 1993).

68. Tebbel and Zuckerman, *The Magazine in America*, 244.

69. Bill Katz, *Magazine Selection: How to Build a Community-Oriented Collection* (New York: R. R. Bowker, 1971), 102.

70. Bill Katz and Linda Sternberg Katz, *Magazines for Libraries*, 8th ed. (New Providence, N.J.: R. R. Bowker, 1995), 806.

71. Katz, *Magazine Selection*, 106.

72. Fredric Wertham, *The World of Fanzines: A Special Forum of Communication* (Carbondale, Ill.: Southern Illinois University Press, 1973), 38, citing Linda Bushyager in *Granfallon*, no. 9, and Robert A. W. Lowndes in *Algol*, no. 17, as his sources.

73. J. Peder Zane, "Now, the Magazines of 'Me,' " *New York Times* 144 (May 14, 1995): sec. 4, p. 4.

74. Chris Dodge, "Pushing the Boundaries: Zines and Libraries," *Wilson Library Bulletin* 69 (May 1995): 27.

75. Zane, "Now, the Magazines of 'Me,' " citing R. Seth Friedman, publisher of *Factsheet Five*.

76. David M. Gross, "Zine Dreams," *New York Times Magazine* 145 (December 17, 1995): 72.

77. Based on scanning recent issues of *Folio: The Magazine for Magazine Management*.

78. Tebbel and Zuckerman, *The Magazine in America*, 243-44.

79. Lisa E. Phillips, "Battle for the Newsstand," *Folio: The Magazine for Magazine Management* 23 (March 15, 1994): 66. The number had increased from 1,800 in 1982.

80. Deirdre Carmody, "On the Annual Scoreboard of New Magazines, It's Sports 67, Sex 44," *New York Times* 144 (June 12, 1995): D5. The report, entitled *Samir Husni's Guide to New Consumer Magazines,* was published in book format by Hearst Magazine Enterprises in 1994 and by *Folio: The Magazine for Magazine Management* in earlier years.

81. Bill Katz and Eric Bryant, "The 10 Best Magazines of 1993," *Library Journal* 119 (May 1, 1994): 52, citing Samir Husni as quoted in Phillips, "Battle for the Newstand," 66-67, 103.

82. Carmody, "On the Annual Scoreboard of New Magazines."

83. William H. Huff, "Serial Subscription Agencies," *Library Trends* 24 (April 1976), 688.

84. Ibid., 685-86.

85. The Faxon Company. *Faxon Company Background*. Available: http://www.faxon.com/html/ab_back.html (Accessed February 15, 1998).

86. Blackwell's. *About Blackwell's Information Services.* Available: http://www.blackwell.co.uk/journals/about/index.html (Accessed April 9, 1998).

87. Lenore Rae Wilkas, *International Subscription Agents*, 6th ed. (Chicago: American Library Association, 1994).

88. Marcia Tuttle, *Managing Serials* (Greenwich, Conn.: JAI Press, 1996), 59.

89. Jim E. Cole, "ISDS: The Unfinished Revolution," in *Advances in Serials Management: A Research Annual*, vol. 4, ed. Marcia Tuttle and Jean G. Cook (Greenwich, Conn.: JAI Press, 1992), 65-89.

90. National Serials Data Program, "How to Obtain an ISSN," in *Bowker Annual: Library and Book Trade Almanac, 1997*, 42d ed. (New Providence, N.J.: R. R. Bowker, 1997), 577-78.

91. Ibid.

92. National Serials Data Program, Library of Congress. *ISSN for Electronic Serials*. Available: http://lcweb.loc.gov/issn/e-serials.html (Accessed February 15, 1998).

93. R. Russell Neuswanger, "ISSN WEB Pages Now Available," *Acqnet* (April 2, 1995).

94. ISSN International Centre. *List of ISSN National Centers / Liste des Centres Nationaux de Reseau ISSN*. Available: http://www/issm/org/fic.html (Accessed February 15, 1998).

95. Cole, "ISDS," 66-67.

96. Neuswanger, "ISSN WEB Pages Now Available."

97. ISSN International Centre. *Statistics of the ISSN Register at the End of 1996*. Available: http://www.issn.org/stat95.html (Accessed February 15, 1998).

98. Cole, "ISDS," 71.

99. Association for Library Collections and Technical Services, *Serials Acquisitions Glossary* (Chicago: Association for Library Collections and Technical Services, 1993), 21.

100. Judith A. Segal, "Journal Deselection: A Literature Review and an Application," *Science and Technology Libraries* 6 (spring 1986): 27.

101. Susan J. Webreck, "National Periodicals Center," *Encyclopedia of Library and Information Science* 40, supplement 5 (1986): 321-38.

102. Paul R. Green, John Merriman, and David P. Woodworth, "The United Kingdom Serials Group: Its History, Development, and Future," *Serials Librarian* 9 (summer 1985): 107-11.

103. Mary Ellen Soper, "The Education of Serials Catalogers," *Serials Librarian* 12, nos. 1/2 (1987): 176.

104. Marcia Tuttle, "Serials Management," in *Guide to Technical Services Resources*, ed. Peggy Johnson (Chicago: American Library Association, 1994), 126.

105. *Report of the ARL Serials Prices Project* (Washington, D.C.: Association of Research Libraries, 1989), from unnumbered overview and summary.

106. Okerson, "Of Making Many Books There Is No End," 41-45.

107. Margo Sassé and B. Jean Winkler, "Electronic Journals: A Formidable Challenge for Libraries," *Advances in Librarianship* 17 (1993): 153.

108. Ibid.

109. Ibid., 154.

110. Ibid., 154-55.

111. Anne B. Piternick, "Electronic Serials: Realistic or Unrealistic Solution to the Journal 'Crisis,' " *Serials Librarian* 21, nos. 2/3 (1991): 23.

112. Murray Turoff and Starr Roxanne Hiltz, "The Electronic Journal: A Progress Report," *Journal of the American Society for Information Science* 33 (July 1982): 195-202.

113. Bruce Morasch, *"Electronic Social Psychology,"* *Serials Review* 12 (summer and fall 1986): 113-17.

114. Jane Hugo and Linda Newell, *"New Horizons in Adult Education:* The First Five Years (1987-1991)," *Public-Access Computer Systems Review* 2, no. 1 (1991): 77-78. Available: http://info.lib.uh.edu/pr/v2/n1/hugo.2n1 (Accessed February 15, 1998).

115. Richard Entlich and others, "Testing a Digital Library: User Response to the CORE Project," *Library Hi Tech* 14, no. 4 (1996): 99.

116. Charles W. Bailey Jr., "Electronic (Online) Publishing in Action . . . *The Public-Access Computer Systems Review* and Other Electronic Serials," *Online* 15 (January 1991): 28-35.

117. Lon Savage, *"The Journal of the International Academy of Hospitality Research,"* *Public-Access Computer Systems Review* 2, no. 1 (1991): 54-66. Available: http://info.lib.uh.edu/pr/v2/n1/savage.2n1 (Accessed February 15, 1998).

118. Eyal Amiran and John Unsworth, "Postmodern Culture: Publishing in the Electronic Medium," *Public-Access Computer Systems Review* 2, no. 1 (1991): 55-62. Available: http://info.lib.uh.edu/pr/v2/n1/amiran.2n1 (Accessed February 15, 1998).

119. Edward M. Jennings, "*EJournal*: An Account of the First Two Years," *Public-Access Computer Systems Review* 2, no. 1 (1991): 91-100. Available: http://info.lib.uh.edu/pr/v2/n1/ jennings.2n1 (Accessed February 15, 1998).

120. David F. W. Robison, "The Changing States of *Current Cites*: The Evolution of an Electronic Journal," *Computers in Libraries* 13 (June 1993): 21-23, 26.

121. Frances A. Brahmi and Kellie Kaneshiro, "The *Online Journal of Current Clinical Trials* (OJCCT): A Closer Look," *Medical Reference Services Quarterly* 12 (fall 1993): 29.

122. Rick Noble, "Document Delivery and Full Text from OCLC," *Electronic Library* 14 (February 1996): 59.

123. Eyal Amiran, Elaine Orr, and John Unsworth, "Refereed Electronic Journals and the Future of Scholarly Publishing," *Advances in Library Automation and Networking* 4 (1991): 29.

124. Linda Langschied, "Electronic Journal Forum: *VPIEJ-L*: An Online Discussion Group for Electronic Journal Publishing Concerns," *Serials Review* 20, no. 1 (1994): 90-91.

125. For papers from the seminar, see Brian Cook, ed., *The Electronic Journal: The Future of Serials-Based Information* (New York: Haworth Press, 1992). Also issued as *Australian and New Zealand Journal of Serials Librarianship* 3, no. 2 (1992).

126. For summaries of the topics discussed at this conference, see H. Julene Butler, "Abstracts of Papers Presented at the International Conference on Refereed Journals, October 1993," *Serials Review* 20, no. 4 (1994): 21-30.

127. Marcia Tuttle, "The *Newsletter on Serials Pricing Issues*: Teetering on the Cutting Edge," in *Advances in Serials Management: A Research Annual*, vol. 4, ed. Marcia Tuttle and Jean G. Cook (Greenwich, Conn.: JAI Press, 1992), 37-63.

128. Ibid., 40.

129. Ibid., 49.

130. Birdie MacLennan, "*SERIALST* Scope and Purpose," *SERIALST* (August 2, 1994).

131. Ann Shumelda Okerson and James J. O'Donnell. *NewJour: Electronic Journals Newsletters*. Available: http://gort.ucsd.edu/newjour/ (Accessed July 3, 1998).

132. Cliff McKnight, "Electronic Journals—Past, Present . . . and Future?" *Aslib Proceedings* 45 (January 1993): 7-10.

133. Entlich and others, "Testing a Digital Library," 100.

134. Discussed on October 27, 1993, in "Online Primary Science Journals: An Experimental System and a Production System," a session at the 56th Annual Meeting of the American Society for Information Science, held in Columbus, Ohio, October 24-28, 1993, and attended by the author.

135. Karen A. Butter, "Red Sage: The Next Step in Delivery of Electronic Journals," *Medical Reference Services Quarterly* 13 (fall 1994): 76.

136. Sally Taylor, "AT&T, Springer, Wiley in Document Delivery Project," *Publishers Weekly* 240 (October 18, 1993): 7.

137. Win-Shin S. Chiang and Nancy E. Elkington, eds., *Electronic Access to Information: A New Service Paradigm: Proceedings from a Symposium Held July 23 Through July 24, 1993, Palo Alto, California* (Mountain View, Calif.: Research Libraries Group, 1994), 73-74.

138. Jaco Zijlstra, "*The* University *Licensing Program* (TULIP): Electronic Journals in Materials Science," *Microcomputers for Information Management* 12, nos. 1/2 (1995): 99-102.

139. Nancy Gusack and Clifford A. Lynch, "Special Theme: The TULIP Project," *Library Hi Tech* 13, no. 4 (1995): 7-74.

140. Karen Hunter, "Publishing for a Digital Library—What Did TULIP Teach Us?" *Journal of Academic Librarianship* 22 (May 1996): 209-10.

141. Elsevier Science. *TULIP Final Report: Overview*. Available: http://www.elsevier.nl/inca/homepage/about/resproj/trmenu.htm (Accessed February 15, 1998).

142. Leigh Hafrey, "At Cyberspace University Press, Paperless Publishing Looks Good," *New York Times Book Review* 144 (October 30, 1994): 32.

143. Jack Meadows, David Pullinger, and Peter Such, "The Cost of Implementing an Electronic Journal," *Journal of Scholarly Publishing* 26 (July 1995): 227-33.

144. David J. Pullinger, "Learning from Putting Electronic Journals on SuperJANET: The SuperJournal Project," *Interlending and Document Supply* 23, no. 1 (1995): 20-27.

145. Kevin M. Guthrie and Wendy P. Lougee, "The JSTOR Solution: Accessing and Preserving the Past," *Library Journal* 122 (February 1, 1997): 42-44; JSTOR. *Welcome to JSTOR*. Available: http://www.jstor.org (Accessed February 15, 1998).

146. Donice Cochenour, "Project Muse: A Partnership of Interest," *Serials Review* 21 (fall 1995): 75-81.

147. Johns Hopkins University Press. *Project Muse Home Page*. Available: http://muse.mse.jhu.edu/muse.html. (Accessed February 15, 1998).

148. "Newsweekly Tries On-Line Delivery," *USA Today* (November 26, 1993): B5.

149. David Landis, "Quick Bits: Mags on CD," *USA Today* (July 14, 1994): D8.

150. Steve Lohr, "A CD-ROM Magazine with a Difference: More Ads," *New York Times* 144 (May 8, 1995): C6.

151. *Ulrich's International Periodicals Directory, 1988-89*, 27th ed. (New York: R. R. Bowker, 1988), 1:vii.

152. *Ulrich's International Periodicals Directory, 1998*, 1:vii.

153. Lisabeth A. King and Diane Kovacs, *Directory of Electronic Journals, Newsletters and Academic Discussion Lists*, 5th ed., ed. Ann Okerson (Washington, D.C.: ARL Office of Scientific and Academic Publishing, 1995), iii-iv.

154. MaryLou Hale, "Announcing *The Olive Tree*," *ACQflash* (March 19, 1995).

155. Sassé and Winkler, "Electronic Journals," 155.

156. Stephen P. Harter and Hak Joon Kim, *Electronic Journals and Scholarly Communication: A Citation and Reference Study*. Available: http://php.indiana.edu/~harter/harter-asis96midyear.html (Accessed February 15, 1998).

157. Ellen Duranceau and others, "Electronic Journals in the MIT Libraries: Report of the 1995 E-Journal Subgroup," *Serials Review* 22 (spring 1996): 49-50.

158. *Ulrich's International Periodicals Directory, 1989-90*, 28th ed. (New York: R. R. Bowker, 1989), 1:vii.

159. *Ulrich's International Periodicals Directory, 1998*, 1:vii.

160. Philip Elmer-Dewitt, "First Nation in Cyberspace," *Time* 142 (December 6, 1993): 63.

161. William Miller, "Troubling Myths About On-Line Information," *Chronicle of Higher Education* 43 (August 1, 1997): A44.

162. Michael Strangelove and Diane Kovacs, *Directory of Electronic Journals, Newsletters and Academic Discussion Lists*, 3d ed., ed. Ann Okerson (Washington, D.C.: Association of Research Libraries, 1993), i.

163. Osborn, *Serial Publications*, 24, 45.

164. Luke Swindler, "Serials Publishing Trends," in *Managing Serials*, by Marcia Tuttle (Greenwich, Conn.: JAI Press, 1996), 16.

165. *Ulrich's International Periodicals Directory, 1994-95*, 1:vii.

166. *Ulrich's International Periodicals Directory, 1998*, 1:viii.

167. Miller, "Troubling Myths About On-Line Information."

168. Adrian W. Alexander and Brenda Dingley, "U.S. Periodical Price Index for 1997," *American Libraries* 28 (May 1997), 76.

169. Kent Halstead, "Price Indexes for Public and Academic Libraries," in *Bowker Annual of Library and Book Trade Information, 1997*, 42d ed. (New Providence, N.J.: R. R. Bowker, 1997), 447.

170. The Faxon Company. *Foreign and Domestic Periodicals Price Index for Canada: 1995*. Available: http://www.faxon.com/html/new_cp95.html (Accessed February 15, 1998).

171. Robert E. Molyneux, *The Gerould Statistics, 1907/08-1961/62* (Washington, D.C.: Association of Research Libraries, 1986).

172. *Academic Library Statistics, 1963/64 to 1971/72: A Compilation of Statistics from the Seventy-Eight University Library Members of the Association of Research Libraries* (Washington, D.C.: Association of Research Libraries, 1972), unnumbered pages.

173. Martha Kyrillidou, Ken Rodriguez, and Kendon Stubbs, comps. and eds., *ARL Statistics, 1995-96: A Compilation of Statistics from the One Hundred and Twenty Members of the Association of Research Libraries* (Washington, D.C.: Association of Research Libraries, 1997), 28, 57.

174. Suzanne Frankie, comp., *ARL Statistics, 1975-1976: A Compilation of Statistics from the One Hundred and Five Members of the Association of Research Libraries* (Washington, D.C.: Association of Research Libraries, 1976), 6-15.

175. Kyrillidou, Rodriguez, and Stubbs, *ARL Statistics, 1995-96*, 36, 67.

176. Robert E. Molyneux, comp., *ACRL/Historically Black Colleges and Universities Library Statistics, 1988-89* (Chicago: American Library Association, Association of College and Research Libraries, 1991).

177. Julie A. C. Virgo, Sarah How, and Annette Fern, comps., *ACRL University Library Statistics, 1978-1979: A Compilation of Statistics from Ninety-Eight Non-ARL University Libraries* (Chicago: Association of College and Research Libraries, 1980), 10-11. Expenditures for reporting libraries ranged from $26,312 to $755,901, and the number of subscriptions ranged from 1,028 to 23,470.

178. Hugh A. Thompson, project coordinator, *ACRL University Library Statistics, 1994-95: A Compilation of Statistics from One Hundred Sixteen University Libraries* (Chicago: Association of College and Research Libraries, 1996), 8, 16. Expenditures ranged from $17,610 to $3,215,682, and the number of subscriptions ranged from 140 to a reported figure of 493,886 (which might be questioned, as it seems unduly high).

179. Thomas G. Kirk, "Periodicals in College Libraries: Are the Challenges of Rising Subscription Costs Being Met?" *College and Research Libraries News* 53 (February 1992): 96-97.

180. Association of Academic Health Sciences Library Directors, *Annual Statistics of Medical School Libraries in the United States and Canada*, 3d ed. (Houston, Tex.: Houston Academy of Medicine-Texas Medical Center Library, 1980), 24, 125. Expenditures ranged from $4,182 to $446,600, and the number of serials received ranged from 126 to 8,000.

181. Association of Academic Health Sciences Library Directors, *Annual Statistics of Medical School Libraries in the United States and Canada, 1995-96*, 19th ed. (Seattle, Wash.: Association of Academic Health Sciences Library Directors, 1997), 3:6. The range for expenditures was $102,618 to $1,734,155 and for subscriptions, 353 to 5,415.

182. *Bowker Annual of Library and Book Trade Information, 1978*, 23d ed. (New York: R. R. Bowker, 1978), 238, 240. The data were compiled from the *American Library Directory, 1976-1977* 30th edition, ed. Jacques Cattell Press (New York: R. R. Bowker, 1976). This figure represents 1974-1975 data in some cases and 1975-1976 data in others.

183. *Bowker Annual: Library and Book Trade Almanac, 1995*, 40th ed. (New Providence, N.J.: R. R. Bowker, 1995), 449.

184. *Bowker Annual: Library and Book Trade Almanac, 1996*, 41st ed. (New Providence, N.J.: R. R. Bowker, 1996), 455.

185. *Bowker Annual: Library and Book Trade Almanac, 1997*, 42d ed. (New Providence, N.J.: R. R. Bowker, 1997), 437.

186. Halstead, "Price Indexes for Public and Academic Libraries," 445.

187. Marilyn L. Miller and Marilyn L. Shontz, "Expenditures for Resources in School Library Media Centers, FY 1993/94: The Race for the School Library Dollar," *School Library Journal* 41 (October 1995): 24.

188. Alfred N. Brandon and Dorothy R. Hill, "Selected List of Books and Journals for the Small Medical Library," *Bulletin of the Medical Library Association* 85 (April 1997): 115.

189. Michael R. Kronenfeld, "Update on Inflation of Journal Prices in the Brandon-Hill List of Journals," *Bulletin of the Medical Library Association* 84 (April 1996): 260-63.

190. C. Trenton Boyd and others, "Basic List of Veterinary Medical Serials," 2nd Edition, 1981 with revisions to April 1, 1986, *Serials Librarian* 11 (October 1986): 5-39.

191. Naomi P. Fackler, "Journals for Academic Veterinary Medical Libraries: Price Increases, 1983-1996," *Serials Librarian* 31, no. 4 (1997): 44-45.

192. John O. Christensen, "Cost of Chemistry Journals to One Academic Library, 1980-1990," *Serials Review* 18 (fall 1992): 19-34.

193. Okerson, "Of Making Many Books There is No End," 7.

194. This percentage is my own calculation from the raw data in Kyrillidou, Rodriguez, and Stubbs, *ARL Statistics, 1995-96*, 36.

195. Kirk, "Periodicals in College Libraries," 96.

196. Okerson, "Of Making Many Books There is No End," 15.

197. The 21,007 total current serials listed for the median ARL university library in Kyrillidou, Rodriguez, and Stubbs, *ARL Statistics, 1995-96*, 28, was divided by the approximately 154,000 active titles listed in *Ulrich's International Periodicals Directory, 1996*, 34th ed. (New Providence, N.J.: R. R. Bowker, 1995), 1:vii.

198. Chandra Prabha and John E. Ogden, "Recent Trends in Academic Library Materials Expenditures," *Library Trends* 42 (winter 1994): 502-3, 507.

199. Kyrillidou, Rodriguez, and Stubbs, *ARL Statistics, 1995-96*, 8-13.

200. Molyneux, *ACRL/Historically Black Colleges and Universities*, 20. The average proportion devoted to serials was 42 percent.

201. Kendon Stubbs, introduction to *ARL Statistics, 1992-93: A Compilation of Statistics from the One Hundred and Nineteen Members of the Association of Research Libraries*, compiled by Nicola Daval and Patricia Brennan (Washington, D.C.: Association of Research Libraries, 1994), 7.

202. Anna H. Perrault, "The Changing Print Resource Base of Academic Libraries in the United States: A Comparison of Collection Patterns in Seventy-Two ARL Academic Libraries of Non-Serial Imprints for the Years 1985 and 1989," (Ph.D. diss., Florida State University, 1994). Her data was summarized in handouts at her presentation at the ALISE Annual Conference on February 2, 1995, in Philadelphia and published as "The Shrinking National Collection: A Study of the Effects of the Diversion of Funds from Monographs to Serials on the Monograph Collections of Research Libraries," *Library Acquisitions: Practice and Theory* 18 (spring 1994): 3-22.

203. Kyrillidou, Rodriguez, and Stubbs, *ARL Statistics, 1995-96*, 9,11,13.

204. Ann Okerson and Kendon Stubbs, "The Library 'Doomsday Machine,'" *Publishers Weekly* 238 (February 8, 1991): 36.

205. Peter Applebome, "Profit Squeeze for Publishers Makes Tenure More Elusive," *New York Times* 146 (November 18, 1996): A1.

206. *Report of the ARL Serials Prices Project*, unnumbered overview and summary.

207. Charles A. Hamaker, "Costs and the Serials Information Chain: Containing the Impact on Library Budgets," *Journal of Library Administration* 10, no. 1 (1989): 99-113.

208. Sandra R. Moline, "The Influence of Subject, Publisher Type, and Quantity Published on Journal Prices," *Journal of Academic Librarianship* 15 (March 1989): 12-18.

209. Herbert S. White, "Scholarly Publishers and Libraries: A Strained Marriage," *Scholarly Publishing* 19 (April 1988): 125-29.

210. Ron Akie, "Faxon's 1996 Subscription Price Preliminary Projections," *Newsletter on Serials Pricing Issues,* no. 133 (February 20, 1995).

FURTHER READING

Serials History

Davinson, Donald. "The History of Periodicals." In *The Periodicals Collection*, 19-32. Rev. and enl. ed. Boulder, Colo.: Westview Press, 1978.

Ginsburg, David D. "Rock Is a Way of Life: The World of Rock 'n' Roll Fanzines and Fandom." *Serials Review* 5 (January/March 1979): 29-46.

Houghton, Bernard. *Scientific Periodicals: Their Historical Development, Characteristics, and Control*. Hamden, Conn.: Linnet Books, 1975.

Krieger, Michael T. "The History and Collection of Popular American Catholic Periodicals." *Serials Librarian* 30, no. 2 (1996): 45-65.

Kronick, David A. "Anonymity and Identity: Editorial Policy in the Early Scientific Journal." *Library Quarterly* 58 (July 1988): 221-37.

———. *A History of Scientific and Technical Periodicals: The Origins and Development of the Scientific and Technical Press, 1665-1790*. 2d ed. Metuchen, N.J.: Scarecrow Press, 1976.

———. "Medical 'Publishing Societies' in Eighteenth-Century Britain." *Bulletin of the Medical Library Association* 82 (July 1994): 277-82.

Mott, Frank Luther. *A History of American Magazines*. Cambridge, Mass.: Harvard University Press, 1938-68.

Osborn, Andrew D. "Historical and Statistical Background." In *Serial Publications: Their Place and Treatment in Libraries*, 24-48. 3d ed. Chicago: American Library Association, 1980.

Osburn, Charles B. "The Place of the Journal in the Scholarly Communications System." *Library Resources and Technical Services* 28 (October/December 1984): 315-24.

Peterson, Theodore. *Magazines in the Twentieth Century*. Urbana, Ill.: University of Illinois Press, 1964.

Richardson, Lyon N. *A History of Early American Magazines, 1741-1789*. New York: Octagon Books, 1966.

Tebbel, John. *The American Magazine: A Compact History*. New York: Hawthorn Books, 1969.

Tebbel, John, and Mary Ellen Zuckerman. *The Magazine in America, 1741-1990*. New York: Oxford University Press, 1991.

Veaner, Allen B. "Into the Fourth Century." *Drexel Library Quarterly* 21 (winter 1985): 4-28.

Wood, James Playsted. *Magazines in the United States: Their Social and Economic Influence*. New York: Ronald Press, 1949.

Electronic Journal History

Amiran, Eyal, and John Unsworth. "*Postmodern Culture*: Publishing in the Electronic Medium." *Public-Access Computer Systems Review* 2, no. 1 (1991): 55-62. Available: http://info.lib.uh.edu/pr/v2/n1/amiran.2n1 (Accessed February 15, 1998).

Bailey, Charles W., Jr. "Electronic (Online) Publishing in Action . . . *The Public-Access Computer Systems Review* and Other Electronic Serials." *Online* 15 (January 1991): 28-35.

Brahmi, Frances A., and Kellie Kaneshiro. "*The Online Journal of Current Clinical Trials (OJCCT)*: A Closer Look." *Medical Reference Services Quarterly* 12 (fall 1993): 29-43.

Butter, Karen A. "Red Sage: The Next Step in Delivery of Electronic Journals." *Medical Reference Services Quarterly* 13 (fall 1994): 75-81.

Chen, Ching-chih. "How TULIP Is Implemented at MIT: Additional Comments from the Journal Editor." *Microcomputers for Information Management* 12, nos. 1/2 (1995): 113-20.

Clement, Gail. "Evolution of a Species: Science Journals Published on the Internet." *Database* 17 (October/November 1994): 44-54.

Cochenour, Donnice. "Project Muse: A Partnership of Interest." *Serials Review* 21 (fall 1995): 75-81.

Collier, Harry R. "Learned Information's Electronic Magazine: A Case Study." *Serials Review* 12 (summer and fall 1986): 69-82.

Collins, Mauri P., and Zane L. Berge. *"IPCT Journal*: A Case Study of an Electronic Journal on the Internet." *Journal of the American Society for Information Science* 45 (December 1994): 771-76.

Dworaczek, Marian, and Victor G. Wiebe. "E-Journals: Acquisition and Access." *Acquisitions Librarian,* no. 12 (1994): 105-21.

Entlich, Richard. "Electronic Chemistry Journals: Elemental Concerns." *Serials Librarian* 25, nos. 3/4 (1995): 111-23.

Entlich, Richard, and others. "Making a Digital Library: The Contents of the CORE Project." *ACM Transactions on Information Systems* 15 (April 1997): 103-23.

———. "Testing a Digital Library: User Response to the CORE Project." *Library Hi Tech* 14, no. 4 (1996): 99-118.

Gusack, Nancy, and Clifford A. Lynch. "Special Theme: The TULIP Project." *Library Hi Tech* 13, no. 4 (1995): 7-74.

Hitchcock, Steve, Leslie Carr, and Wendy Hall. "A Survey of STM Online Journals, 1990-95: the Calm Before the Storm." In *Directory of Electronic Journals, Newsletters and Academic Discussion Lists*, compiled by Dru Mogge and Diane K. Kovacs, edited by Dru Mogge, 7-32. 6th ed. Washington, D.C.: Association of Research Libraries, 1996. Available: http://journals.ecs.soton.ac.uk/survey/survey.html (Accessed February 15, 1998).

Hugo, Jane, and Linda Newell. *"New Horizons in Adult Education*: The First Five Years (1987-1991)." *Public-Access Computer Systems Review* 2, no. 1 (1991): 77-90. Available: http://info.lib.uh.edu/pr/v2/n1/hugo.2n1 (Accessed February 15, 1998).

Hunter, Karen. "Publishing for a Digital Library—What Did TULIP Teach Us?" *Journal of Academic Librarianship* 22 (May 1996): 209-11.

Jennings, Edward M. *"EJournal*: An Account of the First Two Years." *Public-Access Computer Systems Review* 2, no. 1 (1991): 91-100. Available: http://info.lib.uh.edu/pr/v2/n1/jennings.2n1 (Accessed February 15, 1998).

Keyhani, Andrea. "The *Online Journal of Current Clinical Trials*: An Innovation in Electronic Journal Publishing." *Database* 16 (February 1993): 14-23.

Killion, Vicki J. *"Information Resources for Nursing Research*: The Sigma Theta Tau International Electronic Library and Online Journal." *Medical Reference Services Quarterly* 13 (fall 1994): 1-17.

Langschied, Linda. "Electronic Journal Forum: *VPIEJ-L*: An Online Discussion Group for Electronic Journal Publishing Concerns." *Serials Review* 20 (spring 1994): 89-94.

Lucier, Richard E., and Robert C. Badger. "Red Sage Project." *Serials Librarian* 24, nos. 3/4 (1994): 129-34.

McKnight, Cliff. "Electronic Journals—Past, Present . . . and Future?" *Aslib Proceedings* 45 (January 1993): 7-10.

Meadows, Jack, David Pullinger, and Peter Such. "The Cost of Implementing an Electronic Journal." *Journal of Scholarly Publishing* 26 (July 1995): 227-33.

Morasch, Bruce. *"Electronic Social Psychology."* *Serials Review* 12 (summer and fall 1986): 113-17.

Naylor, Bernard, and Marilyn Geller. "A Prehistory of Electronic Journals: The EIES and BLEND Projects." In *Advances in Serials Management: A Research Annual.* Vol. 5, edited by Marcia Tuttle and Karen D. Darling, 27-47. Greenwich, Conn.: JAI Press, 1995.

Pullinger, David J. "Learning from Putting Electronic Journals on SuperJANET: The Super-Journal Project." *Interlending and Document Supply* 23, no. 1 (1995): 20-27.

Robison, David F. W. "The Changing States of *Current Cites*: The Evolution of an Electronic Journal." *Computers in Libraries* 13 (June 1993): 21-23, 26.

Robison, Elwin C. "Architecture, Graphics, and the Net: A Short History of *Architronic*, a Peer-Reviewed E-Journal." *Public-Access Computer Systems Review* 7, no. 3 (1996): 5-12. Available: http://info.lib.uh.edu/pr/v7/n3/robi7n3.html (Accessed February 15, 1998).

Sassé, Margo, and B. Jean Winkler. "Electronic Journals: A Formidable Challenge for Librarians." *Advances in Librarianship* 17 (1993): 149-73.

Savage, Lon. "*The Journal of the International Academy of Hospitality Research.*" *Public-Access Computer Systems Review* 2, no. 1 (1991): 54-66. Available: http://info.lib.uh.edu/pr/v2/n1/ savage.2n1 (Accessed February 15, 1998).

Seago, Brenda L. "*Online Journal of Current Clinical Trials*: Issues for the 1990s and Beyond." *Medical Reference Services Quarterly* 12 (spring 1993): 1-6.

Turoff, Murray, and Starr Roxanne Hiltz. "The Electronic Journal: A Progress Report." *Journal of the American Society for Information Science* 33 (July 1982): 195-202.

Tuttle, Marcia. "The *Newsletter on Serials Pricing Issues.*" *Public-Access Computer Systems Review* 2, no. 1 (1991): 91-105. Available: http://info.lib.uh.edu/pr/v2/n1/tuttle.2n1 (Accessed February 15, 1998).

———. "The *Newsletter on Serials Pricing Issues*: Teetering on the Cutting Edge." In *Advances in Serials Management.* Vol. 4, edited by Marcia Tuttle and Jean G. Cook, 37-63. Greenwich, Conn.: JAI Press, 1992.

Willis, Katherine, and others. "TULIP—The University Licensing Program: Experiences at the University of Michigan." *Serials Review* 20 (winter 1994): 39-47.

Zijlstra, Jaco. "*The University Licensing Program (TULIP): Electronic Journals in Materials Science.*" *Microcomputers for Information Management* 12, nos. 1/2 (1995): 99-111.

Serials Costs and Impact on Libraries

Christensen, John O. "Cost of Chemistry Journals to One Academic Library, 1980-1990." *Serials Review* 18 (fall 1992): 19-34.

Kirk, Thomas G. "Periodicals in College Libraries: Are the Challenges of Rising Subscription Costs Being Met?" *College and Research Libraries News* 53 (February 1992): 94-97.

Kronenfeld, Michael R. "Update on Inflation of Journal Prices in the Brandon-Hill List of Journals." *Bulletin of the Medical Library Association* 84 (April 1996): 260-63.

Prabha, Chandra, and John E. Ogden. "Recent Trends in Academic Library Materials Expenditures." *Library Trends* 42 (winter 1994): 499-513.

Report of the ARL Serials Prices Project. Washington, D.C.: Association of Research Libraries, 1989.

Chapter Three

Collection Management of Serials: Part 1

Collection management is now frequently used to describe the specialty previously called *collection development,* although both terms are still used, sometimes almost interchangeably, with their precise meanings and connotations varying among authorities. *Collection management* was chosen for the chapter title because it implies the management of scarce financial resources to obtain—through a variety of means—information resources that meet patron information needs.

The focus of serials collection management has shifted over the last several decades. During the 1960s, the profession devoted much attention to selection for collection building and microform conversion. Beginning sometime in the 1970s or early 1980s, deselection and budgeting strategies to meet exploding serials costs became major issues. In the late 1990s, the management of electronic journals, the implications of the World Wide Web (WWW), and the effective use of document delivery services are the dominant topics. Ironically, even though new issues rise to the forefront of professional attention, most of the earlier issues must still be confronted.

Collection management is probably both the most important and the most challenging serials function, although this statement might reflect the author's personal bias as a collection development specialist. Undoubtedly, interest in serials collection management has increased in recent years because of continuously escalating serials costs in tandem with stagnant library budgets, the emergence of new electronic formats, and an increased emphasis on access rather than ownership.

Collection management takes place in both a micro and a macro sense. *Micro* refers to a title-by-title approach, whereas *macro* refers to broad, across-the-board decisions or the entire collection. The micro and macro concepts can be applied to evaluation, criteria, and decision making. This distinction may be somewhat artificial in regard to serials because the whole serials collection is often evaluated on a title-by-title basis, but it offers a useful framework for discussion.

This chapter emphasizes serials microevaluation criteria and the basic serials collection management functions: selection; deselection (i.e., cancellation), weeding, and relegation to remote storage; document delivery; the concept of access versus ownership; and budgeting for serials. Chapter 4 addresses such serials collection management functions as filling gaps in backruns, treatment of unbound issues, and multiple copy and location decisions; serials decision models; core lists of serials; and serials macroevaluation methods. See also chapter 5, which addresses the application of citation analysis to journal collection management; chapter 6, which is devoted to periodical use studies; chapter 7, which covers journal ranking methods; chapter 8's section about copyright law's implications for serials management; and chapter 9, which contains analysis of electronic journal management.

SERIALS MICROEVALUATION CRITERIA

All the crucial serials collection management decisions require evaluative judgments about specific serial titles—in other words, *microevaluation*. The criteria for making these judgments are outlined and discussed below. This section does not distinguish between strictly evaluative criteria relating to a particular title's intrinsic merits and selection or deselection criteria (or both) on a title's appropriateness for a particular library. The criteria are listed in alphabetical rather than priority order.

Alternate Format Availability

An increasing number of journals are published in both print and electronic format. This situation creates a complex set of options, as the library faces four choices for such titles: a print subscription only; an electronic subscription only; simultaneous print and electronic subscriptions; or no subscription—presumably relying on a document delivery service or interlibrary loan (ILL) to meet user needs. Similarly, a title's availability as part of a full-text collection the library subscribes to or is considering, such as EBSCO's *MasterFile FullText* series (described in chapter 9), might influence decisions regarding the print version.

Authors

The stature of authors can be useful for assessing a journal's scholarly quality. Author names can be obtained from the table of contents, and institutional affiliation is usually indicated in the bylines for specific articles. Use of this criterion presupposes some level of knowledge concerning the leading scholars in the journal's discipline. However, the title, rank, and institutional affiliation of authors can offer helpful clues concerning their stature. In some disciplines (e.g., library and information science), the institutional affiliation of authors will also help indicate whether the journal is oriented toward scholars or practitioners. The extent of international authorship can also serve as a significant indicator of a journal's basic character, if not quality. A caveat should be noted: New titles may artificially recruit big-name scholars for initial issues, creating an artificial illusion of the authors' stature.

Citation Record

Citation analysis is predicated on the assumption that citation of an item by a researcher indicates that it has been used in the research process. Accordingly, citation data, although controversial, can provide clues about a journal's usefulness to researchers. This criterion is primarily applicable to academic and research libraries because support of the research process is a major component of their mission. Basic citation data (i.e., total citations received, impact factor, and comparison to other journals in the same discipline) are readily available for thousands of journals if a library has access to the *Science Citation Index* (SCI) or *Social Sciences Citation Index* (SSCI) *Journal Citation Reports* (JCR). Also, the Institute for Scientific Information (ISI), the JCR's publisher, can provide customized reports about faculty citation patterns at a particular university.

Collecting Priorities

A library's collecting priorities regarding a title's subject, audience, purpose, and so forth are undoubtedly some of the most important criteria. Serials collecting priorities should be outlined in the library's collection development policy, assuming it has one. In cases where no written collection policy exists, staff with collection management responsibilities usually possess an informal perception of collecting priorities, although informal perceptions are so unstable they may have little practical value—hence, the desirability of a written policy. Margaret Hawthorn's 1990 survey of more than 200 North American academic libraries revealed that 51 percent of large and 48 percent of small academic libraries have unwritten policies on serials selection and cancellation, whereas only 14 percent of large and 25 percent of small academic libraries have written policies.[1]

Collecting priorities often take the form of an across-the-board macro-decision. For example, G. Edward Evans's textbook, *Developing Library and Information Center Collections,* outlines but not necessarily endorses a number of such decisions for serial selection: subscribe to all journals users request if in a collected subject area, any journal requested on ILL more than *X* times, and all core titles; do not subscribe to unindexed periodicals or unrefereed journals.[2]

Core or Recommended Lists

Whether a particular title is listed on a core or recommended periodical list, such as *Magazines for Libraries*, can, in many instances, be a significant factor in collection management decision making. A detailed discussion of the use of these tools, along with an explanation of the core concept, appears in chapter 4.

Cost-Effectiveness

Two other basic criteria, use and subscription cost, can be combined to determine a periodical's cost-per-use or, in other terms, cost-effectiveness. Cost-per-use data are most valuable when used to rank groups of journals—by subject, library location, or possibly the library's complete list (although comparing the cost-effectiveness of journals from different subject areas may result in methodological flaws). Because usage data are required, this criterion would normally be used in cancellation rather than selection decisions. The library would presumably wish to retain the most cost-effective titles and target the least cost-effective ones for review. This is a more valid criterion than cost alone because the most expensive titles can be highly used and thus be more cost-effective than many less expensive periodicals. Most libraries have cost records readily available, but usage data usually require a separate study. For a lengthier discussion, see "Cost Per Use" in chapter 6.

Editor and Editorial Board Membership

This criterion is significant primarily for scholarly journals—most of which have editorial boards. The appropriate names along with their institutional affiliations can usually be obtained from a journal's masthead. The earlier discussion concerning authors' stature and affiliation as evaluative criteria would also apply to the editor and editorial board members.

Geographical Area Availability

This factor frequently affects serials collection management decision making. For example, a serial with one or more other subscriptions within the same library, library system, consortium, or geographical area may, by virtue of this fact, become a more likely candidate for cancellation than a unique subscription that is not available nearby. On the other hand, a title might be selected for subscription because it is not available elsewhere. Finally, many libraries, during their first round of serials cancellations, focus on duplicate copies within the library or system for cancellation.

Grade-Level and Age-Level

These criteria, of course, are limited to children's or young adult magazines and would be of interest only to public, school, or academic libraries supporting education programs that collect for these audiences. Publisher-reported age- and grade-levels for numerous children's magazines can be found in Selma K. Richardson's *Magazines for Children: A Guide for Parents, Teachers, and Librarians*. However, she cautions readers to consider "age- and grade-level designations as rough estimates or general indicators of the reading difficulty."[3]

Indexing

Whether a periodical is indexed is a long-standing evaluation criterion. Yet Hawthorn found that only 19 percent of large libraries and 24 percent of small libraries considered indexing during the selection process. (*Large* libraries were defined as having more than 5,000 current periodical subscriptions, and *small* libraries had between 1,500 and 4,999.)[4] In contrast, an informal survey reported on SERIALST in 1997 revealed that 76 percent of the responding libraries consider indexing a "very important" factor in serials collection management.[5] The conventional wisdom states that an indexed journal is preferable to an unindexed one and that a journal's stature increases with the number of indexes covering it (although a simple count of index coverage would give an unfair advantage to interdisciplinary journals). The validity of indexing and abstracting coverage as a criterion is predicated on two assumptions: the title's selection for coverage testifies to its perceived caliber; and patron demand for the periodical will increase because they will locate citations to it, assuming the coverage is by an index to which the library subscribes or provides access. This criterion penalizes new journals that have not had an opportunity to be picked up by an indexing service.

Ironically, the indexing criterion was once a dual-edged sword. If a library did not hold an unindexed journal in its collection, patron access through ILL would be inhibited because it would be impossible, except through footnotes and bibliographies, to locate citations to specific articles in order to generate ILL requests. Currently, however, citations to a journal not covered by the standard indexes in a library's collection might well be found through CARL's UnCover, accessible for free on the Internet, or a table of contents service.

Interlibrary Loan and Document Delivery Statistics

Because copyright requirements mandate that libraries record serial titles requested on ILL (see "Additional Copyright Issues" in chapter 8), useful evaluation data are provided. As stated in the American Library Association's (ALA) *Guide to the Evaluation of Library Collections*, ILL "loan requests are generally acknowledged to be indicators of unmet research demand on the part of the library's users. These analyses may be used . . . to identify specific current or retrospective journal titles to be purchased."[6] ILL and document delivery data are obviously more useful for selection decisions than for identifying candidates for cancellation. Hawthorn's 1990 survey found that 71 percent of large libraries and 61 percent of small ones incorporated ILL data into selection decisions.[7] Theoretically, there should be no ILL or document delivery requests for a title if a library currently subscribes to it and owns the complete backruns. In such an instance, ILL and document delivery statistics could clearly not be used in cancellation decisions. However, if gaps exist in a library's holdings, ILL and document delivery requests for the missing years would be pertinent to a cancellation decision. Also, ILL and document delivery data can be used for ex post facto monitoring of cancellation decisions.

Language

A journal's language is often not considered a major evaluation criterion because it is such a self-evident factor. For many smaller libraries, language is a criterion only by default, as the collecting emphasis concentrates on English-language periodicals. However, if a significant segment of a public or school library's clientele are nonnative speakers of English, magazines should be collected in the appropriate non-English language. The recent emphasis on multiculturalism in library services and collections implies an increasing need for non-English language periodicals in public and school libraries. Large academic libraries have traditionally collected a substantial number of foreign language periodicals to support research, especially in area studies. The extent to which an academic library should collect foreign language serial publications to support the personal needs of international students is a debatable issue.

Patron Needs

On the surface this seems like a rather simple, straightforward criterion, as meeting client information needs is a fundamental collection development principle. Indeed, many have argued that this should be the most important periodical selection criterion. Beneath the surface, the concept of patron need covers a complex set of issues, including type of need (i.e., research versus teaching); category of patron (e.g., adult versus juvenile or community resident versus nonresident); and the question of need versus demand—a long-standing controversy in collection management thought.

A major, practical question is, How does one determine a particular periodical's relevance to patron needs? A precise scientific approach does not necessarily exist. Most of the other criteria outlined here would be incorporated in reaching the judgment. Helpful strategies include gaining guidance from the collection development policy, informally consulting key patrons, directly examining the periodical in question, reading reviews, and using such tools as *Magazines for Libraries,* by Bill Katz and Linda Sternberg Katz.[8] Often the question boils down to a librarian's professional judgment concerning the match between a periodical and his or her patrons' needs. As Bill Katz stated in 1971, "Selection of any material for the library presupposes some type of judgment."[9] Although the statement is a collection development truism, one can not overemphasize the importance of knowledge concerning the user community and their information needs. Other criteria listed here—use, citation, and ILL and document delivery data—can provide objective indicators of patron demand.

Physical Makeup and Illustrative Material

Public and school libraries attach much greater importance to the physical construction of popularly oriented magazines than academic libraries do for scholarly journals. Major issues relating to physical composition include size, shape, paper quality, binding, typography, and the quantity and quality of illustrative material. These criteria are often mentioned in reviews or can be ascertained through direct examination.

The nature of illustrative matter can be a particularly significant criterion for some serial categories, such as popular magazines, periodicals for a juvenile audience, or art magazines or journals. For example, Phyllis J. Van Orden lists "pertinent and adequately reproduced" illustrations as one of six newspaper and periodical selection criteria for school libraries.[10]

Place of Publication

Place of publication is generally not thought of as a major criterion in serials evaluation and selection. Nevertheless, most libraries tend to emphasize periodicals published in their own country. Moreover, place of publication can be especially important in certain circumstances or for some types of serials.

- *Locally published periodicals.* For public libraries, the fact that a magazine, newspaper, or newsletter was published in its local community or service area would be an important consideration. Likewise, an academic library might place a higher priority on journals published or edited at its institution.

- *Periodicals pertaining to area studies.* Academic libraries supporting area study programs clearly need to collect historical, literary, economic, and political periodicals and newspapers published in the appropriate areas.

- *Newspapers.* The place of a newspaper's publication can be critical for libraries seeking geographical balance in their newspaper coverage or wishing to give either representation or emphasis to particular cities, states, or countries. For example, a library could decide to emphasize newspapers published in its own state or region and select only a single newspaper (presumably the most prestigious) to represent other regions or foreign countries.

- *Political implications associated with place of publication.* Often the place of publication can have political implications (i.e., the knowledge that a periodical is published in a communist regime, a Third World nation, or a military dictatorship would be a valuable indicator of its political stance). For a cogent discussion of the role publication place plays in the selection process, see Ross Atkinson's article "The Citation As Intertext: Toward a Theory of the Selection Process."[11] This factor may now be less significant than in the past, considering the Soviet Union's dissolution in 1991 and the end of the cold war, but nevertheless, it can still be a consideration for some periodicals.

Finally, given fluctuations in international currency exchange rates, the country of publication can have profound implications for a periodical's cost.

Present Holdings

This criterion would obviously apply to cancellation, weeding, and relegation to remote storage but not subscription decisions. Many serials collection managers seem to assume that a long, complete run of a title is positive, whereas a short or incomplete run is negative. Although this premise has some validity, such factors as use, relevance to user need, and the library's collecting priorities should take precedence over the extent of holdings. For canceled titles, the fact that holdings are incomplete and scattered would be a good reason for weeding.

Price

Subscription price is clearly important yet more complex than might be assumed. Some serial titles are deemed so important that librarians feel they must subscribe to them regardless of the price. Hawthorn's research revealed that subscription cost was a much more important criterion in cancellation decisions (with 70 percent of large and 92 percent of small libraries listing it as a factor) than in selecting a new serial subscription, where only 12 percent of large libraries and 9 percent of small ones responded it was a consideration.[12]

Publisher

The publisher's name, a basic evaluative criterion, is readily obtainable by examining the serial and normally included in reviews and advertisements. There are two dimensions to this criterion: the specific publisher's reputation and publisher type—commercial, university press, or society or association. Collection management experience in a subject usually leads to knowledge concerning the reputation of the area's major publishers. Research suggests that periodicals from nonprofit publishers may be more cost-effective than those from commercial ones (see Bernard M. Fry and Herbert S. White,[13] Sandra R. Moline,[14] and others).

Refereed Status

Whether a journal is refereed is an important factor in judging its scholarly quality. For collection management purposes, this criterion would be most important to academic libraries. Apart from libraries, a journal's refereeing status is critical in authors' manuscript submission decisions and in evaluating a scholar's publication record during the promotion and tenure process. Usually (but not always) one can ascertain if a journal is refereed by reading the masthead or the instructions to authors section. Other methods include consulting such standard sources as EBSCO's *Serials Directory*, *Ulrich's*, or *Magazines for Libraries* or telephoning the editor.[15]

Requestor

When a title is under review for cancellation, the name of the individual who originally requested it can be quite useful, especially in an academic setting, where collections have commonly been built in response to faculty demands. For example, a cancellation decision can be much easier if the faculty requestor has left the institution. Obviously, the requestor's name will be available only if the library has maintained a record, which is not always the case. Likewise, when considering titles for subscription, the requestor's status can be significant, with a dean's request carrying more clout than a faculty member's and a faculty member's more than a student's. Based on the author's professional experience in collection management, the requestor's status can sometimes be more critical than the intrinsic merit of the item being requested. Surely political considerations are important in serials collection management, yet there is an ethical dimension to favoring one user over another—raising important and complex issues beyond this discussion's scope.

Subject Focus

A periodical's subject content is obviously one of the most important considerations affecting any collection management decision, especially when placed in the context of the library's collecting priorities and user needs. For academic libraries, the critical factor is the subject's relevance to the curriculum and faculty research interests. Subject focus can normally be ascertained from direct inspection or reading reviews. However, remember that for some periodicals, the subject focus is not readily apparent and, in any case, a title's subject content can change over time.

Subjective Judgment Based on Direct Examination

This criterion differs from most of the others discussed here because it is a technique instead of an intrinsic characteristic of a periodical or library. Nevertheless, a great deal can be learned about a periodical title and many of the other evaluation criteria outlined here can be accessed simply by examining one or more recent issues. Direct examination can verify such basic factual information as the publisher, place of publication, language, and frequency. A quick perusal should reveal the title's subject content and audience (i.e., scholarly journal or popular magazine). For journals, examining the table of contents, scope statement, masthead, and instructions to contributors should indicate whether the journal is refereed, whether there is an editorial board, and the qualifications of authors and editorial board members—thus providing clues to the journal's scholarly quality. For magazines, observe the writing style and physical format as well as the type and quality of illustrative material. Through such perusal, an impressionistic judgment can be made concerning the periodical's scope, intended audience, overall quality, relevance to client information needs, and consistency with the library's collecting priorities.

For cancellation, weeding, and relegation to remote storage purposes, journal issues will obviously be available for examination. Publishers or serial subscription agents frequently provide sample issues to libraries that are considering a title for subscription. With increasing frequency, sample issues can also be examined electronically, such as through the Electronic Newsstand as well as a publisher or journal page on the WWW.

Use

A serial's use record is one of the most decisive criteria, as actual usage is crucial evidence of relevance to patron need. This criterion clearly can not be used for subscription decisions, unless a duplicate is being considered (which is rather unlikely in the present financial environment). Nevertheless, a collection manager's estimation of usage level might affect a selection decision, and actual use is a major consideration in cancellation and weeding decisions. Because of its importance, use is discussed in detail in chapter 6.

User Input

Although a technique instead of a serial or library characteristic, user input counts as an important criterion because it can provide useful information on which to base serials collection management decisions. Input from end users can help access a periodical's relevance to their needs and overall quality as well as provide great political advantages to the library—it is harder for constituents to criticize decisions on which they were consulted.

This approach is most frequently used in academic libraries, where faculty input can be a major—and in some instances, the decisive—criterion. Input can be obtained through both informal (i.e., a personal conversation or telephone call) and formal means (such as a survey).

Writing Style

Writing style is a significant criterion for some types of periodicals, such as literary reviews, popular magazines, and children's and young adult publications. It is used much more frequently by public and school libraries than academic libraries, which would not normally use this criterion in the assessment of scholarly journals. Although judgments about writing style are somewhat subjective, they can be ascertained through direct inspection, reviews, or annotations in recommended lists. Major stylistic issues include clarity, readability, and appropriateness for the intended audience. Because style can vary from article to article within the same magazine, one should base judgments concerning style on more than a single issue.

Summary

A few other possible criteria, not listed above, should be briefly mentioned. A magazine's circulation might be used as a measure of popularity, but it is seldom a critical decision-making criterion. Frequency of publication, although a basic serial characteristic, is usually not a major microevaluation criterion. A serial's age is occasionally considered a criterion, based on the assumption that older titles are more established. A journal's acceptance rate—that is, the percentage of submitted articles accepted for publication—is deemed a measure of scholarly prestige. Acceptance rate and perceived scholarly quality display an inverse relationship—in other words, the lower the acceptance rate the greater the scholarly rigor attributed to a journal. This criterion, primarily of interest to scholars, is seldom used by librarians in serials decision making, partially because it can be difficult to obtain the data. Curricular relevance and quality, frequently stated to be major criteria, are not listed here because *curricular relevance* is covered under the heading "Patron Needs," above, and *quality* represents numerous criteria that have been analyzed under other headings.

Every criteria examined here will not be used in each serials collection management decision. Moreover, their relative importance varies from situation to situation depending upon the type of serial and library and the purpose for which the serial is being evaluated. Methods for combining and assigning relative value to various criteria are discussed in chapter 4, under "Serials Decision Models."

SERIALS COLLECTION MANAGEMENT FUNCTIONS

The basic serials collection management functions are

- selection
- cancellation
- weeding
- relegation to remote storage
- filling gaps in backruns
- treatment of unbound single issues
- multiple copy decisions
- location decisions
- subscription versus document delivery decisions
- budgeting

This section covers the most important functions: selection, deselection (cancellation, weeding, and relegation to remote storage), subscription versus document delivery decisions, and budgeting. The remaining functions are addressed in chapter 4.

Selection

Selection of materials for addition to the collection is probably the oldest and most basic collection management function. For this discussion, *selection* is defined as deciding to place an initial subscription. Although libraries in the present financial environment are more likely to be canceling subscriptions than selecting new ones, some selection is essential to meet new needs of users and to respond to developments in publishing.

Selection can be seen as a three-stage process: identification, evaluation, and selection. *Identification* determines that a periodical actually exists. *Evaluation* assesses the periodical's intrinsic merit or quality. *Selection* entails a library's decision to subscribe to a particular periodical. Each stage will be briefly discussed.

Before an item can be considered for selection, its existence must be identified. Identification can take place through reviews, publisher advertising, or inclusion in core lists or standard tools such as Katz and Katz's *Magazines for Libraries*. For a detailed listing of serials identification tools, see Luke Swindler's chapter on collection development in Marcia Tuttle's *Managing Serials*. He annotates approximately 35 sources for identifying various types of serials, including periodicals, newspapers, and newsletters.[16] Often identification is provided by an individual requesting the subscription. For gifts, identification might take place when the first free issue arrives in the library.

Evaluation focuses on the journal itself and can be either internal or external. In internal evaluation, the collection manager or committee reaches their own assessment of a journal's intrinsic merit. In external evaluation, an evaluation is explicitly supplied by an external third party (e.g., a review of *Magazines for Libraries*). Typical evaluation criteria for a scholarly journal for an academic library would include citation record; indexing; publisher reputation; professional stature of the editor, editorial board members, and contributing authors; and refereed status. In evaluating magazines, a public library would consider writing style, indexing, audience, place of publication, and physical makeup. A school library media center would place emphasis on such criteria as audience, indexing, age and grade level, as well as format and quality of illustrations.

The decision to select a journal for subscription represents the final step in this three-stage framework. Traditional selection criteria include financial considerations, perceived user needs, availability elsewhere in the geographic vicinity, the library's collecting priorities, and such political considerations as the requestor's status. Remember that evaluation and selection do not necessarily correlate with each other. A periodical could be evaluated highly but not selected because the library can not afford it or is not interested in its subject area. For example, a library might decide not to collect the premier dog racing journal because it has no interest in that topic.

The framework of identification, evaluation, and selection represents an idealized intellectual model. In practice, libraries have (or should have) a written procedure for selection of new periodical subscriptions.

Deselection

Three distinct actions—cancellation, weeding, and relegation to remote storage—are grouped under the term *serials deselection*. For the following discussion, *cancellation* is defined as identifying current subscriptions for termination; *weeding* means removing holdings from the collection for disposal or transfer to another library; and *relegation to remote storage* refers to moving materials from the active collection to a less-accessible physical location, internal or external to the library.

Unfortunately, these terms are not always used consistently. Many authorities, including Loriene Roy in her thorough review of the weeding literature in the *Encyclopedia of Library and Information Science*,[17] have used *periodical weeding* to encompass all three types of deselection. The American Library Association's *Guide to Review of Library Collections: Preservation, Storage, and Withdrawal* applies the term *weeding* to both withdrawal and storage.[18] In Great Britain, the term *relegation* is applied to what North Americans call *weeding* or *placement in remote storage*.

In recent years, serials deselection in the majority of libraries tended to concentrate on cancellation rather than weeding or relegation to storage. Most libraries that cancel a current periodical subscription do not immediately weed the backruns from the collection. Periodicals are usually canceled to save money, but typically they are weeded or relegated to remote storage to save space.

Cancellation

As a consequence of library budgets that do not keep pace with serials inflation rates, serials cancellation has become all-too-frequent in innumerable academic libraries throughout North America. In fact, many libraries have faced repeated rounds of cancellations. Thomas E. Nisonger's *Collection Evaluation in Academic Libraries: A Literature Guide and Annotated Bibliography* annotates more than 25 serials cancellation case studies published during the 1980s and early 1990s,[19] thus illustrating the fairly substantial literature on the topic.

In a sense, serials cancellation is easier than selection because more information is directly available upon which to base the decision. Recent holdings are available for inspection; the periodical's actual usage in the library can be accessed; and patrons can provide input based on their experience using the title.

Although budgetary pressures have been the driving force behind most academic library serials cancellations in recent years, responsible serials collection management dictates some cancellation of subscriptions, apart from any financial considerations. The library's collecting priorities or a journal's quality or focus may change so that a subscription to a specific title is simply no longer needed. Furthermore, one can reasonably anticipate a future trend of canceling print subscriptions and replacing them with electronic subscriptions to the same titles. It could be argued, however, that this action represents a shift from one format to another rather than genuine cancellation.

Cancellation Criteria.

Cancellation is the logical opposite of selection—a self-evident observation but one with significant implications for the application of evaluation and selection criteria. The various criteria outlined in this chapter's initial section apply to cancellation as well as selection decisions but generally from the opposite direction—that is, a journal ranking high on a criterion would be selected, whereas one with a low ranking would be canceled. Some of the most important cancellation criteria are summarized below.

- *Use*. Use is the most frequently employed cancellation criterion—a fact verified in Judith A. Segal's review of 53 published items about journal deselection.[20] One should focus attention on the least used titles.

- *Foreign language titles*. Foreign language serials have traditionally been among the first to be canceled.

- *Duplicate subscriptions*. As with foreign language titles, duplicates are traditionally among the first to be deselected.

- *Cost and cost-effectiveness*. Expensive and non-cost-effective titles are usually prime targets for cancellation, with obvious exceptions. Journals that can not be canceled for political reasons, no matter how expensive, are sometimes called "sacred cows."

- *Indexing*. Unindexed titles are major candidates for cancellation.

- *Patron input.* In academic libraries, faculty input is a major, if not decisive, factor.

- *Inclusion on core or recommended lists.* Inclusion on a credible list would be a compelling reason not to cancel a title. This criterion would be most useful for smaller and medium-sized libraries.

The potential value of citation data as cancellation criteria is somewhat controversial. Robert N. Broadus proposes that instead of conducting an expensive use study, a library could check the citation record of its subscription list in the *Journal Citation Reports* and review the bottom-ranking 20 percent for possible cancellation.[21] But Maurice B. Line argues that citation data for low-ranking "fringe" titles are of little decision-making value because a small change in the already limited number of citations received can cause a large fluctuation in rank. Line also asserts that national citation data might not reflect actual usage in a local library.[22] Research on these issues is reviewed in chapter 5. In the final analysis, citation data are valid criteria, but they must be used with caution and with other variables.

Tony Stankus, a prolific author on scientific serials, has proposed canceling and weeding journals in the research areas of faculty members who have ceased publishing. How does one know a faculty member has stopped publishing? Stankus concludes, based on analysis of the publication records of 53 Ph.D.-holding chemists, that "When a faculty member exceeds his own longest previous gap without a paper" he or she has probably ceased publication activity.[23] Although Stankus's technique is intriguing, it is not necessarily recommended, as its implementation could create political problems for a library.

The Serials Cancellation Project.

It is beyond this chapter's scope to present a comprehensive outline for conducting a serials cancellation project. It is difficult, in any case, to generalize about cancellation projects because each one presents unique problems dependent upon the library's circumstances. Nevertheless, some practical considerations, gleaned from the literature and my own professional experience, are listed below.

- *Be prepared in advance.* One cannot overemphasize the importance of advance preparation. Too often serials cancellation projects are carried out in a sense of crisis after unexpected budgetary developments. Have a contingency plan. Keep readily accessible the information you will need, including expenditure records, use studies, collection evaluations, and pertinent correspondence with faculty. Analyze past cancellation projects so that mistakes can be corrected in future projects.

- *Maintain a database of serial records, ideally in electronic form.* The record for each title should, at a minimum, contain basic information—the publisher, holdings, frequency, vendor, yearly costs for the past several years, the requestor, and programs supported by the periodical. Additional information might include circulation, use data, citation data, indexing, coverage in recommended lists, and results of user surveys. Sherrie Schmidt, Jane Treadwell, and Gloriana St. Clair describe the use of database management software to create a serials review list at Texas A&M University.[24]

- *Develop a plan for the project.* The plan should address such issues as the project's goal in terms of the dollar amount or percentage to be cut; the set of steps to be completed; a timetable for the completion of each step and a final deadline; the decision-making methodology to use; who is ultimately responsible for final decisions; a mechanism for communicating with library users; and staff responsibilities.

- *Consult with faculty, but retain final decision-making authority in the library.* Anecdotal evidence from academic librarians indicates that all-too-frequently, decision-making authority is turned over to the institution's faculty. Although this may be politically advantageous, it is also an abdication of professional responsibility. One is tempted to paraphrase the adage "war is too important to be left to the generals" with the statement "serials collection management is too important to be left to the faculty."

- *Be fully aware of the political implications.* This is a self-evident but vital point. Communicate why the project is necessary. Place your library's action in the context of national trends (i.e., innumerable libraries throughout the country are canceling serials). Stress that access to canceled titles can be provided by means other than ownership. Devise a mechanism for faculty input concerning which titles are canceled.

- *Maintain a positive attitude.* Maintaining staff morale can be challenging because a serials cancellation project often requires considerable extra work. Remember, however, that serials cancellation is not inevitably bad. Regular review of serial subscriptions may be viewed as part of responsible collection management, which is why cancellation endeavors are sometimes termed "serials review" projects. In the initial round, these projects often identify numerous periodical titles that should be canceled in any case based on changes in library collecting priorities.

Weeding

Weeding refers to removing items from the collection, much as one excises obnoxious weeds from a garden. A fairly voluminous body of literature concerning weeding has been published, and some explicit weeding methodologies have been proposed. Both the theory and practice of weeding have traditionally tended to focus on monographs, although the concept can be applied to any format collected by the library, including periodicals. The two best-known guides to weeding, Stanley J. Slote's *Weeding Library Collections: Library Weeding Methods,*[25] issued in four editions and arguably the premier work on the topic, and Joseph P. Segal's *Evaluating and Weeding Collections in Small and Medium-Sized Public Libraries: The CREW Method,*[26] concentrate almost exclusively on books, with only limited reference to serials weeding.

Slote lists (but does not necessarily endorse) six periodical weeding criteria applicable to various types of libraries, which he "culled" from the published weeding literature: unindexed titles; ceased-publication titles that have no cumulative index; incomplete runs; early volumes of long runs, especially of 50 or 60 volumes; "journals in English petroleum libraries after 13 years;" and "in school libraries, keep three to five years; one year if not indexed."[27] In the third edition of his work, Slote asserted, "For runs of periodicals, remove all before a specific publication date. This date should be established separately for each run."[28] Segal's CREW Method proposes weeding periodicals that are not indexed in the *Readers' Guide* or other major indexing tools owned by the library. He also states that periodicals and newspapers should be clipped "sparingly" for the vertical file prior to discard.[29]

Periodical weeding differs from monograph weeding in some key respects. Periodical weeding is easier because fewer titles must be reviewed. It is also more complicated because periodical weeding can occur at two levels: the decision to remove the complete holdings or the decision to remove part of the holdings, presumably those older than a particular date.

Major criteria for weeding periodicals are enumerated below (but not in a priority order). These criteria should normally be applied in combination with each other.

- *Physical condition.* As with all formats, periodicals in deteriorating physical condition are good candidates for weeding.

- *Completeness of holdings.* Short, scattered holdings are better candidates for weeding than long, complete runs.

- *Use.* Unused or infrequently used periodical runs are obvious targets for weeding. Use in relation to shelf space occupied has also been suggested as a periodical weeding criterion.

- *Age.* Older periodical runs have traditionally been considered prime targets for weeding. However, the critical variable is use rather than age per se. The concept of "literature obsolescence" relates use to age by demonstrating that older periodical holdings are less frequently used. As explained in chapter 5, obsolescence varies among disciplines.

- *Current collecting priorities.* One of the most compelling reasons for weeding is a change in the library's collecting priorities.

- *Availability elsewhere.* Periodical runs that are available in nearby libraries are clearly stronger candidates for weeding than holdings unique within the geographical area. Likewise, duplicate runs within the same library system may be prime weeding targets. Locally published periodicals should not be weeded to ensure their permanent archiving in at least one library.

- *Cooperative agreements with other libraries and consortiums.* A periodical can be weeded with greater confidence if another library has agreed to maintain the specific title or a strong collection in its subject area.

- *Indexing.* The conventional wisdom asserts that unindexed titles are excellent possibilities for weeding, and indexed ones should be maintained. However, it should be stressed that the critical factor is not current indexing but whether the runs under consideration for weeding were indexed.

- *Core or recommended lists.* Most libraries are reluctant to weed titles on core or recommended lists. Some small libraries use a strict policy: Any title not on a recommended list should be weeded.

- *Whether the library currently subscribes to the periodical under examination.* Lack of a current subscription can be a major factor in deciding to weed the backrun holdings, as they become more obsolete with each passing year.

From a more theoretical perspective, John Urguhart argues that the effectiveness of any weeding criterion can be tested by two measurements: the proportion of weeded items subsequently needed for use and the proportion of total use lost by weeding.[30] However, very little empirical research on periodical weeding criteria effectiveness has been reported in the literature.

For academic and research libraries, citation data can be especially helpful in decisions about weeding as well as relegation to remote storage. When a journal's backruns are no longer cited or cited infrequently, it is presumed that use by researchers has ceased or tapered off. The "cited half-life," available for thousands of journals in the ISI's JCR, is a helpful indicator of how long a particular journal's backruns are cited. Detailed explanations of the cited half-life and the JCR may be found in chapter 5.

From a long-term perspective, the development of electronic journals has potentially profound implications for serials weeding strategy. Disposal of print holdings that are easily accessible electronically might be a logical step. However, there is no present guarantee that electronic holdings will be permanently archived. Finally, canceling and weeding electronic journals per se offers a myriad of unresolved issues that librarians have hardly even begun to address.

Weeding is often the most difficult collection management function. It can be expensive in terms of staff time and requires changing cataloging or holdings records. Moreover, weeding is fraught with political risk, as many patrons do not understand why a library would dispose of holdings. Yet, apart from the space-saving issue, a well-weeded periodical collection should be stronger and more effective at meeting client information needs.

Relegation to Remote Storage

The terms *remote storage, secondary storage,* or simply *storage* may be considered synonyms. The Association for Library Collections and Technical Services' (ALCTS) *Guide to Review of Library Collections* defines *storage* as "the transfer of less-used materials to restricted areas within the library building or to a remote facility."[31] In the following discussion, the concept of remote storage refers to a secondary location facility for material that has been processed and added to the collection. A storeroom housing a backlog of unprocessed materials that are inaccessible to library patrons is not considered remote storage.

Relegation to remote storage represents a compromise between full retention in the active collection and weeding. As with weeding, the primary motivation for placement in secondary storage is usually the conservation of shelf space. A typical remote storage area would receive both books and serials. In some instances, a group of libraries may share a single remote storage facility.

The numerous organizational and technical problems involved in administering a remote storage facility (e.g., regular shelves versus compact shelves, the arrangement of material within the facility, and so on) are beyond this book's scope. The major serials collection management issue concerns determining which titles and runs will be placed in remote storage. Most of the weeding criteria and methods discussed in the preceding section would also be applicable to remote storage decisions and consequently need not be repeated here.

An October 1986 survey of college and small university library directors found that nearly half of their libraries (precisely 49.2 percent) used a "storage or secondary location" for at least some serial titles. In terms of location, 65.6 percent of these facilities were in the library, 25 percent on campus, and 6.3 percent off campus. Moreover, 54.2 percent of those responding to the question indicated periodicals in storage were accessible "within minutes"; 15.3 percent, "within an hour"; 20.3 percent, in 24 hours; and 10.2 percent responded "other"—presumably more than 24 hours. Respondents indicated the following criteria for placement of periodicals in remote storage: a cutoff date, 16.9 percent; use record, 28.8 percent; faculty recommendation or approval, 6.8 percent; and "other" (such as duplicate holdings or items in poor physical condition), 7.6 percent. Moreover, 12.6 percent indicated that canceled journals were placed in storage.[32]

Document Delivery

Traditional collection development postulated that patrons' information needs were to be met by materials owned by and housed in the library. In recent years, a new paradigm emerged, stating that a library's ownership of an item is irrelevant as long as patrons can be provided access to needed documents. The frequently heard but somewhat simplistic slogans "access versus ownership" or "just-in-time versus just-in-case" symbolize this new approach.

The document delivery concept lends itself especially well to journals because individual articles represent distinct units of manageable size that can easily be procured externally. Furthermore, the currently available indexing and abstracting services provide reasonably adequate bibliographical control of the serials literature, thus helping end users identify pertinent articles.

The term *document delivery* is sometimes used in a broad sense to embrace both traditional ILL and commercial document delivery. However, document delivery using the numerous commercial document delivery services that have become major players on the library scene in recent years is usually viewed as a distinct phenomenon from traditional ILL. Dennis P. Carrigan writes:

> It [document delivery] refers to libraries' efforts to secure for their clients copies of materials not available in the libraries, by turning to suppliers that offer the service for a fee. Although the suppliers

receiving the most attention are commercial and not-for-profit firms, there are libraries that, while continuing to perform their traditional roles, have become document delivery agents in this sense of the term. Depending on one's perspective, document delivery and interlibrary loan are complements or competitors.[33]

Document delivery differs from traditional ILL in several respects:

- An ILL item is obtained from the collection of another library, whereas document delivery is usually provided by a commercial vendor.

- ILL is often, but not always, provided free of charge, but there is invariably a fee for document delivery.

- In traditional ILL, a library staff member acts as an intermediary to process the request, but in document delivery the end user often initiates the request.

- Document delivery is generally perceived to be quicker than ILL.

- ILL often supplies the original item, whereas document delivery invariably provides a copy.

- Within specific limitations (see the explanation for the "Rule of Five" in chapter 8's "Copyright" section), articles can be supplied through ILL without payment of a copyright fee, but with document delivery a copyright fee is almost always added. Parenthetically, some librarians have argued that use of document delivery results in the loss of the five free requests per journal that the library would be entitled to receive without paying a copyright fee under ILL.

Numerous entities offer document delivery services to libraries. Some leading services are mentioned in this section, but it is not the author's intention to offer evaluative commentary or endorse one commercial service over another. In the mid-1990s noteworthy document delivery players include national libraries, for example, the Canada Institute for Scientific and Technical Information (CISTI) or the British Library Document Supply Centre; commercial vendors, for example, DIALOG Information Services or EBSCO publishing; and not-for-profit entities such as the Educational Resources Information Center (ERIC) Document service or the Research Libraries Group (RLG). These services typically charge a set fee for each delivered article plus a copyright fee that varies according to the publisher's charge. A 1993 *Library Journal* article by Mounir Khalil summarized 26 document delivery services that were operating or in the planning stage, including ADONIS, the OCLC Dispatch Service, and the UMI Article Clearinghouse. Addresses, phone and fax numbers, coverage, and cost were generally provided for each.[34] Tuttle provides detailed descriptions of seven such services: UnCover, OCLC's ArticleFirst, UMI Infostore, the Genuine Article, Faxon Finder, EBSCODoc, and Swets and Zeitlinger's SwetScan.[35]

Some publishers offer document delivery services for articles from their own publications. For example, Haworth Press advertises in its journals the "Haworth Document Delivery Service" for all Haworth-published articles. The cost is comprised of a "set-up charge per article," photocopying charges per article based on the item's length, an optional "flexicover" charge per article, postage, and handling, and an optional same-day fax service charge based on the number of pages. Likewise, the *New York Times* advertises an "Articles by Fax or Mail" service whereby previously published articles on high-interest topics, such as AIDS, can be ordered for $3.95 each.[36]

An April 1994 survey of 90 Association of Research Libraries (ARL) libraries found that 78 (86.7 percent) used commercial document delivery services to obtain items for their patrons. In terms of the number of supplied items, the most frequently used services were CISTI, 11,630; the Genuine Article, 3,092; UnCover, 3,012; DIALOG, 1,853; the British Library Document Supply Centre, 1,843; and UMI Article Clearing House, 1,776. According to the number of libraries using their services, the top-ranked suppliers were the British Library Document Supply Centre and UMI Article Clearinghouse, both used by 64 libraries; Chemical Abstracts Service, 52 libraries; UnCover, 38 libraries; and the Genuine Article, 30 libraries. Not unexpectedly, given the increased emphasis on access rather than ownership, 73.7 percent (56 of 76 respondents) reported an increased use of document delivery suppliers over the previous fiscal year; 77.8 percent (63 of 81) projected an even greater use of document delivery services in the coming fiscal year.[37]

Document Delivery Versus Subscription

Libraries have traditionally used ILL to procure articles from serials they canceled or never subscribed to in the first place, but commercial document delivery is now a strategic alternative to subscription; and, for a given title, the choice between the two is a fundamental serials collection management decision. The criteria for reaching this decision are examined below.

- *Availability from document delivery services.* Document delivery is not an option for titles that are not offered by document delivery services.

- *Level of use.* Document delivery is most appropriate for infrequently used titles.

- *Need for immediate access.* Subscription is the logical option for titles to which immediate access is required, as most document delivery services take one or two days at a minimum.

- *Purpose of use.* Apart from usage level, the purpose of use is a crucial factor. Titles needed to support the teaching process, which requires rapid access to materials, are better suited for subscription. Moreover, document delivery is not a good option if browsability is an important consideration. In contrast, serials supporting research are strong candidates for document delivery because immediate access is usually not necessary.

- *Political considerations.* This is another self-evident factor. As Bill Coons and Peter McDonald ask, is the decision to use document delivery in place of subscription "likely to adversely affect a powerful department chair?"[38]

- *Cost-effectiveness.* A major question concerns the break-even point at which a library should subscribe to a journal rather than rely on commercial document delivery. If financial considerations are the sole criterion, three major variables would affect the decision: 1) cost of each document delivery; 2) cost of an annual subscription; and 3) number of demands for document delivery within the year. The mathematics are simple, even though the decision making is complicated. If each document delivery costs $9 and an annual subscription $50, it appears cost-effective to subscribe if there will be six or more uses of the journal within a year. (Five uses would cost $45, and six would cost $54.) However, such a crude analysis does not consider the relative staff cost of maintaining a subscription versus reliance on document delivery. In any case, the decision can not be made on cost-effectiveness alone. Unfortunately, one of the most important considerations, user convenience, can not easily be quantified.

Various decision-making policies have been suggested, but there is no consensus. Official standards offer some limited guidance. The 1995 Association of College and Research Libraries (ACRL) standards for college libraries state:

In general it is good practice to consider owning any title that is needed more than five times per year. . . . It may not be necessary to subscribe to certain less frequently used titles if they are available at another library nearby, or if needed articles may be quickly procured through a reliable delivery system or by electronic means.[39]

Coons and McDonald recommend that a subscription be considered in every case where the annual document delivery cost is greater than half the subscription price.[40] A study at the Columbia University Libraries of biology journal requests during 1993 found access through either commercial document delivery or interlibrary loan to be far more cost-effective than subscription for all titles requested 10 or fewer times.[41] Carol Tenopir and Donald W. King likewise assert that ILL or document delivery is less expensive than subscription for journals "read" fewer than 10 times a year.[42] Eleanor A. Gossen and Suzanne Irving conclude that document delivery is preferable for every title used fewer than five times per year regardless of subscription cost.[43]

Bruce R. Kingma and Suzanne Irving's decision model concerns the "economic efficiency" of ILL versus subscription, based on analysis of mathematics and science journals at the State University of New York (SUNY) at Albany, Binghamton, Buffalo, and Stony Brook Libraries during fall 1994. They outline three sets of decision rules:

1. based on the financial cost to the library

2. based on the cost to the library and its patrons

3. based on the cost to the borrowing library, its patrons, and the lending library[44]

Because this relatively sophisticated model does not lend itself well to succinct summary, the interested reader should consult Kingma and Irving's original publication for full details.

Several studies have demonstrated that substantial savings can be derived from substituting document delivery for subscription. The Columbia study found that for the titles from which one article was requested in 1993, the estimated total cost of subscription was $244,917 compared to $11,421 for document delivery.[45] Donna Goehner, dean of libraries at Western Illinois University, revealed at an ALA conference that during an 18-month period, the library had paid $703.70 to access articles through commercial document delivery for faculty requests for items from recently canceled serial subscriptions; the subscriptions for those serials would have cost approximately $50,000.[46] In late 1995 *Forbes* magazine reported that the Louisiana State University Library had paid $25,000 during the preceding two years for commercial document delivery, yet two years earlier $446,000 worth of scholarly journals had been canceled.[47]

The preceding analysis presupposes that the library bears the whole cost of document delivery. Actually, this issue raises a host of questions. Should document delivery costs be recovered, either wholly or partially, from the patron? If the library picks up the cost, which budget should be charged: materials, interlibrary loan, serials, or some other department? Or should a separate line item be created? Should certain categories of patrons receive a higher priority than others? Should a limit be placed on the number of patron requests? Should document delivery be paid for or subsidized for all titles or only certain ones; if the latter, which ones? What criteria are used in determining subsidized and paid-for titles?

Commercial document delivery services available on the Internet, such as UnCover, allow the patron to order articles directly without the intervention of a library staff member. This concept, often termed *disintermediation,* presents an interesting set of issues. One could argue that a library is not necessary if the end user can directly order needed articles. Yet a library can still play a vital role in disintermediated document delivery by paying the fee (either fully or partially). Most of the questions outlined in the preceding paragraph would clearly apply to disintermediated document delivery.

The previously mentioned April 1994 survey of ARL institutions indicated that 54.2 percent of the responding libraries (45 of 83) paid the complete cost of commercial document delivery, whereas 12 percent (10 of 83) passed the full cost on to the patron. Further, 24.1 percent (20 of 83) split the expense between the library and patron, and 9.6 percent (8 of 83) responded "other," which was not explained. Perhaps the latter category included cases where different patron types were treated differently, that is, subsidizing faculty, but not student, requests.[48]

Table of Contents Services

Table of contents services are a relatively new development on the library scene, although they might be viewed as a modified form of Selective Dissemination of Information (SDI) introduced several decades ago. In essence, these services send to designated recipients—usually through Electronic mail (e-mail) or fax, sometimes on tape, disk, or in print—the table of contents of recent journal issues or citations to journal articles based on a subject profile. These services, usually with their own distinctive names, are offered by commercial document suppliers and serial subscription agents. The former includes UnCover Reveal and the latter, Faxon FlashTOC or Swets and Zeitlinger's SwetScan.

Although the precise details vary from service to service, one can cite Un-Cover Reveal as an example. For a $25 annual fee (as of March, 1998), an individual can have the table of contents of 50 journals and the results of 25 search strategies sent to his or her e-mail address. Through the Table of Contents Re-distribution Service, an organization can centrally receive tables of contents for its own redistribution at an annual cost of $10 per title. Institutions (including libraries, universities, and academic departments) can get a site license that allows each user to receive the table of contents for 50 journals of their choice, and the licensing fee is calculated according to a sliding scale based on the number of subscribers. For example, the fee is $750 per year for up to 50 subscribers and $4300 annually if there are more than 400 subscribers.[49]

Table of contents services are inextricably connected to the document delivery concept because many commercial document suppliers also provide this service. For document delivery to work well, library customers must know what articles have recently been published in their areas of interest. Research has yet to be published concerning how libraries actually use table of contents services for serials collection management. Nevertheless, one can speculate that these services

1. provide current awareness that assists access to journals to which the library currently subscribes;

2. help identify articles in journals not subscribed to by the library so they can be obtained through document delivery;

3. sometimes help ordering of documents by the end user without mediation of library staff;

4. as a serendipitous spin-off, provide data about faculty or other patrons' interest in journals.

Key decisions for a library include whether to use a table of contents service, which one to select, and how to finance it. No guidelines or explicit methodologies exist for determining whether a library needs a table of contents service. Basically, the decision is a judgment call. If library staff are satisfied the present journal collection adequately meets patron information needs without procuring documents from external sources, a table of contents service would probably not be especially useful. In contrast, the greater the use of document delivery, the more benefits would be derived from a table of contents service (e.g., identifying articles to be requested and compensating for the fact users can not browse journals to which the library does not subscribe). The budgetary questions about document delivery, discussed in the above section, also apply to table of contents services. Criteria for selecting a table of contents service include cost, coverage, currency, ease of use, and ability to customize service for local needs.

With increasing regularity journals have been making their table of contents available on the WWW or through listservs. Yet it seems doubtful that their separate efforts could be used for systematic serials access with the same effectiveness as a commercial document delivery system.

Access Versus Ownership: The Arguments

This section summarizes the arguments concerning the two basic strategies for meeting patron information needs: access and ownership.

Pro-Access Position.

This position assumes that as long as the library or information center can provide the patron relatively quick access to a document that meets his or her information needs, it is irrelevant whether the item is owned and housed within the institution's four walls or procured from an external source. The ownership concept often wastes scarce financial resources by purchasing materials that are seldom if ever used, as demonstrated by the Pittsburgh study (discussed in chapter 6) and numerous other investigations. Moreover, access through external sources saves shelf space. New technology, including fax machines and the Internet, facilitate access. For example, Ariel, a system developed by the RLG for transmitting documents over the Internet, provides rapid, cost-effective, and high-resolution document delivery. Access proponents often denigrate the ownership concept as "warehousing" and point out that even if a document is owned, it may not be available to patrons.

A distinction between bibliographical access (knowing what has been published) and physical access (having the information source in the patron's hands) should be noted. One of the first consequences of the introduction of electronic media into libraries was that bibliographical access far exceeded immediate physical access, as CD-ROM indexes and abstracts provided citations for serial articles that were not contained in the local collection. This may make patrons more aware of the collection's inadequacies and lead to increased demands for external access through ILL and document delivery.

Pro-Ownership Position.

Ownership represents the traditional paradigm of librarianship. Critics of the pro-access position argue that some of its underlying assumptions—that patrons already know which items will meet their information needs and can wait a reasonable amount of time for access—are not always valid. In reality, patrons sometimes need nearly instantaneous access to information As an extreme example, one sometimes hears the anecdote about the doctor who requested a journal article be delivered to him during surgery and when it was returned to the library, it was covered with blood! Furthermore, clients frequently do not know which documents will meet their information needs. The access concept does not allow for browsing, serendipitously finding relevant items, or directly viewing the range of materials on a particular topic. Although perhaps suitable for supporting research needs, access is less appropriate for such other purposes as teaching, entertainment, or ready reference. Moreover, Rudolf Jacob Penner's research has demonstrated a significant correlation between ownership and accessibility of material.[50]

Analysis.

The "access versus ownership" issue represents a continuum rather than a dichotomy. In other words, it is not a question of wholly one or the other, but rather of the proper balance between the two. It has been observed that the slogan should read "access and ownership," not "access versus ownership." In recent years the balance has clearly been shifting from ownership toward access—a trend that will surely continue. Nevertheless, it seems highly unlikely (at least to this author) that access will totally displace ownership within the foreseeable future.

In the short term, the increasing emphasis on access makes serials collection management more challenging because librarians have more options (e.g., ownership, ILL, or commercial document delivery) in deciding how to best meet patron information needs.

Budgeting for Serials

Budgeting is inextricably connected with collection management. The budget process is traditionally viewed as a mechanism for setting priorities and helping shape the collection, although, as explained below, these concepts may be less applicable to serials budgeting. Nevertheless, many serials collection management decisions (e.g., cancellation projects) are driven by financial decisions. Fundamental budget issues relating to serials are the budget's composition (what budget lines are included) and division (allocation of funds among budget lines); provision for such special categories as new subscriptions, electronic journals, and document delivery; projection of the funds required for the next fiscal year's serials costs; and ex post facto analysis and evaluation of serials expenditure patterns.

This section covers the major budgeting issues pertinent to serials collection management. The effect of the so-called serials crisis on library materials budgets has been analyzed in the preceding chapter. Serials financial accounting is addressed in chapter 8, and budgeting for electronic journals is in chapter 9. In-depth discussion of basic library budgeting principles and procedures is beyond this section's scope. The reader is referred to recent texts on the topic, such as Murray S. Martin's *Academic Library Budgets*,[51] Ann E. Prentice's *Financial Planning for Libraries*,[52] or *Basic Budgeting Practices for Librarians,* by Richard S. Rounds.[53]

The ALA's *Guide to Budget Allocation for Information Resources* lists several intended benefits of a budget document, including translating "collecting priorities into a concrete form," serving as a device for requesting funds, communicating budget information, and acting "as an historical record showing actual expenditures, including variances from the initial budget."[54] Budgeting is commonly viewed as an opportunity for planning and setting priorities, predicated on the assumption that various budget categories will receive support in approximate proportion to their perceived importance. Yet it is questionable whether this assumption applies to serials because of the unique budgeting problems they present.

For most formats, such as monographs or audiovisuals, the library begins with an allocated amount and orders the number of items necessary to expend the allocation. In contrast, a library begins the fiscal year with a set number of serial subscriptions and must expend whatever amount of money is required to meet these ongoing commitments. Thus, serials budgeting is more likely to involve estimating the funds required to pay for the library's serials list than determining the collecting priority of the serials format. This explanation is, of course, an oversimplification, but it helps clarify the inherent dilemma of serials budgeting and the common perception that for academic libraries serials expenditures may be out of control.[55] The fact that a Brown University library budgeting document, reproduced in an ARL SPEC kit, uses the phrase "serials commitment" illustrates the concept.[56]

The Composition of the Serials Budget

The organization of the serials budget is more of an administrative than a collection management issue, so it will only be briefly touched upon here. A fundamental issue concerns what line items are included in the serials budget. Traditional expenditure categories include current periodical subscriptions, memberships, backruns, replacements, newspapers, microformat, reference serials, standing orders, and binding. In the current environment, document delivery, table of contents services, and electronic journals could conceivably have separate budgetary lines. A related issue is the possible breakdown of the serials budget among branches or departments. Inconsistency in the makeup of the serials budget among libraries complicates the comparison of serials expenditures. For example, some libraries count standing orders as monographs, but others consider them serials. (The ARL attempts to address this problem by providing precise instructions to reporting libraries.)

It is not uncommon for a library to have a single periodicals or serials budget or expenditures line, undifferentiated by subject. A 1987 CLIP Note found that only 42.8 percent (50 of 116) of college libraries allocated periodical funds by discipline or department.[57] However, responsible collection management calls for an analysis of serials expenditures by subject. Nearly two decades ago, Edward S. Warner and Anita L. Anker wrote, "It is becoming increasingly desirable—even required, as a result of economic and political imperatives—that the costs of [scholarly journal] collection support be attributed to academic programs."[58] In fact, for many libraries an impending serials review or cancellation project provided the initial impetus for assigning current subscriptions to departmental or subject categories.

Many journals can readily be assigned to subject areas (e.g., the *American Historical Review* to history). For less obvious titles, Library of Congress (LC) classification or Dewey decimal classification (DDC) numbers or subject headings in *Ulrich's* can lend assistance. Warner and Anker describe a method used at the University of North Dakota library in which a journal's cost is apportioned among departments according to their perception of the journal's importance, based on a faculty survey.[59]

Breaking down the serials budget by subject involves some practical problems. Many interdisciplinary journals can not be pigeonholed into specific subject categories. Scholars in one discipline use journals that belong to other disciplines.

Some departments play political games by contriving to have a serial they want charged to another department's budget.

Two theoretical approaches analyze serial support for a subject area—content analysis and component analysis. In a content analysis, every title would be assigned to some subject, but each can be assigned only once. Thus, a journal on economic history would have to be assigned to either economics or history, but not both. In a component analysis, all journals supporting a subject are assigned to it even if it means assigning a single title to multiple subject areas. Accordingly, the title mentioned above would be assigned to both economics and history. Paradoxically, a content analysis may be more practical for serials review projects because each title is sent to a single department; but for collection analysis reasons, component analysis more accurately depicts serials support for various subject areas.[60]

Projection of Funds Required for the Next Year's Serials Expenditures

Estimating the cost for the library's serials subscription list in the forthcoming fiscal year is one of the most difficult serials budgeting functions. Some strategies and tactics are summarized below:

- Take into account changes in the library's subscription list by adding the cost of new subscriptions and subtracting the price of canceled and ceased titles. Do not forget to calculate the cost of serial subscription agent fees.

- Consider the general makeup of your library's subscription list in terms of U.S. versus non-U.S. subscriptions and Science, Technical, and Medical (STM) versus other subjects.

- Be conscious of the most-current pricing trends (appendix 1 annotates several sources of data on serials pricing trends, including the *Bowker Annual* and the ALA and ALCTS Library Materials Price Index Committee's annual report).

- Pay attention to serial subscription agent projections of the year's serials inflation rate, which appear in timely fashion on listservs.

- Ask your serials subscription agent to provide an estimate of the inflation rate for your library's subscription list.

Budgetary Provision for New Serial Subscriptions

Given that new serial titles are constantly coming into existence and that client information needs evolve over time, responsible serials collection management requires that new serials subscriptions be ordered fairly regularly. Hawthorn found that in 1990, 36 percent of larger libraries and 31 percent of smaller libraries had a budget allocation for new serial subscriptions.[61] A number of strategies can ensure funds for new subscriptions.

Many libraries use what might be termed a "cancel to reorder" policy whereby fund managers can generate funds for new subscriptions by canceling present subscriptions. Hawthorn's research indicated that 48 percent of large libraries and

51 percent of small ones spent money from cancellations on new subscriptions, although some permitted only a fraction of the freed-up funds to be so used.[62] As a variation on this theme, the cost of ceased periodical titles might be earmarked for new subscriptions. (For many libraries, however, serials price inflation consumes any savings from cancellation and cessation.)

Some libraries solicit gift or endowment funds dedicated to serials. For example, an "adopt a serial" program allows a donor to sponsor a specific serial subscription.

Academic libraries can allow individual selectors or each academic department to allocate its own materials budget between monographs and serials, thus possibly freeing funds for new serial subscriptions. A 1987 CLIP Note revealed that the Missouri Western State University library in Saint Joseph, Missouri, allowed departments to apportion their annual materials allocation however they wished among formats, provided no more than 60 percent was used for journals.[63] Delegating the responsibility to academic departments would help educate faculty concerning serials budgetary problems and remove some of the political pressure from library staff. However, there would be some associated disadvantages. A considerable amount of professional responsibility for serials management would be transferred to faculty, and interdisciplinary journals might fall through the cracks.

Frederick C. Lynden cited examples at the Cornell, Iowa, and Minnesota university libraries whereby selectors were allowed to apportion budget cuts however they wished among serials and monographs.[64] Beverly P. Lynch reported that bibliographers at the University of Illinois at Chicago are also responsible for dividing their funds between serials and monographs with the stipulation that the library's total serials expenditure does not exceed 50 percent of the materials budget.[65]

Delegation of serials budgeting authority to the selector or bibliographer level offers several advantages, for example, more flexibility in responding to the unique needs of different subject areas than with an "across the board" approach, and the danger of shifting materials funds from the humanities to the sciences would be alleviated.

Budgeting for Document Delivery

Budgeting for document delivery represents a particularly significant issue in the current environment's emphasis on access. It is intimately connected with serials budgeting because one presumes that in most libraries the majority of document delivery requests are for serial items. Because it is a relatively new issue, little has been published on document delivery budgeting. Key questions would concern whether to create a separate document delivery budget line and, if so, how much money to allocate and where to get it.

A serials cancellation project affects these questions two ways: a greater need for document delivery is created because there are fewer current periodical subscriptions, and the project may have freed funds to use for document delivery. The aftermath of a major cancellation project may therefore be an appropriate occasion for creating a document delivery budget line or increasing an already existing one.

A January 1995 SERIALST contribution reported that after a serials cancellation project, an unnamed library used the following formula to calculate the document delivery budget:

Whereby:
X equals the uses of canceled titles
Y equals the amount allocated for serials document delivery
Thus:
$X/2 \times 15 = Y$

In other words, the number of times canceled titles were used is divided by two and then multiplied by 15, equaling the presumed dollar cost of document delivery.[66] No time period for recording use is stated, although one assumes it would be a year. It was stated that any dollar amount for document delivery cost could be plugged into the formula. There may be some flaws in this model (e.g., the presumed 2:1 ratio of canceled journal use to future document delivery request is problematic). Moreover, the model assumes the library will bear the full cost of document delivery for canceled titles. If part of the costs are charged back to patrons, the library's budgetary requirements would be reduced. Nevertheless, the formula represents one of the first primitive attempts to quantify document delivery budgeting—an issue requiring more research before definitive answers are available.

The April 1994 survey of ARL libraries found that 53.6 percent (45 of 84) did not have a separate document delivery budget line. Of the 39 that did, exactly two-thirds (26) allocated the funds from the acquisitions or materials budget or both, one allocated them from general administration funds, and 9 responded "other," which was not explained.[67]

Analysis of Serials Expenditures

Several related questions will be answered in this section: how much to spend on serials, what portion of the total materials budget to devote to serials, and how to analyze the serials-monograph ratio by subject area. The answers to these questions varies depending on such key variables as library type, library size, and subject area. Note that in almost all budget categories the final expenditure figure at the end of the fiscal year will not precisely match the original allocation—a phenomenon that can be particularly pronounced for serials. Obviously, collection management analysis should be based on actual expenditure rather than the budgeted amount.

Many libraries allocate the materials budget by the "historical precedent" method, a type of genetic drift in which each area receives the same proportion of the budgetary pie year after year. Although this approach might work for monographs, it does not lend itself well to serials budgeting. Continuous renewal of all serial subscriptions will eventually shift funding support from the humanities to the sciences because science journals inflate in price at a significantly higher rate than humanities periodicals. Almost inevitably, most libraries (or at least most academic libraries) will sooner or later be forced to examine their serials expenditure patterns. Such analysis often results in serials cancellation projects or reallocation of funds.

Many authors have quite correctly reflected on the difficulty of ascertaining proper serials expenditure patterns. As succinctly observed by Peggy Johnson, "The search for the perfect allocation formula or the ideal ratio between serials and monographs is a frustrating process."[68] Siegfried Feller likewise states, "There can be no definitive answer, even for a given type and size of library."[69] Robin B. Devin asks, "How much is too much?" referring to the proportion of the materials budget devoted to serials.[70] Considerable professional judgment is required. Although there are no right or wrong answers, such methods as standards, comparative data, citation studies, and formulas can provide assistance.

Standards.

For a few libraries, standards provide some insight for evaluating total serials expenditure levels. For illustration, the budget section of the 1994 ACRL, ALA, and Association for Educational Communications and Technology (AECT) standard for junior and community college libraries stipulates that a "minimum" collection (at the 50th percentile) should spend $8.70 per Full Time Equivalent (FTE) student on "current serials," and an "excellent" collection (at the 90th percentile) should spend $22.20 for each FTE student.[71]

Information Power: Guidelines for School Library Media Programs, the 1988 American Association of School Librarians (AASL) and AECT standard for school library media centers, presents as quantitative national guidelines per-pupil current periodical expenditure figures, based on 1985-1986 U.S. Department of Education statistics, for "high service" programs in seven levels and sizes of schools. The expenditure figures summarized in table 3.1 were compiled by the author from the seven tables in *Information Power*'s appendix A, which presents data in four categories covering staff, collections, facilities and equipment, and the budget.[72]

Table 3.1.
Per-Pupil Periodical Expenditures from *Information Power*'s Appendix A

	Percentile Level		
School Level and Size	75th	90th	95th
Elementary Under 500	$1.31	$1.85	$ 2.67
Elementary over 500	$0.88	$1.32	$ 1.70
Middle/Junior Under 500	$3.10	$4.74	$ 5.89
Middle/Junior over 500	$1.71	$2.51	$ 2.97
High Schools Under 500	$4.72	$8.23	$11.36
High Schools Between 500 and 1,000	$3.40	$5.36	$ 7.47
High Schools over 1,000	$2.11	$2.94	$ 4.95

Expenditures per pupil on serials range from $.88 at elementary schools with more than 500 pupils (at the 75th percentile) to $11.36 at high schools with fewer than 500 students (at the 95th percentile). It is noteworthy but not unexpected that smaller schools consistently display larger per-pupil expenditures. For example, for high schools at the 75th percentile, the expenditure decreases from $4.72 to $3.49 to $2.11 as one proceeds from smaller to larger schools.

As an alternative to analysis of expenditures per pupil, *Information Power* includes the cost of current periodical subscriptions as part of a four-factor model (along with replacement books, additional books, and reference materials) for calculating the recommended budget for print materials. Unfortunately, the instructions for calculating the periodicals component are not especially helpful. They merely state one should begin with the number of subscriptions that "need to be renewed or started" and multiply it by the average cost of a periodical subscription (for the appropriate school level) or use the actual subscription cost. The document also asserts that the collection's strengths and weaknesses, changes in the student body's makeup, and inflation should be considered in calculating the periodicals budget.[73] *Information Power* was the current standard when this book was written. A revised edition, issued in the summer of 1998, was unavailable to the author.

Comparative Data.

It might be of some value to compare a library's monographic and serials expenditures with the ratios in other libraries of a similar type, size, and purpose. Comparison could be made with data from specific libraries or collective data from a group of peer institutions. Such data can be found in a variety of sources listed in appendix 1, including *ACRL University Library Statistics* and the *ARL Statistics*. State agencies, as well as regional or local consortiums, might also be a source of data. Alternatively, a library could conduct its own survey. For example, during the 1980s the Indiana University library surveyed expenditure patterns in 80 peer institutions.[74] For libraries not wishing to undertake such an extensive effort, one might obtain expenditure and budgeting data through informal contacts with a small number of similar libraries. It should be noted that a 1990 survey of 34 ARL libraries found that the monographic-serials expenditures ratio ranged from 50:50 to 15:85, with 40:60 the most frequently reported ratio (by eight libraries).[75] Comparative data provide a context for evaluating a particular library's expenditure pattern but not a definitive answer. Each library has its own unique mission. Furthermore, the patterns in other libraries are not necessarily "correct," as they also confront similar pressures from serials price inflation.

Citation Studies.

For university and research libraries, the large number of published citation studies for countless subject areas can provide guidance concerning the materials budgets' division between monographs and serials. Several authors, including Robin B. Devin and Martha Kellogg,[76] Michael Bowman,[77] and Devin,[78] have published tables summarizing the proportion of citations to serials from numerous studies. Chapter 5 presents a more-detailed discussion concerning the pros and cons of using citation data to assist the serials budgeting process. As a slight variation on this theme, Tony Stankus and William Littlefield advocate allocating the science journal budget according to the number of researchers in each specialty and their publication productivity.[79]

Formulas.

A large number of so-called allocation formulas for dividing the monographic budget among subject areas have been published and debated by the profession. These formulas typically incorporate data on student enrollment, faculty, courses, degrees, publication output, cost, circulation, etc. (For more specific details, see the literature reviews by Mary Sellen[80] and John M. Budd.[81]) Similar formulas for serials do not abound in the literature—probably because the unique budgeting problems associated with serials are not conducive to setting priorities among subject areas. As stated by Stankus and Littlefield in 1987, "apart from the voluminous price 'complaint' literature, there is little devoted to actual allocation schemes for serials."[82]

In fact, research indicates that only a minute fraction of academic libraries use allocation formulas in periodicals or serials budgeting. The precise figures were 7.6 percent (9 of 118) in an October 1986 CLIP Note survey;[83] 10.4 percent (37 of 357) in John M. Budd and Kay Adams's 1987 survey of academic libraries with materials budgets exceeding $100,000;[84] and 12 percent (23 of 192) for periodical subscriptions and 13.5 percent (26 of 192) for serials in a December 1994 survey of college and small university libraries.[85] The previously mentioned 1990 survey of ARL libraries found that only 13.9 percent (11 of 79) used a formula in allocating or reallocating materials funds, although specific data for serials were not reported.[86]

A 1987 ACRL CLIP Note contained periodical allocation formulas or budget policies used at some academic libraries (e.g., Franklin and Marshall College, Oberlin College, Missouri Western State College, and Shepherd College).[87] Recent reports include the development of allocation formulas covering both monographs and serials at George Mason University,[88] the University of Southern Mississippi,[89] Central Missouri State University,[90] and Monash University in Australia.[91]

Perhaps the best-known formula pertaining to serials is Charles B. Lowry's so-called matrix formula, used at the University of Texas at Arlington and other institutions. Book and serial funds are distributed to each department according to a formula incorporating 12 variables: FTE faculty, freshman-sophomore credit hours, junior-senior credit hours, master's credit hours, doctoral credit hours, library use, graduate degrees, undergraduate degrees, book cost, serials cost, faculty publications, and faculty external grants. A "Book/Serial Dependency Index" is then used to divide each department's allocation between monographs and serials in proportion to the total cost of current books and serials subscriptions in the area, using Blackwell North America approval plan book statistics and serials data from Faxon.[92] Thus, for a subject where the cost of books was $40,000 and serial subscriptions $60,000, the monograph-serials budgetary ratio would be 40:60 percent.

Benefits of the formula approach are a complex array of variables is considered; a seemingly objective and equitable method is used; favoritism and politics are presumably eliminated from the process, or at least reduced; and, if applied on a regular basis, changing trends in the parent institution and the external environment (i.e., production and cost of materials) can be incorporated. On the negative side, formulas may work better for allocating book funds than serial funds; be time-consuming to implement; fail to adequately address document delivery and electronic journals; and not be appropriate for interdisciplinary subject areas. In support of the last point, a staff member at the University of Texas at Arlington, where the matrix formula was used, once expressed concern on the *COLLDV-L* listserv that the formula was not adequately supporting interdisciplinary subjects.[93]

The methods described above can be used for both budget allocation per se and ex post facto evaluation of expenditures. These processes are really two sides of the same coin, because analysis of previous years' expenditures can lead to future budget reallocations.

NOTES

1. Margaret Hawthorn, "Serials Selection and Deselection: A Survey of North American Academic Libraries," *Serials Librarian* 21, no. 1 (1991): 31. Also, 10 percent of the large and 13 percent of the small libraries reported written policies were under development or revision; 6 percent of the large libraries indicated all serial decisions were under the faculty's control with no policy input from the library. Her figures do not add to 100 percent.

2. G. Edward Evans, *Developing Library and Information Center Collections*, 3d ed. (Englewood, Colo.: Libraries Unlimited, 1995), 188.

3. Selma K. Richardson, *Magazines for Children: A Guide for Parents, Teachers, and Librarians*, 2d ed. (Chicago: American Library Association, 1991), xxiv.

4. Hawthorn, "Serials Selection and Deselection," 37.

5. Steve Black, "Summary: Collection Development and Indexing," *SERIALST* (February 14, 1997). The percentage is my own calculation from the raw data (16 of 21). Black speculates that indexing may increase in significance as budgets tighten.

6. American Library Association, *Guide to the Evaluation of Library Collections*, ed. Barbara Lockett (Chicago: American Library Association, 1989), 12.

7. Hawthorn, "Serials Selection and Deselection," 36.

8. Bill Katz and Linda Sternberg Katz, *Magazines for Libraries*, 9th ed. (New Providence, N.J.: R. R. Bowker, 1997).

9. Bill Katz, *Magazine Selection: How to Build a Community-Oriented Collection* (New York: R. R. Bowker, 1971), 27.

10. Phyllis J. Van Orden, *The Collection Program in Schools: Concepts, Practices, and Information Sources*, 2d ed. (Englewood, Colo.: Libraries Unlimited, 1995), 161. The other five criteria were the contents' interest, appropriateness of format for the magazine's purpose and audience, whether any users require large print items, and indexing.

11. Ross Atkinson, "The Citation As Intertext: Toward a Theory of the Selection Process," *Library Resources and Technical Services* 28 (April/June 1984): 109-19.

12. Hawthorn, "Serials Selection and Deselection," 37, 39.

13. Bernard M. Fry and Herbert S. White, *Publishers and Libraries: A Study of Scholarly and Research Journals* (Lexington, Mass.: Lexington Books, 1976).

14. Sandra R. Moline, "The Influence of Subject, Publisher Type, and Quantity Published on Journal Prices," *Journal of Academic Librarianship* 15 (March 1989): 12-18.

15. Kate McCain, "Refereed Journals," *SERIALST* (March 26, 1996).

16. Luke Swindler, "Serials Collection Development," in *Managing Serials*, by Marcia Tuttle (Greenwich, Conn.: JAI Press, 1996), 65-100.

17. Loriene Roy, "Weeding," *Encyclopedia of Library and Information Science* 54, supplement 17 (1994): 380-82.

18. Association for Library Collections and Technical Services, *Guide to Review of Library Collections: Preservation, Storage, and Withdrawal*, ed. Lenore Clark (Chicago: American Library Association, 1991).

19. Thomas E. Nisonger, *Collection Evaluation in Academic Libraries: A Literature Guide and Annotated Bibliography* (Englewood, Colo.: Libraries Unlimited, 1992), 167-76.

20. Judith A. Segal, "Journal Deselection: A Literature Review and an Application," *Science and Technology Libraries* 6 (spring 1986): 31.

21. Robert N. Broadus, "A Proposed Method for Eliminating Titles from Periodical Subscription Lists," *College and Research Libraries* 46 (January 1985): 30-35.

22. Maurice B. Line, "Use of Citation Data for Periodicals Control in Libraries: A Response to Broadus," *College and Research Libraries* 46 (January 1985): 36-37.

23. Tony Stankus, "Journal Weeding in Relation to Declining Faculty Member Publishing," *Science and Technology Libraries* 6 (spring 1986): 43-53.

24. Sherrie Schmidt, Jane Treadwell, and Gloriana St. Clair, "Using dBaseIII+ to Create a Serials Review List," *Microcomputers for Information Management* 5 (September 1988): 169-82.

25. Stanley J. Slote, *Weeding Library Collections: Library Weeding Methods*, 4th ed. (Englewood, Colo.: Libraries Unlimited, 1997).

26. Joseph P. Segal, *Evaluating and Weeding Collections in Small and Medium-Sized Public Libraries: The CREW Method* (Chicago: American Library Association, 1980).

27. Slote, *Weeding Library Collections*, 4th ed., 26.

28. Stanley J. Slote, *Weeding Library Collections: Library Weeding Methods*, 3d ed. (Englewood, Colo.: Libraries Unlimited, 1989), 15.

29. Segal, *Evaluating and Weeding Collections*, 15.

30. John Urquhart, "Relegation," in *Periodical Administration in Libraries: A Collection of Essays*, ed. Paul Mayes (London: Clive Bingley; Hamden, Conn.: Linnet Books, 1978), 117-18.

31. Association for Library Collections and Technical Services, *Guide to Review of Library Collections*, 26.

32. Jamie Webster Hastreiter, Larry Hardesty, and David Henderson, comps., *Periodicals in College Libraries*, CLIP Note 8 (Chicago: Association of College and Research Libraries, 1987), 9-10. Some of the percentages are my own recalculations from their raw data.

33. Dennis P. Carrigan, "From Just-in-Case to Just-in-Time: Limits to the Alternative Library Service Model," *Journal of Scholarly Publishing* 26 (April 1995): 178.

34. Mounir Khalil, "Document Delivery: A Better Option?" *Library Journal* 118 (February 1, 1993): 43-47.

35. Marcia Tuttle, *Managing Serials* (Greenwich, Conn.: JAI Press, 1996), 314-20.

36. *New York Times* 143 (January 10, 1994): A5.

37. Mary E. Jackson and Karen Croneis, comps., *Uses of Document Delivery Services*, SPEC Kit 204 (Washington, D.C.: Association of Research Libraries, Office of Management Studies, 1994), 3-4. The percentages are my own calculations from the raw data.

38. Bill Coons and Peter McDonald, "Implications of Commercial Document Delivery," *College and Research Libraries News* 56 (October 1995): 627.

39. Association of College and Research Libraries, College Libraries Section, Standards Committee, "Standards for College Libraries, 1995 Edition," *College and Research Libraries News* 56 (April 1995): 247.

40. Coons and McDonald, "Implications of Commercial Document Delivery," 626.

41. Paul McCarthy, "Serial Killers: Academic Libraries Respond to Soaring Costs," *Library Journal* 119 (June 15, 1994): 44, citing Anthony W. Ferguson, Kathleen Kehoe, and Barbara A. List, *Columbia University Scientific Information Study* (New York: Columbia University Libraries, 1993).

42. Carol Tenopir and Donald W. King, "Setting the Record Straight on Journal Publishing: Myth vs. Reality," *Library Journal* 121 (March 15, 1996): 32.

43. Eleanor A. Gossen and Suzanne Irving, "Ownership Versus Access and Low-Use Periodical Titles," *Library Resources and Technical Services* 39 (January 1995): 43.

44. Bruce R. Kingma with Suzanne Irving, *The Economics of Access Versus Ownership: The Costs and Benefits of Access to Scholarly Articles via Interlibrary Loan and Journal Subscription* (New York: Haworth Press, 1996), 39. Also issued as *Journal of Interlibrary Loan, Document Delivery and Information Supply* 6, no. 3 (1996).

45. McCarthy, "Serial Killers," 41.

46. Thomas E. Nisonger, "Access and Holdings: Integrating Issues of Access and Collection Development," *Library Acquisitions: Practice and Theory* 19 (spring 1995): 118-19. I summarized Goehner's presentation at the ALA 1994 Annual Conference.

47. John R. Hayes, "The Internet's First Victim," *Forbes* 156 (December 18, 1995): 200-201.

48. Jackson and Croneis, *Uses of Document Delivery Services*, 5-6. Again, the percentages are my own calculations from the SPEC Kit's raw data.

49. CARL. *Reveal Home Page*. Available: http://uncweb.carl.org/reveal/index.html (Accessed March 8, 1998).

50. Rudolf Jacob Penner, "Measuring a Library's Capability," *Journal of Education for Librarianship* 13 (summer 1972): 17-30.

51. Murray S. Martin, *Academic Library Budgets* (Greenwich, Conn.: JAI Press, 1993).

52. Ann E. Prentice, *Financial Planning for Libraries*, 2d ed. (Metuchen, N.J.: Scarecrow Press, 1996).

53. Richard S. Rounds, *Basic Budgeting Practices for Librarians*, 2d ed. (Chicago: American Library Association, 1994).

54. American Library Association, *Guide to Budget Allocation for Information Resources*, ed. Edward Shreeves (Chicago: American Library Association, 1991), 1-2.

55. Beverly P. Lynch, "A Library Director's Perspective on Collections and the Library User," in *Collection Management for the 1990s: Proceedings of the Midwest Collection Management and Development Institute, University of Illinois at Chicago, August 17-20, 1989*, ed. Joseph J. Branin (Chicago: American Library Association, 1993), 14. Lynch asserts, "Libraries must get control of their serials budgets."

56. Frederick C. Lynden, "Preliminary Estimate of the 1991/92 Serials Commitment," in *Materials Budgets in ARL Libraries*, SPEC Kit 166, comp. Peggy Johnson (Washington, D.C.: Association of Research Libraries, Office of Management Studies, 1990), 97-104.

57. Hastreiter, Hardesty, and Henderson, *Periodicals in College Libraries*, 7. One library (0.8 percent of the respondents) reported it allocated periodical funds per faculty member.

58. Edward S. Warner and Anita L. Anker, "Utilizing Library Constituents' Perceived Needs in Allocating Journal Costs," *Journal of the American Society for Information Science* 30 (November 1979): 325.

59. Ibid., 325-29.

60. The distinction between content and component analysis is briefly discussed by Thomas E. Nisonger, "Editing the RLG Conspectus to Analyze the OCLC Archival Tapes of Seventeen Texas Libraries," *Library Resources and Technical Services* 29 (October/December 1985): 322, based on Glyn T. Evans, Roger Gifford, and Donald R. Franz, *Collection Development Analysis Using OCLC Archival Tapes: Final Report* (Albany, N.Y.: SUNY Office of Library Services, 1977). ERIC Document ED 152 299.

61. Hawthorn, "Serials Selection and Deselection," 33.

62. Ibid.

63. Hastreiter, Hardesty, and Henderson, *Periodicals in College Libraries*, 69.

64. Frederick C. Lynden, "The Impact of the Rising Costs of Books and Journals on the Overall Library Budget," *Journal of Library Administration* 10, no. 1 (1989): 89.

65. Lynch, "A Library Director's Perspective," 7.

66. Jeanie M. Welch, "Document Delivery," *SERIALST* (January 31, 1995). Unfortunately, the posting is ambiguous in regard to whether X represents the number of times canceled titles were used, or the number of canceled titles multiplied by the number of their uses.

67. Jackson and Croneis, *Uses of Document Delivery Services*, 5-6. Again, the percentages are my own calculations from the SPEC Kit's raw data.

68. Peggy Johnson, "Materials Budgets in ARL Libraries," *SPEC Flyer* 166 (July 1990): 2, in *Materials Budgets in ARL Libraries*, SPEC Kit 166, comp. Peggy Johnson (Washington, D.C.: Association of Research Libraries, Office of Management Studies, 1990).

69. Siegfried Feller, "Developing the Serials Collection," in *Collection Development in Libraries: A Treatise*, pt. B, ed. Robert D. Stueart and George B. Miller Jr. (Greenwich, Conn.: JAI Press, 1980), 508.

70. Robin B. Devin, "Who's Using What?" *Library Acquisitions: Practice and Theory* 13, no. 2 (1989): 169.

71. "Standards for Community, Junior, and Technical College Learning Resources Programs," *College and Research Libraries News* 55 (October 1994): 577. [Prepared by a joint committee at the Association for Educational Communications and Technology (AECT) and ACRL, co-chairs, Marilyn McDonald and Gretchen H. Neill.]

72. American Association of School Librarians and Association for Educational Communications and Technology, *Information Power: Guidelines for School Library Media Programs* (Chicago: American Library Association; Washington, D.C.: Association for Educational Communications and Technology, 1988), 117-23.

73. Ibid., 127-30.

74. Stella Bentley and David Farrell, "Beyond Retrenchment: The Reallocation of a Library Materials Budget," *Journal of Academic Librarianship* 10 (January 1985): 323.

75. Johnson, "Materials Budgets in ARL Libraries," 2.

76. Robin B. Devin and Martha Kellogg, "The Serial/Monograph Ratio in Research Libraries: Budgeting in Light of Citation Studies," *College and Research Libraries* 51 (January 1990): 46-54.

77. Michael Bowman, "Format Citation Patterns and Their Implications for Collection Development in Research Libraries," *Collection Building* 11, no. 1 (1991): 2-8.

78. Devin, "Who's Using What?" 167-70.

79. Tony Stankus and William Littlefield, "One Researcher, One Journal, One Research Paper: Workable Budgeting Schemes at the Science Departmental Level," in *Scientific Journals: Issues in Library Selection and Management*, ed. Tony Stankus (New York: Haworth Press, 1987), 199-208.

80. Mary Sellen, "Book Budget Formula Allocations: A Review Essay," *Collection Management* 9 (winter 1987): 13-24.

81. John M. Budd, "Allocation Formulas in the Literature: A Review," *Library Acquisitions: Practice and Theory* 15, no. 1 (1991): 95-107.

82. Stankus and Littlefield, "One Researcher, One Journal, One Research Paper," 208.

83. Hastreiter, Hardesty, and Henderson, *Periodicals in College Libraries*, 7.

84. John M. Budd and Kay Adams, "Allocation Formulas in Practice," *Library Acquisitions: Practice and Theory* 13, no. 4 (1989): 383-85. However, 145 (40.6 percent) used a formula for materials fund allocation, primarily for books.

85. Jane H. Tuten and Beverly Jones, comps., *Allocation Formulas in Academic Libraries*, CLIP Note 22 (Chicago: Association of College and Research Libraries, 1995), 16, 21. The percentages are my own calculations from the raw data. In total, 40 percent (76 of 192) of the responding libraries used an allocation for at least some type of information resource.

86. Peggy Johnson, comp., *Materials Budgets in ARL Libraries*, SPEC Kit 166 (Washington, D.C.: Association of Research Libraries, Office of Management Studies, 1990), 13. Four additional libraries had future plans to use a formula.

87. Hastreiter, Hardesty, and Henderson, *Periodicals in College Libraries*, 66-74.

88. Laura O. Rein and others, "Formula-Based Subject Allocation: A Practical Approach," *Collection Management* 17, no. 4 (1993): 25-48.

89. Carol Cubberley, "Allocating the Materials Funds Using Total Cost of Materials," *Journal of Academic Librarianship* 19 (March 1993): 16-21.

90. Mollie Niemeyer and others, "Balancing Act for Library Materials Budgets: Use of a Formula Allocation," *Technical Services Quarterly* 11, no. 1 (1993): 43-60.

91. Merran Evans, "Library Acquisitions Formulae: The Monash Experience," *Australian Academic and Research Libraries* 27 (March 1996): 47-57.

92. Charles B. Lowry, "Reconciling Pragmatism, Equity, and Need in the Formula Allocation of Book and Serial Funds," *College and Research Libraries* 53 (March 1992): 121-28.

93. Julie Alexander, "Budget Allocation Methodologies," *COLLDV-L* (March 2, 1995).

FURTHER READING

Selection and General Serials Collection Management

Evans, G. Edward. "Serials." In *Developing Library and Information Center Collections,* 186-209. 3d ed. Englewood, Colo.: Libraries Unlimited, 1995.

Feller, Siegfried. "Developing the Serials Collection." In *Collection Development in Libraries: A Treatise.* Pt. B, edited by Robert D. Stueart and George B. Miller, Jr., 497-523. Greenwich, Conn.: JAI Press, 1980.

Hawthorn, Margaret. "Serials Selection and Deselection: A Survey of North American Academic Libraries." *Serials Librarian* 21, no. 1 (1991): 29-45.

Katz, Bill. "Art of Selection." In *Magazine Selection: How to Build a Community-Oriented Collection*, 21-44. New York: R. R. Bowker, 1971.

Osborn, Andrew D. "Principles of Serial Selection." In *Serial Publications: Their Place and Treatment in Libraries*, 77-99. 3d ed. Chicago: American Library Association, 1980.

Stankus, Tony, ed. *Scientific Journals: Issues in Library Selection and Management*. New York: Haworth Press, 1987.

Swindler, Luke. "Serials Collection Development." In *Managing Serials*, by Marcia Tuttle, 65-100. Greenwich, Conn.: JAI Press, 1996.

Urquhart, John A. "The Selection and De-Selection of Serials." In *Serials Management: A Practical Handbook*, edited by Margaret E. Graham and Fiona Buettel, 11-23. London: published by Aslib in collaboration with the United Kingdom Serials Group, 1990.

Cancellation

Association of Research Libraries. Office of Management Studies. *Serials Control and Deselection Projects*. SPEC Kit 147. Washington, D.C.: Association of Research Libraries, Office of Management Studies, 1988.

Bostic, Mary J. "Serials Deselection." *Serials Librarian* 9 (spring 1985): 85-101.

Broadus, Robert N. "A Proposed Method for Eliminating Titles from Periodical Subscription Lists." *College and Research Libraries* 46 (January 1985): 30-35.

Crump, Michele J., and LeiLani Freund. "Serials Cancellation and Interlibrary Loan: The Link and What It Reveals." *Serials Review* 21 (summer 1995): 29-36.

Metz, Paul. "Thirteen Steps to Avoiding Bad Luck in a Serials Cancellation Project." *Journal of Academic Librarianship* 18 (May 1992): 76-82.

Olsrud, Lois, and Anne Moore. "Serials Review in the Humanities: A Three-Year Project." *Collection Building* 10, nos. 3/4 (1990): 2-10.

Perkins, David L. "Weed It and Reap." *Serials Librarian* 18, nos. 1/2 (1990): 131-40.

Stankus, Tony. "New Specialized Journals, Mature Scientists, and Shifting Loyalties." *Library Acquisitions: Practice and Theory* 9, no. 2 (1985): 99-104.

Tucker, Betty E. "The Journal Deselection Project: The LSUMC-S Experience." *Library Acquisitions: Practice and Theory* 19 (fall 1995): 313-20.

Walter, Pat L. "Doing the Unthinkable: Canceling Journals at a Research Library." *Serials Librarian* 18, nos. 1/2 (1990): 141-53.

Wise, Suzanne. "Making Lemonade: The Challenges and Opportunities of Forced Reference Serials Cancellations: One Academic Library's Experiences." *Serials Review* 19 (winter 1993): 15-26.

Weeding

American Library Association. Association for Library Collections and Technical Services. *Guide to Review of Library Collections: Preservation, Storage, and Withdrawal*. Edited by Lenore Clark. Chicago: American Library Association, 1991.

Benedict, Marjorie A., Michael Knee, and Mina B. LaCroix. "Finding Space for Periodicals: Weeding, Storage and Microform Conversion." *Collection Management* 12, nos. 3/4 (1990): 145-54.

Diodato, Virgil P. "Original Language, Non-English Journals: Weeding Them and Holding Them." *Science and Technology Libraries* 6 (spring 1986): 55-67.

Seymour, Carol A. "Weeding the Collection: A Review of Research on Identifying Obsolete Stock. Part II: Serials." *Libri* 22, no. 3 (1972): 183-89.

Slote, Stanley J. *Weeding Library Collections: Library Weeding Methods*. 3d ed. Englewood, Colo.: Libraries Unlimited, 1989.

Stankus, Tony. "Journal Weeding in Relation to Declining Faculty Member Publishing." *Science and Technology Libraries* 6 (spring 1986): 43-53.

Taylor, Colin R. "A Practical Solution to Weeding University Library Periodical Collections." *Collection Management* 1 (fall-winter 1976-1977): 27-45.

Urquhart, John. "Relegation." In *Periodicals Administration in Libraries: A Collection of Essays*, edited by Paul Mayes, 116-26. London: Clive Bingley; Hamden, Conn.: Linnet Books, 1978.

Westbrook, Lynn. "Weeding Reference Serials." *Serials Librarian* 10 (summer 1986): 81-100.

Ownership Versus Access and Document Delivery

Carrigan, Dennis P. "From Just-in-Case to Just-in-Time: Limits to the Alternative Library Service Model." *Journal of Scholarly Publishing* 26 (April 1995): 173-82.

Chrzastowski, Tina E., and Mary A. Anthes. "Seeking the 99% Chemistry Library: Extending the Serial Collection Through the Use of Decentralized Document Delivery." *Library Acquisitions: Practice and Theory* 19 (summer 1995): 141-52.

Coons, Bill, and Peter McDonald. "Implications of Commercial Document Delivery." *College and Research Libraries News* 56 (October 1995): 626-29.

Ferguson, Anthony W., and Kathleen Kehoe. "Access vs. Ownership: What Is Most Cost Effective in the Sciences." *Journal of Library Administration* 19, no. 2 (1993): 89-99.

Gossen, Eleanor A., and Suzanne Irving. "Ownership Versus Access and Low-Use Periodical Titles." *Library Resources and Technical Services* 39 (January 1995): 43-52.

Higginbotham, Barbra Buckner, and Sally Bowdoin. *Access Versus Assets: A Comprehensive Guide to Resource Sharing for Academic Librarians*. Chicago: American Library Association, 1993.

Khalil, Mounir. "Document Delivery: A Better Option?" *Library Journal* 118 (February 1, 1993): 43-47.

Kingma, Bruce R., with Suzanne Irving. *The Economics of Access Versus Ownership: The Costs and Benefits of Access to Scholarly Articles via Interlibrary Loan and Journal Subscription*. New York: Haworth Press, 1996. Also issued as *Journal of Interlibrary Loan, Document Delivery and Information Supply* 6, no. 3 (1996).

Kjaer, Kathryn. "Current Access to Scientific Journals: An Alternative Strategy." *Colorado Libraries* 16 (March 1990): 20-22.

Thornton, Glenda A., and Yem Fong. "Exploring Document Delivery Options: A Pilot Study of the University of Colorado System." *Technical Services Quarterly* 12, no. 2 (1994): 1-11.

Serials Budgeting

Almagro, Bertha R. "Budgeting and Planning: A Tandem Approach." *Serials Librarian* 10 (fall 1985/winter 1985-1986): 173-79.

American Library Association. Association for Library Collections and Technical Services. *Guide to Budget Allocation for Information Resources*. Edited by Edward Shreeves. Chicago: American Library Association, 1991.

Bowman, Michael. "Format Citation Patterns and Their Implications for Collection Development in Research Libraries." *Collection Building* 11, no. 1 (1991): 2-8.

Burdick, Amrita J., Anne Butler, and Marilyn G. Sullivan. "Citation Patterns in the Health Sciences: Implications for Serials/Monographic Fund Allocation." *Bulletin of the Medical Library Association* 81 (January 1993): 44-47.

Bustion, Marifran, and others. "Methods of Serials Funding: Formula or Tradition?" *Serials Librarian* 20, no. 1 (1991): 75-89.

Clack, Mary E., and Sally F. Williams. "Using Locally and Nationally Produced Periodical Price Indexes in Budget Preparation." *Library Resources and Technical Services* 27 (October/December 1983): 345-56.

Devin, Robin B. "Who's Using What?" *Library Acquisitions: Practice and Theory* 13, no. 2 (1989): 167-70.

Devin, Robin B., and Martha Kellogg. "The Serial/Monograph Ratio in Research Libraries: Budgeting in Light of Citation Studies." *College and Research Libraries* 51 (January 1990): 46-54.

Evans, Merran. "Library Acquisitions Formulae: The Monash Experience." *Australian Academic and Research Libraries* 27 (March 1996): 47-57.

Lowry, Charles B. "Reconciling Pragmatism, Equity, and Need in the Formula Allocation of Book and Serial Funds." *College and Research Libraries* 53 (March 1992): 121-38.

Warner, Edward S., and Anita L. Anker. "Utilizing Library Constituents' Perceived Needs in Allocating Journal Costs." *Journal of the American Society for Information Science* 30 (November 1979): 325-29.

Williams, Sally F. "Construction and Application of a Periodical Price Index." *Collection Management* 2 (winter 1978): 329-44.

Chapter Four

Collection Management of Serials: Part 2

This chapter continues the analysis of serials collection management begun in chapter 3. It focuses on filling gaps in backruns, treating unbound issues, multiple copy decisions, location decisions, serials decision models, core lists of serials, and the major approaches to serials macroevaluation.

OTHER SERIALS COLLECTION MANAGEMENT FUNCTIONS

Serial selection, deselection, budgeting, and document delivery are the serials collection management functions that have received the most attention in the literature. Yet a thorough coverage must also address such functions as filling gaps in backrun holdings, treatment of unbound issues, multiple copy decisions, and location decisions.

Filling Gaps in Backruns

For a variety of reasons (e.g., a subscription was not begun until several volumes had already been published, a subscription was canceled and later reinstated, etc.), a library may have incomplete holdings of a particular periodical's backruns. This section focuses on the collection management decision of whether a gap should be completed, with the processing aspects covered in chapter 8. The concept of completing gaps should be differentiated from filling in missing issues at the time of binding. This issue has not received much attention in the literature, so formal guidelines and theoretical discussion are sparse.

Filling in the gap decisions are usually made on a micro (title-by-title) basis. The decision criteria include the journal's intrinsic importance, the length and age of the gap, usage patterns in the library, interlibrary loan (ILL) or document delivery requests for the missing volumes, the journal's cited half-life in the *Journal Citation Reports* (JCR), the availability of the missing volumes in nearby libraries, the cost of completing the gap, and whether the library has a current subscription.

The cited half-life, available for thousands of journals in the JCR, indicates the extent to which older runs are still being cited by researchers and thus has potential application to gap-filling decision making. For a technical explanation of the Institute for Scientific Information's (ISI) calculation of cited half-life, see chapter 5. One doubts whether a great number of librarians consults the JCR while reaching decisions about periodical gaps, yet the potentially useful data contained in this source should be brought to their attention.

Treatment of Unbound Issues

Traditional print periodicals are generally received as single, unbound issues. The old *Horizon* and *American Heritage* magazines are rare examples of periodicals with hardbound single issues. Thus, when the unbound issues accumulate to a certain point, typically a bibliographical volume, a decision must be made about their permanent preservation. Generally, five options are theoretically possible:

1. Discard

2. Binding

3. Microformat in lieu of binding

4. Permanent maintenance in an unbound form

5. Digitization or electronic preservation

Each of these is discussed below. A survey of college and small university library directors found that, on average, 65.6 percent of periodical titles in their libraries were bound, 16.9 percent maintained on microfilm, and 12.2 percent on microfiche.[1]

Discard

Unbound issues can be discarded if the library does not wish to permanently maintain them in the collection. Obvious candidates for discard would be issues that are superseded by a cumulative volume (e.g., indexing or abstracting services such as *Library Literature*). Periodicals whose content is of ephemeral value, for example, providing current awareness, would be strong candidates for discard. Many newsletters would fall into this category. Gift periodicals are often discarded because the library does not wish to commit funds for binding. When the discard option is adopted, a decision should be made to keep issues for a set time period, such as six months, one year, two years, and so forth. Whether a periodical is of temporary or enduring value often requires a subject specialist's judgment.

Binding

Binding is the preferred and most frequently used method for dealing with unbound periodicals. This option reduces the loss of individual issues. A significant portion of library budgets is devoted to periodical binding, but it is a worthwhile expenditure because it more or less adequately protects the library's substantial investment in serial subscriptions.

P. G. Peacock has published a decision table on which periodicals to bind. A scale of one to three is applied to four variables:

Physical condition: good = 1; average = 2; poor = 3

Number of parts issued per year: less than 4 = 1; 5 to 12 = 2; more than 13 = 3

Frequency of use: low = 1; average = 2; high = 3

Value in terms of price, rarity, academic or local interest: low = 1; average = 2; high = 3.

Peacock states that, generally, a title scoring several threes will be bound, but those rating several ones will be left unbound.[2] Unfortunately, he does not precisely outline the definitions for high, average, and low physical condition, use, and value.

Microformat in Lieu of Binding

Use of microform instead of binding saves shelf space, offers protection against mutilation and theft, and is particularly appropriate for serials, which do not lend themselves well to binding because of their size, frequency, and sometimes poor paper quality. Several disadvantages are associated with this option. Both print and microfilm formats must be paid for. Certain periodicals, such as those in which illustrations are a major feature, are unsuitable for microformat. Many readers feel uncomfortable with the microformat (e.g., browsing is difficult); and although there are four ways to put it into the machine, three of them are wrong! Moreover, the microformat requires expensive equipment and storage cabinets, and there is a danger of obsolescence in the format itself or the equipment that runs it. If the microformat option is adopted, there is often a choice between microfilm or microfiche.

Factors in determining whether a title should be preserved in microform are outlined below, but not in priority order:

- *Condition of paper holdings.* If many missing or mutilated issues are in the current holdings, microformat would be preferable to binding, all other factors being equal.

- *Use.* Highly used titles normally should not be preserved in microform because of user resistance to the format.

- *Language.* Foreign language periodicals are often strong candidates for microform because they are less likely to be heavily used.

- *Cost.* There is conflicting evidence in the literature whether binding or microformat is less expensive, but the cost-effectiveness of the two formats should be separately calculated for each periodical under consideration because it will vary among titles.

- *Indexing.* Indexed titles are better candidates for microformat preservation than unindexed ones because microforms are hard to browse and indexing helps users locate needed articles.

- *Illustrations.* Periodicals in which illustrative matter is a major feature are not good candidates for microform.

- *Type of periodical.* Technical titles that contain numerous graphs, maps, scientific illustrations, or statistical tables; quasi-reference journals that emphasize book reviews or other features that would not be indexed; and poetry or short story magazines whose format is part of their "charm" are not good candidates for the microformat.[3] Microform is the recommended preservation method for daily newspapers. Weekly news magazines, such as *Time, Newsweek,* or the *Economist,* are more problematic because their physical size is compatible with binding but several volumes would be required for a single year's run.

- *Article length.* Most authorities contend that periodicals with short articles are more appropriate for microform than those with long articles because the reader will be less inconvenienced. Taking a contrarian position, Helen M. Grochmal argues that whether long-article or short-article periodicals are best suited to microform will depend on user preference and the availability of copy machines.[4]

- *Availability in microformat.* If titles are not commercially available in microformat, the expense of in-house production or on-demand commercial production would probably be prohibitive.

Microform in lieu of binding is a distinct concept from microform conversion, which entails substituting the microformat for periodical runs that are already bound. Nonetheless, the criteria outlined above would apply to both situations.

Permanent Maintenance in an Unbound Form

Theoretically, periodicals could be maintained indefinitely without binding, such as by storing them in a Princeton file—a container especially designed for periodicals. Indeed cogent arguments have been made against binding periodicals. As summarized by Peacock, money is saved; a volume's separate parts can be simultaneously used by more than one patron; volumes are not missing from the shelves while at the bindery; and unbound issues are easier to photocopy.[5] Fortunately, most libraries reject this option. The cost of binding or microformat can reasonably be viewed as a means of protecting the library's already substantial investment in serials.

Digitization or Electronic Preservation

One can easily imagine that at some future point electronic archiving or digitization will be used for the permanent preservation of print periodicals, but this is presently not a feasible solution for most libraries. The Library of Congress's (LC) National Digital Library Program for preserving valuable resources through digitization is focusing on formats other than serials. The JSTOR project, described in chapter 2, is experimenting with digitization of print journal backruns.

Multiple Copy Decisions

Determining the number of copies for a particular title is a basic collection management decision that applies to both monographs and periodicals. In the past libraries have held multiple subscriptions for a variety of reasons, including high usage, the need for the same title in different branches, and the desirability of extra copies for staff use. One presumes, given the current environment, that libraries now seldom place additional periodical subscriptions. In fact, duplicate subscriptions are frequently among the first to be canceled.

Location Decisions

Multibranch libraries, especially university libraries with subject-based branches, often question which branch should house a particular periodical title. Key questions include

Which location should place an initial subscription?

For locations with duplicate subscriptions or holdings, which one should cancel or weed a title?

Should a particular title be transferred from one location to another?

Location decisions, about which very little has been published, are undoubtedly assuming greater importance as libraries cancel duplicate subscriptions in response to the current serials crunch. The obvious decision criteria would be patron need, a periodical's relevance to a location's subject emphasis, and actual or estimated usage. A collection development policy might help resolve conflicts by explicitly assigning subject responsibilities to the different locations within a library system. However, this tactic will not work for periodicals that legitimately fall within the domain of more than one subject area or whose focus is difficult to ascertain. The issue is complicated by the interdisciplinary nature of modern scholarship as demonstrated by innumerable citation and circulation studies.

SERIALS DECISION MODELS

Many criteria affect serials collection management decisions. Obvious questions concern what weight should be assigned to various factors and how they can be combined to reach a decision. This section reviews some explicit journal decision models that have been proposed in the literature and analyzes the major issues regarding these models.

A decision model may be viewed as a complex journal ranking method. Unlike the standard journal ranking methods (discussed in chapter 7), which are usually based on a single dimension such as citation data or expert perception, or the cost-per-use methodologies (mentioned in chapter 6), which incorporate the two criteria of cost and use, a decision model combines numerous variables. Generally, some type of mathematical formula is used to calculate a numerical score or rating for each journal in the set under evaluation. These ratings are then used to construct a hierarchical rank ordering of the complete set so that all journals can be listed from the most valuable through the least valuable. If the results are used for selection, one would presumably begin with the highest ranking title and work down the list until the budget's limit has been reached. In contrast, one would begin at the bottom for cancellation decisions.

More than a dozen published serials decision models are listed in this chapter's "Further Reading" section. To illustrate the structure and nature of these models, a small number are examined below.

In 1980 S. M. Dhawan, S. K. Phull, and S. P. Jain published a model based on a journal's use, citation record, and coverage by abstracts. Data from the *Science Citation Index* (SCI) JCR, *Physics Abstracts*, and usage in several libraries were used to test the model on a set of 400 physics journals. By combining the three variables noted above, the authors advocated journal acquisition according to five hierarchical categories:

1. Journals that are cited, abstracted, and used.

2. Journals that are abstracted, used, but not cited.

3. Journals that are cited, used, but not abstracted.

4. Journals that are used but neither abstracted nor cited.

5. Journals that are abstracted, cited, but not used.[6]

Logical analysis of this hierarchy indicates that Dhawan, Phull, and Jain place the highest value on use, followed by abstract coverage, then citedness.

At the American Society for Information Science (ASIS)1981 annual conference, Gilda Maria Braga and Cecilia Alves Oberhofer presented a model, developed at the Brazilian Institute for Information in Science and Technology, for decision making about scientific and technical journals published in developing countries and summarized in table 4.1. A five-point rating system (1 = low; 5 = high) was applied to numerous variables grouped under seven broad headings: standardization, duration, frequency of appearance, indexing, dissemination, collaboration and contents division, and authority. Examination of table 4.1, which presents their scoring system, indicates some problems. The assumption that more-frequently issued periodicals are more desirable than less-frequently issued ones is highly questionable. Determining whether the editorial board is composed of "experts of well-established competence" may be difficult. A unique characteristic of this model is that the authors offer a method for interpreting a journal's score, unlike most models, which rank order a journal set. An appended "Valuation Scale" states that 0 to 30 points are "very bad"; 31 to 55, "bad"; 56 to 80, "good"; and 80 plus points, "very good."[7] Although interesting from a theoretical perspective and serving as a good illustrative example, this model would seem to have little practical value for most North American libraries.

Judith A. Segal described a relatively simple deselection model that was used in a cancellation project for behavioral sciences and education journals at Ben Gurion University of the Negev, Israel, in 1984. Her model focused on six variables: completeness of holdings, cost, JCR impact factor, indexing, listing in the Katzes's *Magazines for Libraries,* and relevance to curriculum. It awarded five points for each of the following: complete holdings, a cost at or below average for the discipline, an impact factor at

Table 4.1.

Braga and Oberhofer's Model for Evaluating Scientific and Technical Journals

Criterion	Variable	Condition	Number of Points
1. STANDARDIZATION	1.1 *Journal in the whole* (standard for submitting papers)	• to be explicit in the journal • to be explicit in the journal and following national standards	4 5
	1.2 *Journal issues* 1.2.1 Table of contents 1.2.2 Bibliographical strip 1.2.3 ISSN	• existence • existence • existence	4 1 2
	1.3 *Journal articles* 1.3.1 Author affiliation 1.3.2 Abstracts only in the local language (if not English) 1.3.3 Abstracts only in English 1.3.4 Bilingual abstracts 1.3.5 Descriptors or key-words	• indication • existence • existence • existence • existence	3 2 2 4 2
2. DURATION	2.1 *Continuous time of existence*	• each 2 (two) years of life	1
3. FREQUENCY OF APPEARANCE	3.1 *Regular frequency of issues*	• 2 times per year • 3 times per year • 4 times per year • 6 times per year • 12 times per year	1 2 3 4 5
4. INDEXING	4.1 *Coverage by abstracting and indexing services*	• for each national indexing or abstracting service • for each foreign and/or international indexing or abstrating service	2 5
5. DISSEMINATION	5.1 *Circulation (number of copies per issue)*	• between 1,000 and 2,999 • between 3,000 and 4,999 • 5,000 and above	1 2 3
	5.2 *Existence of reasonably complete collections (at least 75% in local libraries)* 5.3 *Reprints*	• for each library • explicit availability	1 1
6. COLLABORATION AND CONTENTS DIVISION	6.1 *Authorship*	• inclusion of about 20% papers from foreign authors • inclusion of papers from authors of different regions of the country	3 5
	6.2 *Communication of on-going research* 6.3 *Letters* 6.4 *Book Reviews* 6.5 *Review Articles*	• to be a regular section • to be a regular section • to be a regular section • regular inclusion	4 2 2 5
7. AUTHORITY	7.1 *Editorial Board*	• to be formed by experts of well-established competence • to be interinstitutional	5 3

Reprinted with permission of the American Society for Information Science from Gilda Maria Braga and Cecilia Alves Oberhofer, "A Model for Evaluating Scientific and Technical Journals from Developing Countries," in *The Information Community: An Alliance for Progress; Proceeding of the 44th ASIS Annual Meeting, Washington, D.C., October 25-30, 1981*, vol. 18, ed. By Lois F. Lunin, Madeline Henderson, and Harold Wooster (White Plains, N.Y.: published for the American Society for Information Science by Knowledge Industry Publications, 1981), 53.

or above average in the discipline, and inclusion in the Katzes's *Magazines for Libraries*. Five points were also granted if, during three of the preceding four years, the journal directly related to at least one course taught at the university. One point was received for each of the discipline's top five indexes that covered the journal. If no impact factor was available because the journal was not covered in the JCR, this variable was eliminated from consideration. Thus, the maximum point total would be 25 or 30, depending upon whether five or six variables were included. The actual points received were then converted to a percentage of the maximum potential points. Then Segal added five points for journals identified as "top priority" in a faculty questionnaire and subtracted five points for journals that were not used during a brief survey. This is obviously a crude model. For many variables, either five points or nothing is awarded without any intermediate scores. The author does not claim it can be applied in other libraries.[8]

Table 4.2 illustrates a journal decision model developed at the University of Evansville and published in 1986 by Ruth H. Miller and Marvin C. Guilfoyle. This model incorporates seven variables: indexing; ILL data; reviews in core lists or bibliographies; demand; program support; cost; and miscellaneous factors. From 0 to 10 points can be assigned in each category, and the weight attached to each ranges from 0.5 for miscellaneous factors to 2 for program support. The indexing category helps illustrate the model's application. A title covered in a major index receives 8 points; if included in a second index, the title gains an additional 2 points for "multiple indexing," resulting in a score of 10. Titles covered in a less-important secondary index receive 5 points (or 7 points if in two or more secondary indexes), whereas unindexed titles receive no points. Examination of the "miscellaneous factors" category clearly indicates that the model requires considerable subjective judgment (e.g., is the "format appropriate" or the "publisher reputation sound"?). However, as stated by Miller and Guilfoyle, the system turns "subjective judgments into numerical scores."[9]

Edward P. Miller and Ann L. O'Neill proposed in 1990 a model for calculating a journal's "effectiveness factor" to be used for deselection purposes. This model is unique in its flexibility. The library using the model can decide which variables (Miller and O'Neill use the term *elements*) to include as well as the weight assigned to each, ranging from 1 to 10. Miller and O'Neill suggest numerous possible variables: "use, curriculum, indexing, ILL availability, holdings, binding/check-in costs, publishers reputation, format, paper quality, claiming problems, language, microfilm," and JCR impact factor. They also present an instrument for surveying users about their assessments on a 1 to 10 scale of such factors as author prestige, article quality, overall journal rating, and "level of embarrassment to admit ignorance of the journal." A library can use some or all of these variables as well as add others. The authors do not explain, except in a few instances, how the variables can be converted to numerical point scales. In fact, it is the library's prerogative to set the numerical scale for each variable. Although this feature may contribute to the model's flexibility, it might also present some practical difficulties. The authors state that the effectiveness factor should be calculated only for candidates for cancellation.[10]

Table 4.2.
Miller and Guilfoyle's Journal Subscription Model Developed at the University of Evansville

   I. INDEXING (8/5/2 Points)   WEIGHT: 1.5
       1. Primary indexing: ASTI/BPI/CIJE/CINAHL/CLI/EDI
            HUMI/PSYCH/SSI/USPSD/
       2. Secondary indexing available at U.E.
       3. Multiple indexing

  II. INTERLIBRARY LOAN (5/10 Points)   WEIGHT: 1.0
       1. 5-8 requests in last year from multiple requestors
       2. >8 requests in last year from multiple requestors

 III. REVIEW/CORE LIST/BIBLIOGRAPHY (4/3/3 Points)   WEIGHT: 1.5
       1. Strong review
       2. Indication of appropriateness for U.E.
       3. Currency or review or list

  IV. DEMAND (4/4/2 Points)   WEIGHT: 1.0
       1. Faculty
       2. Librarian
       3. Student or other patron

   V. PROGRAM SUPPORT (4/3/3 Points)   WEIGHT: 2.0
       1. Substantial number of students or courses/programs supported
       2. Periodical use by these courses/programs is high
       3. Relative strength of current periodical holdings for these
            courses/programs is low

  VI. COST (4/0/3/3 Points)   WEIGHT: 1.0
       1. <\$75
       2. \$75 +
       3. Amount spent for all subscriptions for this department or area
            (versus other areas) is low in relation to need and use
       4. Amount spent for subscriptions (versus books) for this department
            or area is low in relation to need and use

 VII. MISCELLANEOUS FACTORS (3/3/1/3 Points)   WEIGHT: .5
       1. Format appropriate
       2. Not available locally
       3. Publisher reputation sound
       4. Published longer than one year (an acceptable risk)

Dawn Bick and Reeta Sinha, in 1991, published a sophisticated model that was developed at the Houston Academy of Medicine–Texas Medical Center Library. Twenty factors were used as evaluation criteria, including indexing; impact factor; and holdings in the library, Houston area, or region. An evaluation matrix was then used to determine the importance of the evaluation criteria by comparing all criteria with each other on a one-to-one basis. For example, impact factor would be compared in importance with indexing, using a 3-point scale: "3 for a major difference in importance, 2 for a medium difference, and 1 for a minor difference." The weights are then added to obtain a "score" for each journal under evaluation. Predicated on the assumption that a journal's benefit increases with its use, the journal score is multiplied by the number of uses to obtain a "BENEFIT" factor. The BENEFIT factor is then divided by cost to rank the library's current journals by a cost-benefit ratio.[11]

Additional published descriptions of journal decision models were developed at various libraries, including California State University at Dominguez Hills, by Jeffrey Broude;[12] the Lawrence Livermore National Laboratory Biomedical Library, by Richard K. Hunt;[13] the University of Nijmegen Faculty of Medical Sciences (in the Netherlands), by Rikie Deurenberg;[14] and the University of Maryland at College Park, by Natalie Schoch and Eileen G. Abels.[15] Other models based on theory (without explicitly stating they had been used at a specific library) have been advanced by Eleanor D. Dym and Donald L. Shirey,[16] Donald H. Kraft and Richard A. Polacsek,[17] Roy Rada and others,[18] and Victor A. Triolo and Dachun Bao.[19] Andrew Peters reported use of a modified version of the Kraft and Polacsek model at the Central State University library in Oklahoma.[20]

In summary, the major issues in design of a serials evaluation model concern

1. the number of variables included;

2. which variables are included;

3. the numerical scale;

4. the weight or hierarchical value attached to each variable;

5. the difficulty of implementing the model;

6. the degree of flexibility allowed the implementing library;

7. whether the model is based on theory or actual library practice; and

8. the model's explicit purpose (e.g., selection, cancellation, etc.).

Some concerns about journal decision models should be noted. One might question whether a model developed in the context of a single discipline or library can validly be transported to other disciplines or libraries. Moreover, most models are intended to be used in a cross-disciplinary sense—often for all journals subscribed to by the implementing library. For some variables, cross-disciplinary comparison may be like comparing apples and oranges, as citation and price patterns vary from discipline to discipline. There may be a strong subjective factor in the selection of variables and the weight assigned to them. The conversion of data about a specific journal to a numerical scale could sometimes be problematic. Most models appear to have been developed for academic institutions and may not be applicable to other types of libraries.

Journal decision models are of considerable theoretical importance for serials collection management. Unfortunately, there is little evidence, based on surveying the appropriate literature and listservs, that these models have actually been used to any appreciable extent in libraries other than the library where a particular model was developed. Ironically, many libraries implementing serials cancellation projects often reach their own decision rules for combining journal evaluation variables even though a formal, explicit journal decision model is never published.

CORE LISTS OF SERIALS

The so-called core collection has long been a major concept in collection development thought. The word *core* refers to the most important materials that should form the core or heart of the collection. Such terms as *essential* or *indispensable* have been used to describe core materials. The concept has been applied to subjects, formats, and library types as well as combinations of these categories. Specific examples of the core concept include the core books for a college library (e.g., *Books for College Libraries)* or, more relevant to this text, the core periodicals for a type of library or in a particular discipline.

The most frequently used methods for determining the core are inclusion on recommended lists, subjective judgment, use, and citation data, but overlapping holdings among libraries, indexing, and complex multivariable approaches have also been used. Some of the reported methodologies for identifying core periodicals are described below. Standard lists of recommended journals or magazines are often considered to constitute the core. The best-known list of this type, first published in 1969, is *Magazines for Libraries*, by Katz and Katz. The ninth edition, issued in 1997, lists and annotates more than 7,300 titles deemed "most useful for the average elementary or secondary school, public, academic, or special library."[21] The second edition of Selma K. Richardson's *Magazines for Children: A Guide for Parents, Teachers, and Librarians*, published in 1991, recommends and lists more than 110 magazines for children through age 14 and the 8th grade.[22] Since 1965 Alfred N. Brandon and Dorothy R. Hill have been publishing biannually in the *Bulletin of the Medical Library Association* the so-called Brandon-Hill list of recommended books and serials for small medical libraries. Their April 1997 list contained 141 journals.[23] The *Core Collection of Medical Books and Journals*, compiled by Howard Hague,[24] has been identified as the "British counterpart" to the Brandon-Hill list but with an international focus. The 1994 edition lists 249 journal titles.[25]

Although identification of the core was not their primary intention, Tim LaBorie, Michael Halperin, and Howard D. White's study could be used to determine core journals in library and information science. They analyzed overlapping coverage of Library and Information Science (LIS) journals in ten indexing and abstracting services: Four from the discipline itself (*Abstract Journal: Informatics, Information Science Abstracts, Library and Information Science Abstracts*, and *Library Literature*) and six outside the discipline, such as the *Social Sciences Citation Index* (SSCI) and *The Current Index to Journals in Education*. LaBorie, Halperin, and White then identified the 59 titles covered in five or more of these indexing services as the "*de facto* core journals of library and information science."[26]

James C. Baughman's structural analysis of sociology, based on more than 10,000 citations in 446 articles listed in the 1970-1971 *Social Sciences and Humanities Index*, included an identification of the core sociology journals. He ranked journals according to the number of their articles that were cited at least twice and designated the top ten as representing the core. It is noteworthy that five of these were outside the discipline of sociology, thus illustrating the interdisciplinary nature of the social sciences.[27]

At the University of Delaware library, Linda Lawrence Stein identified 27 core "fashion, textile, and apparel merchandising/manufacturing" periodicals by accessing on the Internet the online public access catalogs (OPACs) of eight other major university libraries known to possess strong collections in that specialty. Titles held by a majority of the other libraries (five of eight) were considered the core.[28] Stein's methodology is particularly interesting because it combines the Internet and a traditional collection management approach—analysis of overlapping library holdings. A possible flaw in this method is that the analysis was limited to the 55 titles already held by the University of Delaware library. Thus, a title meeting the decision criterion to be considered core (appearing in five of the eight OPACs accessed on the Internet) would have been overlooked if it were not initially in the University of Delaware collection.

The core concept has obvious relevance to serials management. In selecting periodicals for a new collecting area, one would logically place the highest priority on core titles. A list of core titles can be used as a checklist for collection evaluation. A core title would not normally be a strong candidate for cancellation, weeding, or relegation to remote storage. In some cases a multibranch system might wish to duplicate core periodicals. Core lists can assist budgeting by indicating the cost of subscribing to the core periodicals in a subject area. Moreover, in an age of increasing emphasis on access over ownership, the core concept assumes greater significance. Libraries would presumably wish to subscribe to the core periodicals and rely on access for noncore titles. Indeed, requests for core lists in various subject areas frequently appear on listservs.

In addition to its practical application in libraries, the core serials concept has been used in the research process. Many scholarly investigations have been based on the core journals of a particular subject. For example, Bluma C. Peritz used the citations in 39 core library science journals for her bibliometric analysis of the discipline.[29] Judith Serebnick and Stephen P. Harter used coverage in each of the three major library and information science indexes to identify 39 core LIS journals so they could survey their editors about ethical practices in journal publishing.[30]

Some limitations to the core concept should also be mentioned. A core list does not consider the unique needs of a specific library and its clientele. Each major method for determining core lists (e.g., citation data, subjective judgment, or indexing) may contain its own methodological flaws. Subject- or discipline-oriented core lists will probably not contain interdisciplinary journals.

MAJOR APPROACHES TO THE MACROEVALUATION OF SERIALS

Most of this chapter focuses on micro treatment of individual serial titles. In the final analysis, the most significant question concerns how well the library is meeting patron needs for serials. Thus, macroevaluation is directed toward the entire collection or the library's performance rather than individual titles. A macroevaluation project can concentrate exclusively on the serials format, but commonly the focus is on a particular subject area or the whole collection. In the latter case, serials are usually evaluated as a component of support. This section introduces some fundamental evaluation concepts, the major collection evaluation approaches, and their application to serials.

Approaches to collection evaluation have been characterized as quantitative versus qualitative or collection centered versus client centered. A quantitative approach concentrates on the number of items held, whereas a qualitative method is concerned with the quality of the holdings. A collection-centered method focuses on the collection itself or compares it with an external standard. In contrast, a client-centered method analyzes how well the collection meets the needs of library patrons.

General evaluation techniques can be characterized according to whether they are objective or subjective, real or simulated, and obtrusive or unobtrusive. An objective method relies on measurable units of analysis, such as the number of current periodical subscriptions; a subjective technique is based on impressionistic perceptions, such as a faculty member's opinion on how well the serials collection is supporting his or her research. A real technique is based on an actual situation (e.g., the proportion of time that serial titles are on the shelf when patrons seek them), whereas a simulated technique is structured on an artificial contrivance for research purposes (checking a list of serial citations that are presumed to be representative of patron information needs). At the risk of oversimplification, the involved human subjects are aware of an intrusive evaluation, but unaware of an unobtrusive one. In practical terms, a periodical use study could be either obtrusive or unobtrusive depending on whether patrons are informed that the study is taking place.

Three distinctive concepts relating to serials macroevaluation are ownership, availability, and accessibility. *Ownership* obviously relates to a library "owning" or holding an item as a permanent part of its collection. *Availability* addresses the question of whether a patron can find an item on the shelf when he or she is seeking it. *Accessibility* concerns the time required to provide a sought-after document to a patron.

A brief introduction to the major collection evaluation approaches, outlining the benefits and drawbacks of each, can be found in the American Library Association's (ALA) *Guide to the Evaluation of Library Collections*. Practical step-by-step instructions about implementing the leading techniques are provided in Blaine H. Hall's *Collection Assessment Manual for College and University Libraries*. Finally, the academic library collection evaluation literature from 1980 to 1991 is surveyed in Thomas E. Nisonger's *Collection Evaluation in Academic Libraries: A Literature Guide and Annotated Bibliography*.[31] The traditional collection evaluation approaches and their relationship to serials are discussed below.

The Checklist Approach

The checklist method represents the oldest and most traditional approach to collection evaluation. Many other methods, such as availability studies or document delivery tests, are simply more sophisticated modifications of the checklist technique. As implied by the term *checklist*, a list of items is checked against the collection and the percentage of items held is then tabulated. The larger the proportion of items held, the better the collection is presumed to be. This is a collection-centered, qualitative technique. (Although the checklist method contains a quantitative aspect in that the number of held items is calculated, it is usually considered a qualitative technique because the list is assumed to represent high-quality items.)

A major issue concerns which list to check. The ALA *Guide to the Evaluation of Library Collections* lists 15 possibilities, including bibliographies; recommended lists; items cited in faculty publications, Ph.D. dissertations, or course reading lists; or titles listed by subject in the JCR.[32]

The unit to be checked against the library's holdings can be either a periodical title or a specific article. The list's format—whether it lists citations to articles or simply titles—might determine the checking strategy used. In article-level checking, the criterion for determining a hit would be whether the specific citation is actually contained in the collection, whereas in title-level checking, one presumes the criterion would be whether the library maintains a current subscription. Checking at the article-level probably provides a more meaningful indication of the serial holdings' depth, but it would tend to overestimate collection strength in libraries that have recently canceled many current periodical subscriptions. In some evaluation studies, one might tabulate the findings by both article and title. Note that a checklist can consist exclusively of serial items or include serials entries with other formats. In the latter, the data can nevertheless be tabulated separately for serials.

Many uses of list checking to evaluate periodical holdings have been reported. For example, the University of California at Berkeley Environmental Design Library checked its periodicals against seven major indexes.[33]

Expert Opinion

This subjective, qualitative, collection-centered approach is often termed "direct examination" or "impressionistic judgment." A presumed expert examines the collection and reaches an impressionistic assessment of its quality. This approach would normally be used for a specific subject rather than the whole collection. In assessing a subject's serial holdings, the expert should consider whether the major titles are included, balance among subareas, currency, language, completeness of holdings, and alternate means of access. This method requires considerable subject expertise.

Compiling Holding Statistics

Compiling statistics on the size and growth of the collection represents one of the older, more-traditional, quantitative, collection-centered approaches to evaluation. For serials the most crucial data are totals of current subscriptions, volumes held, and expenditures. The statistics can be compiled for the complete collection or specific subject areas. In some instances, the number of periodical subscriptions per student or pupil is used as an evaluative measure. Statistical data are especially valuable when placed in a comparative context with other libraries or used for longitudinal comparisons of the same library. Serials data for large U.S. university libraries can be found in the annual Association of Research Libraries (ARL) statistical series. (For details on various statistical sources, see appendix 1.) A major issue, unresolved in the mid-1990s, concerns counting such "virtual holdings" as electronic journals—which are accessible but not owned in the traditional sense—in holding statistics. In light of the increasing emphasis on access rather than ownership, it is probable that holdings data will, in the future, become less significant as a periodicals evaluation measure.

Standards

A standard is typically promulgated by an authoritative organization and covers numerous components of library support such as budgets, staffing, facilities, and collections. The collection section usually addresses periodicals. Although traditionally a collection-centered approach, standards can be quantitative, qualitative, or sometimes both. A quantitative standard specifies a set number of items to be held in the collection or acquired within a year; qualitative standards provide prescriptive statements outlining adequacy or excellence without specifying numbers.

Standards date back more than three quarters of a century. In 1920 the ALA published the National Education Association's standards for senior and junior high school libraries,[34] and standards for junior college libraries were first issued by the American Council on Education and the American Association of Junior Colleges in the early 1930s; for college libraries, by the Association of College and Research Libraries (ACRL) in 1959; and for university libraries, by the ACRL and ARL in 1979.[35] Because many standards have been adopted for practically every type of library, a comprehensive review is beyond this chapter's scope.

The current ACRL, ALA, and Association for Educational Communications and Technology (AECT) standards for junior and community college libraries serve as an example of the quantitative approach.[36] This document contains a table (labeled table E, which is partially reproduced here as table 4.3, on page 108) prescribing a given number of current serial subscriptions for 10 categories of student body size in both a "minimum" and an "excellent" collection on a single campus. The recommended number of current serial subscriptions for a "minimum collection" ranges from 230 when there are fewer than 1,000 full time equivalent (FTE) students to 1,800 for 17,000 to 19,000 FTE students. In contrast, the stipulated numbers for an "excellent collection" range from 400 for fewer than 1,000 FTE students to 2,400 for 17,000 to 19,000 FTE students. Although not illustrated in table 4.3, numbers for volumes; film and video; such "other" items as microforms, maps, etc.; and total collection size are also specified.

Table 4.3.
Number of Recommended Serial Subscriptions from Table E of ACRL-ALA-AECT Standards for Community, Junior, and Technical College Learning Resources Programs

Minimum Collection

FTE Students	Current Serial Subscriptions
Under 1,000	230
1,000-2,999	300
3,000-4,999	500
5,000-6,999	700
7,000-8,999	850
9,000-10,999	900
11,000-12,999	1,000
13,000-14,999	1,200
15,000-16,999	1,500
17,000-19,000	1,800

Excellent Collection

FTE Students	Current Serial Subscriptions
Under 1,000	400
1,000-2,999	600
3,000-4,999	800
5,000-6,999	1,000
7,000-8,999	1,200
9,000-10,999	1,400
11,000-12,999	1,600
13,000-14,999	1,800
15,000-16,999	2,100
17,000-19,000	2,400

Information Power (the AASL-AECT standard for school library media centers, discussed in chapter 3) presents data on the number of serials held and the number of current serial subscriptions per 100 pupils at the 75th, 90th and 95th percentile levels in seven categories of school libraries—to be used as quantitative national guidelines. As of the end of 1985, a high school with more than 1,000 students "held" 145 serials at the 75th percentile level, 198 at the 90th percentile, and 231 at the 95th. (Although not explicitly stated, one presumes these numbers refer to current subscriptions.) Total subscriptions per 100 students were reported as 10 at the 75th percentile, 14 at the 90th, and 15 at the 95th.[37] See *Information Power's* appendix A for corresponding data on other school sizes and levels.

The qualitative approach is used in the ACRL guidelines for university undergraduate libraries, which states, "Reference collections in undergraduate libraries should concentrate on the more standard and interdisciplinary indexes and sources. Periodical collections should emphasize the titles covered by these indexes."[38] The 1995 ACRL standards for college libraries assert that "Institutional needs for periodical holdings vary widely," but, as previously mentioned, they suggest a library consider subscribing to any title needed more than five times per year.[39]

Standards are somewhat controversial. Some critics claim that qualitative standards represent meaningless verbiage that can not easily be applied in practice; others assert that quantitative standards place too much emphasis on numbers at the expense of quality. Moreover, most standards adhere to the traditional ownership paradigm and fail to adequately address electronic journals.

Formulas

Another traditional collection evaluation method is the use of a formula—an objective, quantitative, collection-centered approach. Most formulas begin with a base number of volumes and add additional volumes for such variables as the number of FTE faculty and the number of degree programs to calculate the total volumes a library should contain for hypothetical minimum-level collection adequacy. The best-known and most frequently used example is the Clapp-Jordan Formula, originally published by Verner W. Clapp and Robert T. Jordan in 1965 and reprinted as a classic paper in 1989.[40] (A faculty member once told the author that this formula reminded him of a venereal disease.)

The Clapp-Jordan Formula contains separate components for books, periodicals, and documents. To calculate the required number of periodicals for a senior college or university library, begin with 250 subscriptions and 3,750 volumes, which are asserted to be the appropriate figures for a basic undergraduate collection. To this base, add 1 subscription and 15 titles for each FTE faculty member, 1 volume for each FTE graduate and undergraduate student, 3 subscriptions and 45 volumes for each subject major available to undergraduates, 10 subscriptions and 150 volumes for every master's field, and 100 subscriptions and 1,500 volumes for each doctoral program. As would be expected, lower numbers are stipulated for a junior or community college library: 125 periodical subscriptions and 1,875 volumes for the basic collection plus 1 subscription and 15 volumes for each FTE faculty member, 1 volume for each FTE student, and 3 subscriptions and 45 volumes for each field of study. Note that the ratio of subscriptions to volumes is consistently 1:15.

Clapp and Jordan justified the figure of 250 periodical subscriptions for a basic undergraduate collection by noting that it represented half of the 500 periodicals listed in three standard indexes: *Readers' Guide to Periodical Literature*, *International Index*, and *Applied Science and Technology Index*.

Some lesser-known formulas should be briefly mentioned. The California State Formula is structured on a similar principle to the Clapp-Jordan Formula but uses a different base number along with a different set of weights and variables. Likewise, the Clapp-Jordan Formula itself has been modified by slightly changing the variables and their assigned weights (e.g., the Washington State Formula or the Texas version of the Clapp-Jordan Formula). Finally, the ACRL Standards for College Libraries are modeled on the Clapp-Jordan Formula.

Formulas have been used primarily for evaluating the entire collection by calculating whether it contains the requisite number of volumes. Formulas with a separate periodicals component, such as the Clapp-Jordan Formula, could potentially be used to evaluate the size of a library's whole periodical collection. In contrast, most formulas are not intended to evaluate specific subject areas. The Clapp-Jordan Formula's stipulation of an additional 100 subscriptions and 1,500 periodical volumes per doctoral area represents an average figure and should not be interpreted as applying equally to all subjects. The number of periodicals required to support Ph.D.-level study varies from one subject to another, depending upon the subject's scope and the number of journals published in its area.

Formulas do not consider quality or relevance to user need and may discourage weeding in order to "pad the numbers." Furthermore, like many traditional macroevaluation methods, most formulas are not well suited to the newly emerging paradigm of librarianship because they fail to address virtual holdings, which can be accessed but are not owned.

Availability Studies

The term *availability studies* can be applied to a genre of closely related client-centered techniques, which may also be called "shelf availability studies," "frustration studies," or "failure studies." In essence, these studies focus on the level of user success in locating items on the shelf. (Technically, an availability study focuses on overall level of success, but a frustration or failure study concentrates on the causes of nonsuccess.) Patrons are normally asked to complete forms listing which items they were and were not able to locate, and the library staff does follow-up analysis to determine why the latter were not available.

"The branching technique," developed by Paul Kantor during the 1970s and probably the best-known availability study method, examines four branches:

1. Acquisition—the item must have been acquired by the library

2. Circulation—the item must not be checked out

3. Library operations—the item must not be lost or in processing

4. The user—who must be able to successfully locate the item[41]

For the patron to locate the item on the shelf, success must be achieved in all four branches. Lack of success in any single branch leads to overall failure. Most availability studies conducted in libraries have focused on books. Nevertheless, the method generally lends itself well to serials, except that the circulation branch would not be a factor in libraries where serials do not circulate. It is possible that an OPAC that one can dial in to from home using a modem might skew an availability study's results—patrons might not even come to the library if the item they wanted was not listed in the online catalog. For a detailed description, including flowcharts, of the successful application of Kantor's technique to measure serials availability at the University of New Mexico library, see the study by Jan Bachmann-Derthick and Sandra Spurlock.[42] *Output Measures for Public Libraries: A Manual of Standardized*

Procedures, second edition, by Nancy A. Van House and others, contains instructions for a "Materials Availability Survey," which includes serials along with other formats.[43]

Neal K. Kaske argues that the traditional availability study is no longer relevant in the present environment, where a large proportion of patron needs are met by resources external to the library. Instead, he proposes that a modified availability study could be used to evaluate patron access to Internet resources.[44] One can easily envision this technique's application to electronic journals on the Internet. If a patron were unable to access a networked electronic journal, was it because a file server was down? A password was required? The maximum allowable number of simultaneous users were already logged on? Or the patron did not know how to use the system?

Surveying User Opinion

As previously discussed, user input, a subjective, client-centered approach, can be an important microevaluation criterion, but it is likewise an established approach to macroevaluation. John Budd and Mike DiCarlo's method, tested at the Northeast Louisiana University and the Southeastern Louisiana University libraries, is an example of a user survey. Faculty and students were asked to complete a survey instrument using a 1-to-6 scale to rate the library's performance in 20 different areas as well as each area's perceived importance. Three of the 20 related to serials—local newspapers, out-of-town newspapers, and "journals and magazines meeting your needs."[45] Alain Besson and Ian Sheriff later used Budd and DiCarlo's method to evaluate the journal collection at the University of London's medical college libraries.[46]

Unlike many of the traditional methods, surveying user opinion could be used to measure the effectiveness of document delivery programs and patron access to electronic journals. For instance, Tina E. Chrzastowski and Mary A. Anthes report a survey of user satisfaction with serials document delivery at the University of Illinois at Urbana-Champaign Chemistry Library.[47]

Document Delivery Tests

A document delivery test (DDT) measures a library's speed in providing documents, that is, accessibility, regardless of whether the documents are obtained from the collection or an external source. The best-known DDT was developed by Richard H. Orr and colleagues during the late 1960s for evaluating the performance of medical libraries,[48] and subsequent research by Rudolf Jacob Penner found Orr's technique appropriate for other types of libraries.[49] To implement the test, one calculates the amount of time required to obtain each of 300 periodical citations presumed to correspond to user information needs. Orr proposed a "Capability Index," ranging from 0 (none of the 300 items is obtained within a week or less) to 100 (every item is procured in 10 minutes or less).

More recently, a DDT was included in *Output Measures for Public Libraries*, a manual of standardized procedures for evaluating the performance of small and medium-sized public libraries. In contrast to Orr's use of citations, *Output Measures for Public Libraries'* DDT is based on items actually wanted by patrons. Beginning with a sample of sought-after items that were not immediately available, one calculates the percentage that were provided in 7 days, 14 days, and 30 days. Although developed for all materials, this measure can be separately calculated for periodicals.[50]

A DDT would be considered an objective, qualitative, client-centered approach. It seems probable that this technique will be more frequently used in the future because it tests access rather than ownership.

The Conspectus

Developed by the Research Libraries Group (RLG) beginning in the 1970s, the Conspectus, although quite controversial, has emerged as an internationally recognized collection evaluation instrument. It has been used in evaluation, cooperative collection development, policy making, budgeting, preservation, and grant applications. Two different versions—by RLG and Western Library Network (WLN)—are now available. The RLG Conspectus is organized into 22 divisions corresponding to broad areas of knowledge such as "art and architecture" or "library and information science" and 8,139 specific subject headings. The subject breakdown generally corresponds to segments of the LC classification system. The WLN Conspectus is divided into 24 divisions, 500 categories (somewhat similar to the North American Title Count, which uses approximately 500 segments of the Library of Congress classification system to report library holdings), and approximately 5,000 specific subjects. Libraries applying the WLN Conspectus have the option of using the 500 categories, 5,000 specific subjects, or some combination of both. Accordingly, some observers believe the WLN Conspectus is more appropriate for medium-sized or small libraries and nonacademic institutions. The original RLG Conspectus applied to the subject breakdown a 0 to 5 rating system (0 = "Out of Scope," 1 = "Minimal Level," 2 = "Basic Information Level," 3 = "Study or Instructional Support Level," 4 = "Research Level," and 5 = "Comprehensive Level") for the current collecting activity and existing collection strength. The WLN version introduced a 10-point scale by dividing level one into two categories (even and uneven minimal coverage), level two into introductory and advanced categories, and level three into three divisions (basic, intermediate, and advanced instructional support). WLN gives libraries the option of using either the 6- or 10-point scales, which are applied to three collection aspects: the "collection level," meaning accumulated strength; the "acquisitions commitment," that is, the current collecting intensity or activity; and the "goal level," or desired collecting intensity. Finally, the WLN Conspectus is available in two different versions: one corresponding to the LC classification system, the other to the Dewey decimal classification (DDC).

This qualitative, collection-centered tool has been used in Australia, New Zealand, Canada, the United Kingdom, and continental Europe. The second edition of the ALA's *Guide for Written Collection Policy Statements* recommends use of the Conspectus codes in collection development policies to promote standardization among different libraries.[51] Tools available to assist with implementing the Conspectus include *Using the Conspectus Method: A Collection Assessment Handbook*, by Mary Bushing, Burns Davis, and Nancy Powell,[52] and the *Manual for the North American Inventory of Research Library Collections*, prepared by Jutta Reed-Scott.[53]

The Conspectus must be mentioned because it is a major collection evaluation method even though it does not evaluate serials as a separate format. Instead it considers serial holdings as a component in reaching an overall assessment for specific subject categories. The segments of the WLN Conspectus collecting code definitions pertinent to serials, as reported in the *Guide for Written Collection Policy Statements*, are extracted below.[54] A separate set of language codes describes the English and non-English makeup of the collection, but they do not address serials.

> Level 2, the Basic Information Level—a few major periodicals

> Level 2b "Basic Information Level, Advanced"—"a broader selection of basic . . . periodicals and indexes that serve to introduce and define a subject"

> Level 2c "Basic Information Level, Introductory"—"selective major periodicals"

> Level 3 "Study or Instructional Support Level"—"a selection of representative journals"

> Level 3a "Basic Study or Instructional Support Level"—"a selection of basic representative journals/periodicals, and subject-based indexes"

> Level 3b "Intermediate Study or Instructional Support Level"—"all key journals on primary topics, selected journals . . . on secondary topics"

> Level 3c "Advanced Study or Instructional Support Level"—"a significant number of . . . journals on the primary and secondary topics in the field"

> Level 4 "Research Level"—"is intended to include . . . a very extensive collection of journals and major indexing and abstracting services in the field"

A revised set of Conspectus collecting definitions to address remote-access electronic resources was introduced at the 1997 ALA Midwinter Meeting. Drafted by an international committee of 30 to 40 librarians who work with the Conspectus, the revised definitions state that an electronic journal is equivalent to a print journal if three conditions are met: access to it equals or surpasses access to print journals, the library provides a sufficient number of terminals, and there is no additional cost to the patron. The revised definitions also state that delayed availability through document delivery is not the equivalent of immediate on-site or electronic access.[55]

The Conspectus offers the benefit of a uniform standard for describing collection strength that can be used for collection evaluation, collection development policies, preservation decisions, budgeting, and cooperative collection development. Common criticisms of the Conspectus approach include the subjective nature of the collecting levels assessments, the questionable ability of libraries to apply it consistently, and its possible unsuitability for medium-sized and nonacademic libraries. Many feel that the benefits derived from the Conspectus have not been significant enough to justify the extensive time and effort libraries expended in its implementation. Some have questioned the Conspectus's usefulness for evaluating some subject areas, such as the sciences, where serials form a substantial portion of the support.

Citation Studies

The use of citation data is considered a major approach to collection evaluation. Citation analysis can be collection-centered if citations are used as a checklist or client-centered if citation studies are used as evidence of patron need. Chapter 5 is devoted to citation analysis's application to journal collection management.

Use Studies

Analysis of use has been a long-standing, client-centered approach to collection evaluation. Use is also a major factor in periodical evaluation at both the micro level (a single periodical) and the macro level (use patterns for the whole collection). Use studies can consider circulation or in-house use or both, although most periodical use studies focus on in-house use. Because periodical use studies receive detailed coverage in chapter 6, there is no need for further discussion here.

Summary

The most appropriate method for a particular evaluation project will vary depending on numerous factors such as the project's purpose, the type of library, the available time and resources, and the evaluating librarian's level of subject expertise. Many experts recommend the use of different approaches in a single project to lend greater credibility to the results.

With the exception of DDTs, user opinion surveys, and possibly availability studies, the standard collection evaluation techniques are generally tied to the ownership paradigm and do not address the effects of electronic technology. A major challenge for the profession is to develop new client-centered macroevaluation methods emphasizing access and availability rather than ownership and testing how the library integrates print and electronic serials as well as document delivery services to meet client information needs.

NOTES

1. Jamie Webster Hastreiter, Larry Hardesty, and David Henderson, comps., *Periodicals in College Libraries*, CLIP Note 8 (Chicago: Association of College and Research Libraries, 1987), 9.

2. P. G. Peacock, "The Selection of Periodicals for Binding," *Aslib Proceedings* 33 (June 1981): 258. Peacock states his work is based on a decision table for assessing conservation priorities developed by Nicolas Barker of the British Library.

3. Helen M. Grochmal, "Selection Criteria for Periodicals in Microform," *Serials Librarian* 5 (spring 1981): 16.

4. Ibid.

5. Peacock, "The Selection of Periodicals for Binding," 259.

6. S. M. Dhawan, S. K. Phull, and S. P. Jain, "Selection of Scientific Journals: A Model," *Journal of Documentation* 36 (March 1980): 24-32.

7. Gilda Maria Braga and Cecilia Alves Oberhofer, "A Model for Evaluating Scientific and Technical Journals from Developing Countries," in *The Information Community: An Alliance for Progress; Proceedings of the 44th ASIS Annual Meeting, Washington, D.C., October 25-30, 1981,* vol. 18, ed. Lois F. Lunin, Madeline Henderson, and Harold Wooster (White Plains, N.Y.: published for the American Society for Information Science by Knowledge Industry Publications, 1981), 51-54.

8. Judith A. Segal, "Journal Deselection: A Literature Review and an Application," *Science and Technology Libraries* 6 (spring 1986): 25-42.

9. Ruth H. Miller and Marvin C. Guilfoyle, "Computer Assisted Periodicals Selection: Structuring the Subjective," *Serials Librarian* 10 (spring 1986): 9-22.

10. Edward P. Miller and Ann L. O'Neill, "Journal Deselection and Costing," *Library Acquisitions: Practice and Theory* 14, no. 2 (1990): 173-78.

11. Dawn Bick and Reeta Sinha, "Maintaining a High-Quality, Cost-Effective Journal Collection," *College and Research Libraries News* 52 (September 1991): 485-90.

12. Jeffrey Broude, "Journal Deselection in an Academic Environment: A Comparison of Faculty and Librarian Choices," *Serials Librarian* 3 (winter 1978): 147-66.

13. Richard K. Hunt, "Journal Deselection in a Biomedical Research Library: A Mediated Mathematical Approach," *Bulletin of the Medical Library Association* 78 (January 1990): 45-48. The work was performed under contract from the U.S. Department of Energy.

14. Rikie Deurenberg, "Journal Deselection in a Medical University Library by Ranking Periodicals Based on Multiple Factors," *Bulletin of the Medical Library Association* 81 (July 1993): 316-19.

15. Natalie Schoch and Eileen G. Abels, "Using a Valuative Instrument for Decision Making in the Cancellation of Science Journals in a University Setting," in *ASIS '94: Proceedings of the 57th ASIS Annual Meeting: Alexandria, Va., October 17-20, 1994,* vol. 31, ed. Bruce Maxian (Medford, N.J.: published for the American Society for Information Science by Learned Information, 1994), 41-50.

16. Eleanor D. Dym and Donald L. Shirey, "A Statistical Decision Model for Periodical Selection for a Specialized Information Center," *Journal of the American Society for Information Science* 24 (March-April 1973): 110-19. This model was developed at the University of Pittsburgh's Knowledge Availability Systems Center under contract for the National Library of Medicine's Toxicology Information Program.

17. Donald H. Kraft and Richard A. Polacsek, "A Journal-Worth Measure for a Journal-Selection Decision Model," *Collection Management* 2 (summer 1978): 129-39.

18. Roy Rada and others, "Computerized Guides to Journal Selection," *Information Technology and Libraries* 6 (September 1987): 173-84.

19. Victor A. Triolo and Dachun Bao, "A Decision Model for Technical Journal Deselection with an Experiment in Biomedical Communications," *Journal of the American Society for Information Science* 44 (April 1993): 148-60.

20. Andrew Peters, "Evaluating Periodicals," *College and Research Libraries* 43 (March 1982): 149-51.

21. Bill Katz and Linda Sternberg Katz, *Magazines for Libraries*, 9th ed. (New Providence, N.J.: R. R. Bowker, 1997), ix.

22. Selma K. Richardson, *Magazines for Children: A Guide for Parents, Teachers, and Librarians*, 2d ed. (Chicago: American Library Association, 1991).

23. Alfred N. Brandon and Dorothy R. Hill, "Selected List of Books and Journals for the Small Medical Library," *Bulletin of the Medical Library Association* 83 (April 1995): 151-75.

24. Howard Hague, comp., *Core Collection of Medical Books and Journals*, 2d ed. (London: Medical Information Working Party, 1994).

25. Jonathan Eldredge and Susan Gerding Bader, "Book Reviews: *Core Collection of Medical Books and Journals*," *Bulletin of the Medical Library Association* 83 (October 1995): 523-24.

26. Tim LaBorie, Michael Halperin, and Howard D. White, "Library and Information Science Abstracting and Indexing Services: Coverage, Overlap, and Context," *Library and Information Science Research* 7 (April-June 1985): 183-95.

27. James C. Baughman, "A Structural Analysis of the Literature of Sociology," *Library Quarterly* 44 (October 1974): 293-308.

28. Linda Lawrence Stein, "What to Keep and What to Cut? Using Internet as an Objective Tool to Identify 'Core' Periodical Titles in a Specialized Subject Collection," *Technical Services Quarterly* 10, no. 1 (1992): 3-14.

29. Bluma C. Peritz, "Citation Characteristics in Library Science: Some Further Results from a Bibliometric Survey," *Library Research* 3 (spring 1981): 47-65.

30. Judith Serebnick and Stephen P. Harter, "Ethical Practices in Journal Publishing: A Study of Library and Information Science Periodicals," *Library Quarterly* 60 (April 1990): 91-119.

31. American Library Association, *Guide to the Evaluation of Library Collections*, ed. Barbara Lockett (Chicago: American Library Association, 1989. Blaine H. Hall, *Collection Assesment Manual for College and University Libraries* (Phoenix, Ariz.: Oryx Press, 1985). Thomas E. Nisonger, *Collection Evaluation in Academic Libraries: A Literature Guide and Annotated Bibliography* (Englewood, Colo.: Libraries Unlimited, 1992).

32. American Library Association, *Guide to the Evaluation of Library Collections*, 5-6.

33. Charles Eckman, "Journal Review in an Environmental Design Library," *Collection Management* 10, nos. 1/2 (1988): 79.

34. American Association of School Librarians and Association for Educational Communications and Technology, *Information Power: Guidelines for School Library Media Programs* (Chicago: American Library Association; Washington, D.C.: Association for Educational Communications and Technology, 1988), v.

35. Nisonger, *Collection Evaluation in Academic Libraries*, 83-84.

36. "Standards for Community, Junior, and Technical College Learning Resources Programs," *College and Research Libraries News* 55 (October 1994): 572-85.

37. American Association of School Librarians and Association for Educational Communications and Technology, *Information Power*, 117-23.

38. Ad Hoc Committee to Review Draft Guidelines for University Undergraduate Libraries, "Guidelines for University Undergraduate Libraries," *College and Research Libraries News* 58 (May 1997): 332.

39. Association of College and Research Libraries, College Libraries Section, Standards Committee, "Standards for College Libraries, 1995 Edition," *College and Research Libraries News* 56 (April 1995), 247.

40. Verner W. Clapp and Robert T. Jordan, "Quantitative Criteria for Adequacy of Academic Library Collections," *College and Research Libraries* 26 (September 1965): 371-80. Reprinted in *College and Research Libraries* 50 (March 1989): 154-63.

41. Paul B. Kantor, "Availability Analysis," *Journal of the American Society for Information Science* 27 (September-October 1976): 311-19.

42. Jan Bachmann-Derthick and Sandra Spurlock, "Journal Availability at the University of New Mexico," in *Advances in Serials Management: A Research Annual*, vol. 3, ed. Jean G. Cook and Marcia Tuttle (Greenwich, Conn.: JAI Press, 1989), 173-212.

43. Nancy A. Van House and others, *Output Measures for Public Libraries: A Manual of Standardized Procedures*, 2d ed. (Chicago: American Library Association, 1987), 50-62.

44. Neal K. Kaske, "On My Mind: Materials Availability Model and the Internet," *Journal of Academic Librarianship* 20 (November 1994): 317.

45. John Budd and Mike DiCarlo, "Measures of User Evaluation at Two Academic Libraries: Prolegomena," *Library Research* 4 (spring 1982): 71-84.

46. Alain Besson and Ian Sheriff, "Journal Collection Evaluation at the Medical College of St. Bartholomew's Hospital," *British Journal of Academic Librarianship* 1 (summer 1986): 132-43.

47. Tina E. Chrzastowski and Mary A. Anthes, "Seeking the 99% Chemistry Library: Extending the Serial Collection Through the Use of Decentralized Document Delivery," *Library Acquisitions: Practice and Theory* 19 (summer 1995): 141-52.

48. Richard H. Orr and Arthur P. Schless, "Document Delivery Capabilities of Major Biomedical Libraries in 1968: Results of a National Survey Employing Standardized Tests," *Bulletin of the Medical Library Association* 60 (July 1972): 382-422.

49. Rudolf Jacob Penner, "Measuring a Library's Capability," *Journal of Education for Librarianship* 13 (summer 1972): 17-30.

50. Van House and others, *Output Measures for Public Libraries*, 62-65.

51. American Library Association, *Guide for Written Collection Policy Statements*, 2d ed., ed. Joanne S. Anderson (Chicago: American Library Association, 1996), 3.

52. Mary Bushing, Burns Davis, and Nancy Powell, *Using the Conspectus Method: A Collection Assessment Handbook* (Laly, Wash.: WLN, 1997). This item was not available to the author.

53. Jutta Reed-Scott, preparer, *Manual for the North American Inventory of Research Library Collections*, rev. ed. (Washington, D.C.: Association of Research Libraries, Office of Management Studies, 1988).

54. American Library Association, *Guide for Written Collection Policy Statements*, 13-14.

55. Tony Ferguson, "Collection Assessment in the Age of the Virtual Library" (presentation at the American Library Association Midwinter Meeting, Washington, D.C., February 15, 1997).

FURTHER READING

Other Serials Collection Management Functions

Bailey, Martha J. "Selecting Titles for Binding." *Special Libraries* 64 (December 1973): 571-73.

Grochmal, Helen M. "Selection Criteria for Periodicals in Microform." *Serials Librarian* 5 (spring 1981): 15-17.

Peacock, P. G. "The Selection of Periodicals for Binding." *Aslib Proceedings* 33 (June 1981): 257-59.

Reed, Jutta R. "Collection Development of Serials in Microform." *Microform Review* 9 (spring 1980): 86-89.

Journal Decision Models

Bick, Dawn, and Reeta Sinha. "Maintaining a High-Quality, Cost-Effective Journal Collection." *College and Research Libraries News* 52 (September 1991): 485-90.

Braga, Gilda Maria, and Cecilia Alves Oberhofer. "A Model for Evaluating Scientific and Technical Journals from Developing Countries." In *The Information Community: An Alliance for Progress; Proceedings of the 44th ASIS Annual Meeting, Washington, D.C., October 25-30, 1981.* Vol. 18, edited by Lois F. Lunin, Madeline Henderson, and Harold Wooster, 51-54. White Plains, N.Y.: published for the American Society for Information Science by Knowledge Industry Publications, 1981.

Broude, Jeffrey. "Journal Deselection in an Academic Environment: A Comparison of Faculty and Librarian Choices." *Serials Librarian* 3 (winter 1978): 147-66.

Chudamani, K. S., and R. Shalini. "Journal Acquisition—Cost Effectiveness of Models." *Information Processing and Management* 19, no. 5 (1983): 307-11.

Deurenberg, Rikie. "Journal Deselection in a Medical University Library by Ranking Periodicals Based on Multiple Factors." *Bulletin of the Medical Library Association* 81 (July 1993): 316-19.

Dhawan, S.M., S. K. Phull, and S. P. Jain. "Selection of Scientific Journals: A Model." *Journal of Documentation* 36 (March 1980): 24-32.

Dym, Eleanor D., and Donald L. Shirey. "A Statistical Decision Model for Periodical Selection for a Specialized Information Center." *Journal of the American Society for Information Science* 24 (March-April 1973): 110-19.

Hunt, Richard K. "Journal Deselection in a Biomedical Research Library: A Mediated Mathematical Approach." *Bulletin of the Medical Library Association* 78 (January 1990): 45-48.

Kraft, Donald H., and Richard A. Polacsek. "A Journal-Worth Measure for a Journal-Selection Decision Model." *Collection Management* 2 (summer 1978): 129-39.

Miller, Edward P., and Ann L. O'Neill. "Journal Deselection and Costing." *Library Acquisitions: Practice and Theory* 14, no. 2 (1990): 173-78.

Miller, Ruth H., and Marvin C. Guilfoyle. "Computer Assisted Periodicals Selection: Structuring the Subjective." *Serials Librarian* 10 (spring 1986): 9-22.

Oluić-Vuković, Vesna, and Nevenka Pravdić. "Journal Selection Model: An Indirect Evaluation of Scientific Journals." *Information Processing and Management* 26, no 3 (1990): 413-31.

Peters, Andrew. "Evaluating Periodicals." *College and Research Libraries* 43 (March 1982): 149-51.

Rada, Roy, and others. "Computerized Guides to Journal Selection." *Information Technology and Libraries* 6 (September 1987): 173-84.

Schoch, Natalie, and Eileen G. Abels. "Using a Valuative Instrument for Decision Making in the Cancellation of Science Journals in a University Setting." In *ASIS '94: Proceedings of the 57th ASIS Annual Meeting: Alexandria, Va., October 17-20, 1994.* Vol. 31, edited by Bruce Maxian, 41-50. Medford, N.J.: published for the American Society for Information Science by Learned Information, 1994.

Segal, Judith A. "Journal Deselection: A Literature Review and an Application." *Science and Technology Libraries* 6 (spring 1986): 25-42.

Triolo, Victor A., and Dachun Bao. "A Decision Model for Technical Journal Deselection with an Experiment in Biomedical Communications." *Journal of the American Society for Information Science* 44 (April 1993): 148-60.

Macroevaluation of Serials

Bachmann-Derthick, Jan, and Sandra Spurlock. "Journal Availability at the University of New Mexico." In *Advances in Serials Management: A Research Annual.* Vol. 3, edited by Jean G. Cook and Marcia Tuttle, 173-212. Greenwich, Conn.: JAI Press, 1989.

Besson, Alain, and Ian Sheriff. "Journal Collection Evaluation at the Medical College of St. Bartholomew's Hospital." *British Journal of Academic Librarianship* 1 (summer 1986): 132-43.

Orr, Richard H., and Arthur P. Schless. "Document Delivery Capabilities of Major Biomedical Libraries in 1968: Results of a National Survey Employing Standardized Tests." *Bulletin of the Medical Library Association* 60 (July 1972): 382-422.

Penner, Rudolf Jacob. "Measuring a Library's Capability." *Journal of Education for Librarianship* 13 (summer 1972): 17-30.

Chapter Five

The Application of Citation Analysis to Serials Collection Management

In recent years an increasing number of academic and research librarians have begun to realize the potential use of citation analysis as a tool for serials collection management. This chapter covers the concepts of bibliometrics and citation analysis, their application to serials management and evaluation in libraries, the Institute for Scientific Information's (ISI) *Journal Citation Reports* (JCR) and other citation services, Bradford's Law, and some research on the use of citation data. An effort is made to point out the potential uses, advantages, and limitations of various bibliometric approaches. The use of citation data in journal ranking is analyzed in greater detail in chapter 7.

BIBLIOMETRICS, INFORMETRICS, AND SCIENTOMETRICS

Citation analysis is a component of a larger field of study that has at various times been called *bibliometrics, informetrics,* or *scientometrics.* Just as the term *biometrics* refers to the application of statistical methods in biology, *bibliometrics* is the application of quantitative techniques to bibliographical units, such as books or serial articles. The application of quantitative methods to the study of science is called *scientometrics* and to the study of information, *informetrics.* In reality, there is considerable overlap among bibliometrics, scientometrics, and informetrics, and the boundaries are rather fuzzy. During the 1970s and 1980s, *bibliometrics* was generally used when this approach was applied to libraries. Practitioners of the methodology often referred to themselves as *bibliometricians.*

Indicative of the field's growing academic stature, a series of international bibliometric, informetric, and scientometric conferences have been held biennially beginning in 1987 in Diepenbbek, Belgium; London, Ontario; Bangalore, India; Berlin; Chicago; and Jerusalem. A professional organization, the International Society for Scientometrics and Informetrics (ISSI), was incorporated in the Netherlands in 1995 and founded its own listserv, the *ISSI Distribution List*, the same year.

Robert N. Broadus traces the origin of bibliometrics to the counting of scrolls during the third century B.C. at the Alexandrian Library in ancient Egypt.[1] Various authorities identify the first bibliometric study[2] as an article in the 1917 *Science Progress* by F. J. Cole and Nellie B. Eales counting publications in comparative anatomy issued between 1543 and 1860;[3] P. L. K. Gross and E. M. Gross's famous ranking of chemistry journals in 1927[4] (discussed in chapter 7); or Charles Coffin Jewett's (an illustrious nineteenth-century librarian) use of citations from leading textbooks as a checklist for evaluating the Smithsonian Institute library in 1848.[5] The term *statistical bibliography,* coined by E. W. Hulme,[6] was initially applied to this methodology. In 1969 the term *bibliometrics* was introduced by the British librarian Alan Pritchard in a letter to the editor of *Journal of Documentation.*[7] By the mid-1990s some said that *informetrics and scientometrics* should subsume the term *bibliometrics,* based on the premise that the former is a broader concept that embraces bibliometrics. An electronic journal, *Cybermetrics,* devoted to the quantitative study of scholarly communications on the Internet, was announced in early 1997—causing one to wonder if yet another term is evolving. This chapter uses the term *bibliometrics* because of its familiarity and appropriateness to libraries.

CITATION ANALYSIS

Citation analysis is a major branch of bibliometrics. Its use in collection management is based on the underlying assumption that an author who cites an item must have somehow used it in the preparation of his or her publication. Therefore, analysis of researchers' citation patterns provides clues that help libraries meet users' information needs.

The precise meaning of a citation is unclear because it is unknown exactly how an author used a cited work. The term *ceremonial citation* describes the case in which a recognized authority is cited just to prove the author has done his or her homework, even though the cited work may not have been carefully scrutinized. In fact, it is possible that an author could cite a work without actually consulting it. In both cases, that a work has been cited without serious consultation indicates its status.

Citation analysis has been used for several purposes, including

- depicting the basic structure of a discipline's literature;

- performance evaluation or ranking or both of authors, academic departments, research institutes, or even nations in terms of research productivity;

- demonstrating literature growth, especially in particular disciplines and subject areas;

- indicating cross-citation patterns among disciplines, nations, and languages (i.e., analyzing the proportion of library and information science (LIS) citations to other disciplines versus the proportion of other disciplines' citations to LIS);

- identifying research fronts;

- examining scholarly communication patterns; and

- evaluating the effects of funded versus nonfunded research.

These examples represent some of the best-known uses. Others could be named. Citation analysis can assist librarians with serials management in numerous ways, including

- a journal's citation record, for such collection management decisions as subscription and cancellation;

- citation-based journal rankings;

- Bradfordian analysis, to help assess a journal's relative importance to its discipline;

- identification of core journals in a discipline or subject area;

- JCR cited half-life data, to assist with weeding, relegation to remote storage, and filling in gap decisions;

- citation analysis of a discipline's structure, to aid budget allocation decisions; and

- cited references to serials, used as a checklist for collection evaluation.

Danny P. Wallace states that "data produced by bibliometric studies can be of practical assistance by providing a more scientific basis on which to make decisions regarding the selection, retention, and location of bibliographic items in collections."[8] If the method's validity is accepted, there are numerous advantages to using citation data for journal collection development decisions. It is unobtrusive, based on easily documented objective data, and "not dependent on direct input from the users."[9]

Some limitations to the citation analysis approach should be acknowledged. A citation may be negative: an author may be cited as an incompetent or his or her methodology as an example of the way not to do it. Intuitively, this factor seems less relevant to journal evaluation, where the focus is not on a specific author. The JCR's introduction notes that numerous factors other than scholarly merit can result in high citation counts for a journal, including its circulation, the reputation of its authors, cost, the journal's availability in library collections, availability of indexing, the controversial nature of its subject matter, and national research priorities.[10] Likewise, citation analysis would be irrelevant to the evaluation of certain categories of serials that are seldom cited by researchers, such as abstracts and indexes or newspapers.

JCR citation data may be viewed as reflecting journal usage by researchers at the national and international level. How national citation data correspond to the local needs of a particular library's patrons causes much discussion. In fact,

Maurice B. Line succinctly argued that only local use data have "any significant practical value" for journal collection management.[11] Studies addressing the correlation between citation data and local library usage are summarized in this chapter's subsequent section, "Research on Citation Data and Journals."

Other criticisms on applying citation analysis to collection development include:

- it indicates the obvious (e.g., a student in an Indiana University, School of Library and Information Science collection development class once stated that any savvy person would know that the *American Historical Review* is a premier history journal without having to look up its JCR ranking (although this statement would probably apply to only a small number of top-ranked journals);

- it is not clear what a citation really means;

- citation analysis tabulates what is easy to count, which is not necessarily what is significant;

- the distribution of citations to a journal is highly skewed, with a fraction of the articles receiving a disproportionately large share of the citations.[12]

THE *JOURNAL CITATION REPORTS*

The ISI, located in Philadelphia, was founded by Eugene Garfield, North America's most illustrious proponent of citation analysis. The ISI publishes three major citation indexes covering each of the broad areas of human knowledge: the *Science Citation Index (SCI)*; the *Social Sciences Citation Index* (SSCI); and the *Arts and Humanities Citation Index*.

These three indexes each consist of several major components, including

- the *Citation Index*
- the *Source Index*
- the *Corporate Index*
- the *Permuterm Subject Index*

The *Citation Index* is arranged alphabetically by cited author and lists all citations made during the current calendar year to an author's works published during any year. The *Source Index* is arranged alphabetically by citing author. In short, the *Citation Index* deals with who cited an author and the *Source Index* indicates who an author cited. The Corporate Index lists source articles under the first author's institutional affliction. The *Permuterm Subject Index* provides subject access, as its name implies. The annual cumulations fill numerous volumes, with the precise number varying from year to year.

For this book's purposes, we are primarily concerned with the JCR, a companion volume accompanying the *SCI* (the *SCI JCR*) and the *SSCI* (the *SSCI JCR*). The *Arts and Humanities Citation Index* is not associated with a JCR—presumably because journals are less critical in the humanities. The *SCI* and *SSCI JCR*s tabulate citation data to science and social science journals, respectively, from journals covered in all three major indexes: the *SCI*, *SSCI*, and the *Arts and Humanities Citation Index.*

After some experimentation in the late 1960s and early 1970s, the ISI began issuing on an annual basis the *SCI JCR* in 1975 and the *SSCI JCR* in 1977. Through 1988 the JCR was automatically included as the last bound volume (or volumes) in both the *SCI* and the *SSCI*. Beginning in 1989, both JCRs were sold separately as microfiche products instead of in a paper format. Starting in 1994, the JCR was issued on a CD-ROM (thus providing a more powerful and sophisticated searching capability) containing both the *SCI* and *SSCI* versions, although the microfiche editions also continue to be published.[13] There are more than 4,500 titles in the science edition and more than 1,700 in the social science version. Indiana University's School of Library and Information Science was the site for the beta testing of these products in October 1995. Journals can be "filtered" (i.e., selected—by subject, publisher, country of publication, and other categories created by the researcher—by marking specific titles). Within each filter, journals can be "sorted" i.e., ranked by six variables: Journal abbreviation, in other words, alphabetically; total citations received; impact factor; immediary index; total articles published; and cited half-life. Unfortunately, these variables can not be used in combination with each other.[14] Introductory information concerning the JCR can be found at the ISI's World Wide Web (WWW) page.[15] Detailed instruction on the JCR's use can be retrieved from the CD-ROM version or obtained in the printed booklet accompanying the fiche version.

Citation Data Available in the *Journal Citation Reports*

This section explains four citation measures that are readily available in the JCR: total citations received, impact factor, cited half-life, and immediacy index. Additional data that can be obtained from the JCR are briefly discussed.

Total Citations Received

A count of the total citations received by a journal represents the most basic citation measure. In fact, the earliest citation studies of journals, conducted during the 1920s and 1930s, were based on total citation count.

In the JCR a journal's "total citations" count includes the citations received by any issue (current as well as all backruns) during the current year from all other journals in the ISI's database. The figure counts citations to any type of item, including articles, book reviews, editorials, letters, etc. However, the total does not count citations from books or journals not covered in the ISI database.

The total citations figure has often been depicted as a crude, primitive measure. It advantages both older journals with more backruns to be cited and journals that publish more articles. Accordingly, "impact factor," explained under the next heading, was developed to correct for these factors. Despite these biases, high-citation-count titles may actually be the most important journals in terms of their contribution to scholarly communication over time and the emphasis they deserve in library collection management decisions.

Based on reports in the literature, JCR total citations data have been used by libraries for serials collection management less frequently than impact factor, discussed under the next heading. It has been used by the State University of New York (SUNY) at Albany[16, 17] and the Louisiana State University libraries,[18] among others.

Impact Factor

Impact factor represents a ratio between citations received and citable items published. A new impact factor is calculated each year. Figure 5.1 illustrates the calculation of a journal's 1995 impact factor.

Fig. 5.1. Calculation of Impact Factor

$$1995 \text{ Impact Factor} = \frac{\text{No. of 1995 Citations to 1994} + 1993 \text{ Items}}{\text{No. of Citable Items Published in 1994} + 1993}$$

In essence, impact factor represents the number of times a so-called average article has been cited. It compensates for the advantage that older, larger, or more frequently issued journals would enjoy if the evaluation were based strictly on total citations received. Although ostensibly clear-cut, the above formula contains two ambiguities: the definition of *citation* and the definition of *citable item*. According to the ISI definition, a citation is based on an "article-to-article" link. If a specific article in journal X refers to journal Y 20 times but only 15 different journal Y articles, it counts as 15 citations to journal Y. In other words, *Op cits* and *ibids* do not count as citations. If five different articles in journal X cite the same article in journal Y, it also counts as five citations for journal Y. The 1994 JCR on CD-ROM states, "Editorials, letters, news items, and meeting abstracts are not included in the article count." Some ambiguity of interpretation is probably inevitable.

Impact factor scores vary among disciplines. Generally, journals in scientific disciplines display significantly higher impact factor scores than do social science journals—an easily explained phenomenon. As illustrated above, impact factor scores are calculated solely on the basis of citations made to the two previous years in the journal's backrun. Thus, journals in disciplines that cite more current material, such as the sciences, will obviously have higher impact factors than social science journals, which tend to cite older items. Consequently, for practical collection management purposes, a journal's impact factor should only be compared with other journals in its discipline rather than all journals covered in the *SCI* or the *SSCI*.

Although impact factor offers the advantage of an objective measure, a subjective element is involved in determining how impact factor is calculated. As explained above, the ISI calculates impact factor using data from the two preceding years. Yet, impact factor could be calculated based on three, four, or any number of years. At the *Fifth Biennial Conference of the International Society for Scientometrics and Informetrics*, held in Chicago in 1995, Garfield described an impact factor calculated from 5 years of citation data.[19]

The ISI impact factor is not without controversy and has been subject to considerable debate, often highly technical, in the bibliometric literature. Stephen P. Harter states that the impact factor is "somewhat misnamed . . . it measures not so much the impact of a journal but the impact of the typical article appearing in the journal" and points out that a journal publishing a small number of highly cited articles would enjoy a high impact factor but make a limited contribution to scholarly communications.[20] Christinger Tomer questions the need for impact factor because his research indicates that impact factor-based ranking correlates with ranking by total citations.[21] My examinations of JCR data generally tend to confirm Tomer's contention that rankings by impact factor and total citations tend to correspond with each other.

Numerous alternative forms or modifications of the ISI's impact factor have been proposed over the years. These variations are usually constructed by manipulating the data available in the JCR. For illustration, to rate journals based strictly on citations received from their own discipline rather than in the entire ISI database (which includes interdisciplinary journals and journals from other disciplines), Graeme Hirst and Nadia Talent proposed the "computer science impact factor,"[22] Hirst proposed the "discipline impact factor,"[23] Chunpei He and Miranda Lee Pao proposed the "discipline influence score,"[24] and P. Pichappan proposed the "discipline contribution score."[25] George W. Black Jr. used his own version of the discipline impact factor, based on a starting set of four journals selected by an expert, to identify core journals in the area of behaviorally disordered children.[26] Modifications to help journal comparison across disciplines and subareas include the "average subfield impact factor," by P. Vinkler;[27] the "citation strategy indicator," also by Vinkler;[28] the "relative citation rate," by A. Schubert and T. Braun;[29] and the "normalized impact factor," by B. K. Sen.[30] Thomas E. Nisonger developed an adjusted impact factor, used to rank political science journals, to correct the bias introduced by averaging impact factors from adjacent years.[31] Numerous other examples of alternative impact factors could be cited.

Most of these modifications were proposed to render impact factor a more precise measurement for various research projects by information scientists. There seems little reason for librarians to modify the ISI impact factor for collection management, as the required mathematical manipulations are often quite elaborate and time-consuming.

Thomas E. Smith, in his brief introduction to use of the JCR as a serials cancellation tool, recommends that impact factor be used in the final decision after other methods have identified candidates for cancellation. He asserts that if a journal "is not in the top 60% to 80% [of its subject category ranked by impact factor] a decision to discontinue it is probably sound."[32]

The JCR impact factor—usually in combination with other factors—has reportedly been used for serials collection management at the Houston Academy of Medicine–Texas Medical Center Library,[33] the SUNY at Buffalo Health Sciences Library,[34] the Faculty of Medical Sciences Library at Nijmegen University in the Netherlands,[35] the University of Illinois at Urbana-Champaign Biology Library,[36] and the University of Missouri at Kansas City Medical Library,[37] as well as the libraries of Thomas Jefferson University[38] and Brigham Young University,[39] among other institutions. It is reasonable to assume many libraries have used impact factor without providing reports to the profession.

Apart from a library context, impact factor has been used in numerous research projects—review of which is beyond this book's scope. Nevertheless, it should be briefly noted that Henry H. Barschall[40] and Barschall and J. R. Arrington[41] have related impact factor to the cost per 1,000 characters to determine the cost-effectiveness of physics journals.

Cited Half-Life

A journal's cited half-life is defined as "the number of years going back from the current year which account for 50% of the total citations received by the cited journal in the current year."[42] New half-life data are calculated each year. Figure 5.2 illustrates the calculation of journal *X*'s cited half-life for the year 1990.

Fig. 5.2. Calculation of Journal *X*'s Cited Half-Life for 1990

If in 1990 the following years of journal *X* were cited
by all the journals in ISI's database

1989 = 30
1988 = 20
1987 = 20
1986 = 15
1985 = 14
1980 = 1

Divide the distribution in half to determine the cited half-life

1989 = 30
1988 = 20 = 50
1987 = 20
1986 = 15
1985 = 14
1984 = 1 = 50

Cited half-life equals two because half of all citations received
were within two years back from the present year.

The cited half-life does not normally end in a whole number, but a simplistic example was used to illustrate the fundamental concept. The JCR contains a more complicated formula for calculating a cited half-life ending in a decimal.

As would be expected, journals in the pure sciences tend to have low cited half-lives and humanities journals high cited half-lives, with social science journals in between. Actually, cited half-lives are not available for most humanities journals because the *Arts and Humanities Citation Index* lacks a JCR. Yet history, arguably

factor. The eight columns of data reveal for each title ranking by 1994 impact factor, journal abbreviation, total citations received in 1994 by all issues, 1994 impact factor, 1994 immediacy index, articles published in 1994, and 1994 cited half-life. The top-ranked journal in 1994, *College and Research Libraries*, received 420 citations, had a 1.314 impact factor and .179 immediacy index, published 39 articles, and had a cited half-life of 5.40.

Table 5.1.
"Information and Library Science" Journals Sorted by Impact Factor from the 1994 SSCI JCR on CD-ROM

Rank	Journal Abbreviation	ISSN	1994 Total Cites	Impact Factor	Immed Index	1994 Articles	Cited Half-Life
1	COLL RES LIBR	0010-0870	420	1.314	.179	39	5.40
2	J AM SOC INFORM SCI	0002-8231	725	1.074	.568	74	6.00
3	J DOC	0022-0418	258	1.033	.375	16	>10.0
4	ANNU REV INFORM SCI	0066-4200	128	0.941	.222	9	6.40
5	LIBR QUART	0024-2519	136	0.933	.067	15	>10.0
6	B MED LIBR ASSOC	0025-7338	234	0.897	.119	59	4.00
7	J ACAD LIBR	0099-1333	192	0.833	.021	47	4.80
8	INFORM MANAGE	0019-9966	403	0.808	.267	60	4.60
9	INT J GEOGR INF SYST	0269-3798	206	0.719	.233	30	4.10
10	INFORM PROCESS MANAG	****-****	320	0.670	.000	59	5.10
11	ONLINE	0146-5422	183	0.593	.173	75	2.40
12	SCIENTOMETRICS	0138-9130	414	0.593	.056	90	6.10
13	PROGRAM-AUTOM LIBR	0033-0337	62	0.588	.037	27	
14	DATABASE	0162-4105	150	0.556	.148	81	2.40
15	LIBR INFORM SCI	0373-4447	30	0.533			
16	LIBR INFORM SCI RES	0740-8188	68	0.474	.000	16	
17	CAN LIBR J	0008-4352	37	0.435		00	
18	RQ	0033-7072	127	0.397	.053	38	5.10
19	ONLINE CDROM REV	1353-2642	16	0.389	.056	36	
20	ELECTRON LIBR	0264-0473	52	0.382	0.26	39	

The JCR offers the following benefits for serials collection management:

- Citation data can easily and economically be retrieved for several thousand journals.

- Four different citation measures and a variety of other data are available for each journal.

- The data are "from a variety of sources (users); not just the local library."[47]

- The data are current because an updated version of the JCR is released each year.

- A journal can be compared with its peers, thus providing a context for assessing the data.

- The CD-ROM version allows the data to be manipulated in a variety of ways.

Specific criticisms or limitations of the JCR follow.

- Citations from monographs are not included in the ISI database and thus do not influence a journal's score or ranking.[48]

- The journals one wishes to evaluate may not be contained in the JCR.[49]

- Specific departmental needs are not considered.[50]

- The ISI does not adjust the data for journal self-citation.

- Because of the bias toward English-language titles, significant foreign-language titles or journals from peripheral countries are not readily identified.[51]

- The impact factor is influenced by considerations other than citedness, such as type of article, research style, etc.[52]

- A hypercited article may exaggerate a journal's ranking.[53]

- Journals in existence less than four or five years can not be evaluated.[54]

- Because the citation data are gathered from all journals covered in the ISI database, it does not measure a journal's centrality or importance to its own discipline.[55]

- Anecdotal evidence of errors in the JCR is frequently heard. Paul H. Ribbe calculated an error rate of approximately 5 percent in the JCR impact factor.[56]

- Many libraries do not have access to the JCR.

Some practical tips on collection management use of the JCR are elaborated below:

- A journal's raw citation data may be difficult to interpret unless placed in a comparative context with other journals. It is strongly recommended that journals be compared with other journals in their subject area rather than all the journals covered in the science or social science editions of the JCR. The social science JCR groups journals into more than 50 subject categories, and the science JCR, more than 170. Because citation patterns vary among disciplines, comparing journals from different subject areas may be like comparing apples and oranges.

- Rankings should be examined for several years (preferably at least three years), because a journal's ranking can fluctuate widely from year to year—especially for middle- and lower-ranked titles. Research concerning this issue is reported later in the chapter.

- The JCR can be used for either microevaluation of a specific title or macroevaluation of the library's journal collection in a subject area. In the former, a title's relative rank within its discipline would be ascertained. In the latter, the JCR's list of a subject area's top-ranked journals could be used as an evaluative checklist.

- Impact factor and total citations are the two most critical measures for evaluating journals. In the print version, impact factor rankings by subject area can be found in the section entitled "Journals by Category—Ranked by Impact Factor." If the CD-ROM version is being used, the journals in a subject category can be separately sorted by both impact factor and total citations.

- A journal that has just changed titles will be listed without an impact factor because there are no data from the two preceding years to use in the calculation. However, an impact factor will be listed under the superseded title. In the second year after a title change, an impact factor will be listed for both the new and superseded title forms. (This situation reflects the fact that when there has been a significant title change, the JCR does not combine citation counts for the new and old forms.) The JCR on CD-ROM explains that the new title's impact factor "may be lower than expected" because it is based on the most recent articles, which have had less time to be cited; whereas the superseded journal's impact factor "may be higher than expected" as it is calculated from older articles, which have had more time to receive citations. However, anyone can calculate a combined impact factor using the JCR's data on the articles published and citations received for the old and new titles during the preceding two years. Simply averaging the two reported impact factors would not be technically correct because the pertinent data for the two title forms will probably be unequal.

- Some subject categories, including "business," "economics," "information and library science," "law," "psychiatry," and "psychology," are included in both the science and social science JCR but with a different set of journals. Likewise, some titles, such as the *Journal of the American Society for Information Science*, are listed in both the *SCI* and *SSCI* with identical data. To choose between the *SCI* or *SSCI*, turn first to where the discipline intuitively seems to belong (i.e., economics with social science), but to be thorough, examine both.

- Basic collection management decisions, such as subscription and cancellation, should not be based entirely on JCR data—a point emphasized in the JCR's introduction. Rather, it should be used in combination with the other standard journal microevaluation criteria outlined in chapter 3.

- Librarians who can not afford to buy the JCR should try to locate it in a nearby institution. It is relatively easy and inexpensive to photocopy (from the microfiche copy) or print (from CD-ROM).

- If one has a choice between the microfiche and CD-ROM versions, the latter is clearly preferable because it allows greater flexibility in manipulating the data.

Other Information in the *Journal Citation Reports*

The JCR contains a wealth of additional information with considerable value to researchers even though the direct application to library serials management is less certain. In the CD-ROM version, one can retrieve any title in the system and see the calculation of its impact factor, immediacy index, and cited half-life illustrated. One can also display in rank order the journals that cite and are cited by a particular title, along with a 10-year distribution of publication years for the citing and cited articles. These data can be used to calculate a journal's self-citation rate and are also potentially useful for analysis of *journal networks*—groups of journals that cite each other. Though useful for depicting scholarly communications patterns, journal networks' direct relevance to library serials management is highly questionable. Accordingly, further discussion of journal networks is beyond this chapter's scope.

For each journal, the current year's number can be obtained for: research articles published, nonresearch articles published, and the average number of references in both types of articles as well as in all articles. Finally, the publisher's name and address, ISSN, frequency, language, country of origin, title changes within the last two years, and subject categories can be displayed for each journal.[57]

Most of the data in the CD-ROM JCR are also available in the microfiche edition but can not be filtered in the variety of ways that render the CD-ROM version a potentially powerful collection development and research tool. Through 1988, when the print JCR was discontinued, each yearly JCR contained a useful unannotated bibliography of items dealing with journal citation analysis and its application.

Additional ISI Services

The ISI's Research Services Group offers several products and services based on cumulative data from the ISI database extending back to 1981. Some of these are relevant to journal management in libraries.

The *Journal Performance Indicators on Diskette, 1981-1994* cumulates 14 years of citation data for 2,000 journals. For each journal, the number of published articles, the number of citations received, the average number of citations per article for all articles and for cited articles, and the number of uncited papers can be obtained for the 14-year period, any single year, or any 5-year time frame.

The *Institutional Citation Reports* cumulates data from 1981 to the current year. This product indicates in which journals an institution's faculty have published and the journals that have cited their work. Although ostensibly oriented toward institutional and faculty performance evaluation, the *Institutional Citation Reports* could be used in serials management.

The *Local Journal Utilization Report* is the ISI special report most relevant to university library serials collection management. Two lists are produced for an academic library using this service: journals in which the university's faculty have published and journals cited by the faculty in their articles. Both are ranked by frequency and arranged alphabetically. The database extends back to 1981, but smaller time frames can be used.

A significant limitation is that the ISI database apparently does not reflect faculty turnover or movement from institution to institution. Accordingly, a university's report would include titles published in or cited by former faculty members but exclude titles that current faculty members published in or cited prior to their affiliation with the university.[58]

LOCAL CITATION STUDIES

The preceding discussion has focused on ISI data, which are—unless a library is using customized reports—based on citations from researchers throughout North America and the world. The extent to which national citation data are relevant to the unique needs of a specific library has been debated by specialists. However, local studies can be conducted by analyzing the citations to periodicals (and nonperiodical material as well) in faculty publications, student dissertations, theses and other papers, or course syllabi.

Local citation studies have been published in the literature. Citations from forestry faculty publications at the University of Florida,[59] management and human resources master's theses from the National College of Education's off-campus program,[60] psychology and counseling master's theses and Ph.D. dissertations at St. Mary's University (in San Antonio, Texas),[61] and philosophy Ph.D. dissertations at Purdue University[62] have been used as checklists for evaluating the periodical collections of those institutions' libraries. Belen Altuna Esteibar and F. W. Lancaster identified the most frequently cited serials in faculty publications, Ph.D. dissertations, and course reading lists at the Graduate School of Library and Information Science at the University of Illinois at Urbana-Champaign.[63]

The main benefit of using local citation data instead of JCR data is that relevance to patron need may be presumed. The obvious drawback is that compilation of local citation data is more costly than using the readily available JCR data. Furthermore, local data might be influenced by the library holdings, with a particular periodical cited simply because it was available or not cited because it was unavailable.

Library staff will probably not have the time to compile citation data manually from a large number of documents. However, in some databases, such as SCISEARCH, DIALOG searches can provide data on the journals cited by individuals affiliated with a particular academic institution or department—not only listing the journals but indicating their subject and the age of cited articles. This approach has been used for journal collection management at the Yale[64] and Emory University libraries.[65] For use of DIALOG's RANK command (to place in rank order the journals published in or cited by an institution's faculty), see chapter 7.

BRADFORD DISTRIBUTION

The now well-known British librarian and information scientist, Samuel Clement Bradford, published a paper in 1934 based on analysis of bibliographies in applied geophysics, covering 1928 to 1931, and lubrication, from 1931 through June 1933. He identified a pattern in the production of articles by journals that has become known as Bradford's Law—also referred to as Bradford's Law of Scatter, Bradford's Law of Concentration and Scatter, or Bradford's Law of Dispersion. The two versions of Bradford analysis—the "verbal formulation" and the "graphical formulation"—comprise one of the major laws of bibliometrics and have considerable theoretical relevance to serials collection management. In his verbal formulation, Bradford wrote:

> The law of distribution of papers on a given subject in scientific periodicals may thus be stated: if scientific journals are arranged in order of decreasing productivity of articles on a given subject, they may be divided into a nucleus of periodicals more particularly devoted to the subject and several groups or zones containing the same number of articles as the nucleus, when the numbers of periodicals in the nucleus and succeeding zones will be as $1:n:n^2$.[66]

In essence, a few titles are cited many times, and many titles are cited a few times. This phenomenon is technically termed *concentration* and *scatter*.

Bradford organized the journals he studied into three zones. For applied geophysics, 9 journals produced 429 articles in the first zone, 59 journals accounted for 499 articles in zone 2, and 259 journals produced 404 articles in the third zone. Thus, the ratio of journals in the three zones is 9:59:259, which is reducible to approximately 1:6:29. In the three zones for the subject of lubrication, 8 journals produced 110 articles, 29 journals produced 133, and 127 journals produced 152 articles—for a journal ratio of 8:29:127, which is roughly reducible to 1:4:16. For both subjects, Bradford's formula $(1:n:n^2)$ is generally demonstrated as zone three contains in rough approximation the square of the journals in zone 2. N, which varies among different studies, is often referred to as the Bradford multiplier.

Another aspect of Bradford's analysis is the so-called Bradford curve, which results when data on the number of journals and the articles they produce are plotted on a graph—the graphical as opposed to verbal formulation of his law. In 1967 Ole V. Groos reported that lower-zone journals (i.e., those in zones farther from the nucleus) produce fewer articles than predicted.[67] Substantiated in subsequent studies, this phenomenon has been termed *the Groos droop* because, when plotted, the curve droops at its end, giving it an *S* rather than a *J* shape.[68] Various explanations for the Groos droop have been offered, including larger than expected productivity by nucleus journals, an incomplete search that failed to identify scattered articles in lower-zone journals, and the maturing of a discipline. Yeon-Kyoung Chung summarizes eight theoretical explanations for the Groos droop.[69] This somewhat technical point is probably not of great concern to most serials collection managers, yet it is an important theoretical issue for a full understanding of Bradfordian distribution.

Many other highly technical and mathematical issues relating to Bradford's Law are beyond this book's scope. It should be mentioned that Bradford offered a slightly different formulation in his 1948 book,[70] and his law was later reformulated by B. C. Brookes[71] and Ferdinand F. Leimkuhler.[72] Mary W. Lockett offers a thorough literature review of the numerous technical aspects of a Bradford distribution.[73]

For illustration of a Bradford distribution, table 5.2 is reproduced from James C. Baughman's citation analysis of sociology literature. A total of 3,521 cited articles were published in 612 journals. These articles can be divided into nine zones—each containing approximately 400 articles. In this particular study, only a single journal is in the nucleus—zone one. The number of journals required to produce these articles doubles from zone to zone (i.e., the Bradford multiplier is two for the first seven zones and somewhat higher for zones eight and nine). For example, in zone one, a single title contained 376 of the cited articles; in the second zone, two journals contain 410 articles; and in the third zone, four titles produced 403 articles. By the ninth zone, 368 cited articles are scattered among 345 different journal titles.

Table 5.2.
A Bradford Distribution of Sociology Journals

Zone	Articles	Number of Journal Titles	Bradford Multiplier(b)*
1	376	1	...
2	410	2	2
3	403	4	2
4	405	8	2
5	397	16	2
6	387	32	2
7	398	64	2
8	377	140	2.18
9	368	345	2.46
Total	3,521	612	2.08**

*b is a symbol for the Bradford Multiplier
**Average

Reprinted with permission of the University of Chicago Press from James C. Baughman, "A Structural Analysis of the Literature of Sociology," *Library Quarterly* 44 (October 1974): 301.

Published studies applying Bradford analysis to the journal literature of various subject areas are too numerous to enumerate, but a few pertinent examples from the discipline of library and information science should be noted. Chung partitioned the literature of international classification into 12 Bradford zones based on productivity and another 12 zones based on citations received.[74] Steven R. Kirby partitioned the journals that produced American history book reviews into three Bradford zones. In the first zone, 7 journals accounted for 34 percent of the reviews; in the second zone, 18 journals produced 33 percent; and 120 journals produced 33 percent in zone three. However, Kirby notes that the 7:18:120 ratio for the three zones does not conform to a Bradfordian distribution because it reduces to $1:n:n^3$ rather than $I:n:n^2$.[75] Although the data from this study do not technically conform to Bradford's mathematical formula, they nevertheless confirm the fundamental concept of concentration in a few highly productive journals and scatter among many journals making limited contributions. Moreover, one should remember that Bradford's original data only approximately fitted his formula.

Bradford's original research focused on the production of articles by journals. However, Bradford distribution has also been observed in other journal data, including usage in a library, citation patterns, and interlibrary loan (ILL) and photocopy requests. In fact, the general Bradford pattern has been found in numerous library and social phenomena unrelated to journals, for example, top-hit-producing music artists, by Kevin L. Cook;[76] or firms' research and development expenditures, by H. Eto.[77]

Several authors have proposed use of Bradford analysis for practical journal collection management problems. Robert Sivers employs article productivity data on "remote sensing of earth resources" serials, published from 1977 to 1979, to explain how Bradford zones can be used for assigning journals to the appropriate Research Libraries Group (RLG) Conspectus collecting level. In his scheme, the 763 journals producing 3,465 articles were partitioned into four Bradford zones, with each zone accounting for 25 percent of the articles. The five journals in the first zone are deemed "core" and appropriate for Basic collections (RLG Conspectus level 2). The 17 zone-two journals are considered "major" and suitable for Instructional Support collections (level 3).The 178 third-zone journals are judged to be "supporting" for a Research collection (level 4). Finally, the 563 serials in zone 4 are "peripheral" and consequently appropriate only for Comprehensive collections (level 5).[78]

F. W. Lancaster and collaborators suggest that Bradford zones can be related to the level of journal accessibility. They partitioned into five Bradford zones the 1,322 journals identified in MEDLINE searches for patrons of the Library of the Health Sciences at the University of Illinois at Urbana-Champaign. After checking the availability of the journals at four levels of accessibility (in the department library, the university libraries, elsewhere in the state, and elsewhere in the country), they discovered that journals in the higher zones were more accessible.[79]

Many citation and use studies of journals have found (or claimed to have found) a Bradford distribution. William Goffman and Thomas G. Morris partitioned the journals that circulated at the Allen Memorial Medical Library during March 1968 into eight Bradford zones. The nucleus contained 11 journals that circulated a total of 113 times, whereas the eighth zone was composed of 109 journals that circulated once.[80] Martin Gordon found that "at least through the upper 90% of use," the periodicals used at Franklin and Marshall College during 1979 conformed to a Bradford distribution. Gordon partitioned the titles into 11 zones, with 3 titles accounting for 524 uses in zone 1 and 306 titles contributing 445 uses in zone 11.[81] Allan Davis discovered that the citations retrieved from a ProQuest workstation at the University of Wisconsin at Whitewater library "closely follow Bradford's law," dividing into three zones, with 38 journals producing 3,343 citations, 160 journals producing 3,347 citations, and 955 titles accounting for 3,336 citations.[82] Raymond W. Barber and Jacqueline C. Mancall's analysis of the citations in 270 humanities and science papers by "college-bound" high school sophomores, juniors, and seniors found a Bradford distribution among the cited periodicals; 170 titles were cited 602 times. Three titles (*Newsweek*, *Time*, and *Scientific American*) accounted for 21.7 percent of the total citations; the top 10 represented 41.6 percent; and 91 periodicals were cited only once.[83] Katherine W. McCain and James E. Bobick's examination of citations in faculty publications, Ph.D. dissertations, and doctoral qualifying briefs at Temple University's Biology Department found that about 80 percent were produced by 60 titles (18 percent of the total titles).[84] Larry Hardesty and Gail Oltmanns's study of psychology journals cited in undergraduate senior theses at two educational institutions found that approximately 80 percent of the citations were produced by 19 journals at Indiana University and 20 journals at DePauw University—although they did not partition all the journals into Bradford zones.[85] Similar patterns have been found in innumerable other citation and use studies even though the authors did not cite Bradford.

According to Virgil Diodata, conducting a Bradford analysis involves three steps:

1. identifying the articles,

2. listing in rank order (from most to least) the journals containing the articles, and

3. dividing the listed journals into groups or zones so that each zone produces approximately the same number of articles.[86]

Bibliometrics Toolbox software can partition the ranked journals into Bradford zones,[87] although I understand the program it is no longer supported by its creator.

In summary, Bradford analysis has much potential relevance to serials management in libraries. Some of the most obvious applications are outlined below.

- Selection/deselection decisions—it could assist selection of nucleus and other high-zone journals as well as canceling, weeding, or relegating to remote storage titles from the lower zones.

- Defining the core journals—the journals in the Bradford nucleus, in other words, the first zone, are generally considered to be the subject's core journals.

- Collection evaluation—a Bradford ranking could be used as a weighted checklist for serials collection evaluation with higher zone journals counting more than lower zone journals.

- The law of diminishing returns—Bradford distribution clearly illustrates that the law of diminishing marginal utility applies to journal management. A librarian can cover a large portion of article production or meet a significant segment of user demand by collecting the small number of journals in the nucleus. However, as one proceeds to lower zones, the incremental value offered by collecting each additional journal decreases. Therefore, a larger number of lower zone journals must be collected to derive the same value provided by a higher zone journal. Paul Metz expressed it succinctly:

> The implications of the Bradford distribution for serials collection development may be read optimistically or pessimistically. Optimists may note that a relatively small investment will cover an encouraging percentage of the relevant literature. Pessimists will point out that much desirable literature remains outside the core and that as the library spends more and more to acquire these titles, it achieves fewer and fewer results.[88]

- Calculation of cost at various coverage levels—to elaborate on Metz's point, Bradford distribution can assist in calculating the number of journals (and their cost) required to meet various percentages of user need. There was once considerable discussion about the so-called 90 percent library (i.e., one that could meet 90 percent of patron need with its collection). A Bradford distribution can help calculate the cost for any percentage level library.

- Setting priorities among journals—Bradford zones can, predicated on the assumption that higher zone journals are more important than journals in lower zones, be used to establish priorities among journals. Bradford zones have been correlated with collecting levels. They might be used to help determine which journal holdings are housed in the main collection, placed in a remote storage area, or weeded altogether. In the current access versus ownership environment, Bradford zones could be used to divide journals into three categories:

1. titles subscribed to by the library,

2. titles the library pays to access from external sources, and

3. titles the library does not pay to access from external sources.

Some criticisms or concerns about Bradford analysis should be noted. Actual data usually do not precisely match the theoretical distribution. The most productive journals may not contain the best quality articles. (Research concerning this issue is examined in a subsequent section.) There can be ambiguities in defining the parameters of a subject area and what constitutes an article. A journal that is peripheral for one subject area may be in a higher zone for another subject supported by the library and thus still useful.

Because Bradford analysis requires considerable time and methodological sophistication, its use as a practical serials collection management tool may be limited. Yet Bradfordian analysis is exceedingly important from a theoretical perspective because it illuminates fundamental patterns that have profound implications for collection management of journals.

THE STRUCTURE OF DISCIPLINES

Many reference studies have analyzed the structural characteristics of a discipline or subject area. Technically speaking, an analysis of the documents that cite a particular journal, say *College and Research Libraries*, would be termed a *citation study*. In contrast, an analysis of the documents cited in *College and Research Libraries* would be called a *reference study*. Unfortunately, many authors incorrectly apply the term *citation study* to reference studies. Reference studies are more applicable to serials collection management because they reveal the characteristics of the source materials used by researchers.

Shirley A. Fitzgibbons analyzed 119 such reference studies published from 1938 to 1978.[89] A brief annotated bibliography of 26 additional studies published during the 1980s may be found in Nisonger.[90] Typically, these studies analyze the cited references (either the entire set or a sample) in a group of source documents that are assumed to be representative of the subject under investigation. A journal, a group of journals, one or more textbooks, or indexing or abstracting services or both have been used for source documents. For illustration, Baughman used the *Social Sciences and Humanities Index* to identify source documents for his study of sociology,[91] John Budd used the MLA *International Bibliography* for his study of American literature,[92] Nisonger used the *Canadian Historical Review* for Canadian history,[93] and Benjamin O. Alafiatayo used the monograph *Research on Agricultural Development in Sub-Saharan Africa: A Critical Survey* as the source for his analysis of sub-Saharan African agricultural economics.[94] The items cited in source documents are then tabulated according to such factors as age, format, language, subject, and place of publication to derive an overall profile of the subject's literature. These variables are frequently cross-tabulated in the data analysis.

Table 5.3, page 142, is from Bluma C. Peritz's reference analysis of library science. She tabulated 5,334 citations from 716 English-language research papers published at five and ten-year intervals (1950, 1960, 1965, 1970, and 1975) in 39 core international, British, and North American library science journals. Table 5.3 summarizes her findings according to selected subject areas, format, and publication year.

Not unexpectedly, the vast majority of references were in the field of library and information science. The overall percentage of citations to journals was 54 in library and information science, compared to 31 in the social sciences and 33 in science and technology. Note that in library and information science the proportion of citations to journals increased from 39 percent in 1960 to 60 percent by 1975.[95]

The general findings of reference studies can be summarized as follows:

- The proportion of citations to serials varies significantly among disciplines. The sciences tend to cite the highest proportion and the humanities the lowest, with the social sciences falling between the two.

- Except for the most recent issues, frequency of citation declines with age, although this varies from discipline to discipline. The humanities tend to cite the oldest serials, the sciences cite the most current, with the social sciences in the middle.

Table 5.3.
Citations by Selected Fields and Forms of Publication by Year, Percentages

Library and Information Science (including Printing-Publishing)

Form of publication	1950 %	1960 %	1965 %	1970 %	1975 %	Overall %
Journals	44	39	53	53	60	54
Books	31	45	14	14	14	17
Reports	14	11	19	21	14	17
Other	11	6	14	12	12	12
Total*	100%	100%	100%	100%	100%	100%
Number of Citations	**170**	**314**	**546**	**1039**	**1594**	**3663**

Social Sciences

Form of publication	1950 %	1960 %	1965 %	1970 %	1975 %	Overall %
Journals	--- †	45	10	27	35	31
Books	---	45	55	45	41	44
Reports	---	11	24	13	11	13
Other	---	0	10	14	13	12
Total*	---	100%	100%	100%	100%	100%
Number of Citations	**6**	**38**	**29**	**121**	**189**	**383**

Science and Technology

Form of publication	1950 %	1960 %	1965 %	1970 %	1975 %	Overall %
Journals	--- †	44	33	18	38	33
Books	---	44	30	64	43	46
Reports	---	6	26	6	5	9
Other	---	6	11	13	14	12
Total*	---	100%	100%	100%	100%	100%
Number of Citations	**1**	**36**	**46**	**72**	**121**	**276**

* May not add to 100 because of rounding.

† Total too small for calculation of percentages.

Reprinted with permission of Ablex Publishing Corporation from Bluma C. Peritz, "Citation Characteristics in Library Science: Some Further Results from a Bibliometric Survey," *Library Research* 3 (spring 1981): 57.

- Many of the citations are from other disciplines, thus illustrating the importance of interdisciplinarity.

- English is the predominately cited language.

Because these findings essentially parallel the results of usage studies discussed in chapter 6, one can conclude that citation and library use studies reinforce each other.

In summary, several of the structural characteristics are relevant to library serials collection management because they relate to basic decisions that must be confronted about the language, age, subject, format, and geographical parameters of the collection. These characteristics also help delineate patterns of scholarly communications.

ASSISTANCE WITH BUDGETING

As a serendipitous spin-off of the structural studies discussed above, data on format can provide assistance with serials budgeting. (See chapter 3 for a more detailed analysis of serials budgeting.) Robin B. Devin and Martha Kellogg cogently argue that "funds for each subject should be allocated between serials and monographs in the same proportion as each form of literature is used by the researcher."[96] Accordingly, several authors have prepared concise tables compiling the results of numerous reference studies in many disciplines. Table 5.4, on pages 144-45, reproduces a table from Devin and Kellogg's article that displays the proportion of citations to serials in 66 reference studies (published from the early 1930s to the late 1980s) covering 42 disciplines. The proportion of serial citations ranged from 10.9 percent in Cullars' 1988 study of foreign literature to 93.6 percent in Brown's chemistry reference analysis (published in 1956).

Similar summary tables may be found in articles by Devin, who tabulates 24 reference studies published between 1931 and 1980,[97] and Michael Bowman, who summarizes more than 100 cases in 34 disciplines dating from the late nineteenth-century.[98] Richard Heinzkill also summarized the proportion of citations to journals from 27 reported cases, although his table was not compiled explicitly for serials budgeting.[99]

Amrita J. Burdick, Anne Butler, and Marilyn G. Sullivan found a 88:12 percent serials-monograph citation ratio in leading medical journals and textbooks compared with an actual budgeting ratio of 79:21 percent reported in *Annual Statistics of Medical School Libraries in the United States and Canada*. They then recommend an 88:12 percent budgeting ratio to reflect "actual use of serials and monographs in the health sciences."[100]

How can citation data be used in serials budgeting? It could be used as the sole criterion for allocating a department's budget between monographs and serials, although this tactic is not recommended. Alternatively, it could be used as one factor along with others and perhaps included in a formula. If not directly used in reaching budgetary decisions, citation data could be used for ex post facto evaluation of a library's expenditure patterns. These studies can help answer Devin's previously quoted poignant question, "How much is too much?"[101] In the final analysis, citation data should be viewed as a tool that can assist research libraries with serials budgeting rather than as the definitive authority.

Table 5.4.
Serials Use by Subject

LC Class	Subject	Citation	% Serials Use
A	American Studies	Bolles	42.6
BL-BX	Theology	Whalen	23.3
BL-BX	Theology	Heussman	24.8
D-F	History	Baughman	23.3
DA	English History	Jones	27.1
M	Music	Vaughan	28.2
M	Music	Baker	23.5
N	Fine Arts	Simonton	28.6
P	Philology	Tucker	38.4
PA	Classics	Tucker	28.5
PN	Speech	Broadus (1953)	45.7
P	Literature	Stern	15.0
PR-PS	British and American Literature	Cullars (1985)	13.3
P	English Literature	Chambers	28.1
P	English Literature	Heinzkill	19.9
P	Foreign Literature	Cullars (1988)	10.9
	Social Sciences	Guttsman	36.0
	Social Sciences	Earle	29.0
	Social Sciences	Garfield (1976)	38.0
BF	Psychology	Xhignesse	35.0
GN	Anthropology	Baughman (1977)	42.9
HB	Economics	Fletcher	47.3
HB	Economics	Baughman (1977)	59.0
HD	Agricultural Economics	Littleton	31.4
HD-HJ	Business Administration	Sarle	42.3
HD-HJ	Business	Popovich	58.6
HM-HV	Sociology	Broadus (1952)	46.3
HM-HV	Sociology	Broadus (1967)	38.5
HM-HV	Sociology	Lin	38.8
HM-HV	Sociology	Baughman (1974)	38.5
HM-HV	Sociology	Baughman (1977)	44.4
J	Political Science	Baum	31.5
J	Political Science	Baughman (1977)	34.6
JF	Public Administration	Intrama	26.1
L	Education	Broadus (1953)	42.6
L	Education	Chambers	40.5
L	Education	Mochida	41.7
Z	Library Science	Barnard	52.3
Z	Library Science	Penner	50.7

Z	Library Science	Brace	33.0
Z	Library Science	LaBorie	28.2
	Science	Garfield (1976)	80.0
	Science	Earle	82.0
QA	Mathematics	Brown	76.8
QB	Astronomy	Lang	85.4
QC	Optics	Lin	76.5
QC	Physics	Fussler	89.7
QC	Physics	Brown	88.8
QD	Chemistry	Fussler	92.9
QD	Chemistry	Barker	86.1
QD	Chemistry	Brown	93.6
QE	Geology	Gross	85.4
QE	Geology	Laosunthara	83.0
QE	Geology	Craig	77.4
QE	Geology	Brown	87.2
QK	Botany	Hintz	86.3
QK	Botany	Brown	82.7
QL	Zoology	Brown	80.8
QL	Entomology	Brown	81.2
QP	Physiology	Brown	90.8
QR	Microbiology	Kanasy	93.1
R	Medicine	Sherwood	85.2
T	Technology	Earle	70.0
T	Engineering	Waldhart	72.4
TK	Electrical Engineering	Coile	61.9
TP	Chemical Engineering	Patterson	75.8

Reprinted with permission of the American Library Association from Robin B. Devin and Martha Kellogg. "The Serial/Monograph Ratio in Research Libraries: Budgeting in Light of Citation Studies," *College and Research Libraries* 51 (January 1990): 50.

Yet a few caveats should be noted. The various studies have not used a uniform definition of the term *serial*—some consider annuals and yearbooks serials; others do not. Also, many of the studies are quite old, and citation patterns may have changed since they were published. Studies are not available for all subjects. Because citation data measure use by researchers, their potential value as a serials budgeting tool is limited to research libraries. Finally, it should not be used to allocate funds for such nonresearch materials as newspapers, indexes, and abstracts, which are seldom cited.

Contending that proportioning the total costs of current books and serials for a subject area is a better budgeting guide, Lowry states,

Devin and Kellogg fall into the logical fallacy *pro hoc, propter hoc*—putting the effect before the cause. Distributing material funds based on citation studies will not produce the same citation patterns. It may well disturb the collection patterns that led to the citation proportions.[102]

Although not fully elaborated, Lowry's argument seems to be that instead of using citation patterns to determine library collections, other factors, such as "the actual publication of monographs and serials in a discipline" and, presumably, library collecting patterns themselves, really shape citation patterns.

Further research is required before a definitive answer can be given to these issues. It is unclear how much budgeting based on the relative cost of book and serials production would actually differ from budgeting based on citation data. The extent to which libraries have used citation data for budgeting purposes is also unknown.

RESEARCH ON CITATION DATA AND JOURNALS

As citation analysis achieves greater acceptance in recent decades, considerable research offers implications for using citation analysis as a library collection management tool. Space limitations prohibit a full review. This section offers a highly selective summary of the salient research addressing certain issues: the consistency of citation data, the correspondence between citation data and local usage data, and the question of whether the most productive journals in a Bradfordian distribution contain the best quality articles.

The stability, that is, year-to-year consistency, of JCR citation rankings is a major issue of both theoretical and practical concern. If a journal ranked 3rd within its discipline one year and 37th the next year, neither year's position would be reliable for practical decision making. Two methods are available for investigating the stability of journal rankings based on citation data: the "year-by-year" approach and the "journal-by-journal" method. The former analyzes year-to-year ranking changes in a set of journals, usually the journals in a specific discipline. The latter method analyzes changes in the rankings of specific journals over a range of years.

Using the year-by-year method, Louis C. Buffardi and Julia A. Nichols found a .91 correlation between the 1977 and 1978 *SSCI JCR* impact factor scores of 96 psychology journals,[103] and Michael D. Gordon's research based on 59 sociology journals revealed a .844 correlation between their 1977 and 1978 impact factor scores.[104] Nisonger used the year-by-year method to analyze the stability of library and information science, economics, and geography journal rankings in the *SSCI JCR* from 1980 to 1990. He found that in all three disciplines highly ranked journals are more stable than middle or lower ranked ones. Moreover, journals from large disciplines were found to be more unstable than those from small ones (*discipline size* is defined as the number of journals covered in the JCR).[105]

Employing the journal-by-journal method to analyze the 1979 through 1986 rankings of *Online* and *Online Review*, MaryEllen C. Sievert found that *Online* ranged from 1 (among library and information science journals covered in the *SSCI JCR*) in 1981 to 8 in 1982, and *Online Review* ranged from 1 in 1980 to 26 in 1984 (rebounding to 2 in 1986).[106] Nisonger also used a journal-by-journal approach to analyze the stability of the *SSCI JCR* rankings for library and information science journals from 1980 through 1992. His research revealed that the average year-to-year change in rank for all library and information science journals was slightly more than eight ranking positions. Moreover, from 1980 to 1992, 11 journals changed rank between two adjacent years by at least 30 positions on at least one occasion; 26 journals moved 20 or more positions in rank at least once; and 50 journals moved more than 10 positions on at least one occasion. To cite an extreme example, *Serials Librarian* changed positions from 38th among JCR-listed library and information science journals in 1989 to 6th in 1990.[107]

What are the practical implications of this research for librarians and scholars using the JCR? One can not rely on a single year's ranking data for reaching decisions about journals. A journal's ranking can fluctuate dramatically from one year to the next, as a relatively small change in the number of citations received can result in a much larger change in ranking position. Unfortunately, no generally accepted decision rules or guidelines state how many years of JCR data should be considered, but I would recommend examining data from the three most recent years.

The extent to which citation data correspond to actual usage in a local library has major implications about their practical utility for librarians. A high correlation between citation and use data suggests that citation data can be used with some degree of confidence as a surrogate for the latter, whereas a low correspondence implies that citation data are less useful for journal collection management. Studies investigating the relationship between these variables have found somewhat contradictory results. Elizabeth Pan compared journal usage in six U.S. biomedical libraries with *SCI JCR* citation data.[108] She found no correlation between use and impact factor but a statistically significant correlation (0.47) between use and total citations. In a particularly rigorous study, Pauline A. Scales compared a ranked list of journals used at the National Lending Library (in the United Kingdom) with the most frequently cited journals in the *SCI JCR*. For the 50 most frequently used journals, the correlation between the two lists was 0.42; the correlation was 0.26 for the top 50 journals by citation. Only 16 of 50 most-cited titles were among the top 50 in use. She concluded, "Journal citation rankings are not good indicators of actual use, and as such do not constitute valid guides for journal selection."[109] More recently, Michael D. Cooper and George F. McGregor found "no relationship" between impact factor ranking and photocopy requests at the Cetus Corporation's Information Services Center in Emeryville, California.[110] Stephen J. Bensman also found that faculty rating of chemistry journals at Louisiana State University correlated much higher with total citations in the *SCI JCR* (0.66) than with impact factor (0.25).[111]

After analyzing JCR citation data and use at the SUNY at Albany library for biochemistry, cell biology, ecology, geosciences, and mathematics journals, Tony Stankus and Barbara Rice concluded that both JCR total citations and impact factor data correlate well with use for similar journals—the same scope, purpose, subject, and language—that are used at least 25 times per year, although precise correlations were not presented. They asserted that impact factor is preferable for new journals or those publishing a small number of articles.[112] In another report of the same study, Rice stated "relative positions [in rankings by use and JCR total citations] . . . are quite similar." She also noted that current awareness journals tend to be highly used but not cited.[113]

These contradictory findings suggest that the correlation between citation data and actual library usage will vary among different library contexts. Consequently, citation data should be used in combination with other evaluative measures rather than as the sole decision-making criterion.

Some researchers have analyzed whether the most productive journals in a Bradford distribution contain the best quality articles—and found conflicting results. Gertrude House Lamb's 1971 Ph.D. dissertation examined in mathematics a comprehensive bibliography representing quantity and a select bibliography of quality items (as determined by authors' status) and found a high correspondence between the most productive journals on the two lists.[114] Likewise, Danny P. Wallace and Susan Bonzi discovered, based on citations in the *SCI* and *SSCI* to journal articles listed in a bibliometrics bibliography, that the core journals in a Bradfordian distribution are more frequently cited than journals in lower zones, thus implying a higher quality.[115] In contrast, Bert R. Boyce and Mark Funk found "no significant correlation" between journal productivity and "quality weight" (a citation measure similar to impact factor) in experimental extinction—a subfield of psychology.[116] Boyce and Pollens later compared Lamb's list of mathematics journals with "quality weight" and *SCI JCR* citation data. Finding "little correlation," they concluded the most-productive journals do not guarantee high-quality papers.[117]

If the most-productive journals do not offer high-quality articles, the practical value of Bradfordian analysis as a journal selection tool would be significantly diminished. Nevertheless, productivity alone—apart from quality considerations—might be a basis for selection. Boyce and Pollens note that use of a Bradford distribution does not ensure acquiring the best quality papers, but selection of high-ranking journals will "obtain the greatest coverage of the topic for the least cost."[118]

CONCLUSION

Most bibliometric and citation analysis has been applied to traditional print journals. Yet the fundamental concepts are equally applicable to electronic publications. In recent years a small number of electronic journals have been included in the JCR, for example, *The Online Journal of Knowledge Synthesis for Nursing*.[119] It seems highly probable that future bibliometric studies will be used for the evaluation and selection of electronic publications as well as for accessing the role of electronic publications in the scholarly communications process. Bibliometric research can address such issues as how often print journals cite electronic ones and vice versa[120] and when electronic journals' citation rates will equal or surpass their print counterparts.

Because they measure what researchers use, citation data are of value primarily to research libraries. They have considerably less relevance for nonresearch libraries, although the literature includes some examples of their application to college libraries and, in at least one case, to a school library. Moreover, citation analysis is controversial. Many scholars and librarians question its validity. The author neither endorses citation analysis as infallible nor advocates reaching major serials collection management decisions based solely on citation data. Rather, citation data represent a tool that should be used with other indicators.

NOTES

1. Robert N. Broadus, "Early Approaches to Bibliometrics," *Journal of the American Society for Information Science* 38 (March 1987): 127.

2. Thomas E. Nisonger, *Collection Evaluation in Academic Libraries: A Literature Guide and Annotated Bibliography* (Englewood, Colo.: Libraries Unlimited, 1992), 97-98.

3. F. J. Cole and Nellie B. Eales, "The History of Comparative Anatomy," *Science Progress* 11 (April 1917): 578-96.

4. P. L. K. Gross and E. M. Gross, "College Libraries and Chemical Education," *Science* 66 (October 28, 1927): 385-89.

5. C. C. Jewett, "Report of the Assistant Secretary Relative to the Library, Presented December 13, 1848," in *Third Annual Report of the Board of Regents of the Smithsonian Institution to the Senate and House of Representatives* (Washington, D.C.: Tippin and Streeper, 1849), 39-47.

6. E. W. Hulme, *Statistical Bibliography in Relation to the Growth of Modern Civilization* (London: Grafton, 1923).

7. Alan Pritchard, "Statistical Bibliography or Bibliometrics?" *Journal of Documentation* 25 (December 1969): 48-49.

8. Danny P. Wallace, "A Solution in Search of a Problem: Bibliometrics and Libraries," *Library Journal* 112 (May 1, 1987): 43-47.

9. Katherine W. McCain and James E. Bobick, "Patterns of Journal Use in a Departmental Library: A Citation Analysis," *Journal of the American Society for Information Science* 32 (July 1981): 258.

10. *Social Science Citation Index Journal Citation Reports: 1988 Annual* (Philadelphia: Institute for Scientific Information, 1989), 6A.

11. Maurice B. Line, "Rank Lists Based on Citations and Library Uses as Indicators of Journal Usage in Individual Libraries," *Collection Management* 2 (winter 1978): 313.

12. Per O. Seglen, "The Skewness of Science," *Journal of the American Society for Information Science* 43 (October 1992): 628-38.

13. "*Journal Citation Reports* on CD-ROM," an advertising flyer distributed by the Institute for Scientific Information (ISI).

14. "ISI to Release *Journal Citation Reports* on CD-ROM," an ISI press release dated May 2, 1995, and distributed at the 1995 ALA Conference in Chicago.

15. Institute for Scientific Information (ISI). *ISI Products and Services: Journal Citation Reports*. Available: http://www.isinet.com/prodserv/citation/jcr.html (Accessed March 8, 1998).

16. Barbara A. Rice, "Science Periodicals Use Study," *Serials Librarian* 4 (fall 1979): 35-47.

17. Barbara A. Rice, "Selection and Evaluation of Chemistry Journals," *Science and Technology Libraries* 4 (fall 1983): 43-59.

18. Stephen J. Bensman, "The Structure of the Library Market for Scientific Journals: The Case of Chemistry," *Library Resources and Technical Services* 40 (April 1996): 145-70.

19. This statement is based on my attendance of the conference—Garfield's paper was not included in the official proceedings.

20. Stephen P. Harter, "The Impact of Electronic Journals on Scholarly Communication: A Citation Analysis," *Public-Access Computer Systems Review* 7, no. 5 (1996): 11. Available: http://lib-04.lib.uh.edu/pacsrev/1996/hart7n5.htm (Accessed March 1, 1998).

21. Christinger Tomer, "A Statistical Assessment of Two Measures of Citation: The Impact Factor and the Immediacy Index," *Information Processing and Management* 22, no. 3 (1986): 251-58.

22. Graeme Hirst and Nadia Talent, "Computer Science Journals—An Iterated Citation Analysis," *IEEE Transactions on Professional Communication* PC-20 (December 1977): 233-38.

23. Graeme Hirst, "Discipline Impact Factor? A Method for Determining Core Journal Lists," *Journal of the American Society for Information Science* 29 (July 1978): 171-72.

24. Chunpei He and Miranda Lee Pao, "A Discipline-Specific Journal Selection Algorithm," *Information Processing and Management* 22, no. 5 (1986): 405-16.

25. P. Pichappan, "Identification of Mainstream Journals of Science Specialty: A Method Using the Discipline-Contribution Score," *Scientometrics* 27 (June 1993): 179-93.

26. George W. Black Jr., "Core Journal Lists for Behaviorally Disordered Children," *Behavioral and Social Sciences Librarian* 3 (fall 1983), 31-38.

27. P. Vinkler, "Evaluation of Some Methods for the Relative Assessment of Scientific Publications," *Scientometrics* 10, nos. 3/4 (1986): 157-77.

28. P. Vinkler, "A Quasi-Quantitative Citation Model," *Scientometrics* 12, nos. 1/2 (1987): 47-72.

29. A. Schubert and T. Braun, "Relative Indicators and Relational Charts for Comparative Assessment of Publication Output and Citation Impact," *Scientometrics* 9, nos. 5/6 (1986): 281-91.

30. B. K. Sen, "Normalized Impact Factor," *Journal of Documentation* 48 (September 1992): 318-25.

31. Thomas E. Nisonger, "A Ranking of Political Science Journals Based on Citation Data," *Serials Review* 19, no. 4 (1993): 7-14.

32. Thomas E. Smith, "The *Journal Citation Reports* as a Deselection Tool," *Bulletin of the Medical Library Association* 73 (October 1985): 388.

33. Dawn Bick and Reeta Sinha, "Maintaining a High-Quality, Cost-Effective Journal Collection," *College and Research Libraries News* 52 (September 1991): 485-90.

34. Theresa Dombrowski, "Journal Evaluation Using *Journal Citation Reports* as a Collection Development Tool," *Collection Management* 10, no. 4 (1988): 175-80.

35. Rikie Deurenberg, "Journal Deselection in a Medical University Library by Ranking Periodicals Based on Multiple Factors," *Bulletin of the Medical Library Association* 81 (July 1993): 316-19.

36. Diane Schmidt, Elisabeth B. Davis, and Ruby Jahr, "Biology Journal Use at an Academic Library: A Comparison of Use Studies," *Serials Review* 20, no. 2 (1994): 45-64.

37. Gary D. Byrd and Michael E. D. Koenig, "Systematic Serials Selection Analysis in a Small Academic Health Sciences Library," *Bulletin of the Medical Library Association* 66 (October 1978): 397-406.

38. Kate Herzog, Harry Armistead, and Marla Edelman, "Designing Effective Journal Use Studies," *Serials Librarian* 24, nos. 3/4 (1994): 189-92.

39. John O. Christensen, "Cost of Chemistry Journals to One Academic Library, 1980-1990," *Serials Review* 18 (fall 1992): 19-34.

40. Henry H. Barschall, "The Cost-Effectiveness of Physics Journals: A Survey," *Physics Today* 41 (July 1988): 56-59.

41. H. H. Barschall and J. R. Arrington, "Cost of Physics Journals: A Survey," *Bulletin of the American Physical Society* 33 (July-August 1988): 1437-47.

42. *Journal Citation Reports on CD-ROM, 1994 Annual* [CD-ROM] (Philadelphia: Institute for Scientific Information, 1995). System Requirements: IBM PC/compatible PC 386 or higher; minimum 6MB free hard disk space; minimum 4MB RAM (8MB recommended); MS-DOS 3.3 or higher (5.0 or higher recommended); MS-Windows version 3.1 or higher; DC-ROM drive; EGA monitor (VGA recommended); mouse; printer (optional).

43. B. Bargagna, "Controllo di qualita e rilevanza scientifica" (Quality control and science journals), *Biblioteche Oggi* 11 (September 1993): 24-7. This item, in Italian, was not available to the author but is cited based on an abstract in *Library and Information Science Abstracts*.

44. Deurenberg, "Journal Deselection in a Medical University Library," 316-19.

45. Journal Citation Reports on CD-ROM.

46. Bert R. Boyce and Janet Sue Pollens, "Citation-Based Impact Measures and the Bradfordian Selection Criteria," *Collection Management* 4 (fall 1982): 32.

47. Robert N. Broadus, "The Measurement of Periodicals Use," *Serials Review* 11 (summer 1985): 60.

48. Pauline A. Scales, "Citation Analyses As Indicators of the Use of Serials: A Comparison of Ranked Title Lists Produced by Citation Counting and from Use Data," *Journal of Documentation* 32 (March 1976): 21; and Judith A. Segal, "Journal Deselection: A Literature Review and an Application," *Science and Technology Libraries* 6 (spring 1986): 36.

49. Numerous authors have noted this fact. Charles Eckman, "Journal Review in an Environmental Design Library," *Collection Management* 10, nos. 1/2 (1988): 76, reports that 8 of the 21 most-used journals (38 percent) in the University of California at Berkeley's Environmental Design Library were not indexed in the *Science Citation Index*. He does not address the question of whether they could have been in the *Science Citation Index*. See also Segal, "Journal Deselection," 36.

50. Barton M. Clark and Sharon E. Clark, "Core Journals in Anthropology: A Review of Methodologies," *Behavioral and Social Sciences Librarian* 2 (winter 1981/spring 1982): 109.

51. Ibid.

52. Brian D. Scanlan, "Coverage by *Current Contents* and the Validity of Impact Factors: ISI from a Journal Publisher's Perspective," *Serials Librarian* 13 (October/November 1987): 65.

53. McCain and Bobick, "Patterns of Journal Use in a Departmental Library," 265. They mention Hamburger and Hamilton's classic study of chick embryo development, which skews the citation pattern to *Journal of Morphology*.

54. Broadus, "The Measurement of Periodicals Use," 60.

55. Nelson C. Dometrius, "Subjective and Objective Measures of Journal Stature," *Social Science Quarterly* 70 (March 1989): 200-201.

56. Paul H. Ribbe, "Assessment of Prestige and Price of Professional Publications," *American Mineralogist* 73 (May/June 1988): 449-69.

57. *Journal Citation Reports on CD-ROM: A Quick Reference Guide*. (Philadelphia: Institute for Scientific Information, 1995).

58. This section's information is from an ISI flyer distributed at the Fifth Biennial Conference of the International Society for Scientometrics and Informetrics, held at Rosary College, River Forest, Illinois, June 7-10, 1995.

59. Stephanie C. Haas and Katie Lee, "Research Journal Usage by the Forestry Faculty at the University of Florida, Gainesville," *Collection Building* 11, no. 2 (1991): 23-25.

60. Carol M. Moulden, "Evaluation of Library Collection Support for an Off-Campus Degree Program," in *Off-Campus Library Services Conference Proceedings: Charleston, South Carolina, October 20-21, 1988*, ed. Barton M. Lessin (Mount Pleasant, Mich.: Central Michigan University, 1989), 340-46.

61. Margaret Sylvia and Marcella Lesher, "What Journals Do Psychology Graduate Students Need? A Citation Analysis of Thesis References," *College and Research Libraries* 56 (July 1995): 313-18.

62. Jean-Pierre V. M. Herubel, "Philosophy Dissertation Bibliographies and Citations in Serials Evaluation," *Serials Librarian* 20, nos. 2/3 (1991): 65-73.

63. Belen Altuna Esteibar and F. W. Lancaster, "Ranking of Journals in Library and Information Science by Research and Teaching Relatedness," *Serials Librarian* 23, nos. 1/2 (1992): 1-10.

64. Lori Bronars and Katherine Branch, "Cost-Cutting Uses of New SCISEARCH Feature," *Database* 13 (December 1990): 53-58.

65. Robert J. Greene, "Computer Analysis of Local Citation Information in Collection Management," *Collection Management* 17, no. 4 (1993): 11-24.

66. S. C. Bradford, "Sources of Information on Specific Subjects," *Engineering: An Illustrated Weekly* 137 (January 26, 1934): 85-86. Reprinted in *Journal of Information Science* 10, no. 4 (1985): 178.

67. Ole V. Groos, "Bradford's Law and the Keenan-Atherton Data," *American Documentation* 18 (January 1967): 46.

68. Virgil Diodata, *Dictionary of Bibliometrics* (New York: Haworth Press, 1994), 72-73.

69. Yeon-Kyoung Chung, "Core International Journals of Classification Systems: An Application of Bradford's Law," *Knowledge Organization* 21, no. 2 (1994): 77.

70. S. C. Bradford, *Documentation* (London: Crosby Lockwood, 1948).

71. B. C. Brookes, "The Derivation and Application of the Bradford-Zipf Distribution," *Journal of Documentation* 24 (December 1968): 27-59.

72. Ferdinand F. Leimkuhler, "The Bradford Distribution," *Journal of Documentation* 23 (September 1967): 197-207.

73. Mary W. Lockett, "The Bradford Distribution: A Review of the Literature, 1934-1987," *Library and Information Science Research* 11 (January-March 1989): 21-36.

74. Chung, "Core International Journals of Classification Systems," 75-83.

75. Steven R. Kirby, "Reviewing United States History Monographs: A Bibliometric Survey," *Collection Building* 11, no. 2 (1991): 13-18.

76. Kevin L. Cook, "Laws of Scattering Applied to Popular Music," *Journal of the American Society for Information Science* 40 (July 1989): 277-83.

77. H. Eto, "Bradford Law in R and D Expending of Firms and R and D Concentration," *Scientometrics* 6 (May 1984): 183-88.

78. Robert Sivers, "Partitioned Bradford Ranking and the Serials Problem in Academic Research Libraries," *Collection Building* 8, no. 2 (1987): 12-19.

79. F. W. Lancaster and others, "The Relationship Between Literature Scatter and Journal Accessibility in an Academic Special Library," *Collection Building* 11, no. 1 (1991): 19-22.

80. William Goffman and Thomas G. Morris, "Bradford's Law Applied to the Maintenance of Library Collections," in *Introduction to Information Science*, comp. and ed. Tefko Saracevic (New York: R. R. Bowker, 1970), 200-203.

81. Martin Gordon, "Periodical Use at a Small College Library," *Serials Librarian* 6 (summer 1982): 63-73.

82. Allan Davis, "Database Usage and Title Analysis on a CD-ROM Workstation," *Serials Review* 19 (fall 1993): 91.

83. Raymond W. Barber and Jacqueline C. Mancall, "The Application of Bibliometric Techniques to the Analysis of Materials for Young Adults," *Collection Management* 2 (fall 1978): 229, 240.

84. McCain and Bobick, "Patterns of Journal Use in a Departmental Library," 257-67.

85. Larry Hardesty and Gail Oltmanns, "How Many Psychology Journals Are Enough? A Study of the Use of Psychology Journals by Undergraduates," *Serials Librarian* 16, nos. 1/2 (1989): 133-53.

86. Diodata, *Dictionary of Bibliometrics*, 16-17.

87. Chung, "Core International Journals of Classification Systems," 78.

88. Paul Metz, "Bibliometrics: Library Use and Citation Studies," in *Academic Libraries: Research Perspectives*, ed. Mary Jo Lynch and Arthur Young (Chicago: American Library Association, 1990), 151.

89. Shirley A. Fitzgibbons, "Citation Analysis in the Social Sciences," in *Collection Development in Libraries: A Treatise*, pt. B, ed. Robert D. Stueart and George B. Miller Jr. (Greenwich, Conn.: JAI Press, 1980), 291-344.

90. Nisonger, *Collection Evaluation in Academic Libraries*, 111-18.

91. James C. Baughman, "A Structural Analysis of the Literature of Sociology," *Library Quarterly* 44 (October 1974): 293-308.

92. John Budd, "Characteristics of Written Scholarship in American Literature: A Citation Study," *Library and Information Science Research* 8 (April-June 1986): 189-211.

93. Tom Nisonger, "The Sources of Canadian History: A Citation Analysis of the *Canadian Historical Review*," *Manitoba Library Association Bulletin* 11 (June 1981): 33-35.

94. Benjamin O. Alafiatayo, "The Research Literature of Agricultural Economics," *International Library Review* 21 (October 1989): 465-79.

95. Bluma C. Peritz, "Citation Characteristics in Library Science: Some Further Results from a Bibliometric Survey," *Library Research* 3 (spring 1981): 47-65.

96. Robin B. Devin and Martha Kellogg, "The Serial/Monograph Ratio in Research Libraries: Budgeting in Light of Citation Studies," *College and Research Libraries* 51 (January 1990): 53.

97. Robin B. Devin, "Who's Using What?" *Library Acquisitions: Practice and Theory* 13, no. 2 (1989): 167-70.

98. Michael Bowman, "Format Citation Patterns and Their Implications for Collection Development in Research Libraries," *Collection Building* 11, no. 1 (1991): 3-5. The table displays the number of citations in the sample as well as the percentage of citations to books, journals, conference proceedings, government documents, theses, reference works, and miscellaneous formats.

99. Richard Heinzkill, "Characteristics of References in Selected Scholarly English Literary Journals," *Library Quarterly* 50 (July 1980): 357.

100. Amrita J. Burdick, Anne Butler, and Marilyn G. Sullivan, "Citation Patterns in the Health Sciences: Implications for Serials/Monographic Fund Allocation," *Bulletin of the Medical Library Association* 81 (January 1993): 44-47.

101. Devin, "Who's Using What?" 169.

102. Charles B. Lowry, "Reconciling Pragmatism, Equity, and Need in the Formula Allocation of Book and Serial Funds," *College and Research Libraries* 53 (March 1992): 130.

103. Louis C. Buffardi and Julia A. Nichols, "Citation Impact, Acceptance Rate, and APA Journals," *American Psychologist* 36 (November 1981): 1454.

104. Michael D. Gordon, "Citation Ranking Versus Subjective Evaluation in the Determination of Journal Hierarchies in the Social Sciences," *Journal of the American Society for Information Science* 33 (January 1982): 57.

105. Thomas E. Nisonger, "The Stability of *Social Sciences Citation Index Journal Citation Reports* Data for Journal Rankings in Three Disciplines," *JISSI: International Journal of Scientometrics and Informetrics* 1 (June 1995): 139-49.

106. MaryEllen C. Sievert, "Ten Years of the Literature of Online Searching: An Analysis of *Online* and *Online Review*," *Journal of the American Society for Information Science* 41 (December 1990): 562.

107. Thomas E. Nisonger, "Impact-Factor-Based Ranking of Library and Information Science Journals in the *Social Sciences Citation Index Journal Citation Reports*, 1980 to 1992," in *Fifth International Conference of the International Society for Scientometrics and Informetrics: Proceedings—1995; June 7-10, 1995*, ed. Michael E. D. Koenig and Abraham Bookstein (Medford, N.J.: Learned Information, 1995), 393-402.

108. Elizabeth Pan, "Journal Citation As a Predictor of Journal Usage in Libraries," *Collection Management* 2 (spring 1978): 29-38.

109. Pauline A. Scales, "Citation Analyses As Indicators of the Use of Serials: A Comparison of Ranked Title Lists Produced by Citation Counting and from Use Data," *Journal of Documentation* 32 (March 1976): 17-25.

110. Michael D. Cooper and George F. McGregor, "Using Article Photocopy Data in Bibliographic Models for Journal Collection Management," *Library Quarterly* 64 (October 1994): 386-413.

111. Bensman, "The Structure of the Library Market for Scientific Journals," 157.

112. Tony Stankus and Barbara Rice, "Handle with Care: Use and Citation Data for Science Journal Management," *Collection Management* 4 (spring/summer 1982): 95-110.

113. Barbara A. Rice, "Selection and Evaluation of Chemistry Periodicals," *Science and Technology Libraries* 4 (fall 1983): 43-58.

114. Gertrude House Lamb, "The Coincidence of Quality and Quantity in the Literature of Mathematics," (Ph.D. diss., Case-Western Reserve University, 1971). Her dissertation is

summarized in Boyce and Pollens, "Citation-Based Impact Measures and the Bradfordian Selection Criteria," 30-32.

115. Danny P. Wallace and Susan Bonzi, "The Relationship Between Journal Productivity and Quality," in *ASIS '85: Proceedings of the 48th ASIS Annual Meeting; Las Vegas, Nevada, October 20-24, 1985*, vol. 22, ed. Carol A. Parkhurst (White Plains, N.Y.: published for the American Society for Information Science by Knowledge Industry Publications, 1985), 193-96.

116. Bert R. Boyce and Mark Funk, "Bradford's Law and the Selection of High Quality Papers," *Library Resources and Technical Services* 22 (fall 1978): 390-401.

117. Boyce and Pollens, "Citation-Based Impact Measures," 29-36.

118. Ibid., 36.

119. Blaise Cronin and Kara Overfelt, "E-Journals and Tenure," *Journal of the American Society for Information Science* 46 (October 1995): 700.

120. The first attempt to address this issue may be found in Harter, "The Impact of Electronic Journals on Scholarly Communication."

FURTHER READING

Citation Analysis

Barber, Raymond W., and Jacqueline C. Mancall. "The Application of Bibliometric Techniques to the Analysis of Materials for Young Adults." *Collection Management* 2 (fall 1978): 229-45.

Bowman, Michael. "Format Citation Patterns and Their Implications for Collection Development in Research Libraries." *Collection Building* 11, no. 1 (1991): 2-8.

Broadus, Robert N. "A Proposed Method for Eliminating Titles from Periodical Subscription Lists." *College and Research Libraries* 46 (January 1985): 30-35.

Burdick, Amrita J., Anne Butler, and Marilyn G. Sullivan. "Citation Patterns in the Health Sciences: Implications for Serials/Monographic Fund Allocation." *Bulletin of the Medical Library Association* 81 (January 1993): 44-47.

Devin, Robin B. "Who's Using What?" *Library Acquisitions: Practice and Theory* 13, no. 2 (1989): 167-70.

Devin, Robin B., and Martha Kellogg. "The Serial/Monograph Ratio in Research Libraries: Budgeting in Light of Citation Studies." *College and Research Libraries* 51 (January 1990): 46-54.

Dombrowski, Theresa. "Journal Evaluation Using *Journal Citation Reports* as a Collection Development Tool." *Collection Management* 10, nos. 3/4 (1988): 175-80.

Gross, P. L. K., and E. M. Gross. "College Libraries and Chemical Education." *Science* 66 (October 28, 1927): 385-89.

Haas, Stephanie C., and Kate Lee. "Research Journal Usage by the Forestry Faculty at the University of Florida, Gainesville." *Collection Building* 11, no. 2 (1991): 23-25.

Herubel, Jean-Pierre V. M. "Philosophy Dissertation Bibliographies and Citations in Serials Evaluation." *Serials Librarian* 20, nos. 2/3 (1991): 65-73.

———. "Simple Citation Analysis and the Purdue History Periodical Collection." *Indiana Libraries* 9, no. 2 (1990): 18-21.

Lewis, D. E. "A Comparison Between Library Holdings and Citations." *Library and Information Research News* 11 (autumn 1988): 18-23.

Line, Maurice B. "Use of Citation Data for Periodicals Control in Libraries: A Response to Broadus." *College and Research Libraries* 46 (January 1985): 36-37.

McCain, Katherine W., and James E. Bobick. "Patterns of Journal Use in a Departmental Library: A Citation Analysis." *Journal of the American Society for Information Science* 32 (July 1981): 257-67.

Neeley, James D., Jr. "The Management and Social Science Literatures: An Interdisciplinary Cross-Citation Analysis." *Journal of the American Society for Information Science* 32 (May 1981): 217-23.

Nisonger, Thomas E. "A Test of Two Citation Checking Techniques for Evaluating Political Science Collections in University Libraries." *Library Resources and Technical Services* 27 (April/June 1983): 163-76.

Pan, Elizabeth. "Journal Citation as a Predictor of Journal Usage in Libraries." *Collection Management* 2 (spring 1978): 29-38.

Peritz, Bluma C. "Citation Characteristics in Library Science: Some Further Results from a Bibliometric Survey." *Library Research* 3 (spring 1981): 47-65.

Scales, Pauline A. "Citation Analyses as Indicators of the Use of Serials: A Comparison of Ranked Title Lists Produced by Citation Counting and from Use Data." *Journal of Documentation* 32 (March 1976): 17-25.

Smith, Thomas E. "The *Journal Citation Reports* as a Deselection Tool." *Bulletin of the Medical Library Association* 73 (October 1985): 387-89.

Subramanyam, Kris. "Citation Studies in Science and Technology." In *Collection Development in Libraries: A Treatise*. Pt. B, edited by Robert D. Stueart and George B. Miller Jr., 345-72. Greenwich, Conn.: JAI Press, 1980.

Bradford's Law

Boyce, Bert R., and Janet Sue Pollens. "Citation-Based Impact Measures and the Bradfordian Selection Criteria." *Collection Management* 4 (fall 1982): 29-36.

Boyce, Bert R., and Mark Funk. "Bradford's Law and the Selection of High Quality Papers." *Library Resources and Technical Services* 22 (fall 1978): 390-401.

Bradford, S. C. "Sources of Information on Specific Subjects." *Engineering: An Illustrated Weekly* 137 (January 26, 1934): 85-86. Reprinted in *Journal of Information Science* 10, no. 4 (1985): 176-80.

Chung, Yeon-Kyoung. "Core International Journals of Classification Systems: An Application of Bradford's Law." *Knowledge Organization* 21, no. 2 (1994): 75-83.

Lancaster, F. W., and others. "The Relationship Between Literature Scatter and Journal Accessibility in an Academic Special Library." *Collection Building* 11, no. 1 (1991): 19-22.

Sivers, Robert. "Partitioned Bradford Ranking and the Serials Problem in Academic Research Libraries." *Collection Building* 8, no. 2 (1987): 12-19.

Chapter Six

Study of Periodical Use

Most serials textbooks do not devote separate chapters to the study of periodical use despite the topic's importance. Extrapolating from the first of S. R. Ranganathan's five laws of librarianship, "books are for use,"[1] it logically follows that serials are also for use and that use analysis is central to serials management—a contention supported by the fact that 35.9 percent of college and small university libraries, surveyed in the late 1980s, used periodical use studies.[2] This chapter covers the purposes of use studies, methods for conducting them, their design, analysis of cost-per-use, and previously published periodical use studies.

Periodical use covers an extensive range of activity. Periodicals are used for leisure reading, scholarly research, teaching, professional reasons, and hobbies, to name only their most obvious purposes. In libraries, use of library materials, including periodicals, is usually divided into two major categories: circulation and in-house use. *Circulation*, of course, refers to the official charging out of an item by a patron. *In-house use* generally means consulting an item in the library without actually charging it out on a patron card. The majority of periodical use studies reported in the literature focus on in-house use rather than circulation. Other types or indicators of periodical use are photocopying, interlibrary loan (ILL) or document delivery requests, routing to staff members, and reading outside a library context, i.e., one's personal subscription. Citations to periodicals, covered in chapter 5, serve as indicators of use by research scholars. Finally, a distinction should be made between a *use* and a *user* study. The former focuses on what materials are used; the latter addresses who uses the material. In practice, the two are often combined in a single study.

Periodical use can be analyzed at the title, volume, issue, and article level. Most studies analyze use by title. Analysis at the volume level indicates usage patterns by age and assists in weeding and relegation to remote storage. Usage data at the issue level would normally be compiled only for unbound, current issues and would usually be aggregated into volumes and titles before used in decision making. Article-level analysis is used primarily in interlibrary loan or document delivery studies.

For many reasons, it is more complicated to analyze periodical use than book use. In many libraries, periodicals do not circulate. A book use study generally focuses on a single item, whereas a periodical use study might deal with an entire run composed of numerous separate pieces that may even be found in different formats—unbound current issues, bound volumes, and microformat.

PURPOSES, BENEFITS, AND DRAWBACKS

Why should a library invest the time and effort to conduct a periodical use or user study? The reasons why libraries have done so are summarized below.

- *To identify low-use or nonused titles.* This is probably the most-frequent reason for doing a use study. Low-use or unused titles have been traditionally considered for cancellation, and low-use volumes are candidates for weeding or placement in remote storage. In the past, libraries have identified low-use periodicals to switch to a less-expensive binding or microformat.[3] During the late-1990s, low-use periodicals might be canceled as part of a strategy to provide patrons access through document delivery rather than subscription.

- *To identify high-use titles.* In bygone days of more-generous library funding, high-use titles might be duplicated. From a theoretical perspective, data on highly used titles are often used to help define the core.

- *To determine cost-per-use.* These data—often used in cancellation review projects—can be especially critical in subscription-versus-document-delivery decisions.

- *To determine what materials are used by various user categories.* In effect, this purpose combines a use and user study. A periodical used mainly by a library's secondary rather than primary clientele might be a more likely candidate for cancellation. These data also help decide which library branches should subscribe to particular titles.

- *To determine general usage patterns.* Rather than identifying specific high- or low-use titles, a periodical use study can provide valuable information about overall usage patterns, including the percentage of unused titles; what portion of titles satisfy various percentages of total use; and analysis of use by age, subject, user category, or library location.

- *To determine total use of library materials as part of a broader study.* For example, periodical circulation and in-house use are included in "Circulation per Capita" and "In-Library Materials Use per Capita," from *Output Measures for Public Libraries: A Manual of Standardized Procedures.*[4] Likewise, Virginia A. Walter's *Output Measures for Public Library Service to Children: A Manual of Standardized Procedures* contains two parallel measures: "Circulation of

Children's Materials per Child" and "In-Library Use of Children's Materials per Child."[5]

One of the major benefits of a use study is that objective, quantifiable data are provided. Not only do these data help periodical collection management decision making, but they give greater authority and political clout to the decisions that are made. For illustration, many academic librarians comment that their faculty are more willing to accept periodical cancellations if they are presented data indicating little or no usage.

Some disadvantages, outlined below, are generally associated with library use studies—both circulation and in-house use. Most of these limitations would also apply in varying degrees to use studies for both periodicals and books.

- *All uses are usually counted equally.* Consequently, the amount of value or benefit derived from a particular use is often not considered. Furthermore, Roger R. Flynn points out that some journals, some users, and some purposes of use are "more valuable" than others.[6] This issue would not be a concern in studies seeking to identify low-use or nonused titles for cancellation purposes.

- *They reflect success but ignore failure.* If a patron used an item, he or she probably found something of at least some potential value or interest. A patron's failure to locate the specifically sought item or anything of interest—or both—would not be evident from usage counts.

- *"They measure not what should have been used, but what was used."*[7] This quotation from Robert N. Broadus addresses at least two issues: "need versus want" and the question of availability. "Need versus want," sometimes termed "quality versus demand," is a recurring controversy in collection development thought. Usage counts are more representative of what patrons wanted to use than what was in their best interest. This issue is undoubtedly more relevant to the use of popular magazines in a public library than scholarly journals in an academic or research environment. Alternatively, a patron may have used an item simply because it was available.

- *The needs of nonusers of the library are ignored.* F. Wilfrid Lancaster has succinctly argued that use studies "focus only on the expressed needs of those people who are currently active users of a library."[8] Indeed, the author once heard a speaker at an American Library Association (ALA) meeting proclaim that library use data are like U.S. government unemployment statistics—they do not reflect people who have given up.

- *The results in a particular library are probably not applicable to other libraries.* Each library has its own set of clients with unique information needs. Consequently, although citation studies, journal rankings, or core lists are transferable, a library almost invariably must conduct its own periodical use study rather than rely on published studies from other libraries.

For obvious reasons, periodical use studies tend to focus on in-house use rather than circulation. Some difficulties specific to in-house studies follow.

- *It can be difficult to define what constitutes* use. This consideration would not apply to circulation studies in which an item's check out serves as an unambiguous unit of analysis. However, it is a major issue in the study of in-house use. "Use" of a periodical might include reading it carefully, casually flipping through the pages, checking a citation, or merely scanning the title page. Sharon L. Baker and F. Wilfrid Lancaster note that many researchers have defined in-house use as the removal of an item from its usual shelf location—a method that will underestimate total usage because some items will be reshelved by patrons but offers the advantage of an objective measure.[9]

- *Implementing the study can be expensive and time-consuming.* This point is illustrated by Dorothy Milne and Bill Tiffany's report that a three-year study of periodical use at the Memorial University of Newfoundland Library during the late 1980s cost $30,000.[10]

- *Most use studies depend on user cooperation.* Not only does this consideration complicate data gathering, but noncooperative users can skew or even sabotage the results—as has been reported with some regularity in the literature.

METHODS FOR MEASURING USE

This section describes the major approaches for measuring periodical use. Many can be used for books and other formats, but all are applicable to periodicals. Citation data, traditionally considered a measure of journal use, are covered in chapter 5.

Circulation Data

Prior to automation, circulation analysis was usually based on samples. Two sampling approaches are described by Lancaster. A "circulation sample" examines the entire circulation history of a randomly selected portion of the collection. A "checkout sample" analyzes every circulation during a predetermined time period, such as two months.[11] In effect, it offers a snapshot of circulation at a particular moment.

Extracting global circulation data from an automated system is relatively easy, so sampling becomes less significant. However, many libraries do not circulate serials. If they do, it is often restricted to certain classes of patrons or types of serials. In any case, circulation data would not capture the full range of use because periodicals are frequently used in-house. Although most periodical use techniques and actual studies are oriented toward in-house use, some studies incorporate circulation data (e.g., at the National Oceanic and Atmospheric Administration

Library in Boulder, Colorado).[12] Circulation data for journals requested from reserve, rare books, or storage have been used at the University of California at Berkeley Environmental Design Library.[13]

Table Count

In this method, as the name implies, items that require reshelving—whether they were left on tables, book trucks, reshelving areas, or wherever—are counted. Data are gathered and recorded by staff as part of routine reshelving operations. This approach is sometimes referred to as the *sweep* method because items are counted as they are swept up. This technique is straightforward to carry out and offers a seemingly unambiguous definition of use that can easily be understood by non-professional staff recording the data.[14] However, as reported at the Chalmers Institute of Technology in Gothenburg, Sweden, there can still be an ambiguity in the count itself: If a box containing three unbound issues is removed from the shelf, does it count as one use or three uses?[15] Frequent table counts can record two patrons using the same periodical volume during a day. According to Baker and Lancaster, major disadvantages of the table count method are results may be distorted by such environment factors as the proximity of shelves and tables; a costly staff effort might be required to implement it on a long-term basis; and actual usage may be underreported because of patron reshelving.[16] To alleviate the latter issue, most libraries implementing the method prominently display signs requesting patrons not to reshelve items.

This is probably the most frequently used method for measuring in-house periodical use. Some practical "how-to" manuals on library evaluation, *Output Measures for Public Libraries*,[17] *Output Measures for Public Library Service to Children*,[18] and *Measuring Academic Library Performance: A Practical Approach*, by Nancy A. Van House, Beth T. Weil, and Charles R. McClure,[19] recommend the table count method (although they do not always use the specific term) for measuring in-house use of library materials, including periodicals. The literature contains reports of its use for measuring periodical use at the University of Illinois at Urbana-Champaign,[20] the University of South Florida,[21] the Chalmers University of Technology,[22] Franklin & Marshall College,[23] Indiana University,[24] State University of New York (SUNY) at Albany,[25] SUNY at Buffalo,[26, 27] Auburn University,[28] and Oregon State University,[29] among other libraries.

Slip Method

In the slip method, a piece of paper is inserted into or around a volume in such a manner that it will be obviously displaced from its original position if a patron picks up the item. Library staff subsequently examine the volumes on a regular basis (perhaps daily) to determine which volumes were used, based on displacement of the slip, and to insert a new slip in used items. Sometimes a message is printed on the slip asking patrons to place it in a designated box, to prevent cluttering. This technique was reportedly developed at the Newcastle upon Tyne Polytechnic Library in the United Kingdom. Based on its use at the Plymouth Polytechnic Library in the United Kingdom, Su Rooke concluded it is "easy to administer," "does not make large demands on staff time," and is "reasonably reliable in that it does not rely on the co-operation of the user." The method is useful for identifying little-used or non-used titles, but it does not work well for heavily used titles because multiple uses may be missed.[30] Although appropriate for targeted titles or segments of the collection, the slip method would seemingly be quite labor-intensive if applied to the entire collection. Baker and Lancaster state that this technique may overestimate use due to accidental displacement of the slip.[31] The British Library's Science Reference Library also employed the slip method to study periodical use.[32]

Questionnaires or Surveys

This method embraces two separate but related techniques: distribution of questionnaires in the library or surveying patrons external to the library. A questionnaire might be attached to separate items or handed to patrons at a library entrance. Academic libraries frequently survey faculty concerning their periodical use, especially during cancellation projects. This approach can gather data about the type and purpose of use, the benefit derived from the use, and user categories (i.e., who is using what), thus combining a use and user study. Faculty are often asked to evaluate titles as well as to indicate their degree of use. Titles not held by the library can be recommended for possible subscription. Ambiguously worded questions can create a problem, especially on the definition of use. Librarians designing a use survey should consult a social science methodology textbook. User cooperation is required, as survey results may be invalid due to a small response rate. In an academic setting, the faculty may exaggerate usage to protect periodicals in their subject areas. Indeed, conflicting research concerns the extent to which survey results correspond to actual use determined by other methods. For example, Wenger and Childress reported "insignificant correlation" between a use study and questionnaire results,[33] yet Miriam Lyness Sheaves observed that actual and reported use "closely . . . corresponded."[34] Overall, more studies report the former than the latter. Reported surveys on periodical use are too numerous to summarize, but note entire articles devoted to such surveys at the University of Michigan[35] and the University of Illinois at Urbana-Champaign.[36]

Direct Observation

Sometimes termed *unobtrusive observation* if the patrons are unaware of being studied, this technique entails the direct viewing of periodical use. One of this technique's major advantages is that patron cooperation is not required. Consequently, uses not recorded by other methods, such as when a patron reshelves an item or fails to check an inserted slip, would be counted. Also, the length and type of use can be observed. A precise set of decision rules on the definition of use is necessary. Numerous disadvantages to this approach follow: it is costly, considerable staff training is required, both the observing staff member and the observed patron may feel uncomfortable, and the method is prone to observer error.[37] Because of its labor-intensive nature, direct observation is usually conducted on a short-term basis, often at randomly selected locations and times. Marifran Bustion, John Eltinge, and John Harer suggest the technique may be more suitable for use in the Current Periodicals Room than the general stacks, where it would be difficult to distinguish use of periodicals from books.[38] Direct observation can be used with other methods. For instance, it can determine how frequently patrons reshelve items when asked not to do so, to calculate a correction factor for use of the table count method. The use of direct observation of periodical usage at the Texas A&M University library has been reported.[39]

Call Slip Analysis

In a closed stack library, call slips submitted by patrons can be used to analyze periodical use. This method has been used in the New York Public Library's Slavic and Baltic Division,[40] the Washington University Freund Law Library,[41] the University of Bergen School of Dentistry library (in Norway),[42] and the Lancaster-Lebanon Intermediate Unit 13 Library Consortium (in Pennsylvania and composed primarily of school libraries).[43] This technique is unobtrusive and, depending upon the call slip's design, provides information about users. Obvious drawbacks to the call slip method are that it can only be used by libraries with closed access to periodicals, and it requires preservation of request records for a considerable time. Compiling the slips could be tedious and time-consuming.

Photocopy Request Analysis

As with call slip analysis, this technique can only be used under certain conditions: the library must have a photocopying center, and photocopying request records must be preserved. If a library has both a photocopying center and open-access photocopying machines, records from the former would not capture the full range of photocopying. Photocopying represents a specialized category of use. Presumably, the user deemed the article of value if he or she expended the time and money to photocopy it. Yet some question whether these data indicate actual use or patron "photocopying habits."[44] At the University of Connecticut Health Center, a closed stack library where photocopying represented most use, it was possible to obtain a list of titles that had not been photocopied during the preceding two years.[45] The analysis of photocopy requests has also been reported at the Cetus Corporation's Information Services Center[46] and the University of Bergen.[47]

ILL and Document Delivery Request Analysis

Although most of the other techniques measure use in the library, this approach measures use of periodicals external to the library's collection. Therefore, this technique would be useful for selecting or validating cancellation decisions. The method's advantages are nonintrusion on library operations and the data's ready availability. Some periodical use studies (e.g., at the Massachusetts General Hospital Library[48] and the University of South Florida[49]) incorporated ILL data along with data gathered through other methods to capture the full range of patron demand for periodicals.

Adhesive Labels

In the late 1970s W. M. Shaw Jr. proposed "a practical journal usage" technique developed at Case Western Reserve University.[50] When staff members reshelve a bound volume, they attach an adhesive label to its spine. The technique can be applied to current periodicals by applying the label to the appropriate space on the shelf. At various intervals, library staff count the number of titles and volumes with labels to divide the collection into two categories: "used" and "not used." The cumulative fraction used can be calculated for increasingly longer time periods (i.e., after one month, two months, three months, etc.). Shaw states that the fraction used will initially increase rapidly, then more slowly, then level off at what approaches a "constant fraction." He concludes, "When the constant fraction condition is reached, there is a high probability that those volumes or titles that have not been used will not experience significant use in the foreseeable future."[51] Blaine H. Hall recommends use of Shaw's approach until the constant fraction is reached. He states that reaching the constant fraction will probably require a minimum of two years, but "less conclusive results could be obtained in a shorter time."[52]

This technique offers an efficient way to identify nonused titles for weeding and canceling, but an obvious disadvantage is that it indicates nothing about relative use or highly used titles. Noreen S. Alldredge observes this technique may be easier to carry out than other methods, because when a title has been used once, it is eliminated from further investigation.[53] As with the table count method (of which it is sometimes considered a version), results can be affected by patron reshelving. However, one could modify Shaw's method by attaching another label with each reshelving or adding a hash mark to the original label to count the number of uses. In another variation, color-coded dots can be used to distinguish different dates or number of uses.[54] The adhesive label technique has been used at the Texas A&M University[55] and the University of North Carolina at Chapel Hill libraries.[56] This technique has also been called the *dotting* or *spine-marking* method.[57]

Check-Off Method

In this technique, a tag, label, or slip is attached to the front of a periodical bound volume or current issue, so patrons can self-report their use. This method is sometimes referred to as *tagging*. Library patrons are requested to mark on the tag each time they use the item. The tag may contain a list of consecutive numbers, say, 1 through 20. With each usage, the patron marks off the largest unmarked number. Or patrons may write the use date on a blank slip. The patron can be asked to indicate additional information concerning his or her status (i.e., faculty, graduate, or undergraduate) or type of use (browsing, photocopying, etc.). Although this approach is relatively inexpensive to administer, it relies heavily on patron cooperation. Use data could be overreported by patrons with a vested interest in particular titles; for example, faculty members wishing to protect journals in their specialty might deliberately exaggerate the usage level. Indeed, so-called blitz ticking, overticking, and tag removal reportedly took place at the Memorial University of Newfoundland library.[58] Indifferent patrons, however, may fail to check off when actually using an issue, resulting in underreporting. Milne and Tiffany[59] as well as Maiken Naylor[60] conclude that the check-off method significantly underestimates actual usage. Use of this technique has been reported at the University of Illinois at Urbana-Champaign,[61] the Memorial University of Newfoundland,[62] Leeds University,[63] SUNY at Buffalo,[64] and SUNY, College at New Paltz.[65]

Subjective Impression of Use

One can ask library staff responsible for reshelving for their impressions, based on memory, concerning how often they reshelve a specific periodical title. Another version of this method has been facetiously termed 'the dust test.' If you can pick up the volume and blow dust off it, it is probably not highly used.[66] These techniques should never be used as part of a systematic study and are not recommended because they lack rigor, objective data, and authoritativeness. Nevertheless, they can some-times be useful when "quick and dirty" usage information is needed for a particular title or a relatively small number of titles. These methods have been used (but not published) during the author's career as a librarian.

Other Methods

Some other methods should by briefly mentioned. Patrons might be in-terviewed concerning their use of periodicals. Baker and Lancaster describe a tech-nique whereby randomly selected patrons are interviewed about book use—an approach that could be applied to periodicals as well.[67] The interview approach combines a use and user study and provides information about the type of use, its purpose, and the benefit received. The technique can, however, be time-consuming, labor-intensive, expensive, and require considerable staff training.

Robert Goehlert used data from a library-run faculty document delivery service to measure use of political science and economic journals at the Indiana University Libraries.[68] Broadus analyzed the periodicals requested by humanities scholars at the National Humanities Center in Research Triangle Park, North Carolina.[69] Journals used to answer reference questions have been investigated at Iowa State University,[70] and journals used to answer clinical medicine questions studied at the Medical College of Pennsylvania.[71] ILL lending to other libraries has occasionally been included in periodical use analysis.[72] Although technically consti-tuting journal use, these data do not indicate expressed demand on the part of the library's own patrons.

Summary

Although a variety of methods are available for analyzing periodical use, each offers advantages and disadvantages. As stated in *Measuring Academic Library Performance*, "Different methods give different results . . . and it is not clear which is the most accurate."[73] It is questionable whether any method will capture all uses with 100 percent accuracy. Criteria for selecting methods include the project's objec-tive, the available time, staff training and effort required, and expense. The use of multiple methods in a single project is often advisable, as has been done in some of the most rigorous studies. For instance, Wenger and Childress's frequently cited periodical use study at the National Oceanic and Atmospheric Administration Library combined the table count technique, direct observation, a patron questionnaire, circulation data, and ILL requests.[74] A multimethod approach can capture different use categories and employ one technique to access the accuracy of another technique (direct observation to verify table count data or table count data to assess survey results).

Periodical use analysis is closely tied to the traditional ownership paradigm. Ironically, as collections become smaller with an increasing emphasis on access, the question of which titles are actually used or not used in the library assumes greater significance in serials collection management decision making.

Automation and Periodical Use

Finally, it should be emphasized that automation offers a not-yet fully utilized potential for analysis of periodical use. Automated circulation systems can provide information on high-, low-, and noncirculating titles; user categories; and patterns of use; although the reports generated will vary among systems. As previously noted, the fact that most libraries place restrictions on periodical circulation limits the value of these data.

Recent technological innovations allow the reading of bar codes as items are reshelved to tabulate in-house use. In some cases these statistics can be uploaded to the automated circulation system and be included in the reports it produces. Because this process is essentially an automated version of the table count method, the results can be affected by patron reshelving. Use of this approach has been reported at the George Washington University Medical Center,[75] Houston Academy of Medicine–Texas Medical Center,[76] Thomas Jefferson University,[77] and Northern Illinois University libraries—where details concerning the hardware and software are reported.[78]

Some online or CD-ROM indexing, abstracting, and full-text services can provide statistics tabulating the number of times periodical titles have been hit in the database by patron searches. This information's extraction from UMI's ProQuest at the University of Wisconsin at Whitewater[79] and EBSCO's *Magazine Articles Summaries* at the University College of Cape Breton Library[80] has been reported. *SERIALST* recently included postings on data from UMI's ProQuest indexes at Loyola University library in New Orleans[81] and EBSCO's Academic Abstracts CD-ROM at the College of Saint Rose library in Albany, New York.[82] The extent to which database hits correspond to actual library usage is uncertain, but it seems axiomatic that they measure user demand. Librarians should consult vendors about the generation of data from their services, because products vary in this rapidly changing arena.

The methods discussed above have been developed for print serials. World Wide Web (WWW) servers can generate log reports on the number of times the site has been accessed, which files were accessed, who accessed them (thus combining a use and user study), and where they were accessed from. Some log management utilities can sort and tabulate these data. Thus, if an electronic journal is mounted on a library's Web server, usage data should be available, but there is no guarantee because the systems administrator can turn off the function.[83] Some

Web sites even reveal to users the number of times the site has been accessed. Librarians should consult their systems administrator about extracting electronic journal usage data, because they will vary from configuration to configuration. Libraries participating in Project Muse, JSTOR, and OCLC FirstSearch Electronic Collections Online can receive electronic journal usage reports on the part of their patrons.

To date, articles concerning methods for analyzing the use of electronic journals do not abound in the literature. Tova Stabin and Irene Owen described the various software and statistical programs used to gather usage data for the University of Washington Department of Environmental Health Library WWW site.[84]

DESIGNING A PERIODICAL USE STUDY

This section addresses designing a periodical use study. Any library evaluation project (use studies are legitimately considered a type of evaluation) can be thought of as a multistage process: problem definition, design, implementation, data tabulation, interpretation of findings, and action or recommendations. Each of these stages is briefly discussed below. Readers wishing more details are referred to Hall's *Collection Assessment Manual for College and University Libraries*, *Measuring Academic Library Performance*, *Output Measures for Public Libraries*, plus *Output Measures for Public Library Service to Children*. Meredith Butler and Bonnie Gratch's article on planning a user study should also be mentioned.[85]

Problem Definition

In this stage, one asks such questions as, why is the study being conducted? What does one want to find out? What type or types of use are being analyzed? Is the study focused on the entire collection or limited to a subset such as certain subject areas, active titles, low use titles, etc.? What types of serials (e.g., periodicals, newspapers, abstracts and indexes, etc.) will be included? Use studies most commonly occur as part of a broader serials review or cancellation project, but, as previously discussed, there may be a variety of other reasons for a periodical use study.

Design

This is probably the most critical stage, because a poorly designed study can result in flawed or invalid findings. Simply put, the problem definition stage answers *what* and *why,* and the design stage answers *how.* Although the design might include a pilot study or pretest, there are essentially two major aspects to designing the study: determining the methodology and planning its implementation. Significant methodological and planning issues are outlined below.

Method or Methods for Counting Use

Numerous methods were described in a preceding section. More than one method can be used in a single study, such as the table count approach for bound volumes and the check-off technique for current issues.

Length of the Study

The study's length is an especially critical issue. Shaw states that "it is difficult to determine how long such a study should be conducted before reliable results can be obtained" and that most periodical use studies last no longer than four months or one semester.[86] Wenger and Childress concluded that a three-month period is sufficient to identify low-usage titles.[87] Robert J. Veenstra and James C. Wright analyzed 15 published journal use studies conducted in academic, special, and public libraries between 1958 and 1987 and reported time spans between three months and four years, although more than two-thirds were of a year's duration or more.[88] *Output Measures for Public Libraries* recommends a one-week period,[89] and *Output Measures for Public Library Service to Children* recommends two weeks.[90] There may be a fundamental trade-off between the effort required and the precision of the results. A longer study demands greater effort but should produce more accurate results, whereas a shorter study obviously requires less effort, but the findings may be less valid.

Timing of the Study

When a study will be done represents a separate issue from its duration. Usage levels fluctuate throughout the year in accordance with the academic calendar and other variables. An investigation at the SUNY at Buffalo Science and Engineering Library found the highest periodical use in October and February and the lowest in August.[91] Accordingly, a short study must be conducted during periods of normal activity so the findings will be representative of overall usage. One would clearly not want to carry out a use study on the day of the Superbowl!

A study does not necessarily have to be carried out during a continuous period. *Output Measures for Public Library Service to Children* recommends conducting the study during one summer week and one school-year week to account for different usage patterns during the two time periods.[92] Many periodical use studies have been conducted during randomly selected, nonconsecutive days or times. Some techniques, such as direct observation, that can not be sustained on a long-term basis, can be done during randomly selected hours.

Timetable

Another related issue concerns setting a timetable for completion of each step in the project. Even if a project runs behind schedule, a timetable helps the planning process by listing in order the tasks that must be completed.

Statistical Analysis

Statistical issues need to be addressed during the design phase. Discussion of statistical methods is beyond this book's scope. Consulting a statistics textbook or even a statistician is advisable for projects using sampling or sophisticated statistical analysis.

Staffing

Planning a strategy for doing the study requires answering such questions as which staff members will be involved in the study? (Different staff will probably be involved in the various stages of the study, for example, design, implementation, or data analysis.) How much staff training will be necessary? Certainly, all library staff should be informed that the study is taking place. Committees are often appointed to plan and implement use studies, but it helps to designate one staff member to be in charge of the project. The investigation should be designed to minimize the impact on normal staff and patron activities.

Informing Users

A basic planning issue concerns whether library users should be informed about the study. In many cases it will be necessary to inform them. Several methods, for example, check-off, interviews, and questionnaires, almost inevitably require that patrons know about the study. The table count approach works best if patrons are requested not to reshelve items—although a sign could make such a request without stating a formal study is in process. Some techniques—such as adhesive labels, circulation, and ILL and document delivery data use—do not require patron notification.

Users uninformed of a study might claim its results are invalid because they would have cooperated (not reshelving a volume or ticking a tag) had they known it was taking place.[93] Yet the danger of an obtrusive approach is that knowledge a study is taking place may affect the users' actions and thus skew the results. In fact, there is some evidence that this has happened during periodical use studies. Each library will have to resolve this question based on such local considerations as the methods used and the study's purpose.

Implementation

During this stage, the project is carried out and the data actually gathered. Further discussion is not necessary because such major issues as length of study, methods used, etc. have previously been addressed.

Data Tabulation

This step entails compiling the data into useful categories for analysis. Data might be combined from different use categories (such as circulation, in-house use, and ILL and document delivery requests) or from different formats (i.e., unbound issues, bound volumes, and microform). Total usage data can then be analyzed by such variables as title, date, location, user category, etc. The data can also be broken down by time of use (i.e., quarterly, annually, etc.), to track longitudinal trends. Use data for specific titles should be prorated to a yearly total. All studied titles are frequently ranked according to use, although limiting the rankings to titles within a subject or department would offer more valid comparisons. A ranked list indicates the number of titles required to meet various percentages of use (e.g., 90 percent, 99 percent, etc.). It is preferable to tabulate data by publication date rather than volume number. Title changes create a data-tabulation problem. Many libraries combine the data for the new and old title forms, but this should be done with caution. In some studies, data might be cross-tabulated (i.e., which periodicals are used by what user categories).

Data tabulation can be done manually, but software is available, including the Statistical Package for the Social Sciences (SPSS) and various database management or spreadsheet programs. Kate Herzog, Harry Armistead, and Marla Edelman suggest creating a database by downloading records from a bibliographic utility or the library's Online Public Access Catalog (OPAC).[94] Another database issue concerns the fields to create for each record. The fields would address two elements: the periodical—title, publisher, cost, frequency, International Standard Serial Number (ISSN), language, holdings, indexing, fund code, classification number, and status (active or dead), etc.—and the use—date, bound or unbound, etc.[95]

Also, for some projects it might be beneficial to adjust the data to compensate for noncooperating users. Baker and Lancaster suggest that table count statistics can be multiplied to reflect items reshelved by patrons—after estimating the proportion of used items actually reshelved based on unobtrusive observation during a trial period.[96]

Interpretation of Findings

Interpreting the findings can be one of the most challenging aspects of a periodical use study. Absolute level of use may not be the most important factor. Maurice B. Line and Alexander Sandison argued that in weeding (and presumably remote storage) decisions, the critical variable is use in proportion to the amount of occupied shelf space.[97] In a similar vein, Carole J. Mankin and Jacqueline D. Bastille analyzed the journals used at the Massachusetts General Hospital library according to "density of use" (i.e., total use divided by the shelf space occupied).[98] However, in the current environment's concern with serials costs, it has been observed that questions involving shelf space or use density are of secondary interest.[99] Paul Robert Green has described a "usage index" that divides the use count by the number of months an issue was available on the shelves.[100] Another variable that can affect usage figures is the length of a title's backrun—the more volumes owned, the greater the opportunity to be used.[101] As discussed in the next section, the relation of use to cost determines a journal's cost-effectiveness, which offers a more accurate decision-making criterion. Many of the serials decision models analyzed in chapter 4 combine use data with a variety of other variables.

Action or Recommendations

Periodical use studies generally lead to specific actions—a list of current subscriptions to cancel or back volumes to weed. Again, serials collection management decisions should not be made on a single criterion, be it use or any other variable. Rather, use data should be used with other factors during the decision-making process. Action recommendations are not an inevitable requirement of a periodical use study; it can be advantageous to have the data on file for future reference.

Finally, a formal report may be written (for the administration of the library, its parent organization, or other interested parties) or the findings published. Typically a report would cover the study's purpose, the length and timing of the investigation, the methodology, the results obtained, and specific recommendations. It has been suggested that a well-designed periodical use study should include a plan for disseminating the results.[102]

COST-PER-USE

Once a library obtains periodical use data, it can calculate cost-per-use. Such data indicate a periodical's cost-effectiveness (i.e., how much a library must spend for each occasion a periodical title is actually used). Typically, a cost or usage study (or a combined study) ranks a library's current subscriptions from the most to the least cost-effective—in other words, the lowest to the highest cost-per-use. This analysis usually shows that many expensive journals are cost-effective, although some inexpensive titles may not necessarily be cost-effective. In sum, cost and cost-effectiveness are two separate dimensions. Cost-effectiveness data are particularly helpful for decisions on cancellation and subscription versus document delivery—two related concepts, as a library might cancel a title with the intended objective of relying on document delivery to meet future patron need. The least cost-effective journals in the lower portions of the ranking would normally be the prime candidates for cancellation. Through a cost-per-use ranking, one can calculate the portion of the budget required to pay for a specific percentage of use. The concept of journal cost-effectiveness assumes greater significance in an era of tightened budgets, increased accountability, and increased emphasis on access as an alternative to ownership.

In essence, calculating cost-per-use requires combining two bits of data for each title: cost and the number of uses. Although it seems simple, more complex methodological questions must be asked. What elements are included in the calculation of cost: subscription, processing, binding, housing, the subscription agent's fee? How is use defined? For what time period is use data gathered? What range of journal holdings (i.e., the current year, the most recent five volumes, the entire run) is included in the analysis?

The issues involved in defining what constitutes use have been previously discussed. Line and Sandison contend that a periodical's full cost includes ordering, subscription, accounting, claiming, receiving and processing, preparation for and actual binding, and storage.[103] Subscription cost and the subscription agent fee are usually readily ascertainable, but calculation of processing costs requires time, effort, and resources that may not be available to many libraries. Estimating a constant, across-the-board processing cost to apply to all titles would simplify the calculation, but it is clear that actual processing costs vary among titles. The information's ultimate use is an important consideration. Subscription cost alone may be sufficient for calculating relative cost-effectiveness, but for reaching decisions on subscription versus ILL and document delivery for individual titles, overall costs would be the critical factor—an issue already mentioned in chapter 3. Note that cost-per-use can not be calculated for titles that have not been used.

Outlining a precise formula for calculating cost-per-use is beyond this book's scope because the most appropriate method will vary among libraries depending upon the project's purpose and the available resources. Readers interested in detailed descriptions of cost-per-use methodologies are referred to Milne and Tiffany[104] or, for a more rigorous approach, Bruce R. Kingma and Suzanne Irving.[105]

Carole Francq described the Usage/Cost Relational Index (UCRI) developed since 1992 at the Indiana University School of Medicine Library. This technique divides a journal's current annual subscription cost by the number of uses within a given time period to calculate a UCRI Number. The library may select whatever time period it wishes, ranging from several years to less than a year. The journals are then rank ordered according to the Index Number to identify less-cost-effective titles that would be candidates for cancellation. This method does not calculate cost-per-usage data unless one has the subscription cost and complete use data for every year covered in the analysis.[106] Francq's technique provides greater flexibility than a conventional cost-per-use study while accomplishing the same objective: ranking journals according to their cost-effectiveness. Because the method does not necessarily generate cost-per-use data, it would be less useful for subscription-versus-document-delivery decisions.

A survey reported by Tony Schwartz on *SERIALST* in late 1995 revealed that 55 of 60 libraries responding to an inquiry had carried out cost-per-use studies of low-use periodicals. (This proportion can not be extrapolated to all libraries because the survey responses were obviously skewed toward libraries that had conducted such studies.) Not surprisingly, most libraries used the results strictly for cancellation purposes rather than reinvesting the savings in new titles. Some libraries limited the study to expensive titles, which Schwartz believes undermines systematic cost-per-use analysis because, he asserts, most high cost-per-use periodicals tend to have average subscription prices.[107]

Note that dividing the current year's cost by the current year's usage of all or some back volumes—a method used in many studies—may contain some subtle methodological flaws. The actual cost-per-use will be underestimated because only the current subscription price is considered, but volumes that have been paid for in previous years contribute to the usage count. Such an approach also disadvantages journals for which the library holds short backruns versus journals with long backruns because they would have fewer opportunities to be used. A rigorous analysis would require total usage for all years since the subscription began, divided by the cumulative total of each year's cost for the journal, although, as a practical matter, the necessary data might not be available.

Cost-per-use data are not readily comparable among libraries because innumerable variables—including date of study, methodology used, and the mix of titles and subject areas covered—affect the results. With this caveat in mind, some studies that have reported specific figures will be mentioned. The Pittsburgh study (explained in the next section) calculated the per-use-cost for the six branch libraries it examined using two approaches: subscription cost only and total cost, which included storage, processing, staff expenditures, etc. The average cost-per-use, based solely on subscription price, ranged from $2.25 to $7.54, and the range increased to $3.30 to $10.07 when all costs were taken into account.[108]

A 1975 analysis of the subscription and processing costs of political science journals requested by faculty at Indiana University revealed that the cost-per-request ranged from $.17 to $4.98.[109] At the Memorial University of Newfoundland, cost-per-use was calculated by dividing the current subscription cost by a title's estimated total lifetime uses. The periodical cost ranged from $.03 to more than $1,000 per use. Any title costing more than $14 per use was considered a candidate for cancellation.[110] The average cost-per-use for current journals was $3.53 in the University of Illinois at Urbana-Champaign Chemistry Library in 1988.[111] A 1989 study of selected current periodicals at the Freshwater Institute Library, in Winnipeg, Manitoba, Canada, reported that cost-per-use ranged from $1.92 to $26.11.[112] A study of *Beilsteins Handbuch der Organischen Chemie* at two university libraries found that in 1990 the average cost-per-use was $960.75 at the University of Illinois at Urbana-Champaign and $1,494.50 at the University of Delaware.[113] Cost-per-use studies of serial subscriptions at two University of Illinois at Urbana-Champaign departmental libraries led Tina E. Chrzastowski and David Stern to conclude that duplicate subscriptions are cost-effective, as the average cost of a duplicate subscription was $6.31 in the Chemistry Library and $2.86 in the Physics/Astronomy Library.[114]

Cost-per-use studies are usually oriented toward the library's cost, and most do not assign value to the time or convenience of patrons. Cost-effectiveness, as indicated by cost-per-use, is a one-dimensional measure, albeit an important one, that should be used with other considerations when reaching journal collection management decisions.

SUMMARY OF PERIODICAL USE STUDIES

This section discusses some of the major periodical use studies as well as their salient findings. No attempt at comprehensiveness is made because of the large number of published studies.

In 1996, *Library Journal* reprinted a classic article from 1895, "Use of Periodicals," although this item did not report a formal use study.[115] Herman H. Fussler and Julian L. Simon's *Patterns in the Use of Books in Large Research Libraries*, a major study carried out in the University of Chicago library during the 1950s, addressed the use of serials as well as books.[116] In 1958, at the International Conference on Scientific Information, D. J. Urquhart reported a periodical use study at the Science Museum Library in the United Kingdom.[117] Several periodical use studies were published during the 1960s, and the number increased during the 1970s and again in the 1980s. By the late 1990s, published periodical use studies numbered in the hundreds.[118]

The Pittsburgh study, although now more than two decades old, is still the most famous use study in library history. The study is best remembered for its controversial finding that approximately 40 percent of the books acquired by the University of Pittsburgh's Hillman Library in 1969 did not circulate even once during the next seven years. The study of journal use was also a major component of this study.[119] The study analyzed journal use at six departmental libraries on the University of Pittsburgh campus (Physics, Life Sciences, Engineering, Chemistry, Computer Science, and Mathematics) based on samples during one or two trimester periods from autumn 1975 to winter 1977.[120]

Richard W. Trueswell, an industrial engineer who published a series of library use studies during the 1960s, promulgated the famous "80-20 Rule." The rule postulated that 80 percent of book and serial circulation is accounted for by 20 percent of the items in the collection. Trueswell found this pattern applied in all types of libraries.[121] Subsequent research has demonstrated the principle applies to in-house use as well as circulation. In fact, the "80-20" principle applies to many diverse phenomena and has been attributed to the Italian political economist Vilfredo Pareto, who discovered the pattern in income distribution. It should come as no surprise that the percentages "80" and "20" seldom hold up precisely. Yet many studies confirm the fundamental concept that a fraction of the periodical collection accounts for the majority of usage. For example, 16 percent of the titles accounted for 80 percent of the use in a multiyear study at Clarkson College of Technology;[122] 10 percent of the titles fulfilled 72 percent of demand in a four-month study at the Chalmers University of Technology;[123] 35 percent of the current periodical subscriptions accounted for three-quarters of total use in Indiana University's Fine Arts Library during 1979 and 1980;[124] 19.8 percent of the titles accounted for 80.1 percent of the use in a yearlong study at Auburn University's Veterinary Medical Library;[125] 17.1 percent of the titles provided 80 percent of the use during 1979 at Franklin & Marshall College;[126] 26 percent of the subscriptions accounted for 80 percent of the use in a six-month study at the University of Illinois at Urbana-Champaign;[127] and 20 percent of the titles produced 86 percent of the use in a three-month study at the University of California at Berkeley Environmental Design Library.[128] Moreover, 36 of 1,673 journals accounted for half the 48,192 articles requested for photocopying at the Cetus Corporation's Information Services Center from 1987 to 1989.[129]

Many studies likewise demonstrate that a significant portion of the periodical titles were not used during the study period. As illustration, 37.8 percent were unused during 12 months at Washington University Freund Law Library[130] and 11.6 percent in two years at Texas A&M University.[131] Veenstra and Wright found in the 15 studies they analyzed that the percentage of unused titles ranged from 14 to 80 percent, with a mean of 41 percent. As one might suspect, they found that the larger the collection, the smaller the proportion of titles actually used.[132] A more recent study at the SUNY at Buffalo library found only 4.8 percent of the titles were unused.[133] One speculates that the countless serials review projects identifying low-use titles for cancellation may be resulting in a lower proportion of unused titles in academic library collections, but further research on this question is necessary.

As we enter the electronic age, the "80-20 Rule" has clear implications for serials collection management by libraries. Identifying the fraction of journals that make up the lion's share of use helps, from a theoretical perspective, to define the core collection. One presumes that all other factors being equal, a librarian would wish to maintain these highly used journals in the local collection rather than cancel them to rely on access from an external source.

Not unexpectedly, preliminary research indicates that the "80-20" principle also applies to the use of electronic resources. It was found that of 1,325 Internet sites available to users at the University of Toronto library, 10 sites accounted for 33 percent of the Internet connections made by patrons, and 80 percent of the connections were to 13 percent of the sites.[134] This study was based on all sites, but one surmises future research will confirm the "80-20 Rule" in the use of electronic serials on the Internet. At the University of Wisconsin at Whitewater, between 29.5 percent and 47.0 percent, depending upon which database was searched, of the journals accounted for approximately 80 percent of the citations retrieved from CD-ROM databases,[135] and at the University College of Cape Breton, 16.4 percent of the indexed journals provided precisely 80.0 percent of the printed citations.[136]

Age is another variable often addressed in periodical use studies. The term *literature obsolescence* has been applied to the well-documented pattern of declining use of aging periodicals. Literature growth may exaggerate this effect (i.e., current periodicals may appear to be used more simply because there are more current periodicals than older ones), but decline in use with age is a genuine phenomenon.[137] As with interdisciplinarity, these results generally tend to reinforce the patterns found by citation studies. The Pittsburgh study found that generally 60 percent of periodical use was attributed to the most recent 5 volumes and 90 percent to the most recent 15 volumes.[138] Eve-Marie Lacroix's article-level analysis of 4 million ILL requests entered into DOCLINE (the National Library of Medicine's ILL routing system) in the 24-month period ending September 30, 1992, found that 95 percent of the requests were for items published since 1970, 85 percent for articles published in the most recent ten years, and 67 percent in the most recent five years.[139] Because obsolescence varies among subject areas and specific titles, weeding periodical backruns must be done on a title-by-title basis.

Another important use pattern concerns *interdisciplinarity*—defined as use of periodicals in one discipline by members of other disciplines. Most periodical use investigations have not directly addressed interdisciplinarity because a use study per se says nothing about who is using the periodicals. Rather, a combination use and user study is necessary to analyze interdisciplinarity. A survey at the University of Sussex, in which each faculty member could distribute 100 votes among the library's journals, graphically demonstrated interdisciplinarity in the importance attached to journals.[140] Numerous other measures, including citation studies, index coverage, and faculty publication patterns, have illustrated interdisciplinary use of periodicals. Interdisciplinarity often creates problems in serials management, such as which branch should house a journal or which department's budget it should be assigned to.

Several studies (for example, those conducted at Franklin & Marshall College,[141] the British Library's Science Reference Library,[142] the National Lending Library for Science and Technology (in the United Kingdom),[143] and the University of California at Berkeley[144]) indicate that non-English periodicals are used less frequently than English-language ones. Lacroix discovered that 92 percent of the articles supplied on DOCLINE were from English-language journals.[145] These results, which are probably no surprise to most librarians, are consistent with Ruth B. McBride's finding that fewer than 40 percent of University of Illinois social science faculty read non-English serials.[146]

Other reported findings of periodical use studies should be briefly noted: titles covered in indexing services owned by the library display a higher usage rate;[147] if a title's current issues are not used, its bound and microformat volumes probably will not be used;[148] cost-per-use does not necessarily correspond to cost-per-page;[149] heavily used titles are often not covered in the *Journal Citation Reports* (JCR);[150] there is "considerable consistency" between semesters for heavily used titles;[151] and periodicals have higher usage than monographic series.[152]

In summary, the salient patterns indicated by periodical use studies are outlined below:

- Use declines with age.

- A fraction of the titles accounts for a disproportionately large share of total use.

- There is an inverse relationship between collection size and the portion of unused titles.

- English language titles are used much more than non-English ones (based on studies in English-speaking nations).

- Scholars use titles outside their own discipline.

Again, this section has mentioned illustrative examples of these patterns rather than presented a comprehensive review; accordingly, many other studies could have been cited. Although Line's frequently quoted statement "No measure of journal use other than one derived from a local use study is of any significant practical value to librarians"[153] undoubtedly applies to the use of specific titles, these patterns have been reported with enough regularity that their general accuracy can be accepted. Periodical use patterns have obvious implications for their management in libraries, which need not be further elaborated upon here. The patterns are not unique to periodicals, as they have also been observed in book use. One might conclude these patterns would also apply to electronic publications: as noted above, preliminary evidence indicates the "80-20 Rule" holds up in cyberspace.

Note that a research genre addresses interlibrary loan or document delivery requests for periodicals. For example, studies analyze the periodicals or articles requested at the National Library for Science and Technology (in the United Kingdom),[154] the British Library Document Supply Centre,[155, 156] and entered into DOCLINE.[157] These studies contain a systematic bias because they measure demand for items not available in the end user's local library; nevertheless, they indicate broad patterns of periodical usage on a national basis. It is possible they will assume greater significance in the future because of the increasing emphasis on access.

NOTES

1. S. R. Ranganathan, *Library Book Selection* (New Delhi: Indian Library Association, 1952), quoted in G. Edward Evans, *Developing Library and Information Center Collections*, 3d ed. (Englewood, Colo.: Libraries Unlimited, 1995), 111.

2. Jamie Webster Hastreiter, Larry Hardesty, and David Henderson, comps., *Periodicals in College Libraries*, CLIP Note 8 (Chicago: Association of College and Research Libraries,

1987), 10. They report 35.6 percent, but my calculation from their raw data indicates 35.9 percent.

3. W. M. Shaw Jr., "A Practical Journal Usage Technique," *College and Research Libraries* 39 (November 1978): 479.

4. Nancy A. Van House and others, *Output Measures for Public Libraries: A Manual of Standardized Procedures*, 2d ed. (Chicago: American Library Association, 1987), 42-47. These measures are calculated by dividing the total yearly figure by the population of the library's legal service area. The manual provides explicit instructions on how to gather and analyze the data.

5. Virginia A. Walter, *Output Measures for Public Library Service to Children: A Manual of Standardized Procedures* (Chicago: Association for Library Service to Children, Public Library Association, American Library Association, 1992), 34-39.

6. Roger R. Flynn, "The University of Pittsburgh Study of Journal Usage: A Summary Report," *Serials Librarian* 4 (fall 1979): 32.

7. Robert N. Broadus, "The Measurement of Periodicals Use," *Serials Review* 11 (summer 1985): 58.

8. F. Wilfrid Lancaster, "Evaluating Collections by Their Use," *Collection Management* 4 (spring/summer 1982): 39.

9. Sharon L. Baker and F. Wilfrid Lancaster, *The Measurement and Evaluation of Library Services*, 2d ed. (Arlington, Va.: Information Resources Press, 1991), 124.

10. Dorothy Milne and Bill Tiffany, "A Cost-per-Use Method for Evaluating the Cost-Effectiveness of Serials: A Detailed Discussion of Methodology," *Serials Review* 17 (summer 1991): 19.

11. F. W. Lancaster, *If You Want to Evaluate Your Library*, 2d ed. (Champaign. Ill.: University of Illinois, Graduate School of Library and Information Science, 1993), 53.

12. Charles B. Wenger and Judith Childress, "Journal Evaluation in a Large Research Library," *Journal of the American Society for Information Science* 28 (September 1977): 293-99.

13. Charles Eckman, "Journal Review in an Environmental Design Library," *Collection Management* 10, nos. 1/2 (1988): 73.

14. Baker and Lancaster, *The Measurement and Evaluation of Library Services*, 125.

15. Rolf Hasslöw and Annika Sverrung, "Deselection of Serials: The Chalmers University of Technology Library Method," *Collection Management* 19, nos. 3/4 (1995): 157. They counted it as one use if the issues were in the box but three uses if they were removed from the box.

16. Baker and Lancaster, *The Measurement and Evaluation of Library Services*, 125-26. They offer, pp. 125-34, excellent summaries of five approaches to measuring in-house use: table count, the slip method, patron questionnaires, patron interviews, and unobtrusive observation.

17. Van House and others, *Output Measures for Public Libraries*, 44-47.

18. Walter, *Output Measures for Public Library Service to Children*, 37-38.

19. Nancy A. Van House, Beth T. Weil, and Charles R. McClure, *Measuring Academic Library Performance: A Practical Approach* (Chicago: American Library Association, 1990), 55-59. Although advocating the table count method, they briefly mention some other approaches.

20. Tina E. Chrzastowski, "Journal Collection Cost-Effectiveness in an Academic Chemistry Library: Results of a Cost/Use Survey at the University of Illinois at Urbana-Champaign," *Collection Management* 14, nos. 1/2 (1991): 85-98.

21. Josephine King Evans, "Tracking Periodical Usage in a Research Library," *College and Research Libraries News* 51 (November 1990): 958-59.

22. N. Fjällbrant, "Rationalization of Periodical Holdings: A Case Study at Chalmers University Library," *Journal of Academic Librarianship* 10 (May 1984): 77-86.

23. Martin Gordon, "Periodical Use at a Small College Library," *Serials Librarian* 6 (summer 1982): 63-73.

24. Betty Jo Irvine and Lyn Korenic, "Survey of Periodical Use in an Academic Art Library," *Art Documentation* 1 (October 1982): 148-51.

25. Barbara A. Rice, "Science Periodicals Use Study," *Serials Librarian* 4 (fall 1979): 35-47.

26. Maiken Naylor, "Assessing Current Periodical Use at a Science and Engineering Library: A dBASE III+ Application," *Serials Review* 16 (winter 1990): 7-19.

27. Maiken Naylor and Kathleen Walsh, "A Time-Series Model for Academic Library Data Using Intervention Analysis," *Library and Information Science Research* 16 (fall 1994): 299-314. Weekly time series analysis is applied to 8.4 years of periodical use data, based on the table count method.

28. Robert J. Veenstra, "A One-Year Journal Use Study in a Veterinary Medical Library," *Journal of the American Veterinary Medical Association* 190 (March 15, 1987): 623-26.

29. Hugh Franklin, "Comparing Quarterly Use Study Results for Marginal Serials at Oregon State University," *Serials Librarian* 16, nos. 1/2 (1989): 109-22.

30. Su Rooke, "Surveying Non-Usage of Serials," *Serials Librarian* 18, nos. 1/2 (1990): 81-96. Staff monitoring of slip displacement took 10 minutes per day.

31. Baker and Lancaster, *The Measurement and Evaluation of Library Services*, 127.

32. A. Sandison, "The Use of Scientific Literature at the Science Reference Library for Updating Searches," *Journal of Documentation* 35 (June 1979): 107-19.

33. Wenger and Childress, "Journal Evaluation in a Large Research Library," 299.

34. Miriam Lyness Sheaves, "A Serials Review Program Based on Journal Use in a Departmental Geology Library," in *The Future of the Journal: Proceedings of the Sixteenth Meeting of the Geoscience Information Society, November 2-5, 1981*, ed. Mary Woods Scott (n.p.: Geoscience Information Society, 1983), 66.

35. Stephen L. Peterson, "Patterns of Use of Periodical Literature," *College and Research Libraries* 30 (September 1969): 422-30.

36. Patricia Stenstrom and Ruth B. McBride, "Serial Use by Social Science Faculty: A Survey," *College and Research Libraries* 40 (September 1979): 426-31.

37. Baker and Lancaster, *The Measurement and Evaluation of Library Services*, 134.

38. Marifran Bustion, John Eltinge, and John Harer, "On the Merits of Direct Observation of Periodical Usage: An Empirical Study," *College and Research Libraries* 53 (November 1992): 539.

39. Ibid., 537-50.

40. Wojciech Siemaszkiewicz, "The Readership of the Current Periodical and Newspaper Collection in the Slavic and Baltic Division of the New York Public Library," *Serials Librarian* 20, nos. 2/3 (1991): 131-49.

41. Margaret A. Goldblatt, "Current Legal Periodicals: A Use Study," *Law Library Journal* 78 (winter 1986): 55-72.

42. Paul J. Riordan and Nils Roar Gjerdet, "The Use of Periodical Literature in a Norwegian Dental Library," *Bulletin of the Medical Library Association* 69 (October 1981): 387-91.

43. Debra E. Kachel, "Improving Access to Periodicals: A Cooperative Collection Management Project," *School Library Media Quarterly* 24 (winter 1996): 93-103.

44. Eckman, "Journal Review in an Environmental Design Library," 72.

45. Joan Ash and James E. Morgan, "Journal Evaluation Study at the University of Connecticut Health Center," *Bulletin of the Medical Library Association* 65 (April 1977): 297-99.

46. Michael D. Cooper and George F. McGregor, "Using Article Photocopy Data in Bibliographic Models for Journal Collection Management," *Library Quarterly* 64 (October 1994): 386-413.

47. Riordan and Gjerdet, "The Use of Periodical Literature in a Norwegian Dental Library," 387-91.

48. Jacqueline D. Bastille and Carole J. Mankin, "A Simple Objective Method for Determining a Dynamic Journal Collection," *Bulletin of the Medical Library Association* 68 (October 1980): 357-66.

49. Evans, "Tracking Periodical Usage in a Research Library," 958-59.

50. Shaw, "A Practical Journal Usage Technique," 479-84.

51. Ibid., 481.

52. Blaine H. Hall, *Collection Assessment Manual for College and University Libraries* (Phoenix, Ariz.: Oryx Press, 1985), 67.

53. Noreen S. Alldredge, "The Non-Use of Periodicals: A Study," *Serials Librarian* 7 (summer 1983): 62.

54. Sheaves, "A Serials Review Program," 59-75.

55. Alldredge, "The Non-Use of Periodicals," 61-64.

56. Sheaves, "A Serials Review Program," 59-75.

57. Lancaster, *If You Want to Evaluate Your Library*, 81.

58. Milne and Tiffany, "A Cost-per-Use Method for Evaluating the Cost-Effectiveness of Serials," 13-14.

59. Dorothy Milne and Bill Tiffany, "A Survey of the Cost-Effectiveness of Serials: A Cost-per-Use Method and Its Results," *Serials Librarian* 19, nos. 3/4 (1991): 139.

60. Maiken Naylor, "Comparative Results of Two Current Periodical Use Studies," *Library Resources and Technical Services* 38 (October 1994): 373.

61. Katherine Konopasek and Nancy Patricia O'Brien, "Undergraduate Periodicals Usage: A Model of Measurement," *Serials Librarian* 9 (winter 1984): 65-74.

62. Milne and Tiffany, "A Cost-per-Use Method for Evaluating the Cost-Effectiveness of Serials," 7-19.

63. Paul Robert Green, "Monitoring the Usage of Science and Engineering Journals at the Edward Boyle Library, University of Leeds," *Serials Librarian* 25, nos. 1/2 (1994): 169-80.

64. Naylor, "Comparative Results of Two Current Periodical Use Studies," 373-88.

65. Jean S. Sauer, "Unused Current Issues: A Predictor of Unused Bound Volumes?" *Serials Librarian* 18, nos. 1/2 (1990): 97-107.

66. Elizabeth McKenney Titus, Wallace C. Grant, and Lorraine J. Haricombe, "Barcoding As a Tool for Collection Use Analysis: A Pilot Project," *Information Technology and Libraries* 13 (December 1994): 258.

67. Baker and Lancaster, *The Measurement and Evaluation of Library Services*, 129-33.

68. Robert Goehlert, "Periodical Use in an Academic Library: A Study of Economists and Political Scientists," *Special Libraries* 69 (February 1978): 51-60.

69. Robert N. Broadus, "Use of Periodicals by Humanities Scholars," *Serials Librarian* 16, nos. 1/2 (1989): 123-31.

70. Daniel R. Arrigona and Eleanor Mathews, "A Use Study of an Academic Library Reference Collection," *RQ* 28 (fall 1988): 71-81. This study also included the use of books.

71. Naomi Miller, "Journal Use in a Clinical Librarian Program," *Bulletin of the Medical Library Association* 72 (October 1984): 395-96.

72. Tina E. Chrzastowski, "Where Does the Money Go? Measuring Cost Effectiveness Using a Microcomputer to Analyze Journal-Use Data," in *Building on the First Century: Proceedings of the Fifth National Conference of the Association of College and Research Libraries, Cincinnati, Ohio, April 5-8, 1989*, ed. Janice C. Fennell (Chicago: Association of College and Research Libraries, 1989), 201-22.

73. Van House, Weil, and McClure, *Measuring Academic Library Performance*, 56.

74. Wenger and Childress, "Journal Evaluation in a Large Research Library," 293-99.

75. Shelly A. Bader and Laurie L. Thompson, "Analyzing In-House Journal Utilization: An Added Dimension in Decision Making," *Bulletin of the Medical Library Association* 77 (April 1989): 216-18.

76. Dawn Bick and Reeta Sinha, "Maintaining a High-Quality, Cost-Effective Journal Collection," *College and Research Libraries News* 52 (September 1991): 485-90.

77. Kate Herzog, Harry Armistead, and Marla Edelman, "Designing Effective Journal Use Studies," *Serials Librarian* 24, nos. 3/4 (1994): 189-92.

78. Titus, Grant, and Haricombe, "Barcoding As a Tool for Collection Use Analysis," 257-65.

79. Allan Davis, "Database Usage and Title Analysis on a CD-ROM Workstation," *Serials Review* 19 (fall 1993): 85-93.

80. Ian R. Young, "The Use of a General Periodicals Bibliographic Database Transaction Log as a Serials Collection Management Tool," *Serials Review* 18 (winter 1992): 49-60.

81. Rosalee McReynolds, "ProQuest," *SERIALST* (November 26, 1996).

82. Steve Black, "Re: ProQuest," *SERIALST* (November 26, 1996).

83. Lincoln D. Stein, *How to Set Up and Maintain a World Wide Web Site: The Guide for Information Providers* (Reading, Mass.: Addison Wesley, 1995), 115-18.

84. Tova Stabin and Irene Owen, "Gathering Usage Statistics at an Environmental Health Library Web Site," *Computers in Libraries* 17 (March 1997): 30-37.

85. Meredith Butler and Bonnie Gratch, "Planning a User Study—the Process Defined," *College and Research Libraries* 43 (July 1982): 320-30.

86. Shaw, "A Practical Journal Usage Technique," 479-80.

87. Wenger and Childress, "Journal Evaluation in a Large Research Library," 299.

88. Robert J. Veenstra and James C. Wright, "A Review of Local Journal Use Studies: An Investigation of Possible Broader Applications," *Collection Management* 10, nos. 3/4 (1988): 167.

89. Van House and others, *Output Measures for Public Libraries*, 45.

90. Walter, *Output Measures for Public Library Service to Children*, 37.

91. Naylor, "Assessing Current Periodical Use at a Science and Engineering Library," 12.

92. Walter, *Output Measures for Public Library Service to Children*, 37. One multiplies the usage during a summer week by 12 and during a school year week by 40 to obtain the yearly total.

93. Herzog, Armistead, and Edelman, "Designing Effective Journal Use Studies," 191.

94. Ibid., 190.

95. Chrzastowski, "Where Does the Money Go?" 202. She states that at the University of Illinois at Urbana-Champaign library, their 19-field journal database became "the most valuable part of our entire study."

96. Baker and Lancaster, *The Measurement and Evaluation of Library Services*, 124.

97. Maurice B. Line and Alexander Sandison, "Practical Interpretation of Citation and Library Use Studies," *College and Research Libraries* 36 (September 1975): 394.

98. Carole J. Mankin and Jacqueline D. Bastille, "An Analysis of the Differences Between Density-of-Use Ranking and Raw-Use Ranking of Library Journal Use," *Journal of the American Society for Information Science* 32 (March 1981): 224-28.

99. Bustion, Eltinge, and Harer, "On the Merits of Direct Observation of Periodical Usage," 538.

100. Green, "Monitoring the Usage of Science and Engineering Journals," 169-80.

101. Maurice B. Line and Alexander Sandison, "Practical Interpretation of Citation and Library Use Studies," *College and Research Libraries* 36 (September 1975): 393, assert "Ranked lists of crude 'uses' are valueless; most do not even take into account the length of time each journal has been in existence." This issue was addressed at Memorial University of Newfoundland by limiting the study of bound volumes to the most recent five years. See Milne and Tiffany, "A Cost-per-Use Method for Evaluating the Cost-Effectiveness of Serials," 11.

102. Herzog, Armistead, and Edelman, "Designing Effective Journal Use Studies," 191.

103. Line and Sandison, "Practical Interpretation of Citation and Library Use Studies," 396.

104. Milne and Tiffany, "A Cost-per-Use Method for Evaluating the Cost-Effectiveness of Serials," 7-19.

105. Bruce R. Kingma with Suzanne Irving, *The Economics of Access Versus Ownership: The Costs and Benefits of Access to Scholarly Articles via Interlibrary Loan and Journal Subscription* (New York: Haworth Press, 1996), 35-38.

106. Carole Francq, "Bottoming Out the Bottomless Pit with the Journal Usage/Cost Relational Index," *Technical Services Quarterly* 11, no. 4 (1994): 13-26.

107. Tony Schwartz, "Summary of Survey Responses re. 'A Show of Hands?'" *SERIALST* (December 18, 1995).

108. Flynn, "The University of Pittsburgh Study of Journal Usage," 25-33.

109. Robert Goehlert, "Journal Use per Monetary Unit: A Reanalysis of Use Data," *Library Acquisitions: Practice and Theory* 3, no. 2 (1979): 93. The cost analysis covered ordering, subscription, accounting, receiving, processing, and shelving.

110. Milne and Tiffany, "A Survey of the Cost-Effectiveness of Serials," 142-43.

111. Chrzastowski, "Where Does the Money Go?" 202.

112. K. Eric Marshall, "Evaluation of Current Periodical Subscriptions in the Freshwater Institute Library," in *IAMSLIC at a Crossroads: Proceedings of the 15th Annual Conference*, ed. Robert W. Burkhart and Joyce C. Burkhart (n.p.: International Association of Marine Science Libraries and Information Centers, 1990), 117-22.

113. Tina E. Chrzastowski, Paul M. Blobaum, and Margaret A. Welshmer, "A Cost/Use Analysis of Beilstein's *Handbuch der Organischen Chemie* at Two Academic Chemistry Libraries," *Serials Librarian* 20, no. 4 (1991): 73-83.

114. Tina E. Chrzastowski and David Stern, "Duplicate Serial Subscriptions: Can Use Justify the Cost of Duplication?" *Serials Librarian* 25, nos. 1/2 (1994): 187-200. The average cost of a duplicate subscription was $6.31 in the Chemistry Library and $2.86 in the Physics/Astronomy Library.

115. William Howard Brett, "Use of Periodicals," *Library Journal* 121 (March 1, 1996): S1-S2.

116. Herman H. Fussler and Julian L. Simon, *Patterns in the Use of Books in Large Research Libraries* (Chicago: University of Chicago Press, 1969).

117. D. J. Urquhart, "Use of Scientific Periodicals," in *Proceedings of the International Conference on Scientific Information: Washington, D.C., November 16-21, 1958* (Washington, D.C.: National Academy of Sciences—National Research Council, 1959), 287-300.

118. Based on searching *Library Literature* [CD-ROM] (Bonx, NY: H. W. Wilson, 1997.) System Requirements: IBM PC, PS/2 or compatible; 640 K RAM; hard disk; DOS 3.1 or higher; compact disc drive.

119. Allen Kent and others, *Use of Library Materials: The University of Pittsburgh Study* (New York: Marcel Dekker, 1979).

120. Ibid., 57-104.

121. Richard W. Trueswell, "Some Behavioral Patterns of Library Users: The 80/20 Rule," *Wilson Library Bulletin* 43 (January 1969): 458-61.

122. Jacqueline A. Maxin, "Periodical Use and Collection Development," *College and Research Libraries* 40 (May 1979): 248-53.

123. Fjällbrant, "Rationalization of Periodical Holdings," 82.

124. Irvine and Korenic, "Survey of Periodical Use in an Academic Art Library."

125. Veenstra, "A One-Year Journal Use Study in a Veterinary Medical Library."

126. Gordon, "Periodical Use at a Small College Library," 66.

127. Chrzastowski, "Journal Collection Cost-Effectiveness in an Academic Chemistry Library," 90.

128. Eckman, "Journal Review in an Environmental Design Library," 74.

129. Cooper and McGregor, "Using Article Photocopy Data," 386.

130. Goldblatt, "Current Legal Periodicals," 55.

131. Alldredge, "The Non-Use of Periodicals," 63.

132. Veenstra and Wright, "A Review of Local Journal Use Studies," 168.

133. Naylor, "Assessing Current Periodicals Use at a Science and Engineering Library," 13.

134. Joy Tillotson, Joan Cherry, and Marshall Clinton, "Internet Use Through the University of Toronto Library: Demographics, Destinations, and Users' Reactions," *Information Technology and Libraries* 14 (September 1995): 192-93.

135. Davis, "Database Usage and Title Analysis on a CD-ROM Workstation," 92.

136. Young, "The Use of a General Periodicals Bibliographic Database Transaction Log," 54.

137. This somewhat technical question has been debated in the scholarly literature. For example, see Maurice B. Line and A. Sandison, " 'Obsolescence' and Changes in the Use of Literature with Time," *Journal of Documentation* 30 (September 1974): 283-350; or Michael V. Sullivan, "Obsolescence in Biomedical Journals: Not an Artifact of Literature Growth," *Library Research* 2 (spring 1980-81): 29-45.

138. Flynn, "The University of Pittsburgh Study of Journal Usage," 29.

139. Eve-Marie Lacroix, "Interlibrary Loan in U.S. Health Sciences Libraries: Journal Article Use," *Bulletin of the Medical Library Association* 82 (October 1994): 367.

140. Adrian N. Peasgood and Peter J. Lambert, "Multi-User Subjects, Multi-Subject Users: Reader-Defined Interdisciplinarity in Journals Use at the University of Sussex," *British Journal of Academic Librarianship* 2 (spring 1987): 20-36.

141. Gordon, "Periodical Use at a Small College Library," 71.

142. Sandison, "The Use of Scientific Literature at the Science Reference Library," 115.

143. D. N. Wood and C. A. Bower, "The Use of Social Science Periodical Literature," *Journal of Documentation* 25 (June 1969): 111.

144. Eckman, "Journal Review in an Environmental Design Library," 75.

145. Lacroix, "Interlibrary Loan in U.S. Health Sciences Libraries," 363.

146. Ruth B. McBride, "Foreign Language Serial Use by Social Science Faculty: A Survey," *Serials Librarian* 5 (summer 1981): 30.

147. Gordon, "Periodical Use at a Small College Library," 70.

148. Sauer, "Unused Current Issues: A Predictor of Unused Bound Volumes?" 100.

149. Goehlert, "Journal Use per Monetary Unit," 94-97.

150. Eckman, "Journal Review in an Environmental Design Library," 76.

151. Rice, "Science Periodicals Use Study," 40.

152. Nancy J. Butkovich, "Reshelving Study of Review Literature in the Physical Sciences," *Library Resources and Technical Services* 40 (April 1996): 139.

153. Maurice B. Line, "Rank Lists Based on Citations and Library Uses As Indicators of Journal Usage in Individual Libraries," *Collection Management* 2 (winter 1978): 313.

154. Wood and Bower, "The Use of Social Science Periodical Literature," 108-18.

155. Ann Clarke, "The Use of Serials at the British Library Lending Division in 1980," *Interlending Review* 9 (October 1981): 111-17.

156. Karen Merry and Trevor Palmer, "Use of Serials at the British Library Lending Division in 1983," *Interlending and Document Supply* 12 (April 1984): 53-56.

157. Lacroix, "Interlibrary Loan in U.S. Health Sciences Libraries," 363-68.

FURTHER READING

Alldredge, Noreen S. "The Non-Use of Periodicals: A Study." *Serials Librarian* 7 (summer 1983): 61-64.

Alligood, Elaine C., Elaine Russo-Martin, and Richard A. Peterson. "Use Study of *Excerpta Medica* Abstract Journals: To Drop or Not to Drop." *Bulletin of the Medical Library Association* 71 (July 1983): 251-59.

Bader, Shelley A., and Laurie L. Thompson. "Analyzing In-House Journal Utilization: An Added Dimension in Decision Making." *Bulletin of the Medical Library Association* 77 (April 1989): 216-18.

Baker, Sharon L., and F. Wilfrid Lancaster. "Evaluation of In-House Use." In *Measurement and Evaluation of Library Services*, 123-42. 2d ed. Arlington, Va.: Information Resources Press, 1991.

Bremer, Thomas A. "Assessing Collection Use by Surveying Users at Randomly Selected Times." *Collection Management* 13, no. 3 (1990): 57-67.

Broadus, Robert N. "The Measurement of Periodicals Use." *Serials Review* 11 (summer 1985): 57-61.

———. "Use of Periodicals by Humanities Scholars." *Serials Librarian* 16, nos. 1/2 (1989): 123-31.

———. "The Use of Serial Titles in Libraries with Special Reference to the Pittsburgh Study." *Collection Management* 5 (spring/summer 1983): 27-41.

Bustion, Marifran, and Jane Treadwell. "Reported Relative Value of Journals Versus Use: A Comparison." *College and Research Libraries* 51 (March 1990): 142-51.

Bustion, Marifran, John Eltinge, and John Harer. "On the Merits of Direct Observation of Periodical Usage: An Empirical Study." *College and Research Libraries* 53 (November 1992): 537-50.

Butkovich, Nancy J. "Reshelving Study of Review Literature in the Physical Sciences." *Library Resources and Technical Services* 40 (April 1996): 139-44.

Chrzastowski, Tina E. "Journal Collection Cost-Effectiveness in an Academic Chemistry Library: Results of a Cost/Use Survey at the University of Illinois at Urbana-Champaign." *Collection Management* 14, nos. 1/2 (1991): 85-98.

———. "Where Does the Money Go? Measuring Cost Effectiveness Using a Microcomputer to Analyze Journal-Use Data." In *Building on the First Century: Proceedings of the Fifth National Conference of the Association of College and Research Libraries, Cincinnati, Ohio, April 5-8, 1989,* edited by Janice C. Fennell, 201-4. Chicago: Association of College and Research Libraries, 1989.

Clarke, Ann. "The Use of Serials at the British Library Lending Division in 1980." *Interlending Review* 9 (October 1981): 111-17.

Cooper, Michael D., and George F. McGregor. "Using Article Photocopy Data in Bibliographic Models for Journal Collection Management." *Library Quarterly* 64 (October 1994): 386-413.

De Klerk, Ann, and Roger Flynn. "A Comparative Periodical Use Study." In *The Information Community: An Alliance for Progress; Proceedings of the 44th ASIS Annual Meeting, Washington, D.C., October 25-30, 1981*. Vol. 18, edited by Lois F. Lunin, Madeline Henderson, and Harold Wooster, 15-18. White Plains, N.Y.: published for the American Society for Information Science by Knowledge Industry Publications, 1981.

Dole, Wanda V., and Sherry S. Chang. "Survey and Analysis of Demand for Journals at the State University of New York at Stony Brook." *Library Acquisitions: Practice and Theory* 20 (spring 1996): 23-34.

Fjällbrant, N. "Rationalization of Periodical Holdings: A Case Study at Chalmers University Library." *Journal of Academic Librarianship* 10 (May 1984): 77-86.

Flynn, Roger R. "The University of Pittsburgh Study of Journal Usage: A Summary Report." *Serials Librarian* 4 (fall 1979): 25-33.

Francq, Carole. "Bottoming Out the Bottomless Pit with the Journal Usage/Cost Relational Index." *Technical Services Quarterly* 11, no. 4 (1994): 13-26.

Franklin, Hugh. "Comparing Quarterly Use Study Results for Marginal Serials at Oregon State University." *Serials Librarian* 16, nos. 1/2 (1989): 109-22.

Gammon, Julia A., and Phyllis O'Connor. "An Analysis of the Results of Two Periodical Use Studies: How Usage in the 1990s Compares to Usage in the 1970s." *Serials Review* 22 (winter 1996): 35-53.

Goehlert, Robert. "Journal Use per Monetary Unit: A Reanalysis of Use Data." *Library Acquisitions: Practice and Theory* 3, no. 2 (1979): 91-98.

———. "Periodical Use in an Academic Library: A Study of Economists and Political Scientists." *Special Libraries* 69 (February 1978): 51-60.

Goldblatt, Margaret A. "Current Legal Periodicals: A Use Study." *Law Library Journal* 78 (winter 1986): 55-72.

Gordon, Martin. "Periodical Use at a Small College Library." *Serials Librarian* 6 (summer 1982): 63-73.

Green, Paul Robert. "Monitoring the Usage of Science and Engineering Journals at the Edward Boyle Library, University of Leeds." *Serials Librarian* 25, nos. 1/2 (1994): 169-80.

Holland, Maurita Peterson. "Machine-Readable Files for Serials Management: An Optimizing Program and Use Data." *College and Research Libraries* 44 (January 1983): 66-69.

Irvine, Betty Jo, and Lyn Korenic. "Survey of Periodical Use in an Academic Art Library." *Art Documentation* 1 (October 1982): 148-51.

Kachel, Debra E. "Improving Access to Periodicals: A Cooperative Collection Management Project." *School Library Media Quarterly* 24 (winter 1996): 93-103.

Kent, Allen, and others. *Use of Library Materials: The University of Pittsburgh Study*. New York: Marcel Dekker, 1979.

Konopasek, Katherine, and Nancy Patricia O'Brien. "Undergraduate Periodicals Usage: A Model of Measurement." *Serials Librarian* 9 (winter 1984): 65-74.

Lacroix, Eve-Marie. "Interlibrary Loan in U.S. Health Sciences Libraries: Journal Article Use." *Bulletin of the Medical Library Association* 82 (October 1994): 363-68.

Lenahan, Nancy M. "Use of Periodicals and Newspapers in a Mid-Sized Public Library." *Serials Librarian* 16, nos. 3/4 (1989): 1-7.

Line, Maurice B., and Alexander Sandison. "Practical Interpretation of Citation and Library Use Studies." *College and Research Libraries* 36 (September 1975): 393-96.

Mankin, Carole J., and Jacqueline D. Bastille. "An Analysis of the Differences Between Density-of-Use Ranking and Raw-Use Ranking of Library Journal Use." *Journal of the American Society for Information Science* 32 (March 1981): 224-28.

Merry, Karen, and Trevor Palmer. "Use of Serials at the British Library Lending Division in 1983." *Interlending and Document Supply* 12 (April 1984): 53-56.

Miller, Naomi. "Journal Use in a Clinical Librarian Program." *Bulletin of the Medical Library Association* 72 (October 1984): 395-96.

Millson-Martula, Christopher. "Use Studies and Serials Rationalization: A Review." *Serials Librarian* 15, nos. 1/2 (1988): 121-36.

Milne, Dorothy, and Bill Tiffany. "A Cost-per-Use Method for Evaluating the Cost-Effectiveness of Serials: A Detailed Discussion of Methodology." *Serials Review* 17 (summer 1991): 7-19.

———. "A Survey of the Cost-Effectiveness of Serials: A Cost-per-Use Method and Its Results." *Serials Librarian* 19, nos. 3/4 (1991): 137-49.

Naylor, Maiken. "Assessing Current Periodical Use at a Science and Engineering Library: A dBASE III+ Application." *Serials Review* 16 (winter 1990): 7-19.

———. "Comparative Results of Two Current Periodical Use Studies." *Library Resources and Technical Services* 38 (October 1994): 373-88.

———. "A Comparison of Two Methodologies for Counting Current Periodical Use." *Serials Review* 19 (spring 1993): 27-34, 62.

Naylor, Maiken, and Kathleen Walsh. "A Time-Series Model for Academic Library Data Using Intervention Analysis." *Library and Information Science Research* 16 (fall 1994): 299-314.

Peterson, Stephen L. "Patterns of Use of Periodical Literature." *College and Research Libraries* 30 (September 1969): 422-30.

Rice, Barbara A. "Science Periodicals Use Study." *Serials Librarian* 4 (fall 1979): 35-47.

Riordan, Paul J., and Nils Roar Gjerdet. "The Use of Periodical Literature in a Norwegian Dental Library." *Bulletin of the Medical Library Association* 69 (October 1981): 387-91.

Rooke, Su. "Surveying Non-Usage of Serials." *Serials Librarian* 18, nos. 1/2 (1990): 81-96.

Sandison, A. "The Use of Scientific Literature at the Science Reference Library for Updating Searches." *Journal of Documentation* 35 (June 1979): 107-19.

Sauer, Jean S. "Unused Current Issues: A Predictor of Unused Bound Volumes?" *Serials Librarian* 18, nos. 1/2 (1990): 97-107.

Schmidt, Diane, Elisabeth B. Davis, and Ruby Jahr. "Biology Journal Use at an Academic Library: A Comparison of Use Studies." *Serials Review* 20, no. 2 (1994): 45-64.

Shaw, W. M., Jr. "A Practical Journal Usage Technique." *College and Research Libraries* 39 (November 1978): 479-84.

Sheaves, Miriam Lyness. "A Serials Review Program Based on Journal Use in a Departmental Geology Library." In *The Future of the Journal: Proceedings of the Sixteenth Meeting of the Geoscience Information Society, November 2-5, 1981*, edited by Mary Woods Scott, 59-75. N.p.: Geoscience Information Society, 1983.

Siemaszkiewicz, Wojciech. "The Readership of the Current Periodical and Newspaper Collection in the Slavic and Baltic Division of the New York Public Library." *Serials Librarian* 20, nos. 2/3 (1991): 131-49.

Titus, Elizabeth McKenney, Wallace C. Grant, and Lorraine J. Haricombe. "Barcoding As a Tool for Collection Use Analysis: A Pilot Project." *Information Technology and Libraries* 13 (December 1994): 257-65.

Trueswell, Richard W. "Some Behavioral Patterns of Library Users: The 80/20 Rule." *Wilson Library Bulletin* 43 (January 1969): 458-61.

Veenstra, Robert J. "A One-Year Journal Use Study in a Veterinary Medical Library." *Journal of the American Veterinary Medical Association* 190 (March 15, 1987): 623-26.

Veenstra, Robert J., and James C. Wright. "A Review of Local Journal Use Studies: An Investigation of Possible Broader Applications." *Collection Management* 10, nos. 3/4 (1988): 163-73.

Wenger, Charles B., and Judith Childress. "Journal Evaluation in a Large Research Library." *Journal of the American Society for Information Science* 28 (September 1977): 293-99.

Chapter Seven

Journal Ranking Studies

A fairly large genre of studies is devoted to the hierarchical ranking of journals. Although nearly three-quarters of a century have passed since the first journal ranking was published, the potentially valuable information contained in journal ranking studies remains underused by librarian serial managers. This chapter explains the concept of journal ranking, the various methods used to rank journals, the benefits and drawbacks associated with the major approaches, and the potential uses of journal ranking; it also examines some specific studies. Bradford distribution is not discussed here, as a detailed examination was included in chapter 5.

THE CONCEPT OF JOURNAL RANKING

A journal ranking, as the name implies, rank orders a set of journals (often within a discipline or subject area) according to some criterion of value. The journals are usually listed in descending order beginning with number one. Journal ranking is presumably predicated on two assumptions: that significant variation exists among journals in terms of usefulness, prestige, cost-effectiveness, and other criteria of value; and that knowing a journal's hierarchical position within a group of similar journals assists practical decision making.

Journal ranking is controversial, yet we live in an age that emphasizes ranking. Universities, academic programs, football teams, and basketball teams—to name only the most obvious examples—are constantly ranked. At Indiana University, the School of Library and Information Science faculty are annually ranked on research, teaching, and service. This enthusiasm for ranking is a logical outgrowth of two other phenomena presently emphasized in society: evaluation and competition. Once the members of a particular category have been numerically evaluated, it is an easy and logical step to place the evaluative scores in a comparative context and create a ranking. Furthermore, a ranking supports competition by allowing competitors to be viewed in a comparative perspective.

Ranking is fundamental to journal collection management (although this idea is not always understood by collection managers). The essence of collection management entails assigning hierarchical value to journals. Therefore, an analysis of the various journal ranking methods, along with the salient methodological issues, is important for a full understanding of the serials evaluation process.

For purposes of library serials management, a journal ranking can be classified according to at least eight dimensions.

1. the ranking method used

2. whether it is explicit (a ranking) or implicit (a rating)

3. whether it is internal or external

4. whether it is based on local, national or international data

5. whether it is published or unpublished

6. whether it is a stand-alone ranking or part of a broader study

7. the degree of subject specificity

8. the purpose for which the ranking was conducted

Each of these dimensions is discussed below.

The Ranking Method Used

F. W. Lancaster lists and briefly discusses seven methods for ranking journals:

1. use in a library

2. use data from another library

3. opinion

4. total citations

5. impact factor

6. cost-effectiveness

7. the number of articles contributed to a subject

Journals can also be ranked according to readership, the number of subscribers (subtly different concepts because one can read a journal without subscribing to it), *exclusivity* (defined by Lancaster as "the proportion of all articles published by a journal that deal with some subject of interest"),[1] citations received in proportion to words published annually,[2] and complex formulas that combine numerous variables (i.e., decision models). Citation data and subjective judgment are the two most frequent ranking methods used in stand-alone studies external to libraries. The considerable debate concerning the relative merits of these two approaches is analyzed in a subsequent section. Use and cost-effectiveness rankings are commonly used in internal studies by libraries for collection management reasons.

Ranking Versus Rating

The concept of a journal ranking has already been explained. Closely related yet theoretically distinct is a *journal rating*. A rating assigns a numerical value for each journal in the set, but the journals are not arranged in rank order—typically alphabetical order would be used. Obviously, with a relatively minimal effort, an implicit ranking can be constructed from the rating data. One can consider a *ranking* study to represent an *explicit* ranking and a *rating* to constitute an *implicit* ranking. Consequently, journal ratings can fairly easily be used for the same serials collection management purposes as a ranking. In fact, many experts do not concern themselves with this somewhat technical distinction.

Internal Versus External Rankings

From the perspective of serials management in an individual library, an *internal ranking* is one that has been locally compiled by library staff, whereas an *external ranking* has been created elsewhere—by another library, an independent scholar, or an entity such as the Institute for Scientific Information (ISI) through its *Journal Citation Reports* (JCR). In terms of Lancaster's above-cited outline, use in one's own library would be internal; use in another library would be external. Most internal rankings focus on journals to which the library subscribes, although it is possible to compile rankings of journals cited in faculty research or in which faculty members publish.

Local Versus National or International Data

The preceding dimension (internal versus external) refers to where the ranking was compiled, whereas this dimension concerns the source of the data. Most internal studies are based on local data, such as cost or cost-effectiveness in one's own library, but the two dimensions (internal studies with local data, external studies with national or international data) do not always synchronize. A library could conceivably compile its own ranking based on national data (i.e., tabulating the titles cited in a national journal). A majority of external rankings would seemingly be constructed on national or international data, but some could be based on local data from another library. Choosing between a local or national or international ranking forces a trade-off between two significant factors: the effort required and relevance to patron needs. A ranking based on national or international data usually requires less labor (because someone else has compiled it), but its relevance to local patron needs might be questionable; a local ranking in one's own library necessitates greater effort but is clearly pertinent to patron needs.

Published Versus Unpublished

This self-evident distinction requires no explanation. Libraries creating their own internal rankings generally do not publish them. Most published rankings are by scholars, often outside the field of library and information science.

Stand-Alone Rankings Versus Rankings As Part of Broader Studies

The ISI's JCR and numerous scholarly studies are exclusively devoted to journal ranking as an end in itself, yet many journal rankings are embedded in large-scale studies. Libraries conducting studies of journal usage or cost-effectiveness commonly create a ranking as an end product of the project. Innumerable bibliometric studies and many library and information science Ph.D. dissertations contain journal rankings even through creating such a ranking was not the project's primary objective. As one example among many, Yeon-Kyoung Chung's dissertation, analyzing the international literature of classification, includes a ranking of the top 25 journals in citations received and the leading 13 journals in terms of article productivity.[3] Stand-alone rankings are easier to locate in the literature and consequently of more potential value for serials collection management.

A Ranking's Degree of Subject Specificity

Journals can be and have been ranked along a broad continuum of subject specificity covering

1. all knowledge without any subdivision; this approach is used when a library ranks all of its current journal subscriptions;

2. broad divisions of knowledge (the JCR contains rankings for all the science journals and all the social science journals that it covers);

3. disciplines; many published journal rankings are at the disciplinary level. The JCR ranks journals in categories corresponding to disciplines, such as "information science & library science," "political science," "chemistry" or "biology";

4. subdisciplines (i.e., many rankings have been published in such business subareas as accounting or marketing). The JCR also ranks journals in many categories at the subdisciplinary level (e.g., "Chemistry, Organic," "Computer Science, Hardware & Architecture," and "Marine & Freshwater Biology") ; and

5. relatively narrow, specialized areas; for example, Bernd Frohmann ranked journals dealing with cataloging and classification.[4]

The appropriate degree of specificity is related to the ranking's purpose. Most scholars would be interested in a journal's ranking within its discipline or subarea. For collection management purposes, libraries sometimes rank all the journals to which they currently subscribe. However, it is often not advisable to include journals from different disciplines within a single ranking. As explained in chapter 5, varying citation patterns among disciplines render cross-disciplinary comparison with citation data invalid. Indeed, some question whether citation data can be used to compare journals from different subareas of the same discipline. Ranking by use in a library would disadvantage journals that support departments with a small number of faculty and students. Likewise, cross-disciplinary rankings by cost or cost-effectiveness would be compromised by the fact that average journal costs vary widely from discipline to discipline. In short, multidisciplinary journal rankings should be undertaken with extreme caution, if at all; yet subject-based rankings disadvantage interdisciplinary journals.

The Ranking's Purpose

Journal ranking has been conducted for a wide variety of reasons. In general terms the two most frequent purposes are library collection management and use by scholars. Many rankings have been for exceedingly narrow, specific purposes (e.g., to determine if practitioners and educators rank journals differently). I contend that most rankings can be used for library collection management even if they were compiled for other purposes.

A Ranking Versus a Core List of Journals or a Journal Decision Model

An obvious question concerns the difference between a journal ranking and a core list of journals or a journal decision model—both of which were discussed in chapter 4. Although similar in concept, some differences between a journal ranking and these two other phenomena can be noted.

Some core lists are ranked, and some journal rankings are considered to define the core. Nevertheless, journal rankings and core lists usually differ in the following respects:

1. A journal ranking offers a hierarchical distinction among the covered titles (either by explicitly listing them in rank order or with a numerical score from which an implicit ranking can be constructed), whereas a core list often presents the titles in alphabetical order without any hierarchical distinction among them.

2. Generally, every title on a core list is theoretically recommended and is thus desirable for collection management purposes, whereas journals in the lower portions of a journal ranking are not necessarily recommended as strong candidates for the collection.

3. Core lists are generally compiled by librarians for explicit serials collection management use, but ranked lists are frequently created by scholars outside the library and information science (LIS) discipline for nonlibrary objectives, such as assistance with manuscript submission decisions and evaluation of faculty research performance by indicating the status of journals in which they published.

Likewise, some distinctions can be made between a journal ranking and a decision model.

1. A journal ranking is a finished product that lists a group of journals in explicit or implicit hierarchical order, but a decision model is a methodology for creating a journal ranking. (Most decision models create a rank-order list of journals to assist the decision process).

2. A journal ranking is usually based on one or a few variables, whereas most decision models incorporate numerous variables.

3. A published journal ranking covers a predetermined set of journals, but a decision model can be applied to any group of journals, such as those subscribed to by a particular library.

EXAMPLES OF JOURNAL RANKING STUDIES

Some journal ranking studies, chosen because of their historical importance or to illustrate basic approaches, are reviewed in this section. These rankings represent a select sample from the hundreds that have been published.

A now-classic study by two chemistry professors at Pomona College, P. L. K. Gross and E. M. Gross,[5] is generally acknowledged as the first journal ranking. It was based on citation data. The Grosses counted every citation in the 1926 volume of the *Journal of the American Chemical Society*, identifying 247 journals among the 3,633 citations. Seven journals received more than 15 citations, whereas 99 were cited only once. The top 28 journals are listed, by abbreviation, in a table. The authors' assertion that they wished to determine which chemistry journals are "needed in a college library" is quite significant because it illustrates that serials collection management in libraries was an original impetus for journal ranking studies. Some might consider this a truly gross study as it is by Gross and Gross and based on the gross number of citations received. Somewhat ironically, this study—the earliest known use of citation data for library serials management—was done for teaching purposes in a college library, even though the conventional wisdom asserts that citation analysis is most appropriate for research libraries.

The late 1920s as well as the 1930s and 1940s witnessed numerous citation-based journal rankings modeled on the approach of Gross and Gross (i.e., total citations received in one or more source journals). Most of these rankings were in the natural sciences, covering electrical engineering,[6, 7] geology,[8] dentistry,[9] and mathematics,[10] among others. The introduction of the *Science Citation Index (SCI)* and *Social Sciences Citation Index (SSCI) JCR* by the ISI in the mid-1970s helped citation-based rankings, as researchers no longer had to laboriously tabulate citations. Accordingly, these tools have been used in many published journal ranking studies.

To cite a typical example, Harold Colson ranked 35 public administration journals according to three different citation measures based on JCR data: the average number of citations received per year in the *SSCI JCR* for 1981 through 1986; the average *SSCI JCR* impact factor for 1981 through 1986; and the total number of citations received in five major public administration journals from 1981 to 1986, using *SSCI JCR* statistics.[11]

Some rankings come from manipulated forms of JCR impact factor data. For illustration, Thomas E. Nisonger used an "adjusted citation impact factor" for 1987, 1988, and 1989 to rank 65 political science journals.[12] He developed an "adjusted citation impact factor" to correct a subtle methodological bias introduced when one averages JCR impact factors for a range of consecutive years—as was done in the Colson study (discussed above) and many others to compensate for year-to-year fluctuations in the data. Because impact factor is calculated from the number of citations made in the current year to a journal's last two years, averaging impact factors from two or more consecutive years counts data from the middle years twice and the extreme years only once. For example, the following data are considered when a journal's 1995 and 1994 impact factors are combined:

$$1995 \text{ Impact Factor} = \frac{1995 \text{ citations to } 1994 + 1993}{1994 + 1993 \text{ articles published}}$$

$$1994 \text{ Impact Factor} = \frac{1994 \text{ citations to } 1993 + 1992}{1993 + 1992 \text{ articles published}}$$

Thus, 1993 data are counted two times (first for the 1995 impact factor, again for the 1994 impact factor), but 1992 and 1994 data are considered only once. No matter how many consecutive years are averaged, the middle years will be counted twice and the extreme years once. This error has been explained in detail by Nisonger.[13] He calculates his "adjusted citation impact factor" as follows from data available in the JCR:

$$1995 \text{ Adjusted Citation Impact Factor} = \frac{1995 \text{ Citation to } 1993}{1993 \text{ articles published}}$$

As reviewed in chapter 5, the impact factor has been modified numerous times to correct perceived deficiencies, such as the fact that it is based on citations from all journals in the ISI database rather than limited to ones from a journal's own discipline.

Even after ISI began publishing the JCR, some journal rankings were constructed from data compiled by the investigators. For example, Arthur D. Sharplin and Rodney H. Mabry ranked management journals based on citations during the years 1980 to 1983 in two of the field's leading journals: *Administrative Science Quarterly* and the *Academy of Management Journal*. They ranked the top 20 journals according to three citation measures they devised for the study: "simple impact"—total citations received; "article impact"—the mean number of citations per article published annually; and "impact efficiency"—citations received per 10,000 words published annually.[14]

Few published rankings are based on local citation data. One study, by Belen Altuna Esteibar and F. W. Lancaster, conducted at the Graduate School of

Library and Information Science at the University of Illinois at Urbana-Champaign, ranked the leading 20 journals according to five methods:

1. the number of times cited in 131 course reading lists, to measure "teaching relatedness";

2. the number of citations received in 41 doctoral dissertations, to measure "research relatedness";

3. the number of citations in 114 faculty publications, also to measure research relatedness;

4. the unweighted total of numbers 1, 2, and 3 above, with each counting equally; and

5. the weighted total of numbers 1, 2, and 3, using the ratio 10:5:1 for citations in faculty publications, doctoral dissertations, and course reading lists, respectively.[15]

A fundamentally different approach involves ranking a subject's journals based on the opinion of specialists regarding their quality, prestige, importance, influence, etc. Many such studies, variously termed *subjective, perception,* or *reputational rankings,* had appeared by the 1970s, especially in the social sciences. Indeed, during recent decades the overwhelming majority of published journal rankings external to libraries have been based on either citation data or the perceptions of experts.

One typical example of a subjective-based journal ranking is the study of political science journals by Michael W. Giles, Francie Mizell, and David Patterson.[16] Replicating a 1975 study of Giles and Gerald C. Wright Jr.,[17] they sent, during the summer of 1988, a questionnaire to 550 randomly selected political science faculty members listed in the 1986 American Political Science Association *APSA Guide to Graduate Study.* Respondents were asked to rate an alphabetical list of 78 journals (56 still in print from the earlier study plus 22 additional titles) in terms of the general quality of their articles using a 0 to 10 scale: 0 = poor; 2 = fair; 4 = adequate; 6 = good ; 8 = very good; and 10 = outstanding. They were instructed not to rate journals with which they were unfamiliar, and space was provided to write in titles and ratings for additional journals not included on the original list. Respondents were also asked to indicate their specialization areas and publications in journals.

The 78 journals were then ranked in a table according to their mean quality rating. Table 7.1 reproduces the table's portion covering the leading 23 journals (4 journals are tied for 20th, 21st, 22d, and 23d place). Reading left to right after the journal title, the columns present data on the percentage of respondents familiar enough with the journal to rate it, the journal's mean quality rating, the standard deviation (S.D.), and (for journals in specialized areas) the mean quality rating by specialists in the same subfield. *World Politics,* with a mean quality rating of 7.9, is the top-ranked journal. Giles, Mizell, and Patterson report that in 80 percent of the cases respondents gave a journal in their own subfield a higher rating than did the total pool of all respondents. For instance, international relations specialists gave *World Politics* an 8.0 rating, compared to 7.9 by all the raters. Also, 87 percent of the time respondents who had published in a journal rated it higher than those who had not done so—suggesting the possibility of subjective bias in the ratings. Some of the top-ranked journals in this study were from disciplines other than political science (e.g., *American Sociological Review* and *American Journal of Sociology*), once again demonstrating the importance of interdisciplinarity to scholarly communications.

Table 7.1.
Political Scientists' Ratings of Selected Journals

Journal*	% Familiar	Mean Rating	S.D.	Specialists
World Politics	59.5	7.9	1.4	8.0
American Sociological Review	54.9	7.6	1.8	
American Political Science Review	98.6	7.6	2.3	
American Journal of Sociology	50.2	7.5	1.6	
American Journal of Political Science	83.2	7.5	1.8	
Journal of Politics	91.1	7.4	1.6	
American Journal of International Law	18.6	7.3	1.6	
Soviet Studies	9.3	7.2	1.4	7.4
International Organization	37.7	7.1	1.8	7.2
Comparative Politics	55.3	7.0	1.5	7.3
Slavic Review	7.4	7.0	1.5	7.1
Administrative Studies Quarterly	42.8	6.9	1.9	7.2
British Journal of Political Science	58.1	6.8	1.7	
Journal of Political Economy	23.8	6.8	2.8	
China Quarterly	14.9	6.6	1.8	7.0
Political Theory	28.0	6.6	2.0	
Public Administration Review	57.7	6.6	2.1	7.1
Comparative Political Studies	46.0	6.5	1.5	6.7
International Studies Quarterly	41.9	6.5	1.9	6.7
Journal of Conflict Resolution	57.5	6.4	1.8	
Foreign Affairs	75.8	6.4	2.3	6.8
Journal of Latin American Studies	13.1	6.4	1.6	6.8
Public Opinion Quarterly	60.5	6.4	1.6	6.4

*Those journals with which at least 50% of the sample are familiar are italicized.

Reprinted with permission of the American Political Science Association from Michael W. Giles, Francie Mizell, and David Patterson, "Political Scientists' Journal Evaluations Revisited," *PS: Political Science and Politics* 22 (September 1989): 614.

A perception study conducted by David F. Kohl and Charles H. Davis is undoubtedly the best-known ranking of library and information science journals. In fall 1982 they surveyed 66 deans of North American Library Association (ALA) accredited library schools and the 85 directors of Association of Research Libraries (ARL) libraries, asking them to rate a list of journals using a 1-to-5 scale on "how important publication in that journal was for the consideration of promotion and tenure at their institution." They were also asked to list the five "most prestigious" journals in the discipline without specifying any particular order—what Kohl and Davis term the "top five" method.

Kohl and Davis created their list by beginning with 31 "hard-core" library journals compiled by the esteemed Jesse H. Shera, then adding new publications and deleting "special-interest" and Canadian titles. Respondents were given the opportunity to add other titles not on the original list. Kohl and Davis name 10 titles added by ARL library directors and 15 by library school deans.

Four rankings of library and information science journals resulted from their research: 31 journals based on mean rating by ARL library directors; 31 based on the same rating system by library school deans; 18 according to the "top five" method by ARL library directors; and 21 based on the "top five" method by library school deans.[18] Table 7.2 illustrates the first two. ARL library directors ranked *College and Research Libraries* number 1, with a mean 4.7381 rating on a 1 to 5 scale, and *Library Quarterly* was ranked in second position, with a 4.4048 quality rating. Library school deans, however, ranked *Library Quarterly* (4.5106) in first place and the *Journal of the American Society for Information Science* (4.3830) second.

Donald A. Nielsen and R. Wayne Wilson used the Delphi method (a technique for establishing consensus among experts) to rank real estate journals. They initially surveyed 130 instructors in U.S. college and university real estate programs, asking them to rate on a 1 to 20 (high) scale a list of 9 journals, "identified through . . . standard library aids." Respondents were instructed to rate only the journals they were familiar with and given the option of adding titles. The results of the initial rating were reported and eight write-in titles added to the list for a second round of rating. Finally, 17 journals were ranked based on their mean quality rating from the second round. Nielsen and Wilson also calculated a "familiarity index," the proportion of respondents familiar enough with each journal to rate it, and a "prestige index," which represents the "familiarity index" multiplied by the mean quality rating. For illustration, *Appraisal Journal's* 16.5 mean quality rating times its .92 familiarity index resulted in a 15.2 prestige index.[19]

A smaller number of studies have ranked journals according to readership. For illustration, Robert Swisher and Peggy C. Smith ranked the 26 journals most frequently read by academic librarians, using a 1978 survey of Association of College and Research Libraries (ACRL) members then employed in academic libraries.[20]

An annotated bibliography of the most important journal ranking studies conducted during the 1980s appears in Nisonger's *Collection Evaluation in Academic Libraries: A Literature Guide and Annotated Bibliography*.[21] Mary K. Sellen's *Bibliometrics: An Annotated Bibliography, 1970-1990*[22] contains a separate index that directs the reader to more than 200 bibliometric studies that include journal rankings. Selected journal ranking studies are cited in this chapter's "Further Reading" section.

Table 7.2.

Average Ranking of Journal Prestige in Terms of Value for Tenure and Promotion

ARL directors		Library School Deans	
JOURNAL TITLE	AVERAGE RANKING	JOURNAL TITLE	AVERAGE RANKING
College and Research Libraries	4.7381	Library Quarterly	4.5106
Library Quarterly	4.4048	Journal of the American Society for Information Science (formerly ASIS Journal)	4.3830
Journal of Academic Librarianship	4.3810	College and Research Libraries	4.2128
Library Resources and Technical Services	4.3810	Library Trends	4.1489
Library Trends	4.2381	Journal of Education for Librarianship	3.8511
Information Technology and Libraries (formerly Journal of Library Automation)	4.1429	Library Resources and Technical Services	3.7872
Journal of the American Society for Information Science (ASIS Journal)	4.0952	Drexel Library Quarterly	3.5745
Library Journal	3.8571	Special Libraries	3.4255
American Libraries	3.5000	Information Technology and Libraries (formerly Journal of Library Automation)	3.4043
RQ	3.3810	Library and Information Science Research (formerly Library Research)	3.4043
Special Libraries	3.1667	Journal of Academic Librarianship	3.3830
Wilson Library Bulletin	2.9762	Journal of Library History, Philosophy & Comparative Librarianship	3.3191
Library and Information Science Research (formerly Library Research)	2.8810	Library Journal	3.2128
Journal of Library History, Philosophy & Comparative Literature	2.6667	RQ	3.1277
Journal of Education for Librarianship	2.5714	School Library Media Quarterly (formerly School Media Quarterly)	3.0426
Collection Management	2.5238	American Libraries	3.0213
Library of Congress Quarterly Journal	2.5238	School Library Journal	2.8298
Drexel Library Journal	2.4524	Collection Management	2.8085
Harvard Library Bulletin	2.3571	Wilson Library Bulletin	2.8085
Microform Review	2.2619	Information Processing and Management	2.7872
Reference Services Review	2.2143	Law Library Journal	2.5957
Online	2.1667	Harvard Library Bulletin	2.4468
Library Acquisitions: Practice and Theory	2.0000	Microform Review	2.4043
Information Processing and Management	1.9286	Public Libraries	2.3404
Public Libraries	1.7381	Library of Congress Quarterly Journal	2.2979
School Library Journal	1.7381	Online	2.2979
International Library Review	1.5714	Library Acquisitions: Practice and Theory	2.2128
Micrographics Today	1.5714	International Library Review	2.1915
School Library Media Quarterly (formerly School Media Quarterly)	1.5714	Micrographics Today	1.9574
International Journal of Law Libraries	1.5476	Reference Services Review	1.7660
Law Library Journal	1.5238	International Journal of Law Libraries	1.7021

Reprinted with permission of the American Library Association from David F. Kohl and Charles H. Davis, "Ratings of Journals by ARL Library Directors and Deans of Library and Information Science Schools," *College and Research Libraries* 46 (January 1985): 42.

CITATION VERSUS SUBJECTIVE JOURNAL RANKINGS

Numerous studies compare citation and subjective rankings of journals in the same subject. To cite a few examples, James A. Christenson and Lee Sigelman[23] reported citation rankings based on *SSCI JCR* data displayed a .526 correlation with Norval D. Glenn's[24] subjective ranking of sociology journals and a .572 correlation with Giles and Wright's[25] subjective ranking of political science journals. Nisonger[26] found his citation-based ranking of political science journals displayed a .71 correlation with the subjective ranking of Giles, Mizell, and Patterson.[27] Studies too numerous to summarize found relatively modest correlations between citation and subjective journal rankings, suggesting the two approaches may be measuring subtly different things. (The correspondence between citation rankings and usage in a library was addressed in chapter 5.)

A considerable debate, which is sometimes highly technical, concerns the relative merits of citation versus subjective journal ranking. The major arguments, pro and con, are summarized in this section.

Arguments in Favor of Citation Journal Rankings

- Objective data are provided, thus lending greater credibility to the ranking.

- Data for rankings can be easily obtained from the JCR.

- Citation data may reveal changes in journals' status before the changes would become apparent through perception studies.

- The rankings are not influenced by individual bias.

Arguments Against Citation Journal Rankings

- A self-fulfilling prophecy takes place, with older, established, and better-known journals more likely to be cited for these very reasons.

- Many journals are not included in the JCR. (This argument applies only to rankings based on the JCR.)

- Journals that are older, publish longer articles, or have a larger audience have more opportunities to be cited.

- Citation count can be exaggerated by journal self-citation.

- Citation data may not be available for new journals.

- There may be a time lag of a few years before the most recent trends are reflected in citation data.

- It is uncertain what citation data actually measure.

- Several different citation methods have been used for journal ranking; different methods produce different rankings, and there is no consensus about which method is the most valid.

- Most citation data do not measure a journal's value for nonresearch purposes.

Arguments in Favor of Subjective Journal Rankings

- "Journal stature is a complex concept whose subtle nuances are better captured by subjective evaluations than by counting citations."[28]

- It is based on the authority of presumed experts in the subject area.

Arguments Against Subjective Journal Rankings

- A self-fulfilling prophecy takes place, with older, established, and better-known journals more likely to be highly rated for these very reasons. (This argument applies to both citation and subjective rankings.)

- Important journals may have been omitted from the original list being rated. (To address this point, many survey instruments permit respondents to add journals to the list. However, it is questionable whether this tactic adequately addresses the concern. A journal not on the original list would still face a considerable disadvantage. After all, how often does a write-in candidate win an election?)

- Respondents may not be familiar with the journals they are rating. (This criticism is often addressed by asking respondents not to rate journals with which they are unfamiliar.)

- Respondents may be biased in favor of journals in which they have published or in their own specialty area. Alternatively, a respondent might be biased against a journal that had rejected his or her submission.

- Respondents' perceptions of a journal may be outdated, not reflecting recent changes in its actual quality.[29]

- Rankings by different categories of respondents (i.e., practitioners versus educators) can vary significantly.

- Ratings are usually based on somewhat amorphous concepts such as "prestige" or "scholarly quality" for which the precise meaning may be unclear and subject to individual interpretation.

- There can be considerable methodological problems involved in conducting a subjective ranking, including determining who will be surveyed, deciding what rating instrument will be used, and coping with nonresponse.[30]

Analysis

Neither an absolutely right or wrong approach nor a perfect ranking method exists. Each approach offers advantages as well as methodological flaws. In my opinion, when all factors are considered, citation rankings are preferable to subjective ones. Many of the issues discussed in this section can be applied to other contexts, such as the ranking of academic programs.

In a sense, the citation versus subjective journal ranking issue is a reflection of the idealistic-versus-materialistic question in philosophy: If a tree fell in the forest and no one was nearby to hear it, would there still be a sound? The materialistic philosopher or citation journal ranking proponent would posit that ultimate reality lies in the objective world, whereas the idealistic philosophical position and the subjective-based journal ranking adherent would argue that ultimate truth resides in the human mind's perceptions.

LOCAL JOURNAL RANKINGS

A major caveat about journal ranking studies constructed from national or international data is that they may not reflect the unique needs of a particular library's clientele. However, except for ones based on use or cost-effectiveness, relatively few rankings constructed from local data have been described in the literature. Most of those, such as Altuna Esteibar and Lancaster's previously discussed ranking at the University of Illinois at Urbana-Champaign, were apparently done as research projects rather than for serials collection management.

The DIALOG RANK command, introduced in February 1993, allows the relatively inexpensive compilation of local journal rankings through online searching. Once search strategies (often restricted by subject and publication date) have been devised to retrieve the source articles written by authors affiliated with a particular institution or the articles cited in those source articles or both, the RANK command lists and displays in rank order the journals containing the articles retrieved in the search. The command can list the top 50 journals or all journals up to 50,000 (or any specified number) and also indicate the ranking position and number of occurrences for each. When used for collection management, book reviews, columns, and letters to the editor should probably be excluded from the search set. In-depth discussion of online searching techniques is clearly beyond this book's scope, but technical details concerning the RANK command's use have been provided by Bonnie Snow.[31] Parenthetically, note that in the early 1980s Howard D. White advocated creation of such a command, arguing it would allow "Bradfordizing" of search results.[32]

Stephanie C. Haas and Vernon N. Kisling Jr. describe the RANK command's application to search results in the *Scisearch* and *Agricola* databases to rank the journals published in and cited by University of Florida agriculture and science researchers. Although they assert "the implications for quantifying collection development decisions using this technique are tremendous," they note that problems with variant forms of identical journal titles had to be corrected. Haas and Kisling also list the 50 most-cited titles.[33] A similar technique was used to rank the journals published in and cited by Indiana University Biology Department faculty, with a search costing approximately $80.[34] In my opinion, final judgment on the benefits and pitfalls of the RANK command's use should be reserved until more evidence is available, although it appears to be a potentially valuable tool.

COLLECTION MANAGEMENT USES OF JOURNAL RANKINGS

Generalizing about the collection management applications of journal ranking is difficult, as testified to by the eight variables outlined above. Statements applicable to one type of ranking may not necessarily be valid for other types. Because use and cost-effectiveness have been covered in chapter 6, this section's discussion will focus on citation and subjective rankings.

Except for the JCR's citation rankings, little evidence exists that librarians actually use formal published ranking studies in serials collection management. Consequently, these studies constitute sources of underutilized information with considerable potential application to serials collection management in university or research libraries. The published studies' focus on scholarly journals makes them less useful for school or public libraries.

Potential Uses

A journal ranking could be used from both the micro and macro level. In a micro sense, it could assist with a subscription or cancellation decision for a specific title. A journal's relative rank among other journals in its discipline or subject area would be useful information to consider, along with other more traditional factors. If the information is used for selection, it would be desirable for the title to rank high on the list; if used for cancellation, to rank in the lower portions. If a journal were not included in a ranking of its discipline's journals, that could be a valid indicator of a journal's status or lack thereof.

An external ranking can be used for selection with greater confidence than for deselection because, as revealed in chapter 5, higher-ranking journals are more stable. Yet, paradoxically, deselection is now a higher priority for most libraries. From a macro perspective, an external list could be used as a collection evaluation tool, serving as a checklist for evaluating a library's journal subscriptions in a subject.

Kris Subramanyam is one of the few authors to explicitly address the collection management uses of journal rankings. He lists four.

1. Calculating the cost of collecting all journals relevant to a subject

2. Determining the fraction of coverage that could be obtained for a given expenditure figure

3. Determining the "optimal distribution of journal collections" between a central and departmental locations

4. Dividing the collection into "primary, secondary, and tertiary relevance or into stores requiring frequent, occasional, or only rare access."

Subramanyam's first two points presuppose the ranking gives total coverage to the subject.[35] However, most journal rankings, including those in the JCR, do not cover all the journals in a field.

Opposing Views on the Value for Libraries of Journal Ranking Studies

Some prominent authors question the value of journal ranking studies for library serials collection management. Maurice B. Line, in a public exchange with Robert Broadus on the pages of *College and Research Libraries* on the usefulness of *ISI JCR* data for libraries, argued that for most decision-making purposes libraries are primarily interested in noncore journals at the fringe. (The library presumably wishes to collect the core titles). Because noncore titles in the middle and lower ranks receive fewer citations, a relatively small change in the number of citations received can cause a large fluctuation in ranking from one year to the next—an issue explored in chapter 5. Line concludes that "librarians may as well rely on what users say they want" rather than use citation-based rankings.[36]

William E. McGrath, in a 1985 letter to the editor of *College and Research Libraries* commenting on Kohl and Davis's perception-based ranking of library and information science journals, stated that "ranking average ratings without submitting them to appropriate tests of significance cannot be trusted." Although he aims his technical argument at the statistically sophisticated, in essence he contends that if the difference between the mean scores for two adjacently ranked journals is not statistically significant, one can not validly conclude that one journal actually ranks higher than the other. Applying an advanced statistical test to the findings of Kohl and Davis, he identified two "possible clusters" of higher-ranking and lower-ranking journals, but the mean scores for the journals within each cluster were not statistically different from each other. He also argues that an average rating "can hide a great diversity of opinion." An average of three could mean every respondent rated the journal three or that half the respondents rated it one and the other half rated it 5.[37] McGrath's argument would apply to most subjective-based journal rankings. In almost all cases, authors of these studies have not conducted tests of statistical significance.

Lancaster, citing Line's work, argues that journal rankings have little value for deselection purposes because of inconsistencies among different studies in positioning lower-ranking journals—the titles that would be evident candidates for deselection. He comments that a journal consistently at the bottom of all rankings "would have little reason to exist."[38]

Another contrarian view on citation-based journal ranking studies was expressed to the author by Ronald Rousseau, a world renowned bibliometrician, at the Fourth International Conference on Bibliometrics, Informetrics, and Scientometrics, held in Berlin in September 1993. He argued that librarians should pay primary attention to a journal's raw impact factor score rather than the rank within its discipline because random fluctuations in raw impact factor score could cause significant shifts in rank from year-to-year.

Moreover, there is a personal aspect to journal value. For any given scholar, a lowly ranked journal in his or her specialty would be more valuable than a more highly ranked journal in another subfield. Furthermore, the quality of articles in the same journal can vary significantly. A ranking focusing on a specific discipline can undervalue interdisciplinary journals. Rankings can quickly become outdated.

OTHER USES OF JOURNAL RANKINGS

A large proportion, if not the majority, of ranking studies have been conducted by scholars outside the field of library and information science, reflecting the obvious importance of journal ranking for nonlibrary purposes. Knowledge about the status of journals within their field is clearly important to scholars. It can provide guidance in manuscript submission decisions and in evaluating research performance for purposes of promotion, tenure, and annual salary increases—on the premise that publication in a high-ranking journal counts more than in a lowly ranked one. Furthermore, the status of journals their faculty publish in can be a criterion in the assessment of academic departments.

Journal ranking studies have been used to answer specific research questions. As discussed earlier, Kohl and Davis compared the journal perceptions of ARL library directors and library school deans as well as the degree of internal consensus in the ratings of both groups.[39] Thomas P. Howard and Loren A. Nikolai compared the ranking of accounting journals by faculty at Ph.D.-granting institutions versus non-Ph.D.-granting ones and by full professors versus assistant professors.[40] Jean-Louis Malouin and J.-Francois Outreville contrasted the ranking of economics journals by academic economists from four different geographical areas: the United States, the United Kingdom, France, and Quebec.[41] These studies generally show noteworthy variation in rankings by different categories of respondents, suggesting the possibility of bias, the complexity of journal ranking, and that journals may have relative rather than absolute value, depending on the needs of a particular constituency.

A few studies address the attributes associated with journal rank, such as indexing, circulation, age, etc. Mary T. Kim's detailed analysis of library and information science journals found that indexed journals were generally more highly ranked, and library school deans gave research-oriented journals higher rankings.[42] More research is needed on the characteristics associated with high- and low-ranking journals.

To date, journal ranking studies have focused on print journals, although the fundamental principle could be applied to electronic journals or a set of both print and electronic journals. Furthermore, at some future point a ranking (citation, subjective, or some other approach) of a particular subject's journals, both print and electronic, could be used to test the scholarly acceptance of electronic journals.

CONCLUSION

In an abstract theoretical sense, most serials collection management boils down to the ranking of periodicals, even if a library never uses published studies. Stated simplistically, most libraries want the "best" or higher-ranking journals in terms of whatever criteria they deem important. Moreover, ranking provides a context for assessing data about a journal by providing comparison with similar titles. The fact that the chapter entitled "Evaluation of Periodicals" in Lancaster's seminal textbook *If You Want to Evaluate Your Library* deals primarily with journal ranking, illustrates the concept's centrality to journal collection management.

Little evidence suggests that libraries use published journal rankings for collection management, except for JCR citation data. A 1995 posting on *SERIALST* from the University of Tasmania requested a ranked list of journals dealing with "Antarctica and the Southern Ocean," but it was for a research student rather than journal collection management.[43] Consequently, published journal rankings represent an untapped information resource with much potential application to evaluating scholarly journals, yet, many libraries have conducted unpublished, internal rankings based on use or cost-effectiveness.

Journal rankings are clearly controversial. Some authorities question their validity for any purpose, not to mention library serials management. Even if one accepts McGrath's assertion that a journal ranking is valid only for dividing journals into "higher ranking" and "lower ranking" categories, this division would still be useful because serials collection management often involves binary decisions: to select or not select (from the universe of titles to which the library does not currently subscribe) or to cancel or not cancel current subscriptions.

NOTES

1. F. Wilfrid Lancaster, *If You Want to Evaluate Your Library*, 2d ed., (Champaign, Ill.: University of Illinois, Graduate School of Library and Information Science, 1993), 89.

2. Arthur D. Sharplin and Rodney H. Mabry, "The Relative Importance of Journals Used in Management Research: An Alternative Ranking," *Human Relations* 38, no. 2 (1985): 139-49.

3. Yeon-Kyoung Chung, "The International Literature of Classification Systems During the Period 1981-1990" (Ph.D. diss., Indiana University, 1993).

4. Bernd Frohmann, "A Bibliometric Analysis of the Literature of Cataloguing and Classification," *Library Research* 4 (winter 1982): 355-71.

5. P. L. K. Gross and E. M. Gross, "College Libraries and Chemical Education," *Science* 66 (October 28, 1927): 385-89.

6. J. K. McNeely and C. D. Crosno, "Periodicals for Electrical Engineers," *Science* 72 (July 25, 1930): 81-84.

7. Charles F. Dalziel, "Evaluation of Periodicals for Electrical Engineers," *Library Quarterly* 7 (July 1937): 354-72.

8. P. L. K. Gross and A. O. Woodford, "Serial Literature Used by American Geologists," *Science* 73 (June 19, 1931): 660-64.

9. Ingo Hackh, "The Periodicals Useful in the Dental Library," *Bulletin of the Medical Library Association* 25 (September 1936): 109-12.

10. Edward S. Allen, "Periodicals for Mathematicians," *Science* 70 (December 20, 1929): 592-94.

11. Harold Colson, "Citation Rankings of Public Administration Journals," *Administration and Society* 21 (February 1990): 452-71.

12. Thomas E. Nisonger, "A Ranking of Political Science Journals Based on Citation Data," *Serials Review* 19 (winter 1993): 7-14. The author ranked 65 of the 78 journals covered in the reputational study of Michael W. Giles, Francie Mizell, and David Patterson, "Political Scientists'

Journal Evaluations Revisited," *PS: Political Science and Politics* 22 (September 1989): 613-17. Two of their journals had ceased publication, and 11 were not covered in the *SSCI JCR*.

13. Thomas E. Nisonger, "A Methodological Issue Concerning the Use of *Social Sciences Citation Index Journal Citation Reports* Impact Factor Data for Journal Ranking," *Library Acquisitions: Practice and Theory* 18 (winter 1994): 447-58.

14. Sharplin and Mabry, "The Relative Importance of Journals Used in Management Research," 139-49.

15. Belen Altuna Esteibar and F. W. Lancaster, "Ranking of Journals in Library and Information Science by Research and Teaching Relatedness," *Serials Librarian* 23, nos. 1/2 (1992): 1-10.

16. Giles, Mizell, and Patterson, "Political Scientists' Journal Evaluations Revisited," 613-17. They received 215 usable responses—a 39.1 percent response rate.

17. Michael W. Giles and Gerald C. Wright Jr., "Political Scientists' Evaluations of Sixty-Three Journals," *PS: Political Science and Politics* 8 (summer 1975): 254-56.

18. David F. Kohl and Charles H. Davis, "Ratings of Journals by ARL Library Directors and Deans of Library and Information Science Schools," *College and Research Libraries* 46 (January 1985): 40-47. Usable responses were received from 50.6 percent of ARL library directors (43 of 85) and 71.1 percent of library school deans (47 of 66).

19. Donald A. Nielsen and R. Wayne Wilson, "A Delphi Rating of Real Estate Journals," *Real Estate Appraiser and Analyst* 46 (May-June 1980): 43-48. They received 100 responses from the first round (a 76.9 percent response rate). These 100 individuals were surveyed in the second round, for which 60 responses were received (a 60 percent rate).

20. Robert Swisher and Peggy C. Smith, "Journals Read by ACRL Academic Librarians, 1973 and 1978," *College and Research Libraries* 43 (January 1982): 51-58. Their response rate was 83.2 percent (357 of 429).

21. Thomas E. Nisonger, *Collection Evaluation in Academic Libraries: A Literature Guide and Annotated Bibliography* (Englewood, Colo.: Libraries Unlimited, 1992), 177-208.

22. Mary K. Sellen, *Bilbiometrics: An Annotated Bibliography, 1970–1990* (New York: G. K. Hall, 1993).

23. James A. Christenson and Lee Sigelman, "Accrediting Knowledge: Journal Stature and Citation Impact in Social Science," *Social Science Quarterly* 66 (December 1985): 964-75.

24. Norval D. Glenn, "American Sociologists' Evaluations of Sixty-Three Journals," *American Sociologist* 6 (November 1971): 298-303.

25. Giles and Wright, "Political Scientists' Evaluations of Sixty-Three Journals."

26. Nisonger, "A Ranking of Political Science Journals Based on Citation Data," 11.

27. Giles, Mizell, and Patterson, "Political Scientists' Journal Evaluations Revisited."

28. Nelson C. Dometrius, "Subjective and Objective Measures of Journal Stature," *Social Science Quarterly* 70 (March 1989): 197.

29. Giles, Mizell, and Patterson, "Political Scientists' Journal Evaluations Revisited," 614.

30. Ralph A. Weisheit and Robert M. Regoli, "Ranking Journals," *Scholarly Publishing* 15 (July 1984): 313-25.

31. Bonnie Snow, "Rank: A New Tool for Analyzing Search Results on DIALOG," *Database* 16 (June 1993): 111-18.

32. Howard D. White, " 'Bradfordizing' Search Output: How It Would Help Online Users," *Online Review* 5 (February 1981): 47-54.

33. Stephanie C. Haas and Vernon N. Kisling Jr., "The Use of Electronic Ranking to Analyze Scientific Literature Used in Research at the University of Florida," *Collection Management* 18, nos. 3/4 (1994): 49-62.

34. Conversation with Steven Sowell, Indiana University biology librarian, on December 9, 1994. Stephen P. Harter, Indiana University, School of Library and Information Science, and Patricia Riesenman, Indiana University Libraries Reference Department, also provided information about the RANK command.

35. Kris Subramanyam, "Citation Studies in Science and Technology," in *Collection Development in Libraries: A Treatise*, pt. B, ed. Robert D. Stueart and George B. Miller, Jr. (Greenwich, Conn.: JAI Press, 1980), 362-63.

36. Maurice B. Line, "Use of Citation Data for Periodicals Control in Libraries: A Response to Broadus," *College and Research Libraries* 46 (January 1985): 36-37.

37. William E. McGrath, "Ratings and Rankings: Multiple Comparisons of Mean Ratings," *College and Research Libraries* 48 (March 1987): 169-72.

38. Lancaster, *If You Want to Evaluate Your Library*, 90.

39. Kohl and Davis, "Ratings of Journals by ARL Library Directors and Deans of Library and Information Science Schools."

40. Thomas P. Howard and Loren A. Nikolai, "Attitude Measurement and Perceptions of Accounting Faculty Publication Outlets," *Accounting Review* 58 (October 1983): 765-76.

41. Jean-Louis Malouin and J.-Francois Outreville, "The Relative Impact of Economics Journals—A Cross Country Survey and Comparison," *Journal of Economics and Business* 39 (August 1987): 267-77.

42. Mary T. Kim, "Ranking of Journals in Library and Information Science: A Comparison of Perceptual and Citation-Based Measures," *College and Research Libraries* 52 (January 1991): 24-37.

43. Paul Reynolds, "Antarctic Serials," *SERIALST* (August 19, 1996).

FURTHER READING

General Discussions

Archibald, Robert B., and David H. Finifter. "Biases in Citation-Based Ranking of Journals." *Scholarly Publishing* 18 (January 1987): 131-38.

Beed, Clive, and Cara Beed. "Measuring the Quality of Academic Journals: The Case of Economics." *Journal of Post Keynesian Economics* 18 (spring 1996): 369-96.

Cnaan, Ram A., Richard K. Caputo, and Yochi Shmuely. "Senior Faculty Perceptions of Social Work Journals." *Journal of Social Work Education* 30 (spring/summer 1994): 185-99.

Dometrius, Nelson C. "Subjective and Objective Measures of Journal Stature." *Social Science Quarterly* 70 (March 1989): 197-203.

Gordon, Michael D. "Citation Ranking Versus Subjective Evaluation in the Determination of Journal Hierarchies in the Social Sciences." *Journal of the American Society for Information Science* 33 (January 1982): 55-57.

He, Chunpei, and Miranda Lee Pao. "A Discipline-Specific Journal Selection Algorithm." *Information Processing and Management* 22, no. 5 (1986): 405-16.

Lancaster, F. Wilfrid. "Evaluation of Periodicals." In *If You Want to Evaluate Your Library*, 87-108. 2d ed. Champaign: University of Illinois, Graduate School of Library and Information Science, 1993.

Line, Maurice B. "Changes in Rank Lists of Serials over Time: Interlending Versus Citation Data." *College and Research Libraries* 46 (January 1985): 77-79.

McAllister, Paul R., Richard C. Anderson, and Francis Narin. "Comparison of Peer and Citation Assessment of the Influence of Scientific Journals." *Journal of the American Society for Information Science* 31 (May 1980): 147-52.

Nisonger, Thomas E. "A Methodological Issue Concerning the Use of *Social Sciences Citation Index Journal Citation Reports* Impact Factor Data for Journal Ranking." *Library Acquisitions: Practice and Theory* 18 (winter 1994): 447-58.

Taylor, Roger. "Is the Impact Factor a Meaningful Index for the Ranking of Scientific Research Journals?" *Canadian Field-Naturalist* 95 (July-September 1981): 236-40.

Teevan, James J. "Journal Prestige and Quality of Sociological Articles." *American Sociologist* 15 (May 1980): 109-12.

Todorov, Radosvet. "Evaluation of Scientific Journals: A Review of Citation-Based Measures." In *Information Research: Research Methods in Library and Information Science; Proceedings of the International Seminar on Information Research, Dubrovnik, Yugoslavia, May 19-24, 1986*, edited by Neva Tudor-Šilovič and Ivan Mihel, 212-24. London: Taylor Graham, 1988.

Urquhart, John A. "Has Poisson Been Kicked to Death?—A Rebuttal of the British Library Lending Division's Views on the Inconsistency of Rank Lists of Serials." *Interlending Review* 10 (November 1982): 97-99.

Weisheit, Ralph A., and Robert M. Regoli. "Ranking Journals." *Scholarly Publishing* 15 (July 1984): 313-25.

Wiberley, Stephen E., Jr. "Journal Rankings from Citation Studies: A Comparison of National and Local Data from Social Work." *Library Quarterly* 52 (October 1982): 348-59.

Journal Rankings in Business

Albert, Joe, and P. R. Chandy. "Research and Publishing in Real Estate: A Survey and Analysis." *Akron Business and Economic Review* 17 (winter 1986): 46-54.

Brink, David R., and Karl A. Shilliff. "Journal Preferences of Management Teaching Faculty." *Library Acquisitions: Practice and Theory* 13, no. 4 (1989): 391-99.

Browne, William G., and Boris W. Becker. "Perceptions of Marketing Journals: Awareness and Quality Evaluations." *AMA Educators' Proceedings* 51 (August 1985): 149-54.

Coe, Robert K., and Irwin Weinstock. "Evaluating Journal Publications of Marketing Professors: A Second Look." *Journal of Marketing Education* 5 (spring 1983): 37-42.

———. "Evaluating the Accounting Professor's Journal Publications." *Journal of Accounting Education* 1 (spring 1983): 127-29.

———. "Evaluating the Finance Journals: The Department Chairperson's Perspective." *Journal of Financial Research* 6 (winter 1983): 345-49.

———. "Evaluating the Management Journals: A Second Look." *Academy of Management Journal* 27 (September 1984): 660-66.

Cooper, Randolph B., David Blair, and Miranda Pao. "Communicating MIS Research: A Citation Study of Journal Influence." *Information Processing and Management* 29 (January-February 1993): 113-27.

Doke, E. Reed, and Robert H. Luke. "Perceived Quality of CIS/MIS Journals Among Faculty: Publishing Hierarchies." *Journal of Computer Information Systems* 27 (summer 1987): 30-33.

Extejt, Marian M., and Jonathan E. Smith. "The Behavioral Sciences and Management: An Evaluation of Relevant Journals." *Journal of Management* 16 (September 1990): 539-51.

Fry, Elaine Hobbs, C. Glenn Walters, and Lawrence E. Scheuermann. "Perceived Quality of Fifty Selected Journals: Academicians and Practitioners." *Journal of the Academy of Marketing Science* 13 (spring 1985): 352-61.

Howard, Thomas P., and Loren A. Nikolai. "Attitude Measurement and Perceptions of Accounting Faculty Publication Outlets." *Accounting Review* 58 (October 1983): 765-76.

Luke, Robert H., and E. Reed Doke. "Marketing Journal Hierarchies: Faculty Perceptions, 1986-87." *Journal of the Academy of Marketing Science* 15 (spring 1987): 74-78.

Mabry, Robert H., and Arthur D. Sharplin. "The Relative Importance of Journals Used in Finance Research." *Journal of Financial Research* 8 (winter 1985): 287-96.

Nielsen, Donald A., and R. Wayne Wilson. "A Delphi Rating of Real Estate Journals." *Real Estate Appraiser and Analyst* 46 (May-June 1980): 43-48.

Nobes, Christopher W. "International Variations in Perceptions of Accounting Journals." *Accounting Review* 60 (October 1985): 702-5.

Outreville, J. Francois, and Jean-Louis Malouin. "What Are the Major Journals That Members of ARIA Read?" *Journal of Risk and Insurance* 52 (December 1985): 723-33.

Sharplin, Arthur D., and Rodney H. Mabry. "The Relative Importance of Journals Used in Management Research: An Alternative Ranking." *Human Relations* 38, no. 2 (1985): 139-49.

Smith, Charles A., and George D. Greenwade. "The Ranking of Real Estate Publications and Tenure Requirements at AACSB Versus Non-AACSB Schools." *Journal of Real Estate Research* 2 (winter 1987): 105-12.

Weber, Richard P., and W. C. Stevenson. "Evaluations of Accounting Journal and Department Quality." *Accounting Review* 56 (July 1981): 596-612.

Journal Rankings in the Social Sciences

Altuna Esteibar, Belen, and F. W. Lancaster. "Ranking of Journals in Library and Information Science by Research and Teaching Relatedness." *Serials Librarian* 23, nos. 1/2 (1992): 1-10.

Bayer, Alan E. "Multi-Method Strategies for Defining 'Core' Higher Education Journals." *Review of Higher Education* 6 (winter 1983): 103-13.

Blake, Virgil L. P. "In the Eyes of the Beholder: Perceptions of Professional Journals by Library/Information Science Educators and District School Library Media Center Coordinators." *Collection Management* 14, nos. 3/4 (1991): 101-48.

Buffardi, Louis C., and Julia A. Nichols. "Citation Impact, Acceptance Rate, and APA Journals." *American Psychologist* 36 (November 1981): 1453-56.

Burton, Michael, and Euan Phimister. "The Ranking of Agricultural Economics Journals." *Journal of Agricultural Economics* 47 (January 1996): 109-14.

Christenson, James A., and Lee Sigelman. "Accrediting Knowledge: Journal Stature and Citation Impact in Social Science." *Social Science Quarterly* 66 (December 1985): 964-75.

Colson, Harold. "Citation Rankings of Public Administration Journals." *Administration and Society* 21 (February 1990): 452-71.

Ellis, Larry V., and Garey C. Durden. "Why Economists Rank Their Journals the Way They Do." *Journal of Economics and Business* 43 (August 1991): 265-70.

Fabianic, David A. "Perceived Scholarship and Readership of Criminal Justice Journals." *Journal of Police Science and Administration* 8 (March 1980): 15-20.

Feingold, Alan. "Assessment of Journals in Social Science Psychology." *American Psychologist* 44 (June 1989): 961-64.

Garand, James C. "An Alternative Interpretation of Recent Political Science Journal Evaluations." *PS: Political Science and Politics* 23 (September 1990): 448-51.

Giles, Michael W., and Gerald C. Wright Jr. "Political Scientists' Evaluations of Sixty-Three Journals." *PS* 8 (summer 1975): 254-56.

Giles, Michael W., Francie Mizell, and David Patterson. "Political Scientists' Journal Evaluations Revisited." *PS: Political Science and Politics* 22 (September 1989): 613-17.

Glenn, Norval D. "American Sociologists' Evaluations of Sixty-Three Journals." *American Sociologist* 6 (November 1971): 298-303.

Haynes, Jack P. "An Empirical Method for Determining Core Psychology Journals." *American Psychologist* 38 (August 1983): 959-61.

Jones, John F., and Lois M. Jones. "Ranking Journals: A Citation Study of Social Work and Related Periodicals." *Journal of the Hong Kong Library Association,* no. 10 (1986): 9-16.

Kim, Mary T. "Ranking of Journals in Library and Information Science: A Comparison of Perceptual and Citation-Based Measures." *College and Research Libraries* 52 (January 1991): 24-37.

Kohl, David F., and Charles H. Davis. "Ratings of Journals by ARL Library Directors and Deans of Library and Information Science Schools." *College and Research Libraries* 46 (January 1985): 40-47.

Laband, David N. "Measuring the Relative Impact of Economics Book Publishers and Economics Journals." *Journal of Economic Literature* 28 (June 1990): 655-60.

Laband, David N., and John P. Sophocleus. "Revealed Preference for Economics Journals: Citations as Dollar Votes." *Public Choice* 46, no. 3 (1985): 317-24.

Laband, David N., and Michael J. Piette. "The Relative Impacts of Economics Journals: 1970-1990." *Journal of Economic Literature* 32 (June 1994): 640-66.

Lee, David, and Arthur Evans. "American Geographers' Rankings of American Geography Journals." *Professional Geographer* 36 (August 1984): 292-300.

————. "Geographers' Rankings of Foreign Geography and Non-Geography Journals." *Professional Geographer* 37 (November 1985): 396-402.

Liebowitz, S. J., and J. P. Palmer. "Assessing the Relative Impacts of Economics Journals." *Journal of Economic Literature* 22 (March 1984): 77-88.

Malouin, Jean-Louis, and J.-Francois Outreville. "The Relative Impact of Economics Journals—A Cross Country Survey and Comparison." *Journal of Economics and Business* 39 (August 1987): 267-77.

McBride, Ruth B., and Patricia Stenstrom. "Psychology Journal Usage." *Behavioral and Social Sciences Librarian* 2 (fall 1980/1981): 1-12.

Nelson, T. M., A. R. Buss, and M. Katzko. "Rating of Scholarly Journals by Chairpersons in the Social Sciences." *Research in Higher Education* 19, no. 4 (1983): 469-97.

Nisonger, Thomas E. *Collection Evaluation in Academic Libraries: A Literature Guide and Annotated Bibliography*. Englewood, CO: Libraries Unlimited, 1992, 177-208.

———. "Impact-Factor-Based Ranking of Library and Information Science Journals in the *Social Sciences Citation Index Journal Citation Reports*, 1980 to 1992." In *Fifth International Conference of the International Society for Scientometrics and Informetrics: Proceedings—1995; June 7-10, 1995*, edited by Michael E. D. Koenig and Abraham Bookstein, 393-402. Medford, N.J.: Learned Information, 1995.

———. "A Ranking of Political Science Journals Based on Citation Data." *Serials Review* 19 (winter 1993): 7-14.

Peery, J. Craig, and Gerald R. Adams. "Qualitative Ratings of Human Development Journals." *Human Development* 24, no. 5 (1981): 312-19.

Poole, Eric D., and Robert M. Regoli. "Periodical Prestige in Criminology and Criminal Justice: A Comment." *Criminology* 19 (November 1981): 470-78.

Sellen, Mary K. *Bibliometrics: An Annotated Bibliography, 1970–1990*. New York: G. K. Hall, 1993.

Shichor, David, Robert M. O'Brien, and David L. Decker. "Prestige of Journals in Criminology and Criminal Justice." *Criminology* 19 (November 1981): 461-69.

Stack, Steven. "Measuring the Relative Impacts of Criminology and Criminal Justice Journals: A Research Note." *Justice Quarterly* 4 (September 1987): 475-84.

Swisher, Robert, and Peggy C. Smith. "Journals Read by ACRL Academic Librarians, 1973 and 1978." *College and Research Libraries* 43 (January 1982): 51-58.

Tahai, Alireza, and G. Wayne Kelly. "An Alternative View of Citation Patterns in Quantitative Literature Cited by Business and Economic Researchers." *Journal of Economic Education* 27 (summer 1996): 263-75.

Tjoumas, Renee. "Professional Journal Utilization by Public Library Directors." *Serials Librarian* 20, nos. 2/3 (1991): 1-16.

Tjoumas, Renee, and Virgil L. P. Blake. "Faculty Perceptions of the Professional Journal Literature: Quo Vadis?" *Journal of Education for Library and Information Science* 33 (summer 1992): 173-94.

Vocino, Thomas, and Robert H. Elliott. "Journal Prestige in Public Administration: A Research Note." *Administration and Society* 14 (May 1982): 5-14.

———. "Public Administration Journal Prestige: A Time Series Analysis." *Administrative Science Quarterly* 29 (March 1984): 43-51.

Journal Rankings in Science

Chandran, D. "Evaluation of Biochemical Journals by Citation Indexing." *IASLIC Bulletin* 27 (1982): 121-26.

Dame, Mark A., and Fredric D. Wolinsky. "Rating Journals in Health Care Administration: The Use of Bibliometric Measures." *Medical Care* 31, no. 6 (1993): 520-24.

Fang, Min-Lin Emily. "Journal Rankings by Citation Analysis in Health Sciences Librarianship." *Bulletin of the Medical Library Association* 77 (April 1989): 205-11.

Singleton, Alan. "Journal Ranking and Selection: A Review in Physics." *Journal of Documentation* 32 (December 1976): 258-89.

Chapter Eight

Serials Processing in Libraries

This chapter addresses the major serials processing functions: acquisition, check-in, claiming, payment, fund accounting, routing, replacing missing issues, binding, and cataloging. These functions are often collectively referred to as *serials control*—"A general term used to encompass the many aspects of managing a serials collection."[1] The duplicate exchange of serials; housing, arrangement, and circulation; serial subscription agents; vendor evaluation; organization of serials work; and impact of copyright on serials are also covered in this chapter.

ACQUISITION

The logical first step in serials processing for libraries is acquiring the serials. This section focuses on the major components of the acquisitions process (in a broad sense): acquiring the serial, check-in, claiming, payment, and fund accounting.

Methods of Acquiring Serials

Traditionally, the majority of serials are acquired through subscription, although serials are also acquired through such other means as gifts, exchange, or deposit. This section discusses the basic methods whereby libraries acquire serials, except the exchange of serials is covered in more detail later in the chapter.

Subscription

Subscription is the most frequently used serial order method. The *Serials Acquisitions Glossary* defines *subscription* as "the arrangement by which, in return for a sum paid in advance, a periodical, newspaper, or other serial is provided for a specified number of issues or a specified period of time."[2] Typically, a serial subscription begins in January or covers a bibliographical volume[3] (which often but not always corresponds to a calendar year) or both. A *rolling-year subscription* is for a consecutive 12-month period, beginning with the month the subscription is placed.[4] A *bulk subscription* is for a large number of copies (usually 10 or more, according to the *Serials Acquisitions Glossary*) of a particular title to be sent to a single address, often for further distribution.[5]

Membership

A serial subscription is occasionally obtained through membership in a society, association, or organization. To cite a well-known example, *National Geographic* is acquired through membership in the National Geographic Society. In some cases, membership is required to procure the subscription; in other instances, optional membership provides a lower-cost subscription or some other benefit, such as the right to purchase the organization's monographic publications at a discount. Some memberships receive all an organization's publications, both monographic and serial, and thus may be considered the equivalent of a *blanket order*.

Standing Order

A *standing order,* sometimes called a *continuation order,* is officially defined as "a general order to a vendor or publisher to supply the volumes or parts of a particular title or type of publication as they appear, until notified otherwise."[6] The terms *Until Forbidden* or *Til Forbidden* are practically synonymous with standing order. In other words the library is telling the vendor to continue sending the item until told to stop, i.e., until the standing order is canceled. A standing order is not normally used for periodicals but is used for annuals, monographic series, and such law serials as pocket parts. Two crucial elements distinguish a standing order from a subscription. A subscription must be renewed (usually on an annual basis), whereas a standing order, once placed, remains in force until canceled or the ordered item ceases publication. Moreover, subscriptions are paid in advance, but standing orders are paid after each item is received.

Firm Order

A one-time, definite order for one or more items, the *firm order* is closed after the ordered material has been supplied. This order type is often contrasted to an approval plan (discussed below), subscription, or standing order. Firm orders are commonly used to acquire monographs. They are generally unsuitable for serials (because of the format's characteristic of continuing indefinitely), but in certain circumstances, firm orders are used in serial acquisitions. For example, single serial issues (needed for idiosyncratic collection development reasons or, more commonly, to replace missing copies) or a so-called nonsubscription serial (defined as one for which the publisher refuses to accept subscriptions or standing orders)[7] might be acquired through firm orders.

Gifts

Both solicited and unsolicited gifts may include serials. Examples of the latter would be

- newly founded serials that publishers send without charge to entice a library's interest;

- publications by political groups that are more concerned with disseminating their viewpoints than with financial remuneration; and

- individuals "cleaning out their closets."

Unsolicited serials whose sources are not readily apparent can create numerous processing problems, i.e., it is unclear why they arrived, there is no check-in record for them, etc.[8]

Solicited gifts include

- complimentary copies of journals published by the library itself or its parent organization and

- items subscribed to by benefactors and turned over to the library.

Chiou-sen Dora Chen classifies serial gifts into three categories: backfiles, continuous donations, and miscellaneous.[9] In the past many libraries have assigned a staff member to handle gifts or had a combined "gifts and exchange unit." Libraries should avoid giving the donor a statement of the gift's value for income tax purposes because under Internal Revenue Service regulations the donor rather than the recipient is supposed to evaluate the gift. Also, ascertaining a gift's fair market value requires much time and effort.

Approval Plans

Approval plans were developed in the 1960s as a method for quickly and efficiently bringing books into the library and giving overall direction to the collection's development. The library writes a profile with the vendor indicating the subject areas and nonsubject parameters (language, level, publisher type, etc.) in which it is interested in receiving material. Books matching the profile are shipped to the library on a regular basis (typically weekly) for review. The library is free to return unwanted items—thus the name *approval*. Periodicals are not received on approval plans, but such serials as annuals, yearbooks, and numbered monographic series can be included.

Deposit

The U.S. Federal Depository Program, whose purpose is to make federal government documents available to the citizenry, was formally established in 1895 and included 1,400 libraries by the early 1990s.[10] Both monographic and serial items are available. Participating libraries may be full depository or select depository. A full depository library receives all documents distributed by the Government Printing Office. For select depository libraries, the Government Printing Office provides a list of available items and the library creates a profile of what it wishes to receive, often listing specific serial titles. Select depository academic libraries must consider the information needs of local community members when selecting material. That the federal government is shifting toward the electronic distribution of information will have a profound effect on the depository system. Most states have depository programs for state documents. Government document serials are typically administered by a government documents unit rather than a serials unit.

Check-In

Check-in entails maintaining a record that a particular periodical issue has been received. Prior to automation, a Kardex file was traditionally used for serials check-in. Normally a Kardex is arranged alphabetically. Each entry might hold such basic information as title, place of publication, frequency, the vendor, the order type, the date the order was placed, the original requestor's name, routing instructions, binding instructions, payment record, and each number's receipt date. (The precise information will vary from library to library.) Check-in achieves the following objectives: inventory control for currently received periodicals, identification of missing or late issues for claiming, and tracking of payment records. Discussion on *SERIALST* concerns whether the old Kardex file should be retained after automation. Marcia Tuttle notes that in an integrated, automated system, a check-in record need contain only details on receipt because it can be linked to order and bibliographic records that contain the other information traditionally found in the Kardex.[11]

Claiming

In essence, a *claim* is a gentle little reminder to the vendor asking, "Where the heck is my serial issue?" or pointing out some other problem. Yet serials claiming is more complex than is initially apparent. Six types of serial claims or reasons for claiming have been defined by J. Travis Leach and Karen Dalziel Tallman and in the Association for Library Collections and Technical Services (ALCTS) *Guidelines for Handling Library Orders for Serials and Periodicals*.

1. A skipped issue. If issue number 4 arrives before number 3 was received, it is evident that an issue was skipped.

2. A lapsed subscription. In this instance, issues stop arriving because the subscription has expired.

3. A dormant standing order. The major question, of course, concerns how much time must have elapsed before a standing order is considered dormant.

4. An inactive new order. Although a subscription has been placed, the issues do not arrive.

5. A replacement. An issue actually received requires replacement because it is defective or was damaged in the mail.

6. An incorrect number of copies supplied. No further explanation is required.[12]

How long should one wait before placing the claim? Tuttle states, "There is no agreement among vendors or among librarians as to timing of claims."[13] The ALCTS *Guidelines for Handling Library Orders for Serials and Periodicals* recommends a library wait 45 to 60 days after the anticipated publication date before submitting a claim for a new subscription.[14] The B. H. Blackwell's Periodicals Services recommended the following guidelines for ongoing subscriptions: for daily publications, wait ten days since receipt of the last issue; wait two weeks for weekly publications, two months for monthlies, and five months for quarterlies.[15] Tuttle provides a table of recommended claiming periods, ranging from 30 days for a domestic daily to 300 days for a foreign semiannual. If the first claim is not successful, she recommends a second claim after six to eight weeks for domestic publications and three months for foreign ones.[16] Claiming policy and practice vary significantly among libraries and are influenced by such factors as available staff time and the automated system.

According to the ALCTS *Guidelines for Handling Library Orders for Serials and Periodicals*, five factors should be considered prior to placing a claim: the title's publication frequency; the issue's anticipated receipt date; vendor reports; a subscription's beginning date; and other considerations "such as country of origin, method of delivery (air or surface mail), external matters (strikes, political developments, etc.)."[17]

In the past claims were usually sent through the regular mail system. Now Electronic mail (e-mail) is increasingly used to transmit claims as more and more publishers develop electronic capacity. In mid-1996 an Indiana University claims specialist reported that she sent half her claims through e-mail.[18]

Payment

Payment may be viewed as a final step in serials acquisition. It involves processing publisher or subscription agent invoices, a function often termed *payment authorization*. Tuttle stresses this should be done promptly, with careful checking and in accordance with accounting principles.[19] Checks are normally issued by an accounting office outside the library to ensure a librarian does not go to Argentina or Brazil on the serials budget!

Periodical orders are normally renewed each year and paid in advance. A library typically receives an annual invoice during the late summer or early fall. Added charges through supplemental invoices have traditionally caused much consternation to librarians. Reasons for added charges include a price increase by the publisher after the subscription agent sent the invoice, a fluctuation in foreign currency exchange rates, and additional volumes issued by the publisher.[20] Tuttle emphasizes linking order, receipt, and payment records to, among other things, support claiming and create an audit trail[21] to demonstrate that the serials librarian really did not go to Argentina on the serials budget.

Periodicals are sometimes paid for through a *depository account,* in which a sum of money is paid in advance. The cost of subsequent orders is then deducted from the account's balance. Normally, a depository account would not be exclusively for serials.

One occasionally hears that libraries—to take advantage of subscription prices that are less expensive for individuals than institutions—should reimburse supporters who subscribe to journals in their own names and then turn over the received issues. This tactic entails both practical and ethical problems, however, and should be avoided. Such a tactic should not be confused with an "Adopt-a-Serial" program, in which a benefactor pays the subscription cost for a particular serial title, because, in the latter situation, the order would be placed through the library.

Fund Accounting

Sometimes termed *budget control, fund accounting* entails keeping track of serial expenditures as the library progresses through the fiscal year. Serials budgeting issues have been addressed in chapter 3.

Traditional financial accounting categories for library materials include allocation, encumbrance, expenditure, and balance. *Allocation* represents the initial amount of budgeted money. *Encumbrance* refers to funds that have been committed but not yet actually spent. The term *expenditure* is self-explanatory, as it reflects funds that have been paid out. *Balance* refers to the amount still available when encumbrances and expenditures are subtracted from the allocation. A related concept, sometimes termed *free balance,* reflects all unexpended funds.

Monthly financial reports according to these categories, which have been traditionally used for monographs, do not lend themselves especially well to serials for a variety of reasons, including add-on charges, the fact that serials expenditures are driven by a renewal cycle rather than uniform expenditures throughout the fiscal year, and the problem discussed in chapter 3—that the major serials budgetary issue concerns advance prediction of the current subscription list's inflation rate.

Many libraries find it helpful to keep track of serials expenditures according to such variables as subject or department; vendor; publisher; time period (e.g., on a monthly basis); country of origin; and expenditure category (i.e., current subscriptions, standing orders, replacements, etc.).

Automated serials control systems generally include a budgeting and financial accounting system. Serial subscription agent reports can provide assistance. Various software programs can support serials budgeting and financial control. Lynne Myers Hayman describes the use of dBase III+ at Beaver College library,[22] and Helen M. Shuster depicts the use of dBase III+ and Lotus 1-2-3 at Worcester Polytechnic Institute.[23]

Other Acquisitions Functions

Because of space limitations and the fact that this book emphasizes serials collection management rather than processing, other serials acquisitions issues will be noted but not discussed, including preorder searching and verification, order preparation, maintaining invoice files, renewals, cancellation, and mail sorting. Two textbooks, Chen's *Serials Management: A Practical Guide*[24] and Tuttle's *Managing Serials*,[25] offer thorough discussions of these issues as well as the entire serials acquisitions process.

CATALOGING OF SERIALS

This section introduces the important tools and major issues for serials cataloging and briefly describes the Cooperative Online Serials Program (CONSER) project plus union lists of serials. The machine readable cataloging (MARC) record and format integration are discussed in chapter 10. Frieda B. Rosenberg's chapter on serials cataloging in Tuttle's *Managing Serials* offers an excellent analysis of contemporary serials issues.[26]

Cataloging Tools

As stated in a recent cataloging textbook, "in current United States cataloging practice there is no comprehensive code of rules" that covers all aspects of cataloging.[27] Yet some tools are available for serials cataloging.

Codes for descriptive cataloging are often traced to Anthony Panizzi's so-called 91 Rules, published in 1841.[28] The code currently in force is the revised version of the *Anglo-American Cataloguing Rules*, second edition, issued in 1988, amended in 1993, and often abbreviated AACR2R. Descriptive cataloging of serials is covered in AACR2R's chapter 12, organized according to the eight areas of International Standard Bibliographic Description: title and statement of responsibility; edition; numeric/alphabetic/chronological or other designation; publication and distribution or both; physical description; series; note; and standard number and terms of availability. Chapter 21 covers choice of access points (i.e., ascertaining main and added entries). A vital supplement to the AACR2R is the *Library of Congress Rule Interpretations* (LCRI), published in its *Cataloging Service Bulletin*. As promised by its title, the LCRI outlines Library of Congress (LC) interpretations of the cataloging code as well as LC policies, which are generally followed by North American libraries.

Specific tools for serials cataloging have been produced by the CONSER project, described in a subsequent section. The *CONSER Editing Guide* provides practical instruction on MARC "tagging" (i.e., use of MARC fields and application of codes). Its companion piece, the *CONSER Cataloging Manual*, may be viewed as a training guide and reference source for serials catalogers. Also of use are some cataloging textbooks, such as Carol L. H. Leong's *Serials Cataloging Handbook*,[29] Bohdan S. Wynar and Arlene G. Taylor's *Introduction to Cataloging and Classification*,[30] and *Maxwell's Handbook for AACR2R: Explaining and Illustrating the Anglo-American Cataloguing Rules and the 1993 Amendments*.[31] The latter two contain a chapter on serials. The CONSER World Wide Web (WWW) site provides e-mail addresses for submitting serials cataloging questions to the LC.[32]

Bibliographic utilities, which offer databases of cataloging records, might also be viewed as cataloging tools. William Saffady has thoroughly documented the history of these organizations, which originated during the 1960s.[33] The OCLC Online Computer Library Center (OCLC), originally founded in 1967 to support the cataloging function among academic libraries in Ohio,[34] was providing services to 24,000 libraries in 63 countries by 1997. In January 1997 the WorldCat database of items cataloged through OCLC contained 34,378,135 unique records, of which 1,786,063 were for serials.[35] The two other major U.S. bibliographic utilities are the Western Library Network (WLN) and the Research Libraries Information Network (RLIN). The fourth North American bibliographical utility, Utlas International Canada (formerly the University of Toronto Library Automation System) was purchased by ISM Information Systems Management Corporation[36] in December 1992 and renamed the ISM Library Information Services.[37] Bibliographic utilities support serials cataloging in a variety of ways, including providing cataloging records, retrospective conversion, authority control, and creating union lists. CONSER records, discussed below, are available through OCLC. Problems with bibliographic utility databases include duplicate records for the same title, substandard records input by members, and the fact a serial may have changed (title, frequency, publisher, etc.) since a record was input.

Issues in Serials Cataloging

Instruction on cataloging serials is clearly not this chapter's purpose. Readers interested in practical guidance are referred to the various tools mentioned above. This section discusses some major serials cataloging issues.

- *To Catalog or Not*: Whether serials need to be cataloged has been a long-debated issue, with Andrew D. Osborn taking an ambivalent position.[38] Arguably, the major cataloging purpose—helping patrons access the collection—can be accomplished by creating a serials holding list rather than cataloging. In fact, holdings were often not included with the bibliographic record in the old card catalog and early OPACs. However, because OPACs can now easily link bibliographic records with holdings statements, cataloging of serials would be the desirable option.

- *Extent of Cataloging*: Even cataloged serials may not receive complete cataloging treatment (i.e., subject headings and classification numbers in addition to descriptive cataloging). Libraries that shelve serials alphabetically may not perceive a need to assign classification numbers. Ironically, Wynar and Taylor state that determining classification numbers and subject headings for serials may be less complex than for monographs because they are assigned at a more general level.[39]

- *Unit That Is Cataloged*: Cataloging of periodicals could theoretically focus on any of three units: title, issue, or article. For fairly obvious reasons, serials cataloging has usually focused on the title. It would be highly expensive to catalog issues or articles. Moreover, access to specific issues can be provided through holdings statements, and indexing and abstracting services provide access to individual articles. However, some academic libraries (e.g., the College of Charleston and Carnegie-Mellon University) plan to catalog individual articles.[40]

- *Level of Cataloging*: The AACR2R offers three levels of cataloging. The higher the level, the more detail included in the cataloging record. The LC uses an "augmented" level one for serials. The following is added to the bare-bones first-level description: A "general material designation" when appropriate (a serial computer file would be designated as such), parallel title or titles, the first statement of responsibility, the first place of publication, the first publisher, additional physical details, and series.[41] In practice, the amount of detail in the bibliographic description of serials varies widely among libraries.[42]

- *Source of Information for Cataloging*: AACR2R specifies that the chief source of cataloging information for a print serial is the title page of the first issue. If the cataloger does not have access to the first issue, the first available issue can be used. Prior to AACR2, cataloging was based on the latest issue. If there is no title page, as is often the case in a serial's first issue, an alternate title page, cover, caption, masthead, editorial pages, colophon, or other pages can be used.[43]

- *Choice of Entry*: Only infrequently is a serial's main entry an individual author. Thus, the usual choice is between title and corporate author (e.g., is the *Bulletin of the American Cat Fanciers Society* entered under title or the American Cat Fanciers Society?). In the 1970s considerable debate in the profession concerned a proposal to catalog all serials under title main entry, but the proposal was rejected by the Joint Steering Committee for revision of AACR in 1976.[44] However, AACR2 (published in 1978 and implemented by the LC in 1981) did restrict corporate author main entry in favor of more entries under title. In accordance with rule 21.1B2 of AACR2R, a serial is entered under corporate author only if it "emanates" from the corporate body and more than 50 percent of its content deals with the body's policies, procedures, and operations. In contrast, pre-AACR2 policy allowed corporate main entry based on wording in the title.[45]

- *Latest Entry Versus Successive Entry*:[46] Because serials frequently change title and, thus, form of entry, a long-standing issue that is still debated concerns which form should be used in the catalog. Three major options exist: earliest entry, latest entry, and successive entry cataloging. In *earliest entry cataloging*, a serial is cataloged under the earliest or original form of entry—an approach broached by Charles A. Cutter in 1876 and adopted in the United Kingdom in 1908. This approach offers the advantage of a single, consistent form of entry. The clear disadvantage is that a periodical could be entered under a vastly outdated title.[47] *Latest entry cataloging* lists a periodical under its most current title. This option was included in the 1908 and 1949 cataloging codes. A "Title Varies" note is used to link the current title with previous titles by presenting the history of title changes. *Successive entry cataloging* uses a separate catalog record for each significant title change.[48] Successive entry cataloging, which conforms to international standards, was contained in the 1967 Anglo-American Cataloguing Code and adopted by the LC in 1971. Notes, such as "Continues" and "Continued by," connect a title with its immediate preceding title and its immediate following title. This arguably constitutes a more economical, efficient approach than latest entry cataloging because no attempt is made to trace a journal's entire history in a single "Title Varies" note.[49] Successive entry cataloging can lead to a proliferation of records in the catalog, although this is not a significant issue in an automated environment. The Northwestern University Library began using a modified form of latest entry cataloging in 1985 because "meaningless title changes" required new successive entry records.[50] A fourth theoretical possibility is to catalog under the "best known title." This approach has not received much attention in the literature or actual practice because of the strong subjective and relativistic element in determining which title is the "best known."[51]

- *Electronic Journals and Access Versus Ownership*: Chapter 9 addresses electronic journal cataloging issues and the associated question on whether items not physically housed in the library should be entered into the OPAC.

- *Format Integration*: The question of format integration—consolidating seven separate MARC records for different formats (e.g., book, serials, computer files, etc.) into a single record—has received considerable attention from serials catalogers in recent years. Because this issue relates to the structure of the MARC record, it's discussion is deferred until chapter 10.

The CONSER Project

The CONSER project deserves attention because of the important role it has played in serials cataloging during the last two decades. The project began during the early 1970s under the auspices of the Council on Library Resources as a major cooperative effort to support serials retrospective conversion by creating MARC records, but it later shifted emphasis to support the cataloging of current serials. The acronym CONSER originally stood for Conversion of Serials Project, but in 1986 the name was changed to Cooperative Online Serials Program to reflect its new focus. According to the current CONSER mission statement, the program "facilitates identification of and access to serials by cooperatively building and maintaining a database of authoritative bibliographic records."[52] Useful histories or descriptions of the CONSER project have been written by a number of authors, including Suzanne Striedieck[53] and Bill Anderson.[54]

Since its inception, the number of CONSER members has increased. As of December 17, 1996, there were 31, organized into five membership categories. The three U.S. national libraries and the National Library of Canada are considered "National Members." The 16 "Full Members" include the Center for Research Libraries; the U.S. Government Printing Office; Harvard, Cornell, and Indiana Universities; and the University of Pittsburgh. The remaining categories are "Associate" (four members), "Affiliate" (three members), and "Enhanced" (four members). The U.S. Newspaper Program, jointly administered by the LC and the National Endowment for the Humanities, contributes records for U.S. newspapers to the CONSER database.

Prior to 1984 cataloging records from CONSER members were authenticated by the National Library of Canada (for Canadian records) and the LC for all other records. Once authenticated, a record could only be changed by these two national libraries. Due to the backlog caused by these policies, self-authentication by CONSER members was introduced in 1984, except for certain fields.[55]

A few CONSER projects should be noted. The A & I Coverage Project adds abstracting and indexing notes to bibliographic records. A large number of records have been contributed by the U.S. Newspaper Program. A Subject and Classification Task Force was appointed in 1988 to development CONSER guidelines for subject analysis (the majority but not all CONSER records contain subject headings).[56] CONSER is presently addressing cataloging issues posed by electronic serials.

The CONSER database contained about 260,000 records in January 1980,[57] 437,623 "fully authenticated" records at the end of 1988,[58] and 697,000 authenticated records by the beginning of 1995.[59] The database is contained within the OCLC Online Union Catalog. Each week OCLC sends tapes containing authenticated CONSER records to the LC and the National Library of Canada, who distribute them through their MARC services. The entire CONSER database is available in CD-ROM through *CD-MARC Serials*, which can be purchased from the LC. The National Library of Canada distributes CONSER records in microfiche through *CONSER Microfiche*. Paper-format CONSER records appear in *New Serial Titles*, except those contributed by the U.S. Newspaper Program.

Beginning in 1976 a newsletter, *Conser*, provided news about the project. In January 1994 this newsletter was renamed *Conserline* and converted to electronic-only format to be distributed free of charge on a semiannual basis in January and June.[60] Two major publications are the previously mentioned *CONSER Editing Guide* and the *CONSER Cataloging Manual*.

Although a major thrust of the CONSER project has been editing or updating records to reflect title changes, it has also addressed the issue of duplicate serial records in the OCLC database. The project's obvious benefit is the provision of reliable serials cataloging records that can be used for copy cataloging and retrospective conversion. CONSER records also support numerous other serials functions, such as collection management, library automation, interlibrary loan, the creation of union lists, and check-in. Furthermore, CONSER has played an important role in developing and maintaining serials cataloging standards. The CONSER project is generally viewed as a successful cooperative effort that created a high-quality national database of bibliographic records for serials. Striedieck asserts, "Most references to the CONSER database generally express satisfaction with the size and scope (with some notable gaps), though some have decried inconsistencies among records."[61]

Union Lists of Serials

A union list contains the holdings of two or more libraries. According to the *Serials Acquisitions Glossary*, it lists "items of a given type, in a certain field, or on a particular subject."[62] The list can assume a paper or electronic format. In recent decades considerable effort has been devoted to creating union lists of serials. These lists typically contain the periodical holdings of a consortium of libraries or the libraries in a geographical region such as a metropolitan area or a state.

The world's first serials union list was supposedly a 20-page pamphlet issued in Milan, Italy, in 1859; the initial American list, *Check List of Periodicals*, was published by Johns Hopkins University in 1876. In 1927 the American Library Association (ALA) published the *Union List of Serials in Libraries of the United States and Canada*, for which a second edition was published in 1943 and a third in 1965.[63]

In 1981 the *Directory of Union Lists of Serials* identified 60 separate serials union lists. The number had increased to 137 by 1988 when the *Directory*'s second edition was published.[64] The second edition, based on a survey conducted in spring 1986, summarized serials union list projects in 37[65] different states and the District of Columbia as well as Canada, Belgium, and India.

Union lists can contain bibliographic data and holdings or location data (or both)[66] while serving as a "finding" tool. A serials union list can support serials collection development and management and resource sharing by indicating a title's availability elsewhere. Such lists can also support a variety of other library functions, including technical services, interlibrary loan, and reference.

OTHER PROCESSING FUNCTIONS

The serials processing functions previously discussed are arguably the most important. This section directs attention to some additional functions (e.g., routing, replacing missing issues, and binding).

Routing

Distributing a serial issue to a select group of individuals is termed *routing*. Typically, library science journals are routed to staff members, who use them for selection or general professional development. Occasionally, an academic library will route journals to faculty as a form of current awareness or Selective Dissemination of Information (SDI). Special libraries often route journals to their clients because they tend to emphasize customized service. An issue is usually routed before being placed on the shelves for use by patrons, although in some cases libraries may purchase duplicate subscriptions for routing. The major processing issues concern maintaining a list of individuals to whom the issue is to be circulated, integrating routing into the serials work flow, and retrieving issues.

A system for routing new journal issues to faculty at the University of New Hampshire's Biological Sciences Branch Library has been described in the literature.[67] Deborah Naulty has explained the use of Lotus 1-2-3 software to support routing.[68]

Replacing Missing Issues

A replacement issue has been defined by Beth Holley and others as "a substitute for an item once purchased and received, which now requires reordering/repurchasing to complete a binding unit."[69] The term *replacement* is also applied to purchasing issues that were never received (i.e., the claim period lapsed or a subscription began after the first issue).[70] A periodical issue may be missing because it was lost, stolen, or damaged after receipt. Mutilation by patrons who cut out pages or articles (inexcusable behavior in the age of photocopying machines) represents a major cause of damage. To share an anecdote from the University of Manitoba during the 1970s, a patron once entered the Current Periodical Reading Room and asked for a pair of scissors. When asked why he needed them, he replied, "To cut an article out of a magazine!"

Issues are commonly identified as missing through the check-in and claiming process (if they were never received), during preparation for binding (for numbers that were lost, stolen, or damaged), or the public service function (if patrons can not locate a desired issue). In some instances, a library may decide not to replace the issue (e.g., it is superseded by a later cumulation or from a low-priority title).[71] To help, one can compile a list of missing items to replace, arranged by title and number, termed a *Desiderata* or *Want* list.

Options for obtaining missing issues include purchase (from the publisher, a serials subscription agent, or a periodical backrun dealer), duplicate exchange, gifts, microform, or getting a reprint. Under certain circumstances, copyright law allows photocopying an item from another library for replacement purposes—see the later section on copyright. The most appropriate option will vary depending upon the missing item and the resources (i.e., funds plus staff time) available to the library.

As Geraldine F. Pionessa comments, "Special procedures must be followed to handle the idiosyncrasies of replacement orders since they are more like monographic firm orders than subscriptions or standing orders."[72] Her article contains a more-detailed discussion. A replacement program at the University of Alabama library has been briefly depicted in the literature.[73]

Binding

Binding is a major and labor-intensive operation in many libraries. During 1995-96 Association of Research Libraries (ARL) libraries spent more than $25 million on contract binding[74]—of which approximately two-thirds was spent for serials.[75, 76] This section addresses the processing aspects of binding after the collection management decision to bind a particular title (discussed in chapter 4) has been reached. The discussion assumes that serials are bound at a commercial bindery rather than in-house. Major steps in the binding process are briefly outlined below:

- *Identifying titles ready for binding.* A binding schedule should be established for each title. Most periodicals are bound once a year, when a complete bibliographical volume is bound as a physical volume. Frequently issued titles that will be bound in more than a single physical volume may be sent to the bindery two or more times per year. Some libraries avoid sending the most recent issue to reduce patron inconvenience. Instructions on the binding schedule and binding requirements for periodical titles can be kept in a check-in file, a bindery file, or an automated system.[77] Some automated systems contain a "Binding Information File" that serves as a master file of pertinent binding data.[78]

- *Preparing binding shipments.* This is the process's most labor-intensive aspect. The issues are pulled from the shelves and taken to the binding preparation area. Generally a bibliographical volume should be bound as a physical volume, although Milan Milkovic states a thickness greater than $4\frac{1}{2}$ inches is undesirable.[79] The contents are checked for completeness and collated. Tables of contents and indexes would normally be included. Whether to bind covers and advertising is debatable, although the front cover should definitely be bound if it has artistic value or contains bibliographic information. The contents to be bound as a physical volume will be tied or bundled together. (A bottle of aspirin may be needed in cases where a title has switched size or when issues or pages are missing.) The shipment is normally packed in boxes, which are often supplied by the bindery. A binding ticket is printed or written in duplicate (one copy for the library, the other for the bindery) containing instructions for each volume to be bound. Typically, this includes the title, an identification number, account number, the date sent, type of binding, binding style, buckram color, lettering color, spine information (i.e., title, volume, date), slot (location on spine where information appears), and special instructions—often codes are used to save time and space.

- *Bindery pickup.* Generally, commercial binderies pick up and deliver binding shipments on a predetermined schedule. In some cases commercial trucking companies or the post office might be used. A binding or packing list of the included titles and volumes (arranged in alphabetical or some other systematic order) is usually created to accompany the shipment. The number of items in a shipment should be tabulated for record keeping.

- *Keeping record of volumes at bindery.* A temporary record of volumes sent for binding, the date sent, and the expected return date can be quite important for public service purposes. Some automated systems contain a "Binding Shipment File" and can print an "at bindery" list. Many integrated automation systems indicate items at the bindery and the return date in the OPAC.

- *Receiving shipments from binding; reshelving items; adjusting records to indicate return from bindery; preparing bindery invoice for payment.* These self-evident steps require little elaboration. The invoice and the bindery's packing slip should be checked for accuracy. Final processing steps, such as marking with the library's ownership stamp or inserting security strips may be performed prior to reshelving, although, depending upon contractual terms, the bindery might perform these steps.

During the last two decades, automated binding preparation systems have been developed by binderies and marketed by automation vendors (including subscription agents and bibliographic utilities) as part of serials control systems. Moreover, serials control systems that lack a separate binding module can sometimes be manipulated to support the binding process.[80] These systems can make binding procedures easy by automating record keeping and billing and printing binding slips. Yet much of the labor involved in the binding process, such as carrying items to and from the shelves and transporting items back and forth from the bindery, can not be eliminated by automation. Toby Heidtmann described the University of Cincinnati's use of Help-Net, a microcomputer-based binding preparation system from the Heckman Bindery,[81] and Harry H. Campbell and Wesley L. Boomgaarden wrote about the Ohio State University library's use of the General Bookbinding Company's automated binding system.[82]

Other issues include selecting and negotiating terms with a bindery, deciding whether to sign a contract or use a profile, determining standards of acceptable workmanship and service, budgeting for binding and keeping track of expenditures, ascertaining what type of binding is most appropriate for a particular periodical, migrating from a manual to an automated binding system, evaluating the interface between the binding component of one's automated system and the requirement's of one's commercial bindery, and handling incomplete volumes. A detailed discussion of binding may be found in Tuttle's *Managing Serials*.[83]

DUPLICATE EXCHANGE OF SERIALS

Exchange of materials (often duplicate or unneeded items) among libraries has been a long-standing practice. Although most types of material can be exchanged, serials are a major focus of duplicate exchange activity.[84] For illustration, at the University of California at Berkeley Library in the mid-1980s, 90 percent of exchange activity involved serials.[85] During the 1990 fiscal year, 75.8 percent (387,651 of 511,139) of the pieces acquired by the LC Exchange and Gift Division were serials.[86] Generally, either subscriptions or replacement issues are exchanged.

Library exchanges have usually been organized according to two models: one-on-one exchanges between libraries and organized exchange unions. The LC's Surplus Book Program does not precisely correspond to either model. Both organizational models and the LC program will be discussed separately.

Direct Exchanges Between Libraries

As implied, this organizational model refers to an explicit exchange agreement between two libraries (or other educational entities, such as museums or scholarly societies). The exchange can be with domestic or foreign institutions, although the latter is more common. These exchanges are usually for ongoing subscriptions rather than replacement issues, and nonserial items can also be included. Material published by the library or its parent university are frequently offered in the arrangement.

The three types of direct exchange used by the LC Exchange and Gift Division illustrate different theoretical approaches: priced, piece-for-piece, and open. In a *priced exchange,* the partners agree to provide each other materials of a set monetary value within a particular time period. Considerable bookkeeping is obviously required. A *piece-for-piece exchange* tabulates the number of specific items that have been exchanged, usually similar type items (i.e., "book for book, pamphlet for pamphlet, microform for microform"). The LC uses this approach to acquire serials, usually published by the exchange partner, that are not available through regular market channels. In an *open exchange,* libraries donate and receive without recording the number of exchanged pieces or their monetary value.[87]

The traditional motivations for entering direct exchanges follow:

- to obtain journals inexpensively;

- to obtain journals that are difficult or impossible to procure through regular subscription[88] (for example, in the late 1970s only 8 of the 555 serial titles received on exchange by the Johns Hopkins University Library were available through regular subscription channels);[89] and

- in a more idealistic sense, to contribute to a wider dissemination of publications from one's institution or country.

The origin of direct exchange between libraries has been traced to an 1840 Joint Resolution of the U.S. Congress authorizing the LC to exchange materials with foreign libraries. During the late nineteenth century, many U.S. academic libraries established exchanges with foreign institutes.[90] For example, in 1882 the Johns Hopkins University library instituted an exchange with the Royal Swedish Academy of Sciences' Mathematics Institute.[91] The University of California at Berkeley Library began its exchange program in the 1880s.[92] The number of exchange programs between U.S. and foreign libraries expanded in the post-World War II period.[93]

Considerable evidence suggests libraries have been scaling down or eliminating their exchange activities. In the early 1970s the Johns Hopkins Library had 390 exchange agreements, from which they received more than 800 serial titles and provided 660; but by the late 1970s, the figures had been reduced to 555 titles received and 325 supplied, based on 250 exchange agreements.[94] In 1995 it was reported that the Ohio State University libraries had recently eliminated 500 exchanges, keeping only a small number for such crucial areas as the former Soviet Union.[95]

Organized Exchange Unions

In contrast to direct agreements between two libraries, exchange can be organized among a large number of libraries, often under the auspices of a professional organization. Although precise details vary among exchange unions, material may be offered for free, for a set fee, or for reimbursement of postal costs. Typically, lists of materials available for exchange are circulated to members.

Perhaps the best-known duplicate exchange union is the United States Book Exchange (USBE). The USBE, originally termed the Universal Serials & Book Exchange and located in Washington, D.C., was founded in 1948 to help acquire material for European libraries that were damaged or destroyed in World War II. The USBE relocated to Cleveland, Ohio, in spring 1990.[96] A duplicate exchange program among libraries in the greater Dallas–Fort Worth area was run for a brief period during the mid-1980s by the University of Texas at Dallas Library.[97]

The ALA's Library Collections and Technical Services Division manages an exchange program termed the Duplicates Exchange Union.[98] This exchange operates the DEU-L listserv. The material is provided free except for postage reimbursement.[99]

Some more-specialized duplicate exchange unions are briefly summarized below:

> ASEE/ELD Duplicates Exchange. (for engineering materials)
> This exchange union is managed for the American Society for Engineering Education Engineering Libraries Division (ASEE/ELD) and coordinated at the North Carolina State University libraries. Lists of available materials along with claiming instructions can be sent to the coordinator, who will post them to members and on BACKSERV (see below).[100]
> In the last few years, several Internet-based listservs have been created for exchanging serials and other materials among libraries.

> BACKSERV. In autumn 1994 the serial subscription agent Readmore announced a new listserv, entitled BACKSERV, for the exclusive purpose of exchanging serials back issues among libraries.[101] BACKSERV's scope was soon expanded to include books.[102]

> BACKMED. In July 1995 BACKSERV was split in half when Readmore founded a second list, BACKMED, for the exchange of medical serials and books.[103] Both BACKSERV and BACKMED are now administered by Blackwells, which recently merged with Readmore.

> DUPSTM-L. This list offers STM journals and backruns for exchange among Australian libraries.

> COLLIBS. Although not explicitly created for exchange purposes, COLLIBS, a list for academic and research libraries in Australia, frequently offers serial backruns for exchange among Australian libraries.

> EUROBACK. This French-language list is for the exchange of serial backruns and books among European libraries.[104]

LIS-MEDJOURNAL-DUPLICATES. This list is primarily for the exchange of medical and health science journals among medical libraries in the United Kingdom, although non-U.K. libraries can also participate.[105]

NEEDSANDOFFERS-L. This listserv is for the exchange of legal materials, including law serials.

Subscription addresses for most of the above lists can be found in the WWW site "Back Issues & Exchange Services."[106]

Lydia A. Morrow's 10-week study of the ALA's Duplicates Exchange Union, conducted at the Governors State University library in Illinois, indicates that procuring missing serial issues through exchange is inexpensive but highly labor-intensive. She found that 33 hours and 22 minutes were required to review 66 lists (30.33 minutes per list), resulting in the procurement of 45 items (out of 183 requested). Although not stated by Morrow, the required staff time for reviewing lists averaged 44.5 minutes for each item obtained. However, the total out-of-pocket expense of $16.23 for postage reimbursement to the supplying library amounted to only 36 cents per item.[107]

The Library of Congress Surplus Book Program

A surprisingly large proportion of librarians are unaware that the LC acts as the official disposal agent for books and serials that have been discarded from U.S. federal libraries. Often termed the Surplus Book Program, the procedure apparently dates from the post-World War II period. This rather obscure program, administered by the LC Exchange and Gift Division's Receiving and Routing Section, has rarely been described in the literature (e.g., by A. Aime Deschamps,[108] R. Neil Scott,[109] and Thomas E. Nisonger[110]).

More than two million items per year are normally transferred from other federal libraries to the LC for disbursement through this program.[111] The LC uses a seven-level hierarchy for disposing of the material:

1. Selection for its own collection

2. Transfer, whereby federal libraries and agencies select items for transfer to their collections

3. International Exchange, in which staff select material for use in the LC's exchange agreements with overseas libraries, universities, museums, and scholarly societies

4. Domestic Exchange, in which LC staff select items for exchange with such U.S. partners as universities, museums, and historical societies

5. Project Ex, in which book dealers and libraries select sets of material and submit financial bids; if the bid is accepted, the money is used to purchase microfilming services for the LC, which are given "in exchange" for the selected items

6. Domestic Donation, whereby any tax-exempt U.S. library can select free material for its own use

7. Final Disposition, that is, the remaining items are contracted out for paper recycling

Federal libraries select free material at level two. Most other libraries take part at level six, in the Domestic Donation program; although they are also eligible to bid on material at level five, through Project Ex. The Domestic Donation program is open to U.S. university, college, school, and public libraries that qualify as tax-exempt institutions. However, special libraries attached to for-profit corporations as well as non-U.S. libraries are ineligible.

Serials represent a significant portion of the available material. Most of what the LC selects for its own use at level one in the disposal hierarchy are bound serials volumes, which are used to replace missing issues. During the mid-1980s the University of Texas at Dallas Library successfully filled numerous gaps in periodical backruns through the Domestic Donation program. The LC stresses that one should not make a trip to Washington, D.C., simply to select material because no guarantees exist about how much useful material will be available at any particular time.

Summary

The exchange function is closely tied to the paradigm of traditional librarianship, which focuses on the ownership of materials. Moreover, exchange can be costly because of its labor-intensive nature—although exchange listservs on the Internet should reduce the required labor. As noted above, considerable evidence shows libraries are downsizing their exchange operations; and with the increasing emphasis on electronic resources and access, one can assume this trend will continue. Yet a need for a limited number of serials exchanges, especially on the part of large research libraries seeking material from such locations as the former Soviet Union, will probably continue indefinitely.

HOUSING, ARRANGEMENT, AND CIRCULATION

Within the traditional library paradigm, a strategy must be adopted for housing and arranging serials (articles acquired through ILL or document delivery as well as electronic journals do not require housing or arranging in the library).

Several issues will be discussed here:

1. alphabetical versus classified arrangement,

2. integrated versus separate shelving,

3. open versus closed access,

4. other formats, and

5. circulation.

These issues often interconnect with each other as well as with other questions about cataloging policy (e.g., whether journals are classified).

Alphabetical Versus Classified Arrangement

These two basic approaches to the arrangement of periodicals[112] do not require explanation. According to Glenda Ann Thornton, who offers a well-done review, this issue has been debated in the library literature since at least the 1940s.[113] It is argued that an alphabetical arrangement offers the following advantages:

- The patron can retrieve periodicals more directly because it is not necessary to first look up a classification number.

- Processing costs are less expensive because classification numbers do not have to be assigned.

- Rearrangement is easier because periodicals will not be interfiled with books.

The disadvantages associated with an alphabetical approach follow:

- Titles dealing with the same subject will not be grouped together.

- Seemingly insignificant words in the middle of the title—such as *the, of, for,* etc.—can influence the arrangement and confuse the patron.[114]

- Generic titles—such as *Journal of, Transactions, Proceedings,* or *Bulletin*—may cause many different but similar-sounding titles to be grouped together, possibly confusing patrons.[115]

- Different titles from the same organization (e.g., *Journal* and *Bulletin)* would be shelved apart (this could be remedied by shelving under corporate author, although AACR2R has moved in the direction of title main entry).

- The patron may not know whether to look under a periodical's title or corporate author (e.g., would the *Journal of the American Society for Information Science* be shelved under *J* or *A*?).

- Title changes may cause the splitting of backruns (although using cross-reference shelf "dummies," i.e., wooden blocks representing journal titles, can help rectify this problem).

- Unindexed titles "tend to be more or less overlooked."[116]

A classified approach offers these benefits:

- Periodicals on the same or similar subjects will be grouped together, thus making browsing easy.

- The current and superseded forms of a journal's title will be grouped together (unless the title's subject focus has changed).

- Periodicals issued by the same corporate body would normally be collocated.

- Similar-sounding titles are usually scattered, thus possibly reducing patron confusion.

- Insignificant words in the middle of the title will not confuse patrons.

On the negative side, a classified approach does have disadvantages:

- Patrons can not go directly to periodicals because they must locate the call number.

- Assigning classification numbers requires staff time and processing costs.

- Indexing and abstracting may be more important than subject classification for providing access to periodicals.[117]

Numerous surveys exist on how libraries arrange their periodicals. Although their results are somewhat inconsistent, these surveys generally indicate that a majority of libraries use the alphabetical method, larger libraries are more likely to use a classified approach, and that a slight trend toward the classified arrangement exists.

Integrated Versus Separate Shelving

Classified bound periodical volumes can either be housed in a separate area or integrated with the book collection.[118] Integration with the book collection means books and periodicals on the same subject will be housed close to each other, thus making browsing easy. However, integration with the books means that periodicals will be dispersed throughout the collection and thus may be located a significant distance from the periodical indexes, which are required to access their content. Nancy Jean Melin even suggests that interfiling books and periodicals may require "extensive duplication" of periodical indexes.[119] Also, interfiling can complicate stack maintenance by requiring frequent reshifting caused by the rapid growth rate of periodicals. A survey conducted at the 1990 North American Serials Interest Group (NASIG) Conference revealed that of 50 libraries classifying periodicals, 28 (56 percent) intershelved them with monographs, 18 (36 percent) did not, and 4 (8 percent) used both methods.[120]

In their 1989 survey of American academic libraries, Jim Segesta and Gary Hyslop identified three basic patterns for arranging periodical backruns:

1. alphabetical—used by 59 percent;

2. classified and integrated with monographs—used by 21 percent; and

3. classified and separately shelved—used by 15 percent.

They also found that about three percent of the responding libraries, half of which were associated with community colleges, maintained periodical backruns only as unbound issues or on microfilm.[121]

Open Versus Closed Access

The terms *open access* and *closed access* are fairly self-explanatory. In open access the patrons directly retrieve items from the shelf, whereas in closed access the library employs a paging system to retrieve material for the patron. Open periodical stacks obviously offer greater patron convenience and allow browsing. Closed stacks may cost more because it is necessary to staff a paging system for retrieving patron requests. Melin notes that closed stacks can create political problems because inevitably some patrons will request special access.[122] From the positive perspective, closed stacks are presumed to reduce loss, theft, and mutilation. It is easier to conduct a use study in a closed-access setting. Moreover, incomplete volumes can be tied together on the shelves. If access is closed, a classified arrangement is not needed, and an alphabetical sequence makes reshelving by library staff easier.

Other Formats: Unbound Periodicals and Nonperiodical Serials

Most of the professional literature's discussion focuses on bound periodical volumes. Yet the basic issues discussed above also apply to unbound periodical issues and nonperiodical serials.

If bound periodicals are integrated with books, nonperiodical serials would obviously be treated in the same fashion. Tuttle asserts that if periodicals and books are shelved apart, a separate decision should be made for each type of nonperiodical serial. She offers the general guideline that noncirculating materials should be shelved with periodicals, and circulating items, such as analyzed monographic series, should be housed with books.[123]

Segesta and Hyslop's survey identified four approaches for unbound periodical issues:

1. alphabetically on open shelves in a current periodicals collection—used by 41 percent of responding libraries;

2. interfiled with bound volumes—used by 33 percent;

3. maintained in a closed area—used by 13 percent; and

4. an open shelf classified or subject arrangement in a current periodicals section—used by 11 percent.[124]

This discussion presupposes that serials are maintained as part of the library collection. Some serials are kept in library departments (such as the Cataloging department) for in-house use by staff, and occasionally serials may be located in faculty or administrative offices external to the library. A few additional issues beyond this book's scope include creating and maintaining current periodical reading rooms, handling serials on microform, staffing serials service counters, maintaining stacks, and providing security.[125]

Circulation

Variables affecting the circulation of serials include type of library, patron category, the loan period, type of serial (periodical or nonperiodical), and format (bound, unbound current issues, or microformat). Periodicals are usually circulated on a more restrictive basis than books (presumably because multiple patrons may wish to use the same issue or volume, and photocopying machines make reproduction of needed articles easy). Therefore, their loan period may be shorter or circulation may be restricted to certain patron categories (e.g., faculty or graduate students). Some research libraries don't allow periodicals to circulate. Yet nonperiodical serials are often circulated according to the same policy that applies to books. Given the number of variables, the number of potential circulation policies is so great that it is impossible to summarize them all. Indeed, the various branches and departments of a large library system may have different serials circulation policies.

University libraries sometimes allow periodicals to be checked out to a desk or study carrel with the provision they not leave the building. Melin stresses that the abstracts and indexes, which are necessary for accessing periodicals, should never be allowed to circulate.[126] Tuttle argues that libraries should provide a written statement of their circulation policy for all types of serials.[127] Other issues include policies on renewals, recalls, and fines for overdue items.

Summary

The basic policy issues discussed in the preceding sections all directly or indirectly affect two vital issues: availability and accessibility. *Availability* may be defined as success in finding an item on the shelf when the patron wants it; *accessibility* refers to the length of time required to place the item in a patron's hands. (For a discussion of availability studies as a collection evaluation method, see chapter 4.) Obviously, if an item is available, it is immediately accessible.

Trade-offs do occur between the concepts of availability, accessibility, and patron convenience. Circulating periodicals may be more convenient for the patrons who check them out, but it reduces overall availability and accessibility. Closed access may be less convenient for patrons wishing immediate access, but it probably increases availability.

As with many administrative questions, these fundamental issues do not necessarily have unambiguously right or wrong answers and, as pointed out by Thornton, have not been fully researched.[128] Such factors as library type and size, patron needs and expectations, indexing, available resources, and past practice will determine the best policy in any given case. A library is often "locked in by past decisions. If periodicals have not previously been classified, a major commitment of resources, depending on library size, would be required to change the policy. Thornton describes a proposed periodical reclassification project at the University of North Texas library with an estimated cost of $100,000.[129] According to Segesta and Hyslop's survey, only 5 percent (19 of 377) of U.S. academic libraries changed their basic arrangement of bound periodicals during the 1980s.[130]

SERIAL SUBSCRIPTION AGENTS

According to Tuttle, serial subscription agents are one of six types of vendors that market serials to libraries, along with standing order dealers, back issue dealers, publishers, distributors, and magazine fulfillment centers (see Tuttle for definitions of each of these).[131] Arguably, serial subscription agents are the most important players from the librarian's perspective. As the name implies, this commercial entity acts as a library's agent in acquiring current periodical subscriptions. The origin of subscription agents during the nineteenth century has been sketched in chapter 2.

For exceedingly useful practical guides to selecting and using serial subscription agents, refer to *Buying Serials: A How-to-Do-It Manual for Librarians*, by N. Bernard Basch and Judy McQueen,[132] or, more recently, Tuttle's *Managing Serials*. The latter includes appendixes listing specific telephone questions for subscription agents and other serial vendors about orders, claims, invoicing, management reports, and costs.[133] Arnold Hirshon and Barbara Winters publish a sample Request for Proposal for libraries wishing to select a subscription agent through competitive bidding.[134]

Services performed by serial subscription agents include

- placement of new subscriptions,
- subscription renewal,
- subscription cancellation,
- consolidation of serial orders,
- customized invoicing,
- claiming,
- replacement of missing issues,
- management reports analyzing serial collecting and expenditure patterns,
- projection of future serial costs,
- obtaining sample issues,
- table of content services,
- document delivery, and
- access to electronic journals.

The major benefits of using a serials subscription agent are the economies of scale and service. Perhaps the major drawback associated with agents is the cost of the service. Serial subscription agents are analogous to book wholesalers such as Baker & Taylor or Blackwell North America in that they act as a middle person between the publisher and the library.

However, some differences between serial subscription agents and book wholesalers should be noted. Book wholesalers generally offer a discount, but serial subscription agents often do not. A book wholesaler is a dealer who, like an automobile dealer, purchases the item and then resells it to the customer. A serial subscription agent is a broker who, analogous to a stockbroker, acts as an agent in the purchase of an item but never actually owns it.

Librarians sometimes forget that subscription agents provide services to publishers as well as libraries. Among these services are consolidating subscription payments into large lump sums, listing a publisher's titles in the subscription agent's catalog, and providing sales statistics. Some subscription agents, such as B. H. Blackwell's Periodicals Services, directly market periodical titles for which they receive a discount on the subscription price.[135]

How does a librarian find out about subscription agents and their services? Lenore Rae Wilkas provides a practical guide to serial subscription agents around the world entitled *International Subscription Agents*. Arranged alphabetically by country and by agents within a country, the book lists more than 250 agents in 63 different countries including the United States. All continents except Antarctica are represented. Up to 28 different categories of information are provided for each company, including postal address, cable address, phone number, fax number, the type of materials handled, the ability to support automation, service and handling charges, and invoicing policy.[136] One should also mention *Book and Serial Vendors for Asia and the Pacific*, edited by Thelma Diercks.[137]

Most of the leading serial subscription agents, including Faxon, EBSCO, Readmore, and Swets & Zeitlinger, now have home pages on the WWW that offer useful information on their policies and services. See appendix 3 for a listing of these sites, brief annotations, and their Uniform Resource Locator (URL) addresses.

A survey of 80 ARL university libraries, conducted in 1985 by Jan Derthick and Barbara B. Moran, found that all responding to the question used serial subscription agents, 76 percent of paid periodical subscriptions and 64 percent of paid nonperiodical standing orders were received through serial subscription agents; and that the average library used 17 different agents (ranging from 1 to 60).[138]

In an era that increasingly emphasizes smaller collections, access rather than ownership, and electronic publications, a question might arise about the future need for serial subscription agents. Yet, subscription agents appear to be striving to redefine their role by providing automated services, document delivery of specific articles, table of contents services, access to electronic journals, etc.

A relatively new phenomenon that might rival or eventually transform subscription agents is what Hirshon and Winters term a "pass-through fiscal agent." The agent provides Windows-based software that allows a library to directly order, claim, and transfer payment funds over the Internet using Electronic Data Interchange (EDI)—a concept explained in chapter 10. Furthermore, the library is supposed to receive a discount from list subscription price instead of the surcharge normally added by subscription agents.[139] This service was first introduced by RoweCom, founded in 1994 by Richard Rowe, a former Faxon Chief Executive Officer (CEO). RoweCom offers Subscribe software for conducting serials business transactions over the Internet. By means of a Bank One server, located in Columbus, Ohio, funds are transferred from the ordering library's to the publisher's bank account. In late 1996 the RoweCom WWW page asserted that their service eliminated supplemental invoices because the catalog reflects current prices, customers were paying 8 percent less than with their previous subscription agent, and an agreement had been reached with Ameritech for interfacing Subscribe with the NOTIS system. The University of California at Berkeley, the University of Pittsburgh, and the

Massachusetts General Hospital libraries were listed as major RoweCom customers.[140] In October 1996 *Library Journal* reported that the University of California at Berkeley library had saved more than $200,000 on its periodical subscriptions through this service.[141]

Before using a pass-through fiscal agent service, Hirshon and Winters recommend that a library test a service's software (which usually can be downloaded for free from the Net) and compare the cost of a 625 title sample, taken from its current renewal invoice, with the prices quoted by the pass-through agent. They also warn that any subscription cost savings might be partially offset by the need for more staff at the local library level to handle problems.[142] Because pass-through fiscal agents are a relatively new development, many unanswered questions remain about their benefit to libraries, the ultimate form of their services, and their effect on traditional serial subscription agents. However, these agents clearly represent yet another example of the Internet and WWW's potential impact on serials operations as well as the broader socioeconomic trend toward commerce on the Internet.

VENDOR EVALUATION

The term *vendor* is a derivative of the Latin word *vendēre*, which means "to sell." In a technical sense, a serials vendor is the entity from which the item was purchased and might be a serial subscription agency, a book jobber who sells standing orders, a back issue dealer, or the publisher. However, in common usage, the publisher is not considered a vendor.

A significant body of literature exists concerning book vendor evaluation. In 1988 the ALA issued guidelines for the evaluation of book vendors,[143] and the Vendor Study Group published an annotated bibliography listing more than 15 book vendor evaluation studies.[144] Unfortunately, considerably less has been written about the evaluation of serials vendors. The 1997 ALCTS *Guide to Performance Evaluation of Serials Vendors* states that in late 1994 only four published serials vendor evaluation studies could be identified.[145] In general, vendor evaluations may be conducted for the following purposes: monitoring a vendor's conformance with contract terms, comparatively evaluating different vendors, comparing service quality over a period of time to see whether it is increasing or decreasing, and establishing a benchmark on the level of service that should be expected. More specifically, the *Guide* includes improving vendor performance, providing data for bid situations, improving library procedures, providing management information, and promoting better communications among the library, vendor, and publisher among its reasons for doing a serials vendor study.[146]

A formal vendor evaluation study requires careful planning and implementation. Most of the steps outlined for a periodical use study in chapter 6 (problem definition, design, implementation, data tabulation, interpretation of findings, and action or recommendations) would also be applicable to a vendor evaluation study and need not be discussed here. However, the criteria and methodological techniques would obviously differ. The *Guide* outlines the major criteria for evaluation of serials vendors, including order placement, order renewal, claims, order fulfillment, materials' condition on receipt, accurate pricing, service charge or discount rate or both, invoices and credit, and "database quality and automated services."

The reader is referred to the *Guide* for specific methodological techniques—many of which involve gathering various types of statistics—for evaluating each of these criteria. The *Guide* correctly observes that different approaches may be needed for subscription agents and standing order vendors; one should ensure results are not affected by the library's own operations or factors beyond the vendor's control, such as mail strikes; vendors can be validly compared only if they have received similar order mixes; and study results obtained in one library may not be transferable to another. Moreover, a good study should combine objective and subjective methods: the former for criteria that can easily be measured, the latter for difficult-to-quantify factors such as the expertise and service quality of the vendor's staff.[147] It goes without saying that an automated system can greatly help data gathering.

Vendor evaluation and vendor selection are frequently juxtaposed in the serials literature—presumably because the two are logically connected and use the same criteria. For illustration, Derthick and Moran's 1985 survey of ARL libraries used a modified semantic differential rating scale (in which respondents rated terms from "very important" to "not important") to analyze the importance of 28 factors in the selection of serial subscription agents. They identified six factors as the "most significant:" "prompt renewals," "accurate invoices," "speedy claims," "rapid placement of orders," "country of serial's origin," and "agent experience."[148]

Serials vendor evaluation originally focused on subscriptions or standing orders. In recent years, however, attention has turned to the evaluation of commercial document suppliers, which provide individual articles. The basic evaluative criteria for a document supplier would be fill rate, cost, speed, and quality of reproduction.

Examples of serials vendor evaluations reported in the literature include studies at the University of Leeds (in the United Kingdom)[149, 150] and the University of Kentucky.[151] Evaluations of document delivery supplies have been reported at the University of Tennessee at Knoxville,[152] Iowa State University,[153] and Vassar College,[154] among other institutions.

ORGANIZATION OF SERIALS WORK

Prior to the 1930s most libraries combined the processing of serials and monographs, and only a few major libraries had a separate, centralized serials department.[155] Among the first libraries to create separate serials departments were the Boston Public Library in 1858, the LC in 1897, and the New York Public Library in 1911.[156] A significant movement toward creating separate serials departments can be traced to the mid-1930s, with the Minneapolis Public Library and the New York University library cited as notable examples of the earliest libraries that did so.[157] This movement was apparently given impetus by J. Harris Gable's influential article in the 1935 *Library Journal* advocating the creation of separate serials departments.[158] The development of technical service divisions as an administrative layer between departments and the library director dates to the late 1930s.[159] The prosperous 1960s have been termed the "high point" for the establishment of serials departments,[160] and in 1980 Mitsuko Collver noted a continuing trend toward centralized serials departments.[161] Beginning in the mid-1980s, several authorities (for example, Don Lanier and Norman Vogt[162]) noted a reverse trend toward the decentralization of serials operations, with budgetary concerns and the impact of automation acting as major factors.

The organization of serials work has frequently been couched in terms of "form versus function"—an issue that has received considerable discussion, sometimes highly emotional, in library literature. Note that organization by form implies a separate serials department to which the terms *centralized, integrated,* or *unified* have been applied. Organization by function logically implies a decentralized model, with the handling of serials dispersed through several departments and the absence of a serials department—a reality that exists in many libraries. Arguments in favor of a separate serials department follow.

Serials are important enough to warrant separate treatment.

Specialized knowledge and skill are required to handle serials.

Serials' unique nature requires different treatment than other formats.

Better coordination, cooperation, and communications are fostered.

Duplicate record keeping is avoided.

Arguments against an integrated serials department follow.

A serials "mystique" is created.

Automation can make decentralization of processing activities easy.

Although duplication is avoided in some areas, it may be created in others.

The department assumes a life of its own and protects its turf.[163]

Although recommending a centralized serials department based on the theoretical principle of "reciprocal interdependence" for effectively coordinating interdependent functions, Collver noted three reasons "for remaining unconvinced by arguments that one form is preferable to another": most serials organization has been based on the idiosyncratic requirements of particular libraries rather than long-range planning theory, research is lacking about the two forms' relative effectiveness, and it is uncertain which model will work best for future technological developments.[164] Although written in 1980, her cogent arguments remain valid today.

The slogans "form versus function" or "centralized versus decentralized" significantly oversimplify the issue's complexities. In the absence of a serials department, a serials unit may exist in one or more other departments (e.g., cataloging, acquisitions, or public services). Most unified serials departments do not perform all serials functions. Indeed, the definition of what constitutes a "department" can be ambiguous because such terms as *department, division, section,* and *unit* are used inconsistently among libraries. Moreover, these slogans do not address the relationship between a central library and branch locations or the type of materials handled by the serials department (e.g., periodicals only, periodical plus standing orders, etc.).

Numerous studies address the organization of serials work. Fred B. Rothman and Sidney Ditzion wrote in 1940 that 7 of 22 large academic libraries had independent serials departments, although 12 of 22 had serials units—presumably in other departments.[165] Gloria Whetstone's October 1959 survey found that 6 of 16 college and university libraries reported a separate serials department, 9 reported "separately-administered serials units" in larger departments, and one responded that both the cataloging and acquisitions departments were responsible for serials. However, none of the six serials departments were responsible for all serials functions.[166] Donald H. Dyal revealed in 1976 that 74 percent of 46 academic and large public libraries in Texas had serials departments.[167] In 1981 Diane Stine reported that 67.7 percent (21 of 31) of the medium-sized ARL libraries she surveyed had separate serials departments. In terms of functions handled, she identified seven different patterns:

1. order/payment, check-in/claiming, bindery and serials cataloging

2. order/payment, check-in/claiming, and cataloging

3. order/payment, check-in/claiming, and bindery

4. order/payment, check-in/claiming

5. cataloging, check-in/claiming, and bindery

6. cataloging and check-in/claiming

7. check-in/claiming[168]

Other studies also note the wide diversity of organizational models for serials. A 1990 survey of Canadian university libraries by K. Krishan revealed that 56.1 percent (32 of 57) had a separate serials department.[169]

One of the major unresolved issues concerns whether serials cataloging should be under the jurisdiction of the cataloging or serials department. Almost invariably serials collection management is not under the serials department's direct control.

Many libraries use a structure, which may be variously termed the "Serials Committee," "Periodicals Committee," "Periodicals Review Committee," or some variation thereupon, for formal approval of serials collection management decisions such as subscription and cancellation. These committees often seek to represent diverse interests, such as public and technical services as well as the central library and its branches.

Applying such business concepts as outsourcing, reengineering, downsizing, and the team approach to library management has recently become fashionable—some libraries now accept credit cards for fine payments! *Outsourcing*—when a library contracts with an external agency to perform specific functions—has generated considerable interest and concern within the library community. Although frequently used for cataloging, the concept is clearly applicable to serials processing. For a long time libraries have used commercial binderies to outsource the binding function. In their work on outsourcing, Hirshon and Winters suggest that libraries already outsource serials acquisition through the use of subscription agents.[170] In September 1996 a *SERIALST* posting noted that an unnamed "large university library" was considering outsourcing serials check-in,[171] and a follow-up posting asserted this option was being considered by "many universities."[172] However, Hirshon and Winters state that outsourcing serials check-in and claiming "should probably be done on a limited scale . . . where other attempts to increase in-house productivity failed," with the subscription agent the logical external candidate to perform these functions.[173] The obvious benefit of outsourcing is potential savings in staff cost. A drawback would be loss of local autonomy.

In conclusion, the innumerable models and permutations for the organization of serials work can be partially explained by so many different functional areas being involved with serials. Yet no "ideal" model exists. The most appropriate organizational structure will vary from library to library, depending on the particular needs of each. Moreover, the ultimate impact on serials organization of such factors as electronic journals, commercial document delivery, automation, and the application of business trends to library management can not be predicted. The organization and staffing for the handling of electronic journals will be covered in chapter 9.

COPYRIGHT

This section briefly introduces copyright law and examines its ramifications for handling serials in U.S. libraries. Serials lend themselves to copyright concerns because of the ease with which articles may be photocopied in full. For useful sources of information on U.S. copyright law, the reader is referred to the *Copyright Primer for Librarians and Educators*, second edition, by Janis H. Bruwelheide;[174] *Libraries and Copyright: A Guide to Copyright Law in the 1990s*, by Laura N. Gasaway and Sarah K. Wiant;[175] the section on copyright in the third edition of G. Edward Evans's textbook, *Developing Library and Information Center Collections*;[176] and the Copyright Clearance Center[177] and the U.S. Copyright Office[178] WWW home pages. The full complexity of copyright can not be addressed within this book's confines. Moreover, nothing stated in this section should be interpreted as constituting legal advice, which requires consulting an attorney—a frequently expressed caveat in books that address copyright.

Copyright Law

The copyright concept originated in English statutory and common law. It has been traced to the Court of Star Chamber's Royal Charter to the Stationers' Company in 1557 and the Statute of Anne, enacted in 1710.[179] In 1783 the Continental Congress proposed that the states enact copyright laws, and all but Delaware did so. The legal underpinning for copyright law in the United States may be found in the U.S. Constitution. Article 1, section 8, clause 8, states that Congress has the power "to promote the Progress of Science and useful Arts, by securing for limited Times to Authors and Inventors the exclusive Right to their respective Writings and Discoveries." The first U.S. copyright law was passed in 1790, and major revisions were passed in 1831, 1870, and 1909. The current U.S. copyright law, the Copyright Act of 1976, went into effect on January 1, 1978. The United States adhered to the Universal Copyright Convention in 1955 and the Berne Convention in 1989. (A short summary of U.S. copyright law may be found in Arlene Bielefield and Lawrence Cheeseman's *Libraries and Copyright Law*.)[180]

U.S. copyright law grants the copyright owner "exclusive rights" to derive benefit from the work's reproduction, distribution, adaptation, performance, or display. Yet this right is limited (and photocopying allowed) under the "fair use" concept and the privileges allowed to libraries under section 108 of the 1976 copyright law.[181]

The fair use doctrine dates to the nineteenth century[182] and, according to Clara D. Brown and Lynn S. Smith, was incorporated in the so-called Gentleman's Agreement of 1935 between the National Association of Book Publishers and the Joint Committee on Materials for Research.[183] Although fair use had no statutory basis until the 1976 copyright law, the concept received earlier recognition by the courts. Section 107 of the Copyright Act of 1976 outlines four criteria for determining fair use:

1. the use's purpose (i.e., commercial or educational),

2. the copyrighted work's nature,

3. the amount used in proportion to the whole work, and

4. the effect upon the copyrighted work's potential market value.

Nevertheless, in actual practice considerable ambiguity exists about the definition of fair use. One can not assume that a use for educational purposes automatically qualifies as fair use.

Section 108(a) of the 1976 copyright law allows a library or archives to photocopy one copy of a work under certain conditions: the copying is not done for "direct or indirect" commercial advantage; the library is "open to the public," or available to other researchers not affiliated with its institution; and copyright notice is included on the copied item.[184]

Impact of Copyright on Serials Management in Libraries

This section examines seven areas in which copyright affects serials and their management by or use in libraries:

1. library photocopying for patrons,

2. in-house photocopying by patrons,

3. photocopying for reserve,

4. digitizing for electronic reserve,

5. interlibrary loan borrowing,

6. photocopying to replace damaged or missing periodicals,

7. photocopying for classroom teaching purposes.

Library Photocopying for Patrons

Many libraries operate a photocopying center or otherwise provide photocopying services to their clients. According to section 108(d) a library can make for a patron a single copy of one article per journal issue if four conditions are met: the copy becomes the patron's property; the library has no knowledge the copy will be used for any purpose other than private study, scholarship, or research; a copyright warning is displayed in the area where photocopy requests are accepted; and the warning is also displayed on the request form.[185] Gasaway and Wiant stress that when photocopying requests are telephoned, faxed, or e-mailed to the library, an alternative method must be devised for delivering the warning at that time—such as reading it over the telephone or creating a fax submission form that includes the warning. If the photocopy is faxed to the patron, the library must destroy its copy because only one copy is allowed. No record keeping is required.[186]

In-House Photocopying by Patrons

Most libraries contain public access photocopying machines that patrons use on an unrestricted basis. Section 108(f)(1) states that neither libraries nor their employees will be held legally accountable for unsupervised patron photocopying if an appropriate warning sign is posted nearby photocopying machines.[187] The first edition of the *Copyright Primer for Librarians and Educators* recommended use of a warning worded approximately as follows:

Notice: The copyright law of the United States (Title 17 U.S. Code) governs the making of photocopies or other reproductions of copyrighted material: the person using this equipment is liable for any infringement.[188]

Gasaway and Wiant caution that if a library fails to post a warning notice it might face liability for copyright violations.[189] The *Copyright Primer for Librarians and Educators* recommends that libraries inventory and place appropriate warnings on all their reproducing hardware as well as consider attaching the warning on equipment that circulates to clients.[190]

Photocopying for Reserve

Academic libraries maintain a separate reserve section for teaching materials supporting the institution's courses. For serial materials, photocopies of journal and magazine articles are typically placed on reserve. Unfortunately, as stated by Kenneth D. Crews, "the copyright implications of reserves received little attention in the legislative history of the 1976 Copyright Act."[191] Indeed, section 108 does not mention photocopying for reserve.[192]

To address this dilemma, the ALA published in 1982 the *Model Policy Concerning College and University Photocopying for Classroom, Research and Library Reserve Use*, often termed the *Model Policy*. The policy states that if a faculty member requests only one copy be placed on reserve, the library may photocopy an entire article for that purpose. It also states that requests for multiple copies must conform to the following four guidelines:

1. "The amount of material should be reasonable in relation to the total amount of material assigned," considering the course's nature, subject matter, and level.

2. A "reasonable" number of copies may be made, considering the number of students in the course, the assignment's difficulty, and the number of other courses that use the same item.

3. Copyright notice should be attached to the item.

4. Photocopying should not be "detrimental to the market for the work," and at least one copy of the photocopied material should "generally" be owned by the library.

The *Model Policy* elaborates that "in most instances" a reasonable number of copies is less than six, but in "unusual circumstances" (e.g., considering the number of enrolled students, the assignment's difficulty, and the time available for completion), more are permitted. It also states that several photocopies of copyrighted articles, citing recent issues of *Time* or the *New York Times* as examples, can be placed on reserve if there is not sufficient time to request copyright permission. As with classroom use, "repetitive" photocopying of an item for different courses or successive years of the same course "normally" requires copyright permission.[193]

According to the *Copyright Primer for Librarians and Educators*, a library may place on reserve a photocopy made by a professor—the presumption being that the photocopy was made legally.[194] Gasaway and Wiant state a library can "occasionally" put on reserve a photocopy of an item not held in its collection—one owned by a faculty member or obtained on interlibrary loan (ILL)—so long as this is not a "general practice." They also recommend that the library rather than faculty decide what is a "reasonable" number of copies for reserve.[195]

Crews's study of university copyright policies found wide variety in reserve policies: 21 percent (17 of 80) were based on the ALA's *Model Policy,* described above; whereas 30 percent (24 policies) were based (presumably because reserve is viewed as a teaching function) to some degree on the Classroom Guidelines (discussed later) even though the guidelines do not explicitly address copyright.[196] This diversity in library reserve policies undoubtedly reflects the lack of legislative direction and the numerous issues involved.[197]

Digitizing for Electronic Reserve

In recent years numerous academic libraries have created "electronic reserves," which digitize articles and other documents. An ALA survey indicated that by spring 1996, 27 percent of Ph.D.-granting-institution libraries had an electronic reserve project in process.[198]

The Electronic Reserves working group of the Conference on Fair Use began meeting in September 1994 to develop fair use guidelines for placing material on electronic reserve. After several of their drafts were rejected by some professional organizations (notably commercial publishers),[199] the working group reached the conclusion that consensus was not feasible and that each library will have to develop its own policy.[200] One of these drafts, dated March 5, 1996, appears as an appendix in Bielefield and Cheeseman's *Technology and Copyright Law*.[201] Links to WWW sites addressing electronic reserve copyright issues may be found on Columbia University's Electronic Reserves Clearinghouse (on the Web).[202]

After examining university electronic reserve policies posted on the Internet, Bielefield and Cheeseman identified the following common stipulations: the system is restricted to students, faculty, and staff affiliated with the institution; one article per serial issue can be entered into the system; and items on electronic reserve must contain copyright notice as well as be deleted from the system when each semester is completed.[203]

Interlibrary Loan Borrowing

ILL sharing of journal articles is the aspect of serials management most affected by copyright. Section 108(g)(2)(d) of the 1976 statute authorizes ILL borrowing consistent with 108(d) described earlier, stating "nothing in this clause prevents a library or archives from participating in interlibrary arrangements that do not have, as their purpose or effect, that the library or archives receiving such copies or phonorecords for distribution does so in such aggregate quantities as to substitute for a subscription to or purchase of such work."[204] In 1976, the Commission on New Technological Uses of Copyrighted Works (CONTU), appointed by Congress to address diverse copyright issues, issued a set of guidelines covering ILL borrowing by libraries.[205] The so-called CONTU Guidelines are not statutory law, but they have been used by libraries for the last two decades with no reported case of a library in compliance with them having been sued for copyright infringement. Although some commercial publishers are challenging CONTU as too lenient for libraries, the guidelines remain the only widely accepted standard for ILL photocopying.[206]

If a library does not currently subscribe to a journal, it is limited to five requests per year from the journal's most recent five years. (The presumed rationale for this limitation is that a library is not supposed to use ILL as a substitute for a current subscription.) Termed the "Rule of Five," this policy is based on section 108(g)(2) of the 1976 copyright law, as interpreted by CONTU.[207]

To comply with copyright, the requesting library must keep a written record of each request for an item from the preceding five years of a journal to which it does not currently subscribe. Moreover, the records must be maintained for three years after the end of the calendar year in which the request originated. (As previously noted, these records provide a serendipitous source of potentially valuable serials management data.) The requesting library must state on its request that it is following the CONTU Guidelines. The "Rule of Five" applies regardless of the technology used to copy and transmit the article: photocopying, facsimile machine, or the Internet using Ariel. However, the *Copyright Primer for Librarians and Educators* advises that the photocopy from which a facsimile was transmitted should be destroyed to avoid making two copies.[208] A request for a currently unavailable article from the last five years of a periodical held by the library or to which a subscription has been placed does not count in the total.[209]

Although the "Rule of Five" ostensibly seems clear-cut, some ambiguities exist in its interpretation. Periodicals older than the five-year limit are not explicitly mentioned in the CONTU Guidelines, but, as noted in the *Copyright Primer for Librarians and Educators*, "they are not to be considered as fair game for unlimited copying. Copyright term is still in effect."[210] Does a multicampus library system, such as Indiana University, count as one library, eight libraries (if each campus is counted), or fifty-seven libraries (if each branch is counted)? A library may exceed the annual limit by paying a copyright fee on each request beyond five.

Photocopying for Replacement Purposes

Replacing missing or damaged periodicals is a well-known library problem (discussed earlier in this chapter). Section 108(c) states that a photocopy may be made to replace a "damaged, deteriorating, lost, or stolen" published item if the library, "after a reasonable effort, determined that an unused replacement cannot be obtained at a fair price."[211] The *Copyright Primer for Librarians and Educators* identifies "fair price" as "the prevailing retail price for an unused copy,"[212] although Gasaway and Wiant assert "it is impossible to define for all circumstances." They also state a "reasonable effort" requires contacting "commonly known U.S. trade sources" and the publisher or copyright owner or using an authorized reproducing service. Gasaway and Wiant further advise that a library probably does not need to replace an entire bound periodical volume if a single article has been cut out and that a photocopy for replacement purposes may be requested from another library if the requesting library originally owned the missing item, attempted to obtain a replacement, and certifies conformance with section 108(c).[213]

Photocopying for Classroom Use

Although not strictly a library function, photocopying for classroom use is an important issue that may affect library serials control. On March 19, 1976, the Ad Hoc Committee on Copyright Law Revision, the Author-Publishers Group, and the Association of American Publishers signed the "Agreement on Guidelines for Classroom Copying in Not-for-Profit Educational Institutions with Respect to Books and Periodicals," a document often called the "Classroom Guidelines."

The Classroom Guidelines specify that a single copy of a newspaper or periodical article or a single "chart, graph, diagram, drawing, cartoon, or picture" from a periodical can be made by or at the request of a teacher for research, teaching, or classroom preparation. Multiple copies for classroom teaching or discussion (not to exceed one per pupil) can be made by or for a teacher provided three conditions are satisfied: the brevity and spontaneity tests, the test of cumulative effect, and the placement of copyright notice on each copy. The brevity test allows photocopying "a complete article" of less than 2,500 words and one illustration, such as a chart, graph, diagram, drawing, cartoon, or picture, per periodical issue. The spontaneity test requires the copying be caused by "inspiration of the individual teacher," and "the inspiration and . . . its use for maximum teaching effectiveness are so close in time that it would be unreasonable to expect a timely reply to a request for permission." According to the cumulative effect test

1. an item can be copied for only one course in the school,

2. no more than two articles from the same author or three from the same periodical volume can be copied during a semester, and

3. there shall be no more than nine instances of copying for one course during a semester.

However, newspapers, current news periodicals, or other periodicals' news sections do not count in the limits under two and three. The guidelines conclude that photocopying can not be substituted for purchase of a periodical, a teacher can not repeatedly copy the same item from semester to semester, and students can not be charged a fee beyond the copying cost.[214]

The *Copyright Primer for Librarians and Educators* advises that the term *course* refers to a specific subject, so someone teaching several subjects to the same students can make nine copies a semester for each subject. Moreover, an instructor teaching two sections of the same course can make photocopies for both sections. However, items copied for a fall course can not be used again in the spring course because there would be sufficient time to obtain copyright permission.[215]

Additional Copyright Issues

The above review makes it apparent that to conform with specified conditions and restrictions, periodical articles may be photocopied for a variety of purposes. The question is less clear in regard to newsletters. Gasaway and Wiant assert that photocopying an entire newsletter is not permissible,[216] but Crews states that in some circumstances this might be considered fair use.[217]

The Copyright Clearance Center (CCC), a not-for-profit organization located in Danvers, Massachusetts, was established in 1978 to license photocopying. Its purpose is to make payment of copyright fees easy and to distribute the fees to the appropriate publishers. In 1990 more than 600,000 journals were registered with the CCC,[218] and the figure now approaches two million.[219] The CCC is presently developing the Academic Electronic Reserves program for collecting copyright fees for items placed on electronic reserve by academic libraries.[220] Crews points out some limitations to using the CCC: fees are set by the publishers and thus vary widely; not all journals can be licensed because some publishers do not participate; and "an administrative and financial burden" can result.[221]

Many serial publishers have created a formal provision for directly paying them the copyright fee at the time photocopies are made in the local library. For example, Haworth Press includes a "local photocopying royalty payment form," as part of the Document Delivery Service form reproduced in its publications.

Copyright balances an inherent tension between two conflicting principles: protection of intellectual property rights and provision of access to information. During the twentieth century, technological developments have affected copyright in at least two major ways:

1. they have made copyright infringement progressively easier: photo-copying requires less effort than mimeographing, and contemporary computer networks allow copyright violation with a keystroke; and

2. technology has advanced faster than the statutory law: the 1909 copyright statute did not foresee the influence of photocopying machines, and the current copyright law does not adequately address electronic media.

Considerable ambiguity exists in copyright law, with definitive legal answers lacking for many questions.

NOTES

1. Association for Library Collections and Technical Services, *Serials Acquisitions Glossary* (Chicago: Association for Library Collections and Technical Services, 1993), 27.

2. Ibid., 30. This definition is modified from the *ALA Glossary of Library and Information Science*.

3. A bibliographical volume, in the context of serials, refers to individual issues grouped together in a larger unit that generally corresponds to a year. A bibliographical volume can be distinguished from a physical or material volume, which refers to the items bound together in a single, physical unit.

4. Association for Library Collections and Technical Services, *Serials Acquisitions Glossary*, 26.

5. Ibid., 6.

6. Ibid., 29.

7. Ibid., 21.

8. Mark Kovacic, "Controlling Unsolicited Serial Publications," *Serials Review* 13 (spring 1987): 43-47.

9. Chiou-sen Dora Chen, *Serials Management: A Practical Guide* (Chicago: American Library Association, 1995), 70.

10. Barbara Kile, "Government Documents in Libraries and Society," in *Management of Government Information Resources in Libraries*, ed. Diane H. Smith (Englewood, Colo.: Libraries Unlimited, 1993), 4.

11. Marcia Tuttle, *Managing Serials* (Greenwich, Conn.: JAI Press, 1996), 152.

12. J. Travis Leach and Karen Dalziel Tallman, "The Claim Function in Serials Management," in *Advances in Serials Management: A Research Annual*, vol. 4, ed. Marcia Tuttle and Jean G. Cook (Greenwich, Conn.: JAI Press, 1992), 150-51; and Association for Library Collections and Technical Services, *Guidelines for Handling Library Orders for Serials and Periodicals*, rev. ed. (Chicago: American Library Association, 1992), 6.

13. Tuttle, *Managing Serials*, 178.

14. Association for Library Collections and Technical Services, *Guidelines for Handling Library Orders for Serials and Periodicals*, 7.

15. B. H. Blackwell Ltd. *B. H. Blackwell's Periodicals Services*. Available: http://www.blackwell.co.uk/libserv/periodicals/services/libhow.html#claims (Accessed summer 1997).

16. Tuttle, *Managing Serials*, 178.

17. Association for Library Collections and Technical Services, *Guidelines for Handling Library Orders for Serials and Periodicals*, 6.

18. Conversation with Judith A. Grannon, May 29, 1996.

19. Tuttle, *Managing Serials*, 164-66.

20. Association for Library Collections and Technical Services, *Serials Acquisitions Glossary*, 2, 30-31.

21. Tuttle, *Managing Serials*, 163-66.

22. Lynne Myers Hayman, "Serials Budget Management Using a Microcomputer," *Serials Librarian* 21, no. 1 (1991): 13-27.

23. Helen M. Shuster, "Fiscal Control of Serials Using dBase III+," *Serials Review* 15 (spring 1989): 7-20.

24. Chen, *Serials Management*, 75-98.

25. Tuttle, *Managing Serials*, 149-71.

26. Frieda B. Rosenberg, "Cataloging Serials," in *Managing Serials*, by Marcia Tuttle (Greenwich, Conn.: JAI Press, 1996), 195-234.

27. Bohdan S. Wynar, *Introduction to Cataloging and Classification*, 8th ed. by Arlene G. Taylor (Englewood, Colo.: Libraries Unlimited, 1992), 29.

28. Bohdan S. Wynar, *Introduction to Cataloging and Classification*, 7th ed. by Arlene G. Taylor (Littleton, Colo.: Libraries Unlimited, 1985), 40.

29. Carol L. H. Leong, *Serials Cataloging Handbook: An Illustrative Guide to the Use of AACR2 and LC Rule Interpretations* (Chicago: American Library Association, 1989).

30. Wynar, *Introduction to Cataloging and Classification*, 8th ed.

31. Robert L. Maxwell and Margaret F. Maxwell, *Maxwell's Handbook for AACR2R: Explaining and Illustrating the Anglo-American Cataloguing Rules and the 1993 Amendments* (Chicago: American Library Association, 1997).

32. Library of Congress. *CONSER Program Home Page*. Available: http://lcweb.loc.gov/acq/conser/ (Accessed March 8, 1998).

33. William Saffady, *Introduction to Automation for Librarians*, 3d ed. (Chicago: American Library Association, 1994), 232-57.

34. OCLC. *What is OCLC? / History of OCLC*. Available: http://www.oclc.org/oclc/menu/history.htm (Accessed March 8, 1998).

35. OCLC. *OCLC at a Glance*. Available: http://www.oclc.org/oclc/promo/4968ocgl/4968.htm (Accessed March 8, 1998).

36. "Utlas Purchased by ISM," *American Libraries* 24 (February 1993): 119.

37. ISM Information Services. Brief History of ISM Library Information Services. Available: http://www.ism.ca/lis/history.htm (Accessed March 8, 1998).

38. Andrew D. Osborn, *Serial Publications: Their Place and Treatment in Libraries*, 3d ed. (Chicago: American Library Association, 1980), 216-18, cited in Rosenberg, "Cataloging Serials," 197.

39. Wynar, *Introduction to Cataloging and Classification*, 8th ed., 163.

40. Rosenberg, "Cataloging Serials," 197.

41. Wynar, *Introduction to Cataloging and Classification*, 8th ed., 167.

42. Ibid., 162.

43. Ibid., 163-64.

44. Sally C. Tseng, "Serials Cataloging and AACR2: An Introduction," *Journal of Educational Media Science* 19 (winter 1982): 185.

45. Maxwell and Maxwell, *Maxwell's Handbook for AACR2R*, 274.

46. This issue has been summarized by Ellen Siegel Kovacic, "Serials Cataloging: What It Is, How It's Done, Why It's Done That Way," *Serials Review* 11 (spring 1985): 79-80; and Rosenberg, "Cataloging Serials," 211-15.

47. D. E. Davinson, *The Periodicals Collection: Its Purpose and Uses in Libraries* (London: Andre Deutsch, 1969), 182.

48. Bradley Carrington, Mary M. Case, and Sharon Scott, "Latest Entry Cataloging As an Option," *Serials Librarian* 17, nos. 3/4 (1990): 155.

49. Kovacic, "Serials Cataloging," 80.

50. Carrington, Case, and Scott, "Latest Entry Cataloging As an Option," 155-56.

51. Davinson, *The Periodicals Collection*, 183.

52. This statement and most of this section's factual information is from the Library of Congress, *CONSER Program Home Page*. Available: http://lcweb.loc.gov/acq/conser/ (Accessed March 1, 1998).

53. Suzanne Striedieck, "CONSER and the National Database," in *Advances in Serials Management: A Research Annual*, vol. 3, ed. Jean G. Cook and Marcia Tuttle (Greenwich, Conn.: JAI Press, 1989): 81-109.

54. Bill Anderson, "History of the CONSER Program (1986-1994)," *Serials Review* 21 (summer 1995): 1-16.

55. Ibid., 5.

56. Ibid.

57. Carol C. Davis, "OCLC's Role in the CONSER Project," *Serials Review* 6 (October/December 1980): 77.

58. Striedieck, "CONSER and the National Database," 89.

59. Anderson, "History of the CONSER Program (1986-1994)," 5.

60. "Changes Made to CONSER Newsletter," *OCLC Newsletter,* no. 207 (January/February 1994): 31.

61. Striedieck, "CONSER and the National Database," 94.

62. Association for Library Collections and Technical Services, *Serials Acquisitions Glossary*, 32.

63. Joseph A. Puccio, *Serials Reference Work* (Englewood, Colo.: Libraries Unlimited, 1989), 59-60.

64. American Library Association, "Directory of Union Lists of Serials, Second Edition," *Serials Review* 14, nos. 1/2 (1988): 115-59. Although outdated, this directory lists the beginning date, the number of libraries, the number of titles and holdings, the contact person, and an address for each project.

65. This figure is based on my own count.

66. Elizabeth Hood, "The Catalog Record and Automated Union Listing," *Serials Review* 14, nos. 1/2 (1988): 31, indicates that a union list's precise function (bibliographic versus holdings information) has been a long-debated issue, but the two are not mutually exclusive.

67. David M. Lane, Francis Hallahan, and Constance Stone, "Automatic Circulation of New Journal Issues," *College and Research Libraries News* 51 (December 1990): 1068-70. The authors refer to the system as "special circulation" rather than routing.

68. Deborah Naulty, "Implementing an Internal Routing Sticker System," *Library Software Review* 9 (January-February 1990): 32-33.

69. Beth Holley and others, "Replacement Issues: Where Do You Find Them and at What Cost?" *Serials Librarian* 21, nos. 2/3 (1991): 165-68.

70. Ibid.

71. Geraldine F. Pionessa, "Serials Replacement Orders: A Closer Look," *Serials Review* 16 (spring 1990): 66-67.

72. Ibid., 66.

73. Holley and others, "Replacement Issues," 165-66.

74. Martha Kyrillidou, Ken Rodriguez, and Kendon Stubbs, comps. and eds. *ARL Statistics, 1995-96: A Compilation of Statistics from the One Hundred and Twenty Members of the Association of Research Libraries* (Washington, D.C.: Association of Research Libraries, 1997), 36.

75. Martin Gordon, "Automated Binding Control: Libraries, Binders and Serial Agents," *Serials Librarian* 15, nos. 3/4 (1988): 158, reports a survey that indicates approximately two-thirds of an academic library's binding expenditures are for serials.

76. Dorothy C. Bailey, "Coping with a Binding Crisis," *Serials Review* 13 (winter 1987): 60, reported that 66 percent of binding expenditures at the Georgia Institute of Technology's library during four years were for periodicals and serials.

77. Chen, *Serials Management*, 103.

78. David U. Kim, "Computer-Assisted Binding Preparation at a University Library," *Serials Librarian* 9 (winter 1984): 37.

79. Milan Milkovic, "The Binding of Periodicals: Basic Concepts and Procedures," *Serials Librarian* 11 (October 1986): 107.

80. Marifran Bustion and Anne L. Highsmith, "Incorporating Binding Operations into an Integrated Library System," *Serials Librarian* 20, no. 4 (1991): 25-33. They describe use of the NOTIS system (even though it did not contain a binding module) to support binding at the Texas A & M University library.

81. Toby Heidtmann, "Help-Net Binding Preparation System at the University of Cincinnati," *Serials Review* 15 (spring 1989): 21-26.

82. Harry H. Campbell and Wesley L. Boomgaarden, "The Ohio State University Libraries' Utilization of General Bookbinding Company's Automated Binding Records System," *Serials Review* 12 (winter 1986): 89-99.

83. Tuttle, *Managing Serials*, 257-70.

84. Marion T. Reid, "Exchange History As Found in the Johns Hopkins University Library Correspondence," *Library Acquisitions: Practice and Theory* 8, no. 2 (1984): 99-103.

85. Joseph W. Barker, "A Case for Exchange: The Experience of the University of California, Berkeley," *Serials Review* 12 (spring 1986): 65. Barker states that "all Berkeley partnerships revolve around the exchange of at least one serial."

86. Imre Jármy, "Exchange and Gift: Almost 90 Percent of Permanent Collections Are Acquired Through the Division," *Library of Congress Information Bulletin* 49 (December 17, 1990): 429. The percentage is my own calculation from the raw data. Of these items, 78 percent were obtained by exchange and 10 percent through gifts; 12 percent were purchased.

87. Ibid., 430.

88. Barker, "A Case for Exchange," 64, cites serials published in countries with which U.S. trade is prohibited or that do not accept U.S. currency as examples in this category.

89. Pamela Bluh and Virginia C. Haines, "The Exchange of Materials: An Alternative to Acquisitions," *Serials Review* 5 (April/June 1979): 104.

90. Ibid., 103.

91. Ibid., 104.

92. Barker, "A Case for Exchange," 63.

93. Bluh and Haines, "The Exchange of Materials," 103.

94. Ibid., 104.

95. L. Hunter Kevil, "Summary of Responses to Gifts and Exchange Query," *SERIALST* (January 11, 1995). He cites and quotes Carol Pitts Hawks, the head of acquisitions at Ohio State University.

96. "USBE Rises Again," *American Libraries* 21 (May 1990): 403.

97. Tom Nisonger, "Sharing Books in An Age of Austerity," *Texas Libraries* 48 (spring 1987): 23-25.

98. Lydia A. Morrow, "The Duplicate Exchange Union: Is It Still Viable?" *Technical Services Quarterly* 12, no. 1 (1994): 43.

99. Rebecca H. Stankowski, "Duplicates Exchange/Serials Quest/Faxon Quest—Summary," *SERIALST* (February 14, 1995).

100. Orion Pozo, "Re: Question About Book Disp," *GIFTEX-L* (March 1, 1996).

101. Marilyn Geller, "The Serials Back Issues and Duplicate Exchange List," *ACQNET* 4 (October 19, 1994).

102. Stankowski, "Duplicates Exchange/Serials Quest/Faxon Quest—Summary."

103. Amira Aaron, "Announcing New BACKMED List," *GIFTEX-L* (July 19, 1995).

104. Birdie MacLennan, *Back Issues & Exchange Services.* Available: http://www.uvm.edu/~bmaclenn/backexch.html (Accessed March 8, 1998).

105. Ibid.

106. Ibid.

107. Morrow, "The Duplicate Exchange Union," 46-48. She concluded, "The DEU may not be viable for every institution, but it still remains an option to those institutions with available resources."

108. A. Aime Deschamps, "Free Books, Anyone?" *Catholic Library World* 41 (October 1969): 108-9.

109. R. Neil Scott, "The Duplicate Books Collection of LC's Exchange and Gift Division," *Southeastern Librarian* 30 (summer 1980): 86-90.

110. Thomas E. Nisonger, "The Library of Congress Surplus Book Program—A Single Library's Experience," *Library Acquisitions: Practice and Theory* 15, no. 1 (1991): 85-94. The discussion of the LC Surplus Book Program is based primarily on this article plus the author's personal experience making selection trips to the Library of Congress.

111. Jármy, "Exchange and Gift," 432, reports that approximately 2,250,000 items were transferred to the Library of Congress during the 1990 fiscal year.

112. The discussion of alphabetical versus classified arrangement is based primarily on Joseph C. Borden, "The Advantages and Disadvantages of a Classified Periodicals Collection," *Library Resources and Technical Services* 9 (winter 1965): 122-26.

113. Glenda Ann Thornton, "Physical Access to Periodical Literature: The Dilemma Revisited and a Brief Look at the Future," *Serials Review* 17, no. 4 (1991): 34-35.

114. Nancy Jean Melin, "The Public Service Functions of Serials," *Serials Review* 6 (January/March 1980): 41.

115. Thornton, "Physical Access to Periodical Literature," 34.

116. Borden, "The Advantages and Disadvantages of a Classified Periodicals Collection," 125.

117. Thornton, "Physical Access to Periodical Literature," 34. She cites Herman H. Fussler, "Characteristics of the Research Literature Used by Chemists and Physicists in the United States, Part II," *Library Quarterly* 19 (April 1949): 37, to support this contention.

118. A succinct discussion of integrated versus separate shelving and open versus closed access may be found in Nancy Jean Melin, "The Public Service Functions of Serials," *Serials Review* 6 (January/March 1980): 39-44.

119. Ibid., 40.

120. Thornton, "Physical Access to Periodical Literature," 39-40. When both methods were used, it was primarily because of separate policies at the central library and branches.

121. Jim Segesta and Gary Hyslop, "The Arrangement of Periodicals in American Academic Libraries," *Serials Review* 17 (spring 1991): 23. Their survey, mailed in January 1989, received 384 usable responses.

122. Melin, "The Public Service Functions of Serials," 41.

123. Tuttle, *Managing Serials*, 282.

124. Segesta and Hyslop, "The Arrangement of Periodicals in American Academic Libraries," 24.

125. Several of these issues are covered in the chapter "Public Services Issues" in Chen's *Serials Management*, 122-37.

126. Melin, "The Public Service Functions of Serials," 42.

127. Tuttle, *Managing Serials*, 278.

128. Thornton, "Physical Access to Periodical Literature," 36.

129. Ibid., 37.

130. Segesta and Hyslop, "The Arrangement of Periodicals in American Academic Libraries," 23.

131. Tuttle, *Managing Serials*, 101-3.

132. N. Bernard Basch and Judy McQueen, *Buying Serials: A How-to Do-It Manual for Librarians* (New York: Neal-Schuman, 1990).

133. Tuttle, *Managing Serials*, 101-28.

134. Arnold Hirshon and Barbara Winters, *Outsourcing Library Technical Services: A How-to-Do-It Manual for Librarians* (New York: Neal-Schuman, 1996), 96-104.

135. B. H. Blackwell Ltd. *B. H. Blackwell's Periodicals Services*. Available: http://www.blackwell.co.uk/libserv/periodicals/services/libhow.html#claims (Accessed summer 1997).

136. Lenore Rae Wilkas, *International Subscription Agents*, 6th ed. (Chicago: American Library Association, 1994).

137. Association for Library Collections and Technical Services, *Book and Serial Vendors for Asia and the Pacific*, ed. Thelma Diercks (Chicago: Association for Library Collections and Technical Services, 1995).

138. Jan Derthick and Barbara B. Moran, "Serial Agent Selection in ARL Libraries," in *Advances in Serials Management: A Research Annual*, vol. 1, ed. Marcia Tuttle and Jean G. Cook (Greenwich, Conn.: JAI Press, 1986), 11-12, 18-19.

139. Hirshon and Winters, *Outsourcing Library Technical Services*, 92-93.

140. RoweCom *Welcome to RoweCom*. Available: http://www.rowe.com/ (Accessed March 8, 1998 but the information cited in text has been taken down).

141. Michael Rogers, "RoweCom/Ameritech Enter Online Subscription Deal," *Library Journal* 121 (October 15, 1996): 23.

142. Hirshon and Winters, *Outsourcing Library Technical Services*, 93.

143. American Library Association, *Guide to Performance Evaluation of Library Materials Vendors* (Chicago: American Library Association, 1988).

144. Vendor Study Group, "Vendor Evaluation: A Selected Annotated Bibliography, 1955-1987," *Library Acquisitions: Practice and Theory* 12, no. 1 (1988): 17-28.

145. Association for Library Collections and Technical Services, *Guide to Performance Evaluation of Serials Vendors* (Chicago: American Library Association, 1997), 2.

146. Ibid., 4-5.

147. Ibid., passim.

148. Derthick and Moran, "Serial Agent Selection in ARL Libraries," 26-27.

149. Paul Robert Green, "The Performance of Subscription Agents: A Preliminary Survey," *Serials Librarian* 5 (summer 1981): 19-24.

150. Paul Robert Green, "The Performance of Subscription Agents: A Detailed Survey," *Serials Librarian* 8 (winter 1983): 7-22.

151. October R. Ivins, Mary K. McLaren, and Joyce G. McDonough, "Planning, Conducting, and Analyzing Serials Vendor Performance Studies," *Serials Librarian* 19, nos. 3/4 (1991): 221-23.

152. Alice Duhon Mancini, "Evaluating Commercial Document Suppliers: Improving Access to Current Journal Literature," *College and Research Libraries* 57 (March 1996): 123-31.

153. Wayne Pedersen and David Gregory, "Interlibrary Loan and Commercial Document Supply: Finding the Right Fit," *Journal of Academic Librarianship* 20 (November 1994): 263-72.

154. Kathleen Kurosman and Barbara Ammerman Durniak, "Document Delivery: A Comparison of Commercial Document Suppliers and Interlibrary Loan Services," *College and Research Libraries* 55 (March 1994): 129-39.

155. William Gray Potter, "Form or Function? An Analysis of the Serials Department in the Modern Academic Library," *Serials Librarian* 6 (fall 1981): 85.

156. Rosalee McReynolds, "Serials Librarianship," in *Encyclopedia of Library History*, ed. Wayne A. Wiegand and Donald G. Davis Jr. (New York: Garland Publishing, 1994), 574-75.

157. Potter, "Form or Function?" 86.

158. J. Harris Gable, "The New Serials Department," *Library Journal* 60 (November 15, 1935): 869-87.

159. Potter, "Form or Function?" 85.

160. Valerie J. Feinman, "Factors and Flexibility: The Form vs. Function Dilemma," in *Serials and Microforms: Patron-Oriented Management*, ed. Nancy Jean Melin (Westport, Conn.: Meckler, 1983), 150.

161. Mitsuko Collver, "Organization of Serials Work for Manual and Automated Systems," *Library Resources and Technical Services* 24 (fall 1980): 316.

162. Don Lanier and Norman Vogt, "The Serials Department: 1975-1985," *Serials Librarian* 10 (fall 1985/winter 1985-1986): 7.

163. Potter, "Form or Function?" provides a good overview of the arguments on the two sides of the issue. The arguments presented here are synthesized from Potter and other sources.

164. Collver, "Organization of Serials Work for Manual and Automated Systems," 308.

165. Fred B. Rothman and Sidney Ditzion, "Prevailing Practices in Handling Serials," *College and Research Libraries* 1 (March 1940): 167.

166. Gloria Whetstone, "Serial Practices in Selected College and University Libraries," *Library Resources and Technical Services* 5 (fall 1961): 284-85.

167. Donald H. Dyal, "A Survey of Serials Management in Texas," *Texas Libraries* 38 (winter 1976): 164-65.

168. Diane Stine, "Serials Department Staffing Patterns in Medium-Sized Research Libraries," *Serials Review* 7 (July/September 1981): 83-84. The percentage is my own calculation from Stine's raw data.

169. K. Krishan, "Organization of Serials in the University Libraries in Canada," *Canadian Library Journal* 48 (April 1991): 123.

170. Hirshon and Winters, *Outsourcing Library Technical Services*, 92.

171. Jamie Rowse, "Costing the Check-in Process," *SERIALST* (September 3, 1996).

172. Patricia Barbour, "Re: Costing the Check-in Process," *SERIALST* (September 3, 1996).

173. Hirshon and Winters, *Outsourcing Library Technical Services*, 92.

174. Janis H. Bruwelheide, *Copyright Primer for Librarians and Educators*, 2d ed. (Chicago: American Library Association; Washington, D.C.: National Education Association, 1995).

175. Laura N. Gasaway and Sarah K. Wiant, *Libraries and Copyright: A Guide to Copyright Law in the 1990s* (Washington, D.C.: Special Libraries Association, 1994).

176. G. Edward Evans, *Developing Library and Information Center Collections*, 3d ed. (Englewood, Colo.: Libraries Unlimited, 1995), 487-509.

177. Copyright Clearance Center. *Copyright Clearance Center Online*. Available: http://www.copyright.com/ (Accessed March 1, 1998).

178. Library of Congress. *U.S. Copyright Office Home Page*. Available: http://lcweb.loc.gov/copyright/ (Accessed March 8, 1998).

179. Gasaway and Wiant, *Libraries and Copyright*, 4-5.

180. Arlene Bielefield and Lawrence Cheeseman, *Libraries and Copyright Law* (New York: Neal-Schuman Publishers, 1993), 30-49.

181. Gasaway and Wiant, *Libraries and Copyright*, 20, 26, 43.

182. Ibid., 26-27.

183. Clara D. Brown and Lynn S. Smith, *Serials: Past, Present and Future*, 2d rev. ed. (Birmingham, Ala.: EBSCO Industries, 1980), 343. According to Kenneth D. Crews (in written communication with the author in August 1997), some consider this a pragmatic agreement rather than fair use.

184. 17 U.S.C. § 108(a). Online version available at the Cornell University United States Code Web Site. Available: http://www.law.cornell.edu/uscode/17/108.html (Accessed March 8, 1998). See Kenneth D. Crews, *Copyright, Fair Use, and the Challenge for Universities: Promoting the Progress of Higher Education* (Chicago: University of Chicago Press, 1993), 94-95, for a discussion of the debate over copyright notice's meaning.

185. Gasaway and Wiant, *Libraries and Copyright*, 48-49; and Bruwelheide, *Copyright Primer for Librarians and Educators*, 23-24. The warning's wording, as developed by the Register of Copyrights, should read as follows:
NOTICE: WARNING CONCERNING COPYRIGHT RESTRICTIONS The Copyright law of the U.S. (Title 17, United States Code) governs the making of photocopies or other reproductions of copyrighted material. Under certain conditions specified in the law, libraries and archives are authorized to furnish a photocopy or other reproduction. One of these specified conditions is that the photocopy or reproduction is not to be "used for any purpose other than private study, scholarship, or research." If a user makes a request for, or later uses, a photocopy or reproduction for purposes in excess of "fair use" that user may be liable for copyright infringement.
This institution reserves the right to refuse to accept a copying order if, in its judgement, fulfillment of the order would involve violation of copyright law.

186. Gasaway and Wiant, *Libraries and Copyright*, 49-50.

187. 17 U.S.C. § 108(f). Online version available at the Cornell University United States Code Web Site. Available: http://www.law.cornell.edu/uscode/17/108.html (Accessed March 8, 1998).

188. Mary Hutchings Reed, *Copyright Primer for Librarians and Educators* (Chicago: American Library Association; Washington, D.C.: National Education Association, 1987), 13. The second edition, by Bruwelheide, does not recommend precise wording for the warning.

189. Gasaway and Wiant, *Libraries and Copyright*, 51.

190. Bruwelheide, *Copyright Primer for Librarians and Educators*, 18.

191. Crews, *Copyright, Fair Use, and the Challenge for Universities*, 84.

192. Bruwelheide, *Copyright Primer for Librarians and Educators*, 22.

193. "Model Policy Concerning College and University Photocopying for Classroom, Research, and Library Reserve Use," *College and Research Libraries News* 43 (April 1982): 129. (Prepared by Mary Hutchings, ALA's legal counsel, March 1982.)

194. Bruwelheide, *Copyright Primer for Librarians and Educators*, 38.

195. Gasaway and Wiant, *Libraries and Copyright*, 148.

196. Crews, *Copyright, Fair Use, and the Challenge for Universities*, 88-90.

197. Ibid., 87, outlines 10 policy issues about reserve but concludes the 2 "crucial" issues concern the proportion of an item that can be copied and the number of copies that can be made.

198. Kerry Borchard, "Copyright Implications of Electronic Reserve Services," *Lita Newsletter* 18 (winter 1997): 9.

199. Written communication from Kenneth D. Crews to the author, August 1997.

200. Borchard, "Copyright Implications of Electronic Reserve Services," 9.

201. Arlene Bielefield and Lawrence Cheeseman, *Technology and Copyright Law: A Guidebook for the Library, Research, and Teaching Professions* (New York: Neal-Schuman, 1996), 195-99.

202. Jeff Rosedale. *Electronic Reserves Clearinghouse.* Available: http://www.cc.columbia.edu/~rosedale/ (Accessed March 8, 1998).

203. Bielefield and Cheeseman, *Technology and Copyright Law*, 105.

204. 17 U.S.C. § 108(g). Online version available at the Cornell University United States Code Web Site. Available: http://www.law.cornell.edu/uscode/17/108.html (Accessed March 8, 1998).

205. Texts of the CONTU guidelines may be found, in somewhat different forms, in *American Libraries* 7 (November 1976): 610 and at Coalition for Networked Information (CNI), *Information Policies: CONTU.* Available: http://www.cni.org/docs/infopols/CONTU.html Accessed March 8, 1998).

206. Conversation with Kenneth D. Crews on February 2, 1996.

207. Conversation with Kenneth D. Crews on November 4, 1994.

208. Bruwelheide, *Copyright Primer for Librarians and Educators*, 29.

209. Ibid., 19.

210. Ibid.

211. 17 U.S.C. § 108(c). Online version available at the Cornell University United States Code Web Site. Available: http://www.law.cornell.edu/uscode/17/108.html (Accessed March 8, 1998).

212. Bruwelheide, *Copyright Primer for Librarians and Educators*, 27.

213. Gasaway and Wiant, *Libraries and Copyright*, 47.

214. Texts of the Classroom Guidelines may be found in Crews, *Copyright, Fair Use, and the Challenge for Universities*, 195-97; and Gasaway and Wiant, *Libraries and Copyright*, 231-33, among other places.

215. Bruwelheide, *Copyright Primer for Librarians and Educators*, 34-35.

216. Gasaway and Wiant, *Libraries and Copyright*, 53.

217. Written communication from Crews.

218. Gasaway and Wiant, *Libraries and Copyright*, 68.

219. Written communication from Crews.

220. Copyright Clearance Center. *Electronic Reserves Service.* Available: http://www.copyright.com/stuff/ereserve.html (Accessed March 1, 1998).

221. Crews, *Copyright, Fair Use, and the Challenge for Universities*, 125-26.

FURTHER READING

Acquisitions

Chen, Chiou-sen Dora. "Processing Serials Acquisitions." In *Serials Management: A Practical Guide*, 75-98. Chicago: American Library Association, 1995.

——. "Serials Acquisitions Methods." In *Serials Management: A Practical Guide*, 65-74. Chicago: American Library Association, 1995.

Tuttle, Marcia. "Acquiring Serials." In *Managing Serials*, 149-72. Greenwich, Conn.: JAI Press, 1996.

Binding

Brothers, Rebecca L. "Automating Serials Binding: Guidelines for Customizing the Binding Procedure in INNOPAC." *Technical Services Quarterly* 11, no. 4 (1994): 45-59.

Chen, Chiou-sen Dora. "Preservation and Bindery." In *Serials Management: A Practical Guide*, 99-106. Chicago: American Library Association, 1995.

Kim, David U. "Computer-Assisted Binding Preparation at a University Library." *Serials Librarian* 9 (winter 1984): 35-43.

Milkovic, Milan. "The Binding of Periodicals: Basic Concepts and Procedures." *Serials Librarian* 11 (October 1986): 93-118.

Montori, Carla J. "Managing the Library's Commercial Library Binding Program." *Technical Services Quarterly* 5, no. 3 (1988): 21-25.

Root, Trudie A. "Inhouse Binding in Academic Libraries." *Serials Review* 15 (fall 1989): 31-40.

Check-in and the Kardex

Bardeleben, Marian Z., Martha M. Wilson, and Murray D. Rosenberg. "Off-Site Journal Check-In: An Alternative to Internal Control of Serials." *Serials Review* 9 (winter 1983): 56-62.

Farrington, Jean Walter. "The Serials Visible File: Observations on Its Impending Demise." *Serials Review* (winter 1986): 33-36.

Feick, Tina, and others. "Check-In with the SISAC Symbol (Bar Code): Implementation and Uses for Libraries, Publishers and Automation Vendors." *Serials Librarian* 23, nos. 3/4 (1993): 249-51.

McNellis, Claudia Houk. "A Serial Pattern Scheme for a Value-Added Predictive Check-In System." *Serials Review* 22 (winter 1996): 1-11.

Cataloging

Cole, Jim E., and James W. Williams, eds. *Serials Cataloging: Modern Perspectives and International Developments*. New York: Haworth Press, 1992. Also issued as *Serials Librarian* 22, nos. 1/2 and 3/4 (1992).

Kovacic, Ellen Siegel. "Serials Cataloging: What It Is, How It's Done, Why It's Done That Way." *Serials Review* 11 (spring 1985): 77-86.

Leathem, Cecilia A. "An Examination of Choice of Formats for Cataloging Nontextual Serials." *Serials Review* 20, no. 1 (1994): 59-67.

Leong, Carol L. H. *Serials Cataloging Handbook: An Illustrative Guide to the Use of AACR2 and LC Rule Interpretations*. Chicago: American Library Association, 1989.

Maxwell, Robert L., and Margaret F. Maxwell. "Serials." In *Maxwell's Handbook for AACR2R: Explaining and Illustrating the Anglo-American Cataloguing Rules and the 1993 Amendments*, 271-97. Chicago: American Library Association, 1997.

Mullis, Albert A., with Jenny Gascoigne. "Cataloguing and Classification." In *Serials Management: A Practical Handbook*, edited by Margaret E. Graham and Fiona Buettel, 75-94. London: published by Aslib in collaboration with the United Kingdom Serials Group, 1990.

Rosenberg, Frieda B. "Cataloging Serials." In *Managing Serials*, by Marcia Tuttle, 195-234. Greenwich, Conn.: JAI Press, 1996.

Smith, Lynn S. *A Practical Approach to Serials Cataloging*. Greenwich, Conn.: JAI Press, 1978.

Tseng, Sally C. "Serials Cataloging and AACR2: An Introduction." *Journal of Educational Media Science* 19 (winter 1982): 177-214.

CONSER

Anderson, Bill. "History of the CONSER Program (1986-1994)." *Serials Review* 21 (summer 1995): 1-16.

Bartley, Linda K., and Regina R. Reynolds. "CONSER: Revolution and Evolution." *Cataloging and Classification Quarterly* 8, nos. 3/4 (1988): 47-66.

Striedieck, Suzanne. "CONSER and the National Database." In *Advances in Serials Management: A Research Annual*. Vol. 3, edited by Jean G. Cook and Marcia Tuttle, 81-109. Greenwich, Conn.: JAI Press, 1989.

Union Lists

American Library Association. "Directory of Union Lists of Serials, Second Edition." *Serials Review* 14, nos. 1/2 (1988): 115-59.

Hepfer, Cindy. "Union Listing: A Literature Review." *Serials Review* 14, nos. 1/2 (1988): 99-113.

Schaffner, Ann C., guest ed. "Perspectives on the Future of Union Listing." *Serials Review* 19 (fall 1993): 71-78, 94.

Claiming

Bustion, Marifran, and Elizabeth Parang. "The Cost Effectiveness of Claiming." *Serials Librarian* 23, nos. 3/4 (1993): 297-99.

Carlson, Barbara A. "Claiming Periodicals: The 'Trembling Balance' in the 'Feud of Want and Have.'" In *Legal and Ethical Issues in Acquisitions*, edited by Katina Strauch and Bruce Strauch, 119-27. New York: Haworth Press, 1990.

Leach, J. Travis, and Karen Dalziel Tallman. "The Claim Function in Serials Management." In *Advances in Serials Management: A Research Annual*. Vol. 4, edited by Marcia Tuttle and Jean G. Cook, 149-69. Greenwich, Conn.: JAI Press, 1992.

Lively, Donna Padgett, and Lisa A. Macklin. "Taming the Claims Monster: Some Methods of Measuring and Improving the Efficiency of Claiming Through a Vendor." *Serials Librarian* 24, nos. 3/4 (1994): 245-47.

Copyright

Bielefield, Arlene, and Lawrence Cheeseman. *Libraries and Copyright Law*. New York: Neal-Schuman, 1993.

———. *Technology and Copyright Law: A Guidebook for the Library, Research, and Teaching Professions*. New York: Neal-Schuman, 1996.

Bruwelheide, Janis. *Copyright Primer for Librarians and Educators*. 2d ed. Chicago: American Library Association; Washington, D.C.: National Education Association, 1995.

Crews, Kenneth D. *Copyright, Fair Use, and the Challenge for Universities: Promoting the Progress of Higher Education*. Chicago: University of Chicago Press, 1993.

———. "Copyright Law and Information Policy Planning: Public Rights of Use in the 1990s and Beyond." *Journal of Government Information* 22 (March/April 1995): 87-99.

———. "What Qualifies as 'Fair Use'?" *Chronicle of Higher Education* 42 (May 17, 1996): B1-B2.

Gasaway, Laura N., and Sarah K. Wiant. *Libraries and Copyright: A Guide to Copyright Law in the 1990s*. Washington, D.C.: Special Libraries Association, 1994.

"Model Policy Concerning College and University Photocopying for Classroom, Research, and Library Reserve Use." *College and Research Libraries News* 43 (April 1982): 127-31. (Policy prepared by Mary Hutchings, ALA's legal counsel, March 1982.)

"New Rules on Photocopy Limits and Classroom Use." *American Libraries* 7 (November 1976): 610-11.

Reed, Mary Hutchings. *The Copyright Primer for Librarians and Educators*. Chicago: American Library Association; Washington, D.C.: National Education Association, 1987.

Weil, Ben H., and Barbara F. Polansky. "Copyright, Serials, and the Impacts of Technology." *Serials Review* 12 (summer and fall 1986): 25-32.

Duplicate Exchange of Serials

Barker, Joseph W. "A Case for Exchange: The Experience of the University of California, Berkeley." *Serials Review* 12 (spring 1986): 63-73.

Bluh, Pamela, and Virginia C. Haines. "The Exchange of Materials: An Alternative to Acquisitions." *Serials Review* 5 (April/June 1979): 103-8.

Eggleton, Richard. "The ALA Duplicates Exchange Union—A Study and Evaluation." *Library Resources and Technical Services* 19 (1975): 148-63.

Jármy, Imre. "Exchange and Gift: Almost 90 Percent of Permanent Collections Are Acquired Through the Division." *Library of Congress Information Bulletin* 49 (December 17, 1990): 429-32.

McKinley, Margaret. "The Exchange Program at UCLA: 1932 through 1986." *Serials Review* 12 (spring 1986): 75-80.

Morrow, Lydia A. "The Duplicate Exchange Union: Is It Still Viable?" *Technical Services Quarterly* 12, no. 1 (1994): 43-48.

Reid, Marion T. "Exchange History As Found in the Johns Hopkins University Library Correspondence." *Library Acquisitions: Practice and Theory* 8, no. 2 (1984): 99-103.

Stevens, Jana K., Jade G. Kelly, and Richard G. Irons. "Cost-Effectiveness of Soviet Serial Exchanges." *Library Resources and Technical Services* 26 (April/June 1982): 151-55.

Yu, Priscilla C. "Cost Analysis: Domestic Serials Exchanges." *Serials Review* 8 (fall 1982): 79-82.

——. "Duplicates Exchange Union: An Update." *Serials Review* 11 (fall 1985): 59-64.

Housing, Arrangement, and Circulation

Borden, Joseph C. "The Advantages and Disadvantages of a Classified Periodicals Collection." *Library Resources and Technical Services* 9 (winter 1965): 122-26.

Melin, Nancy Jean. "The Public Service Functions of Serials." *Serials Review* 6 (January/March 1980): 39-44.

Pierson, Robert M. "Where Shall We Shelve Bound Periodicals? Further Notes." *Library Resources and Technical Services* 10 (summer 1966): 290-94.

Segesta, Jim, and Gary Hyslop. "The Arrangement of Periodicals in American Academic Libraries." *Serials Review* 17 (spring 1991): 21-28, 40.

Thornton, Glenda Ann. "Physical Access to Periodical Literature: The Dilemma Revisited and a Brief Look at the Future." *Serials Review* 17, no. 4 (1991): 33-42.

Organization of Serials Work

Buckeye, Nancy. "The Library Serials Committee: How to Balance Decreasing Budgets with Collection Development Needs." *Serials Review* 1 (July-September 1975): 5-7.

Chen, Chiou-sen Dora. "Organization of Serials Management." In *Serials Management: A Practical Guide*, 20-35. Chicago: American Library Association, 1995.

Collver, Mitsuko. "Organization of Serials Work for Manual and Automated Systems." *Library Resources and Technical Services* 24 (fall 1980): 307-16.

Gellatly, Peter, ed. *The Good Serials Department.* New York, Haworth Press, 1990. Also issued as *Serials Librarian*, 19, nos. 1/2 (1990).

Hanson, Jo Ann. "Trends in Serials Management." *Serials Librarian* 8 (summer 1984): 7-12.

Harrington, Sue Anne. "Serials Organization: A Time for Reappraisal." *Serials Librarian* 10, nos. 1/2 (fall 1985/winter 1985-1986): 19-28.

Harrington, Sue Anne, and Deborah J. Karpuk. "The Integrated Serials Department: Its Value Today and in the Future." *Serials Librarian* 9 (winter 1984): 55-64.

Lanier, Don, and Norman Vogt. "The Serials Department: 1975-1985." *Serials Librarian* 10 (fall 1985/winter 1985-1986): 5-11.

Potter, William Gray. "Form or Function? An Analysis of the Serials Department in the Modern Academic Library." *Serials Librarian* 6 (fall 1981): 85-94.

Stine, Diane. "Centralized Serials Processing in An Automated Environment." *Serials Review* 9 (fall 1983): 69-75.

———. "Serials Department Staffing Patterns in Medium-Sized Research Libraries." *Serials Review* 7 (July/September 1981): 83-87.

Weber, Hans H. "Serials Administration." *Serials Librarian* 4 (winter 1979): 143-65.

Replacing Missing Issues

Holley, Beth, and others. "Replacement Issues: Where Do You Find Them and at What Cost?" *Serials Librarian* 21, nos. 2/3 (1991): 165-68.

Pionessa, Geraldine F. "Serials Replacement Orders: A Closer Look." *Serials Review* 16 (spring 1990): 65-73, 80.

Routing

Lane, David M., Francis Hallahan, and Constance Stone. "Automatic Circulation of New Journal Issues." *College and Research Libraries News* 51 (December 1990): 1068-70.

Naulty, Deborah. "Implementing an Internal Routing Sticker System." *Library Software Review* 9 (January-February 1990): 32-33.

Serial Subscription Agents

Barker, Joseph W. "Unbundling Serials Vendors' Service Charges: Are We Ready?" *Serials Review* 16 (summer 1990): 33-43.

Basch, N. Bernard, and Judy McQueen. *Buying Serials: A How-to-Do-It Manual for Librarians.* New York: Neal-Schuman, 1990.

Derthick, Jan, and Barbara B. Moran. "Serial Agent Selection in ARL Libraries." In *Advances in Serials Management: A Research Annual.* Vol. 1, edited by Marcia Tuttle and Jean G. Cook, 1-42. Greenwich, Conn.: JAI Press, 1986.

Hirshon, Arnold, and Barbara Winters. "Outsourcing the Acquisition of Serials." In *Outsourcing Library Technical Services: A How-to-Do-It Manual for Librarians,* 91-105. New York: Neal-Schuman, 1996.

Huff, William H. "Serial Subscription Agencies." *Library Trends* 24 (April 1976): 683-709.

Tonkery, Dan. "Reshaping the Serials Vendor Industry." *Serials Librarian* 25, nos. 3/4 (1995): 65-72.

Tuttle, Marcia. "Subscription Agents and Other Serials Suppliers." In *Managing Serials,* 101-28. Greenwich, Conn.: JAI Press, 1996.

Vendor Evaluation

Association for Library Collections and Technical Services. *Guide to Performance Evaluation of Serials Vendors*. Chicago: American Library Association, 1997.

Bonk, Sharon C. "Toward a Methodology of Evaluating Serials Vendors." *Library Acquisitions: Practice and Theory* 9, no. 1 (1985): 51-60.

Ivins, October. "The Development of Criteria for Evaluating Vendor Performance of Monograph and Serial Vendors." In *Advances in Serials Management: A Research Annual.* Vol. 2, edited by Marcia Tuttle and Jean G. Cook, 185-212. Greenwich, Conn.: JAI Press, 1988.

Ivins, October R., Mary K. McLaren, and Joyce G. McDonough. "Planning, Conducting, and Analyzing Serials Vendor Performance Studies." *Serials Librarian* 19, nos. 3/4 (1991): 221-23.

Kent, Philip G. "How to Evaluate Serials Suppliers." *Library Acquisitions: Practice and Theory* 18 (spring 1994): 83-87.

Kurosman, Kathleen, and Barbara Ammerman Durniak. "Document Delivery: A Comparison of Commercial Document Suppliers and Interlibrary Loan Services." *College and Research Libraries* 55 (March 1994): 129-39.

Chapter Nine

The Electronic Journal

During the 1990s the somewhat diverse phenomena variously termed *electronic journals, electronic serials,* or *electronic publishing* rapidly evolved. Though it may sound trite, the electronic journal may fundamentally transform serials management in libraries.

The electronic journal concept covers a wide variety of diverse phenomena. It has been applied to networked publications available on the Internet through such technological means as e-mail, listservs, anonymous File Transfer Protocol (ftp), gophers, and the World Wide Web (WWW) as well as through such offline technologies as floppy disks, disk cartridges, magnetic tape, or CD-ROM.[1] In 1996 electronic journals on the Internet were available in 23 different data formats, including American Standard Code for Information Interchange (ASCII), HTML, and PostScript.[2] Some electronic journals group articles into issues; others release them separately. Some electronic journals are sent to the library through Electronic mail (e-mail) or listservs, but others must be accessed from remote sites. An electronic journal can be free or fee-based through subscription, licensing, or pay-for-use. Some can only be purchased as part of a multijournal package. The term *electronic journal* has been applied to

1. an electronic version of an established print journal,

2. an electronic only journal,

3. a journal that is issued in both electronic and print format.

Many established print-based journals now also publish an electronic version. Some primarily electronic journals, such as *New Astronomy*, issue a paper version for archiving purposes.[3] Theoretically, an established journal could abandon print and transform to an electronic-only format, or vice versa. Serial types available in electronic format include journals, magazines, newspapers, newsletters, and zines. In this chapter the term *electronic journal* is used for all these categories.

The term *electronic publishing* likewise covers many different things. In regard to serials, indexing information, abstracts, tables of contents, partial text, full text, text and graphics, and such value-added features as keyword searching capacity can be available in an electronic format. Some electronic journals group their contents using the traditional approach of volumes and issues; others disseminate articles separately. Academic conferences or discussion lists, organized around a particular theme, are a major form of electronic publication that does not easily fit into traditional serial classification schemes. Electronic publishing also covers nonserial items such as electronic books or other types of text (e.g., encyclopedias, poetry, etc.). Publisher and journal home pages and preprint servers on the WWW are also significant pieces of the electronic mosaic.

A fairly extensive literature on electronic journals already exists, testifying to the profession's interest in the topic. Through April 24, 1997, 428 items had been published on electronic journals, based on a search of *Library Literature* on CD-ROM. Nevertheless, only a minute portion of these items present empirical-based research.

This chapter focuses on the management of electronic journals in libraries but also addresses the Internet and WWW and their uses in serials management, electronic full-text collections, and the electronic journal's role in the scholarly communications process. However, the myriad of technological details involved in creating and disseminating an electronic journal are beyond the scope of this analysis. Definitional questions relating to electronic publications are covered in chapter 1, the electronic journal's historical development is found in chapter 2, and the electronic journal's potential role in future scholarly communications is discussed in the epilogue.

THE INTERNET

The Internet has been a major impetus to the development of the electronic journal and supports the management of print journals. Meaning "network of networks," the Internet can trace its historical roots to the ARPANET and DARPA Internet founded by the U.S. Department of Defense in the late 1960s and 1970s. In the mid-1980s NSFNET, founded by the National Science Foundation (NSF) to link supercomputers for scientific research, became a major component of the Internet.[4] Not until the early 1990s did the library profession become aware of the Internet and its vast potential for meeting information needs. By the mid-1990s the Internet had practically become a household word. The number of books that have now been published on the Internet is staggering. A keyword search in *Books in Print* + (the CD-ROM version of *Books in Print*) in late 1996 retrieved more than 1,400 titles on the Internet and more than 500 on the WWW.

In October 1996 plans were announced for the creation of Internet 2, a more technologically advanced version to be developed over the next three to five years to meet the needs of researchers and educational institutions. By January 1997, 98 universities had become charter members sponsoring the project.[5]

The last three or four years have witnessed the explosive growth of the WWW, sometimes abbreviated WWW and often termed *the Web*. A major part of the Internet, the WWW is based on hyperlinkages among documents and nontextual multimedia. The WWW's historical origin is attributed to a March 1989 proposal by Tim Berners-Lee at the European Particle Physics Laboratory (abbreviated CERN after its French name), located in Geneva, Switzerland. Although the project "began to take shape" in late 1990, "1992 was a developmental year."[6] By June 1993 there were approximately 100 Hypertext Transfer Protocol (HTTP) servers on the

WWW.[7] Data on the number of Web sites vary from source to source, but there is no question that the WWW has undergone tremendous growth. The number of Web servers was reported at 500 in October 1993,[8] 4,500 in May 1994,[9] 110,000 in October 1995,[10] and 603,367 in December 1996.[11] The Netcraft Web server survey reports there were 2,215,195 Web servers as of April 1, 1998.[12] The figure will be higher by the time this book is published.

The wide variety of information resources available on the Internet include listservs, electronic journals, data files, newsgroups, WWW home pages, and access to Online Public Access Catalogs (OPACs) throughout the world. That the Internet has played a major role in the development of electronic journals hardly needs to be demonstrated.

Use of the Internet in Management of Print Journals

It should be emphasized that the Internet and WWW also support the management of traditional print journals. Some illustrative examples are outlined below.

- *E-mail Communications.* Electronic mail offers a medium for direct communication between librarians, on the one hand, and serial publishers or vendors, on the other, that can be used for innumerable purposes, including claiming, price quotations, and miscellaneous problem solving. Two surveys conducted at the Central Connecticut State University library in May 1994 found that 11.6 percent and 10.0 percent of newly received journals contained publisher e-mail addresses.[13] A list of publisher e-mail addresses can be found on AcqWeb.[14]

- *WWW Home Pages.* Most of the principal players on the serials scene now have WWW pages. The major categories are outlined below.
  Publishers. Nearly 1,000 publishers have WWW home pages. Many publishers have separate pages devoted to their journal division and links to Web sites for specific periodicals they publish. For example, the University of Chicago Press Journals Division home page[15] contains information about the journal division, staff, subscription, and advertising and lists rentals, new titles, and electronic journals. Web pages for the journals it publishes can be accessed by title and subject. Collections of publisher Web pages may be found at AcqWeb[16] or Faxon's site,[17] among other places.
  Journal Home Pages. One typical example is the Web home page for *Library Quarterly*,[18] announced by the University of Chicago Press in March 1995. The information offered includes the journal's history, statement of scope, instructions to authors and book reviewers, policy on books reviewed and books listed, and subscription information. Editorial board members are listed along with their current e-mail addresses and Web home page Uniform Resource Locator (URL), if available. Beginning April 1995, the table of contents and author biographies for each issue have been posted here.[19] *Slavic Review* includes electronic postprints

(i.e., articles from recent issues electronically posted after the print version has been issued).[20] In numerous instances the distinction between a journal Web site and an electronic journal seems to blur because the Web site contains many issues in electronic format. Several collections of journal Web pages are available on the WWW, including the National Library of Australia's, for Australian journals and magazines;[21] the "Index of Law-Related E-Journals and Periodicals,"[22] for law journals; the Electronic Newsstand's,[23] for popular magazines; and MedWeb's,[24] for medical journals.

Vendors. Numerous serials vendors, including subscription agents and back issue dealers, have their own Web sites. These pages normally include information about corporate history and structure, services, policies, and staff and often include forms for submitting orders.

Serial Departments. Not surprisingly, library serials departments were slower than publishers and vendors to establish WWW pages. A posting on *SERIALST* in late 1996 listed eight serials department Web sites, all in academic libraries.[25] It also recommended an article in *RSR: Reference Services Review* on designing a library Web page.[26] Typically, a serials department's Web page is a link on the library's Web site. Serials pages include basic information on staff, hours open, circulation policy, etc.; holdings lists; canceled titles lists; access to electronic journals; indexes and abstracts; departmental annual reports; the department's place in the library's organizational structure; and links to other serials resources available on the Internet. Instructions on designing serials department home pages are clearly beyond this book's scope. Note that home pages can communicate basic serials information to library clients, assist with managing traditional print journals, and provide access to electronic journals.

Serials Cancellation Web Sites. Some academic libraries have created Web pages devoted to serials cancellation projects.[27] For example, the MIT libraries' page includes the final project report, letters about the project, the project plan and calendar, vendors' price projections, cost and expenditure data, and key personnel.[28]

Duplicate Exchange Web Sites. These cites are discussed in chapter 8 and appendix 3.

Miscellaneous. Many important serials players that do not fit into any of the above categories also maintain Web sites, for example, the International Standard Serial Number (ISSN) International Centre or the North American Serials Interest Group (NASIG). See appendix 3 for an annotated listing.

- *OPACs.* Accessing another library's OPAC over the Internet can support serials management in numerous ways, predicated on the assumption the accessed library has cataloged its serials. Linda Lawrence Stein's identification of core periodicals by accessing

OPACs was discussed in chapter 4. Accessing the OPACs of nearby libraries could support serials resource sharing by providing information for subscription and cancellation decisions plus facilitating interlibrary loan. Another library's serial holdings could be accessed via the Internet and used as a checklist for evaluating one's own serials collection. Herb Weinryb, a serials descriptive cataloger at the Library of Congress (LC), described accessing bibliographic and name authority records for European serials in the OPACs of Dutch and Swedish libraries to assist cataloging.[29]

- *Listservs.* Listservs are used for communications among librarians (often including vendors and others) about professional meetings, advertised job openings, pricing trends, missing issues, title changes, automated serials control systems, and innumerable other serials management issues. *SERIALST*, of course, is the listserv most relevant to serials, but numerous other listservs discuss issues pertaining to serials. Several listservs are devoted to the duplicate exchange of serials and other items (see chapter 8 as well as appendix 3 for details).

- *Support of Document Delivery and Interlibrary Loan.* The databases of document delivery vendors (e.g., CARL's UnCover), can be accessed on the Internet to identify article availability. It is also possible to order, pay for, and receive articles over the Internet. In a similar sense, the Research Libraries Group's (RLG) Ariel can be used for faxing articles from one library to another for interlibrary loan.

- *The Electronic Newsstand.* Founded in 1993 and located in Washington, D.C., the Electronic Newsstand provides online samples of articles from such major periodicals as *Business Week*, *Discover*, the *Economist*, and the *New Yorker*.[30] It can be accessed by gopher, telnet, and the WWW. Eight periodicals were originally accessible on this resource, but the number increased to 80 in 1994, 240 by March 1995,[31] 275 in July 1995, and about 2,000 in early 1997.[32] Although established as a marketing tool for publishers, this resource could potentially be used by librarians wishing to browse magazines for selection purposes. Ironically, many of the Electronic Newsstand's periodicals are published only in print format.

Preprint Servers

Electronic media is used for distribution of *preprints* and *working papers* (i.e., copies of a journal article that are made available prior to official publication). Preprints play a role in the scholarly communication process by providing dissemination of work prior to publication and, in some cases, providing feedback to the author that can be incorporated into the final version. In the early 1980s the unsuccessful Birmingham Loughborough Electronic Network Development (BLEND) project in the United Kingdom experimented with electronic distribution of 21 preprints through a system named "Poster Papers."[33]

Ann Okerson states that "preprints began to become popular" on the Internet by 1991;[34] by June 1995 approximately 70 preprint servers were on the Internet.[35] Perhaps the best-known electronic preprint servers are the Los Alamos National Laboratory Physics Service, created by Paul Ginsparg,[36] and the International Philosophical Preprint Exchange, run by the Philosophy Department of the University of Chiba, located in Chiba, Japan, with a branch in Toronto, Canada.[37] Preprint servers can be accessed through the gophers or WWW sites of many libraries or academic departments. Other important Internet preprint servers include the Cambridge Astronomy gopher, the American Mathematical Society gopher, the Economics Working Paper Archive, HNSource (for history), and Scuola Internazionale Superiore di Studi Avanzati (International School for Advanced Studies) (for several physics specialties), located in Trieste, Italy.[38]

Scholars have informally shared preprints with each other for a long time. However, because academic libraries traditionally placed a low priority on collecting preprints in the paper format and many did not collect them at all, preprints were not readily accessible on an organized, systematic basis. The Stanford Linear Accelerator did distribute paper preprints from the late 1960s to 1993 (when it discontinued the practice because 50 percent had already been circulated on the Internet).[39] In many disciplines, however, one usually needed informal contacts in the so-called old boy network to obtain preprints or working papers. That preprints are becoming much more widely available on the Internet—a trend that will accentuate in the future—significantly increases their potential to affect the scholarly communications process.

Summary

The well-known Internet visionary Clifford A. Lynch distinguishes between "modernization" (i.e., doing what libraries have always done "in a more efficient and/or cost-effective way") and "transformation," which changes "processes in a fundamental way."[40] There is no question that the Internet is modernizing serials management in libraries. The real issue concerns how and in what time frame serials management will be transformed by the Internet.

ISSUES IN ELECTRONIC JOURNAL MANAGEMENT IN LIBRARIES

This section addresses the management of electronic journals by libraries. Because electronic journals are undergoing such rapid change, anything written about them may be outdated before publication. The only solution to this problem would be not to write about electronic journals! Statements that apply to first-generation electronic journals might not apply to second-generation journals, and analysis of second-generation electronic journals might be rendered irrelevant by future technological developments. Consequently, the focus is on general analysis of salient issues rather than the provision of concrete practical advice.

Several published surveys reveal that throughout the 1990s an increasing proportion of U.S. libraries offered electronic journals to patrons. A survey conducted at the 1990 NASIG Conference found that 6 of 80 libraries were purchasing online electronic journals, and 16 were purchasing electronic journals in other formats.[41] A January 1994 survey of Association of Research Libraries (ARL) libraries revealed that 35 of 75 respondents (46 percent) were "currently making electronic journals available."[42] Two years later, a major American Library Association (ALA) and Ameritech joint survey found that access to free electronic journals was provided by 71 percent of institutions whose highest degree was the Ph.D. and by 48 percent of libraries associated with Baccalaureate-level institutions.[43] The percentages were lower for fee-based electronic-only journals: 57 percent for Ph.D. institutions and 32 percent for bachelor's level institutions.[44]

In the early 1990s libraries began appointing task forces to address the management of electronic journals. Two of the most famous were the Virginia Polytechnic Institute and State University Task Force, created in the fall of 1990,[45] and an MIT Task Force, set up in July 1991.[46] Other libraries reporting the establishment of such task forces or ad hoc committees during this period included the University of Saskatchewan, in the spring of 1992,[47] and, in the United Kingdom, Loughborough University.[48] A SPEC kit published in August 1994 included electronic journal task force reports from seven major U.S. and Canadian universities, including Cornell and the University of California at Berkeley.[49]

Selection

The basic issues, staffing, and process and criteria for selection of electronic journals are discussed below.

Issues

Five fundamental selection issues for electronic journals exist:

1. What does "selection" of an electronic journal mean?
2. Who will do the selection?
3. What selection procedure is used?
4. How are titles that are candidates for selection identified?
5. What selection criteria will be used?

Although selecting a print journal almost invariably means deciding to subscribe, electronic journal "selection" refers to a variety of actions in different contexts. On a theoretical level, selection might mean deciding to ease patron access to a particular electronic journal. Michael Buckland contends that selection of any Internet resource means "privileging" it by making patron access to the chosen resource easier than to other Internet resources, such as by including it on a Web page.[50] From a practical perspective, selecting an electronic journal could refer to five actions:

1. placing a paid subscription,

2. signing a license agreement,

3. accessing a title on a pay-per-use basis,

4. including a title in a library's gopher, and

5. providing access through a WWW site.

Staffing

There are two theoretical organizational models for selection of electronic journals:

1. selection by the same bibliographers who select print journals, implying a subject-based distribution of responsibility; and

2. selection by specialists in electronic resources, implying a format-based assignment of responsibility. However, these are ideal types that oversimplify reality.

The previously mentioned ARL survey identified seven staffing patterns for selection of electronic journals. Individual bibliographers selected them in 15 libraries (43 percent); committees of librarians in 10 libraries (28 percent); the collection development librarian in 9 libraries (26 percent); the teaching faculty in 7 libraries (20 percent); committees of bibliographers in 5 (14 percent); the acquisitions or serials librarian in 4 (11 percent); and the dean or director of libraries in 2 (6 percent). "Other" unspecified approaches were reported by 13 libraries (37 percent). Percentages do not add to 100 because of multiple responses.[51]

In contrast to subject- or format-based staffing, Samuel Demas described a "genre-based" organizational model used at Cornell University's Albert R. Mann Library. Genre specialists select resources, regardless of format, in various information categories or "genres," such as applications software, bibliographic files, full text, numeric files, or multimedia. Although not explicitly stated by Demas, most electronic journals would presumably fall under the full-text genre, and others would be multimedia. This model's objective is to *mainstream* (i.e., integrate into routine library operations) the selection of electronic resources. Recommendations by genre specialists are reviewed by Cornell's Electronic Resources Council—a standing committee representing all areas of the library.[52] It should be stressed that a library could simultaneously use more than one staffing model. Also, many of these staffing issues would apply to functions other than selection.

Process and Criteria

The same three-stage conceptual process for serial selection outlined in chapter 3 (i.e., identification, evaluation, and selection) can be applied to electronic journals. Identifying electronic journals can be challenging, especially on the Internet, where bibliographical control of resources, although improving, is still far from ideal. Some useful identification tools are available. The ARL's *Directory of Electronic Journals, Newsletters and Academic Discussion Lists* and the listserv NewJour cover networked electronic journals. Numerous Internet resources can assist with the identification (or, using the Net's terminology, the *discovery*) of electronic journals on the Internet. The number of Internet search tools is ever-increasing—including, among the best-known, Yahoo, Lycos, and the WWW Virtual Library. So-called electronic journal collections on the Internet can be exceedingly useful in the identification process. The "Ejournal SiteGuide: A MetaSource"[53] offers links to 36 sites that collect electronic journals. Noteworthy collections include the Committee on Institutional Cooperation (CIC) Electronic Journals Collection[54] (which replaced the earlier CICNet E-Serials Archive[55] and the University of Houston's Scholarly Journals Distributed via the WWW.[56] (See appendix 3 for an annotated listing of several other collections.) Electronic journals on CD-ROM are included in *CD-ROMs in Print*[57] and the *Gale Directory of Databases. Volume 2: CD-ROM, Diskette, Magnetic Tape, Handheld, and Batch Access Database Products*.[58] Other methods for identifying electronic journals on the Internet include the following:

1. serendipity when surfing the Internet,

2. staff or patron suggestions,

3. reviewing the electronic journals provided by other libraries,

4. publisher advertisements, and

5. published reviews.

The microevaluation of electronic journals to determine the item's intrinsic quality and characteristics involves most of the traditional criteria for print journals plus further criteria unique to the electronic format. Traditional criteria would include the authors' credentials, the editor and editorial board membership, refereed status, publisher's reputation, subject content, and scholarly quality. In contrast, such traditional criteria as index coverage and citation record would not be especially applicable to electronic journals because most are too new to have been picked up by indexing services or to have established a citation record. Examples of additional criteria for the electronic format are technical compatibility with the library's hardware, the user interface, the amount of training required, whether the journal is archived, and the journal's data format (ASCII, Postscript, etc.).

The final step entails the actual selection decision. Here user information needs, the level of user technological sophistication, the library's informal collection priorities, and the written collection development policy statement are the dominant considerations. For fee-based journals, the cost and terms of the licensing agreement would be criteria.

Nineteen of 34 ARL libraries (57 percent) reported that the selection criteria for electronic journals were the same as for print ones, and 15 (43 percent) indicated they differed. The responding libraries stated the following factors are considered in the selection of electronic journals: if the journal deals with a subject in which delivery speed is important, 15 (43 percent); "interactive or online format is important," 15 (43 percent); "long-term archival access may not be critical," 7 (20 percent); faculty request, 18 (51 percent); technical compatibility or lack thereof, 22 (63 percent); and other, 18 (51 percent). The figures do not total to 100 because of responses in multiple categories.[59]

A distinct but related issue concerns choice of format. As many commercial and university press publishers offer electronic versions of their established print journals (a trend that as of 1997 is picking up increased momentum), libraries will, for many titles, have three subscription options: print only, electronic only, or both print and electronic.

Option three would seem to offer the best of both worlds. Carl H. Gotsch cogently argues that many scientists prefer their journals to be available in both formats because electronic journals offer superior searching capability, delivery speed, and links to other information sources, whereas print titles provide superior browsability, reading ease, and image quality.[60] Retaining the print subscription would allay concerns about the archiving issue. The obvious disadvantage would be the cost factor. I believe many libraries will experience a transitional phase in which numerous dual print and electronic subscriptions are maintained for a certain time prior to a complete transition to the electronic format. One should note a fourth option for meeting patron information needs: use of commercial document delivery.

Acquisition

This section discusses acquisition procedures, staffing, licensing, and check-in and claiming for electronic journals.

Procedures

First-generation electronic journals could be subscribed to and were often actually sent to the library. However, one might question the traditional serial acquisitions model's applicability to second-generation remote-access electronic journals, especially because the very word *acquisition* logically implies the item is physically acquired by the library. Unlike print journals—which are purchased for permanent ownership—for many fee-based electronic journals, the library is simply licensing access rights.

An MIT subgroup on electronic journals, appointed in 1995, identified five specific acquisition functions for fee-based, later-generation electronic journals:[61]

1. Determining the price
2. Negotiating with the vendor
3. Completing the license agreement
4. Encumbering the funds
5. Recording the order

In addition to these five steps, one might add three more:

1. Verifying the title can be accessed
2. Communicating with the vendor if it can not be accessed (the electronic equivalent of claiming)
3. Preparing an invoice for payment

In January 1994 6 ARL libraries (17 percent responding to the question) reported they acquired electronic journals through the same procedures as print ones,

20 (57 percent) used a modified form of their normal acquisitions procedure, and 8 (23 percent) used separate procedures developed specifically for electronic journals.

Staffing

The basic staffing issue is whether the acquisition functions for electronic journals are performed by the regular acquisitions staff or different staff with expertise in the electronic format. The previously mentioned ARL survey revealed that the staff member "responsible for acquiring/providing access to electronic journals" was a computer professional in 18 libraries (51 percent), the acquisitions librarian in 9 libraries (26 percent), support staff in 8 libraries (23 percent), paraprofessional staff in 4 (11 percent), and "other" in 10 (28 percent). Figures do not add to 100 because of multiple responses by some libraries.[62] In the final analysis, the acquisition of electronic journals requires additional staff skills (e.g., negotiating licenses, familiarity with the electronic format, etc.) on the part of serialists.

Licensing

As stated in *LIBLICENSE: Licensing Digital Information*, a WWW site recently created by the Yale University Library, "A license usually takes the form of a written contract or agreement between the library and the owner of the rights to distribute digital information . . . [and] licensing agreements often are complex, lengthy documents filled with arcane and unfamiliar terms."[63] A major issue for fee-based electronic journals concerns the terms of the licensing agreement. Typical licensing issues include method of calculating payment, restrictions on use, and what happens upon termination. Licensing agreements are generally written for the vendor's advantage rather than the library's, but it is often possible for a library to negotiate more advantageous terms.

Meta Nissley outlined nine electronic materials pricing options used by publishers:

1. A yearly flat fee, which allows unlimited use

2. The augmented price model, in which a library subscribes to a title's print version and pays an additional fee for the electronic format

3. The pay extra for print approach, a flip-flop of number two, in which the library subscribes to the electronic version and pays extra for the print

4. The pay per use model

5. Payment per potential user, based on an institution's size

6. Charge per connect time, which may include additional charges for downloading, etc.

7. Acquisitions on demand, which means on a per-article basis

8. Bundling or packaging, where a group of electronic journals are priced together at a discount price

9.   Consortial pricing, for a group of libraries[64]

The issue is complicated by the fact that no standard pricing model presently exists.

Check-In and Claiming

The concept of check-in is applicable to early generation electronic journals sent to libraries through e-mail or listservs. The Virginia Polytechnic Institute and State University Task Force recommended that the serials department "record the receipt" of electronic journals as is done for their print counterparts.[65] However, the concept breaks down in regard to later-generation electronic journals. The 1995 MIT electronic journal subgroup decided that for journals pointed to on the Web, "the idea of check-in is meaningless, since we have no holdings. Link maintenance would be our quality-control substitute for check-in."[66]

In January 1994, 63 percent (22) of responding ARL libraries indicated they did not check-in electronic journals. Moreover, 94 percent (33) did not check-in electronic journals "not acquired but available through gopher/remote access."[67] The percentage of libraries not checking in electronic journals has perhaps increased since then because of the proliferation of Web-based journals, which do not lend themselves to check-in.

Related to check-in is the question of how to claim nonreceived issues. The previously mentioned Virginia Tech Task Force recommended claiming electronic journal issues that are not received.[68] Yet several problems could be associated with claiming electronic journals, including an unpredictable issuance schedule (for some journals), the release of articles separately rather than grouping them into issues, and the fact that Web-based journals are not actually sent to the library. When a larger proportion of electronic journals become fee-based rather than free, a systematic mechanism will be necessary for ensuring that a library actually has access to what it has paid for.

Budgeting

Throughout the first half of the 1990s most networked electronic journals tended to be free, so budgeting for them was not a major issue. To illustrate the point, in October 1995 Steve Harter found that only 12 of 134 refereed electronic journals (9 percent) were fee-based.[69] The proportion of electronic journals that are free will inevitably decline as more commercial and university press publishers begin offering electronic versions of their established print journals. Moreover, online and CD-ROM journals have traditionally been fee-based.

As with staffing, there are two theoretical approaches to budgeting for electronic journals: the subject-based and the format-based. The former implies electronic journals would be funded from the same budget line as other serials; the latter implies separate budget lines for electronic resources. Both approaches might be used simultaneously, with some electronic journals funded from a separate electronic resources budget line and others from subject allocations. In reality, budgeting is much more complicated because different categories of electronic journals might be paid for from different budget lines (e.g., journals on CD-ROM might be paid from a CD-ROM budget, but full-text journals available through DIALOG might be paid from an on-line searching fund). As of January 1994, only 1 of 34 (3 percent) ARL libraries reported a separate line item for electronic journals in their serials budget.[70] However, electronic journal costs are often paid from a larger budget for electronic resources.

Cataloging

Many of the same cataloging issues confront both electronic journals and print journals: Should they be cataloged at all? If so, what level of cataloging should be used? Should electronic journals be classified? Should they be assigned subject headings? What sources of cataloging records are available? Should a library catalog a title it licenses but does not own?

In addition to the usual questions, a set of unique cataloging issues are associated with electronic journals. Unlike print serials, an electronic journal does not exist in a tangible, physical format and is not shelved in the library. Taemin Kim Park notes that many libraries do not classify electronic journals because one of a class number's major functions is to indicate physical location on the shelf.[71]

It must be stressed that electronic journal cataloging entails some fairly technical issues that will not be discussed here. Examples include the question whether there should be multiple catalog records for journal titles simultaneously available in print and electronic format or different electronic formats as well as the use of the new MARC 856 field, which indicates where a title can be accessed. The Cooperative Online Serials Program's (CONSER) definition of an electronic serial has been noted in chapter 1.

Sources addressing the practical aspects of cataloging electronic journals include Mary Beth Fecko's *Cataloging Nonbook Resources: A How-to-Do-It-Manual for Librarians,* which contains a chapter with practical advice on cataloging early generation electronic journals.[72] Nancy Olson of the OCLC Online Computer Library Center (OCLC) has prepared *Cataloging Internet Resources: A Manual and Practical Guide,* available on the OCLC web site.[73] Module 31 of the *CONSER Cataloging Manual* provides authoritative guidance for cataloging remote access electronic serials,[74] including policies for multiple-format periodicals and the inclusion of location and access information.[75]

From the perspective of library management of electronic journals, a key issue concerns whether records for remote access electronic journals should be entered into the OPAC. A recent *Serials Review* issue contained a discussion of this question.[76] Arguments in favor of doing so follow:

- If a print subscription has been replaced by an electronic one, a cataloging record for the latter helps link the two.[77]

- "OPACs are finding aids and not simple catalogs. . . ."[78]

- The traditional distinction between owned and accessed resources may no longer be relevant.[79]

- It would ease access to remote journals selected specifically to meet local patron need.[80]

Negative arguments included the following:

- The item might cease to be available due to the instability of Web resources.

- The traditional principle that a catalog's purpose is to indicate what a library owns is violated.

- Placing the records in the OPAC may be confusing the functions of a *catalog* (what a library holds) and a *bibliography* (what is available).[81]

- It is questionable whether the present cataloging code can be applied to Internet resources.[82]

Although a definitive answer may be uncertain, this debate illustrates how electronic journals challenge the profession to reexamine traditional library assumptions.

In January 1994, 57 percent of ARL libraries (20 of 33 responding to the question) reported that their level of cataloging for electronic journals was the same as for paper ones.[83] Park's research reveals that in February 1997 cataloging records could be found in OCLC for 153 of 254 (60.2 percent) networked electronic journals. Of these, 67.9 percent (104) had full bibliographical description, 80.3 percent (123) had a LC or Dewey classification number, and 73.8 percent (113) had LC subject headings.[84]

Maintenance

Maintenance is an especially critical issue for electronic journals that are accessed through a library's gopher or Web site. Because the Internet is notoriously unstable, resources are often "here today, gone tomorrow." The address may have changed or the source is no longer updated. Many libraries assign a paraprofessional staff member to continuously check the validity of gopher and Web links, although such a tactic is obviously labor-intensive and expensive. Some software programs available for this function include Linkcheck for gophers and Anchor Checker for Web pages. At the MIT libraries these programs are reported to falsely report dead links, thus resulting in "time-consuming and tedious" staff processing.[85]

Preservation and Archiving

This issue represents one of the major electronic journal problems due to the inherently transient nature of electronic media. Taking a broad perspective, there is a genuine concern that the content of electronic publications will be lost from the scholarly record if appropriate archiving strategies are not developed. From a specific library's viewpoint, guaranteed access to electronic journal back-runs is an important issue. The major questions follow:

1. Which electronic journals will be archived?

2. Who will do the archiving?

3. What format will be used?

Libraries routinely archive print periodicals by binding them. But, as discussed in chapter 3, not all print subscriptions are considered important enough to bind. Likewise, some electronic publications may lack the enduring scholarly value to warrant permanent archiving. Many of the criteria outlined in chapter 3 for microevaluation of serials would be applicable to ascertaining whether a particular electronic journal merits archiving.

As with most questions involving electronic journals, the issue of who bears ultimate responsibility for archiving has not been resolved. Potential solutions are consortial efforts at the regional or national level (either for-profit or nonprofit), local libraries, or journal publishers.

There have been numerous proposals and some notable preliminary efforts to cooperatively archive electronic journals on a regional or national basis. As an example of the former, the creation of a "Central Directory" of abstracts with the full text loaded on "regional servers" has been proposed.[86] The Committee on Institutional Cooperation (CIC), composed of the 11 Big Ten institutions plus the University of Chicago, has been a major player in regional-based cooperative archiving through its CICNet E-Serials Archive[87] and the CIC Electronic Journals Collection—discussed at greater length in a subsequent section. OCLC announced in November 1996 the First Search Electronic Collection Online service. The project's initial objective is to archive a "critical mass" of 500 electronic journals within a year, giving first priority to Science, Technical, and Medical (STM) titles. For a fee, OCLC will provide a library access to the archival record for the titles and specific volumes to which the library held a valid subscription.[88]

Relying on publishers to archive their own electronic journals is another potential strategy. For example, Johns Hopkins University Press is archiving the journals available through Project Muse. Yet Stephen P. Harter and Hak Joon Kim's research revealed that 21.4 percent (28 of 131) of publisher archives on the Internet were incomplete for one or more archiving methods, although it was impossible to determine archive completeness in 12.2 percent of the cases (16 of 131).[89] Also, many librarians question whether publishers can be depended upon for permanent archiving because it may not be financially viable to archive little-used, older backruns.

In the final analysis, a library wishing certain access to an electronic journal's backruns can chose to do the archiving itself. Donnice Cochenour and Tom Moothart outline the following criteria for deciding whether a library should locally archive an electronic journal:

- Whether fee-based or free
- Whether publisher provides authorized archive
- Remote site's menu quality in terms of structure and content
- Currency of remote site's files
- Whether restricted access is required by publisher
- Availability of equipment and staff resources to local library[90]

Theoretically, formats available for archiving purposes include paper, CD-ROM, disk, microformat, optical media, plus electronically on computers—and most of these have been experimented with over the years. For example, it was reported in 1992 that the publisher of *Postmodern Culture* archived that electronic journal on microfiche.[91]

Converting electronic journals to paper format was once considered by some librarians as a possible strategy for preservation and archiving. However, it is now apparent that this is not a feasible solution. Technologically sophisticated electronic journals contain features that do not lend themselves to paper conversion, such as video, sound, external links, etc. In January 1994 only three ARL libraries (8 percent of those responding to the question) reported that they made paper copies of electronic journals available to patrons.[92]

Currently, the guaranteed archiving strategy is for a library to store the electronic backruns on its own server, thus giving it direct control. However, this tactic can be quite expensive. For illustration, in 1995 the MIT libraries calculated the cost of archiving five years of 100 first-generation electronic journals was $435 per title per year, but the equivalent annual archiving cost for second-generation electronic journals was estimated at approximately $1,000 per title.[93]

Electronic journals on the Web can be *mirrored* (i.e., copied onto a library's own computer). The MIT libraries outlined four situations in which mirroring would be an appropriate strategy: the original site's stability is uncertain; the original site's holdings are incomplete; the journal is published by MIT; or it is published by MIT Press and relevant to the library's collection.[94]

In the January 1994 ARL survey, 28 percent (10) relied on obtaining back issues from the publisher, 26 percent (9) maintained their own electronic file in either the library or computer center, 26 percent (9) depended on a consortium that maintained an archive, 6 percent (2) created master copies on diskette, 3 percent (1) maintained a master copy on magnetic tape or cartridge, and 3 percent (1) used a paper copy for archival purposes. Thirty-four percent (12) reported other methods, and 18 percent (6) did not use any archival method.[95]

Staff Training and User Education

A host of training issues arise: Who trains library staff? Which staff are trained? What training methods are employed? What is the content of the training? The January 1994 ARL survey indicated that 43 percent of the libraries (15) trained their staff for Internet use by means of structured classes, and 40 percent (14) employed verbal, one-on-one instruction.[96]

Patron education is also an important issue in electronic journal management, although detailed analysis of the various education strategies are outside this book's scope. User education may become less of an issue in the future as patrons become increasingly more experienced and sophisticated in the use of computer technology.

Statistical Reporting

Most libraries typically record the number of their current periodical subscriptions and the total number of periodical volumes owned. A major unresolved issue in electronic journal management concerns how journals that a library provides access to, but does not "own" and physically house, are counted in periodical statistics. What does a library have to do to count an electronic journal among its holdings? Pay for it? Catalog it? Archive it? It is my understanding that the ARL, which compiles serials holding and expenditure statistics, is addressing this issue.

Policy Making

Electronic journals raise a host of policy issues. In fact, most of the fundamental questions discussed in this chapter—on the selection process, selection criteria, staffing, and budgeting—should, when resolved, be reflected in a library's written policy statement. In early 1995 Elizabeth Futas concluded that librarians "do not yet have a handle on" policy making for electronic journals and Internet resources.[97] Her conclusion is consistent with the findings of the January 1994 ARL survey, which revealed that only 5 of 35 responding libraries (14 percent) had a collection development policy that addressed electronic journals.[98] One often observes postings on listservs asking other libraries to share their collection development policies for electronic resources.

The "Guidelines for Internet Resource Selection," developed at the Houston Academy of Medicine–Texas Medical Center Library, serve as a notable example of successful policy formation.[99] Although devised for all Internet resources, these guidelines are worth examining in detail, as they are generally applicable to networked electronic journals. Six criteria are outlined in this document:

1. quality and content, further subdivided into four categories

   a. credibility—whether the item is peer-reviewed, indexed, or electronically archived

   b. importance of resource as demonstrated by availability (e.g., included in multiple Internet sites or available in multiple formats)

   c. comprehensive or unique content

   d. Internet version is complete or meets client needs

2. relevancy—related to subject, accessed by other libraries, used by patrons

3. ease of use

4. reliability and stability—consistent availability on the Net, taking routine problems into consideration

5. cost and copyright (i.e., reasonableness of cost and complexity of complying with copyright restrictions)

6. hardware and software (i.e., whether access can be provided without significant changes in the library's hardware and software)

Cancellation

Cancellation has not been addressed to any appreciable extent in the now fairly substantial literature dealing with electronic journals. A keyword search in *Library Literature* on CD-ROM under the terms *electronic journal* and *cancellation* did not retrieve a single item. Canceling free electronic journals is not a major concern, but canceling fee-based electronic journal subscriptions is potentially a significant issue. A distinct but related issue—canceling the print version after subscribing to its electronic equivalent—is discussed later in this chapter.

Many librarians have expressed concern about what happens when an electronic journal subscription is canceled. Does a library lose everything or maintain the right to use what has already been paid for? The answer to this question, which represents one of the many presently unresolved issues regarding electronic journals, will vary depending on the title, publisher, and the original contractual agreement. Ideally, a library should be able to keep or maintain the right to access what it has already paid for (as with print subscriptions), although this is not always the case. Before ordering a paid subscription or signing a license agreement, a library should ascertain its rights upon termination.

Most of the selection criteria already outlined would also apply to cancellation, but they would be used from an opposite perspective. In other words, an electronic journal that was highly relevant to patron needs would be selected, but one with low relevance might be canceled.

One can easily imagine a future scenario in which budgetary constraints compel libraries to undertake review and cancellation projects for fee-based electronic journals just as has been done for print journals for more than two decades. Alternatively, if electronic journals were to become *unbundled,* so that each article is separately paid for on a per-use basis, electronic journal cancellation per se could become a moot issue.

Weeding

As with selection, weeding an electronic journal can mean different things in different contexts. It could mean deciding to no longer provide access through a library's gopher or WWW site; to archive a journal on a local computer; or to pay a fee to access an external archive. Theoretically, weeding may be closely related to archiving because the decision to stop archiving an electronic title is the functional equivalent of weeding it. Most libraries have not yet confronted the issue of weeding electronic journals because they are still struggling with more fundamental questions regarding selection and access. Also, because they are a relatively new format, electronic journals do not presently have long backruns, although this situation will obviously change with the passage of time. Print journal backruns are frequently weeded to save shelf space or because older volumes are no longer useful to patrons. When the library profession begins to seriously address strategies for electronic journal weeding, the major criteria will probably be the need to save disk storage space and cost (although disk storage space is becoming increasingly less expensive, it remains a nontrivial issue); the extent to which a journal has enduring scholarly value, and the changing information needs of library clients.

Gordon B. Neavill and Mary Ann Sheblé suggest that as electronic journal backruns increase in length, libraries may have to archive them offline on magnetic data tape, which would be loaded at the computer center only in response to specific patron requests. They assert that offline storage would be "equivalent to having printed journals in closed stacks"[100]—in other words, the electronic version of relegation to remote storage.

Presently unforeseen technological developments could have significant long-term implications for electronic journal weeding. If storage were to become less costly, the need to weed would be reduced.

Cancellation of Print Version

Anecdotal evidence indicates that many libraries maintain dual print and electronic subscriptions for numerous periodicals. For some titles, this is required by the publisher. For the others, a major collection management issue concerns when the print subscription should be discontinued. A library presumably would not wish to cancel the print subscription until it had confidence in an archiving strategy for the electronic version. Other crucial criteria would be the cost differential between an electronic only and a dual electronic and print subscription, the degree of patron comfort with the electronic format, and the extent to which the print version for the period covered by the dual subscription is still being used. As noted in chapter 2, the University Licensing Project (TULIP) concluded that many users are not yet ready for electronic publications and may not be soon. A reasonable policy might specify that all dual subscriptions be maintained for a set minimum time period, such as two years, with the final decision to cancel the print subscription made on a title-by-title basis.

Interlibrary Loan

Articles from early generation electronic journals that were e-mailed to libraries or received through listservs could theoretically be requested and sent through interlibrary loan (ILL) in accordance with the tradition established for print periodicals. In 1991 Charles W. Bailey Jr. reported that the University of Houston Libraries filled ILL requests for articles from the *Public-Access Computer Systems Review*, a free but copyrighted electronic journal it has published since 1990, on the same basis that would be applied to print journals.[101] Now anyone can download *Public-Access Computer Systems Review (PACS Review)* articles from an archival site on the WWW. Remote access electronic journals do not lend themselves to ILL. Indeed many observers believe that the traditional ILL process will not become established for electronic journals. Items from free electronic journals should be obtainable without the intervention of another library. As pointed out by Lynch, fee-based electronic resources are generally licensed, and the license agreement typically prohibits sharing with other libraries.[102]

Provision of Access to Patrons

Access is both a fundamental concept of librarianship and a somewhat overused word with many meanings. Hazel Woodward and Cliff McKnight identify three levels of access to electronic journals: access to basic bibliographical data on titles available in electronic form; access to information about the articles they contain (i.e., indexing); and access to the text of the articles.[103] The third level is our main concern here.

In the traditional library paradigm, patron access to serials is provided primarily by owning, binding, and housing them on shelves and to a lesser extent through ILL and reciprocal borrowing. Access to electronic journals differs in some crucial respects: the journal is often not locally owned or stored; the patron need not come to the library to access the journal; and the precise access mode is usually transparent to the patron, who is unaware whether the title is stored on a local computer or pointed to on a remote one.

Providing access to patrons is one of the biggest challenges associated with electronic journals. Numerous methods used in recent years have changed according to technological developments and the evolving nature of electronic journals themselves. In the early 1990s such technologies as gophers, archie, and Wide-Area Information Servers were used to provide access to electronic journals on the Internet. In the late 1990s the prevalent trend is to provide access through the WWW.

Blackwell's Navigator system, introduced in early 1997, is a vendor service that assists libraries with accessing and managing electronic journals. It provides a single gateway to multiple scholarly electronic journals from different publishers. Indexing, table of contents, and full articles are available for journals from participating publishers. The service covers both subscription (which allows password access to users affiliated with subscribing libraries) and the purchase of specific articles when a subscription is not in force. Blackwell presently plans to provide the most current three years rather than permanent archiving. Navigator helps libraries by negotiating license agreements, offering a searchable user interface, addressing password management, and providing usage reports by title.[104, 105] In effect, this service adapts the subscription agent's traditional role as an intermediary between libraries and publishers to the electronic journal environment.

Another aspect of access concerns the hardware configuration offered to patrons. The previously quoted ALA-Ameritech survey found that U.S. academic libraries were using a variety of methods. For example, of doctoral institution libraries offering full-text electronic journals, 90 percent used hardwired PCs or terminals in the library; 44 percent used such PCs or terminals outside the library; 64 percent provided dial-up access to patrons outside the library; moreover, access was provided through a campus network by 70 percent, a local library consortium by 30 percent, and the Internet by 64 percent.[106]

Key access issues include the search interface used by the patron; the search capabilities (author, subject, keyword, Boolean, etc.); whether a password is required; downloading, e-mailing, and printing capabilities; the source's stability; response time; the access mode used (gopher, WWW, etc.); archiving backruns; which individuals are granted access; the number of individuals allowed simultaneous access; the extent of indexing, abstracting, and table of contents available; and the quality of text and graphics.

In a sense, access is a unifying concept. Most of the other functions discussed in this section—selection, acquisition, cataloging, archiving, and maintenance—relate to providing patrons access to electronic journals.

Summary

A frequently discussed question concerns the applicability of traditional library serials management to electronic journals. Chiou-sen Dora Chen points out three ways in which accessing electronic journals is more complicated than acquiring traditional print journals: electronic journals are not necessarily owned—the library may simply be licensing access rights; computer hardware is needed to run electronic journals; and a consistent publisher policy on marketing electronic journals has not yet been developed (i.e., some sell but others lease).[107]

First-generation electronic journals actually sent to the library via e-mail or listservs lend themselves reasonably well to the traditional model. For example, in 1993 Lawrence R. Keating II, Christa Easton Reinke, and Judi A. Goodman, describing the handling of first-generation electronic journals at the University of Houston libraries, wrote that " e-journals should be treated like any other information resource and incorporated into normal processing routines."[108] In contrast, remote-access journals pointed to on the Web depart from the traditional management model in numerous ways. Rather than being sent to the library, remote-access journals have library patrons sent to them. Accordingly, the concepts of acquisition, check-in, claiming, and holdings hardly seem directly applicable. Nevertheless, such functions as selection, deselection, budgeting, maintenance, and possibly cataloging are still relevant. Also, traditional functions may continue in an altered form (e.g., negotiating a license agreement instead of placing a subscription).

COLLECTIONS OF FULL-TEXT TRADITIONAL JOURNALS IN ELECTRONIC FORM

Since the 1980s innumerable indexes and abstracts have been available on CD-ROM (e.g., *Library Literature).* The concept's extension to the inclusion of periodical full text in CD-ROM or other electronic formats was predictable. This phenomenon is frequently referred to as *full text,* which an ALA survey report recently defined as "material already published in ink on paper and now available in electronic full text from services (such as IAC, UMI, EBSCO, OCLC, DIALOG, NEXIS/LEXIS) for which the library pays a subscription or access fee."[109]

ADONIS is arguably the most famous example. Under development since the late 1970s, this project provides the full text of articles from more than 200 STM journals. For an in-depth analysis of ADONIS, see Barrie T. Stern and Robert M. Campbell.[110]

Permutations on this concept are offered by some serial subscription agents. Full text of periodicals are included in a host of EBSCO databases, many of which are designed for particular types of libraries. Some representative examples, as advertised on the EBSCO WWW page in November 1996, are briefly depicted below.

Academic Abstracts FullTEXT. Advertised as "designed to fit the needs of small colleges," it contains abstracts and indexing for 850 publications, "searchable" full text for 125 journals, and coverage of the *New York Times*.

Academic Search FullTEXT 1,000. It includes abstracts and indexing for 3,100 "scholarly" journals, full text for more than 1,000 journals, and coverage of the *Christian Science Monitor*, the *New York Times*, and the *Wall Street Journal*.

Canadian MAS FullTEXT Elite. It holds abstracts and indexing for more than 400 U.S. and Canadian magazines, with searchable full text for over 140, and is aimed at Canadian high school and junior college libraries. *Canadian MAS FullTEXT Select* is an abbreviated version.

MasterFile FullText 350, MasterFile FullText 650, MasterFile FullTEXT 1,000, and *MasterFile FullTEXT 1,500.* Advertised as suitable for public, academic, and business libraries, they contain indexing and abstracts for more than 3,100 journals and full text for the number of journals in their titles.

Several EBSCO databases with journal full text are oriented toward specific library markets: *Middle Search Plus,* for junior high and middle school students; *Primary Search,* for elementary schools; and *Public Library FullTEXT,* for public libraries. EBSCO also markets *Business Source Elite, Business Source Plus, General Science Source, Health Source, Health Source Plus, Humanities Source, Military FullText*, and *Social Science Source,* all of which contain abstracts, indexing, and full text in the subject areas indicated by their titles. These services are generally available in several formats, including CD-ROM, a local tape load, or through EBSCOhost, although the options vary from title to title.[111]

Because full-text journal collections are rapidly evolving, their ultimate impact on library serials management can not be predicted. They could clearly be used to augment the present collection or as a substitution for canceled titles. Print subscriptions could conceivably be canceled after acquiring the full-text database. When mounted with an OPAC on a campuswide information system, full-text journal databases typically require a password for access (due to licensing restrictions), unlike conventional print journals, which can be used by anyone in open stack libraries.

ELECTRONIC JOURNAL COLLECTIONS

A group of electronic journals systematically arranged on a gopher or Web page could be considered an electronic journal collection. Unlike traditional print journals, the titles in an electronic collection need not be located together on the same server.

The CIC, through its CICNet project, has been a major player in the creation of electronic journal collections. The original CICNet project conceptualized in 1992, termed the Electronic Serials Archive, sought to archive on a gopher all the public domain electronic journals available on the Internet. In 1994 it was proclaimed "the largest and most comprehensive single site for electronic serials in the public domain."[112] In 1994 CICNet contained more than 700 electronic journal titles, organized into 25 broad subject categories, but it was deactivated in May 1996.

Based on the recommendation of a task force appointed in February 1993, CICNet decided to create a "managed" collection to be termed the Electronic Journal Collection (EJC). Unlike the Electronic Serials Archive, which contained many scattered, incomplete, noncurrent holdings (anything that could be obtained for free on the Internet through ftp), the managed collection is to be selected, cataloged, and continuously monitored by professional staff. Rather than being limited to titles available through ftp, it will also include electronic journals accessible through gophers and Web pages. The prototype for the EJC, containing approximately 50 journals as of late 1996, can be accessed on the CIC's WWW home page. CIC was then seeking grant funding to underwrite the project's completion.[113]

Useful reviews of electronic journal collections and resources available on the Internet were provided by Birdie MacLennan in 1994 and 1995, including CICNet, the LC, the MIT libraries, the University of California at Santa Barbara's InfoSurf, and the University of California at Santa Cruz's InfoSlug.[114] Unfortunately, some of the sites annotated by MacLennan have not been kept current. Some electronic journal collections available on the WWW are annotated in appendix 3.

One should mention the so-called Mr. Serials process, developed at the North Carolina State University library, for automated creation of electronic journal collections for a specific library. The program provides a systematic process for selection, storage, access, organization, bibliographic control, and acquisitions of electronic journals that are delivered by e-mail.[115]

What are the implications of electronic journal collections for libraries? They can serve as a form of cooperative collection development among libraries. A library, through its gopher or WWW site, can easily link to an electronic journal collection. In contrast to traditional cooperative collection development, permission or a formal agreement is usually not required for such links, although some proprietary titles requiring passwords may not be available. Although the practical uses will vary among different electronic journal collections (depending upon a particular collection's purpose), such collections can be used for identification of electronic journals in the selection process; as a source of cataloging records (e.g., the CICNet project); or to perform an archival function. From a broader perspective, these collections can contribute to the scholarly communications process by facilitating direct end user access to electronic serials without a library's intervention.

THE ELECTRONIC JOURNAL'S ROLE IN SCHOLARLY COMMUNICATION

The numerous problems associated with the present system of scholarly communication through print journals include high journal cost; the scattering of articles on a subject due to the proliferation of journals; lengthy delays in publication; reviewer bias in the refereeing system;[116] highly specialized, low-circulation journals; a declining revenue base for journal publishers; lack of timely feedback to authors; and the "reselling of scholarly writing" (i.e., university libraries buy back from commercial publishers the research their own faculties publish).[117] Without doubt, the much-lamented "serials crisis" in libraries has been brought on by the traditional system of paper journals.

One major factor in the rise of the traditional journal as a scholarly communications mechanism is that it disseminates information more rapidly than the book. The electronic journal takes this process one step further by disseminating information more rapidly than the traditional journal. As noted above, this issue has been a factor in the decision of some electronic journals to discontinue their paper version. Moreover, the first printed journals evolved from informal communication among scholars, and the earliest electronic publications (e.g., listservs) tended to serve as vehicles for informal discussion among scholars.[118]

A major issue concerns whether the electronic journal merely represents a different format for the traditional journal or an entirely new form of scholarly communication.[119] Because we are in a period of rapid change, the electronic journal's form five or ten years into the future is uncertain. Nevertheless, the electronic format offers potential features that are impossible with conventional print journals:

- Rapid revision
- Insertion of reader commentary
- Online searching and manipulation of text
- Hypertext links to cited documents and databases
- Multimedia features such as video and sound
- The ability to extract and manipulate formulas and graphics
- Notification systems to readers on articles of interest[120]

In addition, electronic journals offer some practical advantages to libraries:

- Quicker article delivery
- No concern about theft or mutilation
- Shelf storage space is not an issue
- Accessibility from outside the library
- Simultaneous use by more than one person (although some license agreements prescribe a maximum number of simultaneous users)

On the negative side, several problems or unresolved issues are presently associated with electronic journals:

- The reluctance of scholars to submit their best quality work to electronic publications
- Questions about full acceptance of electronic publications in the scholarly accreditation process (e.g., promotion and tenure)—related to the preceding point
- Unresolved copyright issues
- Publisher uncertainty about pricing and the subsequent lack of uniform pricing and licensing structures

- Questions about whether and how electronic journals will be permanently archived
- Rapidly changing technological developments
- End-users resisting the format or requiring training
- Hardware and software required for use

The refereeing status of electronic journals is intimately connected with their academic acceptance. Only a small fraction of the first electronic journals were refereed, although the number of refereed electronic journals has been steadily increasing. In 1993 the ARL's *Directory of Electronic Journals, Newsletters and Academic Discussion Lists* included approximately 100 refereed electronic journals.[121] In the United Kingdom, the Joint Funding Council's Libraries Review Group Report recommended in December 1993 that funding councils give refereed electronic journal publications equal weight with peer-reviewed print publications.[122]

SUMMARY

The electronic journal represents one of the largest and most exciting challenges confronting contemporary librarians. This format offers potential threats (e.g., that directly transmitting electronic journals to end users will eliminate libraries from the information loop) and potential opportunities (e.g., reducing serial expenditures and meeting client information needs more efficiently).

Library management of electronic journals is complicated by the rapidly changing external environment in terms of the technology itself, the Internet, the number of available electronic journals, and psychological acceptance of the format. More than one observer has commented that planning for the management of electronic journals in libraries is like shooting at a moving target.[123]

NOTES

1. John B. Black, "So We Have This Great Electronic Journal, Now What? Some Observations on the Practical Aspects of the Distribution of Electronic Journals," *Serials Review* 20 (winter 1994): 24-25. This is a summary of his presentation at the International Conference on Refereed Electronic Journals, at the University of Manitoba, Winnipeg, Manitoba, October 1993.

2. Stephen P. Harter and Hak Joon Kim, "Accessing Electronic Journals and Other E-Publications: An Empirical Study," *College and Research Libraries* 57 (September 1996): 446. The three most frequently used formats were ASCII, by 80 journals; HTML, by 62; and PostScript, by 24.

3. Gary Taubes, "Science Journals Go Wired," *Science News* 271 (February 9, 1996): 764.

4. Dennis G. Perry, Steven H. Blumenthal, and Robert M. Hinden, "The ARPANET and DARPA Internet," *Library Hi Tech* 6, no. 2 (1988): 51. ARPA stands for Advanced Research Projects Agency and DARPA, Defense Advanced Research Projects Agency.

5. Laverna Saunders-McMaster, "Internet 2: An Overview of the Next Generation of the Internet," *Computers in Libraries* 17 (March 1997): 57-59.

6. John December and Neil Randall, *The World Wide Web Unleashed* (Indianapolis, Ind.: SAMS Publishing, 1994), 45-46.

7. David Angell and Brent Heslop, *Mosaic for Dummies, Windows Edition* (Foster City, Calif.: IDG Books, 1995), 19.

8. December and Randall, *The World Wide Web Unleashed*, 46.

9. Angell and Heslop, *Mosaic for Dummies*, 19.

10. "Energizing the 'Net,' " *USA Today,* October 30, 1995, sec. B, p. 1.

11. Netcraft. *The Netcraft Web Server Survey.* Available: http://www.netcraft.co.uk/survey/ (Accessed March 8, 1998). The author thanks Jian Liu, the Indiana University Libraries Reference Department for providing this information.

12. Ibid., (Accessed April 8, 1998).

13. Marie Kascus and Faith Merriman, "Using the Internet in Serials Management," *College and Research Libraries News* 56 (March 1995): 176.

14. Acqweb. *The Acqweb International Directory of Email Addresses of Publishers, Vendors and Related Professional Associations, Organizations, and Services.* Available: http:// www.library.vanderbilt.edu/law/acqs/email-ad.html (Accessed March 8, 1998).

15. University of Chicago Press. *University of Chicago Press Journals Division.* Available: http://www.journals.uchicago.edu/ (Accessed March 8, 1998).

16. Acqweb. *Acqweb's Home Page.* Available: http://www.library.vanderbilt.edu/law/acqs/ acqs.html (Accessed March 8, 1998).

17. The Faxon Company. *Faxon Home Page* Available: http://www.faxon.com (Accessed March 1, 1998).

18. University of Chicago Press. *Library Quarterly Home Page.* Available: http://www. journals.uchicago.edu/LQ/home.html (Accessed March 8, 1998).

19. John V. Richardson, "Library Quarterly Web homepage," *JESSE* (March 13, 1995).

20. American Association for the Advancement of Slavic Studies. *Slavic Review Home Page.* Available: http://harold.econ.uiuc.edu/~slavrev/index1.html (Accessed March 8, 1998).

21. National Library of Australia. *Australian Journals Online.* Available: http://www.nla.gov.au/ oz/pausejour.html (Accessed March 8, 1998).

22. University of Southern California Law School and Law Library. *Legal Journals on the Web.* Available: http://www.usc.edu/dept/law-lib/legal/journals.html (Accessed March 8, 1998)

23. Electronic Newsstand. *Welcome to the Electronic Newsstand.* Available: http://www.enews.com/ (Accessed March 8, 1998).

24. Emory University Health Sciences Center Library. *MedWeb: Electronic Publications.* Available: http://www.gen.emory.edu/MEDWEB/keyword/electronic_publications.html (Accessed March 8, 1998).

25. Gregory Szczyrbak, "Serials Web Page Summary," *SERIALST* (October 27, 1996).

26. Mark Stover and Steven D. Zink, "World Wide Web Home Page Design: Patterns and Anomalies of Higher Education Library Home Pages," *RSR: Reference Services Review* 24 (fall 1996): 7-16.

27. Donna Canevari de Paredes, "Serials Cancellation Projects," *CollDV-L* (March 18, 1997).

28. Massachusetts Institute of Technology Libraries. *1995/96 Serial Review and Cancellation Project*. Available: http://macfadden.mit.edu:9500/sercan/top.html (Accessed March 8, 1998).

29. Herb Weinryb, "Accessing European Serials Cataloging Records Through the Internet," *Serials Librarian* 26, no. 2 (1995): 65-74.

30. Bill Eager, *Using the World Wide Web* (Indianapolis, Ind.: Que, 1994), 10.

31. Birdie MacLennan, "Serials in Cyberspace: Collections, Resources, and Services on the Networks (an Overview As of March 1995)," in *Directory of Electronic Journals, Newsletters and Academic Discussion Lists*, 5th ed., comp. Lisabeth A. King and Diane Kovacs, ed. Ann Okerson (Washington, D.C.: ARL Office of Scientific and Academic Publishing, 1995), 35-36.

32. Electronic Newsstand. *Welcome to the Electronic Newsstand*. Available: http://www.enews.com/ (Accessed March 8, 1998).

33. Anne B. Piternick, "Electronic Serials: Realistic or Unrealistic Solution to the Journal 'Crisis'?" *Serials Librarian* 21, nos. 2/3 (1991): 22.

34. Ann L. Okerson, "The Electronic Journal Environment, 1993," *Serials Review* 20 (winter 1994): 22. This is a summary of her presentation at the International Conference on Refereed Electronic Journals.

35. Joan O'C. Hamilton and Heidi Dawley, "Darwinism and the Internet: Why Scientific Journals Could Go the Way of the Pterodactyl," *Business Week* no. 3430 (June 26, 1995): 44.

36. Bernard Naylor, "Ginsparg Los Alamos Preprint Archive," *Newsletter on Serials Pricing Issues,* no. 134 (March 22, 1995). These preprints are available prior to peer review. The archive was originally limited to high energy physics but expanded to other areas of physics.

37. International Philosophical Preprint Exchange. *IPPE-International Philosophical Preprint Exchange*. Available: http://ds.internic.net/cgi-bin/enthtml/ftpsite/ippe.b (Accessed March 9, 1998).

38. Edward Lim, "Preprint Servers: A New Model for Scholarly Publishing," *Australian Academic and Research Libraries* 27 (March 1996): 30.

39. Ann Okerson, "Introduction," in *Directory of Electronic Journals, Newsletters and Academic Discussion Lists*, 4th ed., comp. Lisabeth A. King and Diane Kovacs, ed. Ann Okerson (Washington, D.C.: Association of Research Libraries, 1994), iv.

40. Clifford A. Lynch, "The Transformation of Scholarly Communication and the Role of the Library in the Age of Networked Information," *Serials Librarian* 23, nos. 3/4 (1993): 8.

41. Glenda Ann Thornton, "Physical Access to Periodical Literature: The Dilemma Revisited and a Brief Look at the Future," *Serials Review* 17, no. 4 (1991): 39, 41.

42. Elizabeth Parang and Laverna Saunders, comps., *Electronic Journals in ARL Libraries: Issues and Trends*, SPEC Kit 202 (Washington, D.C.: Association of Research Libraries, Office of Management Studies, 1994), 4.

43. Mary Jo Lynch, "Electronic Services: Who's Doing What?" *College and Research Libraries News* 57 (November 1996): 662.

44. Mary Jo Lynch, project director, *Electronic Services in Academic Libraries* (Chicago: American Library Association, 1996), 16.

45. The Virginia Tech Task Force has been described by Gail McMillan, "Embracing the Electronic Journal: One Library's Plan," *Serials Librarian* 21, nos. 2/3 (1991): 97-108.

46. Margo Sassé and B. Jean Winkler, "Electronic Journals: A Formidable Challenge for Librarians," *Advances in Librarianship* 17 (1993): 159-61.

47. Marian Dworaczek and Victor G. Wiebe, "E-Journals: Acquisition and Access," *Acquisitions Librarian,* no. 12 (1994): 110.

48. Hazel M. Woodward, "The Impact of Electronic Information on Serials Collection Management," *IFLA Journal* 20 (February 1994): 36. Precise dates are not given, but the Loughborough Task Force apparently issued its report sometime in 1993.

49. Parang and Saunders, *Electronic Journals in ARL Libraries.* The other five were the University of Alberta, the University of Nebraska at Lincoln, the University of Tennessee at Knoxville, and Virginia Polytechnic Institute and State University.

50. Michael Buckland, "What Will Collection Developers Do?" *Information Technology and Libraries* 14 (September 1995): 158.

51. Parang and Saunders, *Electronic Journals in ARL Libraries,* 5. The specific question was, "Who decides which journals are added to the collection?"

52. Samuel Demas, "Collection Development for the Electronic Library: A Conceptual and Organizational Model," *Library Hi Tech* 12, no. 3 (1994): 71-80.

53. Joseph Jones. *Ejournal Site Guide: A Meta Source.* Available: http://www.library.ubc.ca/ejour (Accessed March 1, 1998).

54. Committee on Institutional Cooperation. *CIC Electronic Journals Collection.* Available: http://ejournals.cic.net/ (Accessed March 1, 1998).

55. Committee on Institutional Cooperation. *CIC EJournal Archive.* The CIC Archive. [The archive itself was taken down in May 1996.] Available: gopher://gopher.cic.net:2000/11/e-serials/archive (Accessed March 1, 1998).

56. University of Houston Libraries. *Scholarly Journals Distributed via the World Wide Web.* Available: http://info.lib.uh.edu/wj/webjour.html (Accessed. March 1, 1998).

57. *CD-ROMs in Print* (Westport, Conn.: Meckler, 1987-).

58. *Gale Directory of Databases,* vol. 2: *CD-ROM, Diskette, Magnetic Tape, Handheld, and Batch Access Database Products.* (Detroit, Mich.: Gale Research, 1993-).

59. Parang and Saunders, *Electronic Journals in ARL Libraries,* 5.

60. Carl H. Gotsch, "How Many Online Journals," *ARL-EJOURNAL List* (November 20, 1996).

61. Ellen Duranceau and others, "Electronic Journals in the MIT Libraries: Report of the 1995 E-Journal Subgroup," *Serials Review* 22 (spring 1996): 56-57.

62. Parang and Saunders, *Electronic Journals in ARL Libraries,* 6.

63. Yale University Library. *LIBLICENCE: Licensing Digital Information—Introduction.* Available: http://www.library.yale.edu/~llicense/intro.shtml (Accessed April 6, 1998).

64. Richard P. Jasper, "ALCTS Acquisitions Administrators Discussion Group: Electronic Journal Pricing and Licensing; Where Do Librarians and Publishers Agree?" *Library Acquisitions: Practice and Theory* 20 (fall 1996): 379-81. Jasper summarizes Meta Nissley's presentation at the 1996 ALA Midwinter Meeting.

65. Gail McMillan, "Embracing the Electronic Journal: One Library's Plan," *Serials Librarian* 21, nos. 2/3 (1991): 105.

66. Duranceau and others, "Electronic Journals in the MIT Libraries," 59.

67. Parang and Saunders, *Electronic Journals in ARL Libraries*, 8.

68. McMillan, "Embracing the Electronic Journal," 105.

69. Steve Harter, "Authentication Schemes for Individual Campus Subscriptions," *VPIEJ-L* (October 10, 1995).

70. Parang and Saunders, *Electronic Journals in ARL Libraries*, 5.

71. Taemin Kim Park, "Bibliographic Control and Access of Networked Electronic Journals in OCLC and Local Libraries," 12, unpublished manuscript, which she kindly provided to me.

72. Mary Beth Fecko, *Cataloging Nonbook Resources: A How-to-Do-It-Manual for Librarians* (New York: Neal-Schuman, 1993), 147-60.

73. Nancy B. Olson, ed. *Cataloging Internet Resources: A Manual and Practical Guide, 2nd ed.* Available: http://www.oclc.org/oclc/man/9256cat/toc.html (Accessed March 1, 1998).

74. In essence, CONSER defines "remote access" electronic journals as those available on networks rather than on CD-ROMs or floppy disks.

75. Bill Anderson and Les Hawkins, "Development of CONSER Cataloging Policies for Remote Access Computer Files," *Public-Access Computer Systems Review* 7, no. 1 (1996): 6. Available: http://info.lib.uh.edu/pr/v7/n1/anderson.7n1 (Accessed March 1, 1998).

76. Ellen Finnie Duranceau, ed., "Cataloging Remote-Access Electronic Serials: Rethinking the Role of the OPAC," *Serials Review* 21 (winter 1995): 67-77.

77. Martha Hruska, "Remote Internet Serials in the OPAC?" *Serials Review* 21 (winter 1995): 69.

78. Eric Lease Morgan, "Adding Internet Resources to Our OPACs," *Serials Review* 21 (winter 1995): 70.

79. Hruska, "Remote Internet Serials in the OPAC?" 69.

80. Allison Mook Sleeman, "Cataloging Remote Access Electronic Materials," *Serials Review* 21 (winter 1995): 74.

81. Regina Reynolds, "Inventory List or Information Gateway? The Role of the Catalog in the Digital Age," *Serials Review* 21 (winter 1995): 75-77.

82. Hruska, "Remote Internet Serials in the OPAC?" 68.

83. Parang and Saunders, *Electronic Journals in ARL Libraries*, 6.

84. Park, "Bibliographic Control and Access of Networked Electronic Journals in OCLC and Local Libraries," 9-11. She took a purposeful sample of networked electronic journals that were peer-reviewed or had an ISSN from the 1995 *Directory of Electronic Journals, Newsletters and Academic Discussion Lists*.

85. Duranceau and others, "Electronic Journals in the MIT Libraries," 55.

86. John Dovey, "Archiving in Perpetuo—III," *VPIEJ-L* (July 27, 1995).

87. See note 55 (above).

88. Richard Frieder, "Archiving Electronic Journals," *ARL-EJOURNAL List* (November 20, 1996). OCLC will use software to keep track of the titles and volumes to which a library has subscribed.

89. Harter and Kim, "Accessing Electronic Journals and Other E-Publications," 448.

90. Donnice Cochenour and Tom Moothart, "Relying on the Kindness of Strangers: Archiving Electronic Journals on Gopher," *Serials Review* 21 (spring 1995): 74.

91. D. Scott Brandt, "Campus-Wide Computing," *Academic and Library Computing* 9 (November-December 1992): 18.

92. Parang and Saunders, *Electronic Journals in ARL Libraries*, 7.

93. Duranceau and others, "Electronic Journals in the MIT Libraries," 51.

94. Ibid., 55.

95. Parang and Saunders, *Electronic Journals in ARL Libraries*, 9.

96. Ibid., 8. Other responses were locally developed manuals, 26 percent (9); software tutorial programs, 3 percent (1); programmed instruction, 3 percent (1); and other, 8 percent (3).

97. Elizabeth Futas, *Collection Development Policies and Procedures*, 3d ed. (Phoenix, Ariz.: Oryx Press, 1995), 4.

98. Parang and Saunders, *Electronic Journals in ARL Libraries*, 5.

99. Gregory F. Pratt, Patrick Flannery, and Cassandra L. D. Perkins, "Guidelines for Internet Resource Selection," *College and Research Libraries News* 57 (March 1996): 134-35.

100. Gordon B. Neavill and Mary Ann Sheblé, "Archiving Electronic Journals," *Serials Review* 21 (winter 1995): 15.

101. Charles W. Bailey Jr., "Electronic (Online) Publishing in Action . . . *The Public-Access Computer Systems Review* and Other Electronic Serials," *Online* 15 (January 1991): 31.

102. Clifford A. Lynch, "The Roles of Libraries in Access to Networked Information: Cautionary Tales from the Era of Broadcasting," in *Emerging Communities: Integrating Networked Information into Library Services: Papers Presented at the 1993 Clinic on Library Applications of Data Processing, April 4-6, 1993*, ed. Ann P. Bishop (Urbana-Champaign, Ill.: Graduate School of Library and Information Science, University of Illinois at Urbana-Champaign, 1994), 123-24, 130.

103. Hazel Woodward and Cliff McKnight, "Electronic Journals: Issues of Access and Bibliographical Control," *Serials Review* 21 (summer 1995): 74.

104. Tom Moothart, "Blackwell's Periodicals Entry into E-Journal Distribution," *Serials Review* 22 (winter 1996): 83-86.

105. Michael Rogers, "Electronic Journal Navigator Development Project Launched," *Library Journal* 121 (October 1, 1996): 25.

106. Mary Jo Lynch, *Electronic Services in Academic Libraries*, 17.

107. Chiou-sen Dora Chen, *Serials Management: A Practical Guide* (Chicago: American Library Association, 1995), 68.

108. Lawrence R. Keating II, Christa Easton Reinke, and Judi A. Goodman, "Electronic Journal Subscriptions," *Library Acquisitions: Practice and Theory* 17 (winter 1993): 456.

109. Mary Jo Lynch, *Electronic Services in Academic Libraries*, 6.

110. Barrie T. Stern and Robert M. Campbell, "ADONIS—Publishing Journal Articles on CD-ROM," in *Advances in Serials Management: A Research Annual*, vol. 3, ed. Jean G. Cook and Marcia Tuttle (Greenwich, Conn.: JAI Press, 1989), 1-60.

111. EBSCO Publishing. *EBSCO Publishing Proprietary and Licensed Databases*. Available: http://www.epnet.com/database.html#aae (Accessed March 1, 1998).

112. Birdie MacLennan, "Electronic Serial Sites: Collections, Resources, and Services on the Networks," in *Directory of Electronic Journals, Newsletters and Academic Discussion Lists*, 4th ed., comp. by Lisabeth A. King and Diane Kovacs, ed. Ann Okerson (Washington, D.C.: Association of Research Libraries, 1994), 24.

113. Donnice Cochenour, "CICNet's Electronic Journal Collection," *Serials Review* 22 (spring 1996): 63-68.

114. MacLennan, "Electronic Serial Sites," 23-34; and "Serials in Cyberspace," 11-40.

115. Eric Lease Morgan, "Description and Evaluation of the 'Mr. Serials' Process: Automatically Collecting, Organizing, Archiving, Indexing, and Disseminating Electronic Serials," *Serials Review* 21 (winter 1995): 1-12.

116. Hak Joon Kim, "Electronic Journals As a New Medium for Formal Scholarly Communication and Key Factors That Influence Their Acceptance" (Ph.D. qualifying paper, Indiana University, 1996), 11.

117. Pieter A. van Brakel, "Electronic Journals: Publishing via Internet's World Wide Web," *Electronic Library* 13 (August 1995): 390-91.

118. Ann Okerson, "Electronic Journal Publishing on the Net: Developments and Issues," in *New Technologies and New Directions: Proceedings from the Symposium on Scholarly Communication, the University of Iowa, November 14-16, 1991*, ed. G. R. Boynton and Sheila D. Creth. (Westport, Conn.: Meckler, 1993), 51-64. Okerson states, "I am not alone in the view that a great deal of the informally continuing 'conversations' on the Net are the beginnings of a new kind of journal (or an old one, if you will, the notebooks, conversations, and diaries that were the precursors of today's formal paper journal)."

119. Okerson, "Electronic Journal Publishing on the Net," 53.

120. Karen A. Hunter, "The Changing Business of Scholarly Publishing," *Journal of Library Administration* 19, nos. 3/4 (1993): 28 lists several of these potential features.

121. Woodward and McKnight, "Electronic Journals," 73.

122. Stevan Harnad, "Credit for Electronic Journal Publication in the UK," *VPIEJ-L* (July 26, 1995).

123. Thomas E. Nisonger, "Collection Management Issues for Electronic Journals," *IFLA Journal* 22, no. 3 (1996): 233.

FURTHER READING

Electronic Journals

Amiran, Eyal, Elaine Orr, and John Unsworth. "Refereed Electronic Journals and the Future of Scholarly Publishing." *Advances in Library Automation and Networking* 4 (1991): 25-53.

Anderson, Bill, and Les Hawkins. "Development of CONSER Cataloging Policies for Remote Access Computer Files." *Public-Access Computer Systems Review* 7, no. 1 (1996): 6-25. Available: http://info.lib.uh.edu/pr/v7/n1/anderson.7n1 (Accessed March 1, 1998).

Arms, William Y. "Scholarly Publishing on the National Networks." *Scholarly Publishing* 23 (April 1992): 158-69.

Auld, Larry. "Reader Interaction with the Online Journal." *Serials Review* 12 (summer and fall 1986): 83-85.

Bailey, Charles W., Jr. "Electronic (Online) Publishing in Action . . . *The Public-Access Computer Systems Review* and Other Electronic Serials." *Online* 15 (January 1991): 28-35.

———. "Network-Based Electronic Serials." *Information Technology and Libraries* 11 (March 1992): 29-35.

Barschall, H. H. "Electronic Version of Printed Journals." *Serials Review* 18, nos. 1/2 (1992): 49-51.

Brandt, D. Scott. "Campus-Wide Computing." *Academic and Library Computing* 9 (November-December 1992): 17-20.

Buhsmer, John H., and Andrew Elston. "NewsNet." *Serials Review* 13 (fall 1987): 13-18.

Butler, Brett. "Electronic Editions of Serials: The Virtual Library Model." *Serials Review* 18, nos. 1/2 (1992): 102-6.

Butler, H. Julene, ed. "Abstracts of Papers Presented at the International Conference on Refereed Journals, October 1993." *Serials Review* 20 (winter 1994): 21-30.

Caplan, Priscilla. "Controlling E-Journals: The Internet Resources Project, Cataloging Guidelines, and USMARC." *Serials Librarian* 24, nos. 3/4 (1994): 103-11.

Cochenour, Donnice. "CICNet's Electronic Journal Collection." *Serials Review* 22 (spring 1996): 63-68.

Cochenour, Donnice, and Tom Moothart. "Relying on the Kindness of Strangers: Archiving Electronic Journals on Gopher." *Serials Review* 21 (spring 1995): 67-76.

Cook, Brian, ed. *The Electronic Journal: The Future of Serials-Based Information*. New York: Haworth Press, 1992. Also issued as *Australian and New Zealand Journal of Serials Librarianship* 3, no. 2 (1992).

Craighead, Laura M., and William C. Dougherty. "The Systems Approach to Electronic Journals." *Serials Review* 17 (winter 1991): 78-80.

Drummond, Louis. "Going Beyond Online." *Online* 14 (September 1990): 6-8.

Duranceau, Ellen, and others. "Electronic Journals in the MIT Libraries: Report of the 1995 E-Journal Subgroup." *Serials Review* 22 (spring 1996): 47-61.

Dykhuis, Randy. "The Promise of Electronic Publishing: OCLC's Program." *Computers in Libraries* 14 (November/December 1994): 20-22.

Eisenberg, Daniel. "The Electronic Journal." *Scholarly Publishing* 20 (October 1988): 49-58.

Entlich, Richard. "Electronic Chemistry Journals: Elemental Concerns." *Serials Librarian* 25, nos. 3/4 (1995): 111-23.

Fecko, Mary Beth. "Electronic Serials." In *Cataloging Nonbook Resources: A How-to-Do-It-Manual for Librarians*, 147-60. New York: Neal-Schuman, 1993.

Gardner, William. "The Electronic Archive: Scientific Publishing for the 1990s." *Psychological Science* 1 (November 1990): 333-41.

Grochmal, Helen M. "Selecting Electronic Journals." *College and Research Libraries News* 56 (October 1995): 632-33, 654.

Harnad, Stevan. "Scholarly Skywriting and the Prepublication Continuum of Scientific Inquiry." *Psychological Science* 1 (November 1990): 342-44.

Harter, Stephen P., and Hak Joon Kim. "Accessing Electronic Journals and Other E-Publications: An Empirical Study." *College and Research Libraries* 57 (September 1996): 440-56.

———. *Electronic Journals and Scholarly Communication: A Citation and Reference Study.* Available: http://php.indiana.edu/~harter/harter-asis96midyear.html (Accessed March 1, 1998).

Johnson, Peggy. "Electronic Scholarly Communication." *Technicalities* 10 (June 1990): 4-7.

Jul, Erik. "Electronic Journals in a Print-on-Paper World." *Computers in Libraries* 12 (February 1992): 37-38.

———. "Of Barriers and Breakthroughs." *Computers in Libraries* 12 (March 1992): 20-21.

Keating, Lawrence R., II, Christa Easton Reinke, and Judi A. Goodman. "Electronic Journal Subscriptions." *Library Acquisitions: Practice and Theory* 17 (winter 1993): 455-63.

Lancaster, F. Wilfrid, ed. "Networked Scholarly Publishing." *Library Trends* 43 (spring 1995): 515-756.

Langschied, Linda. "Electronic Journal Forum: VPIEJ-L: An Online Discussion Group for Electronic Journal Publishing Concerns." *Serials Review* 20 (spring 1994): 89-94.

Malinconico, Michael. "Electronic Documents and Research Libraries." *IFLA Journal* 22, no. 3 (1996): 211-25.

Manoff, Marlene, and others. "The MIT Libraries Electronic Journals Project: Reports on Patron Access and Technical Processing." *Serials Review* 19 (fall 1993): 15-40.

Manoff, Marlene, Eileen Dorschner, and Marilyn Geller. "Report of the Electronic Journals Task Force, MIT Libraries." *Serials Review* 18 (spring and summer 1992): 113-29.

McMillan, Gail. "Electronic Journals: Considerations for the Present and the Future." *Serials Review* 17 (winter 1991): 77-86.

———. "Embracing the Electronic Journal: One Library's Plan." *Serials Librarian* 21, nos. 2/3 (1991): 97-108.

———. "Technical Processing of Electronic Journals." *Library Resources and Technical Services* 36 (October 1992): 470-77.

Moothart, Tom. "Providing Access to E-Journals Through Library Home Pages." *Serials Review* 22 (summer 1996): 71-77.

Morgan, Eric Lease. "Description and Evaluation of the 'Mr. Serials,' Process: Automatically Collecting, Organizing, Archiving, Indexing, and Disseminating Electronic Serials." *Serials Review* 21 (winter 1995): 1-12.

Neavill, Gordon B., and Mary Ann Sheblé. "Archiving Electronic Journals." *Serials Review* 21 (winter 1995): 13-21.

Nisonger, Thomas E. "Collection Management Issues for Electronic Journals." *IFLA Journal* 22, no. 3 (1996): 233-39.

———. "Electronic Journal Collection Management Issues." *Collection Building* 16, no. 2 (1997): 58-65.

———. "Electronic Journals: Post-Modern Dream or Nightmare: Report of the ALCTS CMDS Collection Development Librarians of Academic Libraries Discussion Group." *Library Acquisitions: Practice and Theory* 17 (fall 1993): 378-80.

Okerson, Ann. "Electronic Journal Publishing on the Net: Developments and Issues." In *New Technologies and New Directions: Proceedings from the Symposium on Scholarly Communication, the University of Iowa, November 14-16, 1991,* edited by G. R. Boynton and Sheila D. Creth, 51-64. Westport, Conn.: Meckler, 1993.

———. "The Electronic Journal: What, Whence, and When?" *Public-Access Computer Systems Review* 2, no. 1 (1991): 2-17. Available: http://info.lib.uh.edu/pr/v2/n1/okerson.2n1 (Accessed March 1, 1998).

Racine, Drew. "Access to Full-Text Journal Articles: Some Practical Considerations." *Library Administration and Management* 6 (spring 1992): 100-104.

Sassé, Margo, and B. Jean Winkler. "Electronic Journals: A Formidable Challenge for Librarians." *Advances in Librarianship* 17 (1993): 149-73.

Ungern-Sternberg, Sara von, and Mats G. Lindquist. "The Impact of Electronic Journals on Library Functions." *Journal of Information Science* 21, no. 5 (1995): 396-401.

Willis, Katherine, and others. "TULIP—The University Licensing Program: Experiences at the University of Michigan." *Serials Review* 20 (winter 1994): 39-47.

Woodward, Hazel M. "The Impact of Electronic Information on Serials Collection Management." *IFLA Journal* 20 (February 1994): 35-45.

Woodward, Hazel, and Cliff McKnight. "Electronic Journals: Issues of Access and Bibliographical Control." *Serials Review* 21 (summer 1995): 71-78.

The Internet and Serials

Kascus, Marie, and Faith Merriman. "Using the Internet in Serials Management." *College and Research Libraries News* 56 (March 1995): 148-50, 176.

Lim, Edward. "Preprint Servers: A New Model for Scholarly Publishing." *Australian Academic and Research Libraries* 27 (March 1996): 21-30.

Nisonger, Thomas E. "The Internet and Collection Management in Libraries: Opportunities and Challenges." In *Collection Management in the 21st Century: A Handbook for Librarians,* edited by G. E. Gorman and Ruth H. Miller, 29-58. Westport, Conn.: Greenwood Press, 1997.

Pratt, Gregory F., Patrick Flannery, and Cassandra L. D. Perkins. "Guidelines for Internet Resource Selection." *College and Research Libraries News* 57 (March 1996): 134-35.

Stein, Linda Lawrence. "What to Keep and What to Cut? Using Internet as an Objective Tool to Identify 'Core' Periodical Titles in a Specialized Subject Collection." *Technical Services Quarterly* 10, no. 1 (1992): 3-14.

Weinryb, Herb. "Accessing European Serials Cataloging Records Through the Internet." *Serials Librarian* 26, no. 2 (1995): 65-74.

Chapter Ten

Serials Automation

In a strict sense, the term *automation* refers to the application of machinery to perform work that would otherwise be done by human beings. Therefore, the use of photocopiers, facsimile machines, and (in bygone days) typewriters in libraries could technically fall under the rubric *library automation.* Currently, however, *library automation* is generally understood to refer to the use of computers, computer networks, or CD-ROM—the meaning used in this chapter.

Serials automation covers several distinct concepts, including automating serials control procedures in libraries, the electronic journal, automating bibliographic access to serials, and automated vendor services. Some of these topics have been dealt with wholly or partially in other chapters, such as the electronic journal in chapter 9. This chapter discusses the history of serials automation, the role of standards, and steps in the automation of serials processing. The focus is on automation's use for serials management and control rather than technological details about hardware, software, systems specifications, etc. No attempt is made to compare systems, and mention of a particular system should not be interpreted as endorsement.

HISTORY OF SERIALS AUTOMATION

The application of computer technology to library functions is generally considered to have begun during the 1960s or 1970s. Yet as far back as the 1940s, Ralph Parker, at the University of Texas at Austin, reportedly experimented with modifying for serials control his circulation system based on Hollerith punched cards.[1] During the 1950s scattered reports on the application of noncomputer technology to serials management appeared in the literature.[2] For example, in 1953 Ralph R. Shaw described the use of Photoclerk, which made photographic reproductions of serial records, in periodical claiming, routing, ordering, and renewing at 11 U.S. libraries, including Columbia University, the Enoch Pratt Free Library, and the U.S. Department of Agriculture.[3] A Flexowriter Automatic Writing machine was used to create periodical holdings lists at the U.S. Naval Postgraduate School library in Monterey, California.[4]

The earliest computerized serials systems were developed in-house, often by an academic library collaborating with a university computing center. Vendor-supplied systems were not available on the market, so libraries wishing to automate serials had no other option. Frederick G. Kilgour writes that the first computerized serials control system was developed at the University of California at San Diego library in the early 1960s. Prepunched cards corresponding to serials issues were processed at the university computing center. This system produced lists of serials holdings, received items, nonreceived items, claims, and expired subscriptions as well as binding lists.[5]

Gary M. Pitkin notes that certain functions were likely to be automated with each other, such as check-in and claiming, binding and holdings information, and routing and renewal.[6] Moreover, the earliest automated serial systems were rather crude by contemporary standards. They tended to focus on creating lists and operated in a batch mode.

The *Kansas Union List of Serials*, issued in 1965, was reportedly the first computer-produced, multiple-institution serials holding list. It listed 22,000 serial titles held by eight academic libraries.[7] During the 1970s computer technology was used to produce the *Pennsylvania Union List of Serials* and the *Minnesota Union List of Serials* as well as similar lists at the University of California at Los Angeles (UCLA), Stanford, and the University of California at Berkeley.[8]

By 1968 an online serials control system was operating at Laval University in Quebec, Canada.[9] Undoubtedly the most famous in-house serials system was PHILSOM (Periodical Holdings in the Library of the School of Medicine),[10] developed by the School of Medicine Library at the University of Washington (in St. Louis) and originally implemented in 1962.[11] William Saffady lists the San Francisco Public Library and the UCLA Biomedical Library, as well as the libraries at the University of Arizona, the University of Massachusetts, and the University of Washington, as others that implemented their own custom-designed online serials control systems during the early decades of library automation.[12]

Several of the successful systems were adopted for use, often with modifications, in other libraries. For example, the Lister Hill Library of the Health Sciences at the University of Alabama at Birmingham adopted a modified form of the PHILSOM system in the late 1960s and in the mid-1970s implemented a modified version of the UCLA Biomedical Library serials control system.[13]

The late 1960s and early 1970s saw the development of the four major North American bibliographic utilities: OCLC Online Computer Library Center (OCLC), Western Library Network (WLN), Research Libraries Information Network (RLIN), and University of Toronto Library Automation System (UTLAS, now called ISM Library Information Services). Their initial purpose was to support the automation of the cataloging function, but they now offer a wide variety of services, including retrospective conversion, authority control, archiving electronic journals, and so forth. The widespread acceptance during the 1970s of the MARC record (machine readable cataloging), including the MARC-S (machine readable cataloging serials format), was a major boost to library automation. The Cooperative Online Serials Program (CONSER) project (discussed in chapter 8) to create machine readable bibliographic records for serials, became operational in 1973.

During the 1970s many of the in-house serial systems of the 1960s were upgraded and converted to online. During the late 1970s OCLC introduced its serials subsystem for check-in, which Sara Heitshu describes as "never a total success . . . [but] a highly visible project and much discussed by librarians."[14]

However, the decade's major library automation efforts focused on circulation, which, along with cataloging, was one of the first two functions to be automated. According to Saffady, circulation lent itself well to automation because of its labor-intensive nature and because its resemblance to inventory control was easily understood by computer specialists with little knowledge of library operations.[15] Although there is no reason why serial volumes can not be bar coded and circulated, circulation automation was clearly oriented toward monographs.

In the 1980s, vendors began offering a variety of serials automation options to libraries, so that in-house development was no longer a necessity or even a desirable option. Heitshu reports the number of vendors marketing automated serials control systems increased from 4 in 1980 to 60 in 1986.[16] Early in the decade serial subscription agents began offering access to their databases on a time-sharing basis. For example, in 1981 Faxon introduced the LINX system, which offered serials check-in and access to payment records. Its DataLINX provided online access to the Faxon database of more than 200,000 titles. EBSCO also introduced EBSCONET.[17]

The major automation developments of the 1980s were Online Public Access Catalogs (OPACs) and integrated systems—both of which often treated serials as a stepchild. An integrated system uses a single database to perform such basic library functions as cataloging, circulation, acquisitions, and serials control. The same bibliographical record is linked to separate records for ordering, payment, routing, etc. Using of the same record for multiple functions is cost-effective and reduces the probability of inputting errors. When all modules are fully functioning, an integrated system allows exchange of information among the various modules so that received serials issues or new serial titles on order can be displayed in the OPAC. Unfortunately, serials control was all too often among the weakest modules or the last to be fully developed. Many of the initial OPACs did not include serials holdings information. However, serials presented an automation challenge because of their ongoing nature, frequent title changes, and the number of exceptions involved in serials work. Heitshu stresses that academic libraries now had a choice between the serials module of an integrated system (e.g., GEAC or NOTIS) or a stand-alone serials control system, such as B. H. Blackwell's PERLINE.[18]

During the 1980s a number of microcomputer-based serials control systems for small and medium-sized libraries entered the market. Saffady mentions CHECKMATE, marketed by the Cooperative Library Agency for Systems and Services, and the SC350 Serials Control System, developed by OCLC, as examples.[19] In 1982 REMO was developed by Readmore, and in 1986 Faxon introduced Micro-Linx, SMS Canada produced the DavexPC serials management system, and Dawson U.S. acquired PC Max, developed in the early 1980s by Dawson U.K.[20]

Also during the same decade, many libraries began using off-the-shelf word processing or database management software run on microcomputers for a variety of serials management or control functions, such as creating print-format serials holdings lists, budget control, assigning titles to subjects and departments, and organizing data for cancellation projects. Some commercial binderies began marketing their automated binding systems to libraries.[21]

The 1980s witnessed the rise of so-called turnkey vendors, who provided libraries a complete automation system, including hardware, software, installation, staff training, and ongoing maintenance. The term's derivation refers to the library ability to metaphorically "turn a key" and receive an automated system—just as one can turn a key and drive an automobile off a dealer's lot.

In 1987 Roy Rada and his collaborators published a paper about the use of expert systems for journal selection in the field of medicine.[22] However, this was not representative of a major trend of the decade. Indeed, the use of expert systems for library materials selection has only been tentatively explored by a few scholars.

A 1985 survey of college libraries by John A. Camp and others found that only 12.5 percent of the respondents (26 of 208) had online serials control systems: 8 (30.8 percent) were from bibliographic utilities; 7 (26.9 percent) were developed in-house; and 3 (11.5 percent) were obtained from turnkey vendors. At the same time, 35.8 percent (73 of 204) took part in online union lists of serials.[23] A 1986 survey of Association of College and Research Libraries (ACRL) college library directors by Jamie Webster Hastreiter, Larry Hardesty, and David Henderson found that 52.5 percent (62 of 118) had automated at least part of their periodical operations. Specifically, 10.2 percent had automated periodical ordering; 16.9 percent, check-in and claiming; 41.5 percent, holdings and 22.0 percent, periodical cataloging.[24]

The 1990s represent the fourth decade of library automation, yet in 1995 Chiou-sen Dora Chen wrote, "Finally in the 1990s, the time has come for serials automation."[25] A major trend of the mid- to late- 1990s is the shift to client/server integrated systems, although Jeff Barry, José-Marie Griffiths, and Gerald Lundeen wrote in April 1995 that the term *client/server* had become a "buzzword" whose precise meaning is ambiguous.[26]

In the 1990s the vendor market remained somewhat volatile. In 1994 Trisha Davis and James Huesmann wrote, "In the past year, several serials control systems have been phased out of production, others have been replaced or updated by dramatically different versions, and new systems have been introduced. It is a dynamic, growing field."[27] Also system migration (i.e., changing from one automated system to another), and networking among libraries, sometimes on a statewide basis such as the OhioLinks project, continued to increase throughout the 1990s, as did interest in the Serial Item and Contribution Identifier (SICI) standard and X12 for Electronic Data Interchange (EDI), discussed later in this chapter. Web-based OPACs, with direct links to electronic journal Uniform Resource Locators (URLs), which allow the end user to proceed seamlessly from the catalog to the journal itself, represent a significant trend of the late 1990s. The other major automation developments of the 1990s—the Internet, the World Wide Web (WWW), and electronic journals themselves—have been discussed elsewhere in this book.

In summary, the major automation trends affecting serials may be briefly recapitulated as follows. Prior to the 1960s few attempted to apply primitive or noncomputer technology to serials control. During the 1960s a number of systems were developed in-house, first in a batch mode and later online. In the 1970s these systems were further developed and not infrequently adopted or modified by other libraries. The 1980s witnessed integrated systems, off-the-shelf software, OPACs, and stand-alone systems run on microcomputers. The major trends of the 1990s are system migration, the client/server model, the Internet, the WWW, and electronic journals. Who knows what developments the third millennium will bring?

THE ROLE OF STANDARDS IN SERIALS AUTOMATION

Because standards are necessary for automation's effective use in serials management, they require considerable attention. What is a standard? According to the International Organization for Standardization (ISO), "Standards are documented agreements containing technical specifications or other precise criteria to be used consistently as rules, guidelines, or definitions of characteristics, to ensure that materials, products, processes and services are fit for their purpose."[28] There is not always a clear distinction between an automation and nonautomation standard because a single standard, for example, the International Standard Serial Number (ISSN), can be used in both an automated or nonautomated environment. Yet standards are especially critical to automation because they promote compatibility among different hardware, software, and systems. Accordingly, this section discusses the major organizations and standards that affect serials automation.

Standards Organizations

The major standards organizations whose actions affect serials are described below.[29]

American National Standards Institute

The American National Standards Institute (ANSI) describes itself as a "private-sector, nonprofit, membership organization"[30] that serves as "administrator and coordinator of the United States private sector voluntary standardization system."[31] Founded in 1918, ANSI is headquartered in New York City with an additional office in Washington, D.C. ANSI is the U.S. representative in the ISO.[32] This organization is probably familiar to readers because of the ANSI number assigned to adopted standards. ANSI has officially sanctioned at least six major standards pertaining to serials, several of which are discussed later in this chapter.

National Information Standards Organization

The National Information Standards Organization (NISO) is one of almost 300 U.S. organizations involved in developing technical standards for various industrial sectors. NISO specializes in standards pertaining to information. Its constituency comprises publishers, libraries, indexing and abstracting services, other information services, and automation vendors. NISO was founded in 1939 under the name the American National Standards Committee Z39. After some name changes and restructuring, it incorporated as a not-for-profit educational association and assumed its present name in 1984. At present there are more than 55 voting members of NISO, including the Library of Congress, the National Library of Medicine, the American Library Association (ALA), Readmore, Faxon, and EBSCO. NISO publishes a newsletter entitled *Information Services Quarterly*, and NISO Press sells standards and draft statements.[33]

A list of NISO standards may be found in a recent *Bowker Annual*. Among the six standards relevant to serials one should mention: ISSN (Z39.9-1992); SICI (Z39.56-1991); Serials Holding Statements (Z39.44-1986); and Electronic Manuscript Preparation and Markup (Z39.59-1987). The later two are presently under review or revision.[34]

International Organization for Standardization

The ISO (the abbreviation is from the French language, which is also used by this organization), founded in 1947, is a worldwide federation of more than 100 national standards organizations. The ISO Central Secretariat is located in Geneva, Switzerland.[35] A keyword search of the ISO Catalog of Standards on the WWW under the term *serials* retrieved seven items, including ISO/DIS 3297 for ISSN and ISO 9230:1991 for "determination of price indexes for books and serials purchased by libraries."

Book Industry Systems Advisory Committee

Although originally founded in 1974 for promotion of International Standard Book Numbers (ISBNs), the Book Industry Systems Advisory Committee (BISAC) later turned its attention to application of the ANSI Accredited Standards Committee (ASC) X12 standard for EDI in the book industry,[36] explained below. BISAC should be noted because it has been termed a "sister Committee" of the Serials Industry Systems Advisory Committee (SISAC).[37]

Serials Industry Systems Advisory Committee

SISAC was founded in 1982 at the behest of the Book Industry Study Group to develop serials automation standards for presentation to NISO and ANSI. It focused on three areas: computer-to-computer transmission of serials business transactions through the X12 standard for EDI; automation of serials check-in and control through the SICI standard; and standardized coding of articles to ease document delivery and royalty payments.[38]

Its members include publishers, librarians, serial subscription agents, and document delivery vendors. Headquartered in New York City, SISAC publishes the *SISAC Newsletter*, *SISAC News*, and SISAC-L—an Internet listserv for the discussion of SISAC business.[39] Two of its major achievements have been the SICI and the SISAC Bar Code Symbol. In the early 1990s it began to focus on the application of EDI to serials.

Canadian Serials Industry Systems Advisory Committee

Organized in 1991, the Canadian Serials Industry Systems Advisory Committee (CSISAC), is, as the name implies, the Canadian equivalent of SISAC. Through international committees, CSISAC has been collaborating with SISAC and the International Committee on Electronic Data Interchange for Serials (ICEDIS) on the development of EDI. CSISAC has also explored SICI, Standard Generalized Markup Language (SGML), and document delivery.[40]

International Committee on Electronic Data Interchange for Serials

Founded in 1989, ICEDIS's purpose is to foster cooperation between subscription agents and Science, Technical, and Medical (STM) publishers for promoting in the serials industry the use of EDI standards. It works in close conjunction with SISAC and CSISAC. ICEDIS's membership is composed of seven serial subscription agents (Blackwell, EBSCO, Faxon, Harrassowitz, Readmore, SWETS, and Turpin) plus eight scientific, technical, and medical publishers (Carfax, Elsevier Science, Harcourt Brace Jovanovich, Kluwer, the Royal Society of Chemistry, Springer-Verlag, Taylor & Francis, and John Wiley).[41] The committee has endorsed the ANSI ASC X12 standard.[42]

Automation Standards

The major automation standards pertinent to serials are discussed below.

International Standard Serial Number

The ISSN was discussed in chapter 2. Although not exclusively an automation standard, ISSNs contribute to the handling of serials in automated systems by allowing unique identification of a particular title and differentiating between serials with similar titles.

MARC

As stated on the Library of Congress MARC Home Page, "The MARC formats are standards for the representation and communication of bibliographic and related information in machine-readable form."[43] MARC is, in the words of Walt Crawford, "the single most important factor in the growth of library automation in the United States and other countries."[44] Histories of MARC's early development have been written by Henriette D. Avram[45] and Karen M. Spicher.[46] The Library of Congress developed and tested the MARC record during the 1960s. In March 1969 the Library of Congress began weekly distribution of MARC records for English-language books.[47] MARC was adopted by ANSI as a national standard in 1971 and as an international standard by ISO in 1973.[48]

MARC-S was initially published in 1970, and the Library of Congress began distributing MARC serials records in 1973.[49] In 1974 a second edition of the MARC serials format was issued, and in 1977 it was implemented by OCLC.[50]

Especially significant for serials is the MARC standard for holdings data. The Library of Congress published the *USMARC Format for Holdings and Locations* in 1984.[51] The revised version, the *USMARC Format for Holdings Data, Including Guidelines for Content Designation*, was published in 1989.[52] For an in-depth explanation of the MARC holdings format, see Frieda B. Rosenberg's chapter on managing serials holdings in Marcia Tuttle's *Managing Serials*.[53]

By the end of the 1980s, there were nine types of MARC records, for holdings data, authority records, and seven bibliographic formats: books, serials, maps, computer files, music, visual materials, and manuscripts. The *USMARC Format for Classification Data*[54] and the *USMARC Format for Community Information*[55] were issued during the early 1990s.

Detailed examination of the MARC record's structure is beyond this chapter's scope, but the four basic components will be briefly outlined. The "leader," the first 25 characters, contains information about the record itself rather than the bibliographic item being described and allows the computer program to read the record. Next, the "directory" indicates the position of each MARC field within the record, thus allowing the program to quickly locate specific information. The first 9 fields or "tags" of a MARC record (001 through 009) comprise the "variable control fields." These generally use fixed-field codes (i.e., one, two, or three place numerals or characters) to present data about both the record itself and the bibliographic item. As Deborah J. Byrne explains, "The coded information in the fixed field expresses the information explicitly and succinctly. This allows a computer to recognize the information and use it efficiently and effectively."[56] Finally, the "variable data fields" contain the textual information that describes the bibliographic item being cataloged. The number of fields and the length of each will vary from record to record. Tags and subfield codes are used to help the computer program locate specific fields and subfields. For example, tag 247 identifies the field for a former title or title variations. An "indicator" conveys specific instructions to the system about processing or a field's content. The reader is referred to Crawford and Byrne[57] for further explanation of MARC record structure.

MARC's major benefit is the creation of a uniform standard for machine readable cataloging records. It thus promotes the exchange of records among libraries and the use of bibliographic utilities. Moreover, it renders a library's database independent of specific hardware or software (as long as both are MARC compatible), thus supporting system migration. Yet, MARC may not be necessary for every automation objective. Crawford notes that "MARC is not the answer" for projects such as a small library's current periodicals list.[58] It is doubtful that a full MARC record is needed for acquisitions.

MARC "format integration" has recently received considerable attention within the serials community. For well over a decade, the system of different MARC record structures for seven separate bibliographic formats was clearly creating problems, especially for serials. Ostensibly, such nonserial items as maps, videocassettes, sound recordings, and computer files can simultaneously assume a serial form. MARC-S, developed for print serials, did not fully provide for describing the characteristics of nonprint materials.[59] Further difficulties were presented by mixed media items, such as a map or datafile accompanying a periodical.

In 1988 the USMARC Advisory Group approved Proposal 88-1, which established the guidelines for format integration.[60] After some delays, the Library of Congress began implementing format integration in early 1996 and the first records appeared in the MARC Distribution Service in March 1996.[61] With format integration the seven separate MARC records have been replaced by a single record structure. A new 006 MARC field allows the cataloger to indicate an item's secondary aspects (e.g., a datafile accompanying a periodical or the fact that a map is also a serial would be noted here). Also, many other fields, subfields, or indicators in MARC records have been added, deleted, expanded, or made obsolete by format integration.[62]

According to Rosenberg, format integration's practical implication for serials cataloging is that the nontextual format of nonprint serials will be their primary aspect, and seriality will be noted in the 006 field as a secondary characteristic. In other words, a serial computer file will be cataloged primarily as a computer file and secondarily as a serial.[63] Wayne Jones and Young-Hee Queinnec proclaim that format integration's major benefit is "better provision for the recording of data concerning nonprint serials."[64] Format integration should also improve searching and retrieval from online catalogs. Rebecca R. Malek-Wiley asserts, "because the same data should be in the same fields for all types of material, consistency both of indexing and retrieval and of display should be facilitated."[65] Possible disadvantages associated with format integration include the logistics of its implementation, the cost for reconfiguring computer systems, and problems presented by older MARC records predating format integration.[66]

X12 for Electronic Data Interchange

EDI refers to the electronic exchange of business data, such as purchase orders, invoices, etc.[67] EDI offers some advantages over paper communication, including rapid transmission, verification that the message has been received, and reduction of both labor and the possibility of error because trading partners do not have to rekey paper messages into their system. In the United States, EDI was first used in the transportation, pharmaceutical, and electronics industries, as well as in warehousing.[68]

In 1979 ANSI established the ASC X12 for the purpose of developing the EDI standard, which is now referred to by that committee's name—ASC X12 or simply X12. Although Frederick E. Schwartz wrote in 1991 that "in North America and much of the rest of the world, ANSI X12 is synonymous with EDI,"[69] a European standard, the Electronic Data Interchange for Administration, Commerce, and Transport (EDIFACT), promoted by the United Nations Economic Commission for Europe, does exist. Although a scheduled convergence of ANSI X12 and EDIFACT in 1997 was reported in the literature,[70] such an event has not taken place.[71]

Because X12 is a general standard for business shipping, receiving, and invoicing, it does not explicitly address specific needs of the serials industry, such as claiming.[72] Therefore, the SISAC is responsible for X12's customization for serials and, in 1990, appointed five subcommittees for this task.[73] These committees first developed standards for claims, claims responses, and invoices before addressing purchase orders, purchase order acknowledgments, and other functions.[74]

In the summer of 1995 the *SISAC X12 Implementation Guidelines for Electronic Data Interchange* were issued.[75] These guidelines included five transaction sets (elsewhere defined as "highly structured computer messages that correspond to specific workflows"[76]): 810, for invoices; 856, for shipping notice; 869, for order status inquiry (i.e., "claims") ; 870, for order status report (i.e., "claim responses") ; and 997, for functional acknowledgment.[77] Other sets in various stages of testing and development are 832, for price or sales catalog; 846, for inventory inquiry; 850, for purchase order; and 855, for purchase order acknowledgment.[78]

The earliest applications of EDI to librarianship were, according to Linda Richter and Joan Roca, "proprietary," that is, developed by specific organizations for communication with their customers.[79] Because these early proprietary systems did not conform to a uniform national standard, a system used to communicate with one vendor would not work for other vendors.

The first serials vendor to use EDI was Faxon, which decided in the summer of 1989 to experiment with ANSI X12 instead of the ANSI/NISO Z39.55-199X *Electronic Orders and Claims* standard. It began a pilot project involving six publishers plus the Welch Medical Library of Johns Hopkins University, the University of Minnesota library, and the Miles Laboratories Library in Indianapolis.[80] More recently, the literature describes Faxon's experimental use of X12 to communicate with libraries from the Mankato State and North Dakota State Universities,[81] Laurentian University (in Canada),[82] and Dartmouth College.[83] In July 1997 the Faxon Web page asserted the company was sending 7,000 messages a month using X12.[84]

Testifying to EDI's significance, the Faxon WWW site lists nine serial titles devoted exclusively to the topic, including *EDI Forum: The Journal of Electronic Data Interchange, EDI Monthly Report*, and *EDI World: The Source for Electronic Data Interchange Management*. There is also a listserv, EDI-L, devoted to the discussion of EDI issues.[85]

The X12 standard for EDI offers the opportunity for speedier and more-efficient communications among libraries, publishers, and serials vendors. Unlike ISSN and MARC, its full potential has yet to be realized. A related concept, Electronic Funds Transfer (EFT), is sometimes termed "the final stage of EDI"[86] but to date has received considerably less attention in the serials community.

Serial Item and Contribution Identifier and the SISAC Bar Code Symbol

The SICI standard was developed by SISAC for uniquely identifying specific serial issues and articles and has been officially adopted as ANSI/NISO X39.56 (1991). Version 2 was submitted by the SICI Revision Committee to NISO on January 1, 1996.[87] The standard allows creation of the SICI code from either a citation or the serial itself, regardless of whether the publisher has printed it on the item.[88] A SICI code is illustrated in figure 10.1.

Fig. 10.1. Illustration of a SICI Code[89]

Item: "The Compaq Portable II." *Library Systems*, v. 6, no. 6 (June 1986), p. 4
SICI Code: 0277-0288(198606)6:6L.4CP;1-

"0277-0288"	= the ISSN for the serial *Library Systems*
"(198606)"	= identifies the date as June 1986
"6:6"	= identifies the issue as volume 6, number 6
"L.4"	= identifies the item's location as beginning on page 4
"CP"	= the first letters of significant words in the item's title
";1"	= based on version 1 of SICI
"-"	= the final element is a check digit

SICI, when encoded in machine readable form, is known as the SISAC Bar Code Symbol. Because it can be read by a bar code wand, the SISAC Bar Code Symbol would allow more rapid serials check-in of issues marked with it. The SISAC bar code has received considerable support within the serials community. As of the mid-1990s many major publishers, automated library system vendors, and serial subscription agents were committed to supporting the SISAC Bar Code Symbol.

SISAC asserts that SICI has possible application to document delivery, interlibrary loan (ILL), copyright payments, and electronic reserve room use, among other functions. Arnold Hirshon and Barbara Winters conjecture that SICI might eventually allow serial issues to arrive in libraries already checked-in and that it has potential application to other automated serials functions (e.g., ordering and claiming).[90]

Other Standards

Some leading STM publishers have proposed a Publisher Item Identifier (PII) for providing unique identification of documents, such as serial articles, book chapters, or any other unit the publisher wishes to sell. It is based on a 17-character alphanumeric code assigned by the publisher. The PII has been adopted by the American Chemical Society, the American Institute of Physics, the American Physical Society, Elsevier Science, and the Institute of Electrical and Electronics Engineering (IEEE) for all articles published after January 1, 1996. Proponents of this standard assert it is compatible with ISSN and SICI, but, unlike SICI, it can be assigned to an item before it is published and allows a document to stand alone rather then be viewed as part of a serial or book. Moreover, the PII applies to all forms of a document: print or electronic, varying electronic forms, and a serial article reprinted as a book chapter.[91]

The Association of American Publishers has been developing a Digital Object Identifier (DOI) system for uniquely identifying "works which are bought, sold or accessed over digital networks" for such purposes as copyright management, ordering, billing, and bibliographic control. In April 1997 the International Publishers Association decided to support the DOI system. The DOI number consists of two parts: a prefix assigned to the publisher by the DOI agency and a suffix assigned by the publisher. According to the Information Identifier Committee of the International Publishers Association, "the [DOI] system is far from complete" (i.e., an international network of registration agencies must be established and the underlying technology tested). A public presentation of a DOI prototype was scheduled for demonstration at the Frankfurt Book Fair in October 1997.[92]

The PII has not yet been adopted by national agencies, and the DOI system is still under development. Hence, their ultimate acceptance and impact upon libraries and the serials industry can not be predicted. It is also unclear to what extent the PII and DOI system will complement or conflict with each other.

Summary

Standards are important to automation because they support networking, sharing of records, and communications among the major players in the serials arena. Compliance with standards is voluntary. But a standard's widespread adoption is necessary for its ultimate success. In this rapidly changing environment, new standards evolve and older ones become obsolete.

AUTOMATION OF BIBLIOGRAPHIC ACCESS TO SERIALS

Provision of bibliographic access to serials could be viewed as a subset of serials control, yet it is important enough to warrant a separate discussion. In the broadest terms, this heading includes access to

1. serial titles;

2. serial issues, which are often termed "holdings"; and

3. specific articles, which are generally accessed through "indexing."

Some CD-ROM products, such as *Ulrich's Plus* or EBSCO's *Serials Directory* offer bibliographic access to serial titles. Beginning in 1992 the International Serials Data System (ISDS) database has been available in CD-ROM format as *ISDN Compact*.[93]

Bibliographic control at the article level has long been provided by online access to indexes and abstracts through such services as DIALOG. Beginning in the mid-1980s an ever-increasing number of indexing and abstracting services have been issued as CD-ROMs. In the mid-1990s libraries often have three automation options for accessing indexes and abstracts: online access, CD-ROM, or local mounting of the database.

In the past OPACs have provided much better access to monographic holdings than to serials. Basic questions on serials access and the OPAC follow: Are serial titles included in the OPAC? Is holdings information included? Are indexes available through the OPAC? Is dial-in access available? Is a password required for dial-in access?

Serials access will be a major component of an ongoing project, the CIC Virtual Electronic Library. Using the Internet and OCLC WebZ software, the project will eventually allow end users at the CIC institutions to seamlessly search the OPACs of the 12 CIC libraries along with numerous databases. Bibliographical access will be provided to 550,000 serials (along with 60 million books), and end users will be able to initiate ILL and commercial document delivery requests.[94]

Although not traditionally thought of as part of bibliographic control, access to serial collections could be considered a fourth level. Electronic journal collections accessible on the Internet have been discussed in chapter 9.

AUTOMATION OF SERIALS CONTROL PROCEDURES

In the systems analysis approach to automation, one examines the tasks that must be performed and then asks how automation can perform those tasks. The traditional serials control functions discussed in chapter 8 (e.g., ordering, claiming, check-in, fund accounting, etc.) can be performed by an automated system. Indeed automation of each serials function presents its own set of challenges, but a function by function analysis is not within this chapter's scope.

Record keeping represents a major component of serials processing. Indeed, some serials textbooks devote an entire chapter to the discussion of serials records. A group of records organized together constitutes a file. Important files for serials automation include bibliographic, holdings, order, vendor, binding, claims, check-in, and fund accounting records, and (for larger libraries that order abroad) currency conversion. For a useful discussion of file integration in a serials control system, see Trisha Davis and James Huesmann.[95]

The discussion and comparative evaluation of specific serials control systems are beyond this book's scope. An exceedingly valuable source of comparative data on automation vendors and automated systems is the *Library Technology Reports*, published by the ALA. For more than a decade, *Library Journal* has offered an annual automation report in its April 1 issue (this does not, of course, imply that the topic is an April Fools' Day joke). This series has provided a valuable introductory overview of the automation market. Each annual article summarizes major trends of the previous year, profiles major vendors, and provides considerable data on the number of system installations by leading vendors. A particularly useful feature is an appended list of the names, addresses, and telephone numbers of currently active vendors.

A similar annual automation survey has appeared since the mid-1980s in the *Library Systems Newsletter*, published by *Library Technology Reports*. This survey is usually divided into two segments covering 1) PC or MAC-based systems and 2) all others. Market trends and profiles of leading vendors are included. In 1989 John Corbin offered a comparative summary of the serials control functions in 24 automated systems,[96] and in 1992 Richard W. Boss offered a similar functional summary of 26 systems.[97] Davis and Huesmann's *Serials Control Systems for Libraries*, published in 1994, compares five microcomputer-based serials control systems in terms of local files, functionality, and systems requirements: the SC350, Micro-Linx, DavexPC, PC Max, and REMO.[98]

An automated serials system offers the advantages of greater speed, accuracy, efficiency, and the ability to provide new services (e.g., public service access to serials check-in and holdings records). An early impetus to library automation was the desire to reduce staff and increase savings, although it is doubtful that automation results in either.

An automated serials system can generate data that are quite useful in collection management, especially in the areas of macroevaluation and budgeting. A report of serials expenditures by subject or department in a series of previous fiscal years can assist in reaching or evaluating such budgeting issues as the overall serial budget's division among subject areas, the proportion of departmental materials' expenditures devoted to serials, and the projection of budgetary requirements for the forthcoming fiscal year. As a downside, it can sometimes be difficult to extract the needed data from the system or customize it to your library's particular needs.

Data from a serials subscription agent may be limited to the library's subscriptions with that agent. Anecdotal evidence suggests that many librarians feel that automated systems have not lived up to their full potential in providing collection management data.

In addition, an automated system can be quite expensive, and considerable staff time and effort is required to implement it. Vendors may advertise automated products that are not fully developed. An automated system has a finite life expectancy—often estimated at five to seven years. Most present serials control systems are tied to the traditional ownership paradigm and are geared to ordering, claiming, checking-in, etc. serial titles that will be housed in the library's collection rather than handling electronic journals or document delivery of articles. There may be unforeseen and unintended consequences (e.g., automating serials check-in places greater pressure on serials staff to make current periodical issues immediately available).

STEPS IN THE SERIALS AUTOMATION PROCESS

Because many textbooks address automation planning in libraries,[99] a detailed description is unnecessary. Case studies of serials automation projects in specific libraries are too numerous to summarize. The basic steps in implementing an automated system are outlined below. These steps would apply to the automation of any library function, but the discussion addresses issues pertaining to serials. In the current automation environment, a library usually purchases a system rather than developing one in-house. For a library implementing the serials module of its integrated system, several of the steps would be skipped or abbreviated.

Establishing a Timetable

The initial step should entail outlining the tasks that must be accomplished and setting a deadline for each. Various types of planning charts, such as a Gantt chart, can be used. However, as the library proceeds through the project's various stages, revision of the deadlines and addition of new tasks may be required.

Staffing

Staffing arrangements for serials automation should be made fairly early in the planning process, if for no other reason than it is staff who implement the project. Use of a committee or task force represents a standard approach. (A committee is ongoing, whereas a task force disbands when its goals have been achieved. Accordingly, the latter term is technically correct in regard to most library automation projects, although in practice both terms are used.) A large project (e.g., bringing up an integrated system) might use a complex set of task forces and subcommittees covering each module as well as such specific tasks as database content, site preparation, screen design and so forth. The serials control automation task force would typically be chaired by the serials department head or team leader or another key professional staff member. In larger libraries, representatives from other departments with an interest in serials, such as public services, cataloging, or acquisitions, should be included on this task force. Likewise, the serials area would be represented on other task forces whose responsibilities impact serials (e.g., cataloging, design of the OPAC display, etc.).

The serials staff, both professional and nonprofessional, should be involved in planning the system implementation from an early stage. Although the staff may not have computer expertise, they should certainly understand the processes to be automated. Staff involvement will also contribute to their psychological acceptance of the automated system.

A strategy for staff training should be a necessary part of any automation project. Because the serials module of an integrated system is often the last to be implemented, it is likely that serials staff will already have experience using the other modules, thus reducing the required training. Unlike for the OPAC, user education would not be an issue for a serials control system. Hazel Woodward and Margaret E. Graham offer practical tips on staff training for serials automation, including brief sessions, a small number of participants, and hands-on experience.[100]

Analysis of the Library's Needs

This critical step involves analysis of the library's present situation and what it wishes to achieve through automation. One should examine such fundamental factors as the available hardware, library size, financial resources for the project, and the extent of retrospective conversion of serial titles. Based on these considerations, the first decisions concern the basic approach to be used: a stand-alone system versus a module of an integrated system; upgrading the present system or migrating to a different one. The level of automation already achieved will affect serials automation decision making. For example, if a library already has an integrated system, does it wish to install that system's serials models, substitute a stand-alone serials system, or attempt to interface the serials module from a different integrated system?

Also included in needs analysis would be a list of the functions one expects the system to perform and standards to which it must conform. Boss outlines 96 functional requirements recommended for a local library serials control system, specifically listing 10 capabilities: serials holdings display, ordering, claiming, receiving, routing, vouchering, binding preparation, funds accounting, union listing, and notes fields. Boss also recommends the ability to search serial records by 18 different fields (e.g., title, variant title, call number, ISSN, uniform title, etc., and conformance with the SISAC standard).[101] More recently, James R. Mouw outlined more than 60 criteria for selecting a serials system.[102]

One would obviously consider the number of serial titles and projected future changes. Although library automation textbooks stress the importance of projecting future growth trends, this will probably not be a major issue in serials automation because most libraries are unlikely to be anticipating a future increase in the number of their subscriptions.

Identification of Candidate Systems

This step, which logically follows from the needs analysis, might be conceptualized as a two-stage process:

1. identification of the available systems that meet the library's basic specifications; and

2. from the set of systems identified in stage one, selection of a small number of leading candidates.

A possible starting point for gathering the information necessary for this process would be AcqWeb's "Guide to Automated Library Systems, Library Software, Hardware and Consulting Companies," on the WWW.[103] Other tactics include surveying the literature, informal contacts with colleagues, and visiting the exhibition booths at ALA conferences. Sometimes the investigation may reveal that only a few systems meet the library's requirements, so further winnowing of candidates as depicted in stage two is unnecessary.

Selecting a System

An approach to selecting an automated system that has received considerable attention is the Request for Proposal (RFP)—a legalistic document that concisely outlines a library's specifications. Vendor RFP responses can be used to evaluate a candidate system, make a final selection, and to begin negotiations on a contract with the selected vendor. It should be noted, however, that many libraries do not use the RFP approach.

Numerous strategies are available for gathering information to assess candidate systems. A literature review would be advisable. One can request on-site demonstrations by vendors. Informal contact with other librarians using the system can be quite helpful. Many systems have organized user groups that could be a source of information. User listservs for several major systems—including NOTIS-L (for NOTIS), VTLSLIST (for the Virginia Tech Library system), MULTLIS (for MULTILIS), and ADVANC-L (for the GEAC Advance Library System)—and their subscription addresses are included in the *Directory of Electronic Journals, Newsletters and Academic Discussion Lists*.[104] Not infrequently, postings appear on *SERIALST* requesting evaluative comments about a particular automated serials system.

Basic criteria for evaluating a system include functionality, cost, vendor reputation, vendor support, support of standards, documentation, degree of computer expertise and staff training required. Depending on a library's situation, the ability to interface with other systems could also be a criterion.

Most textbooks advocate the development of "decision rules" for system selection. Joseph R. Matthews outlines five specific evaluation methodologies. "Subjective judgement" uses opinion rather than an objective method. The "Cost-only technique" selects the least-expensive system meeting all the library's requirements. In the "Weighted-scoring technique," the library assigns point values to desired system features and selects the system scoring the most points, based on its features. The "Cost-effectiveness ratio" approach uses the weighted-scoring technique but divides each system's total costs by the number of points received to select the most cost-effective vendor. Finally, the "Least total cost method" selects the system meeting all mandatory requirements that is least expensive to install and operate for five to seven years.[105]

Contract or Purchase Agreement

After selection, the next step would be negotiating and signing a contract or purchase agreement with the vendor. Note that vendors' standard contracts are written to their advantage rather than the library's. A library can sometimes negotiate more favorable terms with a vendor. If a library has used an RFP, its provisions might be incorporated into the contract. Most textbooks advise that the library have an attorney review any documents before they are signed. In implementing the serials module of an integrated system already in the library, this step would already have been applied.

Site Preparation

According to David C. Genaway, the two most critical components of implementing an automated system are "people preparation" and "site preparation," which involve "the physical aspects of installing and running a computer-based library system."[106] Site preparation addresses such issues as determining where terminals and printers will be placed; locating power sources (e.g., wiring and electrical outlets); preparing the floor layout; and adding such communications channels as phone lines and port access.[107] Several other major automation issues, including security, file backups, and ergonomics are often considered part of site preparation. Site preparation issues would normally be addressed on a librarywide basis for the entire automation system, but serials automation would entail site preparation for the serials department or work area and possibly for a current periodicals reading room.

Database Preparation

Database creation can be one of the most expensive and time-consuming aspects of serials automation, especially for larger libraries. Two interconnected tasks are involved: retrospective conversion of records and loading the records into the automated system. *Retrospective conversion* has been defined as "the process whereby records only humans can read are transformed so that computers can read them, too."[108] Converting records from one format to another is termed *conversion,* and *retrospective* refers to the conversion of preexisting records. A recent search in the *Library Literature* CD-ROM indicates that 35 articles have been published on serials retrospective conversion since 1984, so a lengthy discussion is unnecessary. Many of the articles published in the 1980s commented on the poor quality of the converted records. If a library is implementing an integrated system's serials module, the retrospective conversion of bibliographic records for serials will probably already be completed.

According to Chen, "the main work" of serials automation is entering the records needed for acquisitions into the system's database. She lists four types of records as the most critical for this function and discusses the problems associated with file creation for each: bibliographic, order, invoice and payment, and check-in. Sometimes a library's subscription agents can electronically load order, invoice, and payment records into the system; otherwise, records must be entered manually—an obviously labor-intensive process. Of the four, loading serials check-in records can be the most difficult[109] and was once compared to growing bananas in Greenland.[110] Jean Walter Farrington notes that loading the serials database is often a two-step process: first the bibliographic records, then order, invoice, and check-in data. She warns, "Be prepared for a more difficult and more time-consuming task than originally anticipated."[111]

Marlene Clayton and Chris Batt list six major issues in database creation: record content, adherence to standards, the source of records, the input method and staff resources allocated to the project, cost, and timing and sequencing logistics.[112] A particularly crucial issue for serials concerns whether records are entered for inactive as well as active titles.

Finally, after the records are loaded, cleanup of problems and continued maintenance work are required. The importance of entering and maintaining accurate records can not be overemphasized. Inaccurate automated records are still inaccurate, despite the mystique computers enjoy. A database of high quality records assumes a life of its own independent of any specific hardware or software, thus facilitating system migration.

Activating the System

As implied, this step entails putting the automated system into operation in place of the previous system. Corbin lists four basic strategies for activating an automated system: total, pilot, phased, and parallel. The total approach completely begins the new system while shutting down the old at a single time. In the pilot method, the serials control module would be tested in one branch or location prior to activation in the entire library system. The phased approach activates one function at a time. For example, serials check-in, ordering, routing, fund accounting, and other functions, would be brought up separately. In the parallel approach, the most conservative and expensive method, the new and old systems are operated simultaneously until one is confident the new system is functioning properly.[113]

Acceptance Tests

After activation, the final step involves verification that the automated system is operating correctly. Corbin outlines three types of acceptance tests: reliability (i.e., measuring downtime), response time, and functionality.[114] Arguably, the functionality test is the most critical for serials. One works down a list of functions advertised by the vendor or included in the vender's RFP response, ascertaining that each is performing correctly.

System Migration

By the late-1990s many libraries were migrating to their second or even third automated systems. Some case studies of serials system migration have been reported in the literature, for example, from MicroLinx to NOTIS at City University of New York's (CUNY) Queens College, by Belinda Chiang;[115] and from an in-house system to Innopac at the University of Massachusetts at Amherst, by Patricia Banach.[116] Margaret Bell Hentz has described the conversion of serials bibliographic and holdings information from Faxon's SC-10 system to a Techlib/Plus OPAC at Boehringer Ingelheim Pharmaceuticals, Inc., in Ridgefield, Connecticut.[117] Other examples could be cited. Grace Agnew and Toni Lambert have recently published a guide-book addressing the technical aspects of system migration.[118]

System migration entails unique problems, but the steps depicted above should remain essentially the same whether a library is moving from a manual to an automated system or migrating from one automated system to another. Yet as William W. Wan observes, "system migration is much more complicated than auto-mating one or two manual procedures."[119]

Major migration problems include staff training for the new system and transfer of data from one system to the other. Carol Pitts Hawks (now Carol Pitts Diedrichs) has noted the problem involved in transferring payment history records as well as frequency and publication pattern data for specific serial titles.[120] Wan, in analyzing the Texas Woman's University library's migration from the GEAC GLIS 8000 to GEAC ADVANCE, comments that serials encountered the most problems, as enumeration and frequency information necessary for check-in was not transferred correctly.[121]

It is advisable, if feasible, to begin the new system at the beginning of the fiscal year to simplify fund accounting. Chen advises that titles should be converted from the old system to the new in alphabetical order.[122] Often a special loader program may have to be written to transfer data from one system to another, but editing of records may be necessary.[123]

CONCLUSION

Because almost every library function deals with serials, most library automation affects serials to some extent.

A number of authorities have outlined a three-stage process in library automation:[124]

1.   print access to print information sources,

2.   automated access to print information sources, and

3.   automated access to automated or electronic information sources.

Because these stages are not always linear, a library could simultaneously be in more than one stage. For example, a library using a print serials holding list because serials are not included in its OPAC (not an uncommon situation in the 1980s) would be classified in stage two for monographs and stage one for serials. At the time of this writing, a majority of libraries (but not all) are at stage two, and libraries providing access to electronic journals are also in stage three.

NOTES

1. Stephen R. Salmon, *Library Automation Systems* (New York: Marcel Dekker, 1975), 2.

2. Gary M. Pitkin, *Serials Automation in the United States: A Bibliographic History* (Metuchen, N.J.: Scarecrow Press, 1976), 1-5. This book provides detailed summaries of 101 items about serials automation published from 1951 to 1974.

3. Pitkin, *Serials Automation in the United States*, 2-3.

4. George R. Luckett, "Partial Library Automation with the Flexowriter Automatic Writing Machine," *Library Resources and Technical Services* 1 (fall 1957): 207-10, summarized in Pitkin, *Serials Automation in the United States*, 4.

5. Frederick G. Kilgour, "History of Library Computerization," *Journal of Library Automation* 3 (September 1970): 223-24.

6. Pitkin, *Serials Automation in the United States*, viii.

7. Kilgour, "History of Library Computerization," 224.

8. Debora Shaw, "A Review of Developments Leading to On-Line Union Listing of Serials," in *The Management of Serials Automation: Current Technology and Strategies for Future Planning*, ed. Peter Gellatly (New York: Haworth Press, 1982), 188.

9. Rosario de Varennes, "On-Line Serials System at Laval University Library," *Journal of Library Automation* 3 (June 1980): 128-41.

10. Pitkin, *Serials Automation in the United States*, 15.

11. William Saffady, *Introduction to Automation for Librarians*, 3d ed. (Chicago: American Library Association, 1994), 368.

12. Ibid.

13. Rick B. Forsman, "EBSCONET Serials Control System: A Case History and Analysis," *Serials Review* 8 (winter 1982): 83.

14. Sara Heitshu, "Serials Automation: Past, Present, and Future," in *Advances in Serials Management: A Research Annual*, vol. 2, ed. Marcia Tuttle and Jean G. Cook (Greenwich, Conn.: JAI Press, 1988), 103-4.

15. Saffady, *Introduction to Automation for Librarians*, 3d ed., 196-97.

16. Heitshu, "Serials Automation: Past, Present, and Future," 106, 109.

17. Ibid., 105, and Saffady, *Introduction to Automation for Librarians*, 3d ed., 368.

18. Heitshu, "Serials Automation: Past, Present, and Future," 106-7.

19. William Saffady, *Introduction to Automation for Librarians*, 2d ed. (Chicago: American Library Association, 1989), 347-48.

20. Trisha Davis and James Huesmann, *Serials Control Systems for Libraries* (Westport, Conn.: Mecklermedia, 1994), 79, 103, 123, 139.

21. Heitshu, "Serials Automation: Past, Present, and Future," 109.

22. Roy Rada and others, "Computerized Guides to Journal Selection," *Information Technology and Libraries* 6 (September 1987): 173-84.

23. John A. Camp and others, "Survey of Online Systems in U.S. Academic Libraries," *College and Research Libraries* 48 (July 1987), 342-43.

24. Jamie Webster Hastreiter, Larry Hardesty, and David Henderson, comps., *Periodicals in College Libraries*, CLIP Note 8 (Chicago: Association of College and Research Libraries, 1987), 12.

25. Chiou-sen Dora Chen, *Serials Management: A Practical Guide* (Chicago: American Library Association, 1995), 138.

26. Jeff Barry, José-Marie Griffiths, and Gerald Lundeen, "Automated System Marketplace 1995: The Changing Face of Automation," *Library Journal* 120 (April 1, 1995): 46-47.

27. Davis and Huesmann, *Serials Control Systems for Libraries*, 1.

28. International Organization for Standardization (ISO). *Welcome to the ISO Online*. Available: http://www.iso.ch/welcome.html (Accessed March 1, 1998).

29. Links to most of the standards organizations discussed in this section are collected on the Faxon Company's Web Site [The Faxon Company. *The Faxon Company and Standards*. Copyright January 1998. Available: http://www.faxon.com/html/ind_lps.html (Accessed March 1, 1998).

30. American National Standards Institute (ANSI). *ANSI Online*. Available: http://www.ansi.org/ (Accessed March 1, 1998).

31. Ibid.

32. Ibid.

33. National Information Standards Organization (NISO). *NISO Home Page*. Available: http://www.niso.org/ (Accessed March 1, 1998).

34. "National Information Standards Organization (NISO) Standards," *Bowker Annual: Library and Book Trade Almanac, 1994*, 39th ed. (New Providence, N.J.: R. R. Bowker, 1994), 795-97.

35. International Organization for Standardization (ISO). *Welcome to the ISO Online*. Available: http://www.iso.ch/welcome.html (Accessed March 1, 1998).

36. Book Industry Study Group, Inc. *Book Industry Systems Advisory Committee (BISAC)*. Available: http://www.bookwire.com/bisg/bisac.html (Accessed March 1, 1998).

37. "SISAC Restructures to Prepare Electronic Communications Standards for Journals," *Technical Services Quarterly* 9, no. 1 (1991), 73.

38. Book Industry Study Group, Inc. *Serials Industry Systems Advisory Committee (SISAC)*. Available: http://www.bookwire.com/bisg/sisac.html (Accessed March 1, 1998).

39. Amira Aaron, "SISAC-L, New Internet List," *SERIALST* (October 10, 1996).

40. Robert Renaud, "A Canadian Perspective on Serials Industry Standards: The Canadian Serials Industry Systems Advisory Committee (CSISAC)," *Serials Librarian* 26, nos. 3/4 (1995): 135.

41. International Committee on Electronic Data Interchange for Serials. *ICEDIS Home Page*. Available: http://www.faxon.com/Standards/icedis.html (Accessed June, 1997).

42. Marcia Tuttle, *Managing Serials* (Greenwich, Conn.: JAI Press, 1996), 58.

43. Library of Congress. *MARC Standards.* Available: http://lcweb.loc.gov/marc/ (Accessed March 1, 1998).

44. Walt Crawford, *MARC for Library Use*, 2d ed. (Boston: G. K. Hall, 1989), 1.

45. Henriette D. Avram, "Machine-Readable Cataloging (MARC) Program," *Encyclopedia of Library and Information Science* 16 (1975): 380-413.

46. Karen M. Spicher, "The Development of the MARC Format," *Cataloging and Classification Quarterly* 21, nos. 3/4 (1996): 75-90.

47. Crawford, *MARC for Library Use*, 208.

48. Ibid., 209.

49. Ibid., 208.

50. Tuttle, *Managing Serials*, 202.

51. Network Development and MARC Standards Office. *USMARC Format for Holdings and Locations: Final Draft* (Washington, D.C.: Library of Congress, 1984).

52. Network Development and MARC Standards Office. *USMARC Format for Holdings Data: Including Guidelines for Content Description* (Washington, D.C.: Library of Congress, 1989).

53. Frieda B. Rosenberg, "Managing Serial Holdings," in *Managing Serials*, by Marcia Tuttle (Greenwich, Conn.: JAI Press, 1996), 243-49.

54. Network Development and MARC Standards Office. *USMARC Format for Holdings Data: Including Guidelines for Content Designation* (Washington, D.C.: Library of Congress, 1990).

55. Network Development and MARC Standards Office. *USMARC Format for Community Information: Including Guidelines for Content Designation* (Washington, D.C.: Library of Congress, 1993).

56. Deborah J. Byrne, *MARC Manual: Understanding and Using MARC Records* (Englewood, Colo.: Libraries Unlimited, 1991), 24.

57. Ibid., 20-27, and Crawford, *MARC for Library Use.*

58. Crawford, *MARC for Library Use*, 303.

59. Ibid., 221.

60. Katherine G. Evans, "MARC Format Integration and Seriality: Implications for Serials Cataloging," *Serials Librarian* 18, nos. 1/2 (1990): 37.

61. "LC Format Integration Completed" (posted to USMARC distribution list, 29 February 1996) [Bob Warwick. *Bob Warwick's Technical and Automated Services Home Page.* Available: http://warwick.rutgers.edu/f-lcfi2.html (Accessed March 1, 1998)].

62. Evans, "MARC Format Integration and Seriality," 37.

63. Frieda B. Rosenberg, "Cataloging Serials," in *Managing Serials*, by Marcia Tuttle (Greenwich, Conn.: JAI Press, 1996), 226-27.

64. Wayne Jones and Young-Hee Queinnec, "Format Integration and Serials Cataloguing," *Serials Librarian* 25, nos. 1/2 (1994): 83-95.

65. Rebecca R. Malek-Wiley, "USMARC Format Integration: An Overview," *LLA Bulletin* 56 (fall 1993): 97.

66. Ibid., 97-99.

67. Linda Richter and Joan Roca, "An X12 Implementation in Serials: MSUS/PALS and Faxon," *Serials Review* 20, no 1 (1994): 13-24.

68. The Faxon Company. *The Faxon EDI Resource Guide for the Serials Community*. Available: http://www.faxon.com/Standards/EDI_guide.html#articles (Accessed June, 1997).

69. Frederick E. Schwartz, "The EDI Horizon: Implementing an ANSI X12 Pilot Project at the Faxon Company," *Serials Librarian* 19, nos. 3/4 (1991): 41.

70. Glen Kelly, "Electronic Data Interchange (EDI): The Exchange of Ordering, Claiming, and Invoice Information from a Library Perspective," *Collection Management* 19, nos. 3/4 (1995): 79-80.

71. Report from Jian Liu, Indiana University Libraries Reference Department, April 1, 1998, after he posted an inquiry on the *EDI-L* Listserv.

72. Wilbert Harri, Alan Nordman, and Fran Fisher, "EDI Implementation: A Discussion and Demonstration," *Serials Librarian* 24, nos. 3/4 (1994): 251.

73. Richter and Roca, "An X12 Implementation in Serials," 15.

74. Joan Griffith, "Electronic Data Interchange: Dartmouth + Faxon + Innopac + SISAC + X12 = Serials Claims Pilot Project," *Serials Review* 21 (fall 1995): 34.

75. Book Industry Study Group, Inc. *SISAC X12 Implementation Guidelines for Electronic Data Exchange—June 1995*. Available: http://www.bookwire.com/bisg/x12-manual-TOC.html (Accessed March 1, 1998).

76. Griffith, "Electronic Data Interchange," 34.

77. Book Industry Study Group, Inc. *SISAC X12 Implementation Guidelines for Electronic Data Exchange—June 1995*. Available: http://www.bookwire.com/bisg/x12-manual-TOC.html (Accessed March 1, 1998).

78. Sandra H. Hurd, "Selection of an Integrated Library System Vendor, an Agent's View," *Serials Review* 22 (summer 1996): 91.

79. Richter and Roca, "An X12 Implementation in Serials," 15.

80. Schwartz, "The EDI Horizon," 48.

81. Richter and Roca, "An X12 Implementation in Serials," 13-24, 42.

82. Kelly, "Electronic Data Interchange (EDI)," 77-94.

83. Griffith, "Electronic Data Interchange," 33-45.

84. The Faxon Company. *The Faxon Company and Standards*. Available: http://www.faxon.com/html/ind_lps.html (Accessed March 1, 1998).

85. The Faxon Company. *The Faxon EDI Resource Guide for the Serials Community*. Available: http://www.faxon.com/Standards/EDI_guide.html#articles (Accessed June, 1997).

86. Kelly, "Electronic Data Interchange (EDI)," 87.

87. ANSI/NISO. *SICI: Serial Item and Contribution Identifier Standard*. Available: http://sunsite.berkeley.edu/SICI/ (Accessed March 1, 1998).

88. Andrew Wells. *38th ABN Standards Committee Meeting: Serial Item and Contribution Identifier (SICI)*. Available: http://www.nla.gov.au/2/abn/committees/sc29.html (Accessed March 1, 1998).

89. This illustration is adapted from one used by the 38th ABN Standards Committee Meeting [Andrew Wels. *38th ABN Standards Committee Meeting: Serial Item and Contribution Identifier (SICI)*. Available: http://www.nla.gov.au/2/abn/committees/sc29.html (Accessed March 1, 1998)].

90. Arnold Hirshon and Barbara Winters, *Outsourcing Library Technical Services: A How-to-Do-It Manual for Librarians* (New York: Neal-Schuman, 1996), 93.

91. Elsevier Science. *Publisher Item Identifier As a Means of Document Identification*. Available: http://www.elsevier.com/inca/homepage/about/pii/ (Accessed March 1, 1998).

92. International Publishers Association. *Information Identifier Committee*. Available: http://www.ipa-uie.org/ipa_iic.html (Accessed March 1, 1998).

93. Saffady, *Introduction to Automation for Librarians*, 3d ed., 362.

94. "Committee on Institutional Cooperation and OCLC Building a Virtual Electronic Library," *OCLC Newsletter,* no. 223 (September/October 1996): 6-7.

95. Davis and Huesmann, *Serials Control Systems for Libraries*, 27-43.

96. John Corbin, *Directory of Automated Library Systems*, 2d ed. (New York: Neal-Schuman, 1989), 176-211. The 24 systems were Advanced Libraries, Carlyle Systems, CLSI, Comstow, Data Research, Data Trek, Dynix, Eyring, Faxon, Follett, GEAC, IBM, Information Dimensions, Inlex, Innovative Interfaces, NOTIS, OCLC, RINGGOLD, Sobeco Group, TCJC, UNISYS, VTLA, Washington University, and Winnebago.

97. Richard W. Boss, "Technical Services Functionality in Integrated Library Systems," *Library Technology Reports* 28 (January/February 1992): 5-109.

98. Davis and Huesmann, *Serials Control Systems for Libraries*, 57-158.

99. Examples of library automation textbooks include John M. Cohn, Ann L. Kelsey, and Keith Michael Fiels, *Planning for Automation: A How-to-Do-It Manual for Librarians*, 2d ed. (New York: Neal-Schuman, 1997); and John Corbin, *Implementing the Automated Library System* (Phoenix, Ariz.: Oryx Press, 1988), among numerous possibilities.

100. Hazel Woodward and Margaret E. Graham, "Serials Automation," in *Serials Management: A Practical Handbook*, ed. Margaret E. Graham and Fiona Buettel (London: published by Aslib in collaboration with the United Kingdom Serials Group, 1990), 127-28.

101. Boss, "Technical Services Functionality in Integrated Library Systems," 41-56.

102. James R. Mouw, "Selecting a System That Will Meet the Needs of Serials Control," *Serials Review* 22 (summer 1996): 83-86.

103. Acqweb. *Acqweb's Guide to Automated Library Systems, Library Software, Hardware, and Consulting Companies*. Available: http://www.library.vanderbilt.edu/law/acqs/pubr/opac.html (Accessed March 1, 1998).

104. Dru Mogge and Diane K. Kovacs, comps., *Directory of Electronic Journals, Newsletters and Academic Discussion Lists*, 6th ed. (Washington, D.C.: Association of Research Libraries, 1996), 634-57.

105. Joseph R. Matthews, *Choosing an Automated Library System: A Planning Guide* (Chicago: American Library Association, 1980), 49-52.

106. David C. Genaway, "Ergonomics; Environment; Energy: A Brief Primer for Site Preparation," *Technicalities* 8 (December 1988): 8-11.

107. Ibid., 9.

108. Cohn, Kelsey, and Fiels, *Planning for Automation*, 73.

109. Chen, *Serials Management*, 145-47.

110. Huibert Paul, "Automation of Serials Check-In: Like Growing Bananas in Greenland?" parts 1 and 2, *Serials Librarian* 6 (winter 1981): 3-16; (summer 1982): 39-62.

111. Jean Walter Farrington, "Selecting a Serials System: The Technical Services Perspective," *Library Resources and Technical Services* 32 (October 1988): 405.

112. Marlene Clayton with Chris Batt, *Managing Library Automation*, 2d ed. (Aldershot, U.K.; Brookfield, Vt.: Ashgate, 1992), 176-77.

113. Corbin, *Implementing the Automated Library System*, 140-42.

114. John Corbin, *Managing the Library Automation Project* (Phoenix, Ariz.: Oryx Press, 1985), 180-84.

115. Belinda Chiang, "Migration from Microlinx to NOTIS: Expediting Serials Holdings Conversion Through Programmed Function Keys," *Serials Librarian* 25, nos. 1/2 (1994): 115-31.

116. Patricia Banach, "Migration from an In-House Serials System to Innopac at the University of Massachusetts at Amherst," *Library Software Review* 12 (spring 1993): 35-37.

117. Margaret Bell Hentz, "Data Conversion from Faxon's SC-10 Serials Control System into Techlib/Plus' On-Line Card Catalog," *Special Libraries* 85 (summer 1994): 162-82.

118. Grace Agnew and Toni Lambert, *Online System Migration Guide* (Chicago: American Library Association, 1996).

119. William W. Wan, "System Migration and Its Impact on Technical Services," *Public Library Quarterly* 13, no. 4 (1993): 13.

120. Carol Pitts Hawks, "Automated Library Systems: What Next?" *Serials Librarian* 21, nos. 2/3 (1991): 91.

121. Wan, "System Migration and Its Impact on Technical Services," 17.

122. Chen, *Serials Management*, 147.

123. Wan, "System Migration and Its Impact on Technical Services," 14.

124. For example, a slightly variant form of this concept may be found in Yuan Zhou, "From Smart Guesser to Smart Navigator: Changes in Collection Development for Research Libraries in a Network Environment," *Library Trends* 42 (spring 1994): 652-57.

FURTHER READING

Boss, Richard W. "Technical Services Functionality in Integrated Library Systems." *Library Technology Reports* 28 (January/February 1992): 5-109.

Boss, Richard W., and Judy McQueen. "The Uses of Automation and Related Technologies by Domestic Book and Serials Jobbers." *Library Technology Reports* 25 (March/April 1989): 125-251.

Chen, Chiou-sen Dora. "Serials Automation." In *Serials Management: A Practical Guide*, 138-51. Chicago: American Library Association, 1995.

Clapper, Mary Ellen. "Standards for Serials." *Serials Review* 12 (summer and fall 1986): 119-31.

Crawford, Walt. "Serials." In *MARC for Library Use: Understanding Integrated U.S. MARC*, 67-76. 2d ed. Boston: G. K. Hall, 1989.

Davis, Trisha, and James Huesmann. *Serials Control Systems for Libraries*. Westport, Conn.: Mecklermedia, 1994.

Farrington, Jean Walter. "Selecting a Serials System: The Technical Services Perspective." *Library Resources and Technical Services* 32 (October 1988): 402-6.

Heitshu, Sara. "Serials Automation: Past, Present, and Future." In *Advances in Serials Management: A Research Annual*. Vol. 2, edited by Marcia Tuttle and Jean G. Cook, 95-115. Greenwich, Conn.: JAI Press, 1988.

Hurd, Sandra H. "Selection of an Integrated Library System Vendor, an Agent's View." *Serials Review* 22 (summer 1996): 89-91.

Martin, Sylvia. "Vanderbilt's Process for Selecting an Integrated Library System." *Serials Review* 22 (summer 1996): 80-83.

Mouw, James R. "Selecting a System That Will Meet the Needs of Serials Control." *Serials Review* 22 (summer 1996): 83-86.

Petersen, Karla D. "Planning for Serials Retrospective Conversion." *Serials Review* 10 (fall 1984): 73-78.

Pitkin, Gary M. *Serials Automation in the United States: A Bibliographic History*. Metuchen, N.J.: Scarecrow Press, 1976.

Richter, Linda. "How an Automated Library System Meets the Needs of Serials Librarians." *Serials Review* 22 (summer 1996): 87-89.

Rush, James E. "Automated Serials Control Systems." *Serials Review* 12 (summer and fall 1986): 87-101.

Saffady, William. "Automated Acquisitions and Serials Control." In *Introduction to Automation for Librarians*, 347-73. 3d ed. Chicago: American Library Association, 1994.

Tonkery, Dan, and Michael Johnson. "Serials Automation Options: Stand-Alone vs. Integrated Systems." *Serials Review* 13 (fall 1987): 25-28.

Tseng, Sally C., and others. "Serials Standards Work: The Next Frontier." *Library Resources and Technical Services* 34 (April 1990): 139-57.

Tuttle, Marcia. "Serials Standards." In *Managing Serials*, 49-63. Greenwich, Conn.: JAI Press, 1996.

Woodward, Hazel, and Margaret E. Graham. "Serials Automation." In *Serials Management: A Practical Handbook*, edited by Margaret E. Graham and Fiona Buettel, 121-44. London: published by Aslib in collaboration with the United Kingdom Serials Group, 1990.

Epilogue

This book addressed the management of serials in libraries during the late 1990s. (The text was completed in August 1997.) Library serials management is taking place in a dynamic, rapidly changing environment. Ironically, many observers have even questioned the future existence of both libraries and the traditional serial. This epilogue examines the future prospects for library serials management.

FUTURE PROSPECTS FOR LIBRARY SERIALS MANAGEMENT

Forecasting future developments is highly perilous. Consequently, this section will minimize explicit predictions, seeking instead to analyze trends that will affect future developments. Innumerable past predictions have succumbed to the pitfall of making quantitative extrapolations from current trends while failing to foresee the effects of qualitative changes. Legend reports that mid-nineteenth-century transportation forecasters predicted carriages drawn by teams of 10 to 12 horses (a quantitative change) but did not envision motorized transportation (a qualitative change).

It should be stressed that the failure to foresee qualitative change is not necessarily the forecaster's fault. When the author began his library and information science career two decades ago, it was generally known that automation and computers would assume greater importance in the future. Yet, I heard no specific predictions of the major impact personal computers, CD-ROMs, or the Internet would have on libraries. Who could have foreseen these particular technologies? The World Wide Web (WWW) has hardly been in existence more than half a decade but is already profoundly influencing serials. Some presently unforeseen technological innovation may surpass the Web in importance and influence serials in ways that can not now be imagined.

In contrast to the defective forecasting alluded to in the preceding paragraphs, other predictions have been remarkably prescient. In a famous 1945 article in *Atlantic Monthly*, Vannevar Bush envisioned a hypothetical personal information system termed the MEMEX.[1] Many subsequent commentators consider the MEMEX a forerunner of such modern information technologies as the personal computer or hypertext.

Will libraries continue to exit in the future? This question relates to a more fundamental issues: What is a library? A library has been defined in terms of place, process, or collection. In the most traditional definition, the term *library* refers to a place—typically a building that contains information resources within its four walls (although the "library as place" can also be a room in a larger building, as was frequently the case for academic libraries in the nineteenth century and is still the case for contemporary school libraries). The "library as process" concept uses the word *library* as a metaphor for the act of accessing information. The "digital library," the "library without walls," and the "electronic library" (poorly defined terms for which there is no consensus about their precise meaning) all appear to accept the "library as process" metaphor. The "library as collection" defines a library as a collection of resources that offer information or entertainment value. When one hears reference to a scholar's "personal library," the phrase usually connotes the scholar's collection of books or other information resources. The video rental store may be viewed as a contemporary version of the paying library (i.e., a collection of videos that circulate for a fee).[2] Presumably, the library as a metaphor for the process of accessing information will continue indefinitely because as long as intelligent and civilized human beings exist on this planet, they will be interested in accessing information. However, the future of the library as a place or a collection of physical items is problematic.

Clifford Lynch's distinction between modernization and transformation, noted in chapter 9, should be reiterated. The use of technology to modernize serials management has been discussed at numerous points throughout this text. Many observers feel that the Internet and electronic journals will ultimately transform the library's role. For example, Gordon B. Neavill and Mary Ann Sheblé envision that future libraries will perform important functions archiving electronic journals and acting as gatekeepers who legitimize the enduring scholarly value of specific electronic titles by providing access to them.[3] Libraries may also play important roles in educating users about electronic resources and deciding which fee-based electronic journals to buy for user access. Libraries could also assume an important role in electronic journal publication—a trend that may already be underway, given the Johns Hopkins University library's participation in Project Muse.

ALTERNATIVE MODELS TO THE TRADITIONAL SERIAL

Just as the continued existence of libraries can be questioned, so can the future existence of the traditional serial. Numerous alternate models to the printed scholarly journal have been envisioned. A few of the leading models are explored in the following discussion.

The Academic Server Model. In this model universities would distribute faculty research publications over the Internet through a WWW server. As research articles would still be submitted for print publication, their peer-review status (submitted, accepted, published, etc.) would be indicated. This system would coexist with printed journals for a period of time, but the ultimate goal would be to replace the traditional print journal. In 1995 the Indiana University School of Library and Information Science began showcasing faculty research on its WWW home page. However, because of copyright concerns, abstracts as opposed to full text were generally mounted on the Web server.

The Prestigious Electronic Journal Model. This model posits mainstream acceptance of the electronic journal. Peer-reviewed electronic journals would maintain high editorial standards. Consequently, publication in electronic format would be rewarded in the academic promotion and tenure system. Scholarly societies and universities would publish electronic journals and sell site licenses to campuses, libraries, and other organizations, allowing full use. These journals would also be available on the WWW. Many of the problems currently associated with electronic journals (e.g., poor indexing, difficulties in use, etc.) would be resolved.[4]

Acquisition-on-Demand Model. Here the focus is on specific articles, which are acquired as needed, rather than the selection of titles for subscription or licensing. The model can be applied to the print as well as the electronic format and take a variety of forms. The familiar document delivery concept constitutes acquisition-on-demand from print titles. Electronic journal articles can be placed on a server for individual access. Carried to the logical extreme, publishers could cease marketing subscriptions or licenses and focus exclusively on selling individual articles. Then there would be no need for grouping articles into issues and volumes—contrivances developed for the print format.

Note Jerome Yavarkovsky's observation, "Scholars don't read journals, they read articles."[5] In 1988 the American Physical Society, a professional organization of physicists, appointed a task force to address information services and publishing in the year 2020. The task force report, published in April 1991, projected that "in the future the document, rather than the journal, will become the primary entity of scientific communication" and noted this would affect "the way collections of documents we now call journals are produced."[6] The task force recommended the creation of a National Physics Database that would contain papers, books, data, conference proceedings and abstracts, and computer software.[7]

Although there has been voluminous discussion on the potentially profound implications of the "digital shift" from print to electronic media, I believe a full shift to the acquisition-on-demand model would have an even greater impact on serials management in libraries. Selection responsibility would be transferred to end users who request specific articles, and cancellation and weeding would no longer be issues.

FUTURE ROLE OF THE ELECTRONIC JOURNAL

Some crucial issues relating to the electronic journal's future are briefly reviewed below.

Scholarly Acceptance

Lack of full acceptance in the academic credit process (i.e., electronic publications counting for promotion and tenure purposes) and the consequent hesitancy of scholars to submit their best work to electronic journals have been viewed as barriers to the electronic journal's development. In 1992 Erik Jul explained that scholars are reluctant to submit their work to electronic journals because of "lack of an audience," "lack of reward," and "fear of transience (electronic files are not considered as 'permanent' as paper)."[8]

In 1992 William Y. Arms wrote, "Widespread acceptance will require more electronic publications"[9]—a trend that is now increasing. As indicated in chapter 2, the number of peer-reviewed scholarly journals is also occurring. After examining nearly 50 university promotion and tenure documents, Blaise Cronin and Kara Overfelt found no official distinction between print-based and electronic publications for promotion and tenure purposes.[10] Therefore, nearly complete scholarly acceptance of the electronic journal (i.e., the "prestigious scholarly journal model" outlined above) is probably simply a matter of time. However, acceptance will undoubtedly be achieved in some disciplines before others, and even within disciplines, the willingness to adapt to the electronic format will vary among scholars.

Economic Implications for Libraries

Whether electronic journals will offer a potential solution to the cost problems associated with print periodicals has caused considerable speculation. In fact, through the mid-1990s many of the electronic journals on the Internet were free, especially those published by individuals or societies. For illustration, as of late 1995 Stephen P. Harter and Hak Joon Kim found that 89.6 percent (112 of 125) of the peer-reviewed journals in their sample were completely free,[11] and Steve Hitchcock, Leslie Carr, and Wendy Hall discovered that 56.6 percent (47 of 83) of science, technical, and medical (STM) journals were free.[12] Yet by 1997 an increasing number of commercial publishers were issuing electronic versions of their print journals. Finding that free electronic journals present more access problems than fee-based ones, Harter and Kim suggest "the idea of free e-journals may be an illusion that cannot be sustained."[13]

Therefore, it seems unrealistic to believe that electronic journals will substantially alleviate library serial costs in the short run. Rather, they will engender even greater costs for libraries that simultaneously subscribe to both the print and electronic versions of a title. From a long-term perspective, the financial implications of electronic journals for libraries can not be predicted. Even though the profit motive on the part of publishers will still exist, electronic journals might result in cost savings to libraries because of cheaper production costs. As previously discussed, it is even possible that the subscription system could be replaced by another model, such as acquisition-on-demand.

Impact on Scholarly Communications

Many commentators predict that electronic journals and similar electronic phenomena will radically impact the scholarly communications process. The University of Pennsylvania classicist James J. O'Donnell has argued that the emergence of the electronic journal will usher in changes as profound as those engendered by the written word, the codex book, or printing.[14] Stevan Harnad has even argued that electronic communication among scholars will constitute the fourth major revolution "in the history of human thought," after language, writing, and the movable-type printing press.[15]

Apart from O'Donnell's and Harnad's sweeping predictions, it seems clear that electronic media are already affecting scholarly communications in numerous ways. Just as the development of scholarly journals three centuries ago speeded communication among scholars in smaller units (i.e., articles rather than monographs), electronic publications also provide quicker scholarly communications in smaller units than do print journals. For example, most contributions on listservs are of a much shorter length than a journal article. Although ostensibly a rather trivial point, this can lead to practical consequences. I originally intended to include a significant number of quotations from listservs in this book. However, I had to eliminate most of them from the final draft because the publisher's policy that quotations not exceed 10 percent of an item (to ensure compliance with copyright) would have been violated because of the short length of many listserv contributions.

In 1990 the National Library of Medicine's Duane Arenales wrote, "During the 1990s, serials, both print and nonprint, will face increasing competition from informal electronic communications."[16] Although one doubts that such informal electronic communications media as listservs actually threaten journals, they certainly represent a new and significant form of scholarly communications.

William F. Birdsall noted that during the 1920s many observers anticipated profound changes would result from the development of microphotography technology.

> These early myth-makers identified microfilm as the most significant innovation in publishing since the invention of movable type in the fifteenth century. Microfilm would revolutionize library services. It would free scholars from the limitations of the printed text and overcome the barriers created by the geographic distribution of printed material. No longer would the book and journal be the sole means of distributing the intellectual record. Furthermore, this technological revolution would lead to a cultural revolution.[17]

Yet the anticipated revolutionary changes engendered by microphotography never materialized, raising the possibility that the cultural impact of electronic media might not be as profound as some visionaries expect.

Archiving

As discussed in chapter 9, archiving represents one of the largest unresolved dilemmas concerning electronic journals. Probably, a systematic solution other than relying on electronic journal publishers will eventually be developed, although the time frame and method are uncertain. Possible solutions include bibliographic utilities—note the November 1996 initiative by OCLC Online Computer Library Center (OCLC)—or cooperative archiving by libraries on a regional or national basis. Cooperative cataloging through bibliographic utilities can be cited as a successful model of library cooperation, although the results obtained from cooperative collection development efforts are less impressive.

Possible Displacement of Print Serials

The number of electronic journals will almost certainly continue to increase exponentially in the future. Not only will new electronic-only journals come into existence, but many print-based scholarly journals will migrate to an electronic format through a three-stage process: print only, simultaneous print and electronic versions, and electronic only.

Will the print-based serial continue to exist in the new electronic environment? One is reminded of F. Wilfrid Lancaster's famous prediction in his *Libraries and Librarians in an Age of Electronics*, published in 1982, that electronic media would replace print on paper by the year 2000.[18]

Analyzing this question concerns whether new technology replaces old technology or whether the new and old technologies continue to exist side by side. Different historical examples can be cited to support either position. As examples of the former, one can mention the replacement of the scroll by the codex book or the automobile's displacement of the horse and buggy. In support of the latter, one can note the fact that radio did not replace newspapers, nor did television replace radio. Rather, television, radio, and newspapers still continue to exist alongside each other. The former perspective implies that electronic journals will, within a reasonable time frame, supplant the traditional version, but the latter viewpoint foresees electronic and print journals coexisting for the foreseeable future.

This framework, although intriguing, oversimplifies reality. Although television has not replaced radio, the qualitative nature of radio broadcasting has been altered since the rise of television (e.g., radio programs such as "The Lone Ranger" or "The Shadow" are no longer carried). Thus, although the question of whether the electronic format will replace print is open to debate, there seems little doubt that scholarly communications will be fundamentally altered by electronic serials.

Even after a full transition to electronic media on the part of scholarly journals, paper will certainly continue to play an important role. Many end users will prefer the paper format for their own personal use. Just as users now photocopy articles from print journals held in libraries, they will print articles from electronic archives—a process that already takes place with electronic indexing and abstracting services or full-text databases. Furthermore, a demand would still exist for entertainment-oriented magazines in a paper format.

Other Issues

A related issue concerns the extent to which conventions developed for traditional print journals will be continued by their electronic counterpart. The concept of refereeing will clearly continue in the electronic age as there is a need for maintaining quality control as well as for establishing the credentials of academic authors for promotion and tenure purposes. Page numbering as well as separate issues and volumes were obviously developed for the print format. Their relevance and continued existence in an electronic environment is certainly questionable.

FUTURE OF SERIALS MANAGEMENT IN LIBRARIES

Although much attention has been devoted to the implications of electronic serials and the so-called digital shift from a print to an electronic environment, I believe that a shift in emphasis from the serial title to the serial article would produce a more profound effect on library serials management. As previously emphasized, many traditional serials management functions are also applicable to full-text electronic journals. In contrast, a complete shift to unmediated document delivery would reduce the need for basic serials collection management decision making, as patrons would decide which documents to order.

The continuing application of current business trends (e.g., downsizing, outsourcing, or reengineering) to library administration will undoubtedly affect the way libraries handle serials, although the full effects can not presently be foreseen. Perhaps an increasing trend toward disintermediated document delivery in lieu of subscription would result in lower serials technical services staffing levels.

SUMMARY AND CONCLUSION

Andrew D. Osborn began and ended the postscript to his classic serials text's final edition with two specific forecasts: "The era of high prices for serials, characterized by the order one, cancel one syndrome, is apt to persist in the decades ahead";[19] and "serials and serial control, in one form or another, are going to be at the heart of the research library for many decades, if not centuries, to come."[20] The last 15 years have borne out his first prediction (which may have been an understatement!), but the verdict remains open on the second.

As discussed above, the long-term outlook for serials collection management in libraries can not be predicted. Electronic journals, the Internet, and the access concept may fundamentally transform the library serials management process. However, in the short term, serials management is becoming increasingly challenging—and thus more important—as librarians must cope with new technological developments and more options for meeting patron information needs. More than one librarian has commented to the author that the digital format creates additional responsibilities on top of the traditional ones, but the traditional duties still must be done.

Ironically, if library collections of print serials continue to shrink (due to some combination of budgetary factors, increased emphasis on access, and greater acceptance of the electronic format), many of the traditional serials management functions discussed in this book (e.g., selecting, canceling, and weeding; defining the core collection; investigating use within the library; and journal ranking) may assume more significance in managing the print collection. Smaller, local print collections may actually require greater intellectual effort in deciding which titles to include. Finally, many (but not all) traditional serials functions are applicable to electronic journals.

NOTES

1. Vannevar Bush, "As We May Think," *Atlantic Monthly* 176 (July 1945): 101-8.

2. Conversation with David Kaser, Distinguished Professor Emeritus, Indiana University, School of Library and Information Science, summer, 1994.

3. Gordon B. Neavill and Mary Ann Sheblé, "Archiving Electronic Journals," *Serials Review* 21 (winter 1995): 19.

4. James G. Neal, then director of the Indiana University Libraries, speaking at an Indiana University Research Forum on November 8, 1994, stated that the "Academic Server" and "Prestigious Electronic Journal" models were discussed by the Columbia Working Group on Electronic Texts in September 1994.

5. Jerome Yavarkovsky, "A University-Based Electronic Publishing Network," *EDUCOM Review* 25 (fall 1990): 15.

6. "Task Force Report Looks at Future of Information Services," *Bulletin of the American Physical Society* 36 (April 1991): 106.

7. Ibid., 105-7.

8. Erik Jul, "Of Barriers and Breakthroughs," *Computers in Libraries* 12 (March 1992): 21.

9. William Y. Arms, "Scholarly Publishing on the National Networks," *Scholarly Publishing* 23 (April 1992): 169.

10. Blaise Cronin and Kara Overfelt, "E-Journals and Tenure," *Journal of the American Society for Information Science* 46 (October 1995): 700-703.

11. Stephen P. Harter and Hak Joon Kim, "Accessing Electronic Journals and Other E-Publications: An Empirical Study," *College and Research Libraries* 57 (September 1996): 450.

12. Steve Hitchcock, Leslie Carr, and Wendy Hall, "A Survey of STM Online Journals, 1990-1995: The Calm Before the Storm," in *Directory of Electronic Journals, Newsletters and Academic Discussion Lists*, 6th ed., compiled by Dru Mogge and Diane K. Kovacs, edited by Dru Mogge (Washington, D.C.: Association of Research Libraries, 1996), 10. Available: http://journals.ecs.soton.ac.uk/survey/survey.html (Accessed March 1, 1998). The proportion free by publisher type were: Commercial—27.3 percent (9 of 33); society—52.2 percent (12 of 23); and "other"—96.3 percent (26 of 27). The percentages are my own calculations.

13. Harter and Kim, "Accessing Electronic Journals and Other E-Publications," 454.

14. James J. O'Donnell, "St. Augustine to NREN: The Tree of Knowledge and How It Grows," in *Directory of Electronic Journals, Newsletters and Academic Discussion Lists*, 3d ed., by Michael Strangelove and Diane Kovacs, ed. Ann Okerson (Washington, D.C.: Association of Research Libraries, 1993), 2-11.

15. Stevan Harnad, "Post-Gutenberg Galaxy: The Fourth Revolution in the Means of Production of Knowledge," *Public-Access Computer Systems Review* 2, no. 1 (1991): 29-41. Available: http://info.lib.uh.edu/pr/v2/n1/harnad.2n1 (Accessed March 1, 1998).

16. Mary Elizabeth Clack and John F. Riddick, with contributions from Richard R. Rowe, Duane Arenales, and Sheila S. Intner, "The Future of Serials Librarianship: Part 2," *Serials Review* 16 (fall 1990): 63.

17. William F. Birdsall, *The Myth of the Electronic Library: Librarianship and Social Change in America* (Westport, Conn.: Greenwood Press, 1994), 8.

18. F. W. Lancaster, *Libraries and Librarians in an Age of Electronics*, 2d ed. (Arlington, Va.: Information Resources Press, 1982).

19. Andrew D. Osborn, *Serial Publications: Their Place and Treatment in Libraries*, 3d ed. (Chicago: American Library Association, 1980), 451.

20. Ibid., 457.

FURTHER READING

Amiran, Eyal, Elaine Orr, and John Unsworth. "Refereed Electronic Journals and the Future of Scholarly Publishing." *Advances in Library Automation and Networking* 4 (1991): 25-53.

Bailey, Charles W., Jr. "Scholarly Electronic Publishing on the Internet, the NREN, and the NII: Charting Possible Futures." *Serials Review* 20 (fall 1994): 7-16.

Birdsall, William F. *The Myth of the Electronic Library: Librarianship and Social Change in America*. Westport, Conn.: Greenwood Press, 1994.

Butler, Brett. "Scholarly Journals, Electronic Publishing, and Library Networks: From 1986 to 2000." *Serials Review* 12 (summer and fall 1986): 47-52.

Clack, Mary Elizabeth, and John Riddick, editors, with contributions from F. Dixon Brooke, Jr., Czeslaw Jan Grycz, Karen Hunter, and Herbert White. "The Future of Serials Librarianship." *Serials Review* 16 (summer 1990): 55-64.

Clack, Mary Elizabeth, and John F. Riddick, with contributions from Richard R. Rowe, Duane Arenales, and Sheila S. Intner. "The Future of Serials Librarianship: Part 2." *Serials Review* 16 (fall 1990): 61-80.

Gorman, Michael. "The Academic Library in the Year 2001: Dream or Nightmare or Something in Between?" *Journal of Academic Librarianship* 17 (March 1991): 4-9.

Grycz, Czeslaw Jan. "Serials Librarians in the 21st Century and What to Teach Them." *Serials Librarian* 22 (summer 1996): 25-31.

Morris, Sally. "The Future of Journal Publishing." *Interlending and Document Supply* 23, no. 4 (1995): 20-22.

Rowe, Richard R. "The Transformation of Scholarly Communications and the Future of Serials." *Serials Review* 22 (summer 1996): 33-43.

Schaffner, Ann C. "The Future of Scientific Journals: Lessons from the Past." *Information Technology and Libraries* 13 (December 1994): 239-47.

Tomajko, Kathy G., and Miriam A. Drake. "The Journal, Scholarly Communication, and the Future." *Serials Librarian* 10 (fall 1985/winter 1985-1986): 289-98.

Upham, Lois N. "The Future of Serials Librarianship Revisited." *Serials Review* 17 (summer 1991): 71-75.

Appendix 1
Sources of Statistical Data on Serials

Statistical data on serials production, prices, and library expenditures and holdings are useful for cost projections, library budgeting, collection evaluation, and a variety of research purposes. Data from an ongoing statistical series can be used for tracking longitudinal trends. This appendix, in the form of an annotated bibliography, serves as a guide to print and information sources for serial statistics. Many of the sources are listed because they contain relevant serials statistics, even though they are not devoted exclusively to serials. For ongoing series or publications, the citations and annotations are based on the most recent available issue prior to this book's submission. The annotations focus on the type and format of data contained in the source rather than trends indicated by the data, which have been discussed in chapter 2.

Many state libraries publish annual statistical reports, such as *Statistics of Indiana Libraries* or *Statistics of Ohio Libraries*. The format and type of material vary from state to state, but these reports usually include data relevant to serials. No attempt is made to list state-level reports in this appendix, but the reader should be aware of their existence. For serials price projections, see the Web sites of the major serial subscription agents, which are annotated in appendix 3.

Likewise, the annual reports of specific libraries usually contain data on their serial holdings. However, these reports are not included here because these data are more readily obtainable through the *American Library Directory*. The *Newsletter on Serials Pricing Issues* (not annotated here) often includes serials price increase projections by subscription agents. Remember that most statistical reports contain a margin of error. Moreover, many of the data contained in the items annotated below are based on library self-reporting.

Alexander, Adrian W. "Periodical Prices, 1992-1994." *Library Acquisitions: Practice and Theory* 19 (spring 1995): 63-82.

This item represents the 21st report (and as of spring 1998, the most recent) in a series of periodical price studies published annually since 1974. The data are calculated from the active titles in the Faxon database. A major table displays—for 59 broad categories of the Library of Congress classification system—the number of priced periodicals in Faxon's database and their average price during each of the last three years along with year-to-year percentage changes. Another table offers weighted average prices based on the number of subscriptions. Identical sets of data are presented by country of publication for nearly 60 countries. Other tables indicate the average subscription cost and the annual percentage change during a 10-year period for academic, medical, special (both governmental and business), and public libraries. The percentage of periodical subscriptions that fall into 12 price ranges (from less than $50 to greater than $1,000) are also analyzed for these five library types. Although the author warns Faxon's data "may not always be related" to a particular library's serials list, this is nevertheless an important source of serials price data.

Alexander, Adrian W., and Brenda Dingley. "U.S. Periodical Prices—1998." *American Libraries* 29 (May 1998): 82–90.

Sponsored by the ALA-ALCTS Library Materials Price Index Committee, this study, based on 3,938 U.S. periodicals, is the 38th in an annual series and the 14th consecutive one using Faxon data. Most of the analysis is structured around title output, average price, and percentage increase for 25 broad categories, e.g., Russian translations, general interest periodicals, and children's periodicals, and 22 subject areas such as engineering or law. Separate tables present the data for each category from 1984 through 1998. Price, output, and percentage increase data for the last three years is also presented for 19 broad and 55 narrow segments of the Library of Congress classification, while other tables rank the 25 categories by average price and percentage price increase for each of the last four years and indicate the proportion of titles increasing in price during each of the last three years. Also, a table summarizes the average percentage price increase for each year from 1989 through 1998 for all categories but Russian translations and presents a total figure termed the "U.S. Periodicals Price Index."

American Library Directory, 1997-98. 50th ed. New York: R. R. Bowker, 1997.

The *American Library Directory* is considered a standard source for the names, addresses, staff members, and basic statistics of U.S. and Canadian libraries. Arranged geographically, approximately 35,000 libraries of all types are included. Four types of periodical data may be included: periodical expenditures, the number of periodical subscriptions, bound periodicals, and periodicals in microformat. However, all four categories are not necessarily reported for each library. This would be an obvious source for locating periodical data pertaining to a particular library.

Association of Academic Health Sciences Library Directors. *Annual Statistics of Medical School Libraries in the United States and Canada, 1995-96.* 19th ed. Seattle, Wash.: Association of Academic Health Sciences Library Directory, 1997.

Published on a near-annual basis since 1978, this standard source of statistical data covers such items as collections, expenditures, staffing, and salaries for libraries affiliated with accredited U.S. and Canadian medical schools. Data on the number of current serial subscriptions and serials expenditures in 1995-96 are presented for 140 libraries as well as summary statistics for all libraries (i.e., maximum, minimum, and mean). Also, 1995-96 data for a "composite" (i.e., average) medical library is compared with 1994-95 composite data. Charts illustrate the average number of serial subscriptions held by medical libraries each year from 1990-91 through 1995-96 and the percentage of the total 1995-96 budget devoted to serials in various types of medical libraries. A data diskette in a pocket part contains most of this data in machine-readable form.

Association of College and Research Libraries. *ACRL University Library Statistics, 1994-1995: A Compilation of Statistics from One Hundred Sixteen University Libraries.* Project coordinator Hugh A. Thompson. Chicago: Association of College and Research Libraries, 1996.

Published biennially since 1978–79 by the Association of College and Research Libraries (ACRL), this series presents statistical data for more than 100 libraries of U.S. and Canadian Ph.D-granting institutions who are not Association of Research Libraries (ARL) members. The report follows almost the identical format of the *ARL Statistics*. In fact, the ARL survey instrument was used to compile the data. Data are presented on the number of current serials purchased, current serials not purchased, and total current serials in addition to the annual expenditures for current serials. Tables rank order the institutions according to total current serials, current serials purchased, and expenditures for serials. A note indicates this data can be obtained in machine-readable form from the ACRL.

Association of Research Libraries. *ARL Academic Law and Medical Library Statistics, 1992-93 to 1994-95.* Compiled and edited by Martha Kyrillidou and Kimberly A. Maxwell. Washington, D.C.: Association of Research Libraries, 1996.

Collection, expenditure, personnel, and interlibrary loan data for law and medical libraries affiliated with ARL academic institutions are contained in this source. It is organized into six major sections: three covering law libraries for 1992-93, 1993-94, and 1994-95; the other three devoted to medical libraries for the same three years. Each section contains data on number of paid subscriptions, nonpaid subscriptions, total subscriptions, and expenditures on current serials—for reporting library and summary statistics. Also, 1986 serials expenditures and costs are compared for ARL medical libraries and all ARL libraries. A data file with this data can be purchased from ARL. This publication, which the introduction states will be published annually in the future, supplements *ARL Academic Law and Medical Library Statistics; 1977-78 to 1991-92*, available as a computer file.

Association of Research Libraries. *ARL Statistics; 1995-96: A Compilation of Statistics from the One Hundred and Twenty Members of the Association of Research Libraries.* Compiled and edited by Martha Kyrillidou, Ken Rodriguez, and Kendon Stubbs. Washington, D.C.: Association of Research Libraries, 1997.

The most recent item in a series published annually since 1961-62 serves as the standard source of statistical data for ARL members and has been used as a model for the ACRL statistics and Molyneux's data on historically black colleges and universities. Tables, which list the ARL members alphabetically, present data on collections, expenditures, personnel, Ph.D. degrees, faculty, and enrollment. Four of the data sets are pertinent to serials: the number of paid serial subscriptions, the number of current serials not purchased, the total number of serials currently received, and expenditures for serial subscriptions. Summary data (high, low, median, and total) for ARL university libraries are also included. Other tables rank order the ARL libraries and group them into broad categories according to total serial subscriptions, paid serial subscriptions, and total serials expenditures, although the introduction cautions these rankings should not be considered "measures of library quality." The rank order tables are summarized so the reader can quickly determine where a specific university ranks in a particular category. Graphs and tables illustrate monographic and serial collecting and cost trends in ARL libraries from 1986 to 1996. These statistics can be obtained in machine readable form from the ARL. The reader is referred to the ARL's interactive statistics WWW site.[1] *ARL Statistics* would be useful for determining trends in serials collecting and expenditures by ARL members as well as for university librarians wishing to compare their serials statistics with those of ARL libraries.

The Bowker Annual: Library and Book Trade Almanac, 1997. 42d ed. New York: R. R. Bowker, 1997.

The well-known *Bowker Annual* offers a wealth of information on librarianship and publishing. Although coverage has changed over the four decades of this tool's existence, current editions include a state-by-state breakdown of periodical expenditures by public, academic, special, and governmental libraries. Data from the U.S. Periodical Price Index and the U.S. Serial Services Index are reprinted here.

Cahalan, Margaret, Elena Hernandez, and Jeffrey W. Williams. *Statistics of Public and Private School Library Media Centers, 1985-86 (with Historical Comparisons from 1958-1985).* Washington, D.C.: Center for Education Statistics, Office of Educational Research and Improvement, U.S. Department of Education, 1987.

This major statistical study of U.S. school library media centers during the 1984-85 academic year contains much information relevant to serials. Numerous tables include mean statistics on total serial expenditures, expenditures per pupil, expenditures per school, the proportion of total expenditures devoted to serials, the number of serial subscriptions per school, and the number of subscriptions per 100 pupils. Data are presented by type (i.e., private versus public), level, and size of school as well as by state. Some comparisons are made with data from earlier years.

Chaffin, Nancy J. "U.S. Serial Services Price Index for 1998." *American Libraries* 29 (May 1998): 91-92.

Sponsored by the ALA-ALCTS Library Materials Price Index Committee in collaboration with Faxon, this entry, the 35th in an annual series, provides price data on serial services, i.e., indexes and abstracts. Seven tables summarize data for all U.S. serials services (1,282 titles in 1998) except Russian translations; business serial services; general and humanities services; law; science and technology; social sciences; and U.S. documents. The tables present for 1984 and 1988 through 1998 the number of titles analyzed, their average price, the average price's percentage change from the preceding year, and the price index using 1984 as a base of 100.

Downs, Robert B. *University Library Statistics: Assembled for the ARL-ACRL Joint Committee on University Library Standards.* By Robert B. Downs, Chairman; assisted by John W. Heussman. Chicago: Association of Research Libraries and the Association of College and Research Libraries by the American Library Association, 1970.

This volume contains 53 tables of statistics, gathered to help develop standards for university libraries. "Raw" data on resources, staff, space, and finances are separately provided for 50 U.S. and Canadian university libraries. Summary data indicate the total, average, high, low, first-quartile, median, and third-quartile figures, and the 50 universities are ranked in each statistical category. Two data sets pertain to periodicals: current periodicals received and periodicals per student. These data are also separately reported for the law libraries and medical libraries affiliated with the universities. Unfortunately, periodical expenditure data are not included because they are grouped into a larger category along with book and binding expenditures. This document's primary value would be for historical research purposes.

Fackler, Naomi P. "Journals for Academic Veterinary Medical Libraries: Price Increases, 1983-1996." *Serials Librarian* 31, no. 4 (1997): 41-52.

Naomi P. Fackler reports the 11th annual study of veterinary medicine journal prices, based on the "Basic List of Veterinary Medical Serials, 2nd edition." The number of paid titles, their total cost, the average cost per title, an index with the 1983 price as a base of 100, and the average increase per year is reported for core journals, adjunct journals, core and adjunct journals, and indexing and abstracting services for the years 1995, 1994, 1993, 1992, and 1983. Average annual prices and yearly price increases from 1983 through 1995 are given for core journals, adjunct journals, and both combined.

Faxon Company. *Foreign and Domestic Periodicals Price Index for Canada*. Available: http://www.faxon.com/html/new_cpi97.html (Accessed March 31, 1998).

This study is the most current edition of the "Foreign and Domestic Price Index," instituted by Faxon Canada in 1989/1990. The analysis is based on 4,444 titles from the Faxon database, with all price calculations in Canadian dollars. The average annual subscription inflation rate for Canadian libraries is presented for each year from 1990 through 1997. A table analyzes average price data for 34 subjects, including the 1989 price, the 1996 and 1997 prices, the 1996 and 1997 percentage increases from the previous year, and 1996 and 1997 index numbers using the 1989 price as a base of 100. Pricing patterns are analyzed for journals published in seven countries and price projections for 1998 are included. The fourth index was published in print format by Mark S. Davies, Nancy McGrath, and Janelle McInnis,[2] and elsewhere in print Davies and McInnis trace this index's history and tabulate data from the first four surveys.[3]

Fortney, Lynn M., and Victor A. Basile. "*Index Medicus* Price Study: Publishing Trends from 1992-1996." *Serials Review* 22 (fall 1996): 99-126.

In the sixth of an ongoing series first published in 1989, Fortney and Basile use EBSCO data to analyze the price of biomedical journals, based on the 3,099 active titles covered in *Index Medicus* as of January 1996 and available through EBSCO. Figures illustrate the yearly average biomedical journal price from 1986 through 1996 as well as worldwide distribution by number of titles and cost of titles. Most of the report is comprised of lengthy tables that present (for 110 biomedical subjects and more than 70 countries of origin) the total number of titles, the number with prepriced annual subscription rates, total cost for all titles, average price per title, and percentage increase in the average price from 1992 to 1996.

Ketcham-Van Orsdel, Lee, and Kathleen Born. "Periodical Price Survey 1998: E-Journals Come of Age." *Library Journal* 123 (April 15, 1998): 40-45.

    This 38th annual survey uses EBSCO price data to analyze 5,208 titles from the three major Institute for Scientific Information (ISI) databases[4] to indicate trends for research libraries. A table presents average cost plus yearly percentage increases for each year from 1994 to 1998 for 31 subjects. Other tables summarize trends by continent, country, and broad areas of knowledge. Data are presented for school and public libraries based on 503 titles in EBSCO's Magazine Article Summaries and for smaller academic libraries based on 2,398 titles in EBSCO's Academic Search. Charts illustrate 1995 through 1998 currency fluctuations, and 1999 price projections are included.

Miller, Marilyn L., and Marilyn L. Shontz. "Expenditures for Resources in School Library Media Centers, FY 1993-94: The Race for the School Library Dollar." *School Library Journal* 41 (October 1995): 22-33. Reprinted in *The Bowker Annual: Library and Book Trade Almanac; 1996*, 462-81. 41st ed. New York: R. R. Bowker, 1996.

    The seventh in a biennial series begun in 1983, this item analyzes data on the collections, expenditures, and staffing of U.S. school library media centers. The report, covering the 1993-94 school year, is based on 674 survey responses from 1,574 sent to school library media centers in all 50 states. Seventeen tables present data, much of which pertains to periodicals. Included are mean and median total expenditures for periodicals by all school library media centers and mean and median periodical expenditures per pupil (based on local funds only). Likewise, mean and median periodical expenditures and expenditures per pupil are also reported by school level, school size, and region of the country. Median periodical expenditures per school, based on local funds only, are reported for six data points between 1984 and 1994. This is probably the most current source of data on periodical expenditures by U.S. school library media centers.

Molyneux, Robert E., comp. *ACRL/Historically Black Colleges and Universities Library Statistics, 1988-89*. Chicago: Association of College and Research Libraries, 1991.

    Modeled on the ARL and ACRL annual statistical reports, this document presents collections, interlibrary loan, personnel, expenditures, Ph.D., faculty, and enrollment statistics for 68 historically black colleges, universities, and community colleges in the U.S. The number of purchased serial subscriptions, current serials not purchased, and total current serials, along with total serial expenditures, is reported. Tables rank order the institutions according to total current serials received, purchased current serials, and serial expenditures. To the best of this author's knowledge, a more current edition has not been published.

"Periodical Prices, 1997." *Library Association Record* 99 (May 1997): 266.

> Oriented toward the needs of U.K. special and academic libraries (prices are given in pounds sterling), this is the most recent installment in an ongoing series published annually since 1966. The study is based on 2,007 journal titles selected by Blackwell's Periodicals Division. Data is presented for more than 60 subject categories in the humanities and social sciences, medicine, and science and technology. The average 1997 price, the percentage increase since 1996, and an index figure using the 1970 price as zero are presented for each subject category.

Serials Prices 1992-1996, with Projections for 1997. Birmingham, Ala., EBSCO, 1997.

> Five-year historical price data, including average cost per title and a typical subscription list's total cost, are provided for nine types of libraries: academic research, college and university, public, law school, law firm, academic medical, hospital, special, and corporate. Price data are given for both U.S. and non-U.S. titles. Charts illustrate five-year price fluctuations for each of the nine library types.[5]

NOTES

1. Association of Research Libraries, *Association of Research Libraries Statistics*. Available: http://www.lib.virginia.edu/socsci/newarl/ (Accessed March 14, 1998).

2. Mark S. Davies, Nancy McGrath, and Janelle McInnis, "Periodicals Price Index for Canada 1994: The Fourth Survey," *Canadian Journal of Information and Library Science* 19 (September 1994): 1-20.

3. Mark S. Davies and Janelle McInnis, "Evolution of the Periodicals Price Index Study," *Serials Librarian* 26, nos. 3/4 (1995): 43-54.

4. The three databases are *Science Citation Index* (SCI), *Social Sciences Citation Index* (SSCI), and *Arts and Humanities Citation Index*.

5. This annotation is based on inspection of the data when it was formerly mounted on the EBSCO Web page plus an advertisement currently on the page rather than direct examination of the print booklet.

Appendix 2
Serials Bibliographies

      This appendix offers an annotated bibliography of print bibliographies or literature reviews pertaining to serials management that have been published since 1990. It does not cover bibliographies of serials in specific subject areas or formats (e.g., a bibliography of political science serials or electronic journals would not be included). The annotations usually do not repeat information that is obvious from the title. The appendix is organized into three sections: general bibliographies, electronic journals, and specialized topics.

GENERAL BIBLIOGRAPHIES

Association for Library Collections and Technical Services. "Selected Bibliography." In *Guide to Performance Evaluation of Serials Vendors*, 33-38. Chicago: American Library Association, 1997.

      Approximately 25 articles, published from the middle 1970s to the early 1990s, are annotated. The bibliography is organized into two parts covering the functions of serial subscription agents and their selection and evaluation.

Chen, Chiou-sen Dora. "Appendix: A Selected Bibliography on Serials Management." In *Serials Management: A Practical Guide*, 169-75. Chicago: American Library Association, 1995.

      Chiou-sen Dora Chen briefly annotates 36 items organized under four broad headings: literature search tools, serials about serials management, books about serials, and bibliographies.

Davis, Susan. "The Year's Work in Serials, 1989." *Library Resources and Technical Services* 34 (July 1990): 313-25.

      From 1958 through 1993 *Library Resources and Technical Services* published annual bibliographic essays describing the previous year's U.S. literature about serials. In the first installment of the 1990s, Susan Davis lists serials pricing, scholarly communications, journal publishing, and access versus ownership as the year's major issues. The essay divides into 10 sections, including cataloging, copyright, automated systems, subscription agents, and CD-ROM and electronic developments. More than 130 unannotated items are listed in alphabetical order in an appended bibliography.

Ginneken, J. van. *770 Articles and Books on Serials*. Wageningen, Netherlands: Library Agricultural University, 1991. 116p.

> One of the few book-length bibliographies dealing with serials annotates 770 books, book chapters, articles, Ph.D. dissertations, and conference proceedings published between 1983 and 1989. Its five major sections cover serials in general, collection development and acquisitions, technical services, finance, and automation. Non-English items and entries published in Europe, India, and Australia are incorporated. An index includes author and subject entries.

Krishan, Kewal. *A Hundred Years of Serials Librarianship in Canada, 1893-1993: A Bibliography*. Saskatoon, Sask.: Cataloguing Department, University of Saskatchewan Libraries, 1994. 127p.

> Kewal Krishan lists more than 700 articles, conference presentations, and unpublished items by Canadians, published in Canada, or having a Canadian content. Only a minute fraction are annotated. The entries are arranged under 13 broad subject headings, with a combined author-subject index appended. Although not especially well-done, this is the only general bibliography on Canadian serials librarianship.

Lonberger, Jana. "The Rise in Consumerism: The Year's Work in Serials, 1990." *Library Resources and Technical Services* 35 (July 1991): 319-31.

> Jana Lonberger begins by identifying librarians' "rising consumerism" in response to the serials pricing crisis as the 1990 serials literature's "overriding theme." This bibliographic essay includes sections dealing with publishing and scholarly communications, cancellation projects, automated systems, claiming and replacement issues, cataloging and classification, and public services. Approximately 125 items published in 1990 are listed in the appended bibliography.

Riddick, John F. "An Electrifying Year: A Year's Work in Serials, 1992." *Library Resources and Technical Services* 37 (July 1993): 335-42.

> John F. Riddick's review of the 1992 serials literature identifies cataloging and the rise of electronic journals as the year's dominant issues. The bibliographic essay is organized into eight topics covering cataloging, electronic publishing, CD-ROM serials, collection development, pricing, serials management, conference reports, and end pieces. More than 120 entries are listed in the "Works Cited" appendix. This item is the last one in the annual series.

Riemer, John J. "A Rising Sense of Urgency: The Year's Work in Serials, 1991." *Library Resources and Technical Services* 36 (July 1992): 361-73.

> After reviewing the 1991 serials literature, John J. Riemer concludes, "Frustratingly few of the service issues in serials librarianship display evidence of established practices that are obviously still working today." The bibliographical essay is organized into 14 sections including evaluation and use studies, electronic serials, conservation and preservation, and international activities. The appended bibliography lists more than 150 items.

Tuttle, Marcia. "Serials Management." In *Guide to Technical Services Resources*, edited by Peggy Johnson, 120-35. Chicago: American Library Association, 1994.

> This chapter in a major technical services guide annotates approximately 135 items organized into sections on general works, management of serials units, serials publishing, serials processing, automation of serials processing, serials pricing, and resource sharing and union listing. Most of the entries were published since 1985 but a few date as far back as 1937. Professional associations are also listed. Although much more selective, this entry may be viewed as supplementing Marcia Tuttle's earlier bibliographical work on serials.

ELECTRONIC JOURNALS

Bailey, Charles W., Jr. "Network-Based Electronic Publishing of Scholarly Works: A Selective Bibliography." *Public-Access Computer Systems Review* 6, no. 1 (1995): 5-21. Available: http://info.lib.uh.edu/pr/v6/n1/bailey.6n1 (Accessed April 6, 1998). Reprinted in *Directory of Electronic Journals, Newsletters and Academic Discussion Lists*, 5th ed. Compiled by Lisabeth A. King and Diane Kovacs, edited by Ann Okerson, 41-50. Washington, D.C.: ARL Office of Scientific and Academic Publishing, 1995.

> Charles W. Bailey Jr.'s unannotated bibliography covers scholarly electronic publishing on the Internet. Items published from 1990 to 1995 are listed. About one-third of the approximately 165 entries deal with electronic journals. The "Electronic Serials" section is subdivided into "Case Studies and History," "Critiques," "Electronic Distribution of Printed Journals," "General Works," "Library Issues," and "Research" (a section of only three entries). Economic issues, electronic books, library-related issues, future scenarios, new publishing models, and copyright questions are also covered. This useful bibliography provides much better coverage of core library and information science journals than do David F. W. Robison's.
>
> Bailey has mounted several updated versions of his bibliography on the World Wide Web (WWW).[1]

Krishan, Kewal. "A Bibliography of Electronic Journals in Canada, 1980-1993." *Serials Librarian* 26, nos. 3/4 (1995): 21-31.

> Nearly 60 items about electronic journals, either published in Canada or having some undefined "Canadian connection," are listed here. Most of the entries have brief annotations. This work is extracted from Krishan's *A Hundred Years of Serials Librarianship in Canada, 1893-1993: A Bibliography*, published in-house by the University of Saskatchewan Libraries Cataloging Department in 1994.

Nisonger, Thomas E. "A Select Bibliography on Electronic Journals." *IFLA Journal* 22, no. 3 (1996): 237-39.

> Appended to the author's article "Collection Management Issues for Electronic Journals," this short, unannotated bibliography lists more than 60 items, mostly published during the mid-1990s. The emphasis is on the management of electronic journals in libraries and descriptions of specific electronic publications.

Robison, David F. W. "Bibliography of Articles Related to Electronic Journal Publications and Publishing." In *Directory of Electronic Journals, Newsletters and Academic Discussion Lists*, 3d ed., by Michael Strangelove and Diane Kovacs, edited by Ann Okerson, 27-38. Washington, D.C.: Association of Research Libraries, 1993.

> This bibliography was compiled specifically for this directory from items listed in the electronic journal *Current Cites* and published under the name of the *Current Cites* editor, although six other contributors are listed in the abstract. Approximately 85 items, published from 1990 to 1993, are briefly annotated. The bibliography covers a wide range of literature, including computer science, information science, the popular press, electronic resources, and, to a lesser extent, core Library and Information Science (LIS) journals.

Robison, David F. W. "Bibliography of Articles Related to Electronic Journal Publications and Publishing." In *Directory of Electronic Journals, Newsletters and Academic Discussion Lists*, 4th ed., by Michael Strangelove and Diane Kovacs, edited by Ann Okerson, 35-43. Washington, D.C.: ARL Office of Scientific and Academic Publishing, 1994.

> Robison offers an updated version of the preceding entry. This bibliography annotates 65 items, mostly published during 1993 and 1994. The *Directory* editor appends an unannotated list of six additional "favorites."

SPECIALIZED TOPICS

Anderson, Bill. "Appendix B: CONSER Bibliography." *Serials Review* 21 (summer 1995): 14-16.

> This appendix to Bill Anderson's article "History of the CONSER Program (1986-1994)" provides an unannotated listing of 64 items, most of which are articles, published between 1973 and 1994 that deal with all aspects of the CONSER Program.

Kelly, Glen. "Appendix: Electronic Data Interchange (EDI); Selective Bibliography." *Collection Management* 19, nos. 3/4 (1995): 89-94.

> An appendix to Glen Kelly's article on Electronic Data Interchange (EDI) lists more than 60 items ostensibly dealing with EDI. However, many of the entries take a broader focus and address automation standards in general or automated acquisitions and serials control.

Wise, Suzanne. "[Reference Serials Cancellation]: Selected Bibliography." *Serials Review* 19 (winter 1993): 22-26, 96.

> Appended to Suzanne Wise's article on the cancellation of reference serials, this bibliography annotates nearly 60 items, most published during the late 1980s or early 1990s, dealing with various aspects of journal collection management. It is organized into seven sections: general, the access model, communicating with patrons, electronic resources, resource sharing, use studies, and user surveys.

Zackey, Christopher A. "Bibliography: Emerging Relationships Between Reference and Serials." *Reference Librarian* nos. 27/28 (1990): 91-104.

This bibliographic essay provides lengthy, detailed annotations for 15 book chapters and articles, published between 1976 and 1987, that address the relationship between the concepts "serials" and "reference." Christopher A. Zackey's argument that since the early 1980s there has been a shift from a "reference serials" perspective in which "serials were absorbed into a unity with reference, under a reference viewpoint" to a "serials reference" perspective that represents "the new serials-oriented consciousness of reference work" is somewhat lacking in cogency.

NOTES

1. Version 19, dated June 18, 1998, is available on the WWW at http://info.lib.uh.edu/sepb/ sepb.html (Accessed April 10, 1998).

Appendix 3
World Wide Web Sites Pertaining to Serials

This appendix offers a highly select, annotated listing of World Wide Web sites that contain information pertinent to serials. Although a much larger number of sites could have been included, the sites listed here represent, in the author's opinion, the most important or noteworthy. Sites for individual publishers and specific journals have been excluded because of the voluminous number on the Web. Readers interested in publisher or journal sites are referred to the various collections available on the WWW (e.g., AcqWeb, Faxon, or the World Wide Web Virtual Library). A different list of serials sources on the WWW has been compiled by Jeanne M. K. Boydston.[1]

The accuracy of the annotations and the URL addresses for these Web sites was verified during the last week of March or early April 1998 (shortly before submission of the copyedited manuscript to Libraries Unlimited). These sites can be accessed by entering the URL into a graphics-oriented Web browser such as Netscape. Most of the sites can also be accessed by a textual-oriented browser such as Lynx.

AcqWeb. *Acqweb's Home Page.* Available: http://www.library.vanderbilt.edu/law/acqs/acqs.html (Accessed March 30, 1998).

> AcqWeb, undoubtedly the best site for Internet resources pertaining to library acquisitions and collection development, contains much of interest to serial specialists. It includes sections on "serial sites," copyright and licensing, and gifts and exchanges.

Alfred Jaeger, Inc. *Alfred Jaeger Home Page.* Available: http://www.ajaeger.com/ (Accessed March 30, 1998).

> This prominent periodical backrun dealer's WWW site contains information on the company's services, policies, and personnel. Separate pages are devoted to the single-issue service, discounts, and the dealer's policy on purchasing duplicate or unwanted journals from libraries. Lists of recent acquisitions can be searched by subject or title and orders directly submitted through a form.

American Journalism Review. *AJR NewsLink.* Available: http://www.newslink.org/ (Accessed April 3, 1998).

> This site provides links to 8,000 newspaper, news service, magazine, and broadcaster Web sites. Newspapers are organized geographically (country and for U.S. newspapers, state) and by frequency of publication, i.e., daily or non-daily. Magazine sites are organized into more than 40 subject categories. The 50 most popular news sites, based on a user poll, are listed. Newslink has received 4 stars from Magellan and has been ranked among the "top 100" Web sites by *PC Magazine.*

American Society for Engineering Education. *Duplicates Exchange*. Available: http://www.ummu.umich.edu/library/ASEE/duplicates.html (Accessed April 2, 1998).

This Web site describes the services offered by the Engineering Libraries Division of the American Society for Engineering Education Duplicates Exchange, which has been operating on the Internet since 1993.

B. H. Blackwell Ltd. *Blackwell's Information Services*. Available: http://www. blackwell.co.uk/journals/ (Accessed April 10, 1998).

Blackwell's recently created site contains information on the company's history and services. Some features, such as ReadiCat, a web-accessible database of over 100,000 journals, are only available to Blackwell's customers. There are external links to sites of interest to serialists, such as publishers' catalogs and electronic journal resources.

Book Industry Study Group, Inc. *Serials Industry Systems Advisory Committee*. Available: http://www.bookwire.com/bisg/sisac.html (Accessed April 5, 1998).

Basic information on SISAC goals, membership, publications, and meetings can be found here. The site contains useful explanations about Electronic Data Interchange (EDI), the Serial Item and Contribution Identifier (SICI), and the SISAC bar code symbol.

CARL. *Welcome to UnCover Web*. Available: http://uncweb.carl.org/ (Accessed April 3, 1998).

This page of CARL's home page provides access to the UnCover database of 17,000 periodicals. The UnCover index can be used for bibliographical searching, free of charge, as well as for the direct ordering of documents. Other links describe such UnCover services as the UnCover Reveal table of contents services, UnCover S.O.S. (Single Order Source) to facilitate the ordering process, and Uncover Desktop Image Delivery which allows end users to download articles directly to their desktop.

Committee on Institutional Cooperation. *CIC Electronic Journals Collection*. Available: http://ejournals.cic.net/ (Accessed March 30, 1998).

The introductory page describes this site as "a prototype electronic journal management system." The project's ultimate goal is to include all electronic serials available for free on the Internet plus those electronic journals licensed only to Committee on Institutional Cooperation (CIC) member libraries (for which access through the CICnet site may be restricted). This collection's journals "will be continually monitored and managed" by CIC university librarians as well as cataloged and added to OCLC Online Computer Library Center (OCLC). The titles can be accessed through a keyword search, subject headings, or an alphabetical list by title. Still in a developmental stage, the CICnet collection contained more than 140 titles in mid-1997. It has not been updated since June 27, 1997.

Copyright Clearance Center. *Copyright Clearance Center Online*. Available: http://www.copyright.com/ (Accessed March 30, 1998).

The Copyright Clearance Center's home page contains information about its history, mission, and services. Since April 1995 registered users can access through this site *CCC Online* to search for titles and royalty fees.

Other features include links to the full text of the Copyright Act of 1976, the CONTU guidelines, and the guidelines for classroom copying (Classroom Guidelines). Copyright Clearance Center corporate information is also given.

EBSCO Information Services. *EBSCO Home Page.* Available: http://www.ebsco.com/ (Accessed April 2, 1998).

> This home page includes typical information about the company's corporate structure as well as products and services (e.g., EBSCONET, EB-SCOhost, and EBSCOdoc). EBSCO serial price projections for the coming year are also available on this site.

Electronic Newsstand. *Welcome to the Electronic Newsstand.* Available: http://www.enews.com/ (Accessed March 30, 1998).

> Founded in 1993, the Electronic Newsstand claims to be "the number-one magazine site on the Web." Nearly 1,000 magazines are covered. The user has the option of directly entering a specific magazine title or searching one of 25 broad subject categories. Basic information about the magazine, advertising, sample table of contents, articles from current issues, and links to the magazine's Web page are available. Subscriptions can be ordered online. As stated by Birdie MacLennan, ". . . the Electronic Newsstand is a useful current awareness tool for individuals and a convenient collection development tool for librarians who are seeking cost and/or contents information for recent issues of current and popular titles."[2]

Emory University Health Sciences Center Library. *MedWeb: Electronic Publications.* Available: http://www.gen.emory.edu/MEDWEB/keyword/electronic_publications.html (Accessed March 30, 1998).

> This page provides access to more than 1,000 medical journals (mostly established print titles) that have some form of presence on the WWW, i.e., full-text, abstracts, table of contents, or a Web page. The titles can be accessed through a single alphabetical sequence, a country index, keywords, or about 300 subject headings.

Ercelawn, Ann. *Tools for Serials Catalogers.* Available: http://www.library.vanderbilt.edu/ercelawn/serials.html (Accessed March 30, 1998).

> Maintained by Ann Ercelawn of Vanderbilt University, this page contains links to sources and sites that support serials cataloging. Noteworthy features include: cataloging documents from CONSER, the Library of Congress, and OCLC; a list of e-mail addresses where cataloging questions or problems can be answered; the text of recently published documents dealing with format integration; links to the archives of such discussion lists as NewJour, SERIALST, and VPIEJ-L; minutes of the ALCTS Committee to study serials cataloging; and links to Cataloging or Technical Services Department WWW pages.

The Faxon Company. *Faxon Home Page.* Available: http://www.faxon.com/ (Accessed March 30, 1998).

> Mounted in February 1995 and reorganized in July 1997, Faxon's Web server offers information about the company's history, corporate structure, services, and staff. There is considerable information about serial

standards and links to standards organizations. Linkages are also provided to approximately 200 publisher home pages. A particularly useful feature provides serials cost data and price projections. Point Communications, a Web evaluation service, has given Faxon's home page a four-star rating and ranked it among the top 5 percent of all WWW sites.

ISSN International Centre. *ISSN and Serial Publications.* Available: http://www.issn.org/ (Accessed March 30, 1998).

An excellent source of basic information about the International Standard Serial Number (ISSN) system may be found on the ISSN International Centre's bilingual (English/French) WWW site. Links provide an explanation of the ISSN and its uses, ISSN network maps, a directory of ISSN International Centres, information on ISSN products, a "genealogical tree" of serials linked by their ISSN, and statistical breakdowns on the number of registered titles.

Johns Hopkins University Press. *Project Muse Home Page.* Available: http://muse.jhu.edu/ muse.html (Accessed April 2, 1998).

This is the home page for the prototype of Project Muse, whereby the Milton S. Eisenhower Library of Johns Hopkins University, the Johns Hopkins University Press, and Homewood Academic Computing are collaborating to make the full-text of all Johns Hopkins University Press journals available electronically. The home page includes a description of journals and subscription and pricing information. A free sample issue is available for each of approximately 40 journals.

Jones, Joseph. *Ejournal Site Guide: A Meta Source.* Available: http://www.library.ubc.ca/ ejour (Accessed March 30, 1998).

Joseph Jones's useful Web page is comparable to a bibliography on bibliographies. It is a collection of links to Web sites that "collect" specific electronic journals, newsletters, newspapers, or zines. Thirty-six sites, both the well-known and the relatively obscure, were included. Thousands of electronic publications can be accessed through these 36 links. The links are initially arranged in a single, unannotated, alphabetical sequence and then grouped by category, e.g., general, academic, etc., with a descriptive annotation for each site. There is also an evaluative narrative guide to all the sites. This would be an excellent tool for identifying electronic serials for collection management purposes. This site's organization was last changed in December, 1995, although most of the sources it links to have been updated.

JSTOR. *Welcome to JSTOR.* Available: http://www.jstor.org/ (Accessed April 2, 1998).

JSTOR (Journal Storage) is a not-for-profit organization devoted to converting scholarly journal print backruns to an electronic form and licensing access to libraries. This site describes JSTOR's history, goals, pricing structure, and library plus publisher licensing terms, while listing available serial backruns. It includes press releases and a small demonstration database.

Kuiper, Todd. *Todd Kuipers' E-Mail-Zines Listing*. Available: http://propogandist.com/ tkemzl/ (Accessed March 30, 1998).

> Maintained by Todd Kuipers, this site lists zines and newsletters that are available through e-mail. Approximately 240 titles, arranged in about a dozen broad subject categories, were listed here in January 1997. Each entry included a brief description, the e-mail subscription address, and other access addresses through the WWW, ftp, or gopher. One could submit an e-mail address to receive updates to this list. Point Communications has rated this among the top 5 percent of Web sites. As of the spring of 1998 this site was "down" in order to be "fully revamped" by the end of April.

Labovitz, John. *John Labovitz's E-Zine List*. Available: http://www.meer.net/~johnl/ e-zine-list/ (Accessed March 30, 1998).

> Founded in 1993, John Labovitz's directory of electronic zines available on the Internet contained 2,103 titles on March 29, 1998. Titles can be located through keyword searching or an alphabetical directory. The entries include such information as: format, for example, hypertext markup language (html) or American Standard Code for Information Interchange (ASCII); frequency; access method, i.e. gophers, File Transfer Protocol (ftp), the WWW, or e-mail; editor's name, address or fax; submission information; and a descriptive annotation. The majority of these titles can be directly accessed through this list, although some are paid subscriptions requiring passwords. Given four stars by the McKinley Group Magellan service for evaluating Web sites, this Web home page could be a useful guide for identifying electronic zines.

Library of Congress. *CONSER Program Home Page*. Available: http://lcweb.loc.gov/acq/ conser/ (Accessed March 30, 1998).

> This site offers much basic information about the Cooperative Online Serials Program (CONSER) project, including its goals, benefits, products, recent annual reports, a list of institutional members, instructions concerning CONSER membership application, and links to the electronic newsletter *CONSERline* and sections of the *CONSER Cataloging Manual*, module 31, pertaining to electronic serials cataloging. There are many external links to Internet resources, library Online Public Access Catalogs (OPACs), and electronic journal collections. Numerous e-mail addresses are given for asking various types of serials cataloging questions.

Library of Congress. *U.S. Copyright Office Home Page*. Available: http://lcweb.loc.gov/ copyright/ (Accessed March 30, 1998).

> The U.S. Copyright Office's page is on the Library of Congress web server because the Office is located in the Library of Congress. A link entitled "Copyright Basics" provides an excellent overview of copyright law. The electronic version of approximately 30 U.S. Copyright Office circulars can be accessed here. Particularly relevant to this book's theme is circular 62 which offers a detailed explanation about registering serials for copyright.

MacLennan, Birdie. *Back Issues & Exchange Services*. Available: http://www.uvm.edu/ ~bmaclenn/backexch.html (Accessed March 30, 1998).

> Organized by Birdie MacLennan, this site lists services on the Internet that offer free exchange of serials and other materials. Included

are ASEE/ELD Duplicates Exchange, BACKSERV, BACKMED, the American Library Association's Association for Library Collections and Technical Services (ALA-ALCTS) Duplicates Exchange Union, EUROBACK, LIS-MEDJOURNAL DUPLICATES, and NEEDSANDOFFERS-L. Links are provided to WWW sites, gophers, and archives (depending on the service), and list subscription addresses are given.

MacLennan, Birdie. *Serials in Cyberspace: Collections, Resources, and Services.* Available: http://www.uvm.edu/~bmaclenn/ (Accessed March 30, 1998).

As indicated by its title, this site provides links to numerous other sites with electronic journal collections, including CICNet, the University of Houston, the World Wide Web Virtual Library, and John Labovitz's E-Zine List. Birdie MacLennan, who maintains this site, has provided print-format annotations for many of these electronic journal collections in the *Directory of Electronic Journals, Newsletters and Academic Discussion Lists*.[3] MacLennan's Web page offers direct access to a select number of electronic journals, e.g., *Citations for Serial Literature* and *Newsletter on Serials Pricing Issues*, and links to other relevant sites.

National Library of Australia. *Australian Journals*. Available: http://www.nla.gov.au/oz/ausejour.html (Accessed March 30, 1998).

Australian electronic journals—defined as those available from electronic mail (e-mail) addresses or WWW sites in Australia or titles published in other countries that have Australian content or authors—are listed here. Each title's entry typically provides the available issues as well as the editor's name, address, and phone and fax numbers, but not direct links to the title itself. Aiming at comprehensiveness, in mid-1997 this site listed more than 1,100 titles (some seemingly obscure from the North American perspective). They can be accessed alphabetically or by subject. A separate listing of Australian journals and magazines that maintain Web pages is provided. This link on the National Library of Australia WWW Home Page is maintained by the Library's Australian Collection Development Unit, although it has not been updated since June 5, 1997.

National Library of Canada. *National Library of Canada Electronic Collection*. Available: http://www.nlc-bnc.ca/e-coll-e/index-e.htm (Accessed March 30, 1998).

This page is an outgrowth of the NLC's Electronic Publications Pilot Project, conducted from June 1994 to July 1995. The Electronic Collection acquires, catalogs, and permanently stores "formally published" Canadian electronic books and serials available on the Internet. The collection contains approximately 50 Canadian electronic journals that can be accessed by title, subject, or keyword. The site was last revised September 21, 1996.

North American Serials Interest Group, Inc. *North American Serials Interest Group*. Available: http://nasig.ils.unc.edu/nasigweb.html (Accessed March 30, 1998).

The premier North American serials group's web page focuses on organizational and membership questions rather than serials issues per se. The site provides information on the North American Serials Interest Group (NASIG) Executive Board, committee structure, bylaws, and conferences as well as announcements for members and an e-mail address for membership information. Serials-related jobs advertised on 10 different listservs are posted here. The full text of NASIG newsletters and conference proceedings and access to NASIG's electronic services and NASIGNET are also available here, but are limited to NASIG members.

Northwestern University Library. *Interactive Electronic Serials Cataloging Aid.* Available: http://www.library.nwu.edu/iesca/ (Accessed March 30, 1998).

Developed and tested by the Northwestern University Library, this page's purpose is to provide interactive training to serials catalogers concerning how to catalog electronic journals available on the Internet. Included are examples of MARC records for an electronic bulletin, electronic digest, electronic journal, and an electronic newsletter; cataloging rules, guidelines, and local interpretations from the *Anglo-American Cataloguing Rules*, 2d edition, 1988 revision (AACR2R), chapters 9, 12, and 25; as well as glossaries of Internet, cataloging, and computing terms. This site was last updated on July 28, 1997.

Okerson, Ann Shumelda, and James J. O'Donnell. *NewJour: Electronic Journals and Newsletters.* Available: http://gort.ucsd.edu/newjour/ (Accessed March 30, 1998).

NewJour, Ann Shumelda Okerson (Yale) and James J. O'Donnell's (University of Pennsylvania) list of new journals and newsletters available on the Internet, is archived here. More than 5,400 titles are archived in alphabetical order, with the 100 most recent titles listed in reverse chronological order. The archive can be searched by keyword or phrase.

SERIALST. Archives of SERIALST@LIST.UVM.EDU. Available: http://list.uvm.edu/archives/serialist.html (Accessed April 5, 1998).

Contributions to *SERIALST*, the major listserv dealing with serials management in libraries, are available here. The archive can be searched by subject, time period, and author. Monthly archives, dating to October 1990, are arranged by title of the contribution, but can be sorted by author or date.

Swets & Zeitlinger, B.V. *Main Entry Page Swets.* Available: http://www.swets.nl/ (Accessed April 2, 1998).

This Web site of a major European serials subscription agent contains the standard information on services and policies. Noteworthy pages are devoted to the SwetScan table of contents service; the Swets Reprint Catalog (searchable by subject or title), which provides availability and price for hundreds of serial reprints; and the annual Serials Price Increase Report, organized by country or region and subject. A password is required to access the DataSwets database of 180,000 journal titles.

United Kingdom Serials Group. *UK Serials Group WWW Page.* Available: http://www.uksg.org/ (Accessed March 30, 1998).

The U.K. Serials Group home page contains information about its membership, organized events, committees, and publications. There are numerous external links to publishers, serial subscription agents, and other serial sites. Other noteworthy features include a detailed list of library, serial, and automation-related abbreviations and acronyms as well as the table of contents for its principal publication, *Serials*, beginning with volume 8, number 1, March 1995.

United States Book Exchange. *USBE: United States Book Exchange.* Available: http://www.usbe.com/ (Accessed March 30, 1998).

Here are policies, procedures, and pricing information of the USBE—the well-known source for periodical back issues now relocated in Cleveland, Ohio from Washington, D.C. One can access a 1600-page "shelflist" of available periodicals. There is also a page for submitting orders and a list of "most wanted" titles.

United States ISSN Center. *US ISSN Center Home Page.* Available: http://lcweb.loc.gov/issn/ (Accessed March 30, 1998).

This is the WWW page for the National Serials Data Program (NSDP), housed in the Library of Congress, which assigns ISSNs for U.S. serials. The site contains an electronic version of a print brochure explaining ISSN as well as general information about ISSN for electronic serials. There are forms here for U.S. publishers to submit electronic ISSN applications for on-line and networked electronic serials and mail ISSN applications for serials in other formats. Links to additional sites include the ISSN International Centre and the American ISSN Friends.

University of Houston Libraries. *Scholarly Journals Distributed Via the World Wide Web.* Available: http://info.lib.uh.edu/wj/webjour.html (Accessed March 30, 1998).

This site provides access to approximately 125 "established Web-based scholarly journals that offer access to English language article files without requiring user registration or fees."

University of Southern California Law School and Law Library. *Legal Journals on the Web.* Available: http://www.usc.edu/dept/law–lib/legal/journals.html (Accessed March 30, 1998).

University of Tennessee Library patrons comprise this site's in-tended audience. Yet this WWW page serves as an outstanding model of how the WWW can be used for the collection management of journals. Separate pages explain the Library's interlibrary loan (ILL), document delivery, journal review, and new subscription policies. A link to the University of Tennessee Library's home page provides access to electronic journals and electronic journal collections at other sites. Journals Online News contains a wealth of serials information of both local and national significance, including an expla-nation of the serials crisis, a glossary of library terms, the names of library selectors, and numerous links to pertinent publications such as the *Mellon Report on University Libraries and Scholarly Communications.*

University of Tennessee, Knoxville. *Journals Online News.* Available: http://toltec.lib.utk.edu/~jon/ (Accessed March 30, 1998).

University of Tennessee Library patrons comprise this site's in-tended audience. Yet this WWW page serves as an outstanding model of how the WWW can be used for the collection management of journals. Sepa-rate pages explain the Library's interlibrary loan (ILL), document delivery, journal review, and new subscription policies. A link to the University of

Tennessee Library's home page provides access to electronic journals and electronic journal collections at other sites. *Journals Online News* contains a wealth of serials information of both local and national significance, including an explanation of the serials crisis, a glossary of library terms, the names of library selectors, and numerous links to pertinent publications such as the *Mellon Report on University Libraries and Scholarly Communications.*

University of Waterloo Electronic Library Scholarly Societies Project. *Full-Text Archives of Publications of Scholarly Societies.* Available: http://www.lib.uwaterloo.ca/society/ full-text_soc.html (Accessed March 30, 1998).

The Scholarly Societies Project provides links to full-text archives of electronic serial publications from scholarly societies in the sciences, social sciences, and humanities. As indicated in this Web page's introduction, most of the archived publications are newsletter-like items, while only a small portion are research publications. In early 1998 more than 160 electronic publications from approximately 145 societies (mostly located in North America with a scattering from Europe and Asia) were archived here.

World Wide Web Virtual Library: Electronic Journals. Available: http://www.edoc.com/ ejournal/ (Accessed April 2, 1998).

The WWW Virtual Library, CERN's collection of Internet resources in all branches of knowledge, has been selected by Point Communications as one of the top 5 percent of all Web sites. The electronic journals page provides access to seven categories of electronic journals (e.g., academic and reviewed journals, political, business/finance, etc.) and Web pages of print magazines. This site provides links to publishers on the WWW and other resources.

Yale University Library. *LIBLICENSE: Licensing Digital Information.* Available: http://www.library.yale.edu/~llicense/index.shtml (Accessed April 2, 1998).

The Yale University Library, supported by the Commission on Preservation and Access plus the Council on Library Resources, created this Web page to provide university and research libraries information on licensing digital information, which includes electronic journals. The site includes definitions of licensing terms, texts of actual license agreements, links to licensing resources, and a bibliography.

NOTES

1. Jeanne M. K. Boydston, "Serial Sources on the Web," *Serials Librarian* 29, nos. 3/4 (1996): 175-87.

2. Birdie MacLennan, "Serials in Cyberspace: Collections, Resources, and Services on the Networks: An Overview as of March 1995," in *Directory of Electronic Journals, Newsletters and Academic Discussion Lists*, 5th ed., comp. Lisabeth A. King and Diane Kovacs, ed. Ann Okerson (Washington, D.C.: ARL Office of Scientific and Academic Publishing, 1995), 35-36.

3. Ibid., 11-40.

General Bibliography

Alexander, Adrian W. "Periodical Prices, 1992-1994." *Library Acquisitions: Practice and Theory* 19 (spring 1995): 63-82.

Alexander, Adrian W., and Brenda Dingley. "U.S. Periodical Prices—1998." *American Libraries* 29 (May 1998): 82-90.

Alldredge, Noreen S. "The Non-Use of Periodicals: A Study." *Serials Librarian* 7 (summer 1983): 61-64.

Allen, Walter C., ed. *Serial Publications in Large Libraries*. Urbana, Ill.: University of Illinois, Graduate School of Library Science, 1970.

Alligood, Elaine C., Elaine Russo-Martin, and Richard A. Peterson. "Use Study of *Excerpta Medica* Abstract Journals: To Drop or Not to Drop." *Bulletin of the Medical Library Association* 71 (July 1983): 251-59.

Altmann, Klaus G., and G. E. Gorman. "Usage, Citation Analysis and Costs as Indicators for Journal Deselection and Cancellation: A Selective Literature Review." *Australian Library Review* 13 (November 1996): 379-92.

Altuna Esteibar, Belen, and F. W. Lancaster. "Ranking of Journals in Library and Information Science by Research and Teaching Relatedness." *Serials Librarian* 23, nos. 1/2 (1992): 1-10.

American Library Association. "Directory of Union Lists of Serials, Second Edition." *Serials Review* 14, nos. 1/2 (1988): 115-59.

Amiran, Eyal, and John Unsworth. "*Postmodern Culture*: Publishing in the Electronic Medium." *Public-Access Computer Systems Review* 2, no. 1 (1991): 55-62. Available: http://info.lib.uh.edu/pr/v2/n1/amiran.2n1 (Accessed February 15, 1998).

Amiran, Eyal, Elaine Orr, and John Unsworth. "Refereed Electronic Journals and the Future of Scholarly Publishing." *Advances in Library Automation and Networking* 4 (1991): 25-53.

Anderson, Bill. "History of the CONSER Program (1986-1994)." *Serials Review* 21 (summer 1995): 1-16.

Anderson, Bill, and Les Hawkins. "Development of CONSER Cataloging Policies for Remote Access Computer Files." *Public-Access Computer Systems Review* 7, no. 1 (1996): 6-25. Available http://info.lib.uh.edu/pr/v7/n1/anderson.7n1 (Accessed March 1, 1998).

Archibald, Robert B., and David H. Finifter. "Biases in Citation-Based Ranking of Journals." *Scholarly Publishing* 18 (January 1987): 131-38.

Arms, William Y. "Scholarly Publishing on the National Networks." *Scholarly Publishing* 23 (April 1992): 158-69.

Arrigona, Daniel R., and Eleanor Mathews. "A Use Study of an Academic Library Reference Collection." *RQ* 28 (fall 1988): 71-81.

Ash, Joan, and James E. Morgan. "Journal Evaluation Study at the University of Connecticut Health Center." *Bulletin of the Medical Library Association* 65 (April 1977): 297-99.

Association for Library Collections and Technical Services. *Guide to Performance Evaluation of Serials Vendors.* Chicago: American Library Association, 1997.

———. *Guidelines for Handling Library Orders for Serials and Periodicals.* Rev. ed. Chicago: American Library Association, 1992.

———. *Serials Acquisitions Glossary.* Chicago: Association for Library Collections and Technical Services, 1993.

Association of Research Libraries. Office of Management Studies. *Serials Control and Deselection Projects.* SPEC Kit 147. Washington, D.C.: Association of Research Libraries, Office of Management Studies, 1988.

Auld, Larry. "Reader Interaction with the Online Journal." *Serials Review* 12 (summer and fall 1986): 83-85.

Bachmann-Derthick, Jan, and Sandra Spurlock. "Journal Availability at the University of New Mexico." In *Advances in Serials Management: A Research Annual.* Vol. 3, edited by Jean G. Cook and Marcia Tuttle, 173-212. Greenwich, Conn.: JAI Press, 1989.

Bader, Shelley A., and Laurie L. Thompson. "Analyzing In-House Journal Utilization: An Added Dimension in Decision Making." *Bulletin of the Medical Library Association* 77 (April 1989): 216-18.

Bailey, Charles W., Jr. "Electronic (Online) Publishing in Action . . . *The Public-Access Computer Systems Review* and Other Electronic Serials." *Online* 15 (January 1991): 28-35.

———. "Network-Based Electronic Serials." *Information Technology and Libraries* 11 (March 1992): 29-35.

———. "Scholarly Electronic Publishing on the Internet, the NREN, and the NII: Charting Possible Futures." *Serials Review* 20 (fall 1994): 7-16.

Bailey, Dorothy C. "Coping with a Binding Crisis." *Serials Review* 13 (winter 1987): 59-62.

Bailey, Martha J. "Selecting Titles for Binding." *Special Libraries* 64 (December 1973): 571-73.

Banach, Patricia. "Migration from an In-House Serials System to Innopac at the University of Massachusetts at Amherst." *Library Software Review* 12 (spring 1993): 35-37.

Barber, Raymond W., and Jacqueline C. Mancall. "The Application of Bibliometric Techniques to the Analysis of Materials for Young Adults." *Collection Management* 2 (fall 1978): 229-45.

Bardeleben, Marian Z., Martha M. Wilson, and Murray D. Rosenberg. "Off-Site Journal Check-In: An Alternative to Internal Control of Serials." *Serials Review* 9 (winter 1983): 56-62.

Barker, Joseph W. "A Case for Exchange: The Experience of the University of California, Berkeley." *Serials Review* 12 (spring 1986): 63-73.

———. "Unbundling Serials Vendors' Service Charges: Are We Ready?" *Serials Review* 16 (summer 1990): 33-43.

Barr, K. P. "Estimates of the Number of Currently Available Scientific and Technical Periodicals." *Journal of Documentation* 23 (June 1967): 110-16.

Barschall, Henry H. "The Cost-Effectiveness of Physics Journals: A Survey." *Physics Today* 41 (July 1988): 56-59.

———. "Electronic Version of Printed Journals." *Serials Review* 18, nos. 1/2 (1992): 49-51.

Barschall, Henry H., and J. R. Arrington. "Cost of Physics Journals: A Survey." *Bulletin of the American Physical Society* 33 (July-August 1988): 1437-47.

Bartley, Linda K., and Regina R. Reynolds. "CONSER: Revolution and Evolution." *Cataloging and Classification Quarterly* 8, nos. 3/4 (1988): 47-66.

Basch, N. Bernard, and Judy McQueen. *Buying Serials: A How-to-Do-It Manual for Librarians*. New York: Neal-Schuman, 1990.

Bastille, Jacqueline D., and Carole J. Mankin. "A Simple Objective Method for Determining a Dynamic Journal Collection." *Bulletin of the Medical Library Association* 68 (October 1980): 357-66.

Beardman, Sue. "The Cost-Effectiveness of Access versus Ownership: A Report on the Virtual Library Project at the University of Western Australia Library." *Australian Library Review* 13 (May 1996): 173-81.

Beed, Clive, and Cara Beed. "Measuring the Quality of Academic Journals: The Case of Economics." *Journal of Post Keynesian Economics* 18 (spring 1996): 369-96.

Benedict, Marjorie A., Michael Knee, and Mina B. LaCroix. "Finding Space for Periodicals: Weeding, Storage and Microform Conversion." *Collection Management* 12, nos. 3/4 (1990): 145-54.

Bensman, Stephen J. "The Structure of the Library Market for Scientific Journals: the Case of Chemistry." *Library Resources and Technical Services* 40 (April 1996): 145-51+.

Bertuca, David J., and Cynthia A. Bertuca. "Is There a Disk Magazine in Your Future?" *Serials Review* 12 (summer and fall 1986): 41-45.

Besson, Alain and Ian Sheriff. "Journal Collection Evaluation at the Medical College of St. Bartholomew's Hospital." *British Journal of Academic Librarianship* 1 (summer 1986): 132-43.

Bick, Dawn, and Reeta Sinha. "Maintaining a High-Quality, Cost-Effective Journal Collection." *College and Research Libraries News* 52 (September 1991): 485-90.

Black, George W., Jr. "Core Journal Lists for Behaviorally Disordered Children." *Behavioral and Social Sciences Librarian* 3 (fall 1983): 31-38

Bloss, Alex. "ASK: a Database for the Analysis of Local Serials Costs." *Serials Review* 22 (spring 1996): 21-32.

Bluh, Pamela, and Virginia C. Haines. "The Exchange of Materials: An Alternative to Acquisitions." *Serials Review* 5 (April/June 1979): 103-8.

Bonk, Sharon C. "Toward a Methodology of Evaluating Serials Vendors." *Library Acquisitions: Practice and Theory* 9, no. 1 (1985): 51-60.

Borden, Joseph C. "The Advantages and Disadvantages of a Classified Periodicals Collection." *Library Resources and Technical Services* 9 (winter 1965): 122-26.

Boss, Richard W. "Technical Services Functionality in Integrated Library Systems." *Library Technology Reports* 28 (January/February 1992): 5-109.

Boss, Richard W., and Judy McQueen. "The Uses of Automation and Related Technologies by Domestic Book and Serials Jobbers." *Library Technology Reports* 25 (March/April 1989): 125-251.

Bostic, Mary J. "Serials Deselection." *Serials Librarian* 9 (spring 1985): 85-101.

Bourne, Ross, ed. *Serials Librarianship*. London: The Library Association, 1980.

Bowman, Michael. "Format Citation Patterns and Their Implications for Collection Development in Research Libraries." *Collection Building* 11, no. 1 (1991): 2-8.

Boyce, Bert R., and Janet Sue Pollens. "Citation-Based Impact Measures and the Bradfordian Selection Criteria." *Collection Management* 4 (fall 1982): 29-36.

Boyce, Bert R., and Mark Funk. "Bradford's Law and the Selection of High Quality Papers." *Library Resources and Technical Services* 22 (fall 1978): 390-401.

Bradford, S. C. *Documentation*. London: Crosby Lockwood, 1948.

————. "Sources of Information on Specific Subjects." *Engineering: An Illustrated Weekly* 137 (January 26, 1934): 85-86. Reprinted in *Journal of Information Science* 10, no. 4 (1985): 176-80.

Braga, Gilda Maria, and Cecilia Alves Oberhofer."A Model for Evaluating Scientific and Technical Journals from Developing Countries." In *The Information Community: An Alliance for Progress; Proceedings of the 44th ASIS Annual Meeting, Washington, D.C., October 25-30, 1981*. Vol. 18, edited by Lois F. Lunin, Madeline Henderson, and Harold Wooster, 51-54. White Plains, N.Y.: published for the American Society for Information Science by Knowledge Industry Publications, 1981.

Brahmi, Frances A., and Kellie Kaneshiro. "The *Online Journal of Current Clinical Trials (OJCCT)*: A Closer Look." *Medical Reference Services Quarterly* 12 (fall 1993): 29-43.

Brandon, Alfred N., and Dorothy R. Hill. "Selected List of Books and Journals for the Small Medical Library." *Bulletin of the Medical Library Association* 85 (April 1997): 111-35.

Brandt, D. Scott. "Campus-Wide Computing." *Academic and Library Computing* 9 (November-December 1992): 17-20.

Bremer, Thomas A. "Assessing Collection Use by Surveying Users at Randomly Selected Times." *Collection Management* 13, no. 3 (1990): 57-67.

Broadus, Robert N. "The Measurement of Periodicals Use." *Serials Review* 11 (summer 1985): 57-61.

————. "A Proposed Method for Eliminating Titles from Periodical Subscription Lists." *College and Research Libraries* 46 (January 1985): 30-35.

————. "Use of Periodicals by Humanities Scholars." *Serials Librarian* 16, nos. 1/2 (1989): 123-31.

————. "The Use of Serial Titles in Libraries with Special Reference to the Pittsburgh Study." *Collection Management* 5 (spring/summer 1983): 27-41.

Brothers, Rebecca L. "Automating Serials Binding: Guidelines for Customizing the Binding Procedure in INNOPAC." *Technical Services Quarterly* 11, no. 4 (1994): 45-59.

Broude, Jeffrey. "Journal Deselection in an Academic Environment: A Comparison of Faculty and Librarian Choices." *Serials Librarian* 3 (winter 1978): 147-66.

Brown, Clara D., and Lynn S. Smith. *Serials: Past, Present and Future*. 2d rev. ed. Birmingham, Ala.: EBSCO, 1980.

Buckeye, Nancy. "The Library Serials Committee: How to Balance Decreasing Budgets with Collection Development Needs." *Serials Review* 1 (July-September 1975): 5-7.

Buhsmer, John H., and Andrew Elston. "NewsNet." *Serials Review* 13 (fall 1987): 13-18.

Burdick, Amrita J., Anne Butler, and Marilyn G. Sullivan. "Citation Patterns in the Health Sciences: Implications for Serials/Monographic Fund Allocation." *Bulletin of the Medical Library Association* 81 (January 1993): 44-47.

Bustion, Marifran, and Anne L. Highsmith. "Incorporating Binding Operations into an Integrated Library System." *Serials Librarian* 20, no. 4 (1991): 25-33.

Bustion, Marifran, and Elizabeth Parang. "The Cost Effectiveness of Claiming." *Serials Librarian* 23, nos. 3/4 (1993): 297-99.

Bustion, Marifran, and Jane Treadwell. "Reported Relative Value of Journals Versus Use: A Comparison." *College and Research Libraries* 51 (March 1990): 142-51.

Bustion, Marifran, and others. "Methods of Serials Funding: Formula or Tradition?" *Serials Librarian* 20, no. 1 (1991): 75-89.

Bustion, Marifran, John Eltinge, and John Harer. "On the Merits of Direct Observation of Periodical Usage: An Empirical Study." *College and Research Libraries* 53 (November 1992): 537-50.

Butkovich, Nancy J. "Reshelving Study of Review Literature in the Physical Sciences." *Library Resources and Technical Services* 40 (April 1996): 139-44.

Butler, Brett. "Electronic Editions of Serials: The Virtual Library Model." *Serials Review* 18, nos. 1/2 (1992): 102-6.

———. "Scholarly Journals, Electronic Publishing, and Library Networks: From 1986 to 2000." *Serials Review* 12 (summer and fall 1986): 47-52.

Butler, H. Julene, editor. "Abstracts of Papers Presented at the International Conference on Refereed Journals, October 1993." *Serials Review* 20 (winter 1994): 21-30.

Butter, Karen A. "Red Sage: The Next Step in Delivery of Electronic Journals." *Medical Reference Services Quarterly* 13 (fall 1994): 75-81.

Byrd, Gary D., and Michael E. D. Koenig. "Systematic Serials Selection Analysis in a Small Academic Health Sciences Library." *Bulletin of the Medical Library Association* 66 (October 1978): 397-406.

Campbell, Harry H., and Wesley L. Boomgaarden. "The Ohio State University Libraries' Utilization of General Bookbinding Company's Automated Binding Records System." *Serials Review* 12 (winter 1986): 89-99.

Caplan, Priscilla. "Controlling E-Journals: The Internet Resources Project, Cataloging Guidelines, and USMARC." *Serials Librarian* 24, nos. 3/4 (1994): 103-11.

Carlson, Barbara A. "Claiming Periodicals: The 'Trembling Balance' in the 'Feud of Want and Have.'" In *Legal and Ethical Issues in Acquisitions*, edited by Katina Strauch and Bruce Strauch, 119-27. New York: Haworth Press, 1990.

Carrigan, Dennis P. "From Just-in-Case to Just-in-Time: Limits to the Alternative Library Service Model." *Journal of Scholarly Publishing* 26 (April 1995): 173-82.

Carrington, Bradley, Mary M. Case, and Sharon Scott. "Latest Entry Cataloging as an Option." *Serials Librarian* 17, nos. 3/4 (1990): 155-57.

Carson, Doris M. "What Is a Serial Publication?" *Journal of Academic Librarianship* 3 (September 1977): 206-9.

Chaffin, Nancy J. "U.S. Serial Services Price Index for 1998." *American Libraries* 29 (May 1998): 91-92.

Chen, Chiou-sen Dora. *Serials Management: A Practical Guide*. Chicago: American Library Association, 1995.

Chiang, Belinda. "Migration from Microlinx to NOTIS: Expediting Serials Holdings Conversion Through Programmed Function Keys." *Serials Librarian* 25, nos. 1/2 (1994): 115-31.

Chiang, Win-Shin S., and Nancy E. Elkington, eds. *Electronic Access to Information; A New Service Paradigm: Proceedings from a Symposium held July 23 through July 24, 1993, Palo Alto, California*. Mountain View, Calif.: Research Libraries Group, 1994.

Christensen, John O. "Cost of Chemistry Journals to One Academic Library, 1980-1990." *Serials Review* 18 (fall 1992): 19-34.

Christenson, James A., and Lee Sigelman. "Accrediting Knowledge: Journal Stature and Citation Impact in Social Science." *Social Science Quarterly* 66 (December 1985): 964-75.

Chrzastowski, Tina E. "Journal Collection Cost-Effectiveness in an Academic Chemistry Library: Results of a Cost/Use Survey at the University of Illinois at Urbana-Champaign." *Collection Management* 14, nos. 1/2 (1991): 85-98.

———. "Where Does the Money Go? Measuring Cost Effectiveness Using a Microcomputer to Analyze Journal-Use Data." In *Building on the First Century; Proceedings of the Fifth National Conference of the Association of College and Research Libraries, Cincinnati, Ohio, April 5-8, 1989*, edited by Janice C. Fennell, 201-4. Chicago: Association of College and Research Libraries, 1989.

Chrzastowski, Tina E., and David Stern. "Duplicate Serial Subscriptions: Can Use Justify the Cost of Duplication?" *Serials Librarian* 25, nos. 1/2 (1994): 187-200.

Chrzastowski, Tina E., and Karen A. Schmidt. "Collections at Risk: Revisiting Serial Cancellations in Academic Libraries." *College and Research Libraries* 57 (July 1996): 351-64.

Chrzastowski, Tina E., and Mary A. Anthes. "Seeking the 99% Chemistry Library: Extending the Serial Collection Through the Use of Decentralized Document Delivery." *Library Acquisitions: Practice and Theory* 19 (summer 1995): 141-52.

Chrzastowski, Tina E., Paul M. Blobaum, and Margaret A. Welshmer. "A Cost/Use Analysis of Beilstein's *Handbuch der Organischen Chemie* at Two Academic Chemistry Libraries." *Serials Librarian* 20, no. 4 (1991): 73-83.

Chudamani, K. S., and R. Shalini. "Journal Acquisition—Cost Effectiveness of Models." *Information Processing and Management* 19, no. 5 (1983): 307-11.

Chung, Yeon-Kyoung. "Core International Journals of Classification Systems: An Application of Bradford's Law." *Knowledge Organization* 21, no. 2 (1994): 75-83.

Clack, Mary Elizabeth, and John F. Riddick, with contributions from Richard R. Rowe, Duane Arenales, and Sheila S. Intner. "The Future of Serials Librarianship: Part 2." *Serials Review* 16 (fall 1990): 61-80.

Clack, Mary Elizabeth and John Riddick, editors, with contributions from F. Dixon Brooke, Jr., Czeslaw Jan Grycz, Karen Hunter, and Herbert White. "The Future of Serials Librarianship." *Serials Review* 16 (summer 1990): 55-64.

Clack, Mary Elizabeth, and Sally F. Williams. "Using Locally and Nationally Produced Periodical Price Indexes in Budget Preparation." *Library Resources and Technical Services* 27 (October/December 1983): 345-56.

Clapper, Mary Ellen. "Standards for Serials." *Serials Review* 12 (summer and fall 1986): 119-31.

Clark, Barton M., and Sharon E. Clark. "Core Journals in Anthropology: A Review of Methodologies." *Behavioral and Social Sciences Librarian* 2 (winter 1981/spring 1982): 95-110.

Clarke, Ann. "The Use of Serials at the British Library Lending Division in 1980." *Interlending Review* 9 (October 1981): 111-17.

Clement, Elaine. "A Pilot Project to Investigate Commercial Document Suppliers." *Library Acquisitions: Practice and Theory* 20 (summer 1996): 137-46.

Cnaan, Ram A., Richard K. Caputo, and Yochi Shmuely. "Senior Faculty Perceptions of Social Work Journals." *Journal of Social Work Education* 30 (spring/summer 1994): 185-99.

Cochenour, Donnice. "CICNet's Electronic Journal Collection." *Serials Review* 22 (spring 1996): 63-68.

——. "Project Muse: A Partnership of Interest." *Serials Review* 21 (fall 1995): 75-81.

Cochenour, Donnice, and Tom Moothart. "Relying on the Kindness of Strangers: Archiving Electronic Journals on Gopher." *Serials Review* 21 (spring 1995): 67-76.

Cole, Jim. E. "ISDS: The Unfinished Revolution." In *Advances in Serials Management: A Research Annual.* Vol. 4, edited by Marcia Tuttle and Jean G. Cook, 65-89. Greenwich, Conn.: JAI Press, 1992.

Cole, Jim E., and James W. Williams, eds. *Serials Cataloging: Modern Perspectives and International Developments.* New York: Haworth Press, 1992. Also issued as *Serials Librarian,* 22, nos. 1/2 and 3/4 (1992).

———. *Serials Management in the Electronic Era: Papers in Honor of Peter Gellatly, Founding Editor of The Serials Librarian.* New York: Haworth Press, 1996. Also issued as *Serials Librarian,* 29, nos. 3/4 (1996).

Collins, Tim, and Beth Howell. "Journal Accessibility Factor: An Examination of Serials Value from the Standpoint of Access and Delivery." *Collection Management* 21, no. 1 (1996): 29-40.

Collver, Mitsuko. "Organization of Serials Work for Manual and Automated Systems." *Library Resources and Technical Services* 24 (fall 1980): 307-16.

Colson, Harold. "Citation Rankings of Public Administration Journals." *Administration and Society* 21 (February 1990): 452-71.

Compaine, Benjamin M. *The Business of Consumer Magazines.* White Plains, N.Y.: Knowledge Industry Publications, 1982.

Cook, Brian. ed. *The Electronic Journal: The Future of Serials-Based Information.* New York: Haworth Press, 1992. Also issued as *Australian and New Zealand Journal of Serials Librarianship* 3, no. 2 (1992).

Coons, Bill, and Peter McDonald. "Implications of Commercial Document Delivery." *College and Research Libraries News* 56 (October 1995): 626-31.

Cooper, Michael D., and George F. McGregor. "Using Article Photocopy Data in Bibliographic Models for Journal Collection Management." *Library Quarterly* 64 (October 1994): 386-413.

Craighead, Laura M., and William C. Dougherty. "The Systems Approach to Electronic Journals." *Serials Review* 17 (winter 1991): 78-80.

Crawford, Walt. "Serials." In *MARC for Library Use: Understanding Integrated U.S. MARC,* 67-76. 2d ed. Boston: G. K. Hall, 1989.

Cronin, Blaise, and Kara Overfelt. "E-Journals and Tenure." *Journal of the American Society for Information Science* 46 (October 1995): 700-703.

Crump, Michele J., and LeiLani Freund. "Serials Cancellation and Interlibrary Loan: The Link and What it Reveals." *Serials Review* 21 (summer 1995): 29-36.

Davinson, Donald E. *The Periodicals Collection*. Rev. and enl. ed. Boulder, Colo.: Westview Press, 1978.

————. *The Periodicals Collection: Its Purpose and Uses in Libraries*. London: Andre Deutsch, 1969.

Davis, Allan. "Database Usage and Title Analysis on a CD-ROM Workstation." *Serials Review* 19 (fall 1993): 85-93.

Davis, Carol C. "OCLC's Role in the CONSER Project." *Serials Review* 6 (October/December 1980): 75-77.

Davis, Trisha, and James Huesmann. *Serials Control Systems for Libraries*. Westport, Conn.: Mecklermedia, 1994.

De Klerk, Ann, and Roger Flynn. "A Comparative Periodical Use Study." In *The Information Community: An Alliance for Progress; Proceedings of the 44th ASIS Annual Meeting, Washington, D.C., October 25-30, 1981*. Vol. 18, edited by Lois F. Lunin, Madeline Henderson, and Harold Wooster, 15-18. White Plains, N.Y.: published for the American Society for Information Science by Knowledge Industry Publications, 1981.

Derthick, Jan, and Barbara B. Moran. "Serial Agent Selection in ARL Libraries." In *Advances in Serials Management: A Research Annual*. Vol. 1, edited by Marcia Tuttle and Jean G. Cook, 1-42. Greenwich, Conn.: JAI Press, 1986.

Deurenberg, Rikie. "Journal Deselection in a Medical University Library by Ranking Periodicals Based on Multiple Factors." *Bulletin of the Medical Library Association* 81 (July 1993): 316-19.

Devin, Robin B. "Who's Using What?" *Library Acquisitions: Practice and Theory* 13, no. 2 (1989): 167-70.

Devin, Robin B., and Martha Kellogg. "The Serial/Monograph Ratio in Research Libraries: Budgeting in Light of Citation Studies." *College and Research Libraries* 51 (January 1990): 46-54.

Dhawan, S. M., S. K. Phull, and S. P. Jain. "Selection of Scientific Journals: A Model." *Journal of Documentation* 36 (March 1980): 24-32.

Diodato, Virgil P. "Original Language, Non-English Journals: Weeding Them and Holding Them." *Science and Technology Libraries* 6 (spring 1986): 55-67.

Dodge, Chris. "Pushing the Boundaries: Zines and Libraries." *Wilson Library Bulletin* 69 (May 1995): 26-30.

Dole, Wanda V., and Sherry S. Chang. "Survey and Analysis of Demand for Journals at the State University of New York at Stony Brook." *Library Acquisitions: Practice and Theory* 20 (spring 1996): 23-34.

Dombrowski, Theresa. "Journal Evaluation Using *Journal Citation Reports* as a Collection Development Tool." *Collection Management* 10, nos. 3/4 (1988): 175-80.

Dometrius, Nelson C. "Subjective and Objective Measures of Journal Stature." *Social Science Quarterly* 70 (March 1989): 197-203.

Domier, Sharon H. "Listservs Within the Pantheon of Written Materials." In *Advances in Serials Management: A Research Annual.* Vol. 5, edited by Marcia Tuttle and Karen D. Darling, 125-38. Greenwich, Conn.: JAI Press, 1995.

Drummond, Louis. "Going Beyond Online." *Online* 14 (September 1990): 6-8.

Duranceau, Ellen, and others. "Electronic Journals in the MIT Libraries: Report of the 1995 E-Journal Subgroup." *Serials Review* 22 (spring 1996): 47-61.

Duranceau, Ellen Finnie, column editor. "Cataloging Remote-Access Electronic Serials: Rethinking the Role of the OPAC." *Serials Review* 21 (winter 1995): 67-77.

Dworaczek, Marian, and Victor G. Wiebe. "E-Journals: Acquisition and Access." *Acquisitions Librarian* no. 12 (1994): 105-21.

Dyal, Donald H. "A Survey of Serials Management in Texas." *Texas Libraries* 38 (winter 1976): 164-72.

Dykhuis, Randy. "The Promise of Electronic Publishing: OCLC's Program." *Computers in Libraries* 14 (November/December 1994): 20-22.

Dym, Eleanor D., and Donald L. Shirey. "A Statistical Decision Model for Periodical Selection for a Specialized Information Center." *Journal of the American Society for Information Science* 24 (March-April 1973): 110-19.

Eckman, Charles. "Journal Review in an Environmental Design Library." *Collection Management* 10, nos. 1/2 (1988): 69-84.

Eisenberg, Daniel. "The Electronic Journal." *Scholarly Publishing* 20 (October 1988): 49-58.

Entlich, Richard. "Electronic Chemistry Journals: Elemental Concerns." *Serials Librarian* 25, nos. 3/4 (1995): 111-23.

Entlich, Richard, and others. "Testing a Digital Library: User Response to the CORE Project." *Library Hi Tech* 14, no. 4 (1996): 99-118.

Evans, G. Edward. "Serials." In *Developing Library and Information Center Collections*, 186-209. 3d ed. Englewood, Colo.: Libraries Unlimited, 1995.

Evans, Josephine King. "Tracking Periodical Usage in a Research Library." *College and Research Libraries News* 51 (November 1990): 958-59.

Evans, Katherine G. "MARC Format Integration and Seriality: Implications for Serials Cataloging." *Serials Librarian* 18, nos. 1/2 (1990): 37-45.

Evans, Merran. "Library Acquisitions Formulae: The Monash Experience." *Australian Academic and Research Libraries* 27 (March 1996): 47-57.

Fackler, Naomi P. "Journals for Academic Veterinary Medical Libraries: Price Increases, 1983-1996." *Serials Librarian* 31, no. 4 (1997): 41-52.

Farrington, Jean Walter. "Selecting a Serials System: The Technical Services Perspective." *Library Resources and Technical Services* 32 (October 1988): 402-6.

————. *Serials Management in Academic Libraries: A Guide to Issues and Practices.* Westport, Conn.: Greenwood Press, 1997.

————. "The Serials Visible File: Observations on Its Impending Demise." *Serials Review* (winter 1986): 33-36.

Fecko, Mary Beth. "Electronic Serials." In *Cataloging Nonbook Resources: A How-to-Do-It-Manual for Librarians*, 147-60. New York: Neal-Schuman, 1993.

Feick, Tina, and others. "Check-In with the SISAC Symbol (Bar Code): Implementation and Uses for Libraries, Publishers and Automation Vendors." *Serials Librarian* 23, nos. 3/4 (1993): 249-51.

Feller, Siegfried. "Developing the Serials Collection." In *Collection Development in Libraries: A Treatise.* Pt. B, edited by Robert D. Stueart and George B. Miller, Jr., 497-523. Greenwich, Conn.: JAI Press, 1980.

Ferguson, Anthony W., and Kathleen Kehoe. "Access vs. Ownership: What is Most Cost Effective in the Sciences." *Journal of Library Administration* 19, no. 2 (1993): 89-99.

Fjällbrant, N. "Rationalization of Periodical Holdings: A Case Study at Chalmers University Library." *Journal of Academic Librarianship* 10 (May 1984): 77-86.

Flynn, Roger R. "The University of Pittsburgh Study of Journal Usage: A Summary Report." *Serials Librarian* 4 (fall 1979): 25-33.

Forsman, Rick B. "EBSCONET Serials Control System: A Case History and Analysis." *Serials Review* 8 (winter 1982): 83-85.

Fortney, Lynn M., and Victor A. Basile. "*Index Medicus* Price Study: Publishing Trends from 1992-1996." *Serials Review* 22 (fall 1996): 99-126.

Francq, Carole. "Bottoming Out the Bottomless Pit with the Journal Usage/Cost Relational Index." *Technical Services Quarterly* 11, no. 4 (1994): 13-26.

Franklin, Hugh. "Comparing Quarterly Use Study Results for Marginal Serials at Oregon State University." *Serials Librarian* 16, nos. 1/2 (1989): 109-22.

Frohmann, Bernd. "A Bibliometric Analysis of the Literature of Cataloguing and Classification." *Library Research* 4 (winter 1982): 355-71.

Fry, Bernard M., and Herbert S. White. *Publishers and Libraries: A Study of Scholarly and Research Journals*. Lexington, Mass.: Lexington Books, 1976.

Gable, J. Harris. *Manual of Serials Work*. Chicago: American Library Association, 1937.

———. "The New Serials Department." *Library Journal* 60 (November 15, 1935): 869-87.

Gammon, Julia A., and Phyllis O'Connor. "An Analysis of the Results of Two Periodical Use Studies: How Usage in the 1990s Compares to Usage in the 1970s." *Serials Review* 22 (winter 1996): 35-53.

Gardner, William. "The Electronic Archive: Scientific Publishing for the 1990s." *Psychological Science* 1 (November 1990): 333-41.

Gellatly, Peter, ed. *The Good Serials Department*. New York, Haworth Press, 1990. Also issued as *Serials Librarian*, 19, nos. 1/2 (1990).

Geller, Marilyn. "A Better Mousetrap Is Still a Mousetrap." *Serials Review* 22 (spring 1996): 72-73.

Giles, Michael W., and Gerald C. Wright Jr. "Political Scientists' Evaluations of Sixty-Three Journals." *PS: Political Science and Politics* 8 (summer 1975): 254-56.

Giles, Michael W., Francie Mizell, and David Patterson. "Political Scientists' Journal Evaluations Revisited." *PS: Political Science and Politics* 22 (September 1989): 613-17.

Ginneken, J. van. *770 Articles and Books on Serials*. Wageningen, Netherlands: Library Agricultural University, 1991.

Glenn, Norval D. "American Sociologists' Evaluations of Sixty-Three Journals." *American Sociologist* 6 (November 1971): 298-303.

Goehlert, Robert. "Journal Use Per Monetary Unit: A Reanalysis of Use Data." *Library Acquisitions: Practice and Theory* 3, no. 2 (1979): 91-98.

———. "Periodical Use in an Academic Library: A Study of Economists and Political Scientists." *Special Libraries* 69 (February 1978): 51-60.

Goffman, William, and Thomas G. Morris. "Bradford's Law Applied to the Maintenance of Library Collections." In *Introduction to Information Science*, compiled and edited by Tefko Saracevic, 200-203. New York: R. R. Bowker, 1970.

Goldblatt, Margaret A. "Current Legal Periodicals: A Use Study." *Law Library Journal* 78 (winter 1986): 55-72.

Gordon, Martin. "Automated Binding Control: Libraries, Binders and Serial Agents." *Serials Librarian* 15, nos. 3/4 (1988): 157-59.

——. "Periodical Use at a Small College Library." *Serials Librarian* 6 (summer 1982): 63-73.

Gordon, Michael D. "Citation Ranking Versus Subjective Evaluation in the Determination of Journal Hierarchies in the Social Sciences." *Journal of the American Society for Information Science* 33 (January 1982): 55-57.

Gorman, G. E. "The Education of Serials Librarians in Australia: A Proposed Course in Serials Librarianship." *Serials Librarian* 17, nos. 1/2 (1989): 45-67.

Gossen, Eleanor A., and Suzanne Irving. "Ownership Versus Access and Low-Use Periodical Titles." *Library Resources and Technical Services* 39 (January 1995): 43-52.

Graham, Crystal, and Rebecca Ringler. "Hermaphrodites and Herrings." *Serials Review* 22 (spring 1996): 73-77.

Graham, Margaret E., and Fiona Buettel. *Serials Management: A Practical Handbook*. London: Published by Aslib in collaboration with the United Kingdom Serials Group, 1990.

Green, Paul Robert. "Monitoring the Usage of Science and Engineering Journals at the Edward Boyle Library, University of Leeds." *Serials Librarian* 25, nos. 1/2 (1994): 169-80.

——. "The Performance of Subscription Agents: A Detailed Survey." *Serials Librarian* 8 (winter 1983): 7-22.

——. "The Performance of Subscription Agents: A Preliminary Survey." *Serials Librarian* 5 (summer 1981): 19-24.

Green, Paul Robert, John Merriman, and David P. Woodworth. "The United Kingdom Serials Group: Its History, Development, and Future." *Serials Librarian* 9 (summer 1985): 107-11.

Grenfell, David. *Periodicals and Serials: Their Treatment in Special Libraries*, 2d ed. London: Aslib, 1965.

Griffith, Joan. "Electronic Data Interchange: Dartmouth + Faxon + Innopac + SISAC + X12 = Serials Claims Pilot Project." *Serials Review* 21 (fall 1995): 33-45.

Grochmal, Helen M. "Selecting Electronic Journals." *College and Research Libraries News* 56 (October 1995): 632-33, 654.

——. "Selection Criteria for Periodicals in Microform." *Serials Librarian* 5 (spring 1981): 15-17.

Gross, P. L. K., and E. M. Gross. "College Libraries and Chemical Education." *Science* 66 (October 28, 1927): 385-89.

Grycz, Czeslaw Jan. "Serials Librarians in the 21st Century and What to Teach Them." *Serials Librarian* 22 (summer 1996): 25-31.

Gunderloy, Mike, and Cari Goldberg Janice. *World of Zines: A Guide to the Independent Magazine Revolution*. New York: Penguin Books, 1992.

Gusack, Nancy, and Clifford A. Lynch. "Special Theme: The TULIP Project." *Library Hi Tech* 13, no. 4 (1995): 7-74.

Guthrie, Kevin M., and Wendy P. Lougee. "The JSTOR Solution: Accessing and Preserving the Past." *Library Journal* 122 (February 1, 1997): 42-44.

Haas, Stephanie C., and Kate Lee. "Research Journal Usage by the Forestry Faculty at the University of Florida, Gainesville." *Collection Building* 11, no. 2 (1991): 23-25.

Haas, Stephanie C. and Vernon N. Kisling, Jr. "The Use of Electronic Ranking to Analyze Scientific Literature Used in Research at the University of Florida." *Collection Management* 18, nos. 3/4 (1994): 49-62.

Hague, Howard, comp. *Core Collection of Medical Books and Journals*. 2d ed. London: Medical Information Working Party, 1994.

Hamaker, Charles A. "Costs and the Serials Information Chain: Containing the Impact on Library Budgets." *Journal of Library Administration* 10, no. 1 (1989): 99-113.

Hanson, Jo Ann. "Trends in Serials Management." *Serials Librarian* 8 (summer 1984): 7-12.

Hardesty, Larry, and Gail Oltmanns. "How Many Psychology Journals Are Enough? A Study of the Use of Psychology Journals by Undergraduates." *Serials Librarian* 16, nos.1/2 (1989): 133-53.

Harnad, Stevan. "Post-Gutenberg Galaxy: The Fourth Revolution in the Means of Production of Knowledge." *Public-Access Computer Systems Review* 2, no. 1 (1991): 29-41. Available: http://info.lib.uh.edu/pr/v2/n1/harnad.2n1 (Accessed March 1, 1998).

———. "Scholarly Skywriting and the Prepublication Continuum of Scientific Inquiry." *Psychological Science* 1 (November 1990): 342-44.

Harri, Wilbert, Alan Nordman, and Fran Fisher. "EDI Implementation: A Discussion and Demonstration." *Serials Librarian* 24, nos. 3/4 (1994): 249-52.

Harrington, Sue Anne. "Serials Organization: A Time for Reappraisal." *Serials Librarian* 10, nos. 1/2 (fall 1985/winter 1985-86): 19-28.

Harrington, Sue Anne, and Deborah J. Karpuk. "The Integrated Serials Department: Its Value Today and in the Future." *Serials Librarian* 9 (winter 1984): 55-64.

Harter, Stephen P. "The Impact of Electronic Journals on Scholarly Communication: A Citation Analysis." *Public-Access Computer Systems Review* 7, no. 5 (1996): 11. Available: http://lib-04.lib.uh.edu/pacsrev/1996/hart7n5.htm (Accessed March 1, 1998).

Harter, Stephen P., and Hak Joon Kim. "Accessing Electronic Journals and Other E-Publications: An Empirical Study." *College and Research Libraries* 57 (September 1996): 440-56.

———. *Electronic Journals and Scholarly Communication: A Citation and Reference Study*. Available: http://ezinfo.ucs.indiana.edu/~harter/harter-asis96midyear.html (Accessed February 15, 1998).

Hasslöw, Rolf, and Annika Sverrung. "Deselection of Serials: The Chalmers University of Technology Library Method." *Collection Management* 19, nos. 3/4 (1995): 151-70.

Hastreiter, Jamie Webster, Larry Hardesty, and David Henderson, comps. *Periodicals in College Libraries*. CLIP Note # 8. Chicago: Association of College and Research Libraries, 1987.

Hawbaker, A. Craig, and Cynthia K. Wagner. "Periodical Ownership versus Fulltext Online Access: A Cost-Benefit Analysis." *Journal of Academic Librarianship* 22 (March 1996): 105-9.

Hawthorn, Margaret. "Serials Selection and Deselection: A Survey of North American Academic Libraries." *Serials Librarian* 21, no. 1 (1991): 29-45.

Hayman, Lynne Myers. "Serials Budget Management Using a Microcomputer." *Serials Librarian* 21, no. 1 (1991): 13-27.

He, Chunpei, and Miranda Lee Pao. "A Discipline-Specific Journal Selection Algorithm." *Information Processing and Management* 22, no. 5 (1986): 405-16.

Heidtmann, Toby. "Help-Net Binding Preparation System at the University of Cincinnati." *Serials Review* 15 (spring 1989): 21-26.

Heitshu, Sara. "Serials Automation: Past, Present, and Future." In *Advances in Serials Management: A Research Annual*. Vol. 2, edited by Marcia Tuttle and Jean G. Cook, 95-115. Greenwich, Conn.: JAI Press, 1988.

Hentz, Margaret Bell. "Data Conversion from Faxon's SC-10 Serials Control System Into Techlib/Plus' On-Line Card Catalog." *Special Libraries* 85 (summer 1994): 162-82.

Hepfer, Cindy. "Union Listing: A Literature Review." *Serials Review* 14, nos. 1/2 (1988): 99-113.

Herubel, Jean-Pierre V.M. "Philosophy Dissertation Bibliographies and Citations in Serials Evaluation." *Serials Librarian* 20, nos. 2/3 (1991): 65-73.

——. "Simple Citation Analysis and the Purdue History Periodical Collection." *Indiana Libraries* 9, no. 2 (1990): 18-21.

Herzog, Kate, Harry Armistead, and Marla Edelman. "Designing Effective Journal Use Studies." *Serials Librarian* 24, nos.3/4 (1994): 189-92.

Hildick, E. W. *A Close Look at Magazines and Comics*. London: Faber Educational, 1966.

Hirshon, Arnold, and Barbara Winters. "Outsourcing the Acquisition of Serials." In *Outsourcing Library Technical Services: A How-to-Do-It Manual for Librarians*, 91-105. New York: Neal-Schuman, 1996.

Holland, Maurita Peterson. "Machine-Readable Files for Serials Management: An Optimizing Program and Use Data." *College and Research Libraries* 44 (January 1983): 66-69.

Holley, Beth, and others. "Replacement Issues: Where Do You Find Them and at What Cost?" *Serials Librarian* 21, nos. 2/3 (1991): 165-68.

Hood, Elizabeth. "The Catalog Record and Automated Union Listing." *Serials Review* 14, nos. 1/2 (1988): 31-42.

Houghton, Bernard. *Scientific Periodicals: Their Historical Development, Characteristics and Control*. Hamden, Conn.: Linnet Books, 1975.

Howard, Thomas P., and Loren A. Nikolai. "Attitude Measurement and Perceptions of Accounting Faculty Publication Outlets." *Accounting Review* 58 (October 1983): 765-76.

Huff, William H. "Serial Subscription Agencies." *Library Trends* 24 (April 1976): 683-709.

Hugo, Jane, and Linda Newell. "*New Horizons in Adult Education*: The First Five Years (1987-1991)." *Public-Access Computer Systems Review* 2, no. 1 (1991): 77-78. Available: http://info.lib.uh.edu/pr/v2/n1/hugo.2n1 (Accessed February 15, 1998).

Hunt, Richard K. "Journal Deselection in a Biomedical Research Library: A Mediated Mathematical Approach." *Bulletin of the Medical Library Association* 78 (January 1990): 45-48.

Hunter, Karen A. "The Changing Business of Scholarly Publishing." *Journal of Library Administration* 19, nos. 3/4 (1993): 23-38.

——. "Publishing for a Digital Library—What Did TULIP Teach Us?" *Journal of Academic Librarianship* 22 (May 1996): 209-11.

Hurd, Sandra H. "Selection of an Integrated Library System Vendor, an Agent's View." *Serials Review* 22 (summer 1996): 89-91.

Irvine, Betty Jo, and Lyn Korenic. "Survey of Periodical Use in an Academic Art Library." *Art Documentation* 1 (October 1982): 148-51.

Ivins, October. "The Development of Criteria for Evaluating Vendor Performance of Monograph and Serial Vendors." In *Advances in Serials Management: A Research Annual.* Vol. 2, edited by Marcia Tuttle and Jean G. Cook, 185-212. Greenwich, Conn.: JAI Press, 1988.

Ivins, October R., Mary K. McLaren, and Joyce G. McDonough. "Planning, Conducting, and Analyzing Serials Vendor Performance Studies." *Serials Librarian* 19, nos. 3/4 (1991): 221-23.

Jármy, Imre. "Exchange and Gift: Almost 90 Percent of Permanent Collections Are Acquired Through the Division." *Library of Congress Information Bulletin* 49 (December 17, 1990): 429-32.

Jennings, Edward M. "*EJournal*: An Account of the First Two Years." *Public-Access Computer Systems Review* 2, no. 1 (1991): 91-100. Available: http://info.lib.uh.edu/pr/v2/n1/jennings.2n1 (Accessed February 15, 1998).

Johnson, Peggy. "Electronic Scholarly Communication." *Technicalities* 10 (June 1990): 4-7.

Jones, Ed. "Serials in the Realm of the Remotely-Accessible: An Exploration." *Serials Review* 22 (spring 1996): 77-79.

Jones, Wayne, and Young-Hee Queinnec. "Format Integration and Serials Cataloguing." *Serials Librarian* 25, nos. 1/2 (1994): 83-95.

Joswick, Kathleen E., and Jeanne Koekkoek Stierman. "The Core List Mirage: A Comparison of the Journals Frequently Consulted by Faculty and Students." *College and Research Libraries* 58 (January 1997): 48-55.

Jul, Erik. "Electronic Journals in a Print-on-Paper World." *Computers in Libraries* 12 (February 1992): 37-38.

———. "Of Barriers and Breakthroughs." *Computers in Libraries* 12 (March 1992): 20-21.

———. "Revisiting Seriality and Periodicity." *Serials Review* 22 (spring 1996): 70-71.

Kachel, Debra E. "Improving Access to Periodicals: A Cooperative Collection Management Project." *School Library Media Quarterly* 24 (winter 1996): 93-103.

Kascus, Marie, and Faith Merriman. "Using the Internet in Serials Management." *College and Research Libraries News* 56 (March 1995): 148-50, 176.

Katz, Bill. *Magazine Selection: How to Build a Community-Oriented Collection.* New York: R. R. Bowker, 1971.

Katz, Bill, and Linda Sternberg Katz. *Magazines for Libraries*. 9th ed. New Providence, N.J.: R. R. Bowker, 1997.

Keating, Lawrence R., II, Christa Easton Reinke, and Judi A. Goodman. "Electronic Journal Subscriptions." *Library Acquisitions: Practice and Theory* 17 (winter 1993): 455-63.

Kelly, Glen. "Electronic Data Interchange (EDI): The Exchange of Ordering, Claiming, and Invoice Information from a Library Perspective." *Collection Management* 19, nos. 3/4 (1995): 77-94.

Kent, Philip G. "How to Evaluate Serials Suppliers." *Library Acquisitions: Practice and Theory* 18 (spring 1994): 83-87.

Ketcham, Lee, and Kathleen Born. "Periodical Price Survey 1997: Unsettled Times, Unsettled Prices." *Library Journal* 122 (April 15, 1997): 42-47.

Khalil, Mounir. "Document Delivery: A Better Option?" *Library Journal* 118 (February 1, 1993): 43-47.

Kilpatrick, Thomas L., and Barbara G. Preece. "Serial Cuts and Interlibrary Loan: Filling the Gaps." *Interlending and Document Supply* 24, no. 1 (1996): 12-20.

Kim, David U. "Computer-Assisted Binding Preparation at a University Library." *Serials Librarian* 9 (winter 1984): 35-43.

Kim, Hak Joon. "Electronic Journals as a New Medium for Formal Scholarly Communication and Key Factors that Influence their Acceptance." Ph. D. qualifying paper, Indiana University, 1996.

Kim, Mary T. "Ranking of Journals in Library and Information Science: A Comparison of Perceptual and Citation-Based Measures." *College and Research Libraries* 52 (January 1991): 24-37.

Kinder, Robin, and Bill Katz, eds. *Serials and Reference Work*. New York: Haworth Press, 1990. Also issued as *The Reference Librarian*, nos. 27/28 (1990).

Kingma, Bruce R., with Suzanne Irving. *The Economics of Access Versus Ownership: The Costs and Benefits of Access to Scholarly Articles via Interlibrary Loan and Journal Subscription*. New York: Haworth Press, 1996. Also issued as *Journal of Interlibrary Loan, Document Delivery and Information Supply* 6, no. 3 (1996).

Kirby, Steven R. "Reviewing United States History Monographs: A Bibliometric Survey." *Collection Building* 11, no. 2 (1991): 13-18.

Kirk, Thomas G. "Periodicals in College Libraries: Are the Challenges of Rising Subscription Costs Being Met?" *College and Research Libraries News* 53 (February 1992): 94-97.

Kjaer, Kathryn. "Current Access to Scientific Journals: An Alternative Strategy." *Colorado Libraries* 16 (March 1990): 20-22.

Kohl, David F., and Charles H. Davis. "Ratings of Journals by ARL Library Directors and Deans of Library and Information Science Schools." *College and Research Libraries* 46 (January 1985): 40-47.

Konopasek, Katherine, and Nancy Patricia O'Brien. "Undergraduate Periodicals Usage: A Model of Measurement." *Serials Librarian* 9 (winter 1984): 65-74.

Kovacic, Ellen Siegel. "Serials Cataloging: What It Is, How It's Done, Why It's Done That Way." *Serials Review* 11 (spring 1985): 77-86.

Kovacic, Mark. "Controlling Unsolicited Serial Publications." *Serials Review* 13 (spring 1987): 43-47.

Kraft, Donald H., and Richard A. Polacsek. "A Journal-Worth Measure for a Journal-Selection Decision Model." *Collection Management* 2 (summer 1978): 129-39.

Krishan, Kewal. "A Bibliography of Electronic Journals in Canada, 1980-1993." *Serials Librarian* 26, nos. 3/4 (1995): 21-31.

———. *A Hundred Years of Serials Librarianship in Canada, 1893-1993: A Bibliography.* Saskatoon, Sask.: Cataloguing Department, University of Saskatchewan Libraries, 1994.

———. "Organization of Serials in the University Libraries in Canada." *Canadian Library Journal* 48 (April 1991): 123-26.

Kronenfeld, Michael R. "Update on Inflation of Journal Prices in the Brandon-Hill List of Journals." *Bulletin of the Medical Library Association* 84 (April 1996): 260-63.

Kronick, David A. *A History of Scientific and Technical Periodicals: The Origins and Development of the Scientific and Technical Press, 1665-1790.* 2d ed. Metuchen, N.J.: Scarecrow Press, 1976.

———. "Medical 'Publishing Societies' in Eighteenth-Century Britain." *Bulletin of the Medical Library Association* 82 (July 1994): 277-82.

Kurosman, Kathleen, and Barbara Ammerman Durniak. "Document Delivery: A Comparison of Commercial Document Suppliers and Interlibrary Loan Services." *College and Research Libraries* 55 (March 1994): 129-39.

LaBorie, Tim, Michael Halperin, and Howard D. White. "Library and Information Science Abstracting and Indexing Services: Coverage, Overlap, and Context." *Library and Information Science Research* 7 (April-June 1985): 183-95.

Lacroix, Eve-Marie. "Interlibrary Loan in U.S. Health Sciences Libraries: Journal Article Use." *Bulletin of the Medical Library Association* 82 (October 1994): 363-68.

Lancaster, F. Wilfrid. "Evaluation of Periodicals." In *If You Want to Evaluate Your Library*, 87-108. 2d ed. Champaign: University of Illinois, Graduate School of Library and Information Science, 1993.

Lancaster, F. Wilfrid, and others. "The Relationship Between Literature Scatter and Journal Accessibility in an Academic Special Library." *Collection Building* 11, no. 1 (1991): 19-22.

Lancaster, F. Wilfrid, ed. "Networked Scholarly Publishing." *Library Trends* 43 (spring 1995): 515-756.

Lane, David M., Francis Hallahan, and Constance Stone. "Automatic Circulation of New Journal Issues." *College and Research Libraries News* 51 (December 1990): 1068-70.

Langschied, Linda. "Electronic Journal Forum: VPIEJ-L: An Online Discussion Group for Electronic Journal Publishing Concerns." *Serials Review* 20 (spring 1994): 89-94.

Langston, Diane Jones, and Adeline Mercer Smith. *Free Magazines for Libraries*. 4th ed. Jefferson, N.C.: McFarland, 1994.

Lanier, Don, and Norman Vogt. "The Serials Department: 1975-1985." *Serials Librarian* 10 (fall 1985/winter 1985-86): 5-11.

Leach, J. Travis, and Karen Dalziel Tallman. "The Claim Function in Serials Management." In *Advances in Serials Management: A Research Annual*. Vol. 4, edited by Marcia Tuttle and Jean G. Cook, 149-69. Greenwich, Conn.: JAI Press, 1992.

Leathem, Cecilia A. "An Examination of Choice of Formats for Cataloging Nontextual Serials." *Serials Review* 20, no. 1 (1994): 59-67.

Lenahan, Nancy M. "Use of Periodicals and Newspapers in a Mid-Sized Public Library." *Serials Librarian* 16, nos. 3/4 (1989): 1-7.

Leong, Carol L. H. *Serials Cataloging Handbook: An Illustrative Guide to the Use of AACR2 and LC Rule Interpretations*. Chicago: American Library Association, 1989.

Lim, Edward. "Preprint Servers: A New Model for Scholarly Publishing." *Australian Academic and Research Libraries* 27 (March 1996): 21-30.

Line, Maurice B. "Changes in Rank Lists of Serials over Time: Interlending Versus Citation Data." *College and Research Libraries* 46 (January 1985): 77-79.

———. "Rank Lists Based on Citations and Library Uses as Indicators of Journal Usage in Individual Libraries." *Collection Management* 2 (winter 1978): 313-16.

———. "Use of Citation Data for Periodicals Control in Libraries: A Response to Broadus." *College and Research Libraries* 46 (January 1985): 36-37.

Line, Maurice B., and A. Sandison. "'Obsolescence' and Changes in the Use of Literature with Time." *Journal of Documentation* 30 (September 1974): 283-350.

Line, Maurice B., and Alexander Sandison. "Practical Interpretation of Citation and Library Use Studies." *College and Research Libraries* 36 (September 1975): 393-96.

Lively, Donna Padgett, and Lisa A. Macklin. "Taming the Claims Monster: Some Methods of Measuring and Improving the Efficiency of Claiming Through a Vendor." *Serials Librarian* 24, nos. 3/4 (1994): 245-47.

Lockett, Mary W. "The Bradford Distribution: A Review of the Literature, 1934-1987." *Library and Information Science Research* 11 (January-March 1989): 21-36.

Loughner, William. "Scientific Journal Usage in a Large University Library: A Local Citation Analysis." *Serials Librarian* 29, nos. 3/4 (1996): 79-88.

Lowry, Charles B. "Reconciling Pragmatism, Equity, and Need in the Formula Allocation of Book and Serial Funds." *College and Research Libraries* 53 (March 1992): 121-38.

Lynch, Clifford A. "The Transformation of Scholarly Communication and the Role of the Library in the Age of Networked Information." *Serials Librarian* 23, nos. 3/4 (1993): 5-20.

Lynch, Mary Jo, Project Director. *Electronic Services in Academic Libraries*. Chicago: American Library Association, 1996.

———. "Electronic Services: Who's Doing What?" *College and Research Libraries News* 57 (November 1996): 661-65.

Lynden, Frederick C. "The Impact of the Rising Costs of Books and Journals on the Overall Library Budget." *Journal of Library Administration* 10, no. 1 (1989): 81-98.

Malinconico, Michael. "Electronic Documents and Research Libraries." *IFLA Journal* 22, no. 3 (1996): 211-25.

Malouin, Jean-Louis, and J.-Francois Outreville. "The Relative Impact of Economics Journals—A Cross Country Survey and Comparison." *Journal of Economics and Business* 39 (August 1987): 267-77.

Mancini, Alice Duhon. "Evaluating Commercial Document Suppliers: Improving Access to Current Journal Literature." *College and Research Libraries* 57 (March 1996): 123-31.

Mankin, Carole J., and Jacqueline D. Bastille. "An Analysis of the Differences Between Density-of-Use Ranking and Raw-Use Ranking of Library Journal Use." *Journal of the American Society for Information Science* 32 (March 1981): 224-28.

Manoff, Marlene, and others. "The MIT Libraries Electronic Journals Project: Reports on Patron Access and Technical Processing." *Serials Review* 19 (fall 1993): 15-40.

Manoff, Marlene, Eileen Dorschner, and Marilyn Geller. "Report of the Electronic Journals Task Force, MIT Libraries." *Serials Review* 18 (spring and summer 1992): 113-29.

Marshall, K. Eric. "Evaluation of Current Periodical Subscriptions in the Freshwater Institute Library." In *IAMSLIC at a Crossroads: Proceedings of the 15th Annual Conference*, edited by Robert W. Burkhart and Joyce C. Burkhart, 117-22. N.P.: International Association of Marine Science Libraries and Information Centers, 1990.

Martin, Sylvia. "Vanderbilt's Process for Selecting an Integrated Library System." *Serials Review* 22 (summer 1996): 80-83.

Maxin, Jacqueline A. "Periodical Use and Collection Development." *College and Research Libraries* 40 (May 1979): 248-53.

Maxwell, Robert L., and Maxwell, Margaret F. "Serials." In *Maxwell's Handbook for AACR2R: Explaining and Illustrating the Anglo-American Cataloguing Rules and the 1993 Amendments*, 271-97. Chicago: American Library Association, 1997.

Mayes, Paul, ed. *Periodicals Administration in Libraries: A Collection of Essays.* London: Clive Bingley; Hamden, Conn.: Linnet Books, 1978.

McAllister, Paul R., Richard C. Anderson, and Francis Narin. "Comparison of Peer and Citation Assessment of the Influence of Scientific Journals." *Journal of the American Society for Information Science* 31 (May 1980): 147-52.

McBride, Ruth B. "Foreign Language Serial Use by Social Science Faculty: A Survey." *Serials Librarian* 5 (summer 1981): 25-32.

McCain, Katherine W., and James E. Bobick. "Patterns of Journal Use in a Departmental Library: A Citation Analysis." *Journal of the American Society for Information Science* 32 (July 1981): 257-67.

McGrath, William E. "Ratings and Rankings: Multiple Comparisons of Mean Ratings." *College and Research Libraries* 48 (March 1987): 169-72.

McKinley, Margaret. "The Exchange Program at UCLA: 1932 through 1986." *Serials Review* 12 (spring 1986): 75-80.

McKnight, Cliff. "Electronic Journals—Past, Present . . . and Future?" *Aslib Proceedings* 45 (January 1993): 7-10.

McMillan, Gail. "Electronic Journals: Considerations for the Present and the Future." *Serials Review* 17 (winter 1991): 77-86.

———. "Embracing the Electronic Journal: One Library's Plan." *Serials Librarian* 21, nos. 2/3 (1991): 97-108.

———. "Technical Processing of Electronic Journals." *Library Resources and Technical Services* 36 (October 1992): 470-77.

McNellis, Claudia Houk. "A Serial Pattern Scheme for a Value-Added Predictive Check-In System." *Serials Review* 22 (winter 1996): 1-11.

Meadows, A. J. *The Scientific Journal.* London: Aslib, 1979.

Meadows, Jack, David Pullinger, and Peter Such. "The Cost of Implementing an Electronic Journal." *Journal of Scholarly Publishing* 26 (July 1995): 227-33.

Melin, Nancy Jean. "The Public Service Functions of Serials." *Serials Review* 6 (January/March 1980): 39-44.

Melin, Nancy Jean, ed. *Library Serials Standards: Development, Implementation, Impact: Proceedings of the Third Annual Serials Conference.* Westport, Conn.: Meckler, 1984.

———. *Serials and Microforms: Patron-Oriented Management.* Westport, Conn.: Meckler, 1983.

Merry, Karen, and Trevor Palmer. "Use of Serials at the British Library Lending Division in 1983." *Interlending and Document Supply* 12 (April 1984): 53-56.

Metz, Paul. "Thirteen Steps to Avoiding Bad Luck in a Serials Cancellation Project." *Journal of Academic Librarianship* 18 (May 1992): 76-82.

Milkovic, Milan. "The Binding of Periodicals: Basic Concepts and Procedures." *Serials Librarian* 11 (October 1986): 93-118.

Miller, Edward P., and Ann L. O'Neill. "Journal Deselection and Costing." *Library Acquisitions: Practice and Theory* 14, no. 2 (1990): 173-78.

Miller, Naomi. "Journal Use in a Clinical Librarian Program." *Bulletin of the Medical Library Association* 72 (October 1984): 395-96.

Miller, Ruth H., and Marvin C. Guilfoyle. "Computer Assisted Periodicals Selection: Structuring the Subjective." *Serials Librarian* 10 (spring 1986): 9-22.

Millson-Martula, Christopher. "Use Studies and Serials Rationalization: A Review." *Serials Librarian* 15, nos. 1/2 (1988): 121-36.

Milne, Dorothy, and Bill Tiffany. "A Cost-per-Use Method for Evaluating the Cost-Effectiveness of Serials: A Detailed Discussion of Methodology." *Serials Review* 17 (summer 1991): 7-19.

———. "A Survey of the Cost-Effectiveness of Serials: A Cost-per-Use Method and Its Results." *Serials Librarian* 19, nos. 3/4 (1991): 137-49.

Mogge, Dru, and Diane K. Kovacs, comps. *Directory of Electronic Journals, Newsletters and Academic Discussion Lists*. 6th ed. Washington, D.C.: Association of Research Libraries, 1996.

Moline, Sandra R. "The Influence of Subject, Publisher Type, and Quantity Published on Journal Prices." *Journal of Academic Librarianship* 15 (March 1989): 12-18.

Montori, Carla J. "Managing the Library's Commercial Library Binding Program." *Technical Services Quarterly* 5, no. 3 (1988): 21-25.

Moothart, Tom. "Blackwell's Periodicals Entry into E-Journal Distribution." *Serials Review* 22 (winter 1996): 83-86.

———. "Migration to Electronic Distribution Through OCLC's Electronic Journals Online." *Serials Review* 21 (winter 1995): 61-65.

———. "Providing Access to E-Journals Through Library Home Pages." *Serials Review* 22 (summer 1996): 71-77.

Morasch, Bruce. "Electronic Social Psychology." *Serials Review* 12 (summer and fall 1986): 113-17.

Morgan, Eric Lease. "Description and Evaluation of the 'Mr. Serials,' Process: Automatically Collecting, Organizing, Archiving, Indexing, and Disseminating Electronic Serials." *Serials Review* 21 (winter 1995): 1-12.

Morris, Sally. "The Future of Journal Publishing." *Interlending and Document Supply* 23, no. 4 (1995): 20-22.

Morrow, Lydia A. "The Duplicate Exchange Union: Is It Still Viable?" *Technical Services Quarterly* 12, no. 1 (1994): 43-48.

Mott, Frank Luther. *A History of American Magazines*. 5 vols. Cambridge, Mass.: Harvard University Press, 1938-68.

Mouw, James R. "Selecting a System That Will Meet the Needs of Serials Control." *Serials Review* 22 (summer 1996): 83-86.

Naulty, Deborah. "Implementing an Internal Routing Sticker System." *Library Software Review* 9 (January-February 1990): 32-33.

Naylor, Maiken. "Assessing Current Periodical Use at a Science and Engineering Library: A dBASE III+ Application." *Serials Review* 16 (winter 1990): 7-19.

———. "Comparative Results of Two Current Periodical Use Studies." *Library Resources and Technical Services* 38 (October 1994): 373-88.

———. "A Comparison of Two Methodologies for Counting Current Periodical Use." *Serials Review* 19 (spring 1993): 27-34, 62.

Naylor, Maiken, and Kathleen Walsh. "A Time-Series Model for Academic Library Data Using Intervention Analysis." *Library and Information Science Research* 16 (fall 1994): 299-314.

Neavill, Gordon B., and Mary Ann Sheblé. "Archiving Electronic Journals." *Serials Review* 21 (winter 1995): 13-21.

Nielsen, Donald A., and R. Wayne Wilson. "A Delphi Rating of Real Estate Journals." *Real Estate Appraiser and Analyst* 46 (May-June 1980): 43-48

Nisonger, Thomas E. "Collection Management Issues for Electronic Journals." *IFLA Journal* 22, no. 3 (1996): 233-39.

————. "Electronic Journal Collection Management Issues." *Collection Building* 16, no. 2 (1997): 58-65.

————. "Electronic Journals: Post-Modern Dream or Nightmare: Report of the ALCTS, CMDS Collection Development Librarians of Academic Libraries Discussion Group." *Library Acquisitions: Practice and Theory* 17 (fall 1993): 378-80.

————. "Impact-Factor-Based Ranking of Library and Information Science Journals in the *Social Sciences Citation Index Journal Citation Reports*, 1980 to 1992." In *Fifth International Conference of the International Society for Scientometrics and Informetrics: Proceedings—1995; June 7-10, 1995*, edited by Michael E. D. Koenig and Abraham Bookstein, 393-402. Medford, N. J.: Learned Information, 1995.

————. "The Internet and Collection Management in Libraries: Opportunities and Challenges." In *Collection Management in the 21st Century: A Handbook for Librarians*, edited by G. E. Gorman and Ruth H. Miller, 29-58. Westport, Conn.: Greenwood Press, 1997.

————. "A Methodological Issue Concerning the Use of *Social Sciences Citation Index Journal Citation Reports* Impact Factor Data for Journal Ranking." *Library Acquisitions: Practice and Theory* 18 (winter 1994): 447-58.

————. "A Ranking of Political Science Journals Based on Citation Data." *Serials Review* 19, no. 4 (1993): 7-14.

————. "The Stability of *Social Sciences Citation Index Journal Citation Reports* Data for Journal Rankings in Three Disciplines." *JISSI: International Journal of Scientometrics and Informetrics* 1 (June 1995): 139-49.

Noble, Rick. "Document Delivery and Full Text from OCLC." *Electronic Library* 14 (February 1996): 57-61.

O'Connor, Brian. "Moving Image-Based Serial Publications." *Serials Review* 12 (summer and fall 1986): 19-24.

Okerson, Ann. "Electronic Journal Publishing on the Net: Developments and Issues." In *New Technologies and New Directions: Proceedings from the Symposium on Scholarly Communication, The University of Iowa, November 14-16, 1991,* edited by G. R. Boynton and Sheila D. Creth, 51-64. Westport, Conn.: Meckler, 1993.

———. "The Electronic Journal: What, Whence, and When?" *Public-Access Computer Systems Review* 2, no. 1 (1991): 2-17. Available: http://info.lib.uh.edu/pr/v2/n1/okerson.2n1 (Accessed March 1, 1998).

Okerson, Ann, and Kendon Stubbs. "The Library 'Doomsday Machine.' " *Publishers Weekly* 238 (February 8, 1991): 36-37.

Okerson, Ann Shumelda, and James J. O'Donnell, eds. *Scholarly Journals at the Crossroads: A Subversive Proposal for Electronic Publishing.* Washington, D.C.: Office of Scientific and Academic Publishing, Association of Research Libraries, 1995.

Olsen, Jan. *Electronic Journal Literature: Implications for Scholars.* Westport, Conn.: Mecklermedia, 1994.

Olsrud, Lois, and Anne Moore. "Serials Review in the Humanities: A Three-Year Project." *Collection Building* 10, nos. 3/4 (1990): 2-10.

Oluić-Vuković, Vesna, and Nevenka Pravdić. "Journal Selection Model: An Indirect Evaluation of Scientific Journals." *Information Processing and Management* 26, no 3 (1990): 413-31.

Orr, Richard H., and Arthur P. Schless. "Document Delivery Capabilities of Major Biomedical Libraries in 1968: Results of a National Survey Employing Standardized Tests." *Bulletin of the Medical Library Association* 60 (July 1972): 382-422.

Osborn, Andrew D. *Serial Publications: Their Place and Treatment in Libraries.* 3d ed. Chicago: American Library Association, 1980.

Osburn, Charles B. "The Place of the Journal in the Scholarly Communications System." *Library Resources and Technical Services* 28 (October/December 1984): 315-24.

Pan, Elizabeth. "Journal Citation as a Predictor of Journal Usage in Libraries." *Collection Management* 2 (spring 1978): 29-38.

Parang, Elizabeth, and Laverna Saunders, comps. *Electronic Journals in ARL Libraries: Issues and Trends.* SPEC Kit 202. Washington, D.C.: Association of Research Libraries, Office of Management Studies, 1994.

———. *Electronic Journals in ARL Libraries: Policies and Procedures.* SPEC Kit 201. Washington, D.C.: Association of Research Libraries, Office of Management Studies, 1994.

Patterson, Charles D. "Origins of Systematic Serials Control: Remembering Carolyn Ulrich." *Reference Services Review* 16, nos. 1/2 (1988): 79-92.

Paul, Huibert. "Automation of Serials Check-In: Like Growing Bananas in Greenland?" Part 1 *Serials Librarian* 6 (winter 1981): 3-16; Part 2 *Serials Librarian* 6 (summer 1982): 39-62.

Peacock, P. G. "The Selection of Periodicals for Binding." *Aslib Proceedings* 33 (June 1981): 257-59.

Peasgood, Adrian N., and Peter J. Lambert. "Multi-User Subjects, Multi-Subject Users: Reader-Defined Interdisciplinarity in Journals Use at the University of Sussex." *British Journal of Academic Librarianship* 2 (spring 1987): 20-36.

Pedersen, Wayne, and David Gregory. "Interlibrary Loan and Commercial Document Supply: Finding the Right Fit." *Journal of Academic Librarianship* 20 (November 1994): 263-72.

Penner, Rudolf Jacob. "Measuring a Library's Capability." *Journal of Education for Librarianship* 13 (summer 1972): 17-30.

Perkins, David L. "Weed It and Reap." *Serials Librarian* 18, nos. 1/2 (1990): 131-40.

Peters, Andrew. "Evaluating Periodicals." *College and Research Libraries* 43 (March 1982): 149-51.

Petersen, Karla D. "Planning for Serials Retrospective Conversion." *Serials Review* 10 (fall 1984): 73-78.

Peterson, Stephen L. "Patterns of Use of Periodical Literature." *College and Research Libraries* 30 (September 1969): 422-30.

Peterson, Theodore. *Magazines in the Twentieth Century*. Urbana, Ill.: University of Illinois Press, 1964.

Pierson, Robert M. "Where Shall We Shelve Bound Periodicals? Further Notes." *Library Resources and Technical Services* 10 (summer 1966): 290-94.

Pionessa, Geraldine F. "Serials Replacement Orders: A Closer Look." *Serials Review* 16 (spring 1990): 65-73, 80.

Piternick, Anne B. "Electronic Serials: Realistic or Unrealistic Solution to the Journal 'Crisis.' " *Serials Librarian* 21, nos. 2/3 (1991): 15-31.

Pitkin, Gary M. *Serials Automation in the United States: A Bibliographic History*. Metuchen, N. J.: Scarecrow Press, 1976.

Potter, William Gray. "Form or Function? An Analysis of the Serials Department in the Modern Academic Library." *Serials Librarian* 6 (fall 1981): 85-94.

Prabha, Chandra, and John E. Ogden. "Recent Trends in Academic Library Materials Expenditures." *Library Trends* 42 (winter 1994): 499-513.

Pratt, Gregory F., Patrick Flannery, and Cassandra L. D. Perkins. "Guidelines for Internet Resource Selection." *College and Research Libraries News* 57 (March 1996): 134-35.

Price, Derek J. de Solla. *Science Since Babylon*. New Haven: Yale University Press, 1961.

Puccio, Joseph A. *Serials Reference Work*. Englewood, Colo.: Libraries Unlimited, 1989.

Pullinger, David J. "Learning from Putting Electronic Journals on SuperJANET: the SuperJournal Project." *Interlending and Document Supply* 23, no. 1 (1995): 20-27.

Quandt, Richard E. "Simulation Model for Journal Subscription by Libraries." *Journal of the American Society for Information Science* 47 (August 1996): 610-17.

Racine, Drew. "Access to Full-Text Journal Articles: Some Practical Considerations." *Library Administration and Management* 6 (spring 1992): 100-104.

Rada, Roy, and others. "Computerized Guides to Journal Selection." *Information Technology and Libraries* 6 (September 1987): 173-84.

Reed, Jutta R. " Collection Development of Serials in Microform." *Microform Review* 9 (spring 1980): 86-89.

Renaud, Robert. "A Canadian Perspective on Serials Industry Standards: The Canadian Serials Industry Systems Advisory Committee (CSISAC)." *Serials Librarian* 26, nos. 3/4 (1995): 133-43.

Report of the ARL Serials Prices Project. Washington, D.C.: Association of Research Libraries, 1989.

Ribbe, Paul H. "Assessment of Prestige and Price of Professional Publications." *American Mineralogist* 73 (May/June 1988): 449-69.

Rice, Barbara A. "Science Periodicals Use Study." *Serials Librarian* 4 (fall 1979): 35-47.

———. "Selection and Evaluation of Chemistry Periodicals." *Science and Technology Libraries* 4 (fall 1983): 43-58.

Richardson, Lyon N. *A History of Early American Magazines, 1741-1789*. New York: Octagon Books, 1966.

Richardson, Selma K. *Magazines for Children: A Guide for Parents, Teachers, and Librarians*. 2d ed. Chicago: American Library Association, 1991.

Richter, Linda. "How an Automated Library System Meets the Needs of Serials Librarians." *Serials Review* 22 (summer 1996): 87-89.

Richter, Linda, and Joan Roca. "An X12 Implementation in Serials: MSUS/PALS and Faxon." *Serials Review* 20, no 1 (1994): 13-24.

Riordan, Paul J., and Nils Roar Gjerdet. "The Use of Periodical Literature in a Norwegian Dental Library." *Bulletin of the Medical Library Association* 69 (October 1981): 387-91.

Robb, David J., and Angela McCormick. "Decision Support for Serials Deselection and Acquisition: A Case Study." *Journal of the American Society for Information Science* 48 (March 1997): 270-73.

Robison, David F. W. "Bibliography of Articles Related to Electronic Journal Publications and Publishing." In *Directory of Electronic Journals, Newsletters and Academic Discussion Lists*, 3d ed., by Michael Strangelove and Diane Kovacs, edited by Ann Okerson, 27-38. Washington, D.C.: Association of Research Libraries, 1993.

——. "Bibliography of Articles Related to Electronic Journal Publications and Publishing." In *Directory of Electronic Journals, Newsletters and Academic Discussion Lists*, 4th ed., by Michael Strangelove and Diane Kovacs, edited by Ann Okerson, 35-43. Washington, D.C.: ARL Office of Scientific and Academic Publishing, 1994.

——. "The Changing States of *Current Cites*: The Evolution of an Electronic Journal." *Computers in Libraries* 13 (June 1993): 21-26.

Robison, Elwin C. "Architecture, Graphics, and the Net: A Short History of *Architronic*, a Peer-Reviewed E-Journal." *Public-Access Computer Systems Review* 7, no. 3 (1996): 5-12. Available: http://info.lib.uh.edu/pr/v7/n3/robi7n3.html (Accessed February 15, 1998).

Rooke, Su. "Surveying Non-Usage of Serials." *Serials Librarian* 18, nos. 1/2 (1990): 81-96.

Root, Trudie A. "Inhouse Binding in Academic Libraries." *Serials Review* 15 (fall 1989): 31-40.

Rothman, Fred B., and Sidney Ditzion. "Prevailing Practices in Handling Serials." *College and Research Libraries* 1 (March 1940): 165-69.

Rowe, Richard R. "The Transformation of Scholarly Communications and the Future of Serials." *Serials Review* 22 (summer 1996): 33-43.

Rush, James E. "Automated Serials Control Systems." *Serials Review* 12 (summer and fall 1986): 87-101.

Saffady, William. "Automated Acquisitions and Serials Control." In *Introduction to Automation for Librarians*, 347-73. 3d ed. Chicago: American Library Association, 1994.

Sandison, A. "The Use of Scientific Literature at the Science Reference Library for Updating Searches." *Journal of Documentation* 35 (June 1979): 107-19.

Sassé, Margo, and B. Jean Winkler. "Electronic Journals: A Formidable Challenge for Librarians." *Advances in Librarianship* 17 (1993): 149-73.

Sauer, Jean S. "Unused Current Issues: A Predictor of Unused Bound Volumes?" *Serials Librarian* 18, nos. 1/2 (1990): 97-107.

Savage, Lon. *"The Journal of the International Academy of Hospitality Research."* *Public-Access Computer Systems Review* 2, no. 1 (1991): 54-66. Available: http://info.lib.uh.edu/pr/v2/n1/savage.2n1 (Accessed February 15, 1998).

Scales, Pauline A. "Citation Analyses as Indicators of the Use of Serials: A Comparison of Ranked Title Lists Produced by Citation Counting and from Use Data." *Journal of Documentation* 32 (March 1976): 17-25.

Scanlan, Brian D. "Coverage by *Current Contents* and the Validity of Impact Factors: ISI from a Journal Publisher's Perspective." *Serials Librarian* 13 (October/November 1987): 57-66.

Schaffner, Ann C. "The Future of Scientific Journals: Lessons from the Past." *Information Technology and Libraries* 13 (December 1994): 239-47.

Schaffner, Ann C., guest ed. "Perspectives on the Future of Union Listing." *Serials Review* 19 (fall 1993): 71-78, 94.

Schmidt, Diane, Elisabeth B. Davis, and Ruby Jahr. "Biology Journal Use at an Academic Library: A Comparison of Use Studies." *Serials Review* 20, no. 2 (1994): 45-64.

Schmidt, Sherrie, Jane Treadwell, and Gloriana St. Clair. "Using dBaseIII+ to Create a Serials Review List." *Microcomputers for Information Management* 5 (September 1988): 169-82.

Schoch, Natalie, and Eileen G. Abels. "Using a Valuative Instrument for Decision Making in the Cancellation of Science Journals in a University Setting." In *ASIS '94: Proceedings of the 57th ASIS Annual Meeting: Alexandria, Va., October 17-20, 1994.* Vol. 31, edited by Bruce Maxian, 41-50. Medford, N.J.: published for the American Society for Information Science by Learned Information, 1994.

Schwartz, Frederick E. "The EDI Horizon: Implementing an ANSI X12 Pilot Project at the Faxon Company." *Serials Librarian* 19, nos. 3/4 (1991): 39-57.

Segal, Judith A. "Journal Deselection: A Literature Review and an Application." *Science and Technology Libraries* 6 (spring 1986): 25-42.

Segesta, Jim, and Gary Hyslop. "The Arrangement of Periodicals in American Academic Libraries." *Serials Review* 17 (spring 1991): 21-28, 40.

Seglen, Per O. "The Skewness of Science." *Journal of the American Society for Information Science* 43 (October 1992): 628-38.

Serebnick, Judith, and Stephen P. Harter. "Ethical Practices in Journal Publishing: A Study of Library and Information Science Periodicals." *Library Quarterly* 60 (April 1990): 91-119.

Seymour, Carol A. "Weeding the Collection: A Review of Research on Identifying Obsolete Stock. Part II: Serials." *Libri* 22, no. 3 (1972): 183-89.

Sharplin, Arthur D., and Rodney H. Mabry. "The Relative Importance of Journals Used in Management Research: An Alternative Ranking." *Human Relations* 38, no. 2 (1985): 139-49.

Shaw, Debora. "A Review of Developments Leading to On-Line Union Listing of Serials." In *The Management of Serials Automation: Current Technology and Strategies for Future Planning*, edited by Peter Gellatly, 185-90. New York: Haworth Press, 1982.

Shaw, W. M., Jr. "A Practical Journal Usage Technique." *College and Research Libraries* 39 (November 1978): 479-84.

Sheaves, Miriam Lyness. "A Serials Review Program Based on Journal Use in a Departmental Geology Library." In *The Future of the Journal: Proceedings of the Sixteenth Meeting of the Geoscience Information Society, November 2-5, 1981*, edited by Mary Woods Scott, 59-75. N.p.: Geoscience Information Society, 1983.

Shuster, Helen M. "Fiscal Control of Serials Using dBase III+." *Serials Review* 15 (spring 1989): 7-20.

Siemaszkiewicz, Wojciech. "The Readership of the Current Periodical and Newspaper Collection in the Slavic and Baltic Division of the New York Public Library." *Serials Librarian* 20, nos. 2/3 (1991): 131-49.

Sittig, Dean F. "Identifying a Core Set of Medical Informatics Serials: An Analysis Using the MEDLINE Database." *Bulletin of the Medical Library Association* 84 (April 1996): 200-204.

Sivers, Robert. "Partitioned Bradford Ranking and the Serials Problem in Academic Research Libraries." *Collection Building* 8, no. 2 (1987): 12-19.

Smith, Lynn S. *A Practical Approach to Serials Cataloging*. Greenwich, Conn.: JAI Press, 1978.

Smith, Thomas E. "The *Journal Citation Reports* as a Deselection Tool." *Bulletin of the Medical Library Association* 73 (October 1985): 387-89.

Snow, Bonnie. "Rank: A New Tool for Analyzing Search Results on DIALOG." *Database* 16 (June 1993): 111-18.

Soper, Mary Ellen. "The Education of Serials Catalogers." *Serials Librarian* 12, nos. 1/2 (1987): 169-79.

Sreenivasan, Sreenath. "As Mainstream Papers Struggle, the Ethnic Press is Thriving." *New York Times* 145 (July 22, 1996): C7.

Stabin, Tova, and Irene Owen. "Gathering Usage Statistics at an Environmental Health Library Web Site." *Computers in Libraries* 17 (March 1997): 30-37.

Stankus, Tony. "New Specialized Journals, Mature Scientists, and Shifting Loyalties." *Library Acquisitions: Practice and Theory* 9, no. 2 (1985): 99-104.

Stankus, Tony, and Barbara Rice. "Handle with Care: Use and Citation Data for Science Journal Management." *Collection Management* 4 (spring/summer 1982): 95-110.

Stankus, Tony, ed. *Scientific Journals: Issues in Library Selection and Management.* New York: Haworth Press, 1987.

Stein, Linda Lawrence. "What to Keep and What to Cut? Using Internet as an Objective Tool to Identify 'Core' Periodical Titles in a Specialized Subject Collection." *Technical Services Quarterly* 10, no. 1 (1992): 3-14.

Stenstrom, Patricia, and Ruth B. McBride. "Serial Use by Social Science Faculty: A Survey." *College and Research Libraries* 40 (September 1979): 426-31.

Stern, Barrie T., and Robert M. Campbell. "ADONIS—Publishing Journal Articles on CD-ROM." In *Advances in Serials Management: A Research Annual.* Vol. 3, edited by Jean G. Cook and Marcia Tuttle, 1-60. Greenwich, Conn.: JAI Press, 1989.

Stevens, Jana K., Jade G. Kelly, and Richard G. Irons. "Cost-Effectiveness of Soviet Serial Exchanges." *Library Resources and Technical Services* 26 (April/June 1982): 151-55.

Stewart, Linda. "User Acceptance of Electronic Journals: Interviews with Chemists at Cornell University." *College and Research Libraries* 57 (July 1996): 339-49.

Stine, Diane. "Centralized Serials Processing in An Automated Environment." *Serials Review* 9 (fall 1983): 69-75.

Stine, Diane, comp. and ed. *Projects and Procedures for Serials Administration.* Ann Arbor, Mich.: Pierian Press, 1985.

——. "Serials Department Staffing Patterns in Medium-Sized Research Libraries." *Serials Review* 7 (July/September 1981): 83-87.

Stoll, Donald R., ed. *Magazines for Kids and Teens: A Resource for Parents, Teachers, Librarians, and Kids.* Glassboro, N. J.: Educational Press Association of America; Newark, Del.: International Reading Association, 1994.

Stoller, Michael A., Robert Christopherson, and Michael A. Miranda. "The Economics of Professional Journal Pricing." *College and Research Libraries* 57 (January 1996): 9-21.

Striedieck, Suzanne. "CONSER and the National Database." In *Advances in Serials Management: A Research Annual*. Vol. 3, edited by Jean G. Cook and Marcia Tuttle, 81-109. Greenwich, Conn.: JAI Press, 1989.

Sullivan, Michael V. "Obsolescence in Biomedical Journals: Not an Artifact of Literature Growth." *Library Research* 2 (spring 1980-81): 29-45.

Swisher, Robert, and Peggy C. Smith. "Journals Read by ACRL Academic Librarians, 1973 and 1978." *College and Research Libraries* 43 (January 1982): 51-58.

Sylvia, Margaret, and Marcella Lesher. "What Journals Do Psychology Graduate Students Need? A Citation Analysis of Thesis References." *College and Research Libraries* 56 (July 1995): 313-18.

Taylor, Colin R. "A Practical Solution to Weeding University Library Periodical Collections." *Collection Management* 1 (fall-winter 1976-77): 27-45.

Taylor, David C. *Managing the Serials Explosion: The Issues for Publishers and Libraries*. White Plains, N.Y.: Knowledge Industry Publications, 1982.

Taylor, Roger. "Is the Impact Factor a Meaningful Index for the Ranking of Scientific Research Journals?" *Canadian Field-Naturalist* 95 (July-September 1981): 236-40.

Tebbel, John. *The American Magazine: A Compact History*. New York: Hawthorn Books, 1969.

Tebbel, John, and Mary Ellen Zuckerman. *The Magazine in America, 1741-1990*. New York: Oxford University Press, 1991.

Teevan, James J. "Journal Prestige and Quality of Sociological Articles." *American Sociologist* 15 (May 1980): 109-12.

Tenopir, Carol, and Donald W. King. "Setting the Record Straight on Journal Publishing: Myth vs. Reality." *Library Journal* 121 (March 15, 1996): 32-35.

Thornton, Glenda Ann. "Physical Access to Periodical Literature: The Dilemma Revisited and a Brief Look at the Future." *Serials Review* 17, no. 4 (1991): 33-42.

Thornton, Glenda A., and Yem Fong. "Exploring Document Delivery Options: A Pilot Study of the University of Colorado System." *Technical Services Quarterly* 12, no. 2 (1994): 1-11.

Titus, Elizabeth McKenney, Wallace C. Grant, and Lorraine J. Haricombe. "Barcoding As a Tool for Collection Use Analysis: A Pilot Project." *Information Technology and Libraries* 13 (December 1994): 257-65.

Todorov, Radosvet. "Evaluation of Scientific Journals: A Review of Citation-Based Measures." In *Information Research: Research Methods in Library and Information Science; Proceedings of the International Seminar on Information*

Research, Dubrovnik, Yugoslavia, May 19-24, 1986, edited by Neva Tudor-Šilović and Ivan Mihel, 212-24. London: Taylor Graham, 1988.

Tomajko, Kathy G., and Miriam A. Drake. "The Journal, Scholarly Communication, and the Future." *Serials Librarian* 10 (fall 1985/winter 1985-86): 289-98.

Tonkery, Dan. "Reshaping the Serials Vendor Industry." *Serials Librarian* 25, nos. 3/4 (1995): 65-72.

Tonkery, Dan, and Michael Johnson. "Serials Automation Options: Stand-Alone vs. Integrated Systems." *Serials Review* 13 (fall 1987): 25-28.

Triolo, Victor A., and Dachun Bao. "A Decision Model for Technical Journal Deselection with an Experiment in Biomedical Communications." *Journal of the American Society for Information Science* 44 (April 1993): 148-60.

Tseng, Sally C. "Serials Cataloging and AACR2: An Introduction." *Journal of Educational Media Science* 19 (winter 1982): 177-214.

Tseng, Sally C., and others. "Serials Standards Work: The Next Frontier." *Library Resources and Technical Services* 34 (April 1990): 139-57.

Tucker, Betty E. "The Journal Deselection Project: The LSUMC-S Experience." *Library Acquisitions: Practice and Theory* 19 (fall 1995): 313-20.

Turoff, Murray, and Starr Roxanne Hiltz. "The Electronic Journal: A Progress Report." *Journal of the American Society for Information Science* 33 (July 1982): 195-202.

Tuttle, Marcia. *Introduction to Serials Management*. Greenwich, Conn.: JAI Press, 1982.

———. *Managing Serials*. Greenwich, Conn.: JAI Press, 1996.

———. "The *Newsletter on Serials Pricing Issues*." *Public-Access Computer Systems Review* 2, no. 1 (1991): 91-105. Available: http:info.lib.uh.edu/pr/v2/n1/tuttle.2n1 (Accessed February 15, 1998).

———. "The *Newsletter on Serials Pricing Issues*: Teetering on the Cutting Edge." In *Advances in Serials Management: A Research Annual*. Vol. 4, edited by Marcia Tuttle and Jean G. Cook, 37-63. Greenwich, Conn.: JAI Press, 1992.

———. "Serials Management." In *Guide to Technical Services Resources*, edited by Peggy Johnson, 120-35. Chicago: American Library Association, 1994.

Ungern-Sternberg, Sara von, and Mats G. Lindquist. "The Impact of Electronic Journals on Library Functions." *Journal of Information Science* 21, no. 5 (1995): 396-401.

Upham, Lois N. "The Future of Serials Librarianship Revisited." *Serials Review* 17 (summer 1991): 71-75.

Urquhart, D. J. "Use of Scientific Periodicals." In *Proceedings of the International Conference on Scientific Information: Washington, D.C., November 16-21, 1958,* 287-300. Washington, D.C.: National Academy of Sciences—National Research Council, 1959.

Urquhart, John A. "Has Poisson Been Kicked to Death?—A Rebuttal of the British Library Lending Division's Views on the Inconsistency of Rank Lists of Serials." *Interlending Review* 10 (November 1982): 97-99.

Van Brakel, Pieter A. "Electronic Journals: Publishing via Internet's World Wide Web." *Electronic Librarian* 13 (August 1995): 389-96.

Veaner, Allen B. "Into the Fourth Century." *Drexel Library Quarterly* 21 (winter 1985): 4-28.

Veenstra, Robert J. "A One-Year Journal Use Study in a Veterinary Medical Library." *Journal of the American Veterinary Medical Association* 190 (March 15, 1987): 623-26.

Veenstra, Robert J., and James C. Wright. "A Review of Local Journal Use Studies: An Investigation of Possible Broader Applications." *Collection Management* 10, nos. 3/4 (1988): 163-73.

Wallace, Danny P., and Susan Bonzi. "The Relationship between Journal Productivity and Quality." In *ASIS '85: Proceedings of the 48th ASIS Annual Meeting; Las Vegas, Nevada, October 20-24, 1985.* Vol. 22, edited by Carol A. Parkhurst, 193-96. White Plains, N.Y.: published for the American Society for Information Science by Knowledge Industry Publications, 1985.

Walter, Pat L. "Doing the Unthinkable: Canceling Journals at a Research Library." *Serials Librarian* 18, nos. 1/2 (1990): 141-53.

Wan, William W. "System Migration and Its Impact on Technical Services." *Public Library Quarterly* 13, no. 4 (1993): 13-20.

Warner, Edward S., and Anita L. Anker. "Utilizing Library Constituents' Perceived Needs in Allocating Journal Costs." *Journal of the American Society for Information Science* 30 (November 1979): 325-29.

Weber, Hans H. "Serials Administration." *Serials Librarian* 4 (winter 1979): 143-65.

Weil, Ben H., and Barbara F. Polansky. "Copyright, Serials, and the Impacts of Technology." *Serials Review* 12 (summer and fall 1986): 25-32.

Weinryb, Herb. "Accessing European Serials Cataloging Records Through the Internet." *Serials Librarian* 26, no. 2 (1995): 65-74.

Weisheit, Ralph A., and Robert M. Regoli. "Ranking Journals." *Scholarly Publishing* 15 (July 1984): 313-25.

Wenger, Charles B., and Judith Childress. "Journal Evaluation in a Large Research Library." *Journal of the American Society for Information Science* 28 (September 1977): 293-99.

Wertham, Fredric. *World of Fanzines: A Special Form of Communication.* Carbondale, Ill.: Southern Illinois University Press, 1973.

Westbrook, Lynn. "Weeding Reference Serials." *Serials Librarian* 10 (summer 1986): 81-100.

Whetstone, Gloria. "Serial Practices in Selected College and University Libraries." *Library Resources and Technical Services* 5 (fall 1961): 284-90.

White, Howard D. " 'Bradfordizing' Search Output: How It Would Help Online Users." *Online Review* 5 (February 1981): 47-54.

Wiberley, Stephen E., Jr. "Journal Rankings from Citation Studies: A Comparison of National and Local Data from Social Work." *Library Quarterly* 52 (October 1982): 348-59.

Wilkas, Lenore Rae. *International Subscription Agents.* 6th ed. Chicago: American Library Association, 1994.

Willis, Katherine, and others. "TULIP—The University Licensing Program: Experiences at the University of Michigan." *Serials Review* 20 (winter 1994): 39-47.

Williams, Sally F. "Construction and Application of a Periodical Price Index." *Collection Management* 2 (winter 1978): 329-44.

Wise, Suzanne. "Making Lemonade: The Challenges and Opportunities of Forced Reference Serials Cancellations: One Academic Library's Experiences." *Serials Review* 19 (winter 1993): 15-26.

Wood, D. N., and C. A. Bower. "The Use of Social Science Periodical Literature." *Journal of Documentation* 25 (June 1969): 108-22.

Wood, James Playsted. *Magazines in the United States: Their Social and Economic Influence.* New York: Ronald Press, 1949.

Woodward, Hazel M. "The Impact of Electronic Information on Serials Collection Management." *IFLA Journal* 20 (February 1994): 35-45.

Woodward, Hazel, and Cliff McKnight. "Electronic Journals: Issues of Access and Bibliographical Control." *Serials Review* 21 (summer 1995): 71-78.

Wynar, Lubomyr, and Anna T. Wynar. *Encyclopedic Directory of Ethnic Newspapers and Periodicals in the United States.* 2d ed. Littleton, Colo.: Libraries Unlimited, 1976.

Young, Ian R. "The Use of a General Periodicals Bibliographic Database Transaction Log as a Serials Collection Management Tool." *Serials Review* 18 (winter 1992): 49-60.

Yu, Priscilla C. "Cost Analysis: Domestic Serials Exchanges." *Serials Review* 8 (fall 1982): 79-82.

———. "Duplicates Exchange Union: An Update." *Serials Review* 11 (fall 1985): 59-64.

Zackey, Christopher A. "Bibliography: Emerging Relationships Between Reference and Serials." *Reference Librarian* nos. 27/28 (1990): 91-104.

Zijlstra, Jaco. "The University Licensing Program (TULIP): Electronic Journals in Materials Science." *Microcomputers for Information Management* 12, nos. 1/2 (1995): 99-111.

Author/Title Index

Subject Index